The
Psychology of
Reading:
An Interdisciplinary
Approach

Second Edition

THE
PSYCHOLOGY OF
READING:
An Interdisciplinary
Approach,
Second Edition

Mildred C. Robeck

University of Oregon

Randall R. Wallace

Central Washington University

LEA LAWRENCE ERLBAUM ASSOCIATES, PUBLISHERS
1990   Hillsdale, New Jersey   Hove and London

Lawrence Erlbaum Associates, Inc., Publishers
365 Broadway
Hillsdale, New Jersey 07642

Library of Congress Cataloging-in-Publication Data
Robeck, Mildred Coen,
    The psychology of reading : an interdisciplinary approach /
Mildred C. Robeck, Randall R. Wallace. — 2nd ed.
        p.   cm.
    Includes bibliographical references.
    ISBN 0-8058-0373-4. — ISBN 0-8058-0374-2 (pbk.)
    1. Reading, Psychology of. I. Wallace, Randall R. (Randall
Reed), 1949– . II. Title.
    BF456.R2R58 1990
    372.4′01′9—dc20   89-49772
                                                                                 CIP

Printed in the United States of America
10 9 8 7 6 5 4 3 2 1

DEDICATION
To Dr. John A. R. Wilson—colleague, mentor, friend

Contents

Preface

Reading can be learned almost as naturally as speech by a few children and is learned only minimally, if at all, by more than a few others who leave school virtually illiterate. We believe every child who has learned to speak through ordinary social intercourse can learn to read with instruction, despite the evidence of an overwhelming national and world problem of illiteracy. Teachers, alone, will not resolve this dilemma. School psychologists and administrators; pediatricians and nurses; child psychologists and psychiatrists; congressional representatives and school board members each need an understanding of the dimensions of the problem. A knowledge of the process of learning to read is needed by, at least, some of these supporting personnel, who may then address the issues of children's literacy. Certainly reading specialist teachers and clinicians will find their work more rewarding when they are able to grasp the psychological significance of their own observations while teaching. This need to know *why* as well as *how* children and youth respond as they do to reading instruction has guided the selection of the content of this book.

In the first edition, *Psychology of Reading: Foundations of Instruction,* we wanted to leave three major ideas with our readers: (1) Reading is a linguistic process; (2) Motivation, the affective domain, may be as important in learning to read as the cognitive domain; and (3) The reality of learning theory is to be found in the mechanisms of the brain where information is mediated and memory traces are stored (Robeck & Wilson, 1974). None of these themes was emphasized in the reading psychologies of the time. This second edition, Robeck and Wallace, *Psychology of Reading: An Interdisciplinary Approach,* has retained the major emphases, which are supported and elaborated by an intervening period of research in reading, neuropsychology, and linguistics.

Our first theme was that reading is a linguistic process. During the 1980s the language arts curriculum was rediscovered and the sequence of difficulty in skill development from listening, to speaking, to reading, and finally to writing was re-established. During 15 years of continuous research on speech and language acquisition, the infant's perception of speech has been demonstrated, the species-specific nature of human speech has been accepted almost universally, the perception of phonemes has been linked to progress in beginning reading, and the understanding of print has been traced to the speech comprehension areas of one hemisphere. Currently, the risk is that reading might again become incidental to the other language arts, and the systematic skill building most young readers need may be neglected. It is now established that proficient readers have surpassed their childhood ability to acquire information aurally. We consider it important that students be instructed to levels of reading proficiency that exceed their comprehension of speech communication. Personal independence and freedom of thought are the potential rewards of conceptual, creative reading. Chapter 3 deals specifically with research on the relationship of speech, reading, and writing. Chapter 15 deals with reading as a motivating force in creative writing.

The second theme of this book is that motivation is learned as an affective component of all reading-related experiences. The act of reading has an emotional effect; if pleasurable the cognitive component tends to be retained, repeated, and remembered. Affects of displeasure or punishment associated with reading, lead to avoidance and forgetting. Chapter 2 introduces the reader to the older and more primitive structures of the brain where motivations are generated and stored. Fortunately, the pleasure effects of learning to read and of sharing books assure a positive experience for most students most of the time.

The third focus is the physical reality of learning. We thought it important for professionals, especially those who work with young people, to know how an individual's brain changes in real and enduring ways from each experience. The cognitive and the affective elements are perceived, mediated, and delegated in ways that are consistent with the existing neural structures of the participants. Part 3 presents the basic aspects of a neuropsychology of reading. The chapter on auditory perception precedes visual perception because speech comprehension precedes and is utilized by print comprehension. We deal with the difficult topic of dyslexia as a problem (if it *is* dyslexia) in a chapter on sensory integration. Some of this material will be a review for students of biology, genetics, and psychology; but for those without background in any of the biological sciences some chapters may require heavy reading. Professional use of the physical evidence of learning has its rewards in understanding and evaluating theoretical models of reading.

Having researched various disciplines for new material to be incorporated into the second edition, what has been deleted? Some of the former bridges from theory to practice have not been included. The chapters on testing, diagnosing, and evaluating reading programs have been cut, while the essence of educational psychology that supports these important procedures has been supplemented and up-dated. In the new edition we anticipate a reader of greater sophistication and psychological background as a result of increased emphasis on reading instruction in teacher education and on more demanding prerequisites for entering these programs. The present content is directed to those who aspire to be reading specialist teachers, speech pathologists, school psychologists, reading consultants, learning-disability clinicians, or informed teachers of teachers. Students of psychology of reading courses should find in this text a comprehensive introduction to the disciplines that contribute research knowledge to this important area.

As we enter the decade of the 1990s, yet another report from Washington deplores the lack of progress in the nation's goal of literacy for all elementary and secondary students of the United States. One favorable note is the improvement of beginning reading skills for the generation of Sesame Street, Head Start, and Follow Through. Your authors have taught children, as well as the teachers and others who serve them. We are persuaded that improvement will come when teaching-adults, whether parent or professional, remain in close personal touch with the learner. Only in this way can reinforcement by recognition of the child's accomplishments be assured. As a nation we need to identify and help poor readers at all ages. We need to extend the comprehension of language at all levels from kindergarten to graduate school. But direct, positive dividends will accrue from prevention of reading problems beginning in the preschool. Methodology, programming, nor facilities can substitute for a teacher who observes and understands the learning that is (or is not) taking place while the reading lesson unfolds. Reading is the challenge of this decade.

Mildred C. Robeck
University of Oregon
Eugene, OR 97403

Randall R. Wallace
Central Washington University,
Ellensburg, WA 98926

I | The Reading Process

*If we accept the belief that drives include the thrill of surmounting diffi-
culties and gaining competence, we can greet, like a breath of fresh air,
the belief that children and others can be motivated by needs other than
those of hunger, thirst, pain, and sex; that they can learn to know and to
value the sweet taste of intellectual achievement.*

—J. P. Guilford

1 Definition of Reading

Information about the reading process comes from many sources. Throughout the last century, contributions from psychology and education have laid a foundation for more recent contributions from psycholinguistics and neuroscience. In this age of shared technology, an increased understanding of the process of reading has occurred through the polygamous marriage of the traditional disciplines of pedagogy, psychology, linguistics, physiology, and neurology. This chapter presents a brief overview of these sources and defines the reading process as viewed from various perspectives.

HISTORICAL PERSPECTIVES

People have been reading as long as ideas have been represented graphically. When the pictographs of primitive cultures became cumbersome, ideographs were adopted because they were simpler to depict. Gradually the symbols that came into use were standardized within cultural groups, thereby making interpretation, or reading, easier. Reading idiographs became increasingly complex until the learner was required to master thousands of characters to understand the author's representations. The last and highest stage in the development of writing was the alphabet, which resolved the written language into a limited number of phonetic symbols and minimized the number of graphic symbols needed to communicate ideas. The word phonetic is derived from the Phoenicians, who passed their alphabet to the Greeks, who later passed it to the Romans. Eventually the invention of paper and the use of the printing press made written materials available thus, creating a need for widespread instruction in reading.

READING PEDAGOGY PRIOR TO 1900

About the turn of the century, reading methodology shifted from a focus on skill instruction to the development of the understanding of the cognitive processes which take place while reading. The impetus originated from the research of Emile Javal, a Frenchman, who published 25 articles on topics of vision, speech, and writing. Of particular interest to other reading theorists were his articles examining the physiological relationship of eye movements to reading and the psychology of communication. The psychology of reading received international attention and Javal's research became the basis for later investigations and discussions conducted by E. B. Huey.

THE PSYCHOLOGY AND PHILOSOPHY
OF HUEY (1870–1913)

Huey spent his early years as a teacher. In 1904, he founded a psychological research laboratory at the University of Western Pennsylvania where he promoted a new scientific movement in reading. His doctoral dissertation, at Clark University, was the basis for his classic work, *The Psychology and Pedagogy of Reading* (1908). Huey's book raised important questions that have challenged reading experts to this time.

Huey viewed reading as a psychophysiological process in which arbitrary, conventional symbols are used to transfer information from individual to individual. His interest in the process of reading led him to explore eye movements, word recognition, information transfer, and text comprehension. He was among the first to discuss the issue of *parallel processing,* a theory still current, which hypothesizes that several pieces of information can be perceived and translated at the same time. Also he conceptualized the theory *automatization of function,* which means that proficient readers obtain the meaning of words automatically without an intermediate step of decoding. Huey's own research and subsequent descriptions of these processes led some investigators to conclude that reading is not necessarily a serial process, but that readers translate information by working back and forth along a line of print.

Huey studied eye movements primarily because he was interested in perception and interpretation. He wondered whether limitations in the physiology of the eye might place some time constraints on reading rate. He designed a device which utilized (1) an eye cap, perforated for seeing, that moved with the eye, (2) an aluminum pointer which traced the sweeps and pauses on smoked paper, and (3) a moving drum-cylinder which recorded the eye-movement sequences while his adult subjects read a paragraph.

This research established that the eye movements along each line of print averaged .04 of a second duration and that the return movement to the next line ranged from .051 to .058 of a second. By contrast, the fixed gazes between movements averaged .19 of a second, almost 5 times the duration of the eye movements. To Huey this meant readers used the pauses to process visual information. The jerky movements, first graphed by Huey, came to be known by reading clinicians as *saccadic movements,* the fixed gazes as *fixations,* and the returns to the next line as *return sweeps.* From his study of the physiology of the eye and his own discovery of saccadic movements, Huey concluded there is more to reading than meets the eye.

The experimental studies available to Huey on visual perception were numerous (Javal, 1879). Primarily the content of these studies measured the timed recognition of words and letters under various conditions. He interpreted this literature as suggesting that total word form was not fixed; rather that the real stimulus (for mature readers) is a series of dominating letters or letter complexes. Also, he noted that visual form seemed to become less important in word recognition as the reader's familiarity with the material increased or whenever the reader's associative connections between letters and words increased. Huey generalized that (1) Perception in reading is an integrated action; (2) Repetition of a reading vocabulary frees the mind from attention to details and reduces concern with the process; (3) Reading is conditioned strongly from within; (4) The person's predisposition,, or *psychological set,* influences the act; and (5) Dominant letters or letter groups set off word recognition.

Another complex aspect of the reading process which Huey studied was information transfer. Although he accepted the psychological consensus of his time that reading *can* be a purely visual process, Huey theorized that most readers verbalize printed symbols, a process he called inner speech. To test this theory he devised an experiment in which he cut and pasted the words of brief selections on separate cards. At widely spaced intervals, he asked the same readers to report their responses to single words (a) when presented in a shuffled order and in isolation, and (b) when presented in sequence while the original text remained exposed to the subject's view. Today these self-reported reader responses would be considered subjective data, but Huey observed that the dawdling associations of randomized words changed to a rich content of imagery when the words were presented in context and when the new words were integrated with preceding words. His subjects reported that, while both visual and auditory images were recalled, printed words frequently translated as speech and visual images were relatively rare and static. This finding emphasized the linguistic aspect of reading.

In another experiment, Huey presented two printed passages of equal difficulty to each of his subjects and asked them to use different approaches: *read the way you like to read* or *read by saying the words to yourself.* Twenty postgraduate students showed little difference in time intervals between their own style and the inner-speech style (5.29 and 5.35 words per second). Huey noted that the disappearance of lip movements did not indicate an absence of inner speech, or subvocalization. He concluded that a considerable amount of what is being read hangs suspended in what he called the primary memory of inner speech. He stated that to read is to translate writing into speech. Somewhat later, Vygotsky (1962) also described the relationship of inner speech and thought with virtually the same conclusions.

Huey believed that various cues from the visual fieldwork simultaneously, but unequally, within the neural system to condition perceptual reactions. He borrowed from William Wundt the idea that inner talk, within the system, results in a general impression of the whole context and subsequent words are interpreted within this total idea. Huey borrowed from William James (1890) a description of the "flow of thought" in which a sentence is a conscious unity. Within this stream of consciousness, each word or word part is analyzed in terms of the situational context and an individual's prior experience. Huey thought of contextual reading as predominantly analysis (the relating of separate parts to the conceptual whole), but involving some synthesis (the combining of separate meanings). This emphasis on analytical versus synthetic processing has influenced reading theory to the present.

More than half of Huey's book was devoted to the history of reading methodology and to pedagogy. At least two precautionary statements he made are particularly apt when applying psychological theory in the classroom: (1) Lacking definitive research we are all working toward daylight,and (2) Individual students vary greatly in their experience and in their habits of perceiving and thinking. Huey was caught in the gap between the answers he had found in the laboratory and the immediate questions about how to teach children to read. Like many before and after him, he resorted to history, philosophy, and contemporary opinion to try to fill this gap.

With reference to beginning reading, Huey has been improperly cited as recommending the postponement of reading instruction until 10 (Kolers, 1968). Rather, Huey suggested that the best way for a child to learn to read was in the home by natural methods, including ABC blocks, word–picture dictionaries, illustrated stories, and labels on objects. He encouraged mothers to involve their 4-year-old children in distributing the family mail, writing picture notes, and reading by imitation. However, he disdained the fetish of reading for its own sake in the primary grades and believed in a language experience approach for teaching. Ideally the school would instruct parents in how to use these natural techniques at home. With this kind of parenting, the child could learn to read at home. Huey suggested that the primary schools of the time could be improved by teaching more physical science, oral expression, manual arts, and foreign language.

Older students, according to Huey, should read for intrinsic interest or value of content rather than as an academic exercise. He believed, like Rousseau, that too much book reading prior to the age of logical thinking could mislead the child into believing that whatever was seen in print was true. His own values for the curricula of older students included library skills, extensive exposure to books as opposed to prolonged analyses of literature, and an emphasis on reading as rapidly as a reader could maintain comprehension.

Huey's pedagogy was instrumental in providing the theory from which the reforms of the 1920s and 1930s evolved. The new methodology emphasized experience-based reading and the development of object–symbol relationships rather than teaching children through abstract symbolism. Many of Huey's major ideas survived while many of his proposed techniques did not. His suggestion that children should learn to read whole sentences silently before reading them orally was supposed to result in expressive oral reading. Directions, which could be acted out, were presented on large strips of tagboard in the teacher's cursive writing. This method was used in the mid-1930s by the senior author, but led to a major problem in trying to determine what the other children might be reading silently while Bobby demonstrated "Hop to the coat room door." In order to teach the prescribed sight vocabulary, many contrived and repetitive lessons were required. Furthermore, cursive writing was more difficult for children to read and to write than conventional manuscript. Huey's point that a word is as easy to identify as a letter applies to the visual perception of mature readers and does not characterize the beginner, who is trying to match the sounds of speech to the alphabet. Nevertheless, Huey delineated a content of the psychology of reading which has persisted for four generations.

Psychological Foundations

The study of how individuals learn has been explained from many different perspectives. Some theorists base learning on stimulus–response patterns while others view it as the formation of cognitive structures to represent ideas. Some theorists count the trials and errors that individuals make while solving problems, while others stress insight or the sudden understanding of an idea. E. L. Thorndike bridged the gap between psychologically based research in the laboratory and the application of learning principles in the classroom setting.

THORNDIKE'S THEORY OF CONTIGUITY AND EFFECT

E. L. Thorndike's (1874–1949) contribution to research on learning has had a profound effect on several aspects of reading. He conceptualized two essential elements in learning: *contiguity* and *effect*. According to the theory of contiguity, associations are formed between events because they occur together in time; and according to the theory of effect, associations are learned because of the pleasantness or unpleasantness that results from the activity.

Thorndike (1913) thought of learning as a process of forming bonds between neurons. His explanation of intelligence was that the more bonds that are formed in the brain, the more intelligent the person becomes. He believed schools should help learners systematically increase the number of bonds formed through experience. To apply his ideas to reading instruction, Thorndike and his students developed dictionaries, spellers, and controlled word lists. He believed that words used frequently should be practiced through stimulus–response strategies for which a pleasure effect was desired over a punishment effect. Thorndike's treatise on reading as a reasoning process has impacted definitions of reading and discussions of reading comprehension. His theoretical base was Pavlov's conditioning, although Thorndike understood and researched the chasm between the conditioning of laboratory animals and the complex process of oral communication.

SKINNER'S THEORY OF OPERANT CONDITIONING

In the late 1950s, B. F. Skinner elaborated Thorndike's principles of learning. Skinner (1953) demonstrated how reinforcement of desired behaviors strengthens the likelihood of their reoccurrence. His research with laboratory animals and people indicated that behavior which is not characteristic of the species can be shaped by conditioning. The operant conditioning model he proposed differed from the classical conditioning model proposed by Pavlov. *Classical conditioning* occurs when a stimulus leading to a well-defined response is replaced with a substitute, or conditioned, stimulus. *Operant conditioning* occurs through the reinforcement of a desired response; a repetition of the behavior can be assured over other possible responses to the same stimulus. According to Skinner's theory: (1) A desired response to a stimulus is substituted for an undesired behavior. Classroom management based on this principle would reward a reluctant reader for taking out the book at reading time rather than going to the restroom. (2) Learning results when a positive reinforcer follows immediately after a behavior. Praising a child for recalling a word would enhance subsequent recall. Skinner, in contrast to Thorndike, did not concern himself with neural connections but was concerned with behaviors that could be observed and controlled.

HULL'S MODEL OF SYSTEMATIC LEARNING

Clark L. Hull (1894–1952) was one of the first psychologists to form a comprehensive system of learning which was both behaviorally and empirically based. Although he was opposed to the subjective notion of consciousness, he argued that the physical events within an individual between a stimulus and the subsequent response could be expressed symbolically without losing objectivity. In his most famous text, *Principles of Behavior* (1943), Hull outlined a unique and powerful model to hypothesize what happens between the stimulus and the response. Based on principles of classical conditioning, he developed 16 postulates of how learning occurs. They were outlined in such precise mathematical terms that discrepancies were quickly located and criticized by other behavioral psychologists. Nonetheless, Hull's is one of the most influential theories on the psychology of learning available in this time.

Hull extended Pavlov's classical conditioning hypothesis by adding the concept of habit through reinforcement. He elaborated Thorndike's *Law of Effect*, which indicated that the effects of reward and punishment are not equal and opposite. Hull used a system of positives or reward to explain purposes, insights, and other thought-related skills which the theory of behaviorism had not addressed. In Pavlovian conditioning, where food was followed by a bell to condition a salivation response, Hull explained that the food not only acted to elicit salivation but also acted to satisfy and reward other concurrent responses. The unconditioned stimuli, the food, served as a reward that produced the correct response, salivation, to occur in close contiguity to the conditioned stimuli, the bell. Hull's research indicated that reinforcement could be perceived as a drive-stimulus reduction which satisfies a psychological need. The child's need to succeed in academic skills, in athletics, and in social situations with peers can be viewed in this context.

TOLMAN'S THEORY OF GOAL-DIRECTED BEHAVIOR

Edward C. Tolman (1886–1959) was a behaviorist who reoriented traditional conditioning theory to include human reasoning. He presented perspectives on learning such functions as thinking, planning, inference, and intention. He viewed classical behaviorism as too restricted to encompass all learning. Although he rejected the notion of introspection as a valid technique for psychological research, he acknowledged the necessity of a conceptual process for the interpretation of observed information. Tolman explained behavior as more than the quantified responses of subjects, and urged psychologists to concern themselves with the purpose and intentions behind the individual's behavior. When a disruptive child has broken a rule, the teacher is concerned with intentions rather than with motor descriptions of the actions.

In his major work, *Purposive Behavior in Animals and Men* (1932), Tolman theorized that behavior is goal directed. Memory is based on mental structures he called "cognitive maps," which the organism uses to select the easiest means to a goal. A rat learning a maze, for example, is directed by both external and internal organization and not solely by a conditioned response. In traditional behaviorism, the organism is moved by a simple stimulus–response paradigm, rather than motivated by a goal. According to Tolman, the learner responds to signals in the environment and by their relation to a goal. A number of studies have demonstrated the accuracy of Tolman's ideas. It has been shown that animals: (1) have an expectancy for rewards, (2) do not follow a fixed sequence of motor movements in maze-type experiments, and (3) can learn by exploring a maze in an unstructured setting (Hilgard & Bower, 1975).

Tolman proposed that problem solving is a process in which the learner creates different hypotheses regarding the problem and checks these hypotheses through systematic guessing. His concept of goal-oriented learning was criticized by many who remained loyal to traditional behaviorism. However, Tolman inspired the emergence of cognitive psychology, including a branch of research called information processing. This current line of investigation links thinking processes to a particular definition of reading which emphasizes comprehension as hypothesis testing.

Principles of behaviorism were based originally on laboratory research and were attractive because the learning they described was distinct, observable, and replicable. In attempting to extend behavioral principles to thinking, researchers such as Hull and Tolman were concerned with measuring internal responses. The results and importance of their work has led to theory and research on processes such as habit, intention, and purpose. These psychological events are important to teachers, even though difficult to define under classroom conditions.

Contributions from Educational Psychology

In this section, selected educational psychologists illustrate a generation of researchers who shifted their interests from laboratory settings to study children's reading in the classroom. Taking a different direction from the experimental work of Hull and others, they focused on the acquisition of reading skills such as word recognition and text comprehension. Generally they were professors who taught the psychology of learning to teachers. Often they were involved in campus reading clinics where they saw the reading failures that accrued from the alphabetic teaching methods, still the predominant teaching strategy in 1920, despite the more advanced positions being advocated by E. B. Huey and John Dewey. This generation of researchers applied the principles of Thorndike, who became known as the father of educational psychology. Their research reorganized individual differences among learners but this variability, inherent in educational settings, complicated the application of their results.

WILLIAM S. GRAY (1885–1960)

Gray was an acknowledged expert on reading for four decades beginning in 1922, when his monograph on the diagnosis and treatment of remedial reading cases was published. He began the practice of preparing summaries of reading research, which were published each February in the *Journal of Educational Research* from 1932 until 1960. Gray criticized the tendency among practitioners to alternate from one extreme of emphasizing phonics as an isolated skill to an opposite extreme of expecting children to guess words from context with little regard to their form.

Gray distinguished between what he called *structural analysis,* word attack based on meaning units within words, and *phonic analysis,* word attack based on sound–letter correspondence. He believed in teaching children to be independent in word recognition, while reading primarily for meaning (*On Their Own in Reading,* 1960). UNESCO (United Nations Educational and Scientific Cultural Organization) commissioned Gray to head an international survey of reading methodology as practiced in various countries (Gray, 1956). He concluded that beginning reading was taught throughout the world either by the *analytical method,* teaching meaning units followed by analysis of sound–letter parts, or by the *synthetic method,* teaching letters and sounds followed by combining them into words. He called for a sophistication in reading instruction that integrated word recognition and meaningful context from the earliest stages of learning to read. Gray's definitions remain basic to current discussions on analytical and synthetic methodology (Vacca, Vacca, & Gove, 1987), developmental reading instruction (Durkin, 1980) and clinical treatment of dyslexia adults (Johnson, 1986).

GATES (1890–1972) AND RUSSELL (1906–1965)

Arthur I. Gates viewed reading as a psychological process in which children's early experiences were significantly related to their subsequent interest in reading. He accepted Thorndike's connectionist theory of learning, but his own research compared the broad implications of different teaching methods on a student's habitual response with reading performance. He measured and analyzed long-term interest in reading, progress at different IQ levels, oral versus silent reading achievement, and the relationship of reading methodology to spelling and writing effectiveness (Gates, 1922).

His early studies—well designed even by modern standards—compared the effects of two categories of analytical phonics he called "modern systematic" versus "opportunistic" methods of teaching word recognition. The modern method, implemented in his own program for teachers, began with a meaning emphasis and whole words, followed by systematic instruction in letters and sounds. Opportunistic methods taught phonics incidentally, as prompted by the interests of the children and the requirements of the context. Gates interpreted the data from his numerous studies to suggest that phonics, taught in isolation, was too tedious for the child of average ability and did not transfer well to the comprehension of text material.

David H. Russell became a collaborator with Gates at a time when intensive phonic systems, taught prior to whole words, were being re-emphasized in American pedagogy. To test the effectiveness of phonics as a separate system, Gates and Russell (1938) added a third category of phonics instruction known as *synthetic phonics*. This method emphasized teaching the alphabetic code first, usually letters associated with names and sounds familiar to the children. After the code was mastered, words were built by combining letters (synthesizing) or by forming letter combinations already known. Unlike some investigators, Gates and Russell found that phonics which were functional and integrated into meaningful text (modern systematic) was equal or superior to phonic systems taught in isolation (synthetic phonics) and that both were superior to the look-say approaches (incidental phonics).

Gates continued to believe in an early emphasis on meaning while assuming that the skillful guidance of the teacher was necessary for the average child to form a "habit of seeing a word as a group of familiar parts" (1922, p. 46). He warned against trial-and-error approaches to teaching, against drilling on sounds already known to the child, and against formal exercises taught merely for the sake of the phonic system. For three decades Gates urged teachers to use word analysis functionally, that is, as a means to comprehensive reading and quality writing.

Russell continued to publish his own research. He became the senior author of a popular basal reading series, along with the teachers manuals which accompanied them, and a number of textbooks on reading pedagogy for teachers. His classic book, *Children's Thinking* (1956), was published at a time when philosophers were questioning whether children could reason logically and when most psychologists were giving little attention to human cognition. Russell's book formed the basis for comprehension levels more varied and more advanced than those being taught in most reading programs. He recommended that teachers could improve the thinking processes of children by following a hierarchical sequence of intellectual development: (1) perceptual thinking, (2) associative thinking, (3) concept formation, (4) problem solving, (5) critical thinking, and (6) creative thinking (Fig. 1.1)

MARION MONROE (1898–1983)

Monroe preceded Fernald (1943), Orton (1937), Vernon (1957), and others in using clinical research to establish a relationship between certain behavioral characteristics and reading disability. She conceived of reading aptitude and reading readiness as being similar with respect to constitutional or physiological factors. This innovative line of research has continued to reappear in clinical literature as *developmental*, opposed to *acquired*, reading disability (Pirozzolo & Wittrock, 1981). She distinguished between physiological defects, such as hearing loss or visual impairment, and perceptual problems, such as lack of discrimination for sounds or letters.

Monroe designed a *Reading Aptitude Test* (1937) which was based on data from 415 clinic subjects. It was more comprehensive than many subsequent works designed to test readiness in educational settings. Her visual subtests

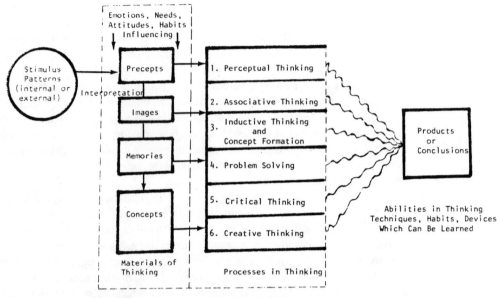

FIGURE 1.1. *Schema for children's thinking. Printed words stimulate linguistic forms which represent concepts already internalized from past experience (From David H. Russell, Children's Thinking, p. 10. Copyright ©️ 1956, Ginn & Company).*

included directional items, ocular-motor control, and memory for complex visual sequences. The auditory tests required the child to match a sound sequence to a picture, to blend sounds into words, and to retell a short story. Fine motor tests included speed and steadiness of hand–eye coordination, and name writing. Language development tests included the reproduction of words that reveal common articulation problems, speed of articulation, naming objects according to class criteria, and sentence length. Lateral dominance and general intelligence were noted and included in the diagnosis. These tests established the use of multiple psychological factors in measuring reading aptitude.

MILES A. TINKER (1893–1977)

Tinker earned his doctorate in psychology and taught introductory courses to undergraduates. While teaching a summer session for educators, he was impressed with their interest in how children learn. This changed the direction of his career toward educational psychology and he began a series of investigations on the psychological bases of reading. He published about 70 articles on visual processing at a time when the devices for photographing eye movements and for timing reading response to print were new. His book, *Legibility of Print* (1963), still remains the handbook of choice for many publishers when designing the format of textbooks.

Tinker's own research was experimentally designed and he was respective of data-based evidence. He was one of the first of his generation to warn that the psychological processes of beginning and proficient readers were different and to suggest that research findings from mature subjects might not apply to young children. During three decades of writing textbooks for teachers and clinicians, he continued to reject a definition of reading as a mere process of changing print into words. To him, reading involved (1) identification and recognition of printed or written symbols which serve as stimuli, (2) recall of meanings built up through experience, and (3) construction of new meanings through the manipulation of concepts already known to the reader.

Considering the depth and breadth of the research generated by these and other educational psychologists it is difficult to understand why such extremes of look-say methodology came to be practiced in many schools from the 1940s to the present time.

Contributions from Psycholinguistics

Psychologists study how people obtain, organize, store, and retrieve knowledge; linguists study the components and production of language. By combining these two disciplines, the field of psycholinguistics describes how language is acquired and expressed. A psychology of language is concerned with three lines of inquiry, each relevant to a psychology of reading: (1) which language abilities are innate, (2) how words relate to one another and to their meanings, and (3) why language disorders occur and how they are treated (Tartter, 1986). Noam Chomsky, still the most influential of linguists, assumed human language to be a creative activity and set about to discover the inherent structure of language, thus rendering it transferable to new expressions and different settings.

CHOMSKY'S IDEAS ON LANGUAGE COMPETENCE

Chomsky formulated a linguistic-oriented theory of language acquisition. Whereas Skinnerian psychology had emphasized the verbal behavior of the speaker, Chomsky was interested in the speaker's intrinsic linguistic abilities. He proposed the existence of universal grammatical rules (syntax) that apply to all human languages, suggesting that everyone is dependent on innate abilities to create coherent speech. In his first book, *Syntactic Structures,* Chomsky (1957) introduced the concept of generative or *transformational* grammar which is a descriptive set of language rules. When systematically applied these rules produce a list of all possible syntactically correct sentences which convey the same thoughts. Chomsky also argued for the independence of syntax and meaning, theorizing that it was possible to discuss the grammatical aspects of language without referring to its semantic content. A refinement of this position resulted in an important new approach which integrated formal grammar and inherent meaning.

In *Aspects of the Theory of Syntax* (1965), Chomsky modified his original theory of language acquisition and constructed what has become known as the Standard Theory. Two new concepts were introduced: *Surface structure* is the relationship between words in a sentence as signaled by syntax. *Deep structure* is the personal interpretation that an individual makes to create meaning from the words in a sentence. Comprehension of what is heard or read occurs when an individual uses prior knowledge or experience (deep structure) to understand the relationship between the words in a sentence (surface structure). Psycholinguists have attempted to determine whether the psychology of Chomsky's theory accounts for competence in oral language and have applied this theory to reading and the instruction of readers.

PSYCHOLINGUISTICS AND READING

During the 1960s and 1970s a number of researchers, analyzed the reading process from the psycholinguistic perspective. Kenneth S. Goodman (1976) popularized a definition of reading that was based on an interaction between thought and language. He referred to reading as a "psycholinguistic guessing game" in which readers use prior information to hypothesize what words will follow and check their guesses according to subsequent text. Proficient readers become skillful in anticipating upcoming print from contextual cues and prior knowledge. Goodman found that disabled readers often do not use context to aid them in identifying words or abstracting meaning. He further suggested that inefficient readers rely too heavily on what he calls grapho/phonic information thus hindering word identification. In Goodman's *Taxonomy of Reading Miscues* (1965), he developed a method of examining reading errors. This taxonomy has been used by many researchers but was found too detailed for practical application in the classroom. Yetta Goodman extended the work of her husband with the *Reading Miscue Inventory Kit* (Goodman & Burke, 1972), which prepared teachers to analyze a reader's strengths and weaknesses through a simplified miscue analysis procedure. She found that young readers typically demonstrate an over-reliance on word-by-word decoding during the early part of their reading development. She hypothesized that this occurred because beginning readers are still learning to coordinate grapho/phonic information with syntactic and semantic information.

Most psycholinguists describe reading as an active process in which the reader interacts with the print through the use of past experience and knowledge of the linguistic system. Phonics is viewed as a cueing system (not a method of reading) which emphasizes word recognition or decoding. Another cueing system is based on the use of context, which is crucial because the meaning of a word can be understood only in relation to surrounding words. A proficient reader uses both syntactic and semantic knowledge to predict upcoming print; phonic cues are used next to eliminate choices between semantically similar words; and finally, context is used again to confirm or reject an individual's prediction.

Weaver (1980) designated some essential components to be implemented in a reading program. These psycholinguistic components are: (1) language experience, (2) immersion, (3) sustaining silent reading, (4) sharing the reading experience, and (5) reading for a specific purpose. The language experience component allows young readers to create their own reading material in order to understand the principle that speech be written. The immersion component has the child read aloud with the teacher, visit the library, and follow printed lines while others read aloud. A crucial aspect of immersion is that the child works with the whole story and not just parts of it. Sustaining silent reading refers to allocating regular class time to silent reading. Sharing the reading experience occurs regularly as students present book reports, poems, and articles, not only through writing, but also through dramatization, demonstration, and drawing. "Reading for a specific purpose" teaches how to vary rate in accordance with the information being sought. Most psycholinguists stress that reading is a communication process. From the child's perspective, the emphasis is understanding the author's message; from the teacher's perspective the emphasis is the student use of both syntactic and semantic knowledge to comprehend the message.

Others besides Chomsky have noted that Skinner's emphasis on observable environmental phenomena fails to consider and explain important observations of language acquisition. (1) Language is species-specific (Brown, 1973; Gleitman, 1986). (2) Children read language milestones at approximately the same ages in many different cultures (Slobin, 1982). (3) Environmental stimulation of language remains relatively stable as individuals mature, but they respond to these same stimuli differently and in accordance with periods of cognitive development from birth to adolescence (Piaget, 1959; Vygotsky, 1962). (4) Language depends on lateralization of the brain hemispheres, indicating a biological basis of linguistic development (Lenneberg, 1967; Best, 1985).

Evidence from Neuroscience

Knowing how the brain processes language is basic to the psychology of reading and learning to read (Fig. 1.2). Brain research has implications for most of the outstanding issues in reading instruction, including the relationship of reading to speaking, the interaction of language and thought in comprehension, and the distinction between poor reading and dyslexia. A knowledge of how the brain is organized to process language reveals that reading is an extension of speech. Printed words seen by the reader are encoded in the visual reception areas, then travel to the auditory areas where the meanings of language are stored. Writing follows reading in linguistic complexity and developmental sequence.

Another line of investigation involves the activities of the neural cells: how they migrate and interconnect during development, how they elaborate in learning, and how they are activated during communication. An internal event, once seen as a psychological process beyond the scrutiny of researchers, has come to be understood as biochemical change in the neural system. Although neuropsychology may seem far removed from the reading lesson, the implications from brain research help clinicians and teachers consider such questions as: How does direct instruction result in learning? Why is attention necessary for long-term retention? What are the neural processes of visual and auditory perception? Is there an optimal age for learning to associate phonemes and graphemes? How do students remember what they read? Neuroscience may not answer questions of methodology directly, but the dialogue among practitioners can take place at a more informed level than without such a background.

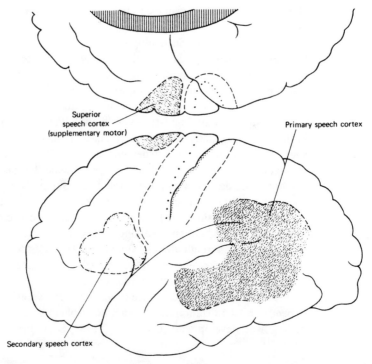

Superior
speech cortex
(supplementary motor)

Primary speech cortex

Secondary speech cortex

FIGURE 1.2. *Language areas of the left hemisphere. Primary speech cortex called Wernicke's area, interprets speech signals. Secondary speech cortex, called Broca's area, directs speech production. Superior speech cortex initiates and coordinates motor functions of the two hemispheres (From W. Penfield & L. Roberts, Speech and Brain Mechanisms, p. 201. Copyright © 1959, Princeton University Press).*

READING AS A LANGUAGE PROCESS

Historically the evidence that language is stored and processed in specific areas of the brain came from the loss of speech, reading, or writing functions in brain-injured patients. As early as the mid-19th century, Pierre–Paul Broca, a surgeon, reported the loss of speech in two patients who both had experienced damage to the same location in the frontal left hemisphere. Two decades later Carl Wernicke separated the functions of speaking and of understanding speech when he located the language interpretation area in the parietal lobe of the left hemisphere; which came to be known as dominant for language. Those exceptional individuals whose right hemisphere is dominant for language were identified much later (Corballis & Beale, 1976).

Clinical Evidence of Brain Organization

Luria created a neuropsychology, probably the first, when he published a model of the integrated brain, based on clinical data from about 200 brain-injured soldiers of World War II. In *The Working Brain* (1973) he reported the results of psychological tests for observing changes in language during therapy. He also studied intellectual activity by analyzing the EEG patterns from an array of electrodes placed on the scalp of patients. By combining surgical and psychological data, he described the functional units of the brain; how they interact to achieve perception and how visual, auditory, and tactile information are integrated.

The speech comprehension area, discovered a century earlier by Wernicke, also has a major role in reading comprehension. By using a painless technique to stimulate the exposed cortical tissues of a conscious patient during surgery, the cortex has been mapped reliably (Penfield & Roberts, 1959). The locations for receiving and processing visual, auditory, and somatic information in the cortex were isolated and their integration while reading from word cards was observed. Geschwind (1974) reported such interesting discoveries as where the recognition of faces occurs, where sensory experiences are templated for long-term memory, and where names of objects are filed. Despite a century or more of clinical experience, the correlation between brain anatomy and specific language disorders has not been widely accepted until recently (Benson, 1982).

Technology for Observing Brain Activity

Recent technology has enabled researchers to study a healthy, normal brain while performing such tasks as naming, reading, and thinking. By injecting a radioactive isotope into the bloodstream, the level of blood flow (which is closely related to brain activity) can be detected and located in a particular cortical area. The procedure called rCBF meaning *regional cerebral blood flow,* utilized an array of 254 detectors placed near the subject's scalp, each capable of scanning one square centimeter of cortical surface. A computer established the resting state of each location, then compared blood flow under test conditions and presented the change in color on a TV screen. High activity was projected as yellows and reds; low activity was shown in greens and blues. When the subject listened to a series of spoken words, the auditory reception and speech comprehension areas of the left hemisphere appeared in orange, pink, and yellow. When the subject read silently, the visual association areas, the frontal eye field, the supplementary motor area, and the speech production area were activated (Lassen, Ingvar, & Skinhj, 1978). Other versions of the rCBF are the PET and the PETT (positron-emission transaxial tomograpy). Improved procedures, including the sniffing of a radioactive gas to replace injection, has enabled researchers to produce a series of precise images during one experimental session (Marshall, 1988).

A new, sophisticated monitor, the CSA (compressed spectral array), uses a computer to analyze EEG frequencies and to project the results in 3 dimensions on a TV screen. The subject's immediate response to language stimuli can be observed (Diagram Group, 1982). The BEAM (brain electrical activity mapping) detects evoked responses to visual and auditory stimuli, averages these potentials by computer, and produces a visual display of neural activity. The BEAM, a noninvasive and painless technique, has been used to study handedness patterns in child dyslexics and in normal readers.

Another class of monitors are the computer assisted scanners which analyze repeated x-ray beams and project an image of brain tissue density. The CT (computerized tomography) and the CAT (computerized axial tomography) are considered to have acceptable levels of radiation for purposes of research on healthy adults. The technique has been used to determine brain asymmetry in dyslexics and in controls. The CAT provides better images of deep brain structures than the CT because it beams a rotation over 180° of the head. A new device, the DSR (dynamic spatial reconstruction) uses multiple x-ray guns to produce 15,000 takes per second, providing a 3-dimensional TV image of an active brain within a controlled sensory environment. Although different laboratories have produced extensive data, the different techniques and devices lack standardization. This causes difficulty for the consumer of the research when comparing results across studies. The cumulative knowledge, however, is impressive.

DEVELOPMENTAL DELAY AND READING

An impressive body of literature has been published on the biological correlates of reading disability in schoolchildren. When children who lack reading skills are identified in large numbers, they can be grouped for differential diagnosis. Pirozzolo and Wittrock (1981) eliminated subjects whose difficulties were explained by factors such as inadequate instruction, below normal intelligence, visual or auditory defects, and sociocultural handicaps. The remaining subjects, became an experimental group labeled "developmental reading disorders." These children were distinct from individuals who had acquired a reading disability through accident or trauma. Subjects with developmental reading disorders showed abnormal responses to a number of neurological tests. Such a diagnosis is extremely useful to a teacher when planning instruction that is responsive to the child's particular characteristics and strengths (Goldberg, Shiffman, & Bender, 1983).

The responsible use of neuropsychological knowledge in school programs has been discussed by Gaddes (1981). Neurological examinations, administered in conjunction with selected psychological tests, reveal strengths and weaknesses in cognitive functioning which are significant in reading instruction. Gaddis estimated that 2% to 3% percent of boys and less than 1% of girls of the school population are developmentally delayed in ways that affect reading.

AN EXTENDED DEFINITION OF READING

A psychology of reading incorporates the affective as well as the cognitive dimensions of language. Nonverbal signs are read at an earlier age than the symbols that appear in print. Young children read picture books and comic strips before they are able to read the words that accompany them. Teachers read the mood of the school principal from body language. Pupils read their teachers, using signals such as posture tension, pace energy, and voice level. Carpenters read blueprints that tell how a house will be constructed. Operators of earth-moving machinery read stakes and flags that tell which mountains to slice and which valleys to fill. All reading uses symbolic representation of reality situations. Reading, as taught in school, is part of a communication sequence that begins with the emotional utterances of infants and develops into a complex lexicon of spoken and written English.

Reading the Emotions of Others

Mothers learned to read the cry signals emitted by their infants whereas other young women could not (Sagi, 1981). John B. Watson found that graduate students in his university—who at the time were unmarried—could not distinguish a pain cry from a rage cry unless they could see the stimulus. Their inability was interpreted to mean that there was no difference in the communication (Watson & Morgan, 1917). Subsequently, it has been found that mothers learn to ignore rage cries, but run to help when they hear a pain cry. Aural discrimination occurs as little differences are noted and associated with the condition parents find when they check the infant.

Very young children learn to read the emotional climate generated by their caregivers. Glaser and Eisenberg (1956), in discussing maternal deprivation, pointed out the effectiveness with which infants come to read their mother's disinterest and to generalize this disinterest to other people. Fantz (1966) demonstrated that during early infancy the visual environment is restricted to near-point accommodation. The neonate's vision is most effective at a distance of 9–12 inches, which enables them to see the facial cues of caregivers. This near-point accommodation assures that the infant will associate visual cues with auditory cues of voice and kinesthetic cues of fondling. The social significance of a smile, which is associated with caressing and a gentle voice, builds a foundation for future interpretation of nonverbal cues.

A significant motivational situation, where children often read emotional responses that are not intended for their viewing, is the start of formal reading. Students who do well get positive reinforcement from the nonverbal signs of their teachers, but not all children are successful. If the teacher thinks, albeit silently, "Oh, another slow one," or "I knew he wasn't ready," the emotional reading by the child is one of nonapproval. Because of the increased tension and nervousness, the child may make unnecessary mistakes, causing the teacher to feel unsuccessful and lowering the spiral of self-expectancy on the part of both. The teacher must be in a position to give honest praise for successful accomplishment, if necessary by arranging learning steps that are small and possible. The alternative to finding a bridge to satisfaction in beginning reading is to perpetuate failure and self-doubt. Teachers rarely show obvious tension, however most adults hide their displeasure more completely when they are working with other adults than when they are working with children.

Language Symbols in the Child's Environment

The first incidental reading learned by many toddlers results from their attention to television, particularly the commercials. A good TV ad is short, having one central message that is usually vocalized while visual cues spell out the name of the product. Young children learn many of these messages by contiguity without any conscious effort on their part.

Sesame Street, a production of public television, introduces prereading skills to preschool, inner-city children. These daily programs accomplish learning by sharp delineation of content, repetition of associations in many contexts, and varied presentation of auditory and visual stimuli. Songs, rhythms, stories, puppetry, and direct instruction are used to teach letter names, beginning sounds, number meanings, and vocabulary. The child's attention is held by rapid pacing and a variety of communicators. An independent evaluation of *Sesame Street* showed the effectiveness of educational television in several ways: (1) Children who watched the most, learned the most. (2) Skills that received the most time and attention on the programs were most often the skills that were learned. (3) Although formal adult supervision was not necessary it enhanced learning (Bogatz & Ball, 1971). Additional conclusions drawn from the study included evidence of transfer of learning to reading itself. Three-year-old children gained the most and 5-year-olds gained the least, suggesting that preschool children are able to learn many skills that traditionally have been introduced in the first grade.

Recent developments in the computer industry have created a new information system that is affordable by many parents. The role that microcomputers will play as young children learn prereading skills is speculative. Although the value and use of computers in producing arcade-style games may be educationally suspect, an abundance of software specifically geared to teaching academic skills is being created. These educational activities come with full color, graphics, and sound. They are aimed at teaching writing, vocabulary, and spelling. The stimulation and immediate feedback that this media provides may be an important component in reading acquisition.

DISCRIMINATION LEARNING IN THE PRESCHOOL

Before learning to read the child must understand that the print of books stands for the same sequence of meaning units that occur in linear speech. The early stages of reading are primarily the matching of print with the words already used in conversation. The conditioning that links the spoken word to the printed symbol on television or in a story book can start the process of discriminating words and their parts. Durkin (1966) found that many children who arrived at school already reading came from homes where parents or older siblings had given favorable attention to the child's spontaneous efforts to pick out words and letters in reading material.

Some investigators believe the *visual discriminations* on which reading is built are expedited by learning the names of the letters before much effort goes into developing a sight vocabulary for words. Gavel (1958) found that in a schoolyear the ability to name letters in September was more highly correlated with reading achievement in June than was mental age. DeHirsch, Jansky, and Langford (1966) found that lack of letter-naming ability was predictive of reading failure. The value to the learner of knowing letter names even when letter names and letter sounds are not identical, appears to be critical in the early stages of reading (Walsh, Price, & Gillingham, 1988).

Another skill basic to learning to read, and one that has not always been emphasized at the prereading level, is the ability to discriminate the sound parts of words. Murphy (1943) reported that exercises designed to develop *auditory discrimination* in young children eliminated the superiority usually found in girls over boys in beginning reading efficiency. Diack (1960) found that discrimination was also enhanced when children were given letter names that enabled them to add an aural discrimination to a visual one. Brady, Shankweiler, & Mann (1983) reported a significant relationship between auditory perception and reading ability. From associations of visual and auditory clues, the child discovers, or conceptualizes, that speech is made up of sound units or words.

The conceptualization that letters and their order are invariate in words is basic to beginning reading. Todd, at age 2½, happily wrote long letters to his grandmother scribbling continuous lines from left to right across the page until it was filled. He insisted these "letters" be mailed. Later he began filling the page with letters placed randomly. At Christmas time he became aware that packages under the tree were specifically designated by labels. He also learned that the name beginning with T was Todd. However, when he mistook "TO DADDY" for TODD, he was energetically corrected by an older sibling. This was his first step in the critical discovery that a particular letter sequence makes a particular word. The format of his letters to grandmother changed again, as he asked how to write words. Todd had conceptualized the invariate structure of words. To do this he must have: (1) discriminated the letters of his name as distinct entities; (2) learned that a group of letters TODD represented himself; and (3) distinguished his name from other words that were similar in appearance. When children do not learn these basic ideas at home or in preschool, they must learn them after arriving at school and before progress in word identification is possible.

DEFINITION OF DECODING

Decoding is the process of translating letter symbols into comprehensible language. Beginning reading, which is primarily learning to decode, is difficult if the words being used are not known in speech. Even when the spoken words are understood, the child must proceed through three steps: (1) the discrimination and identification of each visual unit, (2) the association of correct sound elements with each visual part, and (3) the blending of sound parts to arrive at known words. A variation of this process is used by mature readers when they decode a word that is unfamiliar in speech. The difficulty of the transition from decoding to fluent reading has been overlooked by some mature readers because they see words or parts of words as wholes and may assume that children see them in the same way. During the transitional stage of reading, the child is exposed to basic vocabulary many times, so that words automatically become recognized in units. This fluent stage is the process most people think of as reading, but it is during the early phases, when the skill of recognizing words as wholes is being acquired that many disabilities in reading are created.

IRREGULARITIES AND MULTIPLE MEANINGS

The English language is not easily mastered, partly because linguistic irregularities arise to plague the beginning reader. Despite these hurdles, young children between the ages of 2 and 4 master the grammatical constructions of spoken English. During the acquisition of speech, children form tentative rules or principles of grammar that subsequently are applied when talking (Moskowitz, 1973). Michael, almost 3, generalized that the past tense of a verb is formed by adding "ed." He said, "I goed to the Safeway." His mother imitated, but at a level which recognized the irregular verb. "Yes. Sweetie, you went to the Safeway." The next time he used this construction, he said, "We wented to the store." This, too, was corrected. Apparently children learn the irregularities of syntax on a one-to-one, or association, basis. The persistence of young children and their need to communicate enable them to struggle through this maze of English syntax to master oral language.

Irregularities in the phoneme–grapheme system are one kind of distractor encountered by readers. The graphemes of written communication, which represent the phonemes of speech, are the basic units a reader transcribes when decoding. In English, the regular, or predictable, correspondences between phonemes and graphemes outnumber the irregularities. However, [c] can be like /k/ as in cow, or like [s] as in cent. Unfortunately, many variations cannot be eliminated from meaningful reading because they comprise a common service vocabulary, dating from an Anglo-Saxon or French heritage, when words were spoken differently and spelled the way they were spoken. These discrepancies cause noise in the translation, making it difficult for the learner to formulate a system that is reliable. Unless the teacher helps the child to learn sound–symbol relationships and then to identify inconsistencies, beginning readers must try to build their own system of rules. Many children find the task unmanageable, particularly if the adult models assume that the recognition of word configurations must always precede the discrimination of the parts. Although young children may be engaging in a form of reading when the labels on a package of cereal are recognized, they cannot enter the world of books until they can decode.

Teachers can help children avoid frustration by anticipating the dual function of certain graphemes and the alternate translations. To pursue the previous example, the /k/ in cow and the /s/ in cent are both predictable sounds if one considers the neighboring vowel. The teacher should know the code-breaking sequence well enough to decide when the learner needs to take the step that predicts whether the "hard" or "soft" sound is correct. An essential understanding for the child is that some graphemes systematically represent more than one sound.

A distraction for both readers and speakers is the multiple meaning of words. Adults read common words such as "buy" or "by" and automatically select the correct meaning from context clues. The child who is beginning to read has fewer associations and less flexibility in moving from one meaning to another than mature readers who have learned multiple uses of words. Building concepts such as homonyms, antonyms, and synonyms can ease confusion between words with multiple meanings. Oral word games, played at home or in school, can make the exploration of word meanings a pleasurable experience. Christopher's family enjoyed a game of "Stink Pink," which they played endlessly when touring.

Anyone who had an idea could lead off: "Who can give a stink pink that means an *obese feline?*" The one who guessed *fat cat* got the next turn to ask a rhyming riddle. Unique and difficult rhymes were appreciated by everyone: an intelligent frijole (keen bean), and expiring animal (dyin' lion), or a home for Mickey (mouse house). Because words have multiple meanings, the reader must use context to clarify what specific meaning is being conveyed by the author.

Distinctions between Beginning and Proficient Reading

Young children, for whom mere recognition of words is an accomplishment, must focus their energy on decoding. Singer (1970) analyzed the factors that accounted for individual variability in reading power at intermediate grades, high school, and college levels. He reported that perceptual processes tend to decrease in their relative importance as children progress through the grades, while meaning factors become more significant. Skills which beginning readers need are the following: recognizing sounds in words, structural analysis, and visual-verbal meanings. In older students factors such as vocabulary, intelligence, and fluency in making analogies are positively correlated with reading power. Although Singer tested subjects of different ages, rather than changes in the same subjects over a period of time, his work supports the hypotheses that mental processing differs in unskilled and mature readers. In a discussion of the implications, Singer rejected the idea of teaching beginning reading purely on a decoding basis. Rather, reading is a multidimensional activity requiring affective, motivation, physiological, perceptual, linguistic, and cognitive components. He later concluded that reading instruction is inadequate if one of these components is overemphasized at any level (Singer, 1984).

INHERENT REINFORCEMENTS IN READING

Many people believe that reading, even from the beginning, should be rewarding through the information gained. Although the neophyte experiences satisfaction from a mastery of decoding, payoff from the content is important if skill development beyond simple word recognition is to continue. Most children pass the decoding level of involvement quickly and need to progress to independent, interpretive reading in order to maintain self-motivation.

Comprehension tasks differ according to the purpose of the reader. Purposes vary when the reader looks for a sign marked EXIT, glances through the comics, enjoys a novel, or studies abstract ideas in a textbook. Highly sophisticated skills, as well as motivation, are needed to learn the structure of a neuron or the solution of a quadratic equation. The more complex the task, the more the reader must give of his personal experience, beyond the skills of decoding, to find utility in reading. The materials that students find inherently rewarding must have personal relevance. Most people seek reading situations to expand their private worlds, bringing their fears, hopes, and aspirations into focus. Empathy and understanding are increased by identifying with the character in books. Nostalgic adults may wish in vain for their youngsters to enjoy the same classics they remember, but present-day children may not relate to a world view that is gone. Today's books need to capture and extend the interests of today's children.

LEVELS OF COMPREHENSION

During efficient reading, literal and higher-level comprehension processes occur as written discourse is decoded. LaBerge and Samuels (1974) explained the relationship between decoding and comprehension through a model of automatic information processing. Since reading consists of decoding and comprehension, hypothetically the reader's attention is divided between them. According to this processing model, readers first decode print and then switch their attention to comprehension. Samuels and Eisenberg (1981) make the analogy that this switching process is similar to the case of a student learning a foreign language who must first translate the words, then reread the passage for meaning. Shifting from decoding to comprehension can be time consuming and demands full attention, particularly from beginning readers. Experienced readers, theoretically, decode words automatically and give maximum attention to comprehension. Students who enter the middle and secondary schools still reading poorly may find that integrating the tasks of decoding and comprehension of new subject matter exceeds their capacity to internalize the content.

High-level comprehension processes are closely related to memory processes; most methods measuring comprehension rely on some form of memory task. Samuels and Eisenberg cite recent research indicating that memory occurs as a network of *nodes* and *links,* terms from cognitive psychology. Each node represents a concept which is linked to a large number of other nodes. For example, the concept *dog* includes information common to canines such as their being warm-blooded, feeding their young milk, and walking on four legs. Dog is also linked to features of mammals, such as ears, eyes, and teeth. Concepts usually can be clarified through a network of information stored in long-term memory. *Schemata* (plural for schema) is the term used by cognitive psychologists to represent their notion of memory structures in storage.

Apparently readers do not directly recall everything they have read but actively synthesize incoming information with prior knowledge to form integrated ideas. Proficient readers use schemata to create a framework onto which incoming information is received and stored. The closure, or "aha" experience, when a reader finally grasps a complex idea, occurs as a match is made between a textual thesis and concepts available from personal experiences. High-level comprehension processes depend on an examination of the relationship between linguistic input, prior experience, and the reconstruction of memory when recalling and interpreting what has been read (Bartlett, 1932; Mandler & Johnson, 1977).

A Functional Definition of Reading

What is meant by reading depends on who is using the term and in what context. Erika, 2 years and 4 months old, thinks of herself as "reading" when she turns the pages of a magazine while naming the pictures for herself. Children in reading clinics tend to be quite definitive about the situations in which they "can read" and avoid those in which they have trouble. College students who seek help in reading improvement centers may refer to themselves as "slow readers" but rarely do they call themselves nonreaders. Yet the term nonreader persists in the media, in the literature, and in teacher's rooms with reference to individuals who are unable to function at the levels specified by the curriculum.

READERS AND NONREADERS

Teachers are prone to define readers and nonreaders in terms of their ability to read the material assigned. To the philosophy professor the student cannot read if he is unable to interpret Sartre's *Existentialism*. Middle-school teachers may refer to children who are unable to handle grade-level materials as nonreaders, rather than to determine the readability of the material the student *can* comprehend. The primary teacher is likely to consider the child a nonreader if he or she is unable to work with the slowest reading group. In these and similar situations the teacher defines reading as the child's ability to function in a predefined curriculum.

Students define reading in terms of their own success, which is personal and may be quite different from the definition professionals use. A definition of reading is needed that enables the teacher to communicate with students about their reading progress in a language that avoids the dichotomous and demeaning terminology of reading versus nonreading. The definition should recognize the reader's own purpose as basic to achievement. If teachers can help students define the task to be accomplished, then they can assume much of the responsibility for their own growth.

DEFINITIONS BY EXPERTS

Authorities on the teaching of reading, like students, define reading according to their individual orientations. Stauffer (1969) reviewed numerous descriptions of the reading process and reported universal agreement among authorities on one point only: Comprehension is an invariant condition of reading. However, Reed (1970) disagreed that reading necessarily involved understanding. While repudiating the whole word, or meaning, approach to beginning reading, his definition may seem nearly incomprehensible. "Reading is the identification of linguistic forms from strings of written configurations that represent them, as evidenced by producing the conventional signs for the same linguistic forms in some other system of representation" (pp. 222–223). By this definition it is possible to transliterate language from one form (print) to another (speech) without meanings being known to the reader. By contrast, Carroll expresses the view of most experts on reading when he identifies the "*essential* skill in reading as getting meaning from a printed or written message" (1970a, p. 296).

Some writers have defined reading as interpreting a sequence of cognitive events. Huey (1908) conceptualized a more holistic process, suggesting that when psychologists are able to analyze completely what we do when reading, the most intricate workings of the human mind will be understood. He viewed reading as a reasoning process in which the reader learns and practices accuracy of thought, good judgment, and a feeling of values. Although he thought of the reader as acquiring mental discipline quite directly from the author, rather than constructing his own conceptual framework, Huey grasped the complexity of the reading–thinking relationship and the importance of values as a basis for reading.

Russell (1956) emphasized the prior concepts which the reader brought to the reading process as basic to the interpretations that would be made. To him the comprehension sequence proceeds from *concept formation* to *linguistic form* to *printed words*. Reading was defined as a conceptualized response to a printed word stimulus, emphasizing the importance of associations and conceptualizations within the reader, rather than within the writer of the materials (Fig. 1.1).

Some educational psychologists consider reading a form of problem solving that is learned in much the same way concepts are acquired. According to Stauffer (1970a), reading is an active cognitive process of "seeking relationship to, differentiating from, and reconciling with" existing ideas. "The efficient reader reads with purpose, abstracts information, tests its value, and then accepts or rejects his hypothesis" (p. 135). Bruner, Goodnow, and Austin (1956) and Byers (1961) also expressed the view that thinking and reading strategies are comparable. Goodman (1976) described the act of reading as a selective process in which the reader's own perceptual images and language meanings make up a complex of anticipations that result in hypothesis testing. These definitions refer to readers who have basic word recognition skills and who have achieved sufficient independence to employ context consistency.

Jack A. Holmes (1970), who believed that improvement in teaching depends on a scientific understanding of the reading process, devoted most of his professional life to answering what he considered the basic questions: Just how complex is this ability we call reading? What are its dimensions? How do they operate? He and his research associates isolated many of the significant elements in normal reading through a technique of factorial analysis. Their definition, which evolved from this research, reflects the complexity they observed.

> Reading is an audio-visual verbal-processing skill of symbolic reasoning, sustained by the interfacilitations of an intricate hierarchy of substrata factors that have been mobilized as a psychological working system and pressed into service in accordance with the purposes of the reader. (Holmes & Singer, 1961)

Many authorities were not sufficiently sophisticated to understand the wording of the Holmes–Singer definition and eventually Singer was pressed into giving an explanation in simpler language:

> In reading along a particular sentence, a reader must *retrieve and mobilize systems for recognizing words* and phrases, next *link the recognized words* or phrases *to their corresponding meanings,* and subsequently *utilize various cognitive processes* for inferring, interpreting, and inductively or deductively *arriving at conclusions* or solutions to problems. (1970, p. 157)

The three steps in this process are similar to those described much earlier by Tinker (1952) but reflect a sophisticated knowledge of the reading process accumulated during nearly 20 years of research.

The Holmes substrata-factor theory incorporates a neurological explanation (1957), a statistical description, and a psychological model (1960). He ascribed the uniqueness of readers to differences in neurobiological development, in intellectual organization of related past learning, and in the methodology by which they had been taught to read as children. Holmes stressed the significance of a meaningful sequence of association and conceptualization activities in organizing a classroom lesson. He also understood the private nature of the "mobilizers," which he defined as "deep-seated value systems . . . that the individual holds of himself, and his developing relationship to the environment" (p. 188). He was one of the earliest experts on reading to link functionally the neural organization of the brain to motivation patterns. The Holmes conception of reading as a complex neurophychological process is a useful construct for communication among professionals.

These definitions by experts, selected from hundreds available, indicate a focus, during the 1950s into the 1980s, on reading as a mediation process controlled by semantic-symbolic content emerging from the reader's own motivation when confronting a written message. Current authorities differ in the importance they attribute to comprehension as a criterion behavior, in the context to which they relate reading and linguistics, and in the sophistication of their conception of learning. Most descriptions of the reading process assume a good reader with an unspecified but considerable repertoire of words available, rather than a child in the stages of acquiring word recognition skills. A definition is needed that encompasses reading at all stages by focusing on the learners themselves.

DEFINITION OF READING: A SUMMARY

Reading is a process of translating signs and symbols into meanings and incorporating the new information into existing cognitive and affective structures. Individuals define reading in private ways, depending on the level of functioning and their purpose for reading. Each of the steps in becoming an accomplished reader would be considered reading by a learner who has never experienced the later stages. The teacher's understanding of how students define reading is basic to helping them progress.

Symbolic reading starts with the discrimination of labels and proceeds with the accumulation of many similar labels until further word recognition skills become necessary. The beginning reader combines analytical and synthetic cognition processes in learning to decode. Independence and fluency are possible when the reader has learned to use several strategies for recognizing words: context clues, structural analysis, phonic analysis, and the dictionary. Reading diverse materials gives the student practice in the analysis of meanings and the synthesis of divergent sources. When reading and productive thinking become integrated, the skill achieved and the satisfaction gained provide the motivation to continue.

Purpose and Organization of the Book

The purpose of this book is to help clinicians, reading specialists, and others interested in the bases of literacy to improve their knowledge and professional capacity. Because of an increased understanding of the psychological processes involved they should be better able: (1) develop techniques that build motivation and reduce reading failure, (2) design curricula that emphasize interpretive reading from the beginning, and (3) identify the strengths and needs of each reader in order to create psychologically appropriate sequences.

Part I reviews the historical foundation of a psychology of reading, defines reading from an extended perspective, and presents a learning-motivation model which incorporates major theories of reinforcement and self-direction. Part II shifts to the cognitive components of reading with three chapters on the relationship of reading to language acquisition, the impact of memory and intelligence on reading, and cognitive strategies of individuals. Part III describes the brain functions of reading and reading disabilities. Part IV is concerned with interpreting the instruments of psychological testing and reading diagnosis. Part V relates the learning-motivation theory, presented in Chapter 2, to instruction. The final chapter is about creative readers who would turn their thinking into writing.

2 | Motivation for Reading

Reading processes vary in complexity from the simplest decoding of one-syllable words to a reader's own interpretations of discourse. Reading is affectively loaded with feelings of wonder, surprise, admiration, or dismay. Far too many students have suffered the difficulties of initial reading without the magic that efficient reading releases. When the relationship of pleasurable experience and motivation to read are clear, the cognitive progression from decoding to enjoying literature will seem less formidable to teachers and pupils alike.

A LEARNING-MOTIVATION MODEL

Some years ago, when the differences that separated cognitive psychologists and Skinnerian behaviorists were causing frustration for their students, Wilson, Robeck, and Michael (1969) created a model which placed in relationship the most enduring concepts of learning and of motivation. Their purpose was to help future teachers acquire the techniques of motivation building (from behaviorist psychology), while retaining the upward thrust of human cognition and language learning (from cognitive psychology). The national goals for education, in the aftermath of Soviet space accomplishments, were that students become creative, productive, and inventive. The learning-motivation model incorporates these different pieces of psychological diversity into a working construct. The model is concise enough to be carried around in a teacher's head while planning lessons, interacting with students, and solving problems.

Definition of Learning

Learning is a by-product of an organism's attempt to meet its needs. Each response to a need involves integrated neural activity, which is recorded as a neural pattern, thus modifying the neural system to some extent. These changes in the central nervous system alter the subsequent responses of the individual. An example of the complex interaction of needs is Tony's first day at a new school. He has a need to satisfy his father's expectation that he become a good reader. **29** Another need is to win the respect of the other kids in the class. An opposing need is to allay his fear by running home at recess. Amid these conflicting needs he must decide whether to raise his hand at reading time or sit very still, hoping the teacher will not call on him. If he reads well enough to fulfill his own expectations, several needs may be satisfied, including the dissipation of fear. Whether he decides to withdraw or to participate, he has changed in ways that will affect his future decision making.

Learning is the concomitant of the process of attempting to meet different, and even conflicting, needs. When the result of a choice is satisfying, a connection is made to the neural centers of the brain where pleasure affects are generated. The extra circuit through the pleasure structures tends to ensure that the response pattern will operate again when the same stimulus situation occurs. The student who succeeds in attacking new and bigger words finds pleasure in this new competence and may also strengthen a cognitive strategy of word recognition. When the original response fails, no pleasure circuit is established. In some situations a punishment connection may be established instead, strengthening the tendency toward avoidance or retreat. When a stimulus situation arises that once was punished, a new and different need may be chosen for gratification.

Motivation, like other patterns of behavior, is learned. If students can be motivated, they can be taught. If not, schoolwork is a burden to them and to the teacher as well. The motivated learner becomes self-directing. Motivation is related to attitudes, incentives, and the developing personality. The learning-motivation model maps the interaction between cognitive and affective learning, outlines the steps that will eventuate in a motivated student, and explains the relationship of pleasure to motivation and future cognitive learning.

Levels of Learning

Learning changes the individual as a person and thus changes his or her perception of the world. At the same time, the change in the person makes further learning of the same kind more likely. Humans learn to learn; often by reading. The processes take place at different levels, depending on the presentation of the material, the prior knowledge of the learner, and the motivational strength of the individual for the task. Pleasure reading may be an end in itself and engage the reader at level one functioning. Study reading, on the other hand, may require higher levels of learning (Fig. 2.1).

LEVEL 1: ASSOCIATION

All initial learning consists in the formation of associations, including the *classical conditioning* investigated by Pavlov (1927) and the *operant conditioning* described by Skinner (1953). Most stimulus–response (S–R) learning, which represents nearly all experimental evidence, comes under the rubric of association learning. Most instruction in learning to read is on an association basis. Phoneme–grapheme correspondence, word recognition, and literal comprehension are usually presented as skills to be learned by association. This level of reading is more easily tested and graded than more complex forms. Factual material presented in lectures is often absorbed and recalled by association. Most attitudes are learned by association.

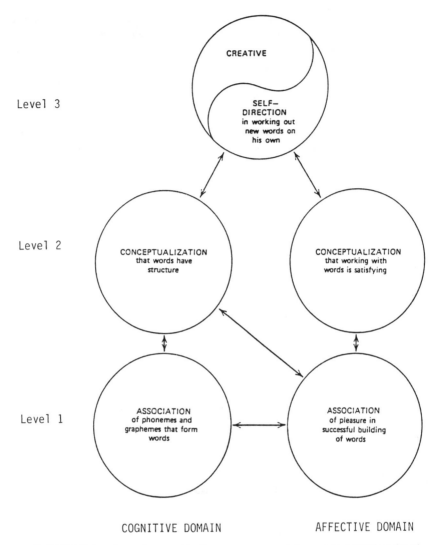

FIGURE 2.1. Learning-motivation processes at the code-breaking level.

Cognitive Associations

Level one learning is the addition of bits of experience, knowledge, or awareness to an existing chain of information or sensitivities. When two sensory events occur together in time, they tend to become associated by a linkage that occurs within the brain (Kendler & Kendler, 1962). When one of the events is remembered, the associated experience also may be recalled. The visual symbol **B** is called by its auditory name, **bee**, and either stimuli can recall the other. The neural connection of two sensory events seems to require nothing more than that they occur together in time, although several such associations may be necessary before recall occurs easily.

The psychological linkage or connection of events that occur together is called *association by contiguity in time.* Pavlov's classical experiments, in which bell ringing and meat powder were linked in the brains of laboratory dogs to produce salivation with bell ringing, are familiar. Watson and Morgan (1917) manipulated the environments of their child subjects to condition emotions, as well as cognitive learning. E. L. Thorndike (1913), who proposed the Law of Associative Shifting, explained: "A response may shift from one situation to anther which is presented at the same time." This law is demonstrated when the child learns sight vocabulary by presenting a picture and a word together. The child is expected to make an associative shift form the picture to the word.

The theory that contiguity affects learning is now generally accepted as fact among educational psychologists (Hilgard & Bower, 1975). A theory of *association by contiguity in space,* which follows logically from this linkage in time, is a potential area of investigation in visual learning. However, reading experiments that test learning by contiguity are difficult to control because the Law of Effect (Thorndike, 1913) may be operating also in unknown ways. The *effect* of the experience on the subject has nearly always been recognized as a factor in experimental responses. The assumption that, when certain things are done to the learner the response can be predicted, is basic to much of the S–R influence on school practice. This view is restrictive if it is the only theory available to the reading teacher.

Affective Association

Not all theorists have differentiated between cognitive and affective learning, although many stimulus–response psychologists consider the most pertinent cause of learning to be the *effect that follows behavior.* Thorndike was one of the first to enunciate the probability of an act being dropped because of the result of the behavior of the learner. His Law of Effect stated that the modifiable bond is strengthened or weakened in accordance with the satisfaction or annoyance that attends its exercise. A student is likely to repeat behaviors that satisfy and not to repeat acts that annoy him or her. Later, Thorndike (1917) found that annoyance did not simply weaken learning, but resulted in different, but unpredictable, behavior. He influenced other educational psychologists by orienting their thinking toward manipulation of the school environment to control student behavior.

The basis for motivation to read or to avoid reading is found in the pleasure or punishment loadings of the reading situation. Early evidence that neural activity in pleasure-producing areas of the brain was associated with learning came from a serendipitous discovery by Olds and Milner (1954). While implanting an electrode in the brain of a laboratory rat to measure neural activity during a learning experiment, they accidentally placed the electrode in contact with subcortical cells that produced pleasure sensations. When mild electrical stimulation was applied to these centers, a rat would repeat an associated behavior (the activity that was going on at the time) rapidly and to the point of exhaustion. Thereafter an experimental apparatus was arranged so that the rat could self-stimulate to receive the pleasure by pressing a bar. Their rats increased the bar-pressing behavior from about 20 presses an hour to thousands of times. Obviously the rats wanted a repetition of this pleasure experience. This tendency to repeat whatever act produced stimulation of pleasure centers has since been established in cats, dogs, monkeys, and human beings. The implication seems clear that *reinforcement,* defined as the tendency to repeat a behavior, occurs in the brain as a pleasure consequence. The brain mechanisms which produce sensations of pleasure have been investigated extensively since the Olds' discoveries and will be presented later in this chapter.

In a reading situation, the student receives pleasure stimulation from successfully breaking the code and from gaining the author's meaning. When success is not obvious to the student, reinforcement must come from affirmation by the teacher, or from built-in feedback from the material, to tell the student that he or she is working in the right direction. The need for external reinforcement occurs when the student's effort is short of the final performance that is intrinsically rewarding. All reading experiences that are rewarding tend to produce repetition of the reading activity that was in process when the pleasure stimulation occurred. This repetition, while attending to the reading act, results in consolidation of the content and the skills being practiced. On the other hand, failures in code breaking, inability to gain the information needed or sought, and displeasure on the part of the teacher all tend to become linked to punishment centers in the same way that success and satisfaction connections are made to the pleasure centers (Fig. 2.2).

Olds (1960) went on to discover centers in the brain that, when stimulated, produced severe reactions to unpleasantness. Electrode stimulation of punishment centers caused shrieks, quivers, biting, and attempts to escape. Brady (1958) designed a test of complex motivation by conditioning his monkeys to operate a lever for hours to minimize punishment stimulation. Pribram (1971), in a discussion of the neurochemistry of reinforcement, mapped the systems of neural connectors where reward and punishment activation was found in rats (p. 274). Teachers and parents should be happy to learn that reward systems extend to the forebrain and are much more extensive than punishment systems.

The effects of pleasure and punishment associations on learning and the affective components of learning can be summarized as follows:

1. Connections to the pleasure generating centers of the brain—*reinforcement*—lead to repetition of the activities involved in learning. This learning tends to be stable and available.
2. No affective or emotional component—*no reinforcement*—tends toward extinction of behavior learned previously. This learning can be restored to performance strength by relatively small amounts of reinforcement, or linkage, to the pleasure-producing system.
3. Connections to the punishment centers—*punishment*—lead to avoidance of the learning or activity. Usually punished behavior is replaced by an activity that is pleasure producing, or reinforcing.

According to B. F. Skinner (1953) *operant conditioning* results from the selective rewarding of actions that occur in increasing approximation to the

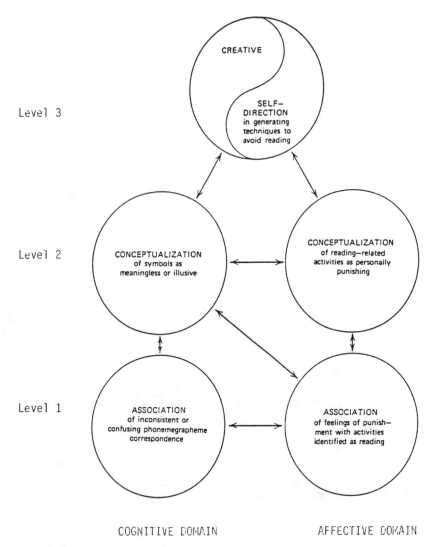

COGNITIVE DOMAIN   AFFECTIVE DOMAIN

FIGURE 2.2. Learning-motivation processes during unsuccessful attempts to learn to read.

desired behavior. In schools the use of electrode stimulation would be frowned upon, but researchers have been evaluating the relative effects of different types of reinforcers: sweets, tokens, and social rewards. Problems develop when the reinforcers being used do not produce pleasure affects for a particular learner. Some programs rely on reinforcers, when cognitive approaches would be more direct and more relevant to the student. The success of reward systems to assure associative learning is an important accomplishment of the behaviorist movement. Forming associations, whether cognitive or affective, is level one learning and basic to more complex functioning.

LEVEL 2: CONCEPTUALIZATION

Human beings are born with a biological necessity to make sense out of the cognitive messages they receive from the environment (Piaget, 1971). They seek to organize, classify, seriate or otherwise relate the ongoing experiential bits and pieces with schemata already built into their neural structures. *Conceptualization* is the psychological act of organizing related bits of experience within a domain of knowledge into an inherent structure. Higher-level thought processes such as generalizing, categorizing, synthesizing, and summarizing nearly always require level two functioning. Young children need to conceptualize the invariate order of letters in words, the relationship of phonemes spoken to words seen, and the syntactic ordering of words to make story books. Older students need to learn how to state the theme of a novel, summarize a chapter, discover the author's purpose in a piece of prose, or synthesize several sources into an integrated report. Helping students generate conceptualizations is more difficult than teaching by association, but conceptualizations are easier to recall and more transferable to other situations.

Cognitive Conceptualizations

The importance of structure in learning was the theme of the early Gestalt psychologists: Werthheimer (1945) on productive thinking, Koffka (1935) on intelligent thought over trial-error learning, and Kohler (1940) on insightful problem solving. Much of their work centered on the nature of visual perception, including the way figure and ground are separated by the individual. In reading print, the words, which change with each fixation as the eye crosses the page, are the figures while the remainder, which the learner should be able to ignore, is ground. They assumed that figure-ground separation was a genetic property and paid little attention to how discriminations are acquired. Their rationalist messages touched a human cord that caught the interest of academia, imbued at the time of connectionist psychology.

One facet of Gestalt psychology that appealed to teachers, because it touched their own experience, was the description of a *gestalt*, the "ah-ha" moment when sudden insight dawns—an understanding is grasped. Another contribution to cognitive theory was the concept of *wholeness*, the idea that the integrated structures that make up experience have specific properties which cannot be identified from its elements, or separate parts. An example in reading is the sentence, which has a meaning not conveyed by the same words when scrambled or reordered. This concept that the whole is greater than the sum of its parts applies to linguistic structures, psychological models, and the brain itself. The Gestalt school experimented with visual forms to suggest how a perceptual experience may be stored in the neural system as a *memory trace*. Their emphasis on human conceptualization was seen as a challenge to behaviorists, and to Thorndike, in particular.

Among those who emerged from Gestalt epistemology to produce a cognitive psychology of his own was Jean Piaget. His structuralism (1970) incorporated the concept of "wholeness," but also included the idea of dynamic transformation (through growth) and the idea of self-regulation. Piaget studied cognitive development from a biological orientation and viewed conceptualization as the child's internal organization of the external world. The child develops this species-specific intelligence through growth of the neural structures (schemata). Sensorimotor knowledge enables a person to assimilate/accommodate (adapt) through subsequent stages of representation, concrete operations and logical thought. For more than 50 years Piaget's qualitative descriptions of human intellectual functioning at different periods in development were the major counterpart to behaviorist psychology.

Piaget's description of a sequence for the development of linguistic representation was used successfully to design an intervention program, the "cognitive curriculum," for disadvantaged preschool children (Weikert et al, 1970). The sequence by which children acquired representations was appropriate for young children of limited experience: (1) Objects of nature were brought into the classroom environment for children to develop sensory-motor knowledge directly. This may be interpreted as associative learning at the *signal level*. Piaget believed the exercise of the internal systems to be pleasurable and self-reinforcing. (2) At the *index level* children explored relationships directly, such the parts of the whole (parts that make a bicycle) or missing parts (the steering wheel on a toy truck). (3) At the *symbol level* children were helped to build mental images through a variety of experiences such as identifying an animal by the sound it makes, making models of objects, and recognizing concrete things in graphics. (4) At the *sign level* words (spoken or written) were related to objects previously experienced directly and concretely through the senses. Most of this learning is associative in nature. The cognitive curriculum grouped experiences in ways that promote subsequent conceptualization, or structuring, to occur. Each sequence of representations covered four content categories: classification, seriation, spatial relations, and temporal relations. Piaget would have said that the child is biologically organized to structure knowledge from sensory experience; this being a human necessity. To Piaget, cognitive development preceded thought and the function of language was to explain knowledge already discovered.

Affective Conceptualizations

One of the most fruitful ways to assure reading progress is to help a student conceptualize the nature of the pleasure to be found in reading. *Affective Conceptualizations* refer to the self-understandings a person derives, primarily about personal needs, goals, attributes, abilities, and motivations. *Self-concept* is the summation of the comparisons each person makes between self and others: a sibling, certain classmates, the real or imagined model among significant adults or peers. Affects are conceptualized from the verbal and nonverbal messages received form others. For young children the messages that matter most come from parents. For primary-aged children the focus may shift to the teacher. By middle grades the comparison that counts is most likely the peer group; by high school it may be the opposite sex. Peer influences dominate the values of many adolescents; therefore it is in their self-interest to become psychologically strong and self-motivated during childhood (Hiebert, 1983).

In the learning-motivation model a distinction is made between levels of affective learning. At level one the emotional state is vague; children, or older persons, may feel good, or pleased in a generalized way after a day at school. They are unconscious of the source of their feelings or of the effect of pleasure rewards on their learning. A student may feel angry, upset, or deflated without identifying the several events that accumulated to produce a down mood. At level two, learners understand the effect of particular events on their feelings. They are in the process of developing a self-concept that is within the reality of their social milieu. Students from a concept of self-as-reader very quickly. The senior author recently completed interviews with 12 intellectually superior adults who had experienced reading difficulty as children (Robeck, 1988). Without exception, they could name a point in elementary schooling when they became aware that they could not read as well as the other kids. Some of them cited the first grade. Fortunately, most students find satisfaction in their accomplishments as readers; for them affective conceptualizations tend to be self-reinforcing.

A cognitive approach to interpersonal relations came from the Gestalt school, of which Kurt Lewin (1935) was at one point a member. Having a propensity for graphic representations, he created a topological theory, or psychology of shifting fields, to show that all psychosocial concepts must be viewed in relationship to the larger context. He wrote of positive valences that made some objects and situations attractive; and of negative valences that, when attached to a task or situation, would cause a student to escape the field psychologically, if physical escape was impossible.

An emphasis in schools on the worth and dignity of the student is healthy. Learning to read is the major cognitive task of the elementary schoolyears. Children who are successful tend to develop feelings of autonomy, mastery of the school environment, positive attitudes toward learning, favorable attitudes toward school and realistic appraisals of their own achievement. They also believe in their own inner control over school success, that effort and their own ability will make the essential difference. [See Chapter 10]. These attitudes combine to produce a positive self-image and continuing motivation.

The affective domain has been researched, usually by comparing poor readers with normal and above-average readers in the same schools. Most poor readers think they are "dumb"; therefore it is not surprising they reveal a low self-esteem (Athey, 1982), and a high anxiety level (Patten, 1983). Their tensions may be acted out in disruptive classroom behavior, in withdrawal or timidity, or occasionally in extraordinary effort. The later may be healthy if accompanied by intervention in reading skill development which is seen as progress by the student. High anxiety often divides the attention of the student between the school task and a preoccupation with how well he or she is doing (Wigfield & Asher, 1984). Efforts directed toward improvement of self-esteem have not been encouraging. To the extent that low self-esteem is caused by poor academic achievement, the obvious approach is a one-on-one program in reading (which eliminates the poor reader's exposure to other students) and frequent feedback for progress. Counseling intervention for student and parents is indicated.

The episodic patterns of real life are neither wholly negative nor wholly positive. Most of the time the momentary bits of experience are mildly to richly satisfying; or somewhat to predominantly punitive. Conventional wisdom once held that most experiences are neutral, the exception being affective loadings of reward or punishment. Current research on the brain mechanisms of motivation suggests a neural linkage through the limbic circuit and the presence of reward–punishment neurotransmitters during all experiences (Stellar & Stellar, 1985). Research on avoidance mechanisms show that punishment effects can be reversed by comparatively brief stimulations to reward mechanisms (Wooldridge, 1963). The effectiveness of this reversal seems most likely to be realized when the learning is still on the association level. Once affective conceptualizations have taken place, reversal appears more difficult. Conceptualizations about self and conceptualizations about content are level two learning which has transfer value and permanence beyond associative-level learning.

LEVEL 3: CREATIVE SELF-DIRECTION

When a person has conceptualized the inherent structure in any body of knowledge, and has conceptualized the sources of satisfaction to be realized from certain activities, a third level of learning may occur, often quite spontaneously. *Creative self-direction* results from a fusion of the motivation that accrues from emotion-laden experience of the affective domain and the uncompleted knowledge from the cognitive domain. *Metacognition,* the awareness of one's own mental processes, at level two is a precursor to creative self-direction. Knowing and appreciating what is known—the eras of history, the format of a sonnet, the periodic table of elements—are examples of structures that creative scholars built upon. Knowing one's own identity, strengths, weaknesses and values is the source of self-motivation and the basis for self-direction.

Active experimentation and the search for novel experience begins very early. Creative, self-directed learning was described by Piaget, in the *Origins of Intelligence in Children* (1952). In the development of sensory-motor intelligence, the toddler of 18 months is described as having discovered new ways to organize actions on objects. Shortly afterward the child invents ways to solve problems, invents make-believe play, and reorganizes space. Children 3 or 4 years old demonstrate their knowledge of linguistic structure to express their wishes in totally new constructions; sometimes inventing the vocabulary they need but do not possess (Brown & Bellugi, 1964). The level of self-mastery that most children achieve in speaking, predates their reading at the independent level by several years. Children must feel the self-mastery of the printed page at some level in order to make the transition to read for their own self-directed purpose.

NEUROPSYCHOLOGICAL BASIS FOR MOTIVATION

Motivation is the psychological power behind a goal-oriented action. It is the inner drive, impulse, or intention that gives a person strength and direction. The neural mechanism for motivation is part of the primitive brain structure of ancient phylogenic origin. Humans have recruited these survival mechanisms to subserve conscious control over their choices and therefore, over their motivations. Although behaviorists have been uncomfortable with the concept of inner direction at any level, they have became very interested in attention, which can be observed in the overt behavior of their subjects. An example of the contributions to attention and reading has been classroom research showing the positive relationship of time-on-task and reading progress. However, teachers who encourage higher levels of student thought and intention want to know how motivations are built within the child so that fostering self-control is possible. Fortunately the current interest in attention and motivation has engaged researchers from several disciplines: cognitive psychology (Posner, 1982); information processing (Schwab & Nusbaum, 1986), educational research (Chall & Peterson, 1986); and neuroscience (Stellar & Stellar, 1985). This section deals with the relationship of attention and motivation. The emphasis is on the neural mechanisms of motivation—the physical realities of internal behavior that neuroscience is in the process of discovering and elaborating.

Relationship of Attention and Motivation

Cultural intuition, as well as developmental psychology, anticipates the gradual extension of children's attention span as they mature. Motivational commitment to productive tasks is expected in most families by adolescence. The school is organized with longer study periods and less teacher direction as students move up the academic ladder. The self-image of the teacher is reinforced by the student who models voluntary reading with his everpresent book, to which he or she returns whenever free of other responsibilities. Motivating students—the continuous concern of the teacher from kindergarten to college—is much easier when the task is directly related to their interests. Despite the effort of most teachers and parents to foster student interest in academic goals, some students find selective attention difficult or impossible.

NEED FOR ATTENTIONAL MECHANISMS

Humans have a limited capacity for attention. H. A. Simon referred to an "attentional bottleneck" of information arriving in the central nervous system (CNS) from multiple sensory systems (Simon, 1986, p. 106). The need for ordering and selecting what the organism will attend to has resulted, during phylogeny, in the conscious and unconscious selection of stimuli from the different modalities and in the serial processing of that information. He has suggested that behavioral and neural research are complimentary, each supplementing the other and both providing cures for education. Simon's cryptic admonition to educators is: *No learning without attention.* The biological requirement of fitness in an organism has evolved the distinctive functions of the human attentional system. Neuroscience and psychology have explored some of the attentional abilities in human subjects: (1) sustaining focus on a task, (2) selecting relevant elements from the sensorial overload, and (3) interrupting an attentional focus to process information having a higher priority.

Sustaining Focus on a Particular Problem

The first function of attention is to select, from a multisensory receiving system, the particular flow of information that an organism needs to sustain an activity.

Humans are continuously surrounded by rich and complex fields of stimuli available to the sensory systems, from which an enormous amount of information could be extracted. Higher organisms have available an even greater store of brain knowledge that could be evoked to impact on the behavior of the moment. The organism needs a mechanism to assure that only a limited amount of sensory stimuli and only the relevant information from long-term memory is brought to bear on an action at any given moment. Without such limitation, thought and behavior would be wildly erratic and lacking direction (Simon, 1986).

One of the neural responses that enables people to screen out irrelevant multisensory stimuli is *habituation*. The term refers to a systematic waning of response activity that occurs during repeated bombardment with a specific stimulus; any change in the parameters of the stimulus (strength, location, or mode) will reinstate the neural response. Most children habituate to the busy noises of the class and are increasingly able to give sustained attention to their own work. A small percentage of school-age children seem unable to attend for more than a few minutes because they are unable screen out the irrelevant sound and sights of the classroom; they are unable to habituate.

A different source of distraction, *attentional deficit,* can impact individuals of any age. It is a preoccupation with personal problems that continue indefinitely without resolution. These personal crises seem to dwarf the immediate task. One of our reading clinic subjects, now an adult, tells of "leaving a battleground" every day he went to first grade, of being "unable to think about anything but the problem at home"—which to this 6-year-old involved real threats to his mother's safety. Despite his native brightness he found himself "hopelessly behind by second grade" and never caught up with his peers or his own potential. Individuals with an attention deficit often escape into an imaginary world they can control; their distraction is from within.

By the 1980s an *attention deficit disorder* had been recognized as a pervasive problem for some children, which probably had organic, rather than behavioral, origin (Dworkin, 1985). Inattention was the major diagnostic criterion for the disorder, although some children were characterized also by impulsivity and/or hyperactivity. The search for a cause of attention deficits in children turned up multiple factors: neurological damage at birth, delayed maturation of the central nervous system, minor physical anomalies, genetic bias toward attention deficit and hyperactivity, biochemical abnormalities (of catecholamine balance) and exposure to toxins. None of these factors has been accepted universally, but most experts agree that combinations of two or three of these conditions in a single child usually calls for diagnosis. When a child brings behavioral patterns such a these to school, can reading disability be far behind? Dworkin considers attentional deficits to result inevitably in poor academic functioning. He recommends thorough assessment, behavior management, environmental manipulation, and academic remediation for children with attention deficit disorders.

Selecting Relevant Elements

The second function of attention is to select from multisensory bombardment and previous stored experience those elements that *could* be relevant to the current problem context (Simon, 1986). Attention brings together the selective information from the senses and associated information from memory into the awareness of the person engaged in the process. Memory retrieval that focuses on potentially relevant elements is a potent factor in information processing. The excitation of sensory subsystems that are relevant to the task and the inhibition of extraneous stimuli are *automatic processes*. They follow sequentially, without effort on the part of the individual, if the motivation to attend is present and the mechanisms of attention are normal. Students who are strong on the selection function bring fresh, but relevant, ideas to a discussion by recalling synonyms, providing examples, or suggesting an alternative analysis of an author's purpose.

Research on selective attention has been conducted by placing electrodes on the scalps of adult subjects and measuring changes in their EEG patterns, while experimentally controlling the stimuli. When subjects were instructed to count light flashes (which were interspersed with auditory clicks) the response spikes in visual reception areas of the occipital lobe were much higher than the limited response spikes in the auditory reception areas. This study made use of the *priming effect,* meaning that the subject was given a prior cue to help facilitate the recognition of the target stimulus. It was shown that central brain mechanisms controlled the selection of stimuli and not the peripheral sense mechanisms. Selective attention implies the cognitive participation of the attender in some goal-oriented context, meaning that attending can be learned and taught.

Interrupting Continuity to Allow Shift

The real-life needs of an organism, such as personal safety and adaptation to the environment, require a mechanism which can interrupt the most absorbing attentiveness to allow a shift of focus (Simon, 1986). The physiology of the eye serves dual functions as selector and interrupter of the stream of conscious thought. The reader's fovea focuses on word, picture, sentence, or the facial communication of another person. The periphery of the eye is designed to pick up changes in the environment and to signal when a different visual focus may be needed. Such interruptions are followed by cognitive evaluation, involving distant cortical areas. Probably the most important skills of a teacher is to control the attentional shifts during the numerous transitions of the schoolday. Teachers cannot prevent disruption; they *can* become skilled at redirecting attention.

The ability to shift attention and to adapt behavior to new conditions is thought to require a second neural mechanism, distinct from the system that achieves attention, and having its own neural complex of excitation and inhibition (Geschwind, 1982). When reading, individuals differ in their flexibility to shift to different codes for different tasks (Posner & Freidrich, 1986). For example, the shift from semantic to syntactic cues is needed to comprehend whether **paint** is a noun or a verb. Young readers may lack flexibility in shifting from phonemic information, which works for **send**, to visual memory when they encounter **sure**. Some readers prefer and persist in one or the other modality (auditory or visual), when the ability to shift strategies would be more efficient (Baron & Strawson, 1976). Proficient readers have learned to shift their rate of reading when they encounter difficult text, thus allowing them the additional time needed for comprehension of complex ideas (Rankin, 1978). High-level processes, such as the integration of information in continuous text, requires three times the commitment of cognitive resources than low-level processes, such as recognizing a familiar word (Graesser, Hoffman, & Clark, 1980). Level one (associative) processing is largely automatic in easy reading, as long as attention is sustained. The higher-level conceptual processes of reading, described in information-processing research, are level two functioning in the learning-motivation model.

NEED TO LEARN SELECTIVE AND SUSTAINED ATTENTION

William James, whose *Principles of Psychology* (1890) is being read and quoted a century later, addressed the topic of attention. "My experience is what I choose to attend to." Attention is a cognitive process that enables us to choose what we perceive and what we think about, thus enabling us to choose the "sort of universe we will inhabit." Teachers, to whom James wrote and lectured in his time, live in a buffer zone where children and youth have gained some control over what they choose to take in perceptually and what they think about, although they are far from being the self-directed individuals whom James described. The great psychologist has confessed to being well into adulthood when he conceptualized the "will to believe" and then only after a prolonged intellectual struggle within himself. Control over attention is an exciting concept because many cognitive psychologists agree that the ability to select and direct one's own attention is a transferable skill, available on demand of the learner, in a variety of study activities.

Developmental growth in the ability to attend selectively to information has been explored by asking children 5 to 15 years old to recall relevant (central) and irrelevant (incidental) stimuli (Hallahan & Reeve, 1980). A dramatic increase was found to occur at about age 12 to 13 in the ability to attend to, and therefore recall, central information. The older children seemed to have learned to ignore incidental information, perhaps by being better able to inhibit attention toward irrelevant information. The researchers also found a developmental lag of 2 to 3 years in selective attention on the part of learning-disabled and mentally retarded children. Research on brain functions in selective and sustained attention of children has neglected the element of *interest* (Simon, 1986). An exception has been Krupski (1980), who reported a series of studies which compared the attentional processes of normal, learning-disabled, and mentally retarded subjects on voluntary and involuntary tasks. She found that the normal group sustained attention longer than the other groups on high-demand tasks, but that the three groups did not differ on voluntary low-demand tasks, nor on short-term attention to involuntary tasks. When reaction time to warning signals (an index of involuntary attention) and action signals (an index of voluntary attention) was compared, the groups did not differ in response to warning signal, but the mentally retarded group was slower to act on the voluntary signal. The same investigator also conducted studies of distractability in classroom settings. She found that normal and reading-disability groups did not differ in attention to task.

However, mentally retarded children 9–12 years old were more easily distracted in an academic setting than either of the other comparison groups. When the experiment was changed to a nonacademic situation, the three groups were comparable. The normal responses of retarded children to signals and their ability to sustain attention in some situations is encouraging to those who expect to teach them to read.

When interpreting research on voluntary attention to reading, a note of caution is warranted. In an impressive work on the determinants of attention, Berlyne (1965) concluded that people give their most persistent attention to stimuli that are neither too simple nor too complex. Very high skill levels are required of teachers to control materials for difficulty in a typical classroom setting. For example, an 11th-grade class is expected to show a reading-grade equivalency range in achievement that reaches from elementary school level into college. It is a rare classroom the meets the Berlyne criteria for sustained interest: Not too easy nor too difficult. Student intention, as well as student attention, may influence the level of arousal that is brought to the reading task.

Arousal, Orientation, and Attention

Attention is the property of all organisms possessing a nervous system (Klivington, 1986). Humans can focus attention both consciously and sub-consciously. They can convert sound signals from the inner ear to linguistic representations in the cortex and can convert light signals from the printed page to visual representations, which in turn access the word bank of speech. The conscious direction readers must sustain for comprehension is built on the primitive, biological structures for arousal. An alerted organism "knows" the source of the sensation through its sensory analyzers and orients toward the object or situation that requires attention. Sustained attention to words and sentences is required while the brain searches for meaning. Although reading behavior is ontogenic and recent, the brain mechanisms of attention are very primitive.

RETICULAR ACTIVATING SYSTEM (RAS)

Arousal begins with a change in sensory signals to the *reticular activating system* (RAS), a structure of neurons in the brain stem. The RAS is a formation of ascending and decending fibers, about the size of a person's little finger, that extends upward from the spinal cord and terminates in the hypothalamus and thalamus at the top of the brain stem (Fig. 2.3). Visual and auditory signals enter the RAS at the midbrain level, where many of the emotion and motivation mechanisms are located. Most of the reticular fibers are undifferentiated, that is, they transmit impulses from more than one sensory system. The explanation of arousal (activation) from classical neuropsychology is that the arousing signal ascends the RAS to the thalamus, where an alerting mechanism is activated. From there a generalized message of arousal is transmitted to the "whole fore-brain" (Beaumont, 1983). This "general alert" disrupts the cortical functions that are in progress and leaves the brain sufficiently disengaged to attend to new information. If the interpretation (based on past experience) signals imminent danger, the motor and endocrine systems are recruited for fleeing the scene.

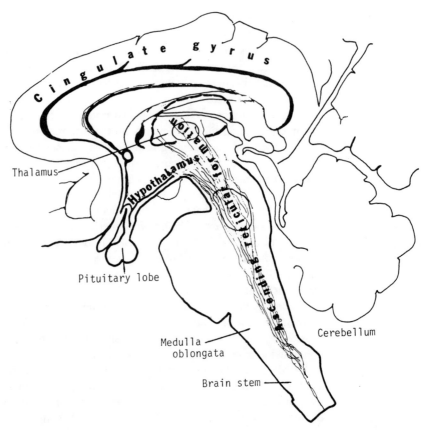

FIGURE 2.3. The brain stem. Reticular activating system (RAS) ascends to level of diencephalon (hypothalamus and thalamus). Two thalami on either side of structures shown in saggital view are indicated by broken lines. Cingulate gyrus (affective cortex) is the inner surface of the cerebral cortex. (Drawing by D. Thompson.)

Arousal (or activation) does not lead inevitably to orientation and attention. Pribram (1971) raised interesting questions about the immediate effect of activation: When does arousal lead to disruption of the organism's *orienting reaction* and when does arousal lead to registration and *habituation?* In other words, how does the person's brain know when to ignore a signal and when to orient for possible action?

ORIENTING REACTION VERSUS HABITUATION

The mechanism of arousal is central to the production of motivation and emotion. Feelings and interests (the appetites and affects) are activated by the affective mechanism, just as perceptual knowledge is activated in processes of cognition. Whether the orienting reaction will occur depends more on the psychological organization of the individual, more on the brain state and the config-uration of expectancies (based on past pleasure–punishment outcomes) than on the level of neural activity. The energy level generated by novel input is less important than a change in the equilibration, or amount of *uncertainty,* created by the new (and incomplete) information. Uncertainty creates disequilibrium and the need for further information, therefore attention is focused on the source of the arousal.

Pribram (1971) explained how the state of disequilibrium occurs at the neural unit level. Arousal is accompanied by changes in *pattern of firing,* both in the reticular formation and at the cortex, but not necessarily by an increase in the amount of firing. During the dissynchronization of uncertainty, neural elements become functionally independent of each other, thus becoming available as sepa-rate information-processing pathways. This enhanced separation, or increased organization within neural units, means increased uncertainty and the need for the organism to attend to the new conditions. To Pribram, arousal represents a state where the independence of the activities of neuronal aggregates in the brain makes for freedom to interact with distant aggregates to retrieve the information needed for action (pp. 206–207). Obviously past learning is critical in the deci-sion that readers make about attending or avoiding.

Habituation is the alternative response of the neural system to arousal. Sokolov (1960) is credited with the original conceptualization and the supporting research. He experienced an incident in his town, where a number of citizens reported unfamiliar noises around 2 A.M. one day. His curiosity was piqued when it was revealed that the train, which usually whistled its approach at that hour, had been taken off the line that night. The townsfolk had habituated to the regular and repeated bombardment of the train whistle. Sokolov, a research psychologist, began measuring people's biological responses to repeated beeps of a horn. He demonstrated that habituation does not indicate a loss of sensitivity in the nervous system, but to an acquired interpretation of the signals. Any change in the frequency, pitch, or regularity of the stimuli re-establishes the orienting response of the subject, as shown by EEG's, galvanic skin reflex, blood flow at fingertips, respiration, and head turning. Sokolov suggested that a *neural model of expectancy* is established in the learner during previous experiences, against which inputs are matched. Arousal wanes when an activation pattern registers a match with a previously stored pattern that was not threatening in its effect, therefore does not require a response.

SELECTIVE ATTENTION BY GATING

The major organizing center of cognitive processing is the *thalamus.* Information from the external senses flows through the thalamus to the cortex and the cortical response to the outside world returns through the thalamus to the systems that perform the action. A pressing question for researchers is: How does this infor-mation come together in coordinated activity? Immediate information from the senses, stored information from past learning, and information about the inten-tions (wants, needs, appetites) of the organism must be integrated. These are the elements of selective attention.

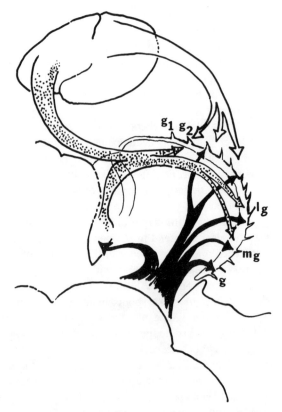

FIGURE 2.4. Simplified model of the gating system in the thalamus. Blackened arrow system shows arrival of sensory information from RAS and adjacent bodies. Gatelets (g1, g2, g . . .) allow or prevent passage of information from sensory receptors. Gates lg and mg represent visual and auditory information. Dotted-arrow system represents projections from the frontal cortex. Clear system, arising in cerebral cortex, represents descending projections. (Redrawn form A. B. Scheibel in The Reticular Formation Revisited, (p. 63.) edited by A. Hobson & M. A. B. Brazier. Copyright © 1980. [Raven Press, by permission])

Current thinking is that a gating mechanism in the thalamus allows or prevents the passage of sensory information to and from cortical areas (Picton, Stuss, Klivington, & Marshall, 1986). The major pathways of the thalamus have been mapped and the interaction of the three information systems has been proposed (Fig. 2.4). Projections from the RAS and other midbrain structures arrive in ordered pathways so that signals are coded in part by their origin in the auditory and visual receptors. These signals provide current information. Projections from association areas in the cortex are relayed through the thalamus and back to the interpretation areas in the cortex, where multisensory information is coordinated. This feedback system makes available stored previous experience. Major pathways from the forebrain, with input from motivation systems, provide the affective information about desires, needs, and the relative strength of these drives.

The thalamus also functions in the control of hemispheric balance by maintaining the activation condition of the dominant hemisphere, while maintaining inhibition of the nondominant hemisphere (Levy, 1980). This balance of functions is important in reading because it is an asymmetrical function controlled primarily in one hemisphere. There is some evidence that some disabled readers lack the midbrain control to achieve this activation–inhibition balance (Gladstone & Best, 1985). An intricate mechanism filters the flow of messages between the frontal cortex and the ancient brain stem to select the object of attention. According to the gating theory, the inhibition, or selective closing of the gates is at least as important as keeping channels open.

For the learner, the basic conditions for selective attention are an appropriate degree of *alertness* to open the thalamic gates together with an *intention* to open the appropriate gate and close all others. Intention is mediated through the frontal cortex, which selects the modality. Alertness, if excessive, is seen by teachers as hyperactive behavior. Inability to sustain attention is seen in pupils as distractability. Lack of alertness is characterized by hypoactivity that ranges from laziness to narcolepsy. Alertness is mediated through the midbrain reticular formation, which is surrounded by structures that control affective responses and gives priority to a certain locus of attention over competing stimuli.

Motivation and Reward

The concept of motivation has been part of the scholar's heritage since the ancient Greeks distinguished between the rational mind-directed behavior of humans and the instinct-driven behavior of lower animals. Neuropsychology has narrowed the gap by discovering the physiological sources of emotion and by establishing the brain as the integrator of all body functions. A neurological substructure subserves all motivated behaviors, all reward and reinforcement, and all feelings of pleasure or satisfaction. The central mechanism for organizing these affective states is the *hypothalamus*. It is a way station of neural aggregates, tucked beneath the two thalami, and having a bundle of anterior extensions to the forebrain. The hypothalamus and the thalamus (the diencephalon) are encircled by a group of structures, called the *limbic system*. These systems together form the mechanisms that build and sustain motivated behavior. Beaumont (1983) suggested that the hypothalamus initiates responses to the current level of motivation, while the surrounding structures control the execution of motivated behavior and record the consequences. This section has two parts: The first describes the limbic circuit that surrounds the hypothalamus and interacts to produce motivation; the second reviews some of the natural chemical stimulants and repressants that produce the reward–punishment effects.

THE LIMBIC CIRCUIT

Not long ago the affective responses that accompanied experiences were thought to be primarily neutral, with only some behavioral effects being associated with feelings of pleasure or punishment. After reviewing the historical and current

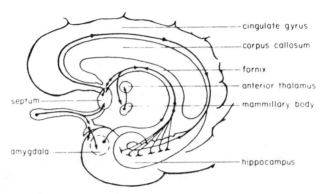

cingulate gyrus
corpus callosum
fornix
anterior thalamus
mammillary body
septum
amygdala
hippocampus

FIGURE 2.5. The limbic circuit surrounding the hypothalamus. Two-way fibers interconnect the hippocampus via the fornix to septal region, to the amygdala. (From Beaumont, Introduction to Neoropyschology, p. 35. Copyright © 1983, Blackwell Scientific Publications.)

work on the neurobiology of motivation, including their own experimental results, Stellar and Stellar (1985) concluded that all activity at the level of the diencephalon has elements of pleasantness or unpleasantness. The neurotransmitters that stimulate the stop-and-go mechanisms, are either inhibitory or excitatory and not neutral in their effect.

The hypothalamus is an area in which slight moves of a stimulating electrode produce opposites in responsive behaviors: aggression versus submission, sleeping and waking, fight or flight, excessive feeding or avoidance of food to the point of starvation. One researcher, Delgado, demonstrated the power of brain stimulation to control behavior. He implanted electrodes in the diencephalon of a bull and entered the ring armed only with a cape and a radio-controlled telemetric stimulator. To the amazement of observers, he succeeded in halting the bull in midcharge. The confused bull merely turned and wandered away. Teachers may sometimes wish they could use these mechanical controls to manage classroom behavior. With understanding of the biological mechanisms that function in motivation they can, over time, teach students to control their own behavior.

The names of the limbic structures are graphically described in Latin (Fig. 2.5). The *fornix* (a vaulted chamber) is a long slender structure that arches the *thalamus* (the inner room) and interconnects the *mammalary bodies* adjacent to the *hypothalamus* (the lower room). The most lateral body, the *hippocampus* (seahorse), is actually embedded in the inner side of the temporal lobe just above and behind the ear. The hippocampus structures on each side of the brain have a vital role in long-term memory. They are generally thought to be the loci where experiences are templated for permanent storage. The intent of a person to remember for a given period of time (until the change is counted out, or until after the final exam) is an important element of motivation.

The *amygdala* (almond) is an oval structure located next to the hippocampus in an anterior (forward) position. It is thought to function in spontaneous behavior since severing its connections to the hypothalamus appears to reduce such behavior (Yim & Morgenson, 1980). A secondary system, concerned with level of *effort,* has been proposed by Stellar and Stellar (1985), which they suggest involves the amygdala. The study of effort, as it relates to motivation, would seem to be a fruitful line of investigation for educational psychologists, who could compare children (over time) on measures of motivation to succeed in school with measures of time on task.

The *cingulate gyrus* is that part of the cortex that faces the inner side of each hemisphere. Sometimes called the affective cortex, these areas are thought to be the long-term storage areas of affective memories. One type of surgery to correct (otherwise untreatable) severe depression has been aimed at the cingulate gyrus. The procedure is to sever its projections to the hypothalamus. Although favorable results for many patients who were otherwise beyond conventional treatment have been reported, any brain surgery to correct psychoses remains controversial (Valenstein, 1980).

The *septal region* is centrally located anterior to the thalamus and superior to (above) the hypothalamus. It shares connections with the RAS (reticular activating system) and the bodies of the limbic circuit. The reader will recall how Olds mislocated an electrical probe, intended for the reticular formation, to stimulate the pleasure centers of the septum accidentally. The thalamus is included in the limbic system in some accounts, and the anterior thalamus does interconnect with the mammary bodies and the septum. However, the evidence is very persuasive that the thalamus is the organizing center for cognitive functions (Beaumont, 1983), while the hypothalamus is the organizing center for affective functions (Stellar & Stellar, 1985). The conditions for stimulating the limbic system are the intricate balance in the biochemistry of the brain.

THE NATURAL REINFORCERS

Electrical stimulation of the brain (ESB), first observed by Olds as a reward so powerful that rats would work to the point of exhaustion to continue the sensation, has become a technique for studying the location of pleasure reinforcement centers and the conditions of motivation. A structure, known as the *medial forebrain bundle* (MFB), has major aggregates of cells in the hypothalamus, particularly in the lateral (outside) areas on both left and right. Long fibers extend from these cells to the neocortex of the forebrain, the amygdala, and the hippocampus. Other fibers project downward (caudally) to the lower brain stem, sending information and control signals from the hypothalamus and also receiving internal body-state information via ascending fibers. Output fibers project from the hypothalamus to all areas of the limbic system. By experimental control of the ESB and by new techniques which locate the electrodes precisely, researchers have produced quantified data of mammal reaction to reward stimulation. These studies have produced persuasive evidence of the effect of pleasure in motivation.

Learning the Effects of Reward

Many researchers now believe that reward effects are learned. When testing ESB reward chemicals against the brain's natural rewards, the behavior extinguishes (disappears) very rapidly during ESB. Researchers have learned they must initiate the pleasure responses of their animals to ES by *priming* them. This means conditioning the animal to the pleasant experience of the stimulation before it will self-stimulate. ESB is thought to activate or increase the arousal level of the animal which then seeks to execute some consummatory act (feeding, for example). The response may be more characteristic of the individual animal's past experience (learning) than the site of stimulation. By changing the location of stimulation from the lateral hypothalamus to a more central and lowered position, the behavior of animals was changed to avoidance or withdrawal, as if the stimulation had been unpleasant. In both pleasant and unpleasant stimulation experiments, individual animals have responded to ESB according to their past conditioning (association learning), rather than by prewired (phylogenic) circuitry.

A hierarchy of functions for the medial forebrain systems has been proposed, based on whether the fibers project upward or downward from the hypothalamus (Stellar & Stellar, 1985). Systems below the hypothalamus serve a major function in general arousal, and perhaps in withdrawal and escape. These are the more primitive, survival response mechanisms. More specific activation, that needed for learned behavior, appears to be directed by structures of the limbic circuitry, under control from centers in the hypothalamus. Major projections to and from the frontal cortex are involved. Activation in the ascending projections seems to be associated with spontaneous activity and investigative behavior (Koob, Riley, Smith, & Robbins, 1978).

Cognitive psychologists point out that the hierarchical organization in learning-directed behavior of laboratory mammals is superseded and greatly enhanced in the motivated actions of children. Gardner (1986) regrets that motivation research has made slight recognition of the ethological study of children carrying out complex actions on *their* natural environment. Lacking such research on human functioning at a conceptualization level, this discussion turns to the chemical basis for reward and motivation.

Pleasure Responses to Dopamine

Neurotransmitters are chemicals that brain cells use to communicate with one another. Brain-altering drugs work because they either *stimulate* the production of natural transmitters or they *mimic* them without being recognized by the brain as imposters. Professionals who deal with children are aware of the controversy over drug treatment in behavioral problems of schoolchildren. Nearly all teachers have been drawn into the political demands for an educational approach to prevention of drug abuse. None of these issues is settled from the point of view of many researchers.

The neurotransmitter dopamine has a major and positive role in the reward-motivation mechanism of the brain. Dopamine is a natural chemical that is associated with pleasure affects. Aggregates of dopamine-releasing cells are found in the lateral hypothalamus, which are stiumlated by ESB pulses to that area. Dopamine release into the MFB has an excitatory effect on some terminals and an inhibitory effect on others. Activation of these dopamine cells has been associated with increased neural activity in the forebrain, the amygdala, the hippocampus, the caudal nucleus, and the ventral tegmental area. These are structures involved in reward and motivation.

Chemicals that Mimic Dopamine

When given the opportunity, laboratory mammals (and humans) will act to promote dopamine release by self-administering it or an agonist, either orally or directly. *Agonists* are mimicking drugs, such as amphetamine or cocaine. Humans report subjective feelings of pleasure associated with dopamine intake, reminding the reader that pleasure feelings must be implied in animals by their behavior. A dopamine-blocking drug, primozide, has been found to decrease the reward effectiveness of ESB. The principal investigators, Wise and Bozarth (1982) proposed the *hedonia hypothesis,* indicating that the hedonistic, or pleasure effect, of dopamine had been eliminated or reduced by the receptor blockage of dopamine sites. Primozide, a neuroleptic, blunts the pleasure of food reinforcers. Self-stimulation studies have shown a reduction in the effort of the animals to reach a goal (a reduction in motivation); but not a reduction in motor ability. The natural opiates, such as the enkephalins, and the imitating drugs are thought to use a common pathway from the lateral hypothalamus to the forebrain and to release the reward-producing chemicals there.

THE PUNISHMENT MECHANISMS

Neuropsychological research has been conducted on the punishment centers in the midbrain and diencephalon, but with less persuasive results than research on pleasure centers. Since the classic studies of Olds and his colleagues, who first discovered sites that caused extreme pain reactions when stimulated, there has been no breakthrough of importance. Small shifts in electrode position alter an animal's behavior from approach to withdrawal and from feeding to food refusal. Pribram (1971) described the punishment mechanism as a medial bundle of fibers, similar to the MFB, yet not as extensive. It projects from the hypothalamus upward to the thalamus and downward to the tectum in the lower brain stem. The finding of a medial thalamic location for adversive learning seems reasonable and has been hypothesized. Although the mechanisms are not yet described adequately, the reality of psychological punishment is known to every person.

INTRINSIC REINFORCEMENT VERSUS INCENTIVES

Anyone who observes people in an airport, on a commuter train, or on a bus may be struck by the number of passengers who are buried in newspapers, magazines, or paperbacks and appear oblivious to their immediate surroundings. Many of these people have experienced enough reinforcement in the act of reading to make the process automatic and self-motivating. Despite the intrinsic rewards of reading, teachers point to young people at every grade level who do not like to read or have not learned to read well enough to experience the pleasure of achievement through study. Should the teacher use a direct approach by providing incentives to arouse the student's active participation? *Intrinsic motivation* is self-motivation; the motive arises from within; the action toward goal fulfillment is self-directed. In neobehaviorist terms, intrinsic motivation is behavior maintained without apparent reinforcement from the outside. *Extrinsic rewards* are designed to inject pleasure into a potential learning situation where self-motivation is lacking. However, rewards are motivating only if the effect is pleasurable to the recipient. This section deals with three applications of motivation theory; (1) the inherent pleasures of reading, (2) the avoidance of reading by some students, and (3) planned reinforcement in teaching reading.

Rewards of Reading

Today's children need to learn to read better than at any previous time in history. The economic reality is that the fastest-growing job categories require literacy skills well beyond the average achievement of today's workers, while the job categories that can be filled by workers with below-average literacy skills are declining, according to a report from the Department of Labor (Gladstone, 1988). The demand is for employees who can not only read and write, but use computers, understand technical concepts, and think independently. Today's youth will meet these criteria with great pain and difficulty unless they become readers before they leave the primary grades. Most poor readers, by middle grades or earlier, spend more effort on covering their disability than on improving their reading skills.

MOTIVATION THROUGH MASTERY

During the initial stages of learning to read, the actual mastery of code breaking generates continuous motivation to tackle other segments of the reading process. In the same way, the failure to master essential parts of the code diminishes motivation and blocks the intrinsic reward of gaining information through reading. A feeling of power comes from control of the mechanics of word recognition, and this feeling increases as individuals shift their motivation to reading for knowing. Six-year-olds exult in the mastery of primer text. The same brain mechanisms are functioning that cause college students to feel exaltation when they master Piaget's *Intelligence and Affectivity* or Dante's *Inferno*.

LUDIC READING

The antecedents of pleasure reading are (1) reading ability, (2) positive expectations, and (3) correct book selection. Nell (1988) studied the psychology of reading for pleasure by comparing the reading practices of a group of typical adult readers and another group that read 10 books or more each month for pleasure. He identified the later group as *ludic readers,* a term derived from Latin, *ludo,* meaning "to play." The pleasure reader is reinforced, not in words and phrases, but in cognitive events that result from interaction between book and reader. For the ludic readers gratification began with the "subjectively effortless" extraction of meaning from the printed page. The subjects reported a feeling of absolute control over their reading; they could slow down for savored parts, skim any parts they found dull, or reread if they so desired. Some of them read to dull their consciousness of an environment they could not escape in real life, while others used reading as a consciousness-heightening activity. Even for readers possessed of skill, motivation, and the appropriate book ludic reading demands attention and comprehension. There is hedonic value in moderate arousal boosts from ludic reading; relief occurs when the plot is resolved. Persons who do not read well enough to pursue pleasure materials at a low level of effort do not experience the physiological and cognitive changes that reward reading and build motivation.

DISTRACTIONS FROM PLEASURE READING

Intrinsic motivation for reading needs to be built before the distractions that characterize later childhood intervene. This means that children need to read fluently by age 8 or 9 in order to capitalize on the positive motivations and avoid the negative motivations of reading. By age 10 or 11 the attractiveness of group games and peer-oriented activities become so strong that reading must be intrinsically rewarding if wide reading is to compete for the child's time.

Television is regarded by popular consensus as the great distracter. The variability from one home to another is so great as to defy conclusions about the viewing habits of particular students. At one extreme are the children who spend more time in front of the tube than they spend in school. The other extreme is parental denial of television viewing. Several positive contributions of TV to reading might be noted: (1) The content of some children's programs, such as "Sesame Street," presents prereading skills to many children whose environment does not otherwise prepare them for school. (2) Many programs, particularly on Public Television System, offer content suitable for viewing at home and reporting at school. (3) Some programs suggest book titles for further information or pleasure reading. (4) Many parents are using the favored TV program as the incentive to be enjoyed when homework is finished, thus providing both intrinsic and extrinsic motivation for schoolwork accomplished.

Negative Motivation

Unpleasant feelings, associated with reading, are pervasive in that the affects generalize to the school setting. In experiments designed to test the power of dopamine-mimicking drugs (amphetamines and cocaine) rats were tested by *place preference* (Goeders & Smith, 1983). The animals were charted for their tendency to remain in one or the other end of a chamber. Then they were assigned to one of the chambers for a series of injections over several days. When an animal was drug-free again it was given access to both chambers. If its preferred place had changed the rewarding and conditioning power of the drug had been demonstrated. The drugs that promote dopamine production in the brain have the opposite effect of dopamine antagonists (neuroleptics), which block conditioning (the reward effect) by the natural dopamine. The basic principles of reward and punishment effects are assumed to affect humans whose motivational systems function with the same neurotransmitters as those of the laboratory mammals.

SUCCESSFUL AVOIDANCE OF READING

Students who are unsuccessful at learning to read over a period of time are almost certain to learn to avoid reading. Mike, age 19, was white, energetic, and personable. Although he was a high school graduate, he had failed the apprentice examination for carpenter's helper. He had lost a job in a filling station because he could not fill out the charge tickets and another job in a supermarket because he could not read the labels well enough to stock shelves. At that point, Mike became so determined to learn to read that he enrolled in the university's reading clinic where he registered a normal IQ and recognized fewer than 10 percent of the Dolch Basic 220 words. His record is a fascinating study in motivation.

Mike saw himself as an amiable avoider who might have learned to read if his parents and teachers had insisted. "I would choose a seat near the back of the room. I would remain as inconspicuous as possible so that the teacher usually would not know me or recognize me much before the end of the term. . . . I never caused trouble. When test forms were passed out, I marked the answers carefully and managed to finish at about the right time along with all the rest. Each term I would sign up for a different teacher, so that I wouldn't be known." He learned enough reading in one quarter at the clinic to pass the tests for painter's helper. In an interview as part of a 25-year follow-up project Mike said he was a successful painter, doing okay. "I don't read much better than I did then, but there are lots of ways to get around it . . . . Sure I'll come in for some tests—it's alright as long as my kids don't hear me." Even successful avoidance has its psychological penalties.

TENSION ASSOCIATED WITH READING

Readers who are highly motivated to improve their reading, and continue over time to feel they are failing, are likely to develop undue tension associated with reading. Robeck (1965) diagnosed 156 children who fell into one of the following classifications: (1) Lacking in word attack skills, but having no unusual emotional complications; (2) Extreme tension associated with reading; (3) Lack of motivation; and (4) Other or unclassified subtypes. Of this clinic sample, tension associated with reading was observed in 44% in the primary-grade children, 15% of those in the upper elementary grades, and 50% of the junior high school group. Bright subjects and those from professional homes were more likely to show tension than lack of motivation.

Adults generally are better prepared to deal with the cognitive than the emotional dimensions of reading disability. Robeck and Wilson (1974) proposed a model of the negative effects of prolonged reading disability (Fig. 2.6). Readers who lack word-attack skills were predicted to follow one of several alternatives: (a) acquire adequate word-recognition skills and become effective readers, or (b) learn decoding skills minimally and become reluctant readers, or (c) fail to learn, while trying, and become tense readers. Tense readers who continue to fail are likely to become avoiders. We are in the process of following reading clinic children, after 25 years, to check out the accuracy of this model. Interviews with a sample of these former subjects points up the destructive effects of reading failure, particularly when neither special programs nor class instruction succeeds in solving the disability.

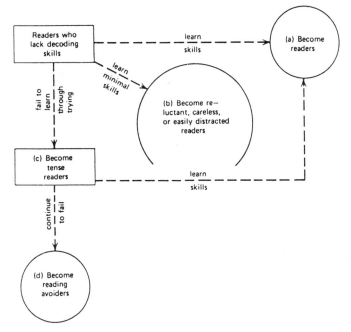

FIGURE 2.6. *Motivational influences on reading progress. The reader who cannot function successfully because of decoding inabilities (a) learns the skills and becomes effective, (b) partly learns and reads enough to get by, or (c) develops tension associated with reading. Under prolonged tension associated with reading, the student either learns the necessary skills or becomes an active avoider of reading.*

Teaching Achievement Motivation

The tendency to think of extrinsic reinforcement as questionable practice in schools has been challenged in recent years by the use of reward strategies to increase learning and effort. The use of reinforcers in classroom management first came in the form of treats; M&M's were favored in part because they were small enough to avoid the satiation of the children. Later token systems were designed which could be cashed for treats or privileges (Walker & Buckley, 1974). These programs focused the teacher's responses on positive recognition of incremental changes in the behavior of students in the direction of classroom goals. In a later study, Walker (1983) tested the effectiveness of different reward systems: treats (appetitive), tokens (symbolic, or deferred), and social. Social reinforcers were designed to provide positive emotional conditioning by praising the child promptly and specifically for persistence in a task as well as its accomplishment. Positive reinforcement was preferred to negative conditioning because researchers assumed that self-esteem would be enhanced by reward and not by punishment.

Most students have learned that if they work hard they can succeed; they are motivated to achieve. Among researchers who believe that success at school results in self-esteem is Becker (1986) who suggested how teachers can promote *positive striving* by students. First, student success can be assured through effective teaching. An academic program that provides a high rate of success and low error ratio is critical in behavior-shaping strategies. Feedback from the program should demonstrate that the student is a capable and competent learner. Second, the model the teacher presents is positive. He or she is clear about the behavior that is expected and lets students know their progress. Competence builds a feeling of confidence, which is associated with particular tasks and therefore is intrinsically rewarding. Third, persistence is reinforced in the face of a difficult task. When a student is having difficulty in a new task, the teacher's focus is to reinforce working hard. "You worked hard, didn't you? This new stuff is hard, and you kept right on with it. You will learn it, too!" In the early stages of *persistence training* the teacher should avoid too much failure, praise frequently for working, then shift to intermittent reinforcement. Fourth, students can be taught to rely on their own judgment, by using games designed for confidence building. Becker emphasized that the persistence behavior a child learns is transferable to other tasks. The learning-motivation model implies that a second, higher level of intrinsic motivation is activated when the learner conceptualizes the sources of his or her pleasure and the relationship of one's action to goals.

Freedom through Access to Ideas

In primitive societies, knowledge was handed down from the shaman to the apprentice, whose training conferred social and personal power along with this knowledge. This neophyte "witch doctor" was highly motivated to learn things that were hidden from the other members of the community. The Egyptian pharaohs preserved their political domination over the priesthood for generations by changing the national gods, thus undermining the priests who were associated with particular deities. When Tutankhamen came into power he re-established old gods, consolidating his power, again by reducing the influence of the men of knowledge and reinstating former priests, who now were beholden to him. Modern rulers surround themselves with persons of knowledge who attempt to control the information that gets to the people through the media. Readers have access to volumes of knowledge that is not available to those who merely listen.

AESTHETIC EXPERIENCES

Aesthetic enjoyment of literature can begin as early as adults begin reading to young children. Sunny, age 4, was twice blessed by having had this exposure to children's literature and the abilities for reading early. She was an overnight guest, along with her mother, who asked whether we happened to have a children's book to read at bedtime. I gave her a teacher's edition of Bill Martin, Jr.'s *Sounds of the Story Teller,* thinking that mother was intending to do the reading. Sunny began at once leafing the pages and settled on Eunice Tietjens's poem, "Moving." She read aloud, to herself as if she were reading discourse:

> I like to move. There's such a feeling
> of hurrying
>   and scurrying.
> And such a feeling

> Of men with trunks and packing cases,
> Of kitchen clocks and mother's *laces,*
> Dusters, dishes, books and **vases**.

Sunny began to chuckle. She read the triplet again, emphasizing the rhymes. She continued the poem in total glee, emphasizing the end of each couplet: forgotten–cotton, handles–sandals. Sunny didn't know that a poem doesn't need to rhyme, but she had discovered that a poem is different from a story.

An aesthetic approach to literature enlists the contributions of both the cognitive and the affective domains. The affective potency of words is a significant variable in their being recognized during brief exposure. Gima (1982) paired potency words (those having high emotional impact) with neutral words and presented them on tachistoscopes to college students. Despite careful control of frequency, word length, and graphic considerations, the high-impact words were remembered best, even under exposure conditions where visual features were emphasized. Conceptualization of both cognitive and emotional content, level two functioning in the model, are antecedents of the appreciative reading of literature.

The appreciation that great writers engender and great teachers generate is the fusion of both creative and self-directing impulses. The understanding of literary structure, at the conceptualization level, can be an engaging experience. For example, a literature class confronted with three sonnets by three authors might be asked: How are they alike? How are they constructed? Could you write a sonnet? By a different approach, the affective impact of a poem may first be heard: rhythm, alliteration, and accent patterns. Do these sonnets sound alike? What words make you feel? What words make you see? Could you write a sonnet? These discoveries (conceptualizations) are quite stimulating, compared with these same principles of poetic form given directly as a lecture. The search to identify beauty in a piece of writing is the essence of literary criticism. There is a tendency to think of criticism as destructive, as pulling something apart, but in good lieterary criticism the analysis enhances the effectiveness of the writing and generates a positive climate for the student's own writing (Chapter 15).

Complaints are perennial that the reading texts supplied to elementary-age pupils are too far removed from the children's world. According to this argument, inner-city children cannot identify with characters and settings that are unlike the homes 'they know. While most professionals approve the attempts made to multiethnic groups, these efforts have resulted in settings that also are suburban, activities that are sterile, and characters that are vague (Blom, Waite, & Zimet, 1970). Much of the content of basic readers is unexciting, primarily because it is devoid of affective significance. The characters in children's classics convey feelings, aspirations, and conflicts that are real to them. The distance between the fictional world and the real world need not be so great that identity cannot take place. *Cinderella, Jack and the Beanstock,* and *The Ugly Duckling* spell out real-life dilemmas to be resolved, yet placed in fanciful settings that do not threaten. The emotional responses to literature are experienced in the same affective mechanisms of the brain that real trauma is processed and recorded for future decision making.

EXPLORING ADULT ROLES

Career choices may be conceived in the life story of some dedicated person in pursuit of a challenge. Paul de Kruif inspired many young people to consider a career in medical research as they read *The Microbe Hunters*. The worlds that were opened to young readers was exciting as they followed the tale of Leeuwenhoek as he revealed the world of the invisible with lenses and microscopes, of Spallanzani as he proved that microbes have parents, and of Koch as he grew the bacilli of anthrax. Similarly, older students decided to become anthropologists after reading Margaret Mead's *Coming of Age in Samoa*. A book engages the reader for sufficient periods of time to allow the response time that fast-paced video experiences do not yield.

Reading provides the possibility of learning roles that are outside the common experience of young people. They can try out different kinds of relationships, as younger children would explore roles through play. They can be "big" and "mean" without having the normal consequences of such acts descend on them, except in imagination, as their roles are being enacted by a character in a book. This vicarious exploration allows young readers to think about the possible consequences and decide how they want their future relationships to proceed.

Adolescence is a stage in growing up when the egocentrism of early childhood returns as self-centered concern with identity, relationships, and the future. In Western cultures this stage has been extended by the need for higher education and by child labor restrictions. Eric Erikson (1963), sees positive advantages in the adolescent's delay of occupational decision, even though he recognizes that emotional costs are involved. When society sanctions indecision and education is available, the young person can explore possibilities and make better choices of a lifework. These advantages accrue only to those who can read well enough to progress academically and enjoy the work of being a student. The adolescent who has resolved the feelings of inferiority during latency by establishing a sense of industry and accomplishment in school is in a good position to deal with the confusing roles of the high school years. The adolescent reader can search for role resolution and explore opportunities through literature.

The changing roles of women in the workplace is another area where reading can help to resolve the sexual identity-role diffusion polarity. Biography may be particularly useful, as great women often become role models for girls and reduce the egocentrism of the boy-men. The stereotypes of sex-appropriate roles in the workplace are quite well established by grade one. Zarry (1978) exposed his first graders to pictures of men and women in unexpected work roles and showed that some change of attitude is possible. If great books on this theme are scarce in the high school, a lively discussion is almost certain to break out if such questions are raised in the literature classes: Would Nora, the misplaced female protagonist of Ibsen's *The Doll House* have a domestic problem today?

Chapter Summary

A learning-motivation model was proposed which places learning by association, conceptualization, and creative self-direction in a hierarchical relationship. If the teacher envisions association learning as basic, and conceptualization as the midstep toward self-direction and creative production, each teaching objective becomes part of a broader perspective. The brain records associations of pleasure and punishment with each act, whether overt or covert. Brain research places the organization of affects, or emotional response, in the hypothalamus at the top of the brain stem. An elegant neural structure, the medial forebrain bundle (MFB), courses through the hypothalamus and connects to the cortical forebrain where actions are initiated. Children who learn to read well are rewarded by a feeling of power that comes from knowledge. Motivation for school achievement requires a conceptualization of the source of personal pleasure, so that rewards from schoolwork can be selected, arranged, and extended by the student. Such engagement in constructive action leads to level three functioning, or creative self-direction.

II | Cognitive Dimensions

Synaptic and growth changes . . . could well be the primary changes constituting the so-called engram or permanent memory trace. At the same time . . . the law of effect . . . says there must be something more than just the use of synapses; . . . Responses that have a good effect tend to be retained, repeated, and remembered, while those that do not fit in are abandoned, lost, and forgotten.

—R. W. Sperry

3 | Reading as a Linguistic Skill

Communication skills develop sequentially from understanding to speaking, to reading, and finally to writing. Babies learn to convey their pleasure or discomfort through prespeech utterances almost as quickly as they are able to distinguish between states of satisfaction and distress. They enjoy listening to their own babble long before they learn to string phonemes into words and they are able to understand words spoken to them before they are able to talk. The nonverbal communication, the phoneme shaping, and the receptive understanding are stages of prespeech, each being a developmental precursor to the emergence of words. The tacit understanding of linguistic structure that toddlers demonstrate in their acquisition of speech is the foundation for the explicit grammar they will use much later when they learn to comprehend written discourse.

Reading is more difficult than listening, although both are classed as *receptive language*. All literate cultures have understood intuitively this order of difficulty and have taught their children to read only after speech is thoroughly established. Reading and writing represent *expressive language*. Both are more difficult than speech, considering the complexity of the cognitive functions that are involved. Bock and Brewer (1985) warn that differences between the spoken discourse children have mastered when they come to school and the written texts they use there have the potential to aggravate comprehension difficulties. Written texts tap a wider range of general knowledge, show different forms of discourse organization, use different anaphoric devices, and provide less contextual support than spoken discourse does. Comprehension of expository prose, which is the major source of information beyond the primary grades, is a crucial step in reading comprehension and needs to be taught to most children.

The order of difficulty in the acquisition of linguistic skills has been inherent in curricular planning since Huey (1908) and probably before that. The evidence is experential and empirical: Children's listening vocabulary exceeds their word usage in speech and their sight vocabulary exceeds the number of words they can spell or write correctly, even when simplified phonetic codes are used. Grade equivalency scores and standardized norms for children and adults reflect these differences in favor of speaking over reading and reading over writing. Children's own writing generally produces a lower readability quotient than their independent readability level in terms of grade equivalency (Barnes, 1983).

In the late 1980s, following more than a decade in which reading programs became very structured and skill-oriented, professional thinking shifted to a focus on linguistic meanings when teaching reading. Recent technical reports reflect new insights on the process of learning to read and its relationship to oral language development and writing (Clark, 1985). Techniques and strategies have been proposed which emphasize the interaction of reading and the other language arts (Britton, 1987). Unfortunately the research on the dynamics of reading and language is less substantive than would seem desirable before widespread changes are instituted (Squire, 1987a). Each linguistic accomplishment in the cognitive development of the child tends to increase competence in literacy, whether the gain is in listening, in speaking, or in writing. The four sections of this chapter are concerned with the psychological implications of the integration of reading and the other language arts.

COMPREHENSION PRECEDES SPEECH

Communication requires a sender and a receiver. Much of the preverbal communication of infants is successful because parents are highly attentive to their baby's needs and strive to understand the cries, gestures, and babbles they produce. An inefficient sender needs a particularly alert receiver if information is to be conveyed. Very young children are inefficient communicators because they have limited control of their expressive mechanisms. By careful attention to the child's early efforts to communicate, caregivers establish "trust" (in the language of Erik Erikson) and "bonds," according to the current conceptualization of attachment. By responding with words of understanding, the adult reinforces the child's efforts to communicate. The child models the language of adults by selectively contracting their speech and the adults model young children by selectively expanding their speech (Brown & Bellugi, 1964). The child says, "We go walk"; the parent replies, "Yes, we will go walking very soon." In this real-life context, spoken words and their meanings are associated.

Biological Predisposition to Language

The spontaneous development of speech in children is impressive, particularly to any adult who has tried to learn a second language. During the 1960s researchers began to describe speech development in individual children and to analyze these observations according to linguistic principles. A predictable sequence of syntactic accomplishments was established which conformed, within acceptable ranges, to the age of the child (McNeill, 1970). Very similar patterns of language learning were found in dozens of languages and in diverse cultures. A conceptualization of a *universality of language acquisition* was widely accepted as species-specific, that is, as innate and uniquely human. This idea of a biological mechanism for language stimulated a multidisciplinary search for the precursors of speech.

PREVERBAL RECEPTIVE PROCESSES

Long before children can speak they have information available that is obscure because they lack the ability to formulate the message in the language of others. One of the challenges to linguists has been to invent ways of measuring and interpreting the auditory receptive abilities of infants. The responses observed have been the infant's attentional shifts during sound stimulation; such as arousal when asleep or awake, vocalization following recorded speech, and heart-rate changes. Evidence of species-specific sensitivity of the auditory receptors to speech sounds was reported by Menyuk (1971). Neonates responded by crying more frequently when another baby cried than when subjected to the same frequency bands of white noise (Simner, 1969). Infants responded differentially to sound frequencies that fell within the speech ranges of 250 to 4000 Hz, as contrasted to sounds outside these ranges; and they attended more to patterned signals, as contrasted to pure tones (Eisenberg, 1965). Older infants, age 11 to 13 months, gave selective attention to both strangers' and mothers' voices when spoken words were tested (Friedlander, 1967). This knowledge of the infant's sensitivity to language has changed the way psychologists think about language perception.

The age at which infants discriminate speech sounds has been revised downward to the first month of life (Eimas, 1974). His research technique used a computer to monitor change in the rate or pattern of nonnutritive sucking by the infant on an electronic pacifier (Chapter 7). The results showed that most infants perceive the change when a repeated vowel sound is shifted to a different vowel. They also discriminate CV (consonant, vowel) pairs, such as /ba/ and /pa/. These and similar findings have stimulated research on the role of speech phonology in reading.

PHONOLOGY AND READING

The human auditory analyzers apparently are phylogenically prepared to perceive speech, but no one has suggested that a similar visual mechanism is biologically inherited for the perception of print. Eyes are specialized for viewing a three-dimensional world of physical events and the brain is organized to interpret the movement of objects and their intention. To read, humans must learn to translate two-dimensional symbols (abstractions) to real-world meanings. Reading requires extraordinary seeing because the meaning of what is seen is linguistic, as contrasted to spatial meanings and survival interpretations of the recent past. In fact, a large part of humanity still does not read, although all normal persons communicate through speech. To extract meaning from print, the visual signal perceived must link up with language centers where linguistic codes are stored. Lenneberg (1967) regarded reading as a special kind of visual perception which requires both linguistic awareness and phonemic maturity.

Linguistic Awareness

Spoken language is fairly impervious to developmental disruption, whereas reading skills are elusive to many children and adults who speak fluently. Fowler

(1981) discussed some of the problems imposed on learners when they attempt to perceive language by eye. Prereading children and illiterate adults have been found to differ in linguistic awareness from skilled readers. *Linguistic awareness* refers to the explicit knowledge of the structure of a language that allows the user to manipulate linguistic units deliberately. For example, nonreaders have difficulty in segmenting words into phonemes, in counting the syllables in a word, in providing rhymes for familiar words, and in acquiring secret languages such as "pig Latin." Correlational studies have shown a closer relationship between linguistic awareness and word-reading skill than between linguistic awareness and listening or speaking skills. Fowler speculates that phonemic knowledge is implicit and automatic in the auditory mechanism of listeners and speakers, while phonemic knowledge must be learned by association when language is perceived in the visual mechanism.

Why young speakers seem not to need an awareness of word segments, while experienced readers seem to have developed this kind of linguistic awareness is an unresolved issue. Some writers think children ought not be encouraged to notice the correspondences between sound and spelling, but to learn words visually, apparently because they adhere to the theory of direct access from print to the mental lexicon (Chapter 9). On the other hand are the researchers who show that many readers become aware of sound units (phonetic, phonological, or morphophonological) without specific instruction and that this knowledge is related to reading skill. Teachers exploit the more or less rule-governed correspondence between the orthographic alphabet and the phonological system of speech to help young readers "sound out" unfamiliar words. The choice for practitioners is how much of this associative relationship will be taught and how much will be left to discovery by young readers. Most reading specialists have found that most young readers succeed better when taught the phoneme–grapheme correspondences, early and specifically (Chall, 1989). Liberman, Mattingly, & Shankweiler (1980) suggest that the innate speech decoder that is responsible for automatic phonetic perception by ear cannot help out when language input is to the eyes.

Phonological Maturity

The distinction between the auditory reception of speech and the visual reception of printed words may not be difficult for children to bridge when learning to read. Chomsky (1970) expressed the view that the stored lexicon of the English speaker is based on morphological features (meaning units), which correspond quite closely to written forms. For example, **heal** and **health** have a meaning, or morphological relationship which is more accessible than the phonological /heel/ and /helØ/. Others have noted that beginning writers spell phonologically more frequently than they spell morphologically. Moskowitz (1978) suggested that a developmental factor is affecting children's associative pairing of visual and phonemic word segments. She found that children beyond the age of 7 or 8, but not before, learn spoken nonsense words more easily if they correspond to orthographic rules than they learn nonsense words that are not rule-based. This could be interpreted as an age-related development of schemata involving morphological rules. The hypothesis could be proposed that individual differences in the age at which morphological relations are conceptualized by children under 7 is a factor in precocious reading.

Fowler (1981) raised the important question whether phonology is eventually bypassed in the development of fluent reading. In other words, does the gradual shift to visual language eventually bypass the auditory language which initially gave the visual words meaning? Language is spoken, as well as written, in sentence or phrase units. Words derive their meaning in relationship to other words. "The family **dog**" carries a very different meaning from "the dirty **dog**" who is probably not a dog but a disliked person. "His **dogged** determination" is pronounced differently than "He **dogged** my every move", which marks one as an adjective and the other as a verb. Linguists cite three defining properties of a word, each having an influence on how its meaning is accessed: a grammatical class (syntax), a meaning (semantics), and the phonological form. If **dog** is the key to the mental dictionary (lexicon) the potential for decision making is still vast: **dog days** (of summer); **dogfight** (brawl); **doggone** (for those not allowed to say damn); **doggy** (of and for little ones); **dog-ear** (the turned down corner of a page); **dogtag** (the visual ID); **dog** paddle (a way to swim); and **dogwood** (the loveliest of flowering trees). There are many other examples, including **dogma**, **dogmatism**, and **doggerel**. These examples imply (1) that single-word letter strings are inadequate for word comprehension, (2) that sight to meaning associations are acquired gradually with experience and within a context. Fowler suggests that a fourth identifying property, *the graphic form,* is added to word comprehension when the speaker learns to read. She doubts that phonology can be bypassed in fluent reading.

The special properties of language—its capacity for generating an indefinite number of communicable messages—make it an available brain mechanism for reading. When language users learn to read they learn a new way that words may be understood; that is, *orthographically.* This means that readers add the new information about orthographic forms to the existing phonological, grammatical, and semantic information that exists in the lexicon. Much of the learning of graphic properties and phonetic units is associative in nature. The mature reader develops priorities when seeking meanings for graphic representations, such as the frequency of their use or the emotional content. When accessing the lexicon, the word that fits the context, or psychological set, may be the first associative link to be activated. The physics student might comprehend **mass** directly and differently from the theological or the sociological student. Over time, reader's recognition priority may give way to the graphic, or the orthographic, form of some words instead of the phonological form. This is a much disputed issue which remains a challenge for researchers of the 1990s.

LANGUAGE-ACQUISITION DEVICE(LAD)

Different child listeners acquire the same relative competence and develop the same set of linguistic rules for speaking despite the fact that they never hear the same set of utterances from which the abstractions of speech are drawn. Modern scholars accept the evidence of an innate mechanism for language processing which Chomsky (1965) called the *language acquisition device* or LAD. The auditory senses of human neonates are selectively responsive to speech sound ranges, the left temporal lobe is targeted during prenatal development to receive spoken language and, later, to interpret it. Cognitive psychology postulates that meanings are built by association with the contiguous input from other senses and their resultant affects of pleasure or displeasure. The word, **bunny**, is heard in the context of a visual toy, with its tactile fuzziness, and its gentle yielding to a hug. The neural system brings together (associates) these stimuli. Biological systems are stimulated in the way phylogeny designed them; and the exercise of these systems, according to Piaget, is self-reinforcing and self-organizing. This internal necessity to organize bits of input is the basis of conceptual thought.

Linguists have emphasized the relationship within spoken language, rather than the multisensory relationships. Chomsky (1965) described the LAD as an innate knowledge of language and an inherited procedure for learning it. There are five components: (1) a technique for representing input (speech) signals; (2) a way of representing structural information about these signals; (3) some delineation of classes of hypotheses about linguistic structure; (4) a method for comparing sentences against hypotheses; and (5) a method for selecting the hypotheses most compatible with the primary linguistic data. Chomsky reasoned that the child's rapid mastery of a complicated syntactic structure was not possible through cognitive learning alone; that the child was born with biological preconceptions of language. The LAD formulation opened the way for the separate components of the device to be isolated and tested; such as the nature of the primary representations, the syntactic structure of children's emerging speech, the kinds of sentences they generate that models do not use, and the nature of lexical organization. The linguistic forms that define speech reflect the sequence by which infants and young children learn to comprehend speakers.

Listening Comprehension

Listening and reading are similar in many ways. Both are receptive processes which gain linguistic information and ideas from other people—the one through visual sensors and the other through auditory sensors. Both sensory systems respond to distant stimuli, which are transduced to the neural code of the central nervous system. Each has its relay pathways from the peripheral sensors to reception areas in the cortex. Both receptor areas process input signals, which activate the recall of past experience and give meaning to the coded sensory signals. The word seen and the word heard may in fact call up the same real-world experiences through associative linkages. Both code systems are made up of elements (phonemes and letters) which can be combined in an infinite number of units, according to a system of rules. The interplay of the knowledge gained by the listener/reader and the knowledge conveyed by the speaker/writer is a major theme in the psychology of communication.

SPEECH RECEPTION AND PRINT PERCEPTION

Obvious differences exist in the format which listeners and readers must interpret. A listener makes use of facial expression and body language, in addition to other techniques of oral communication such as intonation, emphasis, and the prosodic structure of speech. *Prosodic structure* is the pattern of syllable separation and stress which characterizes a language and is thought to be important in the listener's organization of word meanings and subsequent access to this mental lexicon. Readers confront books, which use a different organization of discourse. Capital letters and periods mark the boundaries of sentences; commas signal a pause. Paragraphs, headings, and chapters cue the reader to the writer's organization of the content.

In a discussion of the difference between speech understanding and reading, Nickerson (1981) argued whether reading skills are superimposed on existing understanding/speaking skills. The implication of an interdependent relationship would be that deficiencies in spoken language would need to be remedied as part of the beginning reading program. He cites the advantages within the auditory system for language processing: (1) the biological sensitivity to properties of speech, (2) the availability of a temporary memory for storing speech signals while ambiguous words are reviewed and resolved; (3) the relay of phoneme signals to the ear in correct temporal sequence so that disarrangement is not possible. The visual system has some different advantages which aid readers: (1) The sensory system is more finely tuned, having many more transducers to carry the features of the stimuli, (2) Eye movements are under the control of the individual so that backtracking to clarify ambiguities is possible; (3) The continued availability of text allows for parallel processing of grapheme segments of words and larger meaning units of text. Nickerson's thesis is that speech understanding and reading are multifaceted activities in which interaction occurs between both auditory and visual systems and at more than one level of processing.

SYNTACTIC STRUCTURE AND COMPREHENSION

The understanding of words in context may call for very different processing strategies than single words. Shankweiler, Smith, and Mann (1984) hypothesized that pronoun reference might be difficult for children to interpret in spoken sentences because the pronoun and the noun to which it refers may be separated by many words. This places a special burden on short-term memory while the grammatical relationships are being interpreted. On the knowledge that children who have difficulty learning to read also have problems in recall of verbal materials presented orally, the investigators tested whether the problem was primarily their comprehension or their verbal reproduction of the information contained in the sentences. Matched pairs of good and poor readers were tested on five sentence types, each posing a problem in pronoun reference. These third-grade subjects, grouped for reading ability, were equally skilled at selecting a picture to demonstrate their comprehension. By contrast, the poor readers made significantly more errors when required to repeat the sentences. The investigators' interpretation was that pictures provided cues which lightened the memory load for poor readers. A different interpretation is possible: Many poor readers, at least in sufficient numbers to influence group data, are deficient in sequencing, or the ordered recall of verbal materials. This deficiency would not affect comprehension, wherein speech stimuli is ordered, but could be a problem in recall.

Our own studies of reading clinic children indicated superior comprehension of sentence-length problems presented orally, and significant dysfunction in the ability to repeat meaningless digits in correct sequence.

Children's comprehension of sentences has been analyzed to develop some principles for organizing the reading textbooks in ways helpful to unskilled learners. Snow and Coots (1982) reviewed studies of child speech perception and production for cues to comprehension based on prosodic information, syntactic organization, and information-processing organization. *Syntactic organization* usually refers to a "top-down" strategy in which the context or the meaning cues within the word dictate the word identification and comprehension process. *Information-processing organization* usually assumes a "bottom-up" order for processing in which the elements (phonemes or letter features) activate the recognition of the word or access the memory lexicon. Snow and Coots proposed a complex relationship of prosodic features to explain how the listener/ reader organizes syntactic meanings from continuous sentences.

The child's conceptualization of linguistic structure was outlined in five stages of language acquisition by Chomsky. [See page 68.] Alvermann (1982) used the framework to explore the relationship of syntactic knowledge and reading achievement in normal and disabled readers 6 to 10 years old. Her results showed that poor readers differed significantly from normal readers in the number of subjects who fell into the higher linguistic stages, as well as the number of syntactic structures comprehended. The linguistic state of development correlated highly with the syntactic complexity levels of the material used in the study. No relationship was found between linguistic stages and reading achievement, age, IQ, and socioeconomic status. This study points out the difficulty of direct comparisons between linguistic stages and reading skill because reading levels lag behind speech levels, thus giving readers some lead time in attaining linguistic structures.

CONCEPTUALIZATION OF STORY CLASSES

Children's stories present comprehension barriers for some children as they encounter unfamiliar forms of literary expression. Fantasy presents a kind of story which some pupils have experienced through books whereas others have not. Pellegrini (1983) examined the effectiveness of fantasy play training, a form of dramatic play, on children's immediate comprehension and story memory after 1 week. Nearly 200 kindergarten and first-grade children were assigned to one of four treatment groups. All groups listened to three different books on three occasions, each followed by one of three maintenance treatments or experimental control: (1) adult-directed play, (2) peer-directed play, (3) accommodation questions, or (4) control (no follow-up). The directed play consisted of fantasy enactments of story themes and events not related to everyday experience; for example, acting out a fairy tale. Following the third story, comprehension was measured three ways: by a 10-item criterion-referenced test, by a story recall task, and by a sequential memory task. Maintenance effects (long-term memory) were measured 1 week later with repeats of the test and the story recall test. The results indicated that adult tuition was not an important element, although it may have been a factor in prior play direction to the groups. For immediate comprehension, fantasy reenactment was generally more effective than were follow-up questions. For maintained comprehension, accommodation questions were generally as effective as play conditions. Our interpretation would be that teacher questioning tended to establish story structure in ways that enhanced long-term verbal recall. Apparently dramatic play and story discussion serve different but important functions in extending children's memory for story structure.

Metaphoric language is another source of difficulty for young children in comprehending stories read to them. Vosniadou and Ortony (1984) investigated the hypothesis that children's difficulty in paraphrasing a metaphoric condition may differ from their comprehension of metaphoric language. They read short stories ending with a metaphorical sentence to two groups of 6-year-old children. Half the children were asked to paraphrase the ending, while the other half were asked to act it out with toys in a real-world environment. The children in the enactment group made more correct interpretations than did the children in the paraphrase group. The children's ability to comprehend figures of speech is more advanced than their ability to communicate verbally their understanding of metaphor.

Plausity of the message contributes to children's listening comprehension of story material. Kooney and Murphy (1983) varied the length and plausibility of stories read to children and then tested their ability to "find problems" with the stories. Subjects were 19 third graders and 25 eighth graders who listened to four stories of the following characteristics: long, low plausibility; short, high plausibility; short, low plausibility; or long, high plausibility. Four probe questions of increasing specificity were asked following the presentation of each story. The first two probes were general, preceding and following a request that the child recall the story. The third probe asked for information relating to inconsistency in the story, but did not point it out. The fourth probe explicitly pointed out the inconsistency. Each subject's score was the probe number at which he or she explicitly stated the inference that led to the contradiction in the story. Overall, the length of the story had a small effect. Story concreteness and plausibility had a large effect on the children's ability to monitor their comprehension, that is to state the inference that led to the contradiction.

Some attempts have been made to develop and assess children's listening skills under different experimental conditions. Crowell and Hu-pei Au (1981) tested a hierarchy of comprehension objectives: association, classification, seriation, integration, and extension. They reported that children could be taught increasingly difficult comprehension skills, whether the modality was listening, reading or television viewing. Johnson (1982) tested the recall of children 7 to 9 years old on three language reception modes: listening, oral reading, and silent reading. The difficulty of the material produced significant effects. Boys exhibited very poor recall performance after silent reading, compared with their recall after listening and after oral reading. Girls showed comparable recall performance across all three language reception modes. The implication of this research is that teaching comprehensive listening skills should enhance reading comprehension.

SPEECH AS IMPLICIT KNOWLEDGE

Children acquire speech through a sequence of accomplishments based on implicit, rather than explicit, knowledge of phonemic and syntactic structures. Speech is developmental in the sense that it evolves at predictable times in the maturation of the child, according to an innate neurological blueprint. Speech is learned in the sense that social models are required for the particular language the child acquires and for the communication functions that are served. The child demonstrates *implicit knowledge* of linguistic structures by using correct forms in speech, yet without the ability to explain them. For example, the relationship of noun, verb, and object (NVO) is learned by age 2 or 3. The child expresses this syntactic knowledge very early, "Kitty want mok." even earlier the morphemic significance of the plural **s** is understood, "Two daddy mens." The young child cannot explain these linguistic relationships. Older children acquire *explicit knowledge* of language when they study grammar; but adult illiterates continue to communicate with implicit linguistic knowledge. This section concerns the relationship of speech acquisition to reading.

Stages in the Acquisition of Speech

Infants respond to the speech and facial expression of caregivers from the first week of life. They synchronize their body movements to adult speech (Condon & Sander, 1974). They imitate adult facial expressions, such as opening the mouth and showing the tongue (Field, Cohen, Greenberg, & Woodson, 1982). By 6 months, infants look longer at films when speech and lip movements are synchronized than when they were not; they attend longer to sound films presented to the right visual field (projecting to the left hemisphere); and they babble more to regular speech sound track than to the same track when altered to reduce speech features (Kuhl & Meltzoff, 1982).

FUNCTIONS OF BABBLING

During the infant's first year, the production of prespeech phonemes evolves gradually as communicative crying is supplemented by cooing and babbling. *Cooing* is pleasure-producing vocalization which emerges by the second month and consists primarily of back rounded vowels /u/ and glottal stops that resemble /g/ or /k/. David, a second grader, seemed to be frozen at this level of consonant articulation. He, /Gagi/, used a rapid flowing jargon of CV and CVCV words with some vowel variations and an elaborate repertoire of gestures. His twin, Donald /Gahgo/, was usually at hand to interpret in a slightly more advanced language that could be interpreted by the other children and his teacher with careful listening and some familiarity with his speech. Extensive therapy was required to improve David's speech.

When the infant begins to explore new utterances, at about 4 months old, the babbling stage has begun. *Babbling* produces a variety of speech elements, often in combinations of CV. The most common sequence of consonant practice begins with the labials /b/, /p/, and /m/ (Table 3.1). This early production of "mama," and "papa" resembles what family members are called in many languages. The sequence of consonants that are babbled proceeds backward in the speech mecha-

73 | Speech as Implicit Knowledge

TABLE 3.1. The International Phonetic Symbols for Phonemes of English, Organized with Respect to Articulatory Features. Each Symbol Is Followed by a Word Containing the Sound (Italicized)

		Consonants								
		Labial		Dental		Alveolar		Palatal		Velar
Stops	voiced	b	*b*ill			d	*d*ill			g	*g*ill
	voiceless	p	*p*ill			t	*t*ill			k	*k*ill
Nasals		m	*m*ill			n	*n*ill			ŋ	si*ng*
Fricatives {	voiced	v	*v*eil	ð	*th*e	z	*z*ero	ž	*zh*a-*zh*a		
	voiceless	f	*f*ill	θ	*th*in	s	*s*ill	š	*sh*arp		
Affricates {	voiced							ǰ	e*dge*		
	voiceless							č	*ch*urch		
Liquid/semivowel		w	*w*ill			r,l	*r*ai*l*			h	*h*id

	Vowels		
	Front	Central	Back
High	i b*ee*t		u b*oo*t
	I b*i*t		U b*oo*k
Mid	e b*ai*t	ə sof*a*	o b*oa*t
	ɛ b*e*t		ʌ b*u*t, ɔ b*ough*t
	æ b*a*t		
Low		a b*a*r	

From V. C. Tartter, *Language Processes,* p. 178. Copyright 1986, Holt, Rinehart, & Winston.

nism to palatal and velar sounds. By contrast, the shaping of vowels moves gradually from the back vowels of cooing to the central vowel /a/, and much later to the front vowels /i/, /I/, /e/, and /æ/. During the 6 months or so that the infant babbles, phonemes heard in the native tongue are shaped and those not used in the social ecology are gradually eliminated.

During the cooing and babbling stages, areas of the cortex that subserve speech increase in weight and thickness. The neurons involved in signal transmission and phoneme production elaborate and myelinate (Chapter 6). The pathways that connect speech reception and production areas continue to mature rapidly until age 2, in contrast to the myelination of major visual pathways which tapers off at about 4 months.

The behavioral activities of babbling are evidence of neural linkages that make intentional babbling possible. Two strings of feedback signals are received in the infant's middle ear: one direct from the infant's oral cavity, and the other from the self-initiated voice as received through the outer ears. These signals, attended to by the babbler, are linked associatively in the CNS. The pleasure that infants display during cooing and babbling is reinforcing, that is, strengthening, to the associative linkages between motor and auditory events. An important element in learning and pleasure reinforcement is the infant's gradual control over the voice mechanisms as the ability to make interesting sounds last is learned.

Babies involved with adults in physical activities; babies engaged in face-to-face talking; and babies who are socially reinforced for vocalization will babble more than those who receive less stimulation. Some children do not learn to articulate certain phonemes of spoken English until kindergarten or later. The most likely mispronunciations are /l/, /r/, /w/ which are formed late by most babblers and may not be discriminated by some children when they enter school. Cognitively advanced children who learn to speak very young may substitute /th/ for /s/, perhaps because their knowledge of language precedes the tongue-lip control needed to produce /s/. This "lisp" sometimes continues, uncorrected, into adulthood when it can be a handicap in public appearances.

PHONETIC REPRESENTATION IN READING

The relationship of phonological maturation and skill in reading has been suspected since tutors first observed the inability of some children to make the associative links between printed graphemes and the phonemes of speech. Fox and Routh (1980) reported a strong positive correlation between children's awareness of the phonemic and syllabic structure of words and a successful beginning in reading. Lack of the ability to segment words into syllables at the kindergarten level was predictive of poor reading in first grade. Failure to learn to use phonemic information at that level results in a continuation of reading and spelling problems into adulthood.

Researchers disagree on whether the aural phonetic content of words continues to be activated after a word is established in the sight vocabulary. Perfetti, Bell, and Delaney (1988) addressed this question directly in a series of experiments in which they were able to disrupt the exposure time of a visual word, short of its recognition. The brief stimuli were followed by different masking cues: those having additional phonemic information or those having additional visual information. The question was whether these adult readers had retained in working memory the phonetic or the graphic information on which to complete word recognition. The responses indicated that phonetic activation occurred (1) at the initial stages of print perception, (2) "nonoptionally" without intent or direction on the part of the subject, and (3) "prelexically," that is prior to access in the lexicon. The investigators explained visual word recognition as excitatory links between graphic word forms and phonetic word forms. They suggested that such links allow activation of the system to occur both upward from letter and phoneme units to words (bottom-up theory) and downward from word meanings to letters and phonemes (top-down theory).

Acquisition of Syntax

Following a period of intense babbling, many infants enter into a void of pre-speech at about 10 or 11 months old. When "real" meaningful speech begins, the phonemes spewed forth so playfully may be difficult to articulate. One explanation is that babbling is motor-directed from the bilateral tertiary speech areas of the cortex, while verbal expression is directed from Broca's area in the left frontal lobe (Chapter 6). Certainly new linkages are required between the speech interpretation areas of Wernicke and the speech production areas of Broca. The order of speech acquisition is evidence of the child's natural organization of syntax and one of the great accomplishments of the human species.

ORDER OF SYNTACTIC DEVELOPMENT

Meaningful production of words for most youngsters begins with the use of one-word productions. In the view of some experts, naming, such as "mommy," "papa," and "bobo," is not a stage of speaking because syntactic understanding is not yet demonstrated. They explain "naming" as an associative label function, representing someone or something. When the child says "bobo" to mean "I want my rag doll," most linguists agree that the child has entered the first stage of speech. *Holophrasitic* speech is a one-word expression which stands for a whole sentence or a phrase (Tartter, 1986). The stage when holophrastic speech dominates the child's expressive language begins before the first birthday and evolves into the next stage by the second birthday. A scattering of babbling is expected during this period, especially during solitary play. Some early use of multiple words may be noticed, perhaps because the child perceives them as single word. "Teddybear" may be used as the name of a toy, or "nightnight" as the time to go to bed. The child, however, does not confuse a noun class and a verb class in holophrastic speech. The predominant content of one-word speech is the noun as subject, which most experts concur is the beginning of lexical organization.

Two-word speech expresses a syntactic relationship which may be a noun phrase or a NV sentence. Individual speakers enter this stage in distinctive ways. Michael was fascinated by noun modifiers: "Big truck," "Red truck,", and even "Huge big eno'mous truck." Elyse expanded her speech with "My Marky," "My doll," and "My chair." Two-word speech often begins with a pivot class, combined with an open class, which the child expands rapidly. Both examples reflect the egocentrism of children this age. Michael assumes, "I see . . . " because his perception is limited to his own view and in this construction "truck" becomes the object. Elyse may mean either "Where is . . . " or "I want . . . ," which she communicates by her inflection of **my**. Two-word expressions have been described as *linear syntax,* suggesting a combinational relationship in a word string.

Children very soon experience the need to communicate with NVO (noun–verb–object) relationships. These productions, like the previous stages, are initiated in expressive rather then imitative language (McNeill, 1970). *Telegraphic speech* describes the stage in which two- or three-term relationships are combined to make a skeletal sentence. Modifiers are sparse and sequences are seldom more than three words. Examples are: "Me want banana." "Read book now. " When children begin to use verb phrases, they typically use simple action verbs from their immediate experience: **make, get, do**, which they combine with many different objects. Verbs of location come next (**go, sit, take, put**) and finally verbs of state (**want, see, sleep, is**). Telegraphic speech has a higher-order structure than linear syntax.

At age 3, plus or minus 6 months, the child makes significant semantic advances. More than one proposition is used in a sentence: "I am taking a nap and Pogo is taking a nap." This simple *coordinance* is superseded by causality, priority, or temporal statements. The addition of new meanings, by conjuction, is called *superordinance*. Descriptive clauses that add no new meaning beyond that contained therein, called *subordinance,* are acquired late in speech development. By age 4 the child has mastered these three forms well enough to converse with an adult or another 4-year-old.

INTERACTION OF PHONEMIC AND SYNTACTIC ABILITIES

Ehri (1983) postulated that when a child learns to read and spell, a system of visual representation *for speech* is acquired. The child's competency in speech is likely to improve with these activities, particularly in the discrimination of phonemic segments. When asked to identify the number of phonemes in a word children sometimes resorted to spelling cues, as evidenced by their counting silent letters as phonemes. Ehri observes that phoneme awareness is both antecedent and consequent to the development of reading skill. Phonemic knowledge may be seen in different linguistic subskills, each having a relationship to success in learning to read: ability to segment the speech stream, phonemic synthesis (blending a string of phonemes into a word), identifying the number of phonemes in a word. These findings suggest that phoneme awareness should be taught systematically in conjunction with beginning reading.

NARRATIVE SKILL AND READING SUCCESS

The production of narrative language has been associated with reading success. Feagans and Short (1984) made a cross-sectional and longitudinal study of normally achieving and reading-disabled groups of children in an attempt to understand more clearly the language processes involved in reading achievement. The children were read script-like narratives and asked to demonstrate their knowledge of the story by nonverbal enactment of the narrative. After perfect enactment of the story was assured, the subjects were asked to paraphrase the narratives. Results from both the cross-sectional and longitudinal observations showed that disabled readers comprehended the narratives in a comparable fashion to normally reading peers, but poor readers performed less well on a variety of content and complexity measures derived from the paraphrases. The longitudinal study showed that problems of poor readers persisted over time. These several studies suggest a relationship between expressive language and reading whether the investigators are focusing on phonemic or narrative speech processes.

Science of Phoneme Perception

Psychology and education have been influenced in recent years by the scientific work of linguists, who actively entered the reading professions about 1960. One of their contributions was the table of *international phonetic symbols,* an array of

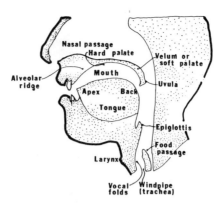

FIGURE 3.1. *Schematic of speech mechanism. Control of air flow through the vocal tract produces various articulatory features of speech (Drawing by Donna Thompson).*

the speech sounds based on the potential of the human articulatory anatomy to produce phonemes. Theoretically any written language could be printed in phonemic transcription and any fluent reader could read it orally, with appropriate pauses and stops. The advantage of having such a tool is obvious in a world of more than 150 countries and many more dialects. Because of variations in stress and aspiration, a modified table of the phonemes of English, organized with respect to its particular articulatory features was presented by Tartter (1986) [Table 3.1]. Descriptions that reflect precise *phonetic* articulations are enclosed in brackets. *Phonemes* and their *allophones* are bordered by a slash. An example of allophones are the medial consonants of latter and ladder, which sound the same and may both be represented by /d/ or /t/.

Although speech is normally produced through vocal articulation, listeners and researchers use several means to record or produce the sounds of language, for example, the tape recorder or the speech synthesizer. Pressure variations in the air that moves through the vocal mechanism produces the sounds of speech (Fig. 3.1). A visual reproduction of the energy flow of a segment of speech is a *spectogram*. The equipment which makes the photographs of phonemes, syllables, and words is a *spectograph*. Technicians who are skilled in reading speech spectograms look for the several formants that make up the photograph (Fig. 3.2). Formants are the dark bands on a spectrogram that represent the force of the resonances from the vocal tract. Formants are usually counted from the lowest frequency to the highest (first, second, third). The time line along the base of the spectogram provides a measure of the response time between changes in the spectrum. This measure is important in describing the voicing features of certain consonants. The voice onset time (VOT) is the interval from when the vocal cords begin to vibrate relative to the release of the consonant. If the vibration starts late, the consonant is classed as voiceless; if it starts early it is seen as voiced. Reading specialists do not need to read spectograms, but they do need to understand the psycholinguistic research on which reading models are based.

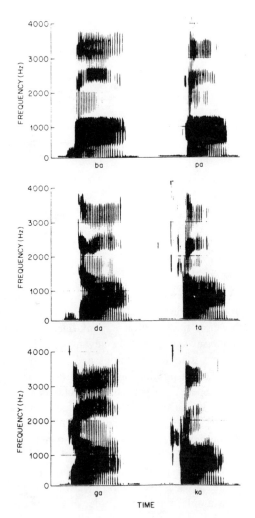

FIGURE 3.2. Spectograms of stop consonants of English in CV syllables with /a/ (From V. C. Tarter, *Language Processes*, p. 198. Copyright 1986, Holt, Rinehart, & Winston).

Speech and Cognitive Processes

An investigation of the role of the working memory in groups of normal and disabled readers was reported by Mann, Shankweiler, and Smith (1984). They tested the ability of grade-three children to comprehend sentences and their accuracy in sentence repetition. It was noted that those subjects with reading disability ordinarily are not impaired in general learning and memory tasks, nor are they retarded in overall language functions. In this comparison of good and poor readers, the researchers were asking whether difficulties with phonetic representation would penalize the children's comprehension of a sentence, as well as their repetition of the same sentences. To maximize complexity, the stimulus sentences had a basic SVO syntax with embedded clauses inserted in various syntactic positions. All four sentences were comprised of the same 10 words. The results showed that good readers were more accurate than poor readers on both repetition and comprehension of complex sentence arrangements. The investigators explained that the successful language learner must assess large parts of the phonetic structure of the utterance at hand, and rely on word order and phonological features to establish the correct syntactic structure when comprehending or repeating sentences. They suggested that "ineffective phonetic representations" may limit the development of syntactic competence and retard the tempo of language development in poor readers. Poor phonetic representation may slow the processing of sentences and become a handicap whenever unusual complexity is built into discourse.

Another study incorporated developmental cognitive psychology in an investigation of the linguistic components of reading. Three Western Australians, Tunmer, Herriman, and Nesdale (1988) followed 118 children from the beginnings of reading in first grade to the end of second grade when appropriate achievement tests were administered. The investigators were interested in "metalinguistic abilities," the children's cognitive operations on language. They used three measures: the Clay prereading tests, which is a comprehensive reading readiness survey; a verbal intelligence test, and some Piagetian measures of concrete operational thought, or *operativity*.

Their longitudinal results suggested: (a) Children's ability to acquire low-level metalinguistic skills depends in part on their level of operativity (cognitive development). In the beginning stages of learning to read, operativity helped children to discover "cryptanalytical intent," which means the conceptualization that print maps onto certain structural features of spoken language. The discovery of the grapheme–phoneme correspondence is basic to the reader's intent when encountering print. The data also suggested: (b) Some minimal level of "phonological awareness" may be necessary for children to profit from letter–name knowledge in the acquisition of phonological recoding skill and (c) Phonological and syntax awareness play more important roles in beginning reading than pragmatic awareness, or practical experience with letter signs. The cognitive development that children demonstrate in the acquisition of speech appears to have long-term consequences in reading acquisition.

READING AS LANGUAGE RECEPTION

The dichotomy between reading as decoding, which usually is emphasized at the beginning stages, and reading for communication may become a source of confusion unless the distinctive goals for each are specified. Word analysis at a mastery level is necessary before word recognition of unfamiliar vocabulary is possible. The sooner word identification becomes automatic the more easily students will be able to read for information. Listening and reading interact in ways that intrigue cognitive psychologists. Tests of listening comprehension are often used as estimates of reading capacity and a discrepancy in favor of listening may signal a specific reading problem in a particular child. Language arts curricula incorporate listening as part of the sequence of communication. Although the relationship of listening and reading has been established many times, the causal effect of one upon the other is difficult to determine because all linguistic systems are activated to some degree when a subject reads. This section explains why reading is more difficult than listening, explores some strategies for improving recall of long passages, and cites some instances of individual differences that call for unusual adjustments in the reading curriculum.

Receptive Processes

Literacy expands a person's horizons beyond the immediate present to encompass the thoughts and experiences of other ages and other places. To some extent the traditional functions of books are being performed by television, movies, radios, and tapes. Degrosky (1982) analyzed the television-viewing habits and reading achievement of seventh and eighth graders. The data showed an average viewing time of more than 17 hours per week, of which 34% was given to situation comedies and less than 1% to documentaries. Reading test scores of the students were significantly were related to grade level, IQ, and quality of television viewing. Reading achievement scores were not correlated significantly with TV-viewing time.

Nevertheless, reading remains the dominant way for students of all ages to obtain information. Reading proceeds more quickly than any form of oral communication similarly detailed; fluent readers comprehend textual materials about twice as rapidly as the typical lecturer speaks. Listening, it should be said, does serve some unique human purposes not achieved through reading, as any student of drama or poetry will be aware. The performing arts convey information through body language and voice that words of print do not. Reading, on the other hand, provides direct access to the author's ideas and permits the reader to take the time required for personal interpretations, without dependence on intermediaries.

PARTICULARIZED HUMAN FUNCTION

Within the present generation, computers have been invented which can be programmed to translate one language into another, although the readout is meaningless without a person to interpret it. A decade ago computer scientists were attempting to interpret brain functions in terms of the mechanisms of digital computers. In the late 1980s they are attempting to model new and more complex computers after the biological brain (Bower, 1988). *Neural networks* is the term used for the system of interconnected computers being programmed to perform memory tasks not possible with previously existing systems. Neurophysiologists point out that the associative connections of computer networks cannot generate information as complex as the linguistic interpretations of the typical 4-year-old. Some philosophers and cognitive psychologists point out that the "connectionist theory of learning" on which neural networks are designed is too simplistic for replicating the thought and language processes of humans. Information processing will continue to improve in complexity, but teachers of reading will want to develop metacognitive responses to reading materials from their students that are not yet envisioned in computer systems.

ABSTRACTION OF THE PRINTED MESSAGE

Most ordinary reading is based on the input of visual symbols that represent auditory signals to the reader. Since there is an extra step in the interpretation process, that of changing the visual stimulus to auditory form, reading is more abstract than listening. Once the visual and auditory language have been used long enough for each to be processed automatically, there may be little difference in the complexity of the neurological processes of reception, transduction, and interpretation in the two modalities. Individual learners, however, may continue to process the input of one modality more efficiently than the other.

To understand text, readers must engage in at least three cognitive activities: recognition, comprehension, and memory. Wilkinson (1982) reported the development of elementary schoolchildren in their understanding of spoken and written discourse. Experiments were conducted to assess individual and developmental differences in speed of word recognition and how these related to performance on a variety of memory tasks. As might be expected, the rapidity of word recognition increased rapidly and consistently from first- to ninth-grade subjects. An unexpected finding was that certain cognitive gains were independent of the child's rate of word recognition. Stated differently, developmental gains in the rapidity of word recognition may have no necessary relation to memory improvement. Individual differences, rather than developmental differences, may characterize the memory skills of individual students. Stable differences were found among individual children in sentence processing that were attributed to the way in which they executed elementary cognitive processes. This would seem to mean that the rate of word recognition is only one of several cognitive processes that must be integrated in the comprehension of discourse.

The ability of proficient readers to manipulate visual symbols without translating them to speech forms in order to abstract meaning is an issue that is under intense investigation by proponents and opponents of this view. Frank Smith (1971) described the process of *immediate comprehension* as going directly from the visual features of print to the message. The fluent reader who has prior knowledge of the concepts recognizes essential words immediately and makes literal interpretation of the author's ideas. Other examples that show nonauditory reading as a possibility are skilled mathematicians who read the language of computers in symbolic rather than semantic terms, and architects or engineers who read drawings and specifications in terms of stress loads. Whenever a reader deals with visual abstractions as meaningful relationships, without auditory activation in motor or speech mechanisms, he or she is reading at this level.

For beginning readers and most adults, speech is the intermediary between ideation and print comprehension. When reading is viewed as a receptive process in which the author, as distinct from speaker, is absent, the child needs continuous verification that the words are correctly recognized and that the meanings are appropriately inferred. When young readers reach the stage where new ideas are encountered, they may want to share the information with others. Oral rereading of story material is one form of verification. At certain stages of word recognition, some children enjoy rereading to parents at home and friends in "playschool" situations. Rereading in class is a challenge to teachers who must decide when and for whom it is needed. Reading a particular selection to answer a question adds a dimension of evaluation to the activity and provides practice in skimming to locate the relevant sentence(s). Children can read to each other in pairs, alternating the paragraphs or taking the role of different characters, without taking the time of the teacher, or the entire class, to hear one child read.

COMPREHENSION OF EXTENDED TEXT

Class discussions about a story read silently can be exciting if the questions are well orchestrated and go beyond the informational level to inferences, character analysis, and moral judgments. Maestas and Croll (1985) found that children were responsive to strategies the authors designed for increasing story comprehension. Children in grades three and four and a group of learning-disabled readers were taught to identify the setting, problem, goal, action, and outcome of a story, according to a procedure called "story mapping." In a follow-up evaluation, the children were tested on free recall of the story and with questions of explicit and implicit comprehension. Both grade-level groups improved their story comprehension in day-to-day lessons. Normal readers were not impeded by the inclusion of low-achieving children in this kind of instruction. This finding that slow readers profited also invites research efforts to use story mapping strategies below and above the third grade for comprehension enhancement.

Individual Differences

Individuals differ in their reading capacity in ways only partly explained by their verbal intelligence. Precocious readers are numerous among intellectually gifted populations, yet about 60% of them are not reading when they arrive at first grade. The abilities of children from educationally disadvantaged families may be misjudged by their use of substandard speech which is assumed to affect school learning adversely, although this relationship has not been established. Children whose native language is other than English may need extra time to learn the new lexicon, yet bilingualism has some advantages in cognitive functioning over monolingualism. Differences such as these require individual attention from the first day the student undertakes a new class assignment.

HYPERLEXIA

Unexpected reading precocity is called *hyperlexia*. Pennington, Johnson, and Welsh (1987) reported a case study of a lefthanded, preschool boy of superior intelligence who read earlier and at a level beyond what his IQ would predict. At age 2 years, 11 months his reading age was 9.3 grade equivalency estimate and at age 4 years, 2 months his reading age was at 11.2. He read nonwords, regular words, and irregular words equally well, indicating to the researchers that his mechanisms for lexical access were similar to those of normal readers. Unlike reports of some hyperlexics, his comprehension of words and sentences was well above age level. When his precocious reading first appeared, he was also advanced in certain reading related skills: phoneme awareness, auditory verbal short-term memory, and word retrieval. He was not similarly superior in visuospatial skills. The child appeared physically normal and without indications of autism or other pathological variations. These data imply that pathological levels of social and language development are not a necessary condition of precocious reading. If this child represents merely extreme variation in a continuum of a reading population, the makers of models must account for hyperlexia, as some of them are currently attempting to account for dyslexia.

SUBCULTURE SPEECH

Children whose spoken language is nonstandard to the extent communication is impaired are likely to have more difficulty in learning to interpret print than those who already use conventional English because they have a larger number of irregularities with which to cope. In standard speech, children are likely to say "hafta" and must learn to read "have to." This kind of irregularity is multiplied for children who say "jaw" instead of "jar," "pin" instead of "pen," and "rat now" instead of "right now." In any patois English, the correspondence between word and utterance and the correspondence between grapheme and phoneme go beyond typical difficulties the child must overcome in going from casual to formal English. Loban (1964), who studied social dialects extensively, designated the stages by which children acquire conformity with adult norms. (1) *Basic grammar* is the level at which children master the major rules in the lexicon of spoken English. (2) The *vernacular* or neighborhood dialect is used to communicate with peers. (3) *Social perception* is the stage at which speech forms correspond to the expectations of the adult world. (4) *Stylistic variation* is used by older children and adolescents to conform with prestige standards in formal versus casual speech. (5) A *consistent standard* is the adherence to valued speech patterns of the group to which an individual aspires, and the ability to maintain the model. (6) The *full range* norm of speech is achieved by a few individuals who master more than one prestige form and apply flexible linguistic styles that enable them to switch downward to their original vernacular when the occasion makes such a switch advantageous. High school students who speak only the vernacular will need a special kind of understanding and rapport on the part of the teacher to accept the more mature stages of *social perception* and *stylistic variation* by which schools and books communicate.

ENGLISH AS A SECOND LANGUAGE

From the time an individual learns to read, the brain links whatever alphabetic code is being learned to its nearest approximation in the phonemic elements of the language spoken. Children who are learning to read a language they do not speak, must learn the new vocabulary in somewhat the same way adults acquire vocabulary in an unfamiliar subject. The brain links English print representations with original language and whatever English meanings that are available. This learning occurs by association because the input and the recall are contiguous in time and/or space. Students who know how to read in English, but do not speak the language they are studying, translate from pronunciation by phoneme–grapheme association to English meanings. Spanish and English, for example, are linked automatically because the alphabetic codes are very much alike and the brain searches out whatever prior learning has relevance. Learning Chinese or Arabic is difficult for English speakers because they cannot link the features of the written language to speech. The point is that persons who have learned to read cannot approach visual language as a novice; nor can they approach speech acquisition as a young child would.

When teaching how to read English as a second language, three dimensions of the task will vary according to the language the student already knows: (a) text comprehension—the effects of one language on the comprehension of the other; (b) the nature of the orthographic code, if the students is literate, and (c) the format of the written language, if different from English. The differences between the native language and English determine the teaching procedures that are most likely to succeed with an individual student or a group of similar linguistic background.

SPANISH–ENGLISH BILINGUALISM

Bilingual education (English and Spanish) has been taught widely in the Southwest. Knowledge available in the child's first language is used to help them acquire the second language, usually English. Most children become bilingual and acquire age-appropriate literacy skills by the time they finish elementary school. The major contingency is mastery of basic auditory and orthographic coding skills early in the study of the second language. When this mastery has been achieved, knowledge used in comprehension of the first language is used automatically to interpret textual material in the second language. Narrative comprehension skills may be transferred from either language to the other and the student shifts easily from one memory system to the other.

Languages which are written from right to left, such as Arabic, Farsi, and Hebrew, appear to be acquired by similar matching strategies and modality integration as English students use when learning to read. Sharon and Calfee (1977) reported that visual–visual matching of print segments was virtually perfect in second- to fourth-grade Hebrew children. Auditory–auditory matching was more difficult than V–V matching or auditory–visual matches when the stimuli were nonverbal. Auditory–visual matching of verbal material for children learning to read in Hebrew was most difficult of these tasks. Hebrew print may look difficult to English readers, but the process of sequencing it to speech appears similar for children of both tongues.

ASIAN LANGUAGES

The influx of Asian children into English-speaking countries and their relative success in academic work has created an International interest in the structure of their language as a basis for cognitive functions in reading. The ancient written language of China, *hanzi,* was a series of logographs or characters written in vertical columns, beginning at the upper right (Wang, 1981). Each frame was aesthetically and asymmetrically constructed to occupy a square and was stroked with a brush from the top downward and from the left. The earliest Chinese logographs date back 6,000 years, true writing at least 3,400 years. By 121 A.D. a dictionary of nearly 10,000 logographs had been compiled. Although the earliest characters were predominantly pictographs, having direct semantic representation; by the Qing dynasty (1644–1911) 82% of the logographs were phonograms, having phonemic representation.

Current logographs are classified as pictographs, simple ideograms, complex ideograms, phonetic loans, and derivatives. Their dictionaries organize *hanzi* characters into classes of "radicals" and subdivide these according to the number of strokes used in constructing the character. Chinese syllables correspond to morphemes and the strokes are made in the precise sequence that they are spoken. The speech and the writing are descriptive: *library* is literally presented as "picture–book–building" and *thirty* as "three-tens." In 1952, the People's Republic simplified the shapes within characters to promote literacy and ease of writing. In addition a Western alphabet was adapted by using diacritic markings to convey the "tones" of the Chinese vowels.

Asian languages are borrowed from the *hanzi,* which is named for the Han people—the majority culture in China (Wang, 1981). The Koreans adapted *hanja* and developed *hangul,* a script that chunks by syllable and visually resembles the strokes of ancient Chinese. Korean script is at once a syllabary, in that its frames correspond to syllables, and an alphabet (in that its letters correspond to segments). Long before phonetics became a science, the shape of some hangul letters resembled tongue shaping in articulation. A sophisticated system of diacritic features represented the features of speech. The Japanese borrowed *kanji,* a basic selection of logographs from hanzi and simplified them. About 1,000 years ago they selected a few dozen logographs for their sound correspondence, stripped them to their graphic elements and developed a system of script called *kana.* Kanji resembles pictographs and is designed to have an iconic relation with the objects they represent. Kana represents speech, employing both single consonants and syllables in a system that is extremely consistent in phoneme–grapheme relationships.

Asian languages are a fertile area for study because the mental processing of pictographic and syllable-based characters is assumed to be processed in different hemispheres of the brain. The dual systems, one semantic and the other phonemic, may be found to contribute to the high rate of literacy in these and some other languages. Extreme disability in learning to read (dyslexia) is about 1% in Japan, whereas it is 4% in Western countries, and much higher than that in some developing nations. Are these differences the result of socialization and acculturation? Does the dual learning of kana and kanji build early associations which reinforce both? Or does this achievement reflect the preschool teaching of letters and reading at home and at an early age? Or are the inheritors of an ancient writing system, also endowed with a mechanism adapted to visual language—a RAD, or reading acquisition device—that beckons little eyes to print. At times your authors have watched the fascination of infants with the figures on crib blankets and wondered.

TURNING SPEECH INTO WRITING

Given the current focus on the reading/writing connection, our readers may find it hard to believe that reading was not always viewed as an integral part of the language arts. Developmental psychologists of the Piagetian persuasion considered speech as culturally imposed and learning to read as education, distinct from the biological blueprint for cognitive development. Vygotsky and Luria thought of language as socialization and literacy as the key to higher levels of logical thought than illiterate people could attain. This section first summarizes Vygotsky's analysis of the differences between speaking and writing for communication. The last part deals with what current theorists call the "wholeness of language."

Vygotsky's Analysis

In his book, *Language and Thought,* Vygotsky anticipated the current interest among linguists and psychologists in understanding how the mind (brain) initiates complex ideas (trans. 1962, original in Russian, 1934). Vygotsky suggested that information is organized into conceptual systems by a developmental progression from *preconceptual perception* to *categorical organization.* He agreed with Koffka that the educational process itself forms new cognitive structures and that instruction in one area can transform the child's quality of thought in another area. In brief, Vygotsky saw development, instruction, and learning as different temporal sequences which were mutually supportive in the larger scheme of a maturation process. This view of cognitive development as qualitative, sequential, and responsive to instruction is important in understanding his views.

In a series of studies Vygotsky (1962) and his colleagues examined the psychological functions requisite for learning the basic school subjects, including reading and writing. He noted that the gap between children's oral language and their written language may be 6 or 8 "linguistic years." He rejected the common notion that such a discrepancy can be explained by lack of vocabulary or grammatical form, since the young child demonstrates these abilities in speech. He rejected mechanics, also, as a reason for the gap, citing Montessori, whose 4- and 5-year-old pupils had adequate small muscle control for writing. Instead he analyzed the unique linguistic demands of composition writing.

According to Vygotsky, composed writing does not repeat the developmental history of speaking: Even at simple levels writing requires a higher level of abstraction. In learning to write, the child must first "disengage himself from the sensory aspect of speech," such as expression and intonation, and "replace words by images of words" (p. 98). Inner speech, that is merely imagined, requires a second order of symbolization when transcribing the sound *images* into written signs. A second consideration is that writing, unlike speech, lacks an interlocutor who creates a dynamic and motivating element in oral communication. Children feel little need to communicate with an absent person. The third reason for the gap between spoken and written expression is that writing requires deliberate analytical action on the part of the child. The unconscious mental operations of speech must be replaced by deliberate cognition of the sound structure of each word, dissection of phonemes, and reproduction in alphabetical symbols. Written language requires conscious work because "its relation to inner speech is different from that of oral speech" (p. 99). Vygotsky notes that thought is speech gone underground; hence inner speech develops later than oral speech. Writing is a longer translation of inner speech, the later being condensed, abbreviated, and syntactically distinct; the writer must change from maximally compact inner speech to maximally detailed explanations for other persons. Vygotsky believed the study of grammar to be paramount in the mental development of the child because it makes conscious the unconscious structure of the native tongue. In current terminology the syntax that was implicit in the child's speech must become explicit in writing.

Wholeness of Language

The "wholeness of language" concept describes the reading–writing relationship and implies that an awareness of the interdependence and commonality among the various forms of communication may provide insights to student learning (Braun, 1986). The goal is to teach students to read like writers and to write like readers. Integrative curricular planning requires unusual commitment of teacher time and, unless well executed, the students may not always understand exactly what they are supposed to be learning. The integrated curriculum cannot be evaluated solely by skill testing; therefore more comprehensive observations of student progress are necessary. Research on methodology is always difficult because it encompasses unmeasured variables of teacher–student interaction. There are inherent problems in evaluating the whole language instruction as Braun indicated: (a) Research problems must be formulated within the context of a holistic approach to language. (b) Research design must provide for observation of the steps in the learning process. (c) Research design must also provide for observation of the cognitive transition from writer-based to reader-based writing. Some research has been reported which meet the first two criteria.

INTEGRATION OF THE LANGUAGE ARTS

Cognitive theorists believe that reading and writing involve similar schema or structures (Whyte, 1987). Observations from pedagogy and research suggest that the processes of reading and writing are mutually reinforcing and should be taught together. While it is assumed on epistemological grounds that reading and writing mutually affect learning, confirming data are difficult to obtain. Pinnell (1988) reported a study in which writing and reading were combined to teach a group of first-grade children at risk for reading failure. The children engaged in "holistic lessons" that included reading and writing, using stories and messages. Descriptions of the reading and writing behavior of a sample ($N = 23$) were drawn from case studies. Teachers kept daily records of their pupil's reading/writing activities and samples of their writing. Eight variables were compared among 133 children who participated in the writing/reading program and 37 who participated in a different program. The results showed that these first-grade children did connect the reading and writing processes in a variety of ways. Although children in the integrated program achieved higher sores on both reading and writing measures than the control subjects, comparable quality of instruction by the other methodologies was not demonstrated.

Native American children have strong receptive skills, but are very selective of situations in which they are expressive. Dooley (1988) facilitated the connection of reading and writing with a third-grade class on an Indian reservation. The pupils were required to keep a dialogue journal in which at least a few lines were entered each day. All the writing was confidential. The teacher answered the entries daily, but did not grade them. Over the 5 months of the project the children's punctuation, grammar, and sentence structure improved in most cases; length of sentences and paragraphs improved in all cases. The project was successful in providing a culture-based learning style which emphasized group cooperation and pragmatic learning experiences. The technique was evaluated favorably by 90% of the students; however it was very pre-emptive of the teacher's time.

Student ability to use sentence combining strategies in writing has been found to correlate with reading comprehension. Evans et al. (1986) studied the effect of sentence combining instruction on tests of sentence structure and reading comprehension. Their subjects were three classes of 6th-grade, 12th-grade, and college students. The results indicated that the experimental treatment most influenced the reading and writing development of students with low abilities. The investigators confirmed previous research suggesting a bond between syntactic construction in reading and writing. Apparently the need for instruction in sentence combining, which is crucial for some students, has minimal value for others. One way to resolve these individual differences would be to incorporate basic instruction into the regular curriculum and to provide special classes for selected students.

The need for special reading and writing courses at the college level was addressed by Malinowski (1988), who advocated further research to proceed simultaneously. Culp and Span (1985) analyzed the progress of two groups of college freshmen enrolled in developmental reading programs. One group had regular writing assignments, while the other group had none. She concluded that writing had a positive effect on reading achievement. Pitts (1986) reported the effect of reading aloud to a class of underprepared college freshmen who followed the text while the instructor read. The students made gains in writing sills, but not in reading. Together, these attempts to correct communication skills at the college level showed positive but inconsistent results from the integration of reading and writing activities.

WRITING TO LEARN READING

Writing creates a purpose for paying attention to features of written language. An informal field study of writing before reading was designed by Connell (1986) for kindergarten. She addressed such questions as how letters should be grouped for early instruction, and what verbal references should be used. Does the teacher take a features approach (l,b,k,d or c,a,o); a pragmatic approach (date, name, lunch option); or a self-selection approach as in writing a note? Are letters identified by name or by sound (emm or m-m-m)? If reference is by sound, should short or long sounds of vowels be used? Connell proposed a modified italic alphabet as providing the easiest transition to cursive writing and/or print. She recommended teaching the association of letter to major sound, rather than teaching alphabet names. The program was used effectively to promote reading readiness in kindergarten.

Whitmer and Miller (1988) explored the relative effectiveness of three programs (a) the IBM Writing to Read program, (b) an experimental classroom writing program, and (c) a control classroom using typical (unchanged) writing activities. The computer-based program (A) used a laboratory setting with voice output and selectric typewriters to encourage writing and reading development. Five hours per week at the computer provided instruction in sound-symbols, followed by structured story-writing and reading. The experimental program (B) provided 4 weekly hours of structured story-writing followed by reading, discussing, and exploring the stories. The control classroom (C) spent approximately 2 hours a week in story writing activities. Test scores showed that mean group gains in reading comprehension were significantly higher for the A-group than for the control group. The writing program B-group scored between the other two groups. Gains for both sexes were highest in the computer program, but boys were lowest in the C program, while girls were lowest in the B program. The investigators concluded that the amount of time scheduled for structured writing emerged as an important factor in writing and reading gains. Evaluations such as these need to explore whether potentially negative effects on oral language expression occur and whether long-term gains in reading are sustained.

Chapter Summary

Psycholinguists generally accept the evidence of a genetic predisposition for speech called the language acquisition device (LAD). The early stages of speech production (*holophrastic speech,* two-word sentences and *telegraphic speech* imply a syntactic organization of the lexicon as it is laid down in the language areas of the left hemisphere. When the child learns to read and spell, a system of visual representation for speech is acquired. Reading is more difficult than listening or speaking, in part because it is more abstract, further removed in time and place from the physical event, and more extended in content. The effect of one communication skill upon the others is difficult to determine, although a linkage is widely accepted among practitioners, linguists, and neuropsychologists. Individual differences make instruction in reading skills extremely challenging because human variability ranges from hyperlexia to dyslexia. The holistic approach to reading implies that the language arts of listening, speaking, reading, and writing are learned (and taught) as integrated functions. In Chapter 15 the reading–writing relationship is presented as a creative and sometimes artistic enterprise.

4 Memory, Intelligence, and Literacy

Reading comprehension is made possible by the recall of stored images that give meaning to print. Memory is embedded in the whole process from perception to resolution. Perception, the immediate interpretation of input from the senses, depends on memory. Memory depends on perception and is influenced by emotion and imagination. Without memory there can be no learning and no retrieval of past experience. *Affective memories* are recalled spontaneously and without conscious attention as the pleasure or punishment concomitant of an experience. Affective memory is consciously engaged by readers of literature to enhance their ludic experience.

Visual memory is dominant in most humans, but images from other modalities are associated and recalled to supplement the thought processes initiated by words in context. The auditory, touch, taste, and other somatic images that support cognition are called *modality-specific memories*. The linkages between the different sensory association areas of the cortex subserve the reading process and assure that integration will occur. Memory retrieval is followed by an impulse to act on the information and, in the case of reading, to reconstruct the new information in some way that meshes with prior cognitive structures. Imagination creates alternative possibilities for dealing with information, whether by action or by reconstruction of the remembered past. This chapter is concerned with (a) the role of memory in reading, (b) the dynamic relationship of intelligence and memory for language, (c) some intellectual characteristics of successful readers, and (d) the relationship of literacy to thought.

MEMORY AND READING

Until about 50 years ago, the concept of a unitary memory prevailed among psychologists. In 1949, Donald Hebb, in the United States, proposed a theory of memory that distinguished between short-term processing and long-term storage. He described short-term memory as an active process of limited duration, leaving no traces, while long-term memory produced structural changes in the nervous system. Hebb proposed the model of a neuronal loop which, when repeatedly

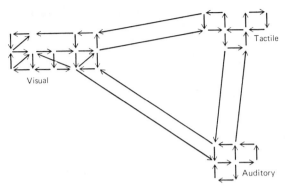

FIGURE 4.1. *Simplified diagram of a cell assembly. Activation by stimulation somewhere in the loop may retrieve memory anywhere in the assembly.*

activated, would cause cells to be functionally connected by growth that linked the cells or by chemical changes that stimulated their activation. He called this processing loop a *cell assembly* (Fig. 4.1). According to Hebb's conceptualization, the excitation of neurons in one area of the brain would activate the entire loop. For example, reading about the tolling of a bell might activate and retrieve the auditory images of grandad's funeral or of Hemingway's novel, *For Whom the Bell Tolls*. A visual word signal would activate pathways through the thalamus, to the forebrain and the auditory cortex and loop back to the thalamus. A memory could be stored and retrieved by any sensation, thought or emotion that activated neurons somewhere in the loop.

Hebb's concept of cell assemblies implied a separation of three processes: acquisition of information, storage of a memory trace, and retrieval of knowledge on demand. Short-term memory provided the discrete pieces of information which the brain organized into frameworks for learning. Memory was viewed as an active process of building neural frameworks and reforming their connections continuously as the brain worked.

Immediate, Short-term Functions

In England, Donald Broadbent (1958) also advocated a dichotomous memory system, based on neurological and psychological evidence. Studies designed to test two-component tasks produced evidence of a relatively stable long-term memory and a much more labile short-term memory. He noted that some amnesic patients are impaired in their ability to store new experience, but their memory of events that occurred some time prior to the trauma remain intact. A different line of evidence came from studies of differentiated *coding* (Baddeley, 1966). Tests of memory span that coding for short-term memory relied heavily on some form of speech or articulatory representation that had little to do with meaning. When long-term learning was required of subjects, their pattern of coding changed to cues which depended on meaning. Rote rehearsal, which helped subjects show effective short-term learning, led to poor long-term retention unless some form of semantic processing was used. Fowler (1981) interpreted her current research with children to suggest that one important difference between good readers and poor readers is the latter's overdependence on phonological short-term memory, and this prolonged attention to word recognition interferes with their comprehension processes.

Short-term memory was described by George Miller (1956) as an immediate mental operation intimately related to general intelligence and maturity. He described the limitation of human short-term memory as 7 ± 2 digits. The number of random letters a person can remember is fewer, 5 or 6, because there are more opportunities in an alphabet to err. Miller proposed the concept of "chunking" by units as a way to extend memory. A telephone number of 15 digits is remembered in chunks: outside line + area code + 7 digits + extension. Miller's experiments showed that almost as many word "units" could be remembered as letter "units." A sentence of 25 words could be remembered better than 25 random words because familiarity with the lexicon and the grammar of language comes to the person's aid. Miller regarded the use of language as a clear example of *transfer of learning* because automatic habits of using the structure of sentences has already been acquired.

Short-term memory tasks are incorporated in most individually administered intelligence tests. Sentence recall is part of some mental tests, including the Stanford–Binet, and digit span subtests are part of the Wechsler children and adult scales. At ages 6 through the teens the ability increases for recalling digits in sequence, when presented orally at 1-second intervals. Experienced psychometrists continue to monitor their own timing of digit presentation because faster presentation produces an inflated score and slower presentation results in fewer digits being remembered. Miller proposed an auditory memory limitation of 13 seconds for pure sequential nonsense symbols, unassisted by mnemonic or semantic cues.

The digit span is used increasingly as an indicator of mental age. Payne and Holtzman (1983) investigated the relationship between reading comprehension, digit span, and memory for temporal patterns similar to the Morse Code. College subjects and fifth graders revealed no relationship between digit span and short-term memory for tonal patterns. However, both tasks discriminated between good and poor fifth-grade readers. Apparently short-term memory for both auditory segments and for auditory patterns are used in contextual reading.

The Working Memory

For more than a decade the concept of a dual system in which a single short-term or immediate memory provided information to a long-term memory has been undergoing revision. Broadbent (1983) proposed a mediation function described as a "temporary memory storage," which processes information without necessarily storing it for long-term use. The term *working memory* has been applied, which Baddeley (1983) defined as "the temporary storage of information in connection with the performance of other cognitive tasks such as reading, problem-solving, or learning" (p. 73). He proposed a model consisting of a "central executive," which functions as the core of a system where information from peripheral subsidiary systems is coordinated (Fig. 4.2). The central executive is assumed to be a limited-capacity attentional mechanism capable of selecting and

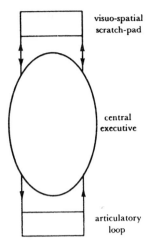

FIGURE 4.2. Simplified representation of the working memory model. (From A. D. Baddeley, *Functional Aspects of Human Memory*, p. 77. Copyright © 1983, The Royal Society. By permission).

controlling the cognitive processes and strategies of the subsystems. The central executive takes advantage of "peripheral" subsystems which themselves are multifunctional. Baddeley has distinguished between *passive storage,* where information is registered and subsequently fades or is displaced, and *active storage,* whereby information is read out in a loop of continuous renewal, perhaps by rehearsal. Although the probability of numerous subsidiary systems is assumed, only two have been researched and described by his group: a "visuospatial scratch-pad" and an "articulatory loop."

THE ARTICULATORY LOOP

Baddeley's conceptualization of a working memory assigns phonological coding to an articulatory subsystem comprised of two components: (a) a phonological input store and (b) an articulatory rehearsal process involving subvocal speech. To him this dual mechanism explains the *word similarity effect*—a term describing why sequences of consonants have similar sounding names (b, g, c, v, p) are harder to remember than dissimilar strings (w, y, k, r, h). His own experiments confirmed the *word-length effect,* which predicts that the number of words remembered will be limited by the time is takes to articulate (rehearse) them. An auditory processing loop, such as that proposed in the model, seemed to explain these effects.

In Baddeley's experiments to test the articulatory loop, subjects remembered fewer multisyllable words than single-syllable words. They remembered fewer two-syllable words that were hard to articulate (harpoon, Friday) than two-syllable words that were spoken quickly (bishop, wicket). Other experiments employed an *articulatory suppression effect* by requiring a subject to articulate a word continuously while doing a visual task of word recall. Memory for words presented visually was consistently impaired because rehearsal is prevented by the continuous, though unattended, involvement of speech. Baddeley's explanation for these effects was that spoken material has obligatory access to the phonological store. Under normal conditions, visually presented items will be recorded phonologically so as to take advantage of the supplementary articulatory storage in the loop. Subvocal transfer of information to the loop is prevented by the pre-emptive use of the articulatory loop by the subject's own speech which has priority access to the subservient (auditory) system.

An undergraduate patient provided one of the Baddeley teams with an unusual opportunity for observing nonspeech articulation. The student had been in a car accident which, initially, left him completely paralyzed. He recovered the use of his upper limbs, but remained totally unable to speak. By typing out his response to questions, he was able to communicate and to demonstrate that he had retained language. He could follow complex instructions, comprehend words, and match synonyms. At issue was whether subvocal rehearsal was occurring, as in normal persons, to produce normal memory span effects while processing words. Results showed that the patient maintained a normal memory span, the phoneme similarity effect, and a clear word-length effect whether words were presented visually or auditorily. The process of subvocal rehearsal appeared to be functioning in the working memory of this subject, independent of the speech musculature. The use of a mechanism for receiving, rehearsing, and holding linguistic information in temporary storage was demonstrated.

The auditory mode has repeatedly shown a *recency advantage* in which words that were heard at or near the end of a string were remembered better than words heard earlier. This observation has been attributed to an *echoic memory* which, until lately, was thought to be short-term and exclusive to auditory processes (Gardiner, 1983). The recency advantage has been observed *also* in long-term memory tests and when items were lip-read or presented in sign-language. Several explanations are possible: (1) Sequential coding is processed by a temporal mechanism which organizes speech whether heard, seen, or signed. (2) The distinctiveness of the message, such as features or emotional content, selects certain parts of the flow of words from a working memory for long-term storage. (3) Echoic memory may be associated with the linguistic mode, enjoying a priority in humans over other modes.

Bertelson (1986) conducted experiments to determine whether echoic memory plays a role in reading by comparing good and poor readers on three listening tasks. Digit sequences were designed to exceed the digit span, or short-term memory, by one digit to test the functioning of a *working memory*. In one task, strings of digits were presented, some being appended by a tone and some by a word, to discover whether either interfered with recall. The poor readers showed a larger deficit in echoic memory than did good readers. Another experiment involved a dichotic listening task in which shadowed words were presented in the attending ear and a series of words interspersed with digits in the nonattending ear. On signal the subjects were asked to recall the last digit they heard. Good and poor readers did not differ when the recall was immediate; but poor readers showed a faster decline as the retention interval was increased. The final experiment was conducted to determine whether the differences in echoic memory were specific to speech or occurred at a more basic aural level. Bursts of white noise were separated by varied intervals of silence (9–400 ms) and subjects were asked to say whether one or two sounds were heard. Good and poor readers showed no differences on this nonlinguistic task of echoic memory. The speech image, but not nonspeech sounds, appears to be retained for longer intervals in the working memory of good readers compared with poor readers.

THE VISUOSPATIAL SCRATCHPAD

The second subsystem of the working memory explored by Baddeley (1983) was hypothesized as a loop specialized for maintaining and manipulating visuospatial images. Like the articulatory loop, it is essentially an input store with active capabilities for regeneration of memory traces by a process external to the store. Baddeley and colleagues required subjects to follow a light dot on a screen with a stylus as interference for memory of numbers on the grid. Their experiments showed that a visuospatial tracking task interfered with memory for visual tasks but not with memory for verbal stimuli. In a series of experiments it was shown that the subsystem was primarily spatial, rather than visual; the scratchpad was much influenced by visual patterns and relationships and very little by eye movements. Baddeley assumed that the working memory uses components of many cognitive systems, including the several perception systems and speech perception in particular.

WORKING MEMORY IN CHILDREN

Child subjects were selected by Hitch and Halliday (1983) as a potential model of how a working memory develops by conducting investigations on children of different ages. Based on the evidence of an increasing memory span during early and late childhood, they sought to determine whether the development of a working memory was based (a) on an increased maturational space for processing (meaning the general capacity for temporary storage improved with age) or (b) on an increased control of the processes with learning. Behind this scholarly language is the perennial issue of genetic maturation versus learning. The investigators were especially interested in age-related limitations for memory retention of reading and arithmetic content. Children in three age groups (8-, 10-, and 12-years) and adults were compared (Fig. 4.3). Words of one to four syllables were presented visually for immediate recall; speed of articulation was assessed by having subjects read aloud from lists of words representing four types of material. The results showed a clear word-length effect in all age groups and a general improvement of recall with age. Surprisingly the data from a study of adult subjects by Baddeley (1983) fit the correlational relationship rather remarkably.

Another investigation by Hitch and Halliday (1983) tested the recall of sequences of either a string of spoken words or corresponding sets of pictures presented at 1- to 2-second intervals. In the picture condition, slides of colored line drawings were presented on a TV screen; in the spoken condition a female researcher recited the word sequences. Children 6, 8, and 10 years old were the subjects. Their task was to repeat the items in correct order; scores were based on items recalled in sequence. In the oldest children, the working memory declined with increasing word length, about equally for auditory and picture presentation.

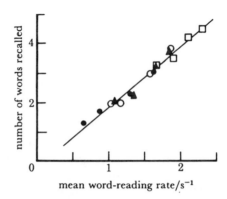

FIGURE 4.3. Relation between number of words recalled and rate at which they had been read aloud in four age groups: ●, 8 years; O, 10 years; △, 12 years; and □, adult. From left to right, the data points for each group correspond to words of four, three, two, and one syllables. (From Hitch & Halliday. In Broadbent (Ed.), *Functional Aspects of Human Memory*, p. 90. Copyright © 1983. By permission of the authors and the Royal Society.

In the youngest children word length had a clear effect for spoken words, but not for pictures. Developmental aspects were confirmed by the intermediate scores of the 8-year olds. In terms of the working memory model, older children appeared to use the articulatory loop to remember both auditory and pictorial items, while young children did not use the articulatory loop to rehearse and remember picture names, even though the names of the objects were familiar and available. Hitch and Halliday cite the theoretical work of Piaget and the experimental work of Flavell to support their findings. They interpreted their data to confirm age differences in the use of an articulatory loop in the service of a visual task.

When compared with competent readers, reading-disabled children do poorly on immediate recall tests such as digit span and visual coding. Cohen, Netley, and Clarke (1984) tested four groups of children on a serial short-term memory task. They presented nine digits, followed by one of three letters: [A] required recall of the first three numerals (primacy effect); [B] required recall of three medial digits; and [C] required recall of the last three numerals (recency effect). The three groups were matched for age and IQ, but differed in reading ability from reading-disabled to average to reading-superior. A fourth group of children, 2 years younger, was matched in IQ to the three other groups and read at a similar level to the older reading-disabled. The immediate memory data showed that (a) differences between the groups were confined mainly to the recall of recency items; (b) within the three older groups, the superior readers excelled over the competent readers, who excelled over the disabled readers; and (c) the youngest group were superior to the disabled readers despite their similarity in reading scores. After discussing several possible explanations, the investigators favored the interpretation that short-term memory and reading are both dependent on some third cognitive operation. The mechanism they seek may be the working memory for articulatory components.

Long-term Memory Storage

The concept of long-term memory as brain storage which endures for hours, or for a lifetime, has been a psychological assumption for a long time and remains essentially unchallenged. Memory in human subjects can be ascertained only by tests of recall. All recall implies linguistic or motor memory and active attention. Research interests of recent decades have focused on different forms of memory retrieval, on the consolidation process by which events are coded in memory, and on the structural changes in the brain that occur with memory storage.

PROCEDURAL AND DECLARATIVE MEMORY

Those who teach find the distinction between procedural and declarative memory a useful conceptualization, supported by brain functions and behavioral research. *Procedural knowledge* is long-term accessibility of information on how to do something. Some examples are the skill to read mirror writing or to solve a complex puzzle. Bloom, Lazerson, and Hofstadter (1985) suggest that procedural learning probably developed earlier in evolution than declarative learning. Simple learning, such as habituation, sensitization, and classical conditioning, take place without individual awareness that learning has occurred, yet long-term storage is involved. Procedural memory involves change in the neural system; the changes may be biochemical or biophysical but they are thought to be limited to the neural circuits that are activated. These changes are less extensive than the remodeling of neural circuitry that declarative memory is thought to require.

The sensorimotor learning of the first 18 months of life is characteristic of procedural knowledge. The infant learns to coordinate movements and deal with gravity, to direct manipulative actions on objects, and to perceive the physical environment through visual, auditory, and somatic senses. Initially these actions, including walking, require concentration of cognitive systems. Gradually the cerebellum takes over the automaticity of physical procedures, freeing the mind-brain for declarative memory processes. Neuroscientists are uncertain about the site of the mechanisms that control automatic language functions, such as the musculature for speech production and the hand–eye coordination of writing.

Declarative knowledge is the long-term accessibility of an explicit record of an individual's previous experiences, together with a sense of familiarity about those experiences. Put another way, declarative memory requires a context to be meaningful. This knowledge of familiarity requires simultaneous processing in many areas of the brain: the temporal region, parts of the thalamus, the sensory association areas where cognitive knowledge is stored. Declarative knowledge is thought to have developed later in the phylogeny of humans and only after many physical procedures have been automatic. A level of self-awareness is considered a precondition for declarative memory. By the age of 2 the child has learned that objects and persons exist apart from the egocentric self and only then is ready to develop the images and representations that cognitive memory requires. Symbolic language forms the schema, or structure, for converting real objects to signals, signs, and symbols. Reading is a declarative process, but the ease with which reading skills are learned and prior knowledge is recalled depends on the primitive structures of pleasure reinforcement.

REGISTRATION AND RECALL

Several retrieval systems are involved in a given learning task. Arnold (1984) explained that tasks involving speech require a motor recall circuit, one or more sensory recall circuits, and an affective memory circuit. A motor analyzer, located in the frontal association cortex, is the storage site for motor memories. The motor activity that accompanies linguistic processes results in an engram in the motor analyzer. An *engram* is the permanent effect in the memory system that results from stimulation. Activation, that is stimulation, in a circuit can be registered by the performance of a motor act, by the imagination of an action being performed, or by the intention to move. Each of these mental manipulations strengthens the potential for performing the task at some future time, whether the motor activity is completed at the time or not.

According to Arnold, the motor analyzer is involved in alteration tasks, hence persons who have damage in this area show right-left and up-down confusion. The impulse to recall something may be *deliberate,* as in mentally constructing a phrase that defines a word; or *spontaneous,* as in recalling the name of a friend at an unexpected encounter. Intentional recall is limited to the auditory and visual modalities or to motor memory. Recall in any memory modality, whether spontaneous or intentional, would be relayed over the same temporal and spatial sequence as the original experience or movement pattern, thus reactivating the engram pattern in the association cortex. The affective circuit provides a sense of the rightness of an activity, which produces an action impulse, and the intention to recall something. Motor circuits have an important function in speech and may be activated in reading silently as well. The linguists have brought speech into the psychology of reading: the neuropsychologists may bring motor memory into the process of reading recall.

Effective recall from long-term storage depends on many factors, including the power of the initial registration of the experience. Some students who do well in examinations have learned how to invent devices for enhancing their recall. *Mnemonic devices* are associative representations which are easier to recall than the target information. Miller (1956) told of his debt to a teacher who saved him endless confusion by telling him that the ordinate of a statistical array was vertical because his mouth went that way when he said it and that the abscissa was horizontal for the same reason. Mnemonic devices are a way of organizing seemingly incoherent material. Children enjoy sharing their "ways of knowing" with each other. A first grader once said, "I always know which way to turn the **d**, I loop it toward the closet door and the **b** turns toward the basket." He solved the problem for a whole class of beginning writers; once the letters were formed automatically the mnemonic was no longer needed. A characteristic of intellectually gifted students is their invention of such devices for remembering critical information.

MEMORY CONSOLIDATION

Changes in the structure of the neural circuitry with learning is an accepted fact of neuropsychology. *Memory consolidation* refers to the physical and psychological changes that occur as the brain organizes and restructures information for

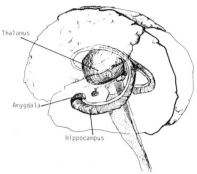

Thalamus

Amygdala

Hippocampus

FIGURE 4.4. Structural site of memory consolidation. Selection and organization of experience occurs in hippocampus and amygdala, through interaction with thalami and adjacent structures. Storage occurs in cortices of cerebral lobes, primarily. Frontal cortex and brain stem are shaded. (Drawing by D. Thompson.)

permanent storage (Bloom, Lazerson, & Hofstadter, 1985). Consolidation is assumed to occur in the hippocampus, the amygdala, and the immediate temporal areas (Fig. 4.4). The hippocampus is a structure about the size of an index finger, lying just beneath the cortex of the temporal lobe. Located in close proximity to its anterior is the amygdala, a spherical structure about the size of a thumbnail. Both are part of the limbic system and are directly connected with natural reward systems. Information is thought to be formulated, converted, or templated at these sites for storage elsewhere, principally in the cerebral cortex and the thalamus. Accidental destruction of the hippocampus results in the loss of knowledge of how to perform a procedure; destruction of the amygdala results in loss of the ability to initiate an action. Experiments with laboratory animals in training have demonstrated some of the conditions that interfere with consolidation. Electric shock, chemicals such as potassium chloride (KCl) in solution, and severe trauma interfere with consolidation and therefore with memory storage. By preventing consolidation at experimentally determined time intervals following learning, researchers have shown that consolidation of learning occurs within a few minutes or a few hours of an experience. Beyond those time frames memory cannot be destroyed by the methods identified in these experiments (Albert, 1966).

Learning effects the microstructure of the neural system. Physical growth occurs in the synaptic connections which strengthens the communication between neurons (Eccles & Robinson, 1984). The numbers of synaptic connections increase with cognitive development and learning. These connections are facilitated by the growth of spurs in the postsynaptic tissue of the receiving neuron which approach the synaptic knobs at the terminals of sending neurons (Fig. 4.5). Other changes, physical and chemical, occur within the cells to enhance transmission.

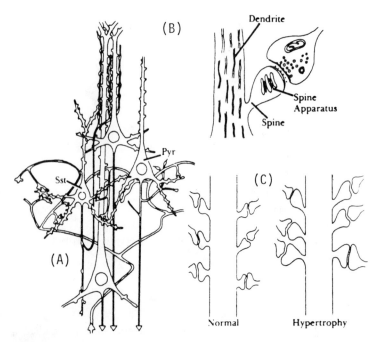

FIGURE 4.5. Synaptic connections between neurons. (A) Shows input fiber from thalamus (white arrow); spiny (stellate) cell has synaptic connections to three pyramid cells which send axons out of cortex (dark arrows). (B) Shows enlarged diagram of dendrital spine in contact with synaptic knob of receiving neuron. (C) Shows normal spines and enlarged growth of hyperactive circuit. (From Eccles & Robinson, p. 130. Copyright © 1984, Free Press. By permission.

RETRIEVAL FAILURE

Failure to retrieve information once stored does not necessarily mean that the knowledge has been lost from long-term storage. Buschke (1974) reported a study in which adult subjects were read a list of words at 2-second intervals, then asked to recall as many as possible of the 20 items. Items that were not retrieved were presented again and the free-recall test was repeated until all 20 items were recalled at least once. Usually this was accomplished by the fourth trial, although not all items were recalled at each trial. Two groups were presented with animal lists; the first group responded by verbal recall and the second by written recall. A third group received a mixed list with sound interference before verbal recall. The major finding was that items not recalled in one trial were spontaneously recalled in a later trial, even though there had been no presentation in the interval. Results were very similar in the three groups. An average of 14 words were recalled on every trial, including the first test; an average of 1 word was lost after one recall and never again remembered. An average of 5 words were recalled, then not retrieved on the next test; but retrieved spontaneously on a subsequent test. The findings indicate that despite restricted exposure the words had been committed to long-term storage. The failures were retrieval failures, rather than loss from long-term memory. The conditions for remembering are obscure, personal, and multifarious.

Some interesting evidence of the location of word banks in the association areas has been gleaned from patients whose damage to certain areas has resulted in amnesia that was specific to certain word categories. Bower (1985) reported a case of stroke in which the victim recovered his memory for words, with the exception of the category of fruits and vegetables. He could name drawings of the objects as unusual as a photograph of a sphinx or as complex as an abacus with near-perfect scores; but he could name common foods only about 65% of the time. He could sort items into classes such as vehicles, animals, shapes, or household articles; but he had trouble with foods. Evidence for such a "thesaurus-like indexing" system is meager, perhaps because knowledge for word categories usually is not probed in patients. Memory research is at an exciting period in the psychology of learning.

COGNITIVE ABILITIES AND READING

Intelligence tests are designed to tap short-term and long-term memory and to present unfamiliar tasks to subjects who then show how they use mental resources to find solutions. The relationship of IQ and reading achievement is positive and consistent if the intelligence quotient is derived from a comprehensive test, is administered individually, and does not require reading. Also, the reading test is assumed to be standardized and selected for a range of difficulty from items that are easy enough to be read by all subjects to items that are complex enough to exceed the ceiling of the top reader's skill (Chapter 11). At lower elementary-school levels the correlations between IQ and reading achievement are moderate to strong; by high school the correlations are moderate; and by graduate school they are consistent but low. The ability factor gradually becomes less important in reading proficiency as prior knowledge, study habits, and motivation become more decisive. In reading programs an assessment of learning ability is necessary if evaluation of an individual's reading progress is a concern. Children of limited ability can become good readers of newspapers and can learn literacy skills adequate to the demands of ordinary work if their early schooling is appropriate and effective. Almost certainly, slow learners will experience self-doubt and failure if held to a standard of early reading performance that is impossible for them. On the other hand, three of five (60%) of the highly gifted children become underachievers in our schools; they meet the minimum standards with very little effort and are not suspected as exceptional by their teachers nor motivated to excel (Robeck, 1968). The following section considers school situations where IQ may be an important factor and explores subskills for reading that can be developed apart from the intelligence quotient.

IQ Estimates and Reading Subskills

Research on the IQ/reading relationship is exceedingly complex, in part because testing for either ability taps memory stores and working strategies common to both. At fourth-grade level, the correlation of IQ and comprehensive reading scores (word identification and comprehension) usually falls between .50 and .55, meaning that 25% to 30% of the variance in reading scores can be attributed to intelligence factors. Goodfriend (1984) studied more than 100 fourth-grade students to determine the effect of classification abilities on reading comprehension. She computed intercorrelations of IQ, story recall, nonverbal classification, and verbal classification. Both nonverbal and verbal classification abilities were found predictive of reading comprehension (story recall) at a significant level *unless the general IQ was controlled statistically.* When the effect of IQ had been accounted for, the classification abilities became insignificant. Measures of the abilities that subserve reading have little predictive value for instruction unless the general factor of intelligence is taken into account.

Recently efforts have been made to identify particular skills that predict reading success (or failure) and to use these measures in combination with IQ scores (Goldstein & Dundon, 1987). Brown and Byrd (1984) compared the accuracy of three formulas for estimating the expected grade-level achievement in reading with a software program that included the student's IQ and chronological age. The regressive equations obtained by a microcomputer program had twice the predictive power when applied to sixth-grade students as the generalized formulas that were being used. Researchers continue to develop better assessment strategies for identifying students with special needs, so that preventive intervention can occur.

PREDICTION AND DIAGNOSIS

The need for IQ measures in special education programs is widely recognized; but better focus on the particular weakness of students is needed. Duane (1986) looked for characteristics that might be shared by 10th- and 11th-grade students who had failed to reach minimum basic standards for reading in their state. They were compared with the general high school population on several variables thought to be related to reading achievement. No significant relationship was found between reading levels and sex, age, age at school entrance, or handedness. A low to moderate correlation was obtained between IQ and reading test scores; further, the IQs appeared to predict success or failure in remedial classes. Curtis (1983) found no significant relationship between IQ and certain citizenship variables such as self-esteem, interest in contemporary problems, concern with civil liberties and critical thinking. Kauffman et al. (1987) studied the characteristics of 250 students from 7 to 19 years old who had been placed in special programs for the seriously emotionally disturbed. They found that a behavior problem index was related to reading achievement in half the subjects; but IQ was not predictive of the amount or kind of behavior problem. It is important to know whether or not IQ is a factor when a student is failing and the reasons are unknown.

The important determinations when diagnosing academic failure are first to establish whether poor reading is the basic cause; and second to distinguish between poor readers exhibiting general reading backwardness and poor readers having specific disabilities. Bloom et al. (1981) tested 80 developmentally disabled children (ages 6 to 10) on the *Woodcock Reading Mastery Tests* and the

Wechsler Intelligence Scale for Children, Revised (WISC–R). The reading test correlated moderately and significantly with IQ; abstract reading skills correlated more fully with the WISC-R Full Scale IQ than did concrete skills. The investigators noted the positive emotional importance of concrete learning to the children. Silva et al. (1985) studied 9-year-old boys to identify the characteristics of those with "general reading backwardness" and those with "specific reading retardation." General reading backwardness was associated with a history of cognitive and motor delay, while the specific reading disability group showed a lower verbal IQ than performance IQ and poor speech articulation. Reading specialists try to differentiate the slow learner who is backward in reading from the student with normal intelligence who has particular cognitive disabilities in areas associated with reading success.

RATE OF MENTAL PROCESSING

Conventional wisdom has assumed that quick thinking is associated with brightness. Since Lindsley in the 1930s, neurologists have attempted to establish the relationship between intelligence and the rate of neural processing as indicated by the average frequencies of the spikes of the EEG. Three tentative correlations were reported over four decades: (1) Alpha frequency is associated with intelligence; (2) Increased EEG activation occurs during mental work; and (3) Greater differential between the hemispheres occurs during mental work.

EEG Frequency and Efficiency

Giannitrapani (1969) employed adult subjects for studying the relationship of three IQ measures (Verbal, Performance, and Full Scale) on the *Wechsler Adult Intelligence Scale* with EEG frequency measures taken from eight locations on the cerebral cortex. An important aspect of his technique was to obtain the differences between a "resting condition" and a "thinking condition." The mental activity measures were taken during problem-solving tasks. Mental arithmetic items requiring a minimum of 5 seconds for solution were used. The highest correlations were obtained from a composite score of EEG frequencies obtained during the thinking condition: with Verbal IQ (.59), with Performance IQ (.78), and with Full Scale IQ (.72). These correlations were disappointing because they were too low to produce viable measures of intelligence; however, the technique was revived (with computerized assistance) in the 1980s to locate the areas of the brain activation during different mental activities.

Another attempt to measure intelligence as brain power, without the involvement of language, was reported by Erdl (1972), called a "neural efficiency analyzer." The technique recorded EEG responses to a series of 200 light flashes and computed an average of the time intervals between the light flash and evoked potentials. Erdl (1968) produced EEG patterns for three subjects with IQs of 137, 100, and 73 which showed the high IQ subject processing at a rate almost double that of the low IQ subject. He was particularly interested in reading and envisioned the use of his test for prereading children, foreign speaking persons, and patients who were aphasic or psychotic. His studies of hemisphere asymmetry created some interest among psychologists and his test was used experimentally in some schools. Correlations from large group studies were low (0.28) to moderate (0.51), too low to be predictive for individual students. This particular device for measuring neural efficiency did not prove practical, perhaps because speed of processing is only one facet of cognitive functioning. Yet the relationship of neural efficiency to IQ measures is consequential and the concept is important for teachers, who must know how to pace learning.

Information Processing

A developmental study was conducted to distinguish two groups of clinic children identified as deficient in reading: one "accuracy-disabled," the other "rate-disabled" (Lovett, 1987). Accuracy-disabled subjects had failed to achieve reliable age-appropriate skills in word recognition. Rate-disabled readers were age-appropriate in word recognition accuracy but deficient in reading speed. Both groups were compared with fluent normal readers selected for reading accuracy similar to rate-disabled children while reading at a significantly faster rate. Results indicated that accuracy-disabled subjects are deficient in all aspects of reading, compared with normal readers and less able to learn new sound-symbol associations. Rate-disabled subjects showed a basic deficit in word recognition speed; they compromised accuracy when reading in context, and compromised spelling when competing visual patterns were part of the task. When disability groups were compared with each other, the accuracy-disabled were low in oral language development, while the rate-disabled were restricted in visual language forms and in naming visual representations. Both groups were impaired in visual naming speed—a task which calls for mediation from visual to auditory symbols, with time being a factor. The study appears to reveal basic differences in cognitive processing which handicap both the inaccurate and the slow processors.

The Lovett study is reminiscent of the impulsivity/reflectivity studies of Kagan and Kogan (1970) and others. Initially the tendency was observed in second-grade children to solve embedded figures tasks quickly and impulsively or slowly and reflectively. In subsequent research the tendency toward long or short decision times was found to be relatively stable in individual children over 2 or 3 years. Response times were found to generalize to cognitive tasks such as figure recognition and hypothesis generating, but correlations with the Wechsler verbal IQ were low and generally not significant. When anxiety was built into the research design, impulsive children were found to increase their errors more than reflective children did. Reading errors were studied extensively among groups of subjects initially classified according to reaction time for visual figures matching. Impulsivity was found to be associated with recognition errors in many children, but attempts to train impulsive children to take more time for responding did not generalize to different teachers and did not reduce the errors. However, training which emphasized accuracy and ignored speed of response resulted in longer reaction time and fewer errors. First-grade children assigned to impulsive/reflective teachers changed in their response rates in the direction of teacher style, the greatest change being found in impulsive boys assigned to reflective teachers.

MEDIATION OF WORDS

Numerous studies have been conducted to discover how different readers mediate a task when the recall of stimulus materials is purposely extended beyond the potential of short-term memory. Bauer and Emhert (1984) compared normal and disabled readers (ages 13–14) on their recall of lists of 10 words presented at intervals of 1, 2, 3, and 4 seconds. Recall of the first few words presented from each list (the primacy effect) produced lower scores in reading-disabled than in nondisabled students; and slower presentation rates increased the primacy effect in both groups, that is, reduced the number of words recalled. The recency effect (recall of last few words presented) was comparable for both groups. The investigators suggested that both normal and reading-disabled children encode and recognize word stimuli, but that the elaborative encoding levels needed for competent reading are deficient in the poor readers. Another interpretation is possible; that recording of verbal material (visual to auditory) is slower in reading-disabled children, producing the primacy effect and not the recency effect.

In a study involving sixth- and seventh-grade students, the investigators attempted to improve rate and efficiency of word recognition through practice exercises in decoding (Hall & Moon, 1986). The theoretical basis was that automatic responses would reduce processing time and improve recall. To add attractiveness to an otherwise monotonous decoding drill, a computer game disk provided the instructions for practice and individual feedback on student success. Treatment was provided in three sessions of 30 minutes involving a visual task, an aural task, and a dual task engaging both visual and aural modes. Reaction times were reduced across the trials, showing increased automaticity of verbal skills. Reaction times for single-modality responses (visual and aural) were briefer than for dual-modality responses. Reading level, number of tasks completed, familiarity of stimuli, and practice accounted for 42% of the variance in reaction time for the aural task. Apparently some skills which distinguish good and poor readers are influenced significantly by direct practice to the level of automaticity.

CHANGES IN IQ WITH LEARNING

The IQ serves as an ability assessment of reasonable consistency and well-constructed tests show resistance to environmental effects. A persistent correlation of specific linguistic subskills with the intelligence quotient raises the question whether acquisition of these subskills is modifiable by instruction. It is noteworthy that many verbal items of the kind that appear in IQ tests are teachable. Validity is maintained, however, because test makers select items to test IQ that can be learned from everyday participation in the culture. Vocabulary, which is part of almost every intelligence test, can be learned in many ways: the words chosen for definition in IQ tests are not particular to a discipline or a profession. Information items can be taught, which is why test makers guard their items from public scrutiny. Despite the technical separation of intelligence and achievement tests, many early childhood education projects claimed IQ changes.

Programs for young children, particularly those in Head Start and Follow Through, were evaluated, in part, on the basis of their success in teaching vocabulary. Direct instruction programs frequently reported gains in IQ for participating children when compared with children who did not participate. Gersten et al. (1981) reported a longitudinal evaluation of a program for low-income children who engaged in the Direct Instruction Follow Through program (DIFT). The program provided daily teacher-directed lessons in reading, language, and arithmetic. The major finding was that little, if any, relationship existed between entry IQ and yearly learning rate in this program. Generally, the students entering the program at higher cognitive skill levels finished the third grade at higher levels, but the growth rates (or amount of academic learning that took place) was not significantly different for the IQ groupings. In a 5-year program for moderately retarded children, Gersten and Maggs (1982) reported significant IQ gains and improvements in language competency. Together, these studies suggest that low-ability students attain cognitive benefits from the carefully programmed instruction of DIFT, which appears to generalize to test situations. Higher-ability children, using the same program, do not appear to improve their skill levels to the extent that their higher potential predicts.

Abilities of Successful Readers

Once in a while a particular child learns to read so early and so spontaneously that the possibility of a reading acquisition device, comparable to the widely recognized language acquisition device (LAD) is attractive. A young graduate student startled his seminar with an extraordinary anecdote about his 18-month-old daughter, Jennifer. Having left most family possessions at home in another country, he checked out a picture book from the library to begin picture-story reading with her. To his astonishment, the child repeatedly took the book from his hands and turned it upside-down. Even when the pages contained only print she persisted in viewing the book in inverted position. He began forthwith to observe his daughter in various situations and noted that when sitting in her highchair she stared downward for extended periods of time at an alphabet and some numerals printed across her bib. She seemed to be studying the letters—upside down. He reached into his wallet for a greenback and placed it on the highchair tray with the words and digits facing Jennifer. She immediately reversed the bill, and looked at it upside down. As a school principal he had discouraged parents from teaching their child to read prior to first grade. "What shall I do?" he asked. The group advised him: Replace the bib. Buy a picture dictionary. When you read to her be sure you view the book together, top-side-up. A few months later he came to the office to say proudly that Jennifer was reading children's story books.

PRECOCIOUS READERS

In her seminal studies of children who come to school already reading, Durkin (1966) identified factors that distinguished them from their nonreading peers. She selected children who passed a criterion word recognition test at the beginning of the first grade in a school district where no reading was taught in kindergarten. Her interviews with parents indicated that these children showed an early interest in reading signs, labels, and in some cases, books. About half of her subjects had begun to copy letters and words on their own initiative and to ask for help with writing. Instruction at home varied from a completely casual approach, such as answering questions, to irregular but systematic lessons. Many children in the sample had older siblings who played school with them. Although the homes varied from upper-lower to lower-upper socioeconomic categories, the families of early readers were supportive of the child in his or her efforts to learn to read. On general ability tests, the range was low average (91 IQ) to very superior (160 IQ) on the Stanford–Binet Intelligence Scales.

Durkin (1970) followed one group of 156 children through the primary grades and another group of 49 early readers through the elementary grades. She found that the best readers, after 5 years in school, were typically the children in the category of earliest readers, aged 3 and 4. Their median achievement was 2.6 reading grade equivalent when they began first grade. At the end of the fifth grade their median grade equivalency was 9.2. By contrast, her early readers who started reading between 5 and 6 showed a median of 1.7 at entrance and 7.6 at the end of fifth grade. Both groups scored significantly higher than a comparison group of classmates matched for sex, age, and IQ. Durkin's studies refuted an opinion long held that a mental age of 6.5 was needed for successful reading. Although Durkin did not claim definitive conclusions about all early readers, she made the following points: (1) The average achievement of pre-school readers over as many as 6 years remains significantly higher than the average achievement of equally bright schoolmates who did not begin to read until after they began first grade. (2) The evidence suggests the possibility that reading earlier than the first grade is valuable for many children. (3) Further experimental programs in teaching reading to first grades could be undertaken since the acceleration of early readers seemed not to be temporary, but long term in its effect, even though little evidence was found that the curriculum had been adjusted to their advanced skills. The investigator suggested that the approach used in homes for teaching early reading might also be used in kindergarten to provide a language-experience program for reading.

STAGES OF READING DEVELOPMENT

Efforts have been made by educational psychologists to match the stages of reading acquisition proposed by Gates and Russell (1938) and Russell (1961) to the periods and stages of cognitive development outlined by Inhelder and Piaget (1958). Chall proposed *Stages of Reading Development* (1983b), which she extended beyond elementary levels and supported with evidence from reading research, developmental psychology, linguistics, and neuroscience. Her six stages and some of the qualitative description follows:

Stage 0: Prereading describes the typical child from birth to age 6, or until the age when reading instruction is begun. During this "pseudoreading" period, the child pretends to read picture-story books, retells familiar stories from picture cues, names letters of the alphabet, writes his or her name, and plays with books and writing materials. Their interest in printed text, understanding of oral language, and perceptual skills suggest readiness for systematic instruction. The child's playful and casual activities give way to the more deliberate skill learning of the next stage.

Stage 1: Initial reading and decoding characterizes the first and second grader who is learning the relation between letters and sounds and between printed and spoken words. At this stage the child masters the ability to combine sight recognition of high-frequency words and sounding skills for phonetically regular words in reading simple text. Skills are acquired by direct instruction in phoneme–grapheme relationships and through practice in oral reading of material within the child's skill levels. Stage 1 readers give more attention to the medium than to the message, using bottom-up strategies to recognize words. By the end of this stage the typical child can read about 600 words, compared with a listening understanding of 4,000 or more. Development of more advanced language syntax, new vocabulary, and complex ideas is achieved through listening to others read. Children whose most significant reinforcement comes from absolute accuracy may remain too long at a word approach, rather than to make the transition to more fluent reading.

Stage 2: Confirmation and fluency is characteristic of the independent reader of second and third grades. This child is able to consolidate basic decoding elements, sight vocabulary and contextual meanings to read increasingly interesting stories and selections outside of reading texts. This newly gained flexibility suggests the use of both bottom-up and top-down strategies. Direct instruction is still needed in advanced decoding skills and comprehension skills. Stage 2 children enjoy being read to and their increased listening vocabulary of about 9,000 words enables them to enjoy stories well above the 3,000-word reading vocabulary they have acquired by the end of this stage.

Stage 3: Reading for learning the new indicates the transition from materials designed for learning to read to materials for gaining knowledge in different subject areas. The stage begins for most students at about the fourth grade (age 9) and continues through grade 8 (age 13). A variety of study materials—reference books, periodicals—are pursued for their content. At the beginning of this stage listening comprehension is more effective than reading comprehension; but by the end of Stage 3 reading and listening are about equal. This age group reads more widely than at any other age from fiction, biography, and nonfiction. It experiences new feelings and explores new attitudes from the relatively safe environment of books.

Stage 4: Multiple viewpoints identifies the transition from reading to gain new knowledge from a single point of view, expressed in elementary school texts, to the more difficult task of comprehending the conflicting views of multiple sources. The stage is indicative of the reading demands of high schools and the skill development is comparable with that of most literate adults. The reader uses top-down strategies of word comprehension and finds silent reading more productive for gaining information than listening. Class discussions which clarify thinking strategies and content organization can help students combine multiple viewpoints into a cohesive report.

Stage 5: Construction and reconstruction describes mature reading, typically of college-level competence. It is purposeful, professional, or personal. Most adults do not reach this stage and not all college course reading calls for this level of reconstruction and integration. At this stage the multiple points of view that were recognized at Stage 4 must be resolved in terms of a personal philosophy, value system, or professional courage. Although Chall recognizes the dynamic quality of individual reading development, the stages provide a theory-based construct for selecting reading materials and activities for students.

Essential Verbal Abilities

Whenever an investigator differentiates between verbal and nonverbal intelligence in the design and the measures used, verbal abilities emerge more highly correlated with reading achievement than nonverbal abilities. Given the positive correlations between different subtests on intelligence measures, a particular verbal ability may be teased out of the data and analyzed for its relationship to reading. Several questions remain: Is the subskill essential to learning to read? If the answer is negative, reading instruction should proceed without intervention. Does low performance in a particular verbal subskill cause reading failure? If the answer is positive, some form of prereading intervention is merited. Is a particular verbal ability acquired during the process of learning to read? This later question focuses on methodology and whether any one method is best for all learners. Developmental psychologists may hope for maturation to resolve all questions of readiness; but the risk in this approach is that a critical period may pass for full development of an essential linguistic ability. The concept of developmental stages in reading implies not only that certain reading accomplishments are basic to more advanced acquisitions, but that neglect at one stage may diminish the learner's potential at subsequent stages.

Certain elemental subskills for reading acquisition appear in kindergarten primary-level studies, but their significance is not confirmed in older readers. Skjelfjord (1976) reasoned that teaching methods alter the importance of pupil readiness for learning to read. The lack of auditory segmenting ability (the inability to discriminate the separate phonemes and the separate syllables in words) may impose impossible psychological demands on a child whose instruction relies on sight word recognition and minimal sound–letter association. Lack of left-to-right sequencing of print may be overcome without stress when assigned to a teacher who systematically orients beginning writers to left-to-right reading and writing until it is an automatic response. This section reviews recent studies of verbal memory and reading achievement in subskills that are considered prerequisite to successful reading.

MEMORY FOR STORIES

The ability to retell a story requires an understanding of the language in which it was communicated, a working memory of sufficient duration to mediate the major events, and a sense of temporal sequence. McNamee (1982) studied the social origins of children's comprehension of stories at a prereading level, testing the theory of Vygotsky that social interaction with adults establishes the patterns of independent thought in the young child. The development of story comprehension and narration skills in preschool children was investigated through two kinds of teacher–child interactions: (1) children individually narrating a story to the researcher, and (2) children dramatizing the story in small groups. The investigator traced the social interaction within and around the four stories, as guided by the teacher, to blueprint the influence of the teacher's guidance over time in the mental constructions and thought processes the children used in story narration. It was concluded that memory for story schemata and comprehension of textual material was being constructed in the dialogues and social interactions. The case studies appeared to confirm the importance of the social interaction between the child and the adult in the development of thought processes and language in the child.

AUDITORY IMAGERY

Auditory imagery refers to the perceptual registration of speech in the brain. Apparently the speech perception of the typical preschool child is focused on words and phrases together with their meaning, rather than on phonemic segments. Yet the ability to discriminate word segments is essential to learning sound–letter correspondence and is positively correlated with reading progress in the primary grades. How the child comes to focus on and discriminate phonemic units is not clear. Maclean et al. (1987) reported a strong, highly specific relationship between young children's knowledge of nursery rhymes and the development of phonological skills in reading. The correlation remained significant when differences in IQ and social background were controlled. This finding leaves open the question whether children with the ability to hear rhyme enjoyed and remembered poems better than most children or whether the ability to hear rhyme and the ability to discriminate phonemes indicate some elemental prerequisite in the auditory modality for processing the visual language.

KNOWLEDGE OF LETTER NAMES

A positive relationship between the knowledge of letter names and progress in learning to read was discovered and reported by Gates (1940). For more than half a century correlative studies have confirmed the Gates finding, but rival views have continued to influence practice. Opposition came initially from proponents of whole word methodology (Witty, 1949), later by some linguists who believed reading acquisition simulated speech acquisition (Smith, 1973), and finally by advocates of a top-down *meaning-driven* emphasis in instruction rather than a bottom-up *code-driven* emphasis. The arguments centered on the lack of a logical need for letter names in reading and the confusion for children when letter names did not conform to letter sounds. Knowledge of letter names persisted, however, as a factor in predictive studies of reading failure. Some explanations for the advantages of letter naming to beginning readers are: (1) The letter symbols become perceptually familiar, and (2) The letter label facilitates long-term storage and retrieval.

As computer technology became available for timing the responses of letter naming, the research took on new sophistication. Walsh, Price, and Gillingham (1988) examined the psychological processes by measuring letter-naming accuracy, letter-naming speed, and picture-naming speed; then distinguished between accuracy and facility in determining whether slow, plodding letter naming hindered progress in reading. Their data were obtained from kindergarten and second-grade children at midyear and from the cohort groups 16 months later. In this context *cohort* indicated the same group of children carrying the same original grade label, but having grown older. Kindergarten children were retested at the end of the first grade and second-grade children were tested at the end of the third grade. A TV-like screen was used to project the letters and pictures, a microphone recorded the naming responses, and a computer timed and calculated the average of response times (reported in reciprocals). Data showed that variance for speed of picture naming was virtually the same for kindergarten and second-grade children. Kindergarten children had an accuracy range from 20% to 100% of 10 letters tested. Second graders were significantly faster than kindergartners in letter naming, although the time variations for processing different letters was related in ways that suggested both age groups were using similar processes. Apparently the differences derived not from superior *strategies,* but from the superior *efficiency* of the second graders.

The investigators discussed their major findings: (1) A strong positive correlation existed in the kindergarten cohort between letter naming speed and subsequent reading development. (2) The association among kindergarten children between letter-naming speed and reading achievement remained strongly positive when the contribution of letter-naming accuracy was controlled (accounted for) statistically. (3) The association among kindergarten children between letter-naming speed and reading achievement remained strongly positive when the contribution of picture naming speed (the domain effect) was controlled statistically. (4) The relation between letter-naming speed and reading achievement was much stronger among kindergartners than among second graders. (5) A threshold effect, initially hypothesized, was not supported by these data. In this study *the threshold effect* referred to a hypothetical level of letter-naming speed beyond which an increase in efficiency would not contribute to improved reading progress. However, some indication of a threshold of 1.1 seconds was indicated at the kindergarten level. The conclusions were drawn that code emphasis should not be overlooked in beginning reading instruction. However, efforts to quicken code processing in children who are no longer slow shows little effect on reading performance. They point out that letter naming improves communication between teacher and child, enabling the adult to identify letter confusions the child may have, and facilitating the teaching of decoding principles. The investigators concluded that the importance of letter naming is critical, but transitory.

An aspect of letter-naming speed that was not addressed in the Walsh et al. (1988) design was the possible relationship to reading achievement at later stages in reading development. Stanovich, Feeman, and Cunningham, (1983) reported significant correlations between letter-naming speed and reading achievement at the first-grade level, nonsignificant correlations at second level, and significant correlations again at the fifth-grade level. In a later study Stanovich, Nathan, and Vala–Rossi (1986) found nonsignificant correlations among third graders and significant correlations in the fifth grade. The question of processing rate and the threshold effect needs to be re-examined. The reading stages of typical primary-age children and the tests by which their achievement is measured do not require rapid reading. By the fifth grade the volume demands of both school subjects and reading tests may again favor the children who process words (and letters) rapidly.

MASTERY LEARNING OF WORDS

The question of a criterion reference for school learning is always important, but uncertainty arises as to the level of mastery to be required. In classroom learning, which involves groups, the fastest learners tend to achieve the highest level of mastery, and the slowest learners may barely reach the minimal standard. An argument could be made that criterion mastery be lowest for fast learners on the grounds that they will remember a higher percentage of whatever has been learned on a long-term basis. The degree of mastery, once studied as overlearning, has received the attention of researchers Chan and Cole (1987). They examined the interactive effect of "cognitive entry behavior" with master-versus-nonmastery learning on reading comprehension. The subjects were 180 third-grade children who were assigned to one of four groups: 90% mastery, 70% mastery, nonmastery, and a nontreatment control group. Experimental groups were individually instructed in three tasks of word recognition, word meaning, and word order. Results indicated that the effects of the training program on immediate achievement varied significantly with the children's initial level of mastery or nonmastery. Subjects who entered with low scores benefited relatively more than high-mastery students. One interpretation is that students with high scores at entry were already achieving beyond the instructional level of the program.

MEMORY AND INFERENTIAL SKILLS

The relation between children's ability to make inferences and their memory for text has received widespread attention. Oakhill (1984) was interested in whether skilled and less skilled text comprehenders answered inferential questions from memory or from available text. The subjects were two comparison groups of 7- and 8-year-olds who were all average or above in two measures of reading: comprehension of printed words and an oral reading index. Two experimental groups were matched for age, sex, and scores on the two reading tests. They differed in text comprehension, one group scoring at or above the screening tests and the other group scoring one-half grade or more below the screening test as measured by a standardized test of paragraph comprehension. The subjects read four stories each and answered literal and inferential questions about each story. The examiner then returned the copy for reference and self-checking and asked the questions again.

Results of the Oakhill study showed that skilled comprehenders were able to answer more questions, both literal and inferential, from memory than were less skillful comprehenders. When the text was made available, less skilled comprehenders improved their literal answers to the level of the comparison group, but their comprehension of implicit inferences remained poor. The main differentiating characteristic of the good comprehenders was their skill at making inferences, which enabled them to relate the ideas within a text and to general knowledge. Since the groups were not matched for IQ, it is unclear whether the skilled comprehenders were also higher in general intelligence, an important factor in inference construction. The investigator reasoned that making inferences provided an additional process that contributed to literal comprehension of the text. This section has explored some of the cognitive abilities that contribute to successful reading. The next section considers two views on the relationship of language and cognition.

LITERACY AND CONCEPTUAL THOUGHT

Jean Piaget changed the way literate people throughout the world think about children's thinking. His "periods" of cognitive development in humans provided a sharp contrast to Pavlovian discoveries of the conditioned reflex and subsequent experimental work on associative learning. Without denying the evidence of connectionist psychology, Piaget went beyond it to describe how intelligent behavior develops in humans by observing children and describing their cognitive functioning in qualitative detail not matched elsewhere in psychology. His work was embraced enthusiastically by two Soviet psychologists, Lev Semenovich Vygotsky and Aleksandr Romanovich Luria, who were colleagues of Pavlov at the faculty of psychology at the University of Moscow. Vygotsky introduced translations of Piaget's early work to Russian psychologists. The three of them came to psychological research from other fields: Piaget from biological science, Vygotsky from medicine, and Luria from neurosurgery.

Species-specific Intelligence: Piaget

The developmental psychology of Piaget is a biologist's description of the intellectual growth of *Homo sapiens*. His lifework was a 50-year production of how the human intellect evolves during ontogeny. He was driven to discover more flexibility in the nature of people than Darwin had described; and more complexity in human learning than Pavlov's connectionist theory allowed. The common links between neurology and intelligence were described as schemata, or *psychological structures,* which assimilated experience and accommodated to it in a dynamic relationship that resulted in cognitive adaptation. Another Piagetian invariant, or principle, was *biological necessity,* seen in humans as a motivating force to understand, to make sense of the bits and pieces of experience. He was influenced by Gestalt psychology, which emphasized the discovery of relationships within an organized "whole" as being a higher knowledge than the properties of the elements. Piaget set out to define the species, albeit on a scale more grand than his doctoral paper on describing a new species of mollusk in a mountain lake of his native Switzerland and hypothesizing how it evolved.

Vygotsky understood and admired Piaget. In the preface to the 1962 translations he wrote:

> Psychology owes a great deal to Jean Piaget. It is not an exaggeration to say that he revolutionized the study of child language and thought. He developed the clinical method of exploring children's ideas which has since been widely used. He was the first to investigate child perception and logic systematically; moreover, he brought to his subject a fresh approach of unusual amplitude and boldness. Instead of listing the deficiencies of child reasoning compared with that of adults, Piaget concentrated on the distinctive characteristics of child thought, on what the child has rather than what the child lacks. Through his approach he demonstrated that the difference

between child and adult thinking was *qualitative* rather than quantitative. (Vygotsky, 1962, p. 9)

Piaget appealed to scholars because of his humane psychology; he appealed to teachers because they could identify with his methodology and apply his findings. Piaget's almost solitary acquisition of intellectual genius, together with his lack of traditional schooling, kept education outside the mainstream of his concern and he continued to distinguish *learning,* which was imposed by culture and the schools, from *development,* which was, to large extent, under the control of the child's own actions. In 1969 at a press conference in Los Angeles, Piaget explained through Inhelder's translation that, of course, a deprived childhood would deprive a child of normal development, but given a "nutritious environment" development would occur in the sequence outlined in the periods and stages.

Language and Intelligence: Vygotsky

Vygotsky's ideas departed from those of Piaget on the function of language as the vehicle for thought. Whereas Piaget described the attributes that all humans share and delineated the principles of intellectual growth in unitary terms, Vygotsky saw the social environment as stimulating or limiting intellectual development and the culture as a heritage for intellectual attainment. Piaget leaned toward genetic explanations while Vygotsky leaned toward environmental explanations. Piaget argued that cognitive advances, such as the concepts of conservation and seriation, occurred independent of language; the child created the language to explain the thought and invented the vocabulary to explain the discovery. Vygotsky believed that language, learned early in childhood from the verbal instructions given by parents, preceded thought, which began when speech went underground. Vygotsky, who had studied linguistics as an undergraduate, adapted Piaget's clinical methods to analyze the function of language in concept development.

Luria, who was Vygotsky's collaborator, described the goals of his mentor:

> In [Vygotsky's] view language is the most decisive element in systematizing perception; insofar as words are themselves a product of sociohistorical development, they become tools for formulating abstractions and generalizations, and facilitate the transition from unmediated sensory reflection to mediated, rational thinking. . . . [He] set out to do a more searching analysis of concept formulation. He wanted to delineate all the stages in which words figure in one's reflections on reality—to observe how the entire, complex process of concept formation is rooted in the use of words which, he maintained, acquire different meanings at successive stages of development. (Luria, 1976, pp. 49–50)

Vygotsky helped to outline Luria's field studies of the effect of literacy on language and thought. Ill with tuberculosis, Vygotsky was forced to stay behind in Moscow when Luria left for the remote villages of Asia to conduct the concept development studies with adults. Vygotsky entered psychology only 10 years before his death at age 38.

Literacy and Intelligence: Luria

Luria's research on cognitive development in adults who were at different levels of literacy was a model for data gathering within a social ecology. Although the data were collected in 1931–1932, the study was not published in the Soviet Union until 1972, followed by publication in English translation in 1974. The 1930s offered a unique opportunity because radical changes were occurring in the remote areas: Agriculture was being collectivized and illiterate young men had been sent to a "short course" to learn minimal reading and writing skills needed to run the operations. Young activists had been sent for schooling, usually a year or more of literacy training to do the political work of the collective. Schools were being opened for children. Young women, previously illiterate, had been sent away to learn basic skills and teaching methods, usually a 2-year program. Three levels of literacy were available to Luria, all within the same social ecology. There remained many peasant women and farmers who were totally illiterate and totally untouched by mass media.

Luria went to live in the villages until he became known and trusted. Most of his data were gathered casually, around a campfire or in a teahouse. His items were designed from the objects used in the village and the vocabulary of the culture. While Luria posed his questions in conversation, an assistant seated nearby took notes, usually verbatim, which he rewrote soon afterward. Women assistants were employed to interview women subjects. His items are still in use for observing children's concept formation and for diagnosing adults who have suffered brain trauma.

PERCEPTION AND CLASSIFICATION

Luria (and Vygotsky) maintained that perception itself changed with literacy, which provided names for categories in addition to concrete experience. Adult subjects were provided with geometrical figures: triangles, circles, trapezoids, and the like. The figures were varied in shading, manner of outlining, and completeness. Table 4.1 shows how different groups responded when asked to name geometrical figures. Unschooled subjects called figures by object-oriented names: "It's a watch." "It's a window-frame." They were unable to group

TABLE 4.1. Naming of Geometrical Figures (in percentages)

Group	Number of Subjects	Object-oriented Names	Categorical Names
Ichkari women	18	100.00	00.0
Women in preschool courses	35	85.3	14.7
Collective farm activists	24	59.0	41.0
Women at teachers' school	12	15.2	84.8

From Luria (1976).

incomplete figures into their appropriate class (a visual perception task) and had difficulty describing how three forms were alike, even by object-oriented labels. One subject described two circles, "No they are not alike, one is a watch and one is a coin." His teacher-trained group used categorical names almost 85% of the time; they grouped figures in categories without difficulty; and they were able to describe the common attributes of figures, using categorical terms, "They are all rectangles."

GENERALIZATION AND ABSTRACTION

In the university studies with children, Vygotsky had determined that concept formation was a gradual acquisition, beginning when the child observed certain attributes of objects as the basis for categorization. By adolescence the child psychologically isolated the distinctive attributes of a category to form "degrees of community." This observation confirmed the hierarchical classification Piaget observed as logical thought. Luria explained that once a person has made the transition to this mode of thought, the focus is on "categorical relationships between objects and not their concrete mode of interaction." Such "taxonomic cognition" differed altogether from the processes at work in "graphic methods" of generalization:

> [Graphic methods of generalization] are based on an individual's practical experience, whereas the core of "conceptual" or "categorical" thinking is the shared experience of society conveyed through its linguistic system. This reliance on society-wide criteria transforms graphic thinking processes into a scheme of semantic and logical operations in which words become the principal tool for abstraction and generalization. (Luria, 1976, p. 52)

Luria's hypothesis was that village adult males would respond to questions of generalization in accordance with their systematic training, indicated by schooling, rather than by their having reached and passed adolescence. He and his assistants prepared charts with drawings of common objects used in the villages and took them to the places that humans gathered for conversation. One chart showed a hammer, a saw, a log, and a hatchet. The subject was asked to tell, "Which of these could you call by one word? The probing technique of the clinical interview, was used to assure that the subject understood the question. "If you call these three a hammer, that won't be right, will it? A fellow told me that the hammer, the saw, and the hatchet belonged together. Why would he say that? A 39-year-old peasant, illiterate, said, "Yes, they all have to work together." "But why then would we take the wood out of the picture?" The man's answer, "Probably he's got a lot of firewood, but if we'll be left without firewood, we won't be able to do anything." The man classified objects not according to verbal and logical principles, but according to practical schemes. Luria's pages of interviews reveal mature syntax in illiterate speakers but their well-articulated answers lacked abstract concepts. Table 4.2 shows the results of interviews with nearly 50 subjects who differed in literacy: Illiterate peasants, collective-farm activists who had had the short-course literacy program, and young men with 2 years' schooling. Luria concluded that thinking limited to

TABLE 4.2. Groupings and Classifications

Group	Number of Subjects	Graphic Method of Grouping	Graphic and Categorical Methods of Grouping	Categorical Classification
Illiterate peasants from remote villages	26	21 (80%)	4 (16%)	1 (4%)
Collective farm activists (barely literate)	10	0	3 (30%)	7 (70%)
Young people with one to 2 years' schooling	12	0	0	12 (100%)

From Luria (1976).

concretes (the graphic method) is neither innate nor genetically determined. It results from illiteracy and the rudimentary types of activity that prevailed in the daily lives of the peasants.

Luria designed and tested mental processes such as self-analysis and imagination. He concluded that cognitive processes, such as generalization, abstraction, deduction, inference, and reasoning, develop through literacy, which provides the words and signs for mental manipulation across experiences. To him, conscious evaluation of one's own cognitive world was the ultimate stage in the development of logical thought. In the late 1980s this process is defined as metacognition. Luria was not prepared for a political climate in Moscow that would bury his study for 30 years because his data had come from one of the Soviet minorities, who were being treated with extraordinary sensitivity at the time. Luria wished he had gone to a remote Russian village instead, where he assumed the findings would have been the same.

Vygotsky and Luria borrowed extensively from Piaget in the formulation of their hypotheses and in the techniques they used in their experiments. They departed from Piaget by assigning a major role to language in the development of concepts, generalizations, and logical reasoning. They also believed that the language from which formulations were derived came initially from the history of the culture, embedded in the language. Vygotsky and Luria tended to ignore the genetic differences within the culture; Piaget tended to ignore the effect of intellectual experience on cognitive development, including the influence of his own probing questions. Vygotsky stated his position:

> The presence of a problem that demands the formulation of concepts cannot in itself be considered the cause of the process, although the tasks with which society faces the youth as he enters the cultural, professional, and civic world of adults undoubtedly are an important factor in the emergence of conceptual thinking. If the environment presents no such task to the adolescent, makes no new demands on him, and does not stimulate his intellect by providing a sequence of new goals, his thinking fails to reach the highest stages, or reaches them with great delay. (Vygotsky, 1963, pp. 58–59)

Teachers who use questioning strategies to stimulate deductive thinking will appreciate the Vygotsky explanation.

Chapter Summary

The distinction between short-term memory and long-term memory implies some form of mediation during which the immediate registration of information is committed to memory storage. This concept of a working memory has been of interest to reading specialists because evidence of an "articulatory loop" and a "visuospatial scratchpad" have been described. Cognitive abilities, as measured by IQ tests, are consistently and positively correlated with reading progress. Inferential skills appear to increase comprehension of literal information, perhaps because the additional process of inferring enhances long-term storage. The evidence favoring literacy in the development of conceptual processes such as classification, generalization, and reasoning was reviewed in the work of Luria. The extent to which memory and intellectual potential can be enhanced through instruction remains a challenge to educators as problems of illiteracy become a national concern.

5 Cognitive Styles and Learning Strategies

Cognitive style is the learner's predisposition to use a particular learning strategy when attending, perceiving, and thinking (Entwistle & Ramsden, 1983). *Strategies,* sometimes referred to as approaches or orientations, are the learner's intentional plans for selecting and combining schema-based skills into routines. *Skills* range from knowledge-based, where access to patterns of stored representations is necessary for identifying the denoted color "yellow," to action-based, where transformation of information is needed for interpreting the connoted meaning of "yellow" as "cowardly" to sync with the context. Whereas skills are related principally to abilities, strategies are related principally to style. In reading, skills include decoding and analyzing words for identification. Once the strategy decision has been made that an inference is needed, making the inference is a skill. Deciding whether to decode or to guess from context or to use both of these skills at once would be a strategy.

A more encompassing term than cognitive style is *learning style,* which is inclusive of cognitive, affective, and physiological processes (Keefe, 1986). This chapter will focus on: (a) the development of cognitive strategies, (b) the theories of intellectual functioning, (c) the conditions of learning to adjust to different cognitive styles, and (d) the qualities of the creative reader.

COGNITIVE STRATEGIES OF READERS

Readers use deep structure strategies when attempting to understand text at its various levels of interpretation; readers use surface structure strategies when memorizing factual information for later recall. Ramsden (1988) suggested that the deployment of these strategies is related to three factors. First, the way the material is taught. An activity which requires recall of steps, rules, and procedures calls for surface reading. Second, how the students anticipate their tests and assignments will be evaluated is important. When students anticipate a multiple-choice exam, they may study differently than when they expect the bluebook. And third, the structure of the content being learned affects the cognitive process as highly structured text is more easily memorized than discursive writing. Ramsden found that most students use surface strategies, while some are more predisposed to deep strategies. Some students, inclined toward surface strategies, stay with them even when they are inappropriate.

Development of Strategies

Piaget observed that young children move from thinking in associations to thinking in structural or operational terms. This change was illustrated in the seriation studies conducted by Inhelder (1969). *Seriation* is defined as the ordering of a number of objects on a particular dimension. In one experiment, children were shown 10 sticks in seriated length from 4 to 10 inches. The children were asked to draw the sticks immediately and at time intervals of 1 month to 6 months. The children who had discovered the essential length relationship were able to draw the sticks in serial representation both immediately and after not having seen the sticks for a long time. According to Piaget (1969), these children had discovered the seriation principle by what he called deductive thinking. Structural analysis, in word attack, can be learned with this kind of focus where the child discovers the structural relationships between prefixes, roots, and suffixes of words.

The nature of the task and the age of the child is often related to the type of strategy used in the learning situation. Elkind and Weiss (1967) studied the responses of children 5 to 8 years old when presented with structured and unstructured arrangements of familiar figures. The children were asked to name the picture while observers recorded their approach to the problem. Responses to unstructured stimuli (pictures pasted in disarray) were compared with responses to structured arrangements (pictures pasted in a triangle). The investigators found that (1) with increasing age the children explored the unstructured array systematically, and (2) all children explored the structure arrays systematically. When the task was presented in an organized form, the younger children demonstrated a similar cognitive strategy to that of the older subjects.

Differences in the way in which initial readers progress through early reading requirements is reported by Biemiller (1970). He observed different strategies in first-grade readers by analyzing the errors they made when reading orally, and reported that changes in the error patterns children made coincided with their reading progress. The young readers progressed through three phases. The first phase was typified by word-substitution errors which were usually semantically and syntactically sound. The second phase consisted of an increase in nonresponding and more errors which were graphically similar to the target word but with a less of semantic convergence. The third phase was characterized by concerns for both graphic similarity and with semantic acceptability. The readers having the most difficulty persisted in continuing to substitute words on the bases of meaning and syntax, and did not attempt to use graphic cues.

The study strategies of secondary and collegiate students were examined by Entwistle (1988). Through factorial analysis data collected from a questionnaire, he isolated three different orientations to studying. First was a *meaning strategy,* wherein the student desired to understand various interpretations, analyzed critically for bias, and extended an interest in the subject area. Students who reported that they were determined to understand thoroughly what they were asked to read, related the ideas in one subject to those in others, justified articles and research with evidence, and continued academic subjects after a course is completed. Second was a *reproducing strategy* wherein the student memorized the material emphasized, wanted to be told precisely what is in an exam, felt pressure by assignment deadlines, and desired a job in the future. And third was an *achieving strategy* wherein the students tried to please the instructor, found it difficult to organize study time, and wanted superior grades. Students reported that they attempted to anticipate what the instructor desired, had difficulty organizing their time effectively, were frequently discouraged and wondered why they were in school, and found it important to do better than their friends. As students mature, strategies develop which lead to their study approach, method of relating ideas, use of evidence, as well as to their perceived reason for learning.

Affective Components

A predisposition to favor one strategy or style over another appears related to learners' affective development, including their upbringing and self- esteem (Ainsworth, Blehar, Waters, & Wall, 1978). Parents who are responsive to the child but not overly protective gradually leave the child feeling competent; the child may develop an early propensity toward both achievement striving and a sensitivity to the feeling of others. Wender, Pederson, and Waldrop (1967) reported that 2½-year-old boys who showed overdependence in nursery school tended to show less ability in abstract cognitive functions when they entered school, perhaps because of their inability to take risks. At age 6½, the same boys showed lower nonverbal intellectual functioning than boys who were considered socially independent in nursery school.

Self-esteem has been associated to the type of learning strategies an individual uses. *Self-esteem* is a personal estimate of the self, seen as higher or lower than someone else in a group. It is the value attached to the private picture that people carry of themselves. After reviewing the literature in this area, McCarthy and Schmeck (1988) concluded that the optimal environment for children is one in which new thoughts, feelings, and actions can be integrated into self-concept without undue risk to the psyche.

Risk taking and elaboration involved in using deep strategies, which require personal thought and judgment, may be rejected if they pose a threat to the self. Dean (1977) investigated preadolescent gifted boys and girls who were classified as having a high or low self-esteem. He reported that children with high self-esteem used more sophisticated learning strategies and adapted them to fit either nonverbal paired association tasks or free-recall tasks. Children with low self-esteem were less flexible in their choice of strategy and preferred more passive, repetitive routines. Black (1974) compared the self-esteem of learning-disabled students classified as retarded readers with learning-disabled readers identified as normal. Self-esteem was not significantly related to IQ, and the negative relationship between self-esteem and reading increased with age and grade suggesting the interdependence of the choice of strategies and self-esteem.

One way teachers can facilitate the use of both surface and deep strategies is to select material of interest to students. Fransson (1977) examined the affective factors behind reading a technical article. He concluded that students who were interested in the article were more apt to employ a deep structure approach, while those who found the reading uninteresting and stressful, employed a surface approach.

DESCRIPTIONS OF INTELLECTUAL STYLE

The predisposition of individuals to function in intellectually consistent ways has been studied extensively. Some investigators have developed and applied dichotomous frameworks; others have developed and applied multifaceted systems; and still others have built hierarchies of intellectual production on a logical basis.

Dichotomies

Research in cognitive style has used different descriptors for similar concepts. Investigators have constructed a number of continuum-based dichotomies, where two extremes are placed at opposite ends of a scale. Global, holistic, field-dependent, reflective, and right-hemisphere describe a style where thinking is characterized by the learner's inclination toward generalities and concepts. Analytical, atomistic, field-independent, impulsive, and left-hemisphere describe a style of thinking characterized by the learner's inclination toward facts and details. This section focuses on the use of dichotomies to describe cognitive style.

STRUCTURE VERSUS DETAIL

Researchers are interested in the tendency of both people who prefer using an inductive strategy (from details to generalizations) and those who do best when functioning deductively (from generalizations to details). Individuals whose cognitive preference is to deal with factual details or specifics tend to be good at storing and retrieving information; spelling and locating resources; sequentially working out a problem one step at a time; but they are less competent at foreseeing how facts can be organized into a concept or generalization. Although the child's beginning reading program should capitalize on their preferred style of learning, success in school and life appears to require a high degree of ability to function in both structural relationships and factual details. The goal of the reading teacher is to help the student function as effectively as possible by relating relevant details to inherent structure.

Students who can adapt their strategies to the learning task exhibit what is referred to as a flexible style. A *flexible cognitive style* is described by Pask (1988) as "versatile" and by Torrance and Rockenstein (1988) as "whole brain"; it depicts the reader who can alternate between extremes of the dichotomy. Santastefano, Rutledge, and Randall (1965) studied cognitive style and reading disability. The subjects and controls had normal vision, no apparent physical defects, and no emotional deficits. Three types of learning tasks were devised to test the relationship between the different cognitive processes and reading success: (1) *focusing-scanning* style, which requires simultaneous attention on two objects being compared; (2) *leveling-sharpening* style, which determines the inclusion or exclusion of past experience, and (3) *constructed-flexible* style, which evaluates the ability to ignore irrelevant details. Only the third variable was related significantly to reading success. Apparently proficient readers are able to move from constructs to details and back to constructs in a flexible way (Schmeck, 1988).

Kirby (1988) points out that three phases of reading development are analogous to three different reading styles which relate to the structure–detail dichotomy. The first phase, called "global," describes the reader who interprets text as a whole rather than a set of words. The early reader, in particular, is encouraged to read pictures and illustrations, and to reconstruct the story on what is thought to be occurring rather than on the printed text. The second phase, "analytical," describes the child who learns to identify words through phonics and structural analysis. The third phase, "synthetic," describes the reader who uses the strengths of both phase 1 and phase 2. An overdependence on the global phase can result in an overreliance on context; an overdependence on the analytic phase can result in word-by-word reading; the synthesis phase leads to proficient, interpretative reading. The teacher's goal is to get the child to move from one phase to the next.

LEFT-BRAIN VERSUS RIGHT-BRAIN

Evidence of brain functioning supports the hypothesis that individuals differ in verbal strengths versus perceptual orientation. On the basis of his studies of brain mechanisms and speech, Penfield (1969) suggested that three areas of the left hemisphere of the cerebral cortex control the interpretation and production of speech (Fig. 1.2). He found that comparable areas in the opposite hemisphere, usually the right, interpret spatial and figural relationships. The implication is that "semantic" and "symbolic" functions are located in the speech areas of one hemisphere. Sperry (1970) found the language and the calculation centers in the speech dominant hemisphere. The "behavioral" and "figural" functions are normally located in the opposite hemisphere, where Sperry found nonverbal ideation, spatial construction, and simple language associations. These opposite sites in the left and right hemisphere coordinate perceptual interpretation of auditory versus visual images.

While evidence of differentiation between individuals has been shown on both physiological and experiential bases, writers since the 1970s have sometimes reduced or simplified the role of the brain functions into right- and left-brain dichotomies. By this simplistic interpretation, creativity supposedly emanates from the right hemisphere; Western societies function from the left hemisphere; some people think from the left-hemisphere and others think from the right; a person uses one side of the brain or the other when solving a particular type of problem. Levy (1982), a distinguished neuropsychologist, expressed concern with the inaccuracy of viewing the organization of the brain as two separate entities. While the two hemispheres differ in important ways, "the nature of these differences has little connection with their popularized picture, however, and the implications for human cognition and emotion are not what has been propagated" (p. 174). Both hemispheres are important in language. Although alexia (loss of ability to read due to brain trauma) occurs more frequently with left-hemisphere damage, it can be also occur when damage is restricted solely to the right side of the brain. One hemisphere may be more influential in processing certain types of information, but trained professionals in music and visual art activate both sides of the brain when listening, viewing, or producing.

While exclusive cognitive activities are not located solely in one hemisphere or the other, each hemisphere is differentiated in function and they emphasize the processing of particular types of information. Moreover, learners appear to have cognitive preferences to the types of information characterized by one of the hemispheres (Sinatra, 1982). Contributions of each hemisphere to reading and writing were outlined by Kane and Kane (1979). They report that the left hemisphere is dominant in these ways: (1) analytical processing of parts to name a word, (2) learning rules of syllabication and structural analysis, (3) naming and describing items through a verbal mode, (4) sequencing events, (5) reading and following verbal direction, and (6) learning subskills through criterion-referenced programs. They report that the right hemisphere is dominant in these ways: (1) learning words holistically through experiences with word meaning, (2) identifying words through figures of speech, metaphor, simile, and analogy, (3) composing and writing sentences through whole composition involvement (prewriting to refining), and (4) synthesizing several selections to relate meaning and create new ideas.

While the left–right dichotomy is one way to describe cognitive style differences, *interhemispheric integration,* whole brain learning, is the instructor's goal as both hemispheres are involved in overall thinking, logic, and reasoning tasks. Levy (1982) suggested that it may be easier for some children to learn to read by phonic approaches and others by sight-word approaches. But the child who learns to read through phonics ultimately needs to use sight words, and the child who learns to read through sight words will still need phonic skills.

FIELD-DEPENDENT VERSUS FIELD-INDEPENDENT

The constructs of field-dependence and field-independence is based on the work of H. A. Witkin in the late 1940s. Witkin originally became intrigued by the knowledge that certain pilots who lost sight of the ground flew their airplanes upside down. Investigation of this phenomenon led to a classification he referred to as field-dependent and field-independent. *Field-dependent* individuals, who are influenced by the overall organization of the background, observe the parts of the field as consolidated. These persons see relationships between skills and concepts, tie material to their own background, and need a well-organized framework for comprehension. *Field-independent* individuals perceive objects and features separate from their surrounding field. They impose structure, make specific concept distinctions, and use hypothesis testing to manipulate concepts (Garger & Guild, 1984). Witkin and his associates developed an instrument, the *Group Embedded Figures Test* (1971) to measure analytical (field-independent) and global (field-dependent) styles by asking students to discover and trace simple forms embedded in more complicated figures.

Bigelow (1967) studied the ability of children to separate figure and ground, and described the differences in this ability according to age, sex, and socioeconomic groups. He separated children on the basis of global versus analytical cognitive styles. By global, he meant an undifferentiated, unsystematic approach to the problem. By analytical, he meant the ability to perceive visually a figure embedded in a complex of irrelevant background. His test was the *Children's Embedded Figures Test*. Bigelow's lower ranking socioeconomic pupils, as a group, were less field-independent, that is, they were less able to pick out form from detail than their higher socioeconomic counterparts. Older children tended to show greater field-independence than younger children. Bigelow concluded that verbal intelligence and the ability to see structure in visual configurations are separate traits. Witkin, Goodenough, and Karp (1967) found that field-dependence increased from ages 8 to 17 and remained relatively stable to age 24, which was the outer limit to their age group. They also found marked individual consistency in field-independence versus field-dependence even in the young children in the study.

Multifaceted Systems

Many researchers developed multifaceted systems to depict the complexity of their findings. Modality preference and transaction profiles have been examined for their role in learning.

PERCEPTUAL MODALITY

Perceptual modality, the tendency of the learner to prefer or learn more efficiently in a particular sensory system, is revealed in neurological functioning and perceptual tests. Educators and psychologists interested in reading usually are concerned with the relative power or dominance of the different sensory systems: visual-spatial, auditory-verbal, and kinesthetic-psychomotor. Long before reading teachers became interested in the neurology of learning, they observed that some children learned words by sight, others sounded the same words repeatedly, while others learned best when they wrote the words. Preference evolves from an orientation toward the kinesthetic modality in infants, to visual organization in childhood, and finally to verbal direction in adulthood. In maturation, all three modes are used with a preference given to one of the areas (Keefe, 1982). Wepman (1968) suggested that instruction be adapted to the preferred modality of the reader. Research supporting or not supporting the matching of learning or reading style to the individual student has been mixed.

Some researchers have tried to match the visual and auditory preferences of students to the method used to teach them reading skills. Robinson (1972) examined 448 first-grade children classified into four groups based on their performance on three visual-discrimination tasks and Wepman's *Auditory Discrimination Test*. Categorized as high visual-high auditory, high visual-low auditory, low visual-high auditory, and low visual-low auditory, word recognition skills were taught by an auditory method or by a visual method. The auditory method produced better results than the visual method in reading and spelling. The group categorized as low visual-high auditory, who were taught aurally, had significantly higher results than those in any groups taught by the visual method.

Some researchers have reported success in matching modality preference with instructional approach. Worden and Franklin (1986–1987) investigated the effect of matching tutorial methods to the perceptual strengths of second- and third-grade, below-average readers. Experimental groups consisted of 24 predominantly visual and 24 predominantly kinesthetic learners while the controls consisted of 24 learners having consistent visual, auditory, and kinesthetic skills. The experimental groups received instruction in two 30-minute tutorial sessions given weekly. Posttest results showed experimental groups made significant gains in word recognition and comprehension.

Antonova (1967) compared concretely oriented and verbal logically oriented pupils when involved in two types of instruction: inductive and deductive. He separated pupils ranked high in intelligence from those ranked low in intelligence. He found that pupils who profited most from deductive instruction were the highly intelligent, concretely oriented; the less intelligent subjects were verbal-logically oriented. Those who profited most from inductive instruction were the highly intelligent, verbal-logically oriented, and the less intelligent were concretely oriented.

On the other hand, Bateman (1968) investigated the question by examining the modality preference of first graders in eight classrooms. She found that the method of instruction accounted for 14% of the variance and individual difference accounted for only 7% of the variance among the children in reading ability. She concluded that matching instruction to perceptual preference did not significantly affect achievement.

Further studies along this line are needed. The failure to find a significant relationship between matching modality and instruction by many researchers invites several explanations: (1) a student may not have one modality preference for all tasks, (2) the degree of preference may be more important, and (3) beginning reading may be more than perceptual activity (Miller, 1979).

From one perspective, matching modality preference to teaching approach is a moot point. The argument has persisted in reading clinics about whether the dominant sensory system should be used to teach reading or whether the weak areas should be strengthened. The physiology of the brain establishes a continuous interaction of motor, visual, and auditory systems. Even if modality strengths can be used in reading instruction, as some have been suggested, the dominant modality should be the basis from which associations to are formed. However, the argument about instruction in the appropriate modality becomes academic because an instructor needs to use the perceptual strengths of the individual student and broaden these to other modalities as the student functions successfully in integrated tasks.

TRANSACTIONAL PROFILES

Two exemplary systems which result in transactional profiles are the *Gregorc Style Delineator* (Gregorc, 1982) and *The Learning Style Inventory* (Dunn & Dunn, 1978; Dunn, Dunn, & Price, 1975). These systems aid in the analysis of individual learning patterns and learning styles.

The *Gregorc Style Delineator* combines two sets of bipolar descriptors: *concrete versus abstract* and *random versus abstract sequential* to construct four learning patterns. Students are categorized as: *concrete sequential* if they are

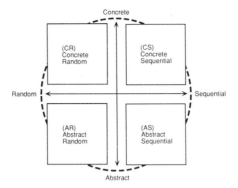

Figure 5.1. Bidimensional matrix of the Gregorc Style Delineator showing the relationship between the concrete-versus-abstract and random-versus-sequential styles. (Adapted from J. W. Keefe, 1982.)

objective, persistent, and concerned with detail; *abstract sequential* if they are logical, analytical, and interested in research; *abstract random* if they are sensitive, aesthetic, and spontaneous; and *concrete random* if they are intuitive, experimental, and risk taking. This is a self-report inventory consisting of 40 words in 10 sets of 4 words per set. Students rank their personal impressions of the words in each set and scores are profiled on a bidimensional matrix to reflect each learner's preferences (Fig. 5.1).

The *Learning Style Inventory* consists of self-report questionnaires generating information from 36 subscales covering 18 elements in five areas:

1. *Environmental stimuli*—light, sound, temperature, and design.
2. *Emotional stimuli*—structure, persistence, motivation, and responsibility.
3. *Sociological stimuli*—pairs, peers, adults, self, group, varied.
4. *Physical stimuli*—perceptual strengths (auditory, visual, tactual, kinesthetic), mobility, intake, time of day.
5. *Physiological stimuli*—global/analytical, impulsive, reflective, and cerebral dominance.

This instrument is intended to delineate the educational conditions in which an individual student is most likely to learn comfortably.

The value of these kinds of transactional profiles in prescribing instructional strategies has been disputed and remains controversial. Kampwirth and Bates (1980) reviewed 22 studies in which only two supported matching teaching method and learning styles. Likewise, Stahl (1988) opposed matching learning styles, including modalities, with instructional approach. He reported that studies supporting the concept of matching learning style to reading method are less numerous than studies reporting negative findings. Also, he was critical of the use of self-report questionnaires to measure learning preferences. He identified many leading questions with obvious answers and objected to the assumption that young children have a metacognitive awareness which enables them to be informative about their own reading behavior.

Other investigators suggest that the negative findings reflect flawed research where small sample sizes were used, brief periods of intervention transpired, or outdated diagnostic tests were employed (Worden & Franklin, 1986–1987). Carbo (1988) cited instances where use of the *Reading Styles Inventory,* an instrument modelled after the *Learning Styles Inventory,* was successful. Many of the investigations, which reported success in matching student style and curriculum, belonged to groups with extreme variability—below-average readers and gifted readers.

Studies of below-average readers frequently select subjects who are substantially lower in their reading skills than would be expected given their age, intelligence, and culture. Poor readers apparently fail to use organized, goal-directed strategies when approaching a specific learning task (Torgesen, 1982). Students in grades 4 through 10 were examined for their spontaneous use of textbook lookbacks, a device which good readers use to monitor their awareness by referring back to the text when discrepancies arose (Garner & Reis, 1981). Students read a narrative passage of three paragraphs with questions following each paragraph. From observations of verbal and nonverbal behaviors, the investigators concluded that most poor comprehenders did not monitor their reading or use lookbacks spontaneously.

Gifted readers are frequently reported as benefiting from matching the style to the curriculum. They accomplish tasks earlier, more quickly, somewhat better, and often a little differently from their peers. Gifted students are reported as being critical, independent of thought and judgment, and persistent (Dunn & Price, 1980). Stewart (1981) administered the *Learning Styles Inventory* and the *Nowicki–Strickland Locus of Control Scale for Children* to approximately 300 fourth-, fifth-, and sixth-grade gifted and talented students and approximately 300 regular students from the same grade levels. She found that gifted and talented students preferred instructional methods which emphasized independence and the general population preferred methods with relatively more structure. Torrance and Rockenstein, (1988) hypothesized that gifted students are capable of using both cerebral hemispheres, both figural and verbal dimensions, interchangeably.

Intellectual Operations

Guilford (1967) developed a Structure of Intellect model (SOI) for describing cognitive functioning. He hypothesized 120 distinct modes of intellectual functioning. By factorial analysis, he and his coworkers have been able to separate, by statistical treatment of the data, more than 100 of the 120 modes projected in the model (Fig. 5.2). These factors are categorized along three dimensions: contents, operations, and products. He found distinct abilities within individuals to deal with different types of *content*: figural, symbolic, and behavioral. Guilford was also interested in the result, or *product,* of the intellectual process. He identified six forms of intellectual outcomes: units, classes, relations, systems, transformations, and implications.

The remaining dimension, one that has the greatest implication for cognitive style, is the intellectual process called *operations*. Statistically, he identified five operations: cognition, memory, convergent production, divergent production, and evaluation. A transcript of a reading discussion by fourth-grade pupils and

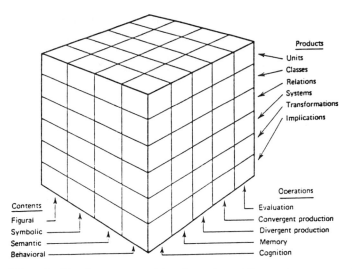

Figure 5.2. Guilford's structure of intellect. A multifaceted construct of cognitive funcioning in which 120 different combinations are possible. (Redrawn from Guilford & Tenopyr, 1969. Implications of the Structure-of-Intellect Model for high school students. In Michael (Ed.), *Teaching for creative endeavor.* Bloomington: Indiana University Press, p. 27, by permission.)

their teacher illustrates each of these operations; each of the questions has a content dimension that is semantic, and product dimension that varies.

The story was "Talking Dog" by Henry Fea. Hugo, the boy, obtained some pills from a man in an alley to make his dog talk. The talking sequence, handled as a fantasy, ends when Hugo cannot tolerate a talking dog and obtains different and more expensive pills to make him stop talking.

Cognition—the first of the Guilford operations—means the immediate discovery, awareness, or recognition, of information. One way to test cognition is by asking for a definition of a word. The teacher wanted the children to understand that the dog really was blackmailing Hugo although the word was not used in the text.

Teacher: How did Sad Sack make Hugo put the whole piece of toast under the table?

Douglas: By talking—to Hugo. He gave it to him so—Sad Sack wouldn't talk out—when his mother came back.

Bobby: Sad Sack says—put more jam on it.

Sandra: Hugo didn't want his mother to hear Sad Sack talking, so he had to give him a piece of toast or Sad Sack would maybe start talking louder and his mother would hear him.

Teacher: What word do we use to mean getting something we want from someone by threatening to tell.

Douglas: Blackmail.

Guilford defines *memory* as the process of retention of information in the same form in which it was committed to storage. Recall is evidence of the memory process. In the story, the teacher asked a question that was designed to help children remember an essential detail of the story problem. Two kinds of pills were involved; the teacher expected the children to remember this from their reading.

Teacher: How much did Hugo pay for the pills?

Douglas: Fifty cents.

Sherry: A dollar.

Douglas: And a half.

Barbara: Fifty cents.

Douglas: A dollar *and* fifty cents. He paid fifty cents for the box and a dollar for the others.

Guilford regarded both divergent and convergent productions as thinking in a generative sense. In *convergent thinking* the necessary information is available to students. They need, however, to select, retrieve, and synthesize the information to build the correct solution. In this kind of problem solving, the mental process generated a structure or relationship that is inherent in the requirements or the problem. There is one right answer in convergent thinking.

In the story sequence, the teacher attempted to bring to the front of children's thinking those relevant bits and pieces of information that would help them generalize that the kinds of things Sad Sack wanted Hugo to do were the kinds of things that dogs do. The author's theme was that the dog had not changed its needs or its motivations because it had learned to talk.

Teacher: What sorts of things did Sad Sack want Hugo to do?

Lillian: All the things that Sad Sack wanted to do, he wanted Hugo to do too.

Brad: Hugo, he wanted to go down to the lake and skate and Sad Sack said that he wanted to chase rabbits and on Saturday he wanted to chase rats and dig.

Bobby: Well, Sad Sack wanted—he always wanted to do things like a dog wanted to do. It didn't change his mind, those pills. He just thought like a dog—still.

Sandra: Maybe Sad Sack wanted to—do everything that dogs do all the time and Hugo didn't want to do everything that Sad Sack wanted to do.

Divergent production makes use of information that has been made available to the learner through previous cognition, memory, and convergent production. These details are transformed, combined, and treated in unique ways to produce new information. In divergent thinking the production is diverse, novel, or original. Usually many answers are possible, hence, the term divergent. This time the teacher's questions are planned to elicit many different answers which had not been stated directly in the story. The teacher sought ideas from the children, based on their private interpretations of the story.

Teacher:	How did this experience help Hugo grow up a little? What do you think he learned?
Gordon:	Well, not to be so foolish, to let his conscience be his guide.
Bobby:	To do things instead of—well not listening to some person—because some person wants you to do it.
Walter:	I think he did a smart thing when he—I'd spend a dollar to stop a dog from talking. I'd take a chance. If I didn't know whether I was getting gypped or not, I would still take a chance, because I wouldn't like a talking dog that can understand me and walk around and blab all the things I do wrong.
Bill:	Well, I think that—when you wish for things, that they aren't always—that you might not really like them as well as you think you do when you are wishing for them.
Mike:	Well, like when he bought the pills he really didn't want to buy them. But you shouldn't just because you don't want to hurt somebody's feelings. That isn't any reason to spend money. I wouldn't buy those pills because it wouldn't be any fun if my dog could talk.
Jeff:	I think it taught Hugo a lesson not to spend his money unwisely. That's what my mama tells me. I go down to the store with some money and I look around and I want something and I buy it and then it's all broken up in a couple of days.

Guilford defined *evaluation* as the process by which judgments are made concerning the goodness, suitability, or adequacy of information. These judgments are made in terms of identity, consistency, and goal satisfactions. Guilford came to believe that evaluations were made during each of the intellectual operations—cognition, memory, and production—but at different levels. Evaluation is seen in the children's arriving at the total cost of the pills, initially introduced in the memory question. It was also seen in the convergent thinking as judgments of what dogs like to do. In the divergent thinking question, the criteria for "growing up" required evaluation. In the following section, evaluation is the major purpose of the question. Although memory is called for in the discussion, the teacher leads the students to discover what is a fantasy.

Teacher:	Tell some of the things that happened in this story that do not happen in real life.
Douglas:	You can't buy pills that would make your dog talk or not talk.
Bobby:	Well, it couldn't happen, but you could just call it like a tale, just like something that somebody made up.
Douglas:	A tall tale—a tall, tall tale.

Sandra:	I don't think a dog could eat a hamburger in one bite, or a whole piece of toast.
Teacher:	How about that—you people who have dogs? Can they eat a piece of toast in one bite?
Sherri:	Well, it depends on how big—
Douglas:	It would have to be a pretty big dog.
Sherri:	How big the dog is. It could be cut in two or it could eat it whole. It could eat it though.
Bobby:	It was a whole piece of bread.
Lillian:	I remember when our dog couldn't eat a whole toast, but he could eat it so fast it would seem like he ate it whole.

By preplanning the major discussion questions, the teacher can use the discussion to stimulate children to use each of the five Guilford operations.

Guilford (1967) discussed the possible relationships between his own construct of intellect and brain functions in learning. He located cognitive evaluation functions within the frontal lobes and their subcortical structures. Eccles and Robinson (1984) reported that sensing errors and incongruities are connected with functions in the frontal lobes. Damage to the frontal lobes has been noted clinically to be affiliated with loss of judgment in social relationships. Guilford hypothesized that empathic relationships also involve cortical and subcortical regions of the frontal lobes. The location of evaluation functions in the same general area of the brain for both cognitive and affective decisions has interesting implications for teaching.

A later version of the SOI model expanded the number of potential abilities for processing different types of information (Comrey, Michael, & Fruchter, 1988). In the dimension *operations,* the category "memory" was divided into memory recoding and memory retention. In the dimension *contents,* the category labeled "behavioral" was divided into visual and auditory components. Instead of 120 cells ($5 \times 4 \times 6$), the revised model consists of 180 cells ($6 \times 5 \times 6$) where each cell represents a unique mental ability. Guilford's extensive testing of this model by factoral analysis reveals the enormous complexity of intelligence.

A Logical Hierarchy

A learning motivation hierarchy presented in Chapter 2 showed how the learner moves from association to conceptualization as the foundation for self-direction. According to this theory, readers can be helped to use the multiple bits of rote learning to build conceptual structures. When teaching proceeds by rote exclusively, the child's tendency to structure his world is frustrated. While visiting schools in Asia and Africa, it was observed that nearly all schools taught English as a second language, using rote methods. Typically one of the pupils would read from a little book and his classmates would repeat the words. (R-A-T) R-A-T spells rat. Rat means ———. (C-A-T) C-A-T spells cat. Cat means ———, and so on. Children learned to speak and to read English by this method. Any conceptualization of language structure (syntax) occurred through the individual's knowledge of a prior language.

By conceptualizing, the learner uses a number of pieces of experience and puts them into a relationship that then may be used more economically in future cognitive operations than associated specifics. One of the most important conceptual strategies that teachers can help children develop is the ability to classify. Sounds are classified into vowels and consonants; books into fiction and nonfiction; and poems into sonnets, ballads, free verse, haiku, limericks, and epics. One way to help young students structure their world is to arrange similar objects together in sets so that similarities and differences are perceived. Preschool children, in learning to speak the language, make this kind of conceptualization when they abstract the essential characteristics of an adjective. At this point in acquiring syntax, they can identify new adjectives from the speech of others and add them or apply them without difficulty. The classification process is extended when the child is able to label a group of things that have common characteristics and represent a grammatical class.

Conceptualizations are extremely useful in thought and communication. Principles, generalizations, laws, models, and formulas are examples of conceptual structures. At the level of formal operations, the adolescent deals with relationships between two or more conceptualizations. Some examples include an understanding of top-down and bottom-up language processing, the relationship among our three forms of government, and the relationship among plot, character, development, and setting in a story.

It is sometimes difficult for a teacher to know whether a student is functioning at the association or conceptualization level. Concepts can be tested for understanding by presenting learning tasks which require application or transfer of the idea to new situations. Children learn to generalize if someone helps them to identify common properties, confirm good guesses, and arrange materials so that similarities and differences are readily perceived. Worthwhile experience for elementary pupils is to select nouns and verbs in sentences, describe their functions, and later define them as syntactic relationships. Going back and forth between specific examples and cognitive structure is the most effective way to learn.

MATCHING STYLE TO CURRICULUM

As Guilford illustrated, cognitive strategies and styles are grounded on multiple intellectual functions which can be identified, defined, and taught. Learning is a complex process, and many ways have been devised to subdivide and name the elements and transactions involved. A complex aspect of instruction is clearly and effectively to address the task of matching the curriculum to the specific needs of each learner.

Ruggiero (1988) developed a "holistic" model which incorporated the principles and strategies of both creative and critical thinking. Creative thinking for producing ideas; critical thinking for evaluating them. This holistic model encourages *student* production and evaluation of ideas, teaches students a sequential approach to productive thinking, and uses decision making, problem solving, and issue analysis. Ruggiero's model is represented by five stages: (1) *exploration* to determine important problems or issues to be raised, (2) *expression* to articulate the problem, (3) *investigation* to examine what information is mean-ingful, (4) *idea production* to examine all possible solutions or arguments, and (5) *evaluation and refinement* to judge and change the solution or arguments if needed. This holistic model, like most models based on inductive thinking, encourages students to learn how to incorporate information autonomously, clas-sify data, and incorporate facts into generalized rules. A teacher who uses a variety of learning models which facilitate learning, from association to creative self-direction, will meet the needs of *most* students.

Conditions of Learning

A classic work, the *Conditions of Learning* by R. N. Gagné (1970), presents a highly regarded description of the principles of learning that are important for teaching students who apply different strategies and prefer different styles. Gagné stressed that it is the learner's activity that facilitates learning; and that the role of the teacher is to create conditions that increase the likelihood that the student will reach a desired outcome level or performance skill. Practice is encouraged to ensure that the child makes the necessary associations but ulti-mately the learners themselves make the essential associations and concep-tualizations even when they are directly pointed out to them. Although Gagné's model appears precise and direct, his goal was to spell out a definition of learning outcomes and a hierarchy of tasks needed for instruction. His description of learning makes it clear that the more complex the model the teacher uses to present a lesson, the greater the likelihood that several types of learning will occur. Gagné developed an eight-level hierarchy of learning which remains pop-ular among teachers at all levels of instruction. The first five levels would be included with association learning as defined in this volume and the other three within conceptualization (Table 5.1). In many cases, Type 6, concept learning, could be built by association responses, but in others a conceptualization occurs that makes the abstraction more easily transferable to other situations. In Type 7, rule learning, Gagné distinguishes this level of learning as understanding rather than mere parroting a rule that has been memorized. In Type 8, problem solving, most of the formulations would be classed as conceptualizations, although some of them would be classified as creative production, depending on the learner's cognitive operation.

Gagné made a strong case for the difference between the types of learning and an even stronger case for the need to develop *all* the lower levels before it is possible to move to a higher type of learning. In discussing foreign-language learning, he cited the use of discovery techniques in learning rules (1970, p. 268). He pointed out that discovery learning may take longer but seems to have advantages of putting principles into long-term memory and in the ultimate generalization of ideas across subject areas. He stressed the importance of basic data on which rules are grounded if the rules are to be established, and suggested teaching problem solving almost exclusively in discovery terms.

Gagné's insistence on the need for building in the preceding types of learning before attempting to achieve a more advanced level has led to the analysis of the concepts that are necessary to solve a problem. Teachers' attention to the neces-sary elements in practical application of these ideas has enabled them to structure

TABLE 5.1. The Eight Types of Learning according to Gagne

Types	Conditions
Type 1: Signal learning—the individual learns to make a *general* diffuse response to a signal. This is the classical conditioning response of Pavlov.	1. The stimulus produces a generalized reaction (contiguity). 2. The stimulus provides the signal. 3. The stimulus must precede the signal.
Type 2: Stimulus–response learning is a type of learning in which a very precise muscular movement in response to a very specific stimulus is formed. It involves operant conditioning, contiguity, and practice.	1. Learning is gradual. 2. Response becomes more sure and precise. 3. Controlling stimulus becomes more sure and precise. 4. Condition 2 plus 3 equals successive approximation. 5. Reinforcement follows the response.
Type 3: Chaining—what is acquired is a chain of two or more stimulus–response connections. (Example: the grip on a bat, the stance and swing in hitting a ball)	1. Individual links must be previously established. 2. There must be contiguity between links.
Type 4: Verbal associations—the learning of chains that are verbal. (Example: English word "match" from the French word "*alumette*"—illuminate—lum—light—match)	1. Learner must know what the word means. 2. He must make a connection between the words. 3. There must be a coding connection. (e.g., be able to associate *lum* with illuminate.)
Type 5: Multiple discrimination—the individual learns to make **n** different identifying responses to as many different stimuli (learning a French vocabulary list or symbols for the chemical elements). The learning of each stimulus–response connection is a simple Type 2 occurrence; the connections tend to interfere with each other's retention.	1. Individual chains between each stimulus and each response must be learned. 2. Steps must be taken to reduce interference.
Type 6: Concept learning—the learner acquires a capability of making a common response to a class of stimuli which may differ widely in physical appear-	1. There is initial coding of property (ballness) plus a response capability. 2. Learner must be able to generalize to a variety of conditions. 3. Learning may be a gradual process.

(continued)

TABLE 5.1. *(Continued)*

Types	*Conditions*
ance (e.g., classifying a football, tennis ball, basketball, and baseball all as balls).	Therefore, there must be the possibility of multiple presentations of examples of the concept.
Type 7: Rule learning—the chaining of two or more concepts. (Example: when water freezes, its volume becomes larger. This principle embodies the concepts of freeze, volume, and larger.)	1. All concepts must have been previously learned. 2. Concepts must be brought together (not necessary that the student do this) 3. Learning takes place in one trial.
Type 8: Problem solving (thinking)—two or more previously acquired principles are somehow combined to produce a new capability that can be shown to depend on a "higher order" principle.	1. Learner must be able to identify the essentials of a solution. 2. He must be able to recall previously learned principles. 3. He must be able to combine the principles so that a new one is formed. 4. There is a sudden solution—repetition will add nothing.

lessons so that problem solving can occur. It may be that the conceptualization of "a conceptualization being possible" is the most critical factor in increasing the effectiveness of classroom procedure. Those who are sure that insight, discovery, or conceptualization is impossible for children will never come across any evidence that contradicts their belief. They will not structure lesson sequences to bring forth conceptualizations they are sure cannot happen.

Curriculum for Creative Readers

This section is concerned with ways the teacher can facilitate the interaction between conceptualization at level two and creative self-direction at level three, to develop a sophisticated reader. Three stages have been proposed in becoming a creative reader (Early, 1960). The first stage is described as unconscious enjoyment where readers use uncritical and subjective surface strategies. They enjoy reading, respond basically to recall questions, and do not examine the text to evaluate for quality and accuracy. The second stage is described as self-conscious appreciation where the reader begins to become objective of the work, comparing it with their own experience and background. They make inferences, question the events that occurred, and begin evaluations based on opinion. The third stage is described as conscious delight, where the reader uses deep strategies in looking at the writing for significance, style, and evaluations based on logical and factual justifications.

Having learned the basic skills, *creative readers* have a number of characteristics that facilitate their becoming unique readers. They become highly absorbed. They use analogies in speech. They have a tendency to burst out with ideas, to challenge, to look closely. They have the urge to tell others, are spontaneous in their use of discovery, show excitement in their voices and boldness about ideas, and have a tendency to lose their awareness of time. They also have an openness to new possibilities. They grasp unique situations, whether concrete or abstract. The teacher can help students move from conceptualization to self-direction as readers by helping them to distinguish the relevant features of both levels. There are distinctions in goals, evaluation, motivation, and production.

GOALS

The learner's goal at the conceptualization level is to understand the real world, to organize and to structure it in ways that can be understood and communicated. As far as reading is concerned, the purpose of a reader might be to conceptualize the author's theme as revealed in a short story. In this situation, the creative reader considers the contributions of the character, plot, and setting; organizes these into a central theme that represents the author's intention; forms a creative structure grounded on his or her view of truth or reality; and may use the short story, for example, to launch a discussion revealing his or her views on the same topic, or even to write a short story that is built around a theme that has become both intimate and vital.

EVALUATION

The reader who evaluates literature at the conceptual level attempts to discover whether it is logically consistent, true to the form the author adopted, and reflects the real world. At conceptualization level, the world of others determines the criteria on which literary criticism is based. The creative reader compares the author's ideas against other sources. A poem might be evaluated or critiqued against the format the poet accepted in the beginning, such as a sonnet. Such an evaluation measures the material read against the literary criteria that are known and understood by the instructor and other members of the class. However, creative evaluation responds primarily to the aesthetic dimension in the poem. "I like it because of the feel it gives me. It says what I feel." In creative evaluation the reader seeks final validation from within rather than from the criteria of others.

MOTIVATION

The conceptualization that is critical to motivation is that reading can be used to resolve an issue, to solve a problem, or to find new evidence. The affects that creative readers conceptualize are the sources of pleasure that come from finding solutions on their own through books. He or she may want answers to such questions as: Why did the Japanese bomb Pearl Harbor? Are there commonalities in the early childhood of eminent persons? Do girls become architects? If the problem is the readers' own choices and they go about in their own way to initiate a search or research procedure, they will have moved into level-three functioning. The motivation of the reader at a self-directing level satisfies a need for some high-level fulfillment.

PRODUCTION

The outcome of the conceptual process is to arrive at some understanding or some relationship that has been devised or predetermined by the culture or the discipline. The conceptualizer adds 2 plus 2 to equal 4. The product of creative self-direction is consciously unique. Creative readers give something of themselves, a plus quality, to their reading that goes beyond the material and the intent of the author. Sometimes this new insight into social or technical problems, and usually some stimulation toward further thought or action results. Such readers do not absorb unthinkingly the premises of another, even though these may be complicated and difficult to conceptualize. When confronted with action, they will say, "Is this right for me?" Essentially, the result of creative reading is a new interpretation or action.

The teacher may encourage creative responses to reading material in many ways, but all of them require imagination as well as understanding. Teachers and students need not get confused over which ideas come from the individual. When the ideas that come from the individual are valued, the level of the children's responses will be lifted. One way to encourage students to read creatively is to let them plan some of their own reading experiences based on what they think they need as readers. Students need to be encouraged to report their own feelings and hunches about a book or a nonbook situation. When children go on their own in reading as in other activities, problems are certain to arise. The teacher who maintains a hopeful outlook will encourage rather than stifle future innovation. Children who have negative reactions toward people in books or toward books themselves should be allowed to express them. In this way the teacher becomes aware of the reality of the student's world and knows better the forces with which he must cope in the classroom. The child who retreats too readily, who gives up his or her idea too quickly, needs support from the teacher to express his or her own ideas. The school should not make the student risk too much as a person to make one's ideas known. Creative reading is stimulated by an early introduction to fantasy and folktales, as well as to factual information. The students who keep discussion problems open and do not work for quick answers are likely to find creative solutions. When the teacher recognizes the student who improvises, other children will try to improvise also.

Chapter Summary

Cognitive style is the learner's predisposition to use a particular learning strategy. Strategies develop as children move from thinking in associations to thinking in structural terms. They are influenced by the child's upbringing and self-esteem. Self-confident learners use deep strategies which require risk taking and elaboration.

Researchers have investigated a number of continuum-based dichotomies: structure versus detail, left-brain versus right-brain, and field-dependent versus field-independent. Multifaceted systems have been developed by those needing a more complex system, than dichotomies, to depict the complexity of their findings. Many studies have attempted to match the learning style of the students to a specifically designed curriculum. While results emanating from this line of research have been mixed, reading lessons built on a solid principles, such as those described by Gagné, are likely to meet the needs of most learners.

Creative readers extend their conceptualization of the author's meaning to expand their own world. Creative readers are motivated by the pleasure and power they get from reading. At the conceptualization level readers evaluate literature by external criteria; at a self-directed level they accept, reject, or modify the standards to fit their own aesthetic values.

III │ Sensory Discrimination of Symbols

But chieflye the anatomye ye oughte to understande;
If ye will cure well anye thinge,
that ey doe take in hande. . .

—John Halle (1529–1568)

141

6 | Brain Functions of Language

The human brain continues to change throughout the lifespan of the individual—from early development through maturation and aging. The brain edits its own activity, using experience to build and revise its own structures, functions, and chemistry. This continuous revision also occurs across generations, meaning that our brain activity changes the culture and the environment which, in turn, alter the brain. The concept of brain change during life experience and across generations is basic to understanding the relationship of speech, a human-specific function, and written communication, a human necessity acquired only recently. The physical structures of perception and memory also change with experience. The interaction of innate (or genetic) influences and acquired (or learned) influences is discussed in the first section of this chapter.

Reading is perhaps the most complex task our culture imposes on its young. Learning to read is a brain-changing experience for which the potential structures are relatively plastic in children (Scheibel, 1985b). Reading begins in the retinas of the eyes, but the light signals received there must be converted to the electrochemical code of the central nervous system before being carried along the optic nerves. Genetically determined pathways lead across the *optic chiasm,* through the *lateral geniculate body,* and on to the *occipital lobes* at the back of the head. Perception of print begins there. At each juncture in this relay, collections of cell bodies perform certain reductions, further converting optic messages for integration with auditory and motor information. Although brain action requires the collaboration of groups of neurons, the transmission process begins with the activation of single cells (Bloom, Lazerson, & Hofstadter, 1985). The structure of cells and their function in learning is explained in the second section.

Reading is a brain function which involves all major areas of the cortex, including the neocortex, a structure highly developed in humans. The mature cortex is so extensive that if spread out it would cover a square meter—more than a square yard. Hence, the reception of word images is some distance and several neural connections away from the word bank of meanings in the auditory language areas. The brain mechanisms of language are explained in the final **143** section.

PHYLOGENIC AND ONTOGENIC
INFLUENCES

The issue of heredity versus environment, or nature versus nurture, shows up in developmental psychology as *phylogenic* versus *ontogenic* influences in learning. Phylogenic behaviors, such as breathing and walking, are controlled by neural systems that stabilize after a certain amount of practice and continue to function without essential change in the neurons. Ontogenically acquired behaviors, such as naming the letters of the alphabet, may also stabilize; but are highly amenable to change through experience. Konrad Lorenz, a zoologist, distinguished between the inner neurological machinery that remains relatively unchanged through repeated performances of a function and those mechanisms that undergo adaptive change through learning (1969). He identified fixed motor patterns, such as orienting and feeding, as phylogenically programmed systems. Such nonadaptive behavior characterizes most of the responses of simple animals. He described how adaptive modification of behavior, which is his definition of learning, is accompanied by physiological changes in the neurological structure of the organism, during its ontogeny, or individual life experience.

This distinction between phylogeny and ontogeny points up the human organism's potential for adaptation. Lorenz believed that the neurological system, including the skin sense organs, develop from a somewhat open program through the reaction of genetically programmed cells to particular environmental influences. The more complex the organism (the higher the species in the phylogenetic hierarchy), the greater the number of systems that are open to modification. In adaptive modification, the organism's way of responding depends on the availability of brain mechanisms to acquire, process, and store information. This concept of the interaction of organism and environment is different from conditioning theory.

Lorenz (1965) identified several kinds of learning that differ from conditioning. One of these, *motor facilitation,* seems to be important in early learning. He cites a study by Hess (1956) in which newly hatched, domestic chicks were fitted with goggles that shifted the image of the food they pecked at. The birds never learned to adjust their aim to the shifted image, but their pecking became surer and more consistently aimed with practice, even though no reinforcement through receiving food had occurred. Motor facilitation is practiced without conscious effort by most beginning readers, but others find the saccadic sweep very difficult to achieve even with adulthood.

Piaget (1971), also a biologist, described adaptation as an interaction of assimilation (the taking in of the environment as allowed by neural structures) and accommodation through growth of those structures (schemata). Although his focus was cognitive development, which he distinguished from learning through education, his notion of biological satisfaction through adaptation is important. He suggested that the exercise of a developing system is an organic necessity, and is self-reinforcing. The visual and auditory systems are examples of phylogenic development, although environmental stimulation is required at critical periods for normal growth. Reading, however, is an example of ontogenic, or individual, learning that is not acquired through maturation but must be learned as adaptive behavior within a particular life environment. Piaget's focus on environmental interaction in human adaptation provides some balance to many researchers of the mid-1980s who leaned toward genetic explanations of child behavior (Witelson, 1985.)

Infant Perception of Speech

Many contemporary linguists have been investigating whether human newborns are phylogenically oriented to speech. The historical view was that children's language dated from the time they began to say words, generally the second year of life. The major concern, *hearing acuity,* was tested in young infants by making a loud noise to see whether it produced a startle. By the 1950s newborns were examined for neurological integrity by presenting a series of pure tones and counting the number of stimuli, usually 1 to 10, required to habituate the infant to the sound. More recently, research on the acquisition of language has analyzed the listening abilities that precede speech (Eisenberg, 1976). Subtle techniques had to be devised to observe these prespeech responses adequately (Schlesinger, 1982).

Various procedures have been utilized to measure the sensitivity of infants to speechlike sounds: changes in heart rate, encephalographic activity in the auditory areas, conditioned responses to phonemes, inhibition of sucking, and habituation of the auditory analyzers to phonemes. For example, changes in the intensity of sound was found to increase the heart rate of neonates (Steinschneider, Lipton, & Richmond, 1966). During the 1970s many studies were launched to determine the receptive language of infants, as distinct from their hearing acuity.

Neonates 1 to 3 days old are able to discriminate their mother's voice when compared with the voices of other mothers in the hospital (DeCasper & Fifer, 1980). Researchers recorded the voices of new mothers while reading orally from a Dr. Suess book. Recordings were switched in order to observe the infant's patterns of disrupted sucking. The investigators suggested that prenatal auditory experience may be a factor in maternal voice discrimination, since some of their newborn subjects had very limited access to their mothers while in the hospital. These findings imply the importance of voice recognition in human bonding and the function of the caregiver's speech in the development of language.

Evidence of voice discrimination in newborns has stimulated research on sounds the fetus has access to, in part to find out whether the auditory system develops by genetic program in the absence of sound or whether environmental stimulation triggers neural growth. The environment of sounds inside the human uterus has been difficult to study for obvious reasons. British psychologists implanted hydrophones inside the amniotic sacs of pregnant ewes to record and transmit sounds from outside the maternal body. The difference in sound levels (attenuation) was determined by a spectrum analyzer which received input from the internal hydrophone and an external microphone attached to the ewe. A difference averaging 30 db was recorded. Conversation at normal voice levels outside the animal could be heard, but not always understood. However, raised voices were distinct. The authors, Armitage, Baldwin, and Vince (1980), suggested that the auditory experience of a fetal mammal may be considerably more extensive and possibly of greater postnatal significance than has been recognized previously.

A breakthrough occurred in the study of infant perception of speech when researchers learned how to synthesize phonemes, to present them as stimuli and to computerize the responses of the subjects. Eric Lenneberg (1967), among others, encouraged research in linguistics and neuroscience by describing speech within a context of communication and language as a biological outcome in humans. Roman Jakobson advanced the science of linguistics by suggesting that the roots of verbal communication might be discovered in the babblings of infants. As a researcher he employed the *spectrum,* which is a visual record of the acoustic characteristics of spoken words. He and his colleagues promoted the idea that the basic requirement for any language-coding system is its capacity to detect the distinctive features of speech (Jakobson, Fant, & Halle, 1967). Lenneberg and Jakobson altered the focus of linguistics by describing speech as communication and the acquisition of language as species-specific.

Sex Differences in Language Structures

The evolutionary function of sex is to provide a population with variability which is not genetically obtainable in asexual reproduction. Although hereditary differences in brain development have been attributed to sex-linked recessive genes (Restak, 1979), the genetic influences of language are probably much more complex. From early in the fetal stage, when the secondary sex characteristics of maleness develop, the potential exists for sex differences in brain differentiation. However, the interaction between gene expression, hormonal modulation, and early environment make it difficult to identify a simple pattern of sex-linked inheritance.

At birth the areas of the cortex that process language (specifically the speech production and the speech reception areas of the left hemisphere) are relatively thicker and heavier in female infants than in males. Conversely the cortical area of the right hemisphere, that specializes in visual-spatial interpretation, is thicker and heavier in males (Fairweather, 1982). Boys have been found to develop right-hemisphere specialization for processing spatial information at an earlier age than girls. Witelson (1976) studied 25 boys and 25 girls between the ages of 6 and 13 years. She tested their ability to discriminate hidden objects with right versus left hands. By the age of 6, boys had established right-hemisphere over left-hemisphere dominance for processing nonlinguistic spatial information. In the case of girls, the right hemisphere did not specialize for spatial perception, as measured by this test, until early adolescence.

In behavioral research involving children, sex differences in cognitive ability have appeared to favor males for spatial and mechanical skills while favoring females for verbal skills (Maccoby & Jacklin, 1974). Kagan (1971) reported that boys and girls of 4 months are equally attentive, visually and vocally, to persons and things. However, differences were observed in the earlier stabilization of social vocalization in girls and their relative precocity in first word usage (Cameron, Livson, & Bayley, 1967). Infant boys showed greater learning increments when a visual reinforcer was used, while girls did better under auditory reinforcement (Watson, 1969).

Men and women who experience brain damage appear to be affected differentially on intelligence test performance. Male patients who suffered left-hemisphere lesions declined significantly in Wechsler Verbal Scale IQs whereas those with right-hemisphere lesions declined significantly in Performance Scale IQs. Female patients suffered declines in both Verbal and Performance Scale IQs following left-hemisphere lesions, but made no significant change in either scale following right-hemisphere lesions, suggesting a linkage of verbal information with a variety of cognitive tasks.

Males, as a group, see better with the right eye and females hear better with the right ear than its opposite (Garai & Scheinfeld, 1968). The right ear and the corresponding left cerebral hemisphere are dominant in most persons for speech detection. Females establish hemisphere asymmetry earlier than males, which appears to give girls earlier precision and stability in acquiring and processing language (Kimura, 1967; Taylor, 1969). These differences, related to sex, suggest that developmental differences in childhood continue to influence hemispheric organization of cognitive processes into adulthood.

CONTROLLED EXPERIMENTS

Research on sex-related differences in the brain was limited to clinical and behavioral research until recently (Diamond, 1985). When rats were found to show structural brain asymmetry, a laboratory model became available for new lines of investigation of learning modes. Dating from the early 1970s, hard data had accumulated to confirm sex differences and, more important, to identify the nature of environmental influences. Diamond (1984) summarized more than a decade of research which we condensed as follows: (1) In male mole rats the right cortex is generally thicker than the left cortex, while the opposite holds true for females. (2) The left-right cortical thickness patterns change in the forebrain areas (but not in visual areas) upon removal of the gonads in males. (3) The left-right cortical thickness patterns change after the removal of ovaries in female neonates, with the right occipital cortex becoming significantly thicker (compared with female littermates). (4) An enriched environment appears to increase the right cortical area which interprets visual information in both sexes. (5) Sex differences in brain asymmetry decrease with age, implying long-term effects of a common environment.

Glick and Shapiro (1984), both recognized for their scientific rigor, reviewed the literature on neurochemical and functional asymmetry. Using laboratory rats whose heredity was known for right-side motor dominance, the investigators imposed biological and environmental controls during a series of experiments. As expected, they discovered sex-related differences based on left-right brain specialization. By sacrificing the animals, they could measure the uptake of certain neurotransmitters which were found to vary in regions which control the handedness functions. The researchers proposed but have not yet conducted new investigations, using radioactive tracers to obtain neurochemical data from a random population of *righthanded humans*. Volunteer subjects could be studied to determine whether the same behavioral and neurochemical relationships existed in humans as those found in right-sided rats. Lefthanded humans were hypothesized to show ambivalent dominance and a failure to confirm the left-right dominance patterns of the more typical population. While the current ideas about the specialization of the left hemisphere for verbal processes and the right hemisphere as the primary organizer for spatial interpretations, it should be remembered that a another view emphasizes the involvement of both hemispheres in complex cognitive functions (Best, 1985).

HUMAN UNIQUENESS AND COMPLEXITY

The high ratio of boys among pupils who experience difficulty in learning to read was discussed by Buffery and Gray (1972). They proposed a model in which males were considered to show less cerebral lateralization than females. The male brain was seen as having language represented more bilaterally (and less specialized) than the female brain. The implied advantage for males was a greater bilateral representation of spatial abilities along with their relative deficit in verbal ability. Females were advantaged (in reading) by greater cerebral lateralization in language. This proposal appears to conflict with those who suggest greater specialization of cognitive functions in males than in females, suggesting that this issue needs further investigation. Beaumont (1983) also cautions that clinical studies of adults on the question of sex differences and brain organization lack investigative controls. According to him a major problem in evaluating the evidence is that most statistical data are collected for other purposes. Few studies are designed to investigate sex differences specifically, yet data are analyzed routinely for the sex variable. Demographic differences, such as the age of patients, the preponderance of males in clinical studies, and unspecified cultural experience may have biased the samples. Beaumont takes the conservative position that the evidence is too thin and inconsistent to include sex differences as a factor in brain organization or cerebral laterality.

In studies which draw from descriptive and clinical evidence, the issue of sex differences will not be resolved soon (McGlone, 1980). Physical evidence of brain differences does not predict cognitive strengths for individuals because data refer to groups. Within-sex variability has been found to be greater than the mean differences between the sexes (Fairweather, 1982). Environmental factors complicate the issue for all older children and adolescents, who increasingly come under the influence of education and life-style. If one accepts the view, widely held among neuropsychologists, of a crowded brain in which potential functions compete for cortical space, the early plasticity for brain development becomes important to practitioners. For example, diagnosing and correcting reading problems is considered easier while the children are still young.

Conclusions from animal research may not be valid for application to humans in the absence of direct research on them, difficult as that may be. The reason for conflicting evidence from clinical sources may be that atypical subjects neither confirm nor negate a typical pattern of sex differentiation. Despite skepticism from some writers, research in the neurosciences shows handedness to be related, at least loosely, to language area locations. Also, language development appears to have some sex-biased differences. In the next section the discussion turns to the basic unit of communication in the central nervous system, the neuron.

STRUCTURE OF NEURAL CELLS

The central nervous system is an interconnected network of receptor, connector, and effector neurons, supported by tissues, fluids, and neuroglial cells. As a biological entity, the human brain is more like a forest than like a computer. The neuron is one living unit in an interdependent ecology that supports its birth, movement, nutrition, and work. Each neuron has a particular role among a ganglion of neurons which have interdependent functions within a relationship with other ganglion. The computer analogy, although simplified, helps us to understand the on-off firing of the action potential of a single neuron. It should be remembered, however, that a continuous electrical slow-wave potential is the physical indicator of a living brain. The language of human beings is made possible by a complex cortical network where the coded symbols of language are processed and where physical events generate thought, speech, and writing.

Prototype of a Neuron

The basic unit of the CNS is the neuron, which consists of a *cell body, dendrites,* and an *axon* (Fig. 6.1). Although the shape and size of neurons vary, according to their location and function within the central nervous system, they are activated and transmit their messages by a common electrochemical code.

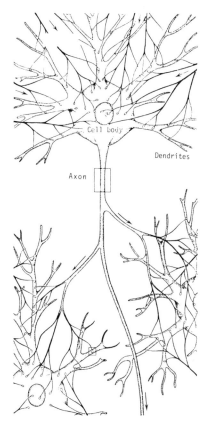

Figure 6.1. Neuron with axon and dendritic processes. Cell body encloses a nucleus, which contains DNA. Impulses from other neurons accumulate to produce an action potential, which may excite or inhibit the neuron. Rectangle (on axon) shown enlarged in Fig. 6.2. Square (on synaptic knob) shown enlarged in Fig. 6.4.

THE DENDRITES: MICRO RECEIVERS

In all neurons, the *dendrites* pick up incoming data from other cells for transmission to the cell body. Dendrites in the retina are equipped with rods or cones that are sensitive to light waves. Dendrites in the inner ear are activated by sound waves. Somatic receptors monitor the organism's own activity by picking up changes in the tension of the articulatory muscles as words being spoken.

THE CELL BODY: MICRO WORKPLACE AND WAREHOUSE

The *cell body* has many functions in addition to the accumulation and transmission of neural impulses. One important function is to produce the intracellular proteins which support intercell communication. The nucleus within the cell body contains the templates or instructions for all biological functions. All such nuclei enclose a full complement of chromosomes, the DNA, or genetic code. In a mature cell the genes are arranged in matched double strands of proteins, each having a particular location on a particular chromosome. Each gene strand is a unique protein, a macro string of animo acids. The sister is a mirror image, bonded by ion attraction and ordered between two relatively stable structures of alternating sugar and phosphate molecules. In an inactive stage the strands spiral to form the familiar DNA helix. To become active, the DNA strands must separate, exposing the code of a single unattached sequence (RNA).

Genes become accessible for transcription under highly controlled conditions. The membrane of the cell nucleus contains the gates which recognize and admit molecules of the particular enzyme that holds the key to enter and stimulate the selected genetic pattern. Transcription begins when the sister strands of the double helix (DNA) separate, and the beginning part of the protein generating sequence is activated. A genetic template (RNA) is assembled along one side of the DNA which represents a mirror image of the particular sequence of amino acids that characterize the gene. This single strand segment is called by a first name, messenger; the mRNA is a pattern for growth.

The nuclear membrane also contains the gates through which the RNA segments move out of the nucleus and into the cytoplasm of the cell body. There the mRNA codes for the assembly (protein synthesis) of another single strand template, *transfer RNA*. During this process, called *translation,* the original molecular order is restored. The RNA moves through the outer cell wall toward the target organ or tissue.

The cytoplasm within the cell body contains minute organisms, called *organelles*. Among them are *mitochrondria,* minute storage batteries which provide the electrical source to activate the cell, to power the assembly of RNA, and to maintain cell functions. The molecules of the amino acids that form from the peptides needed to build proteins are stored in the cell. Ion-bearing molecules (potassium, sodium, and calcium) are present in varied amounts according to the activity level of the cell. These and other components within the cell each have the potential for change in response to other neurons.

One type of organelle, within the cell body, is the *Golgi apparatus* (Rothman, 1985). These tiny membrane compartments, called stacks, keep the different biochemical activities separated and package the enzymes and other proteins for transport to other cells. Camillo Golgi discovered the organelle in 1898 and suspected correctly that it had a role in the secretion of proteins to the outside of the cell. The outer membrane of the cell body also has important functions in communication between cells.

THE AXON: MICRO TRANSPORT SYSTEM

The *axon,* which carries messages away from the cell body, terminates in numerous synaptic knobs (Fig. 6.2). Bundles of axons form the major communication cables from sensory receptive sites to distant reception areas in the brain. The optic and auditory nerves are examples. Axons form the commissures that interconnect the two hemispheres of the brain. They form the arc that interconnects the language reception and language expression areas, the *arcuate fasciculus.*

During brain development, bare primitive fibers grow toward their target cells and make contact with them. Stimulation from the cell body is associated with myelin growth around the axon. *Myelination* occurs as support cells attach to and grow around the axon, insulating it with a sheath of fatty tissue. The sheath is interrupted at intervals along the axon by spaces (nodes) between these cells, where exchange of molecules across the wall of the axon can take place. Myelination in the CNS is formed by *neuroglia,* which differ from the Schwann cells that myelinate the peripheral system (Fig. 6.3).

Myelination speeds the transmission of a neuron, and prevents the diffusion of electrical potential ions through the walls of an axon. It is believed that myelination commits an axon to a particular message bearing function, therefore the process is associated with learning. The timetable for myelination of the major CNS systems has been established by postmortem examination of many samples (Yakovlev & Lecours, 1967).

When a cell is activated the electrochemical message is conveyed from the terminal branches of the sending neuron across a gap, called a *synapse,* to dendrites or other parts of a receiving neuron. A synapse consists of a synaptic knob, a synaptic gap, and the postsynaptic tissue of a receiving neuron (Fig. 6.4). There are approximately 1,000 synaptic connections from one neuron to other neurons, although this number varies from a few to as many as 10,000.

Receptor, Connector, and Effector Neurons

Receptors are sense-gathering units which originate in the eyes, ears, joints, skin, and visceral organs. Distance sensors convert physical information (light, sound, and chemical molecules) into neural impulses. Dendritic fibers, which vary in physical appearance according to the functions they perform, are intimately associated with receptor cells. *Afferent pathways* carry information from sensory receptors through ascending fibers in the spiral column and the brain stem. Sometimes called the input system, the messages are coded and discriminations made in terms of the identity and location of the sensors that are activated.

Connector neurons form the linkages between afferent (input) and efferent (output) neurons as well as between each other. They process information for

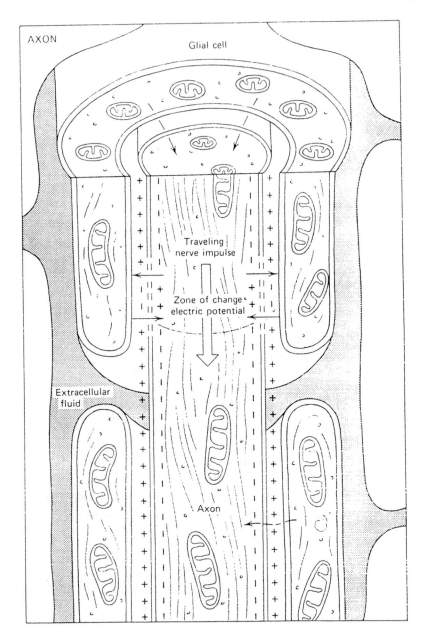

Figure 6.2. Cross-section of an activated axon. Arrow shows direction the impulse travels away from cell body. Exchange of sodium (Na+) for potassium (K+) across axonal membrane creates a traveling zone of millivolt change in electric potential.

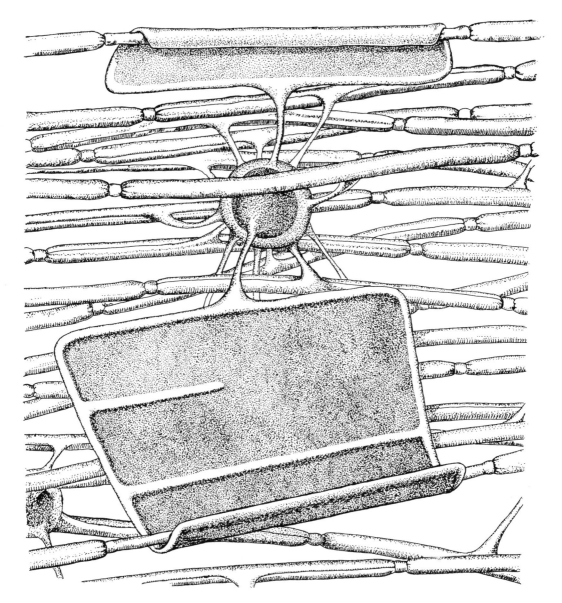

Figure 6.3. Myelination of the axon of a connector neuron. Neuroglial cells grow around bare axons, forming insulation spaced by nodes. (By T. Prentiss from P. Morell & W. T. Norton, Myelin, May, 1980 p. 99. Copyright © *Scientific American*).

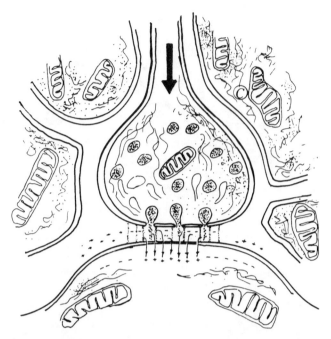

Figure 6.4. Synaptic knob, synaptic gap (cleft), and postsynaptic tissue. Vesicles release neurotransmitter into gap. (Drawing by Donna Thompson).

immediate response, for memory storage, or both. These *interneurons* comprise about 90% of the 14 billion neurons in the adult brain (Stevens, 1979). Connector neurons make up the major sensory nerves, the reticular formation, the limbic system, and the cerebral cortex. *Efferent pathways,* or descending fibers, lead away from central neurons to response systems. Responses are activated by changes in impulse frequency from connector neurons (Sommerhoff, 1974). *Effector neurons* have axons terminating in the muscles, organs or glands where they excite or inhibit an action. Individual neurons are consistent in the particular neurotransmitter they release; it is the receiving neuron that is stimulated or suppressed by a particular chemical message. An activated neuron may have an excitatory effect on one neuron while having an inhibitory effect on an adjacent neuron. These mechanisms coordinate opposing effects such as those required in the saccadic movements of the eyes, where six pairs of muscles must coordinate the tensing and flexing of the muscle pairs for each jerk of the eyeballs. Intricate timing of the neural messages that excite or inhibit each somatic cell is required.

Transmission Processes

The flow of information from sensory receptors to the cortex, from one area of the brain to another, and from the brain to effector cells is carried by electrical impulses generated by chemical exchange. The interpretation of the code, within this neural circuitry, is based on the location of the activated cells from which the message comes and on the frequency of the impulses. How a neuron collects and delivers its messages is basic to the working brain in all cognitive functions.

Message transmission from one neural unit to another requires: (1) the flow of ions within the neuron (the action potential) and (2) the bridging of impulses across numerous synaptic gaps (the synaptic potential). The action potential within the cell is considered primarily an electrical event, and the communication between cells at the synaptic gaps is primarily a chemical event. This section explains the electrochemical activity of single neurons, which together form the complex circuitry involved in brain functions. Variations of these processes are involved in visual and auditory reception and perception.

THE ACTION POTENTIAL

The *resting potential* of a nerve cell is maintained by the membrane which surrounds the cell body. A voltage difference of 60–70 millivolts is sustained in the interior of the cell, which is negative with reference to the exterior environment. Potassium ions (K+) are about 10 times as numerous inside the cell as sodium ions (Na+). The reverse is true of the sodium balance in the fluids outside the cell, resulting in the multivolt differential. During the resting state electrochemical energy is built up in the mitochondria, the minute organelles that function as storage batteries, to provide energy for the activated cell.

The templates (mRNA) for proteins needed during neuronal activation and alteration are transcribed from DNA. These proteins are synthesized and stored in the cytoplasm of the cell body for immediate transfer to the outer membranes. Other proteins function as gates through which selected molecules move in or out of the cell body. Some proteins comprise the structural material of cell growth and maintenance, while still others serve as the pumps that control the potassium-sodium balance within the cell. This later group, often called *sodium pumps,* are the protein molecules responsible for maintaining the resting value of the cell at about -70 millivolts (Stevens, 1979).

The *millivolt exchange* is initiated in the hillock of the axon, located at the opening of the cell body. The voltage difference of 70 millivolts, the resting state, is further reduced by the arrival of nerve impulses through the dendritic knobs (synaptic gaps) of other neurons associated with the cell itself. This voltage reduction, moving across the cell membrane, opens the sodium channels, allowing sodium ions to rush into the axon. The sodium channels close quickly and the potassium channels open, allowing potassium ions to flow outward. Typically this exchange takes place at the nodes of the axon, the gaps between the cells of the myelin sheath. The millivolt differential jumps from node to node away from the cell body along the axon toward the next connecting neuron (Fig. 6.5). The ion movement and the altered charge in the membrane of the axonal walls constitute the action potential. The sending cell is returned to its resting state by a reversal of ion exchanges through the sodium pumps. This electrical impulse is interpreted by the brain according to the pattern of interconnections that are activated and by the duration of the impulse.

The change in millivolt levels when a cell fires appears as a spike on the graph of the electrical impulse. The repeated firings in an activated neuron appear as a

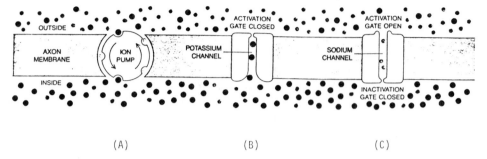

(A)   (B)   (C)

Figure 6.5. *Protein molecules function as sodium pumps and exchange channels. (A) Resting state of cell is maintained at 10 to 1 concentration of K+ ions (large dots) relative to Na+ ions (small dots); pump returns Na+ ions to fluids outside cell, thus maintaining ratio. Activation occurs with arrival of electrical impulse, reducing voltage difference from resting state of about -70 millivolts. (B) Sodium gate opens, allowing infusion of Na+ and closes immediately. Potassium channel opens allowing exit of K+ ions. (C) Sodium channel closes, terminating the action portential. Exchange is repeated along axon to propagate impulse. (By A. Miller from C. F. Stevens, The neuron September, 1989 (p. 20). Copyright © Scientific American).*

series of spikes like the familiar EEG, or electrocephalogram (Fig. 6.6). An individual neuron can fire, recover, and repeat the activation in about 6 msec. Generally, the more frequent the firing, the more urgent the message. The structure of the neuron and its means of electrical exchange are phylogenically ancient, and they function similarly in lower and higher animals.

THE SYNAPTIC POTENTIAL

Communication between neurons takes place at the synaptic gap between the terminal buds of the sending neuron and a site on the transmembrane of the receiving neuron. When a nerve impulse arrives at a nerve terminal, it triggers the secretion of a neurotransmitter that travels across the gap, stimulating the next cell and carrying the message forward.

The role of one transmitter, *acetylcholine,* has been studied and described by Dunant and Israel (1985). At the synapse the exchange is primarily chemical and requires the involvement of yet another common element, calcium (Ca++). Voltage change in the synaptic terminals, stimulated by the arrival of the action potential, causes a change in the membrane of the synaptic knob which allows calcium to enter the terminals. When calcium enters, it triggers the release of acetylcholine, which is present in the cytoplasm, causing it to spurt into the synaptic cleft. When a neuron fires in rapid succession, renewed supplies of acetylcholine are needed to continue the signal. A supply of the neurotransmitter is stored in vesicles, contained in great numbers within the synaptic knob. Dunant and Israel suggest that calcium moves into the vesicles to replace molecules of acetylcholine moving into the gap. Acetylcholine attaches briefly to the

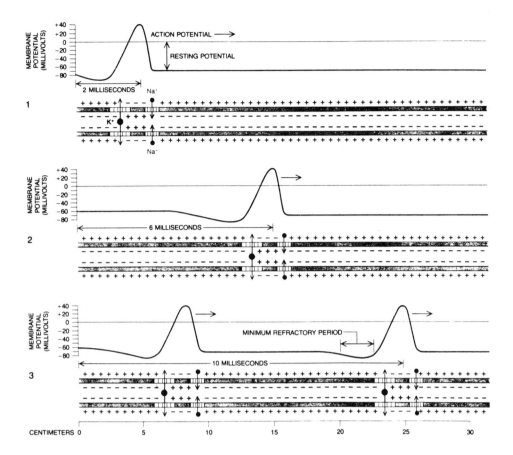

Figure 6.6. Propagation of an impulse. (1) Slight voltage reduction creates exchange of Na+ and K+ ions, which further shifts voltage until inner surface is positive with reference to outer surface. The zone of exchange corresponds to spike on EEG. (2) Action potential travels down axon. (3) Subsequent impulses follow brief recovery period. (By A. Miller from C. F. Stevens, The neuron September, 1979 (p. 20). Copyright © *Scientific American*).

postsynaptic membrane to induce an opening or closing response in the protein gates of the receiving cell. The acetylcholine is then broken down by an enzyme, cholinesterase. Molecules of acetate and choline reenter the cell to be used again. A supply of acetylcholine is available from the cell body, where it is synthesized by a catalyst and floated down the axon to the terminals by a process distinct from the action potential.

Neurons are consistent in the neurotransmitter which they store and release. However, the postsynaptic membranes are selective in the molecules which they accept and attach. A neuron may send an excitatory signal to one receiving neuron, while sending an inhibitory message to another by the same sequence of action potentials. A weak signal normally disperses through the branches of the axon and at the synapses. Given the thousands of synaptic terminals that associate with neighboring neural bodies, it is assumed that many individual synaptic stimulations are needed to activate or inhibit a receiving neuron. Simultaneous messages may enter a cell body from more than one sensory analyzer, from pleasure–punishment centers and from cognitive storage areas.

Biochemical Changes with Learning

The ultimate purpose of research in neuropsychology is to discover the secrets of memory storage and retrieval. Two approaches to this problem have been under way for some time: (1) the biochemical and physical changes within the cell body or its processes, and (2) the grander circuitry within the CNS that interacts across systems to link cognitive experiences and direct behavior. Human learning has not been observed directly, although some of the new technology for scanning brain activity is approaching this goal. The evidence for neuronal change in learning has been obtained from laboratory animal models. Most scholars agree that the biochemistry of the single cell has been conserved through an extended phylogenic period; therefore the basic processes of the cell can be generalized across species. Such generalizations may be limited to a simplistic level of learning. Nevertheless, the structure of cells and their action potential have common features across species, which make some animals appropriate organisms for studying associative learning.

CELL CHANGES IN SIMPLE LEARNING

Experts do not always agree on a definition of *simple learning*. Bloom, Lazerson, and Hofstadter (1985) differentiated simple learning, that occurs without the subject's conscious awareness of a change in behavior, as distinct from the more complex human learning that requires the manipulation of concepts and categories. They identified three forms of simple learning: (1) habituation, (2) sensitization, and (3) classical conditioning.

Habituation occurs when a stimulus is presented so often that the organism stops responding to it. An example from human research is the infant's habituating to a repeated vowel sound, but orienting again when the vowel is changed. During habituation an animal model (the sea snail) was discovered to release decreasing amounts of neurotransmitter into the synaptic gap with each repeated simulation. In habituation (also defined as desensitization), a connection must be formed between the stimulus and response neurons. However, other groups of neurons need not be involved.

CHANGES DURING CLASSICAL CONDITIONING

The reader will recall that classical (Pavlovian) conditioning occurs when a previously neutral stimulus is paired (by contiguity) with an unconditioned (established or natural) stimulus (UCS). The pairing experience is repeated until the organism learns to respond, a conditioned response (CR), to the new stimulus (CS) in the absence of the original stimulus (Chapter 2). Since the sequences of stimulation for habituation and for classical conditioning are opposite in their effect on the organism, one would expect to find differences in the cellular changes during these two learning events.

The neural changes during association learning in a marine snail have been traced and analyzed. Alkon, Lederhendler, and Shockimas (1982) conditioned the snails by classical procedures and studied the physical and biochemical changes that occurred in their neurons. This species naturally moves toward the light at the surface of the water to find food, but moves toward the depths, when the water becomes turbulent, to find a rock to cling to. These are both unconditioned responses (UCR). Under laboratory conditions, the snails were subjected to turbulence in the presence of light. The pairing of light with turbulence trained the snails to slow their rate of movement toward light (CR), an effect which often lasted for weeks. Beginning at the activated cells in the eyes, the researchers traced the neural pathways and analyzed chemical changes in the activated cells.

In the marine snail two sensory systems are involved: (1) the photoreceptor cells of the eyes, (2) the hair cells of a primitive ear. Light generates electrical signals in the snail's eyes; turbulence generates electrical signals in the hair cells. Both systems transmit their coded impulses from the sense receptors to ganglia in the connector system, to motor neurons, and finally to muscle groups. It was discovered that some optic ganglia synapsed with pathways from hair cells. Both sensory systems have two types of cells: A-cells, which are excitatory, and B-cells, which are inhibitory. During conditioning the B-photoreceptor cells became more active, therefore more inhibitory, when two integrated systems were responding than when light alone was the stimuli. The hair cells also contributed to the change in movement. In an unconditioned animal the A-cells of the hair receptors excite the inhibitors attached to the muscles. Turbulence activates the A-cells. When the induced turbulence stopped, cell activity was reduced and a prolonged inhibitory response in the B-cells followed, contributing to further reduction in the snail's movement toward light. In these experiments, associative learning resulted directly from changes in the excitability of particular neurons.

Recently B-cell pathways have been traced to both inhibitory and excitatory cells (Lederhendler & Alkon, 1986). In a series of biochemical analyses, changes in behavior were caused by differences in the $K+$ conductances of the Type B photoreceptors. A reduction in $K+$ within a cell modulated the activity in hair cells, optic ganglia, pedal ganglia, and muscles. Each pathway was found to be responsible for a different behavioral expression of the associative learning. Separate systems were traced for arousal, orientation, and withdrawal behaviors. One explanation for the potassium reduction in the photoreceptor cells is that conditioning changes the protein channels of the cell membranes to allow entry and temporary retention of increased numbers of calcium ions and the exit of $K+$.

Calcium levels are known to increase in the synapse during the release of neurotransmitters. During a process called *phosphorylation* certain enzymes are activated by the calcium ions, causing attachment of phosphate molecules to selected proteins contained in or being synthesized in the cytoplasm of the cell. These altered proteins may become part of the gating structure facilitating the access of neurotransmitters (Alkon, Lederhendler, & Shockimas, 1982).

A different but related explanation of the role of calcium in cellular change following a conditioning experience is the movement of Ca++ down the axon and into the synaptic knobs (Kandel & Schwartz, 1982). There the ions increase the availability of calcium for exchange with neurotransmitter molecules stored in the vesicles of the knobs. The effect could be an increase in the number of times a neuron could fire without depleting the available supply of transmitter molecules.

Calcium has a role in *axonal transport,* the supply system within a neuron that actively moves macromolecules and organelles from their place of synthesis in the cell body to the site of utilization at the synapse. Carafoli and Penniston (1985) proposed that calcium serves as an intracellular messenger. Calcium ions are small, similar in size to sodium ions, but they carry a double charge and bind tightly to large protein molecules. By binding the ion and moving it in and out of the cytoplasm, mechanisms for cellular change are created. These mechanisms include a calcium channel, a sodium-calcium exchange, and a calcium pump. Mitrochondria, found both inside and outside the cell, store calcium when concentrations are high and release it when needed to carry a message.

CONDITIONING BY AVERSIVE STIMULI

Avoidance learning is the elimination or reduction of contact with an object or another organism, following aversive stimulation. Pinel and Treit (1983) departed from tradition laboratory studies of what they called "artificial" conditioning to study neurological changes during "natural" forms of behavior. Their concern was that the underlying mechanisms for learning might be different in contrived and unnatural situations than when the animal was learning the survival behaviors of the wild. They selected a species of rat which engages in "burying behavior." The rats became conditioned in one shock to avoid an electric probe used in the aversive treatment, while ignoring a similar electric probe that was lying in the pen. Aversive learning was shown by efforts to bury the offending probe in each of the rats tested. This consistency enabled the researchers to study the effect of drugs on learning. They discovered that learning was disrupted by anxiolytic drugs (diazepam, chlordiaziepoxide, and pentobarbital) but not by stimulants or by tranquilizers.

Pinel and Treit located the brain mechanism involved in aversive learning by various surgical sections. The removal of the posterior septum eliminated the defensive burying response in the rats. Nevertheless, animals avoided the shock probe, indicating they still associated the object with aversive stimulation. The important difference was that they did not approach and attempt to cope with the punishing object.

These findings about aversive learning have interesting implications. The involvement of deep brain structures (the septum) in associative learning is established in a mammalian species. Aversive conditioning, unlike the shaping strategies of operant conditioning, appears to be learned in a single negative, or punishing, experience and to be remembered on a long-term basis. Any teacher or clinician who has witnessed the array of defensive strategies that problem readers can marshal to avoid reading might be impressed by the durability of this single, negative experience. Most experts agree that cellular change can explain simple learning but look to the interaction of organized groups of cells across various locations in the brain to explain conceptual thought.

BRAIN MECHANISMS OF LANGUAGE

The brain processes language by the same electrochemical code that activates receptor, connector, and effector neurons. The previous section explained the working principles of the neuron, which is the basic unit of the brain. Accounts vary from 10 billion to 14 billion neurons in the central nervous system. When estimates include subunits of neurons such as the rods and cones of the retina and the glial support cells the number becomes 100 billion. How these units are organized to produce thought, speech and written communication has been described by Luria (1973) as the working brain.

The Cortical Map

The brain is generally defined as all of the CNS above the spinal column, including the brain stem. Table 6.1 identifies five major regions and some of the structures within each. Phylogenic progression has created and expanded a mantle, the telencephalon, that covers and encloses the diencephalon (interbrain) and the mesencephalon (midbrain). It is important to remember that the cortical layers are intimately associated with subcortical structures through axonal connections. The *cerebral cortex* consists of six or seven layers of neural cells, numbered as they were initially explored, from the outside inward. The cortex is gray matter, the color of cell bodies. Beneath the bark-like layers of the cortex is

TABLE 6.1. *Regions of the Central Nervous System and Some Major Structures within Each*

BRAIN		TELENCEPHALON	Cerebral cortex
		Rhinencephalon	*Limbic system*
	Forebrain (prosencephalon)	DIENCEPHALON	Thalamus Hypothalamus Basal ganglia Internal capsule
	Midbrain	MESENCEPHALON	Midbrain
Reticular Formation		*Cerebellum*	
	Hindbrain (Rhombencephalon)	METENCEPHALON MYELENCEPHALON	Pons Medulla
SPINAL CORD			

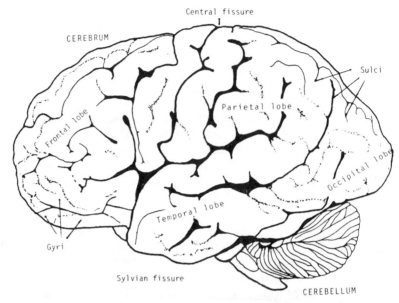

Figure 6.7. Left hemisphere of the brain. Major divisions of cerebrum are central fissure (which separates frontal lobe from posterior lobes). Temporal lobe receives auditory signals; occipital lobe receives visual signals. Convolutions form gyri (bulges); grooves or fissures are sulci.

white matter, consisting primarily of axons sheathed in light-colored myelin. Although different areas of the cerebral cortex have specialized functions, the integrative action of the whole brain is required for complex cognitive activity.

THE CEREBRAL LOBES

The telencephalon (or cortical formation) is divided into left and right hemispheres. Each hemisphere is divided vertically by a deep fissure which separates the *anterior* (front) from the *posterior* (back). The verticle cleft is the *Rolandic,* or *central fissure.* The entire area in the *rostral* (foreward) direction makes up the *frontal lobe* (Fig. 6.7). The areas in the *caudal* direction consist of three lobes. The *temporal lobe,* located behind the outer ear, is bounded by another deep cleft, the Sylvian fissure. The *parietal lobe* extends to the top of the head. The *occipital lobe,* where visual messages are analyzed, lies at the greatest possible anatomical distance from the eyes. The terrain of the two hemispheres is similar but not identical; the lobes are asymmetrical in cortical thickness, in the total area they occupy, and in their functional relationship. Historically the left hemisphere, where language areas were discovered, was called the dominant hemisphere. Major structures, called *commissures,* are formed from bundles of axons that cross the midline of the brain, thus providing communication between the right and left hemispheres. The largest of the commissures, the corpus collosum lies just beneath the fissure that separates the two hemispheres. Cell bodies on both sides send axons to target contralateral locations. Neuroscience seeks to locate areas for specific cognitive functions, to discover how the hemispheres interact and to determine the age at which dominance occurs.

Posterior Lobes: Sensory Integration

The three lobes that are posterior to the central fissure contain the receiving areas of different sensory systems. The *temporal lobes* receive the auditory code for sound messages as varied as the clang of the alarm bell (meaning to vacate the building) or the word *chateau* (meaning a fancy house in France). The *occipital lobes* receive neural messages from the two eyes, after more than half of the fibers cross over (in the diencephalon) to bring right-eye signals to the left hemisphere and vice versa. The *parietal lobes* receive somatic sensory information from different bodily parts to precise locations along the central fissure.

Extending vertically along either side of the central fissure are two extensive convolutions: the *premotor gyrus* of the frontal lobe and the *motor gyrus* of the parietal lobe. Premotor areas show neural activity in specific locations before a voluntary motor act occurs, while motor areas signal feedback of body activity as it occurs. *Gyri* are the coillike bulges on the surface of the brain. The fissures and the smaller grooves between the convolutions are called *sulci*. The major physical features of the brain are recognizable from one human individual to another.

Frontal Lobes: Thought and Initiative

The frontal lobes take up about half of the cortical surface and are relatively recent in evolutionary development. Historically, the frontal lobes have been considered the center of intelligent behavior, but the extent and influence of these lobes within an integrated brain are still being elaborated. By midcentury the accepted view among neurologists was that general intelligence was lowered when a patient suffered injury to a frontal lobe. Hebb (1949) reported that the size and extent of an injury was related to the extent of the impairment. Penfield and Evans (1935) observed that major removal of the anterior part of the frontal lobe reduced the patient's capacity for planned initiative. During the 1950s and 1960s various studies used psychological tests to correlate cognitive functioning with frontal lobe damage in adults. The results, although informative, were less than conclusive by current research criteria. A more precise approach to frontal lobe contributions has become possible by ascribing specific functions to particular subregions of the forebrain (Beaumont, 1983).

The four main divisions of the frontal lobe are: (1) motor and premotor, (2) prefrontal or neocortex, (3) orbital, and (4) Broca's speech production area (Fig. 6.8). Their location and function have been determined primarily by clinical observation of patients with well-defined damage to frontal lobe areas and interpretations from sophisticated psychometric tests.

Motor control areas are organized at three levels. The *primary level of motor control* lies in a strip along the central fissure and has direct connections to spinal motor neurons. Damage to this region is reflected in reduced voluntary control over the precise somatic area that corresponds to the site of the injury along the fissure. A *secondary level of motor control* lies adjacent and anterior to the motor

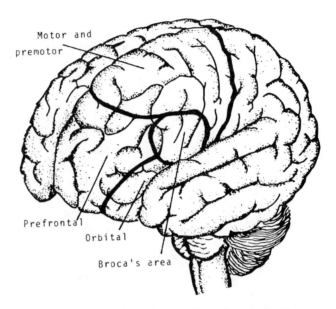

Figure 6.8. Regions of the frontal lobe. (Drawing by D. Thompson.)

cortex. The cells of this *premotor* area connect to lower brain centers, including the thalamus. Premotor areas contribute to the cerebral control of gross body movements, a vital concern of athletes. A *tertiary level of motor control* lies in a rostral direction, extending to the areas of the prefrontal cortex and to Broca's expressive speech areas. Patients with tertiary level damage on the left hemisphere show marked difficulty with verbal fluency, phonetic discrimination, and spelling; with damage on the right hemisphere they show difficulty in abstract design fluency (Beaumont, 1983).

The *prefrontal cortex* consists of convolutions that are phylogenically new and markedly enlarged when compared with other mammals. Penfield (1975) suggested that neocortical areas are uncommitted and unconditioned at birth. Initially they are programmed by experience to specialized functions, then gradually they become employed as mechanisms for high-level functions such as interpretation, evaluation, and transaction. This recruitment of associative structures for conceptual thought processes is a significant contribution to learning theory.

Using a battery of behavioral measures, Beaumont (1983) noted particular deficits in patients with prefrontal anomalies. Various clinical tests revealed a list of deficiencies: (1) planning and programming motor acts, (2) judgment of egocentric space, (3) voluntary eye movements, (4) visual compensation for changes in body position, (5) anticipation of the effect of an action, (6) flexible adaptation to altered circumstances (Wisconsin card sort), (7) programming and planning sequences of behavior (Porteus mazes), (8) spatial problem solving (Block Design), (9) arithmetical problem solving (distinct from computation), (10) visual search (interpretation of illustrations), (11) judgments of recency (time sequence), and (12) self-regulation by covert verbal direction. The basic function of the prefrontal lobes appears to be the generation and operation of strategies for collecting and processing the information needed for intellectual tasks.

The *orbital cortex* subserves aspects of personality and social behavior. A famous example of personality change was the case of Phineas Gage, whose damaged skull (still on display at the Harvard Medical School) shows the location of his injury, suffered in 1848. P.G., the capable and responsible foreman of an excavation crew, was tamping black powder into a drill hole with an iron bar when the explosive detonated. The blast sent the bar into his cheekbone and through the top of his head. Phineas retained his memory and motor skills, but he changed from a respected foreman to an impulsive, inconsiderate, obstinate, and profane man.

Milner (1965) reported that individuals with prefrontal injuries do poorly on cognitive tests because they fail to obey the rules or to make use of suggestive feedback. Orbital damaged patients have been reported to show sexual indiscretions and exhibitionism, although their sexual activity did not increase. Atrens and Curthoys (1982) concurred that sexuality did not increase in their patients, and noted instead that inhibition of unsocial and discretionary behavior was lowered, thus leading to bizarre sexual behavior. Also a lack of emotional expression, of indifference, and loss of drive or initiative were observed. These are characteristics that have been described in pseudodepression.

Frontal lobe damage may affect learning indirectly and therefore may go unnoticed. E. B., a graduate student of ours, came highly recommended as an enthusiastic and innovative teacher, open to new knowledge and new approaches. In private life she was devoutly religious, an exemplary foster parent, and a compassionate friend. She developed an aneurysm behind the right eye, just outside the optic chiasma. Aside from the migraine-like symptoms she reported, her personality changed, to the consternation of colleagues, who noted she was "not at all like herself." She began neglecting the children, attempted a pregnancy with a man she scarcely knew, and fabricated her assignments. Following surgery and recovery, E. B. seemed, at least socially, to have returned to her former enthusiastic and compassionate personality. She wished to return to graduate school, so we questioned her casually, but purposefully during several meetings, to probe her knowledge of coursework taken just prior to surgery. To our surprise, the most significant content from her courses seemed unavailable. Yet her face brightened and she plunged into familiar discourse when people and ideas from prior years came under discussion. The point of this example is that a brain may recover a function, but the clinician or teacher is left to deal with gaps in learning that occurred during trauma, whatever its etiology. Assuming a multifactor approach to diagnosis, several possibilities for E. B.'s memory loss are apparent. Our conjecture is that one factor was her (temporary) change in personality. Attitudes of indifference, lack of initiative, and provocative defenses, instead of openness, deprived her of the motivation needed for long-term memory and professional growth during that period. Following recovery, she continued successfully as a classroom teacher.

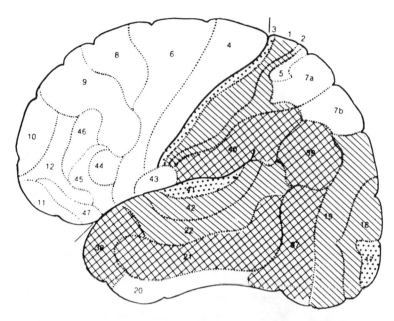

Figure 6.9. Primary, secondary, and tertiary areas for processing sensory information. Numerals represent Brodmann's cortical map. Dotted areas represent auditory, visual, and somatic reception. Diagonal lines represent secondary (association) areas of the three modalities; crossed lines represent tertiary (integration) areas.

SENSORY PROCESSING MODES

The cortical areas posterior to the central fissure receive stimuli from the sensory receptors and generate internal representations of the outside world (Sommerhoff, 1974). The organization of the three lobes (temporal, occipital, and parietal) is similar. Each contains a *primary reception area* where coded messages from the ears, eyes, and somatic sensors are received. Each has an adjoining *secondary association area* where the impulses from the primary areas are compared with stored experience and perceptual interpretations are made, generally within the mode of the initial message. Each has a *tertiary integration area* which overlaps the cortical processes of either or both of the other lobes and performs bimodal integrations. Tertiary areas are phylogenically recent and greatly expanded in humans, compared with other primates (Fig. 6.9).

The *temporal lobe* is unique in humans for its three horizontal strips, or gyri, rather than the two which chimpanzees have. The lobes extend toward the occipital and parietal areas where they integrate in tertiary areas. The cortical map has *Herschl's gyrus* at the top of the temporal lobe, where it wraps around and into the inner surface. This is the primary area on both hemispheres for receiving sound impulses. Primary reception has been pushed backward into the cleft by phylogenic expansion of the three horizontal strips, called the superior, the middle, and the inferior gyri. The *superior gyrus,* next to Herschl's, associates verbal and other sound messages with past experience to give them meaning.

These association areas extend into the *middle temporal gyrus,* which is expansive on the (left) language dominant lobe as well as unique in humans. The posterior end of the gyrus is considered a potential word bank (Benson, 1981). The *inferior gyrus* contains both secondary and tertiary processes, but the later tend to be located in a posterior direction, approaching the occipital cortex. Behind the inferior strip are *mesial* areas, having intimate connections with the limbic system. The *temporal poles,* frontal tips of both lobes, are associated with affective, emotional, and personal experience (Beaumont, 1983). Damage to the auditory cortices of the left hemisphere (in most persons) results in difficulties in language reception and/or comprehension (Penfield & Roberts, 1959).

The *occipital lobes* receive visual sensations in Brodmann's area 17, most of which wraps around the occipital poles of both left and right hemispheres. The primary visual cortex is interesting for its point-to-point array of the visual fields in the two eyes. Besides reduction and relay of visual stimuli, this area perceptually completes images not fully glimpsed. The secondary visual cortex occupies large areas of association cortex, numbered 18 and 19 on both sides. Area 18 performs numerous perceptual functions: converts images into percepts, integrates the association areas in the opposite hemisphere, compensates for the saccadic jerk, fills in visual gaps from stored experience, and relays secondary-level information to area 19. Major connections to and from the thalamus subserve the perception of form, pattern, and color. Other major fibers connect to auditory areas, also via the thalamus. Area 19 performs intersensory integration and certain processes in reading (Beaumont, 1983). The visual analyzers are extremely complex, but extensively studied (Hubel, 1985).

The *parietal lobes* deal with kinesthetic and somatosensory events. They combine information of external space with information from other modalities. The anterior region, which lies posterior to the Rolandic fissure, is the *primary somatosensory cortex.* These areas in both hemispheres receive sensations of touch, temperature and pain, messages from surface sensors in the skin and deep sensors in the muscles, tendons, and joints. Feedback from these sensors is necessary for visual control in reading and finger control in writing. The *secondary somatosensory cortex* lies behind the reception areas and just above the Sylvian fissure. These areas receive feedback from the face, lips, jaw, tongue, and larnyx, during speech.

The posterior regions of the parietal lobes are occupied almost exclusively with integration of somatic, auditory, and visual functions. The right hemisphere (of right-handed persons) is concerned with spatial representation. Patients with damage to this area have interpretation problems, such as left-right confusion, inability to translate designs to their mirror image, and letter reversals and inversions. Difficulties in reading and in arithmetical calculating have been identified as a malfunction of the nondominant parietal area in some patients, perhaps because the spatial representation in initial learning is confused (Beaumont, 1983). The term, *symbolic synthesis,* is used to describe spatial perception of numerals and letters.

The language-dominant left hemisphere (in right-handed persons) is characterized by a greatly expanded posterior parietal, especially adjacent to the *angular gyrus.* This area, which overlaps Wernicke's area for speech comprehension, receives the visual images of printed words and turns them into linguistic meanings. The boundaries between primary, secondary, and tertiary areas of the parietal are highly individual and are correlated with the ontogeny or lifetime experience of the person (Scheibel, 1985a).

Language Areas

The cortical areas for speech and other language functions was discovered in Europe by clinical researchers, more than a century ago. About 1860 Paul Broca, a surgeon, reported his evidence that patients who sustained lesions on the left frontal lobe lost their speech, while those injured on the right frontal lobe did not (Fig. 1.2). In 1874 Karl Wernicke, a medical student, published his dissertation, which contained three enduring contributions: (1) He extended Broca's discovery and reported that patients with frontal damage could understand language, even when they could not speak. (2) He located the reception and comprehension of speech in the left temporal lobe. (3) He diagrammed the long neural connections between the language comprehension area of the temporal lobe and the motor area where speech is produced, a collection of fibers now called the *arcuate fascisculus.*

Norman Geschwind, an American psychologist and health scientist, returned to the early medical papers in search of a holistic approach to the cerebral organization of language. One of his many contributions has been to describe the anatomical relationships among speaking, reading, and writing (Geschwind, 1979). He proposed a model which showed the central role of Wernicke's area in different linguistic processes. When comprehending speech the sounds are received in the primary auditory cortex, then passed through Wernicke's area, where a verbal message is understood (Fig. 6.10). When speaking, the circuitry is as follows: (1) The underlying pattern of an utterance arises in Wernicke's area, (2) The pattern is transferred along the arcuate fascisculus to Broca's area which evokes a program for vocalization, and (3) The program is relayed to the facial areas of the motor control gyrus which activates the appropriate tongue-lip-larnyx muscles of speech. When reading, the visual pattern of print is received in the visual cortex, is transmitted to the angular gyrus which applies a transformation that elicits the auditory form of the word in Wernicke's area. When reading orally, the circuitry is the opposite: Information is passed from auditory reception to Wernicke's and back to the angular gyrus. Laboratory observations are based on reading and writing single words, a simple task when compared with the complex processes of reading text or composing written discourse. Complexities of a different order arise when the person whose language areas are being mapped is not right-handed and whose hemisphere organization is not typical.

Hemispheric Specialization

The asymmetry of the brain is advantageous to individuals and to society because human potential and variability are enhanced by specialization. When primary control for a particular behavior is allocated to one hemisphere, while a secondary or supporting function is located in the contralateral or opposite side, the opportunity for specialization through learning is increased. In this chapter, the anatomy and the functions of the cerebral cortex have been described as they are found in right-handed persons.

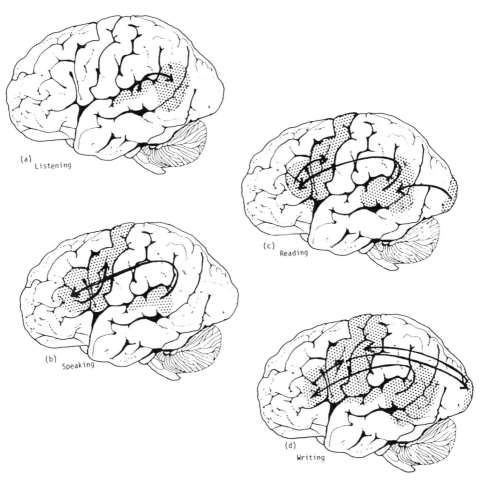

Figure 6.10. Major pathways for linguistic communication. (a) Listening-comprehending; (b) speaking a dictated word; (c) reading a word orally; and (d) writing a dictated word.

Coren and Porac (1977) analyzed samples of art work, dating from 15,000 B.C. to A.D. 1950, to determine how handedness was depicted in unimanual (one-handed) tasks. Their sample of 1,180 scorable instances showed an average of 92.6% dextral (right-handed) use of tools and weapons. There were no significant differences among European, Asian, African, or American sources. This finding supports a biological, rather than a cultural, explanation of handedness. A segment of all populations studied, going back to *Homo erectus,* have been left-handed. A larger segment of these same populations have shown mixed handed preferences for different activities. The term, *mixed-dominance,* has been used by clinicians for decades to describe eye-ear-hand preferences that were not laterally consistent in an individual. One could argue that ambidextrous males would experience social pressure, especially in weapon use, to model the dominant practice. This cultural bias might have been a factor in cross-cultural research, with ambidextrous individuals being shown as right-handed more frequently in artistic representation than was true in life.

Scientists of a neurological or psychological bent have been intrigued by left-handedness for a century or more. Broca's discovery that language resided in the left hemisphere, and his suspicion that this might be true only of the right-handed majority, shook the health professionals of his time and shifted their focus from the hands to the brain. Application lagged behind discovery, however, and a widespread practice, around the turn of the century, was ambidextrous training for the purpose of developing a more symmetrical brain (Harris, 1985).

Hemispheric specialization refers to the neural and functional differences between the two hemispheres in their relative participation in cognitive processes. Hemisphere dominance for handedness and speech are related by a complex circuitry of excitation and inhibition. The location of one function (handedness) predicts the dominant hemisphere for the other function (language) except in a small segment of the population. Contemporary neuroscientists tend to agree that the modern human brain has become increasingly crowded with regard to neuronal space, therefore learning during ontogeny enhances the differentiation with which humans are born (LeMay, 1984).

BIOLOGICAL CORRELATES

Most of the early research on brain laterality came from medical sources. During the last 15 years new techniques have become available for studying brain activity in healthy subjects from infancy to adulthood. Diachotic listening, in which different auditory stimuli are presented through two earphones, have been used to study lateral preference (Beaumont, 1983; Witelson, 1985). Tachistoscopic and dichhaptic tests, which present visual stimuli, accurately timed, have established some of the specializations of the right hemisphere (Cioffi & Kandel, 1979). Individual responses to *brain electrical activity mapping* (BEAM) have shown hemisphere specialization on the left (angular gyrus and Wernicke's) for listening to a sophisticated story. The same techniques have shown specialization on the right central parietal lobe, accompanied by secondary activation in the contralateral cortex, for listening to classical music (Duffy, McAnulty, & Schachter, 1984).

Handedness

In contemporary America, *sinistrality,* or left-handedness, has come to mean individual uniqueness, rather than a sinster handicap, emerging mysteriously in some families. Sinistrals are found in greater proportions among the intellectually gifted, the artistically talented, and professionally trained musicians than in the general population. Left-handedness is considered an asset in certain sports and is a valued trait among many athletes. When studying the clinical correlates of sinistrality, the reader should keep in mind that left-handedness is associated with variability in positive as well as negative ways.

Sinistrality has been correlated with twinning; the inferences from these data having placed the initiation of brain-hand organization to day 7 or 8 following conception (Boklage, 1981). Investigations of groups of nondextral individuals have shown educational handicaps in some individuals. Geschwind and Behan

(1982) compared 500 strong sinistrals with 900 strong dextrals. Significant differences emerged in the sinistral population including: 10 times the rate of learning disabilities, 2.5 times the rate of immune disorders, and higher than normal rates of both anomalies among near relatives. Left-handed and mixed-preference subjects are more numerous in reading clinics than in the general population (Gordon, 1984).

Brain organization is much more complicated for language than for tool use. An estimated 70% of the population have strong left-hemisphere dominance for speech and handedness control (Geschwind & Behan, 1982). This correlation, indicative of rightedness, is also predicative of right ear-eye-hand dominant organization for listening, reading, and writing. The remaining 30% of the general population are what the authors call *anomalous dominance,* meaning they have some deviation from the standard left-hemisphere organization of language and right-hemisphere dominance of visual interpretation. Of this minority group, only about one-third are essentially left-handed, others being generally right-handed, and most showing mixed preferences. According to the authors, these 30% will have some distribution of language in both hemispheres and most will have some degree of developmental learning disorder. Slight language differences may be obscured by other strengths such as strong intellectual power or cultural motivation. Despite their elevated risks of language disorders, many sinistrals have talents which distinguish them from the more common dextrals, particularly in spatial planning and nonverbal communication.

One recent suggestion by Kershner (1985) is that learning-disabled children may be too strongly lateralized. His work is based on dichotic listening techniques which involved giving different oral messages (words and digits) to the two ears. His subjects were groups of normal and learning-disabled children. Previous research has shown that the contralateral connections between the right ear and the left hemisphere are prepotent over ipsilateral (same side) connections (Kimura, 1967). Verbal information arriving at the right ear is easier to perceive, remember, and identify than information arriving in the left ear in most individuals. Kershner (1978) proposed a *developmental balance* hypothesis of cerebral lateralization. According to this model, hemispheric asymmetries are linked initially to genetically programmed perceptual dispositions. The immaturity of the infant's CNS imposes stimulus-bound constraints on its cortical processes. With increasing maturational control and the acquisition of sophisticated learning strategies, the child develops away from a more localized specialization toward an increasing interhemispheric integration and collaboration. Normally, the early imbalance in cerebral processing is replaced in later childhood by higher cognitive determinants of laterality: voluntary attention, response biases, and problem-solving strategies. In learning-disabled children, hemispheric processing was found to be highly unstable, with a tendency for the subjects to switch over to predominantly right-hemisphere processing when the test situation placed heavy demands on the left hemisphere.

Plasticity

Hemisphere specialization is present and functional at birth, according to behavioral and neurological observations. Plasticity research is concerned with the age at which cerebral functions are essentially fixed, when molding by experience is too late. *Functional plasticity* is observed restitution or development of a function after damage to a region of the brain known to interfere with that function. *Neural plasticity* refers to the hypothesized neurobiological changes that underly the recovery of that function. Witelson (1985) makes this distinction to support her theory that hemisphere specialization is consistent throughout the lifespan of the individual, while plasticity declines with the age of the individual at injury. Other research has pushed backward the age of presumed consolidation of hemisphere specialization from adolescence (Lenneberg, 1967) to about 5 years (Krashen, 1973). Witelson attributes the changes in cognitive functioning during development to plasticity, suggesting that the more learning or physiological change that has occurred in a region of the brain the less further neural change is possible.

Another concept, which rounds out Witelson's theory of specialization and plasticity over a lifespan, is the *epiphenomenon* of cognitive development. Cognitive skills showing brain lateralization over a lifespan are expressed in a learning curve which rises sharply from birth, then levels off during childhood. To Witelson the increasing quality of cognitive skills as they are lateralized may be misinterpreted as maturational change, when in fact they result from learning. Her scheme defines hemisphere specialization as a stable factor across a learning graph, plasticity as a declining factor, and the epiphenomenon of cognitive development as an increasing factor. This model has implications for educators. If lateralization is established before the child comes to school, we might try to enhance the specialization, rather than to attempt to change handedness or hemispheric organization. If plasticity is a declining possibility, we might begin early to develop all aspects of language. If cognition changes qualitatively (as Piaget would agree) we might anticipate the higher levels of functioning and teach to them at an earlier age, especially in reading comprehension and evaluation.

CONTRIBUTIONS OF THE RIGHT HEMISPHERE

The role of the nondominant hemisphere for language processing has been examined intensively in recent years. The concept of a passive right hemisphere has been replaced by investigations which reveal hemispheric interaction and collaboration in linguistic tasks. Lezak (1982) presented evidence of mutual inhibition across the corpus callosum which compliments the processing systems of the opposite hemisphere. The language skills of three groups of surgical patients were compared: (1) right-hemisphere-damaged, (b) left-hemisphere-damaged, and (c) a control group of patients who were neither brain-damaged nor depressed (Lezak & Newman, 1979). The patients with right-hemisphere damage were garrulous; they prattled excessively about unimportant matters. Their verbosity extended to paragraph writing in which they produced significantly more words with less content than the other groups. They used long words and elaborate constructions when simpler words and sentences were called for. The evaluative constraints of good composition appeared to be lacking in the expressive language of patients with right-hemisphere damage, although their left hemispheres were intact.

According to Lezak, subjects with right-hemisphere damage did well on structured verbal tasks, but showed marked deficiency when required to organize and construct responses. They made low scores on the Minkus Completion subtest of the Binet, in which a function word must be supplied to a sentence to clarify its meaning. Reading comprehension was adversely affected, as measured by the *Gates–MacGinitie Reading Test,* while vocabulary tested normal. Although both subtests required multiple-choice answers, the comprehension questions required the subjects to bring into the relationship the various elements of the passage. The right-hemisphere-damaged group showed excellent grasp of word meanings on the vocabulary test, while left-hemisphere-damaged subjects did poorly on both word meaning and reading comprehension tests. This study confirmed that the left hemisphere manages the linear and specific aspects of language reception and production. However, brain-damaged individuals lacked the ability to restructure semantic relations without collaboration from the contralateral hemisphere.

The development of hemisphere collaboration is seen in the graphic competence of schoolchildren when drawing complex figures. Kirk (1985) reported increasing accuracy in the copying of the Rey–Oserieth figure, a complex design of line and space relationships. Accuracy was directly related to the strategies the children used: whether piecemeal (ages 6–7), part–whole (ages 8–9), or configural (10 and above). Kirk did not find spurts and plateaus in cognitive development as reported earlier by Epstein (1978) but instead confirmed the progressive reorganization theory of Werner and Kaplan (1963). The evolution of figure drawing in the Kirk studies also conformed with the cognitive development Piaget observed in the children's classification of objects and their constructions of ordered grouping. The importance of left-hemisphere involvement in a task usually attributed to right-hemisphere control became apparent when preplanning the *sequence* was necessary for solving problems of visual alignment and spatial relationships.

Considerable evidence exists that perception precedes production as children develop cognitively. Understanding language precedes speech production, for example. Kirk (1983) conjectured that the gap between young children and adolescents in the ability to solve a complex graphic problem is related to the protracted maturation of neural systems which connect back-to-front and left-right regions of the brain. The right hemisphere is characterized by a high ratio of gray (cell body) matter to white (axonal) matter, indicating extensive within-region integration of multimodal information. The left hemisphere has a greater ratio of white to gray matter, reflecting numerous interconnections of the tertiary areas of the parietal with temporal, occipital, and frontal lobes. The maturation of posterior, anterior, and callosal systems is necessary for children to organize, deploy, and monitor complex reading tasks which have both spatial and sequential components.

Reading and Writing

Reading acquisition is viewed, in this context, as the imposition of a novel visual code on an established auditory-linguistic code. Right-hemisphere involvement in word recognition appears to be substantial during beginning reading when printed letters are intrinsically meaningless visuospatial forms. As auditory–visual associations are learned, a shift toward left-hemisphere specialization occurs (Gladstone & Best, 1985). By age 8, schoolchildren recognize more words presented to the language-dominant left-hemisphere than to the right (Levine, 1985). The left-hemisphere advantage continues to increase through age 11, the range of the experiment.

In children, perception of auditory-linguistic components typically shows a left-hemisphere bias, whereas visuospatial processing shows a right-hemisphere bias (Kimura, 1961, 1966). When given a test that requires them to learn the names for unfamiliar visual symbols, children show a shift from right- to left-hemisphere advantage as they learn the task (Gordon & Carmon, 1976). Together, these studies suggest a strong right-hemisphere contribution in the initial perception of printed words, with increasing specialization in the language-dominant hemisphere as reading skill is attained. The importance of communication across the hemispheres from visuospatial tertiary areas to the angular gyrus appears critical when learning to read.

RH and LH Participation

Right-hemisphere involvement in normal subjects was shown in surface-recorded neuroelectrical activity (EEG) during speech comprehension (Pirozzolo, 1985). Although EEG research has a history of failure to produce clear diagnostic evidence of abnormal patterns in reading disability, recent techniques have shown meaningful results. Electrical potentials that are elicited by sensory stimulation, called event-related potentials (ERPs), have been used along with improved research designs to compare dyslexic children with normals. Support for abnormal laterality in some children who have reading disorders has been discovered and located topologically. Several problems remain: (1) Lack of separation between attentional effects and the reading process; (2) lack of recordings under conditions of active reading; (3) failure to differentiate subgroups of dyslexia, for example, auditory-linguistic and visuospatial; and (4) lack of careful determination of the severity of the reading problem. Recent EEG and ERP studies have tended to support previous research on the importance of neural communication between tertiary areas of the right hemisphere and the angular gyrus of the left hemisphere.

Hemisphere collaboration has been studied much more extensively in children who are retarded than in normal children. Numerous brain correlates of developmental reading disability were reported and interpreted: impaired interhemispheric communications (Gladstone & Best, 1985), developmental absence of normal anterior crossings (Chiarello, 1980), atypical *degrees* of ipsilateral control (Allen & Wellman, 1980), overlateralization (Kershner, 1985; Rudel, 1985), nonstandard writing hand posture (Levy & Reid, 1976), and unstable or inconsistent eye dominance (Stein & Fowler, 1982). Most researchers considered these characteristics, especially in combination, to indicate a child at risk in learning to read.

Nonstandard writing hand posture was studied extensively by Levy and Reid (1976, 1978). They suggested that the hand preferred for fine motor tasks may be predominantly connected either ipsilaterally (same side) or contralaterally (opposite side) to the hemisphere dominant for control of that activity. Individuals who displayed the inverted posture, or "hooked" hand, during writing were thought to have ipsilateral cortical control of the dominant hand. Individuals with normal noninverted posture have typical contralateral control of the hand. Despite some failures to replicate this research, Levy (1982) maintained that individuals who use inverted handwriting posture have atypical neural organization, possibly related to midline development. Allen and Wellman (1980) found strong correlations between reading scores and hand posture in elementary school-children. Gladstone and Best (1985) suggested that the *degree* of ipsilateral control may account for some inconsistency in research findings. Individual variability may affect only a subgroup that is at risk from other factors for developmental reading failure.

The neural pathways in expressive writing are quite different from the mechanics of putting words on paper. Unfortunately the act of creating discourse, has had little attention from neuropsychologists, aside from the work of Lezak and Newman (1979). Vygotsky's analysis, reported in Chapter 3, is based on active involvement of the neocortex, especially the motor areas in the region of speech production (Broca's) and the superior motor areas (Penfield, 1969). According to the pattern of hemisphere specialization and coordination that has been reported for reading, one could speculate that the beginning writing of primary-grade children would be bilateral, with the localization of automatic writing skill becoming established with experience and automization. The bilateral connections of somatic sensory and voluntary motor areas suggest bilateral participation in writing activities.

Major Pathways for Language

The major pathways, which are quite visible to a neuroanatomist, consist of collections of long axonal fibers that connect one functional area of the brain with another. Disruption of neural messages, caused by injury to a major pathway, results in a predictable disruption of function. One major pathway, the arcuate fascusculus, connects the speech reception areas with verbal association areas in the temporal lobe and then arcs to the speech production area of the frontal lobe. Other pathways form ipsilateral connections for visual and motor functions.

The major visual sensory and associative connections for reading have been suggested by Benson (1981). Primary visual reception areas of both hemispheres connect laterally with visual association areas of the same hemisphere (Fig. 6.11). From there visual messages travel to bimodal association areas in the angular gyrus of the left hemisphere, with right-hemisphere pathways crossing over at the splenium, or posterior area of the corpus callosum. Yet another major pathway interconnects the verbal interpretive and spatial interpretive cortices directly. Disruption of these pathways is followed by predictable symptoms of acquired dyslexia or alexia; conversely, neurosurgeons use symptoms of language disruption to locate lesions in the brain.

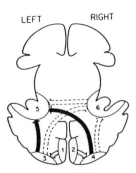

Figure 6.11. Major cross-hemisphere pathways for reading. (1) and (2) indicate left and right primary visual association cortices; (3) and (4) indicate visual association areas; and (5) and (6) indicate cross-modal areas. Heavy lines indicate pathways for verbal-visual associations. (From Benson in *Neuropsychological and Cognitive Processes in Reading.* Copyright © 1981, Academic Press. By Permission).

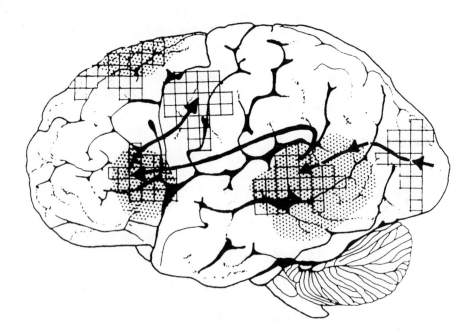

Figure 6.12. Comparison of speech and reading areas from three lines of investigation. Dotted regions indicate speech areas mapped from electrical stimulation of conscious patients by Penfield & Roberts (1959). Arrows indicate major pathways involved in reading, based on anatomical observations in acquired alexia (Geschwind, 1979). Squares show blood flow increases in healthy subject while reading orally (Lassen et al., 1978).

Chapter Summary

Neuroscience has described the major language areas of the cortex and their axonal connections. Remarkable consistency in mapping has been shown by different procedures (Fig. 6.12). Penfield (1969) identified three language areas: the primary speech area extending across Wernicke's area and the angular gyrus, the secondary speech area of Broca, and a tertiary area in the superior premotor gyrus. Geschwind (1979) traced the sequence of neural events during listening, speaking, reading, and writing based on the behavior responses of patients with specific brain injuries. Lassen et al. (1978) used scanning techniques which showed neural activation through detection of blood flow during language functioning. All reading activates these systems.

7 | Speech Perception in Reading

Auditory perception of speech has become an important topic in the psychology of reading, in part because reading and speech comprehension access a common store of words. Several decades of research has established phonemic analysis training as one of the most promising techniques in the improvement of reading skills. Researchers across disciplines have demonstrated the role of prosodic structure in spoken word recognition (Grosjean & Gee, 1987) and the importance of speech acquisition to reading (Gleitman, 1986). Both auditory perception of phoneme units and the comprehension of continuous speech are so directly related to instruction at the beginning stages of reading that knowledge of the mechanisms involved is basic to a psychology of reading.

Auditory discrimination is the process of comparing similarities and differences in auditory stimuli. Phoneme discrimination separates one sound from another, or distinguishes a series of related sounds from surrounding noises. Discrimination of words involves the identification of a pattern of sounds as a configuration against a generalized background of auditory stimulation. During this process, the brain organizes the input for storage, perhaps by some grouping of sound patterns within lexical categories. Part of the memory storage is the affective loading, which accompanies the original discrimination and influences future perception.

Auditory perception is the individual's immediate interpretation of sound stimulation. It involves recognition of a sound pattern as the same or different from patterns previously discriminated and stored. While discrimination builds cognitive structures, perception recognizes the relationship between present and retrieved information. Discrimination sets up the original storage, whereas perception involves taking a sound pattern as a unit, sorting it, and fitting it into an old slot or creating a new one. Perception uses discriminations that have been made in the past. Perceptions are formed within a context of private interpretations, based on past learning, both cognitive and affective. While discrimination and perception are both functions of past learning, perception is more compre-
178 hensive, more complex, and more closely related to conceptualization. *Speech*

perception means the complex processes by which the spoken language is segmented into discernible bits of sound wave energy, transduced into the electrochemical code of the CNS, and finally transformed into the representations of language (Schwab & Nusbaum, 1986). Words are the representations that carry meaning. Auditory word perception is the basis for nearly all visual word recognition during reading. The present chapter focuses on the neuropsychological processes of auditory language. The first section describes the anatomy of the ear, the second deals with current theories of how speech is perceived, and the third reviews research on phonological perception in reading.

NEUROPSYCHOLOGY OF SPEECH RECEPTION

You are walking home from a late-evening lecture, while mentally reconstructing its message. You are alerted by footsteps behind you. The sounds are thumps on the ground, but you interpret them immediately as a person walking behind you. At least two perceptions have already occurred. First, was the location of the sound, facilitated by your outer ear and completed in your auditory analyzers by comparing messages from your two ears. Second, was the recognition of the steps of another person, facilitated by matching the thumps with stored auditory patterns of walking on firm ground. If the darkness is frightening for you, the perception of *loudness* may seem greater than the *intensity* in decibels (dB), the unit that specialists use when testing hearing. Someone says, "Hello, there!" You recognize the voice of your instructor from hundreds of voice patterns you "know" by their unique qualities of articulation and resonance. The world knowledge that readers bring to the printed page is the aesthetics of words, their literal meanings, and the affective associations of a similar experience. Audition begins with a rush (or a whiff) of energy in the outer ear.

Auditory Analyzers

The human voice is superimposed on primitive systems for breathing, swallowing, and coughing. The words have evolved from primitive utterances such as grunts, snarls, squeals, and other nonspeech communication. The inner ear has evolved from primitive clusters of hair follicles. The auditory system of humans has become specialized through phylogeny in the reception and the transmission of speech (Eccles & Robinson, 1984). The auditory analyzers consist of the ears, affector (ascending) and effector (descending) neural systems, and neural cells in the reception areas of the cortex.

OUTER AND MIDDLE EAR
The outer ear consists of a visible appendage (the *auricle*), an *auditory canal,* and the *tympanum* (eardrum), which is its inner boundary. The auricle captures and funnels sound waves to the *tympanic membrane,* causing it to vibrate. The shape of the auricle alters the spectrum of the sound and produces a resonance that increases sound pressure on the tympanum (Pickles, 1982). The anatomy of the outer ear also has a role in selecting particular vibrations for processing through the auditory system (Fig. 7.1).

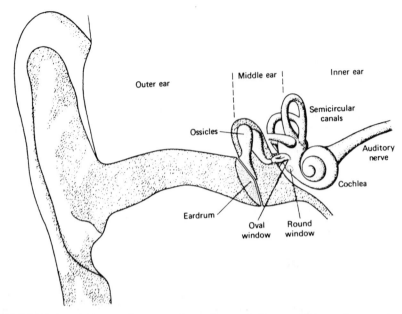

FIGURE 7.1— Organs for reception of sound. Outer-ear funnels sound waves to the eardrum (tympanum). Middle-ear converts airbourne sound to liquid-bourne sound by action of three ossicles. Cochlea of the inner ear contains transducers which code sound signals to neural impulses. (From D. E. Broadbent "Attention and the Perception of Speech" (p. 144) *Scientific American,* April, 1962.) [By permission.]

The middle ear consists of a chamber and three small bones whose intricate movements transmit the vibrations of the tympanic membrane to the oval window of the inner ear (Fig. 7.2). The middle ear functions as a transformer by converting airborne sound vibrations from the other ear to the liquid-borne sound in the inner ear, without significant loss in decibel (db) energy. Ordinarily the loss by reflection, when airborne sound strikes a liquid (such as water), is about 30 db, or 99.9% of the power. The anatomy which helps to accomplish this transformation without such a loss is the three small bones of the *ossicle chain* : the *malleus* (mallet), the *incus* (anvil), and the *stapes* (stirrup).

Three principles of physics are involved in the transmission of sound through the middle ear: (1) The conical shape of the tympanum functions like a mechanical transformer; the buckling motion of the membrane increases the force of the vibrations. (2) The ossicles perform a lever action as the shorter malleus moves the longer incus. (3) The stapes, attached to either end of the *oval window,* transmits vibrations in a surface that is much smaller than the tympanic membrane. Together these three mechanical advantages increase the force of the incoming sound and decrease the velocity, or impact, on the inner ear membrane (Gelfand, 1981).

Two other structures of the middle ear are important. The *intra-aural muscles* contract reflexively to protect the inner ear mechanisms from intensive sound pressure. Unfortunately, the rapid sound of a gunshot and the prolonged sounds

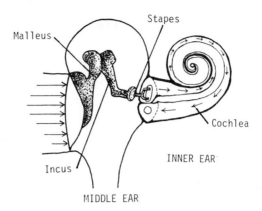

FIGURE 7.2 *Cross-section of the middle and inner ear. Airborne sound energy (large arrows) impinges on the eardrum and moves ossicles (shaded). Vibrations of oval window membrane sends traveling waves (small arrows) through the fluid of cochlean chambers. Sound waves flow up inner canal (scala vestibuli), across small opening at apex (helicotreme) and back through outer canal (scala sympani) to round window. [Drawing by D. Thompson.]*

of heavy metal music are outside the reflexive capabilities of these muscles (Corso, 1981). They also reduce the low-frequency noises from within the body to enhance the perception of speech. The *Eustachian tube,* about 1.5 inches long, connects the inner ear with the upper throat region. This opening serves to equalize the air pressure from within the ear to that of the outside environment. Pressure buildup can be relieved, as when coming down from a flight, by opening the mouth wide and taking a deep breath. Unfortunately, the Eustachian tube becomes a source of infection from respiratory illnesses such as colds, especially in young children whose tensor closure is less precise than that of adults. Middle ear infections reduce auditory acuity. When frequent infections occur during the preschool years of speech acquisition, the result may be limited auditory discrimination and delayed articulation skills.

INNER EAR
The function of the inner ear is to receive sound stimuli at the oval window and to convert the vibrations to the electrochemical code of the central nervous system (CNS). The oval window, which is the outer boundary of the inner ear, opens into a cavity at the base of the *cochlea,* a coiled structure that looks like the shell of a snail. The inner ear also contains the vestibular receptors—three semicircular canala placed at right angles to each other—which are responsive to changes in body balance and orientation. The vestibular receptors have changed very little over phylogeny, but the cochlea has evolved from a simple organ in lower mammals to an elaborate mechanism, suited to speech reception, in humans (Glees, 1988). The vestibular and auditory axons share the *auditory nerve,* the first order of fibers leading away from the ear. The cochlea is directly involved in speech perception; therefore it is the focus of this discussion.

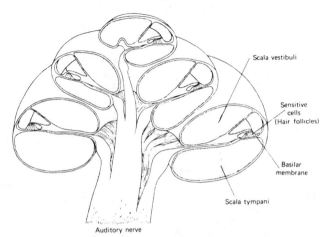

FIGURE 7.3 *Cross-section of a cochlea. Three channels run the length of the coil. Scala media is bounded by membranes which separate endolymph from perilymph fluids in outer scali. Endomorph maintains ion potential of + .80, while perilymph maintains near-zero ion potential (from Broadbent, Scientific American, April, 1962, p. 144). [By permission.]*

The Cochlea

The bony structure of the cochlea houses the sound receptors that transduce sound wave energy into nerve impulses the brain can transmit and interpret. The cochlean coil takes about two and five-eighths turns from its base at the oval window to the apex at its center (Fig. 7.3). Uncoiled it would be about 3 cm. long, increasing in width from its base to its apex. Three unequal channels, filled with fluids, run the length of the cochlea. The two large outer channels are the *scala vestibuli* and the *scala tympani,* separated by a *basilar membrane.* Sandwiched between them and lying along the membrane is a smaller triangular channel, the *scala media.* The outer channels contain perilymph, a typical extracellular fluid that maintains near-zero electrical potential. The scala media contains endolymph, a viscous fluid having a high positive potential (+.80), which is maintained by sodium-potassium pumps in the walls of the basilar membrane. The reader will recognize in this anatomy the conditions for the ion exchange of an action potential.

Organ of Corti

The *organ of Corti* consists of a ribbon-like strip of interconnected sensor cells resting along the basilar membrane that separates the scala media from the scala tympani (Fig. 7.4). Rows of receptor cells run the length of the cochlear coil and respond selectively to the frequency and velocity of the sound waves. When the stapes is moved, as little as the width of an atom, a wave of sound energy travels through the oval window and up the scala vestibula. The receptor cells, called *hair cells,* are capped with bundles of fine projections, the tallest of which reach into the *tectorial membrane.* This exquisite little muscle initiates a shearing

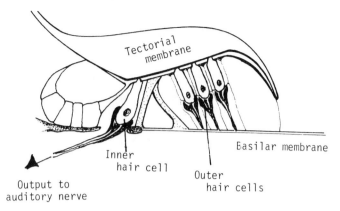

FIGURE 7.4 *Cross section of the Organ of Corti. Inner hair cells respond to sound intensity (loudness). They interconnect with outer hair cells which respond to frequency (pitch). Outer cells have fibers imbedded in tectorial membrane. Inner cells project fibers through the auditory nerve to the brain. Both cell types maintain a resting potential at about −.70 (drawing by Donna Thompson).*

action on selected hair cells as the wave of sound energy flows through the perilymph of the cochlea. High frequencies activate hair cells near the oval window. The waves of lower frequency sounds continue up the channel toward the apex and activate the hair cells within the ranges that are selectively sensitive to them.

A return flow of energy, called the *compression flow,* moves through a gap at the apex (helicotreme), flowing generally backward toward the round window at the base of the scala tympani (See Fig. 7.2.) The communication function of the return channel is not well understood because it has been researched very little. Given the anatomy of the organ of Corti, a possible role of the scala tympanum is the inhibition of noise in the system, a function research has identified with the inner row of hair cells.

Auditory Transducers

Sound receptors are topped by hair-like projections, or *stereocilli,* that pick up wave frequencies to which they are sensitive. There are two types: (1) A single row of *inner hair cells* which runs through the middle of the ribbon-like basilar membrane, and (2) Three to five rows of *outer hair cells* arranged in v- or w-shaped clusters along the outer edge of the ribbon. Although the chambers of the cochlea become smaller toward the apex, the basilar membrane becomes wider and the number of rows of inner cells increases.

Hair cells are activated by the physical energy of sound waves. A shearing action is produced when different time responses occur in the tectorial membrane (where the upper fibers of the hair cells are affiliated), and the basilar membrane (where the lower sections of the hair cells are implanted). This action causes a

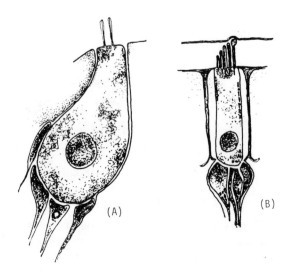

FIGURE 7.5 *Schematic representation of auditory receptors. (A) Flask-like inner hair cell has output to auditory nerve. (B) Shearing action of outer hair cells sets off a chemical exchange which travels the length of the cell and exits as neural impulse which interacts with neighboring cells (drawing by Donna Thompson).*

displacement, or bending of the hair-like fibers, changing the electrical potential within the hair cell body and creating an action potential (Gelfand, 1981). The distance a vibration travels from the oval window is directly related to the length of the wave (frequency), which determines which receptors will respond. The particular cells that are activated transmit a signal pattern, or representation the CNS perceives as pitch. Intensity (loudness) is registered by the numbers of sound waves activated within a time frame, and not by their wavelength. Inner and outer hair cells differ in form, arrangement, and function.

Outer hair cells respond selectively to the traveling waves of sound energy, according to their frequency. Outer cells are numerous (20,000 in each cochlea). The longer fibers project into the tectorial membrane. The length of the hair bundle, as well as its location, determines the sound frequency preferred by a particular cell cluster. Mechanical action, the flexion of stereocilia by the traveling wave, alters the electrical resistance of the membranes at the base of the hair cell, allowing the positive potential of the perilymph to flow through fine tubes in the stereocilia to the cell body (Fig. 7.5). The *resting potential* within a hair cell is −70 mv, a very high-potential difference from the +.80 mv state of the endolymph which bathes the stereocilia. The differential is maintained by sodium and potassium pumps in the membrane of the cell body. They transduce sound energy by chemical exchange and transmit sound signals across synapses at the outlet of the cell body. Their function is sending; they pick up sound stimuli from the outside world for consolidation with information from the inner hair cells.

Inner hair cells are flask-like in contour. They form a single row through the base of the organ of Corti and number only about 3,500 in each ear. They respond to changes in the intensity of sounds. Inner cell bodies have both afferent (sending) and efferent (receiving) nerve endings. They are innervated by fibers that connect to centers in the brain stem. Some of these connections are inhibitory; they release the neurotransmitter, acetylcholine, and perhaps have a function in habituation. Enkephalins, the brain's natural opiates, are present and may contribute to affective associations at the level of the limbic system. The neurotransmitter, GABA, may function as an excitatory transmitter, in contrast to its role in the brain as an inhibitory transmitter (Franklin, 1984). Activation of the auditory transducers is believed to require the combined potential of several processes, with contributions from both inner and outer hair cells (Pickles, 1982). The effect of these summed potentials, called the *cochlear microphonic,* can be measured in the cochlea. These signals enable researchers to plot the frequency limits of hearing within a species or an individual.

CENTRAL AUDITORY PATHWAYS

There are four or five synapses along the ascending pathways from the *cochlear nuclei* to the auditory cortex (Fig. 7.6). At each level, subcortical processing is thought to take place, because the numbers of fibers increase at each junction (Warren, 1982). Contralateral fibers (those leading to the opposite hemisphere) are more numerous than axons at a similar level ascending unilaterally. Fibers from each cochlea number about 31,000, increasing to about 100 million on arrival at the auditory cortex. Pathways lead directly to and from the reticular formation, suggesting continuous communication with the alerting and attention mechanisms. Most of the fibers from the cochlear nuclei are known as the first order neurons of the auditory pathways. Only the major pathways are shown in this simplified diagram of a system which is exceedingly complex.

The second- and third-order neurons comprise separate systems and more than double their axons to 90,000 on each side. They synapse in dorsal nuclei at the reticular level and in the *inferior colliculus* at the midbrain level. The pathways from the dominant right ear to the contralateral side where language resides are more numerous than from left to right, which is evidence from physiology of the contralateral organization of speech perception. The ascending fibers of the reticular formation are difficult to trace, in part because the nuclei located there are nonspecific, meaning that they respond to signals from more than one sensory system. Arousal of the organism to a change in sound levels is a function of the reticular formation (Stellar & Stellar, 1985). Orienting to a particular sound probably takes place at the level of the dorsal and ventral nuclei, where small differences in arrival time at left and right are compared by a listener to identify the spatial location of the sound.

Third- and fourth-order neurons project to the inferior colliculus at the midbrain level and to the thalamus. Some of the fibers of the ascending reticular formation synapse at the midbrain level of the *hypothalamus* where connections are made to the limbic circuit (Chapter 2). These affective structures provide the motivational force, based on past pleasure–punishment reinforcement, for selecting information the organism has learned to be important. Affective loading is

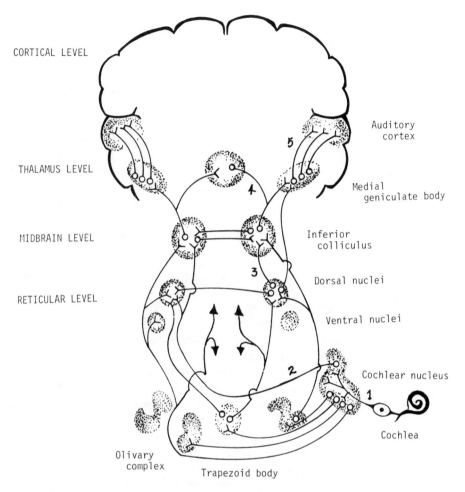

CORTICAL LEVEL

THALAMUS LEVEL

MIDBRAIN LEVEL

RETICULAR LEVEL

Auditory cortex

Medial geniculate body

Inferior colliculus

Dorsal nuclei

Ventral nuclei

Cochlear nucleus

Cochlea

Olivary complex

Trapezoid body

FIGURE 7.6 *Diagram of major ascending pathways from ear to cerebral cortex. Neural processing occurs at each junction. Diagram is extended; compactness may be visualized by locating receiving areas in temporal lobe immediately above and behind the ear (drawing by Donna Thompson).*

relayed via efferent fibers downward to the auditory receptors and upward via afferent fibers to the *thalamus* and to the forebrain where signal selection and attention are controlled. Sustained attention (to auditory messages) almost certainly is centered in or near the thalamus, which has direct connections (not shown) to and from all major areas of the cortex.

Fifth-order neurons project from the *medial geniculate body* to the *auditory cortex* on the ipsilateral side. The auditory processing that takes place at the various synaptic junctures is not well documented as yet. An interesting study of language disorders that resulted from lesions to the thalamus has been reported by Mazaux and Orgogozo (1982). Five patients whose thalamic damage was confirmed by computerized tomography were given diagnostic tests. They showed reduced fluency and impaired articulation of speech. Their reading comprehension appeared normal when reading easy material, but was reduced when material and task difficulty were increased. Only patients with thalamic lesions on the left were affected. This clinic finding suggests (1) that contralateral processes for spoken language are gated at the thalamic level and (2) that language processing and reading are related in ways not yet discovered.

Thresholds for Hearing Speech

The auditory system is suited by phylogeny to process human speech, demonstrating the importance of verbal communication in the enhancement of the species over time. The previous discussion referred to the wavelength of sound as *frequency,* which is conceptually different from *pitch,* the sound as perceived by individuals. Perceived pitch is related to the external stimuli (sound waves), but is altered somewhat by each passage through the auditory analyzers.

Similarly, there are differences between the *intensity* of the external stimulus in decibels and the *loudness* as perceived by individuals, both reported in decibels. Dampening of the original stimuli occurs through the feedback system and through the impact of habituation (the decay of excitation from repeated stimulations). Frequency and intensity are objective measures, while pitch and loudness are considered subjective measures, even though the units are consistently expressed in Hz and db. The sensitivity range of hearing for humans is 20 to 20,000 Hz, or cycles per second (Fig. 7.7). Conversational speech ranges from approximately 125 to 8,000 Hz, well within the hearing threshold of sensitive ears. Comfortable sound pressure levels in db (loudness) vary with the frequency in Hz (pitch). High-frequency sounds require a lower sound pressure level for comfortable listening. Two topics that concern the psychology of speech reception as it affects reading are: (1) the development of phoneme discrimination and speech comprehension, and (2) the prevention of hearing loss.

EFFICIENCY DURING ONTOGENY

A healthy newborn has approximately 20,000 hair cell receptors in each ear and can distinguish loudness, pitch, and tone. Wertheimer (1961) found rudimentary directional oculomotor responses in neonates, starting 10 minutes after birth. Field et al. (1967) reported that full-term neonates could respond to both 70- and 90-decibel sounds, but less well to 70-decibel stimuli. DeCasper and Fifer (1980) discovered that 8 of 10 newborns preferred the voices of their own mothers over the voices of other females at statistically significant levels. Voice discrimination requires associations of rhythmicity, intonation, frequency variation, and phonetic components of speech. Horowitz (1984) warned that the range of individual differences in audition in young children is extensive, which calls for research to determine when a child may be at risk, not only in the development of language, but also in the social relationships that language promotes.

Unless hearing is damaged in some way, children continue to improve their accuracy in hearing words until the age of about 18 (Sterling & Bell, 1930). Part of the improvement may be an increased ability to respond to the test situation. Epstein, Giolas, and Owens (1968) found that children with normal hearing

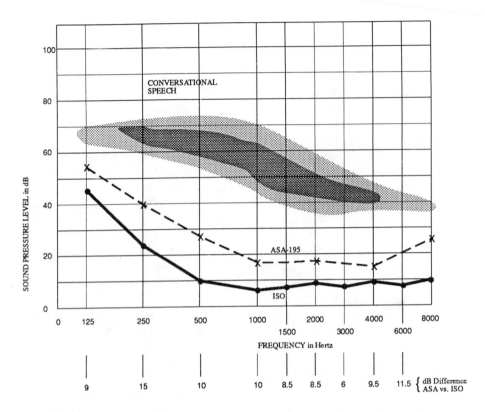

FIGURE 7.7 Audiogram format showing range of speech reception. Middle C of music notation is at Hertz 256.

improved with age in the ability to identify familiar words that were distorted mechanically. However, errors on nonsense words increased as the distortion increased. An improved perceptual strategy may have been available to the older subjects, by which incomplete signals were used to perceive whole words.

According to available data, hearing becomes gradually less effective from age 20 to age 60, particularly in the middle-frequency ranges where speech perception is important (Corso, 1981). Franklin (1984) suggested that living longer in a noise-polluted environment may be the cause of increased deafness in people, rather than their merely getting older. Estimates are that persons living to the theoretical age of 140 in today's environment would become deaf from the wear and tear on the hair cells of the cochlea causing their destruction over time.

Auditory acuity defines the functional efficiency of the hearing apparatus. *Audiograms* chart the points at which a subject responds to a series of frequencies at particular intensity levels. Schoolchildren's hearing acuity is usually determined by a *pure tone audiometer,* which selectively measures their thresholds of pitch and loudness. The test requires a soundproofed room, arranged so that only the intended sound will be available to the subject. Each ear is measured separately, and where a substantial loss is found, a measure using bone conduction, rather than air conduction, is made. Often it is necessary to check an individual's hearing threshold for speech. The best *articulated tests* are phonetically balanced, single syllable words that represent the proportion of phonetic sounds that occur in the language of instruction.

A substantial number of students have partial hearing loss. Lyle, age 7, was proficient at lip reading, having been born with above-average intelligence and having acquired two doting foster parents who spent time talking and reading with him. He had no siblings around with whom they could compare his communication behavior. Lyle could hear the teacher's voice at arm's length, and could perceive speech across the room if he was attending to her lip movements. He read comfortably at grade level; this was accomplished, in part, through articulation therapy and special seating in the classroom. He shared a front desk with an alert classmate, who touched him on the shoulder whenever the teacher needed his attention. Joan, age 9, had more severe loss and marginal learning ability. She responded joyfully to a hearing aid supplied by the speech therapist, but her parents would not allow her to wear it. They did agree to its use during special reading instruction at school, where she made progress in both phoneme perception and word recognition. Children whose hearing loss is in the high-frequency ranges (from 2,000 to 4,000 cps) are likely to hear the voices of men better than women teachers. Many school districts now screen all entering kindergarten children for hearing loss with a pure tone audiometer.

PREVENTION OF HEARING LOSS

The acquisition of language requires accurate reception at the wavelength frequencies that convey speech and at levels of loudness used in conversation. Approximately 80% of hearing loss is the result of deterioration in the hair-like fibers that top the auditory receptors. Prevention of hearing loss is possible by avoiding the loud and prolonged noises that destroy the fragile structure of inner hair cells. Severe injury to a swathe of cells eliminates the signal at that range, followed by deterioration of the receiving neurons. Once destroyed, hair cells and their nerves are not replaced biologically.

Infants left too close to loud music may suffer permanent hearing loss. A recent advertisement in a slick weekly magazine pictured a young father, wearing earphones connected to his stereo, while he played with a happy and sound-protected baby. Franklin (1984) charted the decibel ratings, together with exposure times, that damage hair cells. Her report described noises commonly experienced in the workplace or the home, and were recorded at typical exposure distances. Some examples of exposure conditions that can cause permanent destruction of the affected fibers are: 8 hours of 80 db exposure to heavy city traffic, subways, or factory noise; an extended ring of a loud alarm clock placed at a distance of only 2 feet; 2 hours of 100 db exposure from a chain saw, a boiler shop, or a pneumatic drill; a brief 120 db exposure to a rock concert, a thunderclap, or sandblasting. Current estimates of hearing loss in male adolescents and young adults in the United States run as high as 50%. Although some hearing loss is an inescapable part of life, serious attempts at noise reduction are warranted to protect public health. Individuals can prolong their auditory acuity by avoiding noise pollution, by keeping their distance from hard metal music and by wearing protectors during necessary exposure to loud machines.

One of the motivations for recent research on the neurology of the ear has been the search for better corrective aids for persons with hearing loss. The technology is very far from being able to reproduce a device as efficient as nature's organ of Corti. Some limited success has been reported for mechanical implants into the cochlea which replace some of the damaged hair cells at the high-frequency (outer) end of the basilar membrane. Recipients of this device have experienced improved hearing of high-frequency sounds, which enables them to hear a telephone and certain speech sounds. There are not enough receptors in such a device to reproduce the quality of the normal voice. Some researchers are working with computer-simulated language, with the expectation that precise descriptions of human speech will provide some of the technology for designing better sound receptors.

A hearing device is being tested which is designed to help the persons who have conductive hearing loss. This group makes up approximately 20% of those who have severe hearing loss. Their problem is auditory nerve damage, as distinct from hair cell damage. A tiny magnet is implanted in the skull behind the ear, which keeps in place a detachable sound-processing device. This aid converts sound into vibrations, which are transmitted into the magnet and from there to the inner ear. The next section considers different theoretical models of how normal hearers receive and process the sounds of speech.

COMPREHENSION OF SPEECH

The auditory system is the major organizer of time, and therefore of sequence. The traditional view, and one currently assumed in most reading programs, is that the listener receives a spoken word as a sequence of phonemes and retains this sequence in short-term memory until a match is located in the child's known vocabulary, or lexicon. Although word recognition may require only milliseconds, sequence is important. The four-letter word **stop** contains four phonemes; but reordered, or *permuted,* the letters could say **pots, tops, opts,** or **spot.** But the language of primers is sentences, governed by rules of syntax, and the speech of teachers is continuous discourse. Researchers do not agree on the segment, or basic unit, by which speech is processed. The answers to some of these issues seem to be contained within the phases of perception that begin in the periphery of the auditory system and end with access to the lexical storage areas in the angular gyrus.

Theories of Spoken-word Recognition

Strategies of word perception based on acoustic-phonetic units are referred to as *bottom-up representation.* Strategies which assume that word patterns are recognized as morphemes (meaningful words or syllables) are called *top-down representation.* The question is, does the auditory system recognize a spoken word: (a) as a sequence of sound bursts (bottom-up), or (b) as a meaningful word or morpheme units (top-down)? This distinction is not unrelated to the familiar cleavage between synthetic-versus-analytical methods for presenting printed words to beginning readers. Most of the recent research is theory-based and assumes either a bottom-up or a top-down processing of speech.

BOTTOM-UP STRATEGIES OF REPRESENTATION

Despite three decades of very active research on speech perception, experts have not yet achieved consensus on the basic unit that the brain uses to process words heard. Currently, the question is centered on how speech heard is represented in the neural system. In this context *representation* means the abstraction of the sound wave patterns of speech to linguistic symbols. Three "bottom-up" versions of speech perception as they relate to reading will be described: the phoneme as the "natural" unit of speech, the distinctive features theory, and the motor theory of speech perception (revisited).

Phoneme as Natural Unit of Speech

Most reading methodology is contingent to some extent on the idea that the alphabet originated as graphic representations of individual and identifiable speech sounds. Huey (1908) described the historical sequence by which word-pictographs evolved into written language. Word signs, in which each syllable was represented by its beginning consonant, were the precursors of English alphabetic writing. Vowels were added as further differentiation was required. The system has remained frozen (or nearly so) into a written language that requires vowels (five plus a **Y** or **W** usurped on occasion) to represent multiple and inconsistent vowel phonemes. The abstraction of speech as alphabet came gradually until, in Huey's words, "we have here the use of signs for word-sounds independently of any reference to meanings" (p. 207). The problem did not escape Huey that teachers and pupils must cope with many inconsistencies in matching units of natural speech to print.

The challenge to the alphabet as the basic unit in speech perception has come from linguists, through their scientific analyses of the spectrograms of human speech. Discussed in current literature as the *invariance condition,* the acoustical "pictures" of words failed to show a consistent, discrete unit for representing each phoneme, as the alphabet system implied. In a spectrogram, phonemes assume different forms, largely determined by their position in a word or by their neighboring phonemes (Klatt, 1979). For example, the syllable /di/ rises at the second formant from 2,200 to 2,600 Hz, while the syllable /du/ falls from about 1,200 to 700 Hz during a similar interval (Warren, 1982). Plosive consonants (those which cannot be pronounced in isolation) require a vowel for true articulation. This context sensitivity, or *coarticulation,* produces variants of the same phoneme, called *allophones.* Lack of consistent evidence of the invariance of phonemes is one of the major arguments for the rejection of the theory of alphabet construction.

Although a phoneme may vary from one spoken word to another, comprehension of speech does not seem to be adversely affected. Quite the contrary, according to research that shows such variability to be useful to a listener. Brief phonemic components may be perceived more readily with the added information that comes from the variability caused by adjacent phonemes that are less brief (Wickelgren, 1969). Coarticulation does not seem to interfere with identification of separate phoneme components on the part of adult listeners (Warren,

1982). Wide differences in phoneme discrimination is characteristic of children at school entrance, when some of them still do not hear certain phonemes within words and need to be taught to discriminate them.

In teaching the historical alphabet and letter sounds, schools have employed associative learning strategies. Beginning long before Skinner's operant conditioning techniques became known, phoneme–grapheme correspondence was taught by most teachers to most children and has continued because most children require that the association be precise, even if the spectrogram is not. The view that the phoneme is the natural unit of speech, and the obvious unit of written language, has remained attractive. There are those who still believe reading instruction, at best, is the teaching of the rules of phonics, whereby an appropriate response is learned for each letter or letter cluster. Only minimal instruction is needed for a few children whose language is advanced and who seem to conceptualize the system independently. Erika, age 4 years, 4 months, had heard stories read, had learned the alphabet song, and had acquired some sounds while forming letters. She made the transition to storybooks in the privacy of her own room. Asked by an astonished parent where she learned to read, Erika said, "In my room, by myself." She had the perceptual and comprehension skills to make sound–letter associations from a collage of everyday experiences. This "natural" method of learning to read is not adequate for most primary schoolchildren.

Specialists with background in linguistics and information processing are almost unanimous in rejecting the phoneme as the natural unit of speech, but consensus is lacking among them on which of the other possible units is basic in speech processing. This creates difficulty for reading teachers, who are committed by culture and curriculum to a single, traditional alphabet.

Distinctive Features Theory

Roman Jakobson and his colleagues are generally credited with the conceptualization of spoken language as a sequence of phonemes, each distinguishable from all other phonemes (Jakobson, Fant, & Halle, 1952). According to their *distinctive features* theory, a phoneme is reducible to a small bundle of acoustic features, each corresponding to a contrast of articulation. Jakobson proposed that the development of speech in children can be represented by an ordered sequence of "acquired feature contrasts." The English version of the International alphabet shows how consonant pairs are organized linguistically (See Table 3.1 on p. 73). Consonant contrasts (e.g., voiced, voiceless) lend themselves to direct tests of phoneme discrimination during speech development.

Jakobson brought together the abstract concept of phonetic features and the linguistic information of acoustic features. The precision of the distinctive features approach opened the way to investigate artificial language. Contemporary psycholinguists define *distinctive features* as the acoustic and/or articulatory characteristics by which components of spoken language can be distinguished from each other (Eisenberg, 1976). Using the on-off communication system of digital computers, the contrasting features of speech units can be represented. Despite this progress in representing speech mechanically some problems remain; for example, whether the synthetic stimuli used in some research is generalizable to the natural (more complex) stimuli of human speech.

Some bottom-up theories assume a hierarchy of features, based on their relative importance in the identification of words (Tartter, 1986). Consonants have a higher value in phoneme discrimination than vowels. The research which followed the distinctive features proposals revealed the complexity of phoneme analysis. For example, different speakers produced different band formations (formants) on spectrograms of the same syllable. Also, the same speaker produced formant variations under different psychological conditions or with different facial expressions (Fig. 7.8). Again the criterion of "invariance of the linguistic phoneme" was challenged. Context sensitivity, this time psychological and phonological, challenged the theory. The evidence of coarticulation, that had led to the rejection of the historic alphabet, sent distinctive features advocates in search of more precise technology to analyze the spectrograms. To counter the difficulty of "reading" a spectrogram reliably, it was "decomposed" (Fig. 7.9). Analyses moved from research of "steady-state production" of consonants to the patterns of transition from consonant to target vowel, which meant that hypotheses advanced beyond the single phoneme to the CV relationship.

A significant contribution of distinctive features theory was the concept of voice onset time (VOT), a measure of time lapse between the beginning of the vibration of the vocal cords and the release of the consonant. A breakthrough in the research of speech acquisition was achieved when VOT revealed that very young infants were able to discriminate certain consonant contrasts in CV syllables (Eimas, 1974). However, the same lack of invariance was discovered in the distinctive features of syllable units that had characterized the alphabet and single phoneme proposals.

Distinctive features theory was applied in schools and libraries with the widespread substitution of linguistic phonetic symbols in place of the phonic representations of the old dictionaries. New "linguistic readers" taught families of words that were phonetically consistent to beginners. A difficulty sequence in phoneme discriminations, based on feature contrast information, was implemented in some phonics programs. Those phoneme pairs having many features in

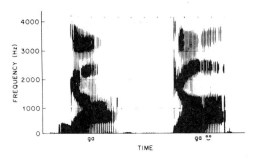

FIGURE 7.8 Spectogram of male voice producing /ga/. Left image shows normal facial condition; right image shows smiling condition (from Tartter, *Language Processes*, p. 217. © 1986, CBS College Publishing).

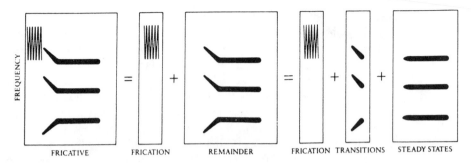

FIGURE 7.9 Decomposition of a spectogram. Cue classes of a fricative are (a) friction, (b) transition, and (c) state of CV syllable (from Tartter, *Language Processes*, p. 217. © 1986, Holt, Rinehart, & Winston [By permission.]

common were conceived as the most difficult and were taught late in the sequence.

Motor Theory of Speech Perception

A view of speech perception, widely accepted in the first half of the century, has been revisited in recent times, in part because neural connections between the motor control areas of speech and the angular gyrus, where visual words are processed, have been discovered. An early proposal by Allport (1924) stated that speech can be understood by the listener through an active matching between his or her own articulatory neural motor commands and speech production. According to the connectionist theory of Watson (1930), speech is recognized by association with the articulatory movements the listener would make to produce the sound(s) heard. Further, the speech musculature responds covertly when speech sounds are heard. Jacobson (1932) tested the notion of covert motor response to language by attaching sensors to particular muscles and giving verbal commands to the subject, "Do not move, but think about hitting a golf ball." The neurons responded in the muscles that would have been needed for a motor response, but at a lower level of activation than the action would have required.

A major criticism of the motor theory of speech perception was the implication, inherent in covert articulation, that listeners need speaking experience before they can understand speech. Lenneberg (1967) had postulated that developmental changes in the ability to perceive phonemic categories would parallel changes in the ability to produce these categories. When studies of infant speech perception showed phoneme discrimination earlier than the onset of speech (Eimas, 1974), the motor theory was discarded by many psycholinguists. A renewal of interest in the 1980s in the motor theory can be attributed in part to the recent and widespread acceptance among scholars of phylogenic preprogramming for the acquisition of speech in humans. If language is phylogenically staged, then the development of articulatory and acoustic mechanisms may parallel, as Lenneberg suggested. More than six decades following Allport's (1924) proposal, a motor theory of speech perception is still a viable position in an unresolved and continuing discussion of how speech perception is learned (Sawusch, 1986).

Whichever model of speech code representation gains favor in the future will need to be consistent with the physical realities of brain functioning during listening (Gerschwind, 1979). Current research from neuroscience shows the activation of the motor areas while merely listening to speech and in the absence of speech production. The prespeech of infants provides an example of how linguistic structures theoretically are exercised initially. Newborns are biologically prepared to hear their own prespeech utterances, which are associated by contiguity with the speech musculature that produces them. Within 3 or 4 months, infants have learned how to make their own interesting sounds last by repeating the tongue-lip-glotteral movements. During the period of babbling, a playing with sounds, has begun. Gradually (from approximately 4 to 11 months) the phonemes heard in the social environment are the phonemes increasingly practiced. This babbling further strengthens the musculature that will one day be used in speech, and sharpens the discriminations the child will need to recognize spoken words. Babies attend to their own babbling, assuring that the productions heard are stored, probably in the association cortex adjacent to the primary auditory reception areas. The economy of biological functioning seems to deny the existence of a two separate systems, one for speech articulation feedback and a second for acoustical messages from others.

There has been a renewal of interest in a *tertiary speech area,* located high on the frontal lobe and adjacent to the motor control gyrus (Eccles & Robinson, 1984). Although the functions of this area were described by Wilder Penfield three decades ago, little attention was given to this third language area until recently. His purpose in mapping the area was to preserve speech following brain surgery. Stimulation of certain parts of the premotor left hemisphere in conscious patients produced vocalizations, but not recognizable speech. Removal of the area in LH produced temporary loss of speech, which patients recovered in about 2 weeks. Eccles reasons that recovery was possible because the superior speech areas, unlike Broca's production area and Wernicke's interpretation area, is bilateral. This makes sense in a system that requires intricate bilateral coordination of the speech-producing muscles on both sides of the lips, mouth, and throat. Recovery occurs as the contralateral side takes over the initiating function of articulatory language. Eccles points out that the *intent* to move is recorded by activation in the nerve cells of the *supplementary motor area* prior to the initiation of a voluntary movement. An angiogram of the cerebral circulation of blood brings out the color coding of orange and red in the tertiary speech area during reading a word, whether silently or aloud (Chapter 6). Eccles concluded that the area controls the inner programming of complex voluntary motor sequences needed in speaking. At last someone has postulated the function of Penfield's tertiary speech area! In doing so the motor theory of speech comprehension has been revisited.

TOP-DOWN STRATEGIES OF PROCESSING

Bottom-up models have generally dealt with elements of words and have limited their investigations to the phoneme unit, the distinctive feature, or the demisyllables CV or VC. Other investigators of spoken-word processing have discovered that word identification is influenced by the context in which it is perceived, suggesting that the semantic level is involved, perhaps initially. An important challenge to bottom-up theory is that words, or morphological units, may be the basic unit of speech perception, indicating that central processing at the cortical level may be controlling perception. These findings have stimulated several lines of research to test a top-down strategy of spoken-word perception. The way was opened for accepting a larger unit as basic in speech processing by Massaro (1974), who showed that the minimal time for processing a sound unit was 250 msec. This was the time required for processing a syllable. He used a *recognition mask* technique in which subjects were asked to identify a speech sound, followed by a noise (mask) which interrupts the processing. When the mask was imposed within 200–250 msec of the speech stimuli, identification of the signal by the subjects was interrupted. When the mask was delayed beyond 250 msec there was no disruption and the sound was identified. Massaro suggested that speech may be heard as a sequence of syllables, each being processed separately.

Evidence of Top-down Processing

The arguments which support top-down processing of speech perception are based on several different techniques which present words or continuous text to the subject (Tartter, 1986). *Noticing errors* was a technique employed to test word perception by distorting the signal with mispronunciations, which listeners were asked to detect. Gross phonetic errors were detected more readily than the substitution of acoustically similar phonemes. Errors in second and third syllables were detected more rapidly than first-syllable errors, suggesting a top-down processing strategy that involved first-syllable representation in the lexicon. First-syllable errors appeared to require extra time for restarting the word recognition process.

Monitoring results is a technique in which subjects are asked to search for a particular signal among the speech signals: a superimposed noise, a speaking error, or a particular segment in the sequence. Monitoring has shown that many segments of the sound stream are available to a subject *at one time* for active perceptual processing. In some tests subjects have processed syllables faster than phonemes, suggesting to some investigators that phoneme discrimination *follows* syllable perception, or perhaps is a parallel process. The concept of *parallel processing* allows the possibility that two mental operations can proceed at the same time, as opposed to the assumption that linguistic operations are serial. Studies which measured reaction time for a monitoring response demonstrated a unit of recognition more expanded than the syllable stimuli often presented. Subjects recognized whole words more quickly than syllables and two-syllable words more quickly than one-syllable words (Foss & Swinney, 1973). These findings, based primarily on speech monitoring by adults, changed the focus of auditory processing from the speech stream per se to focus on meaningful units.

Shadowing mispronounced text is a technique in which subjects are asked to "echo" running speech as they are hearing it. Marslen–Wilson and Welsh (1978) designed syntactic and semantic errors into the sentences presented and recorded the corrections that were made spontaneously during shadowing. Subjects tended to correct the distorted speech to the original pronunciations and word order, so that words and sentences made sense. The time lag of the "shadowing" had no effect on the correcting, nor did subjects pause after correction, as they would be expected to do in a consciously directed correction. One interpretation from this study is that listeners, from the beginning, use syntax and semantics to perceive speech "correctly."

Phonemic restoration is a research technique in which segments are removed or obliterated from continuous speech and subjects are asked to report what they hear. When subjects "hear" intact words wherein phonemes are missing the assumption is that they are using top-down processing to fill the gaps. Samuel (1981) designed a complex presentation of words, using added, deleted, and distorted phonemes within real words and nonwords. He found that subjects were less able to discriminate added or replaced versions of real words than nonwords; suggesting that top-down processing influences isolated words, as well as words in context. Samuel limited his evidence of top-down processing to the syntactic level and not the perceptual level, suggesting the need for researchers to differentiate the *process level* when describing how speech is represented and interpreted by their subjects. The experimental use of meaningful units and continuous speech as stimuli lends credence to top-down strategies because the longer segments more closely resemble natural speech.

Biological Preprogramming

Just as the evidence of phoneme discrimination in young infants revived the theory of bottom-up unit processing of speech, the onset of children's speech has renewed the interest of psychologists in top-down cognitive processing. The one- and two-word sentences of beginning speech suggests a word-unit processing strategy. Also, the young child's selective use of content words suggests a morphemic (meaningful) basis for emerging speech. Gleitman (1986) summarized the evidence for an innate basis for language learning. Children the world over acquire their native tongue at a high level of proficiency and within a narrow developmental time period. This occurs within widely varying child rearing practices, linguistic talent, and cultural motivation. Single words appear at about 1 year of age and two-word sentences at about 2 years. Telegraphic speech, followed by rapid acquisition of functor words, occurs in the third year. By age 4 the normal child speaks much like an adult (Chapter 3). When it was noticed that children emigrating to the United States learned to speak a second language more quickly than their parents did, the search was on for a biologically sensitive period for language learning.

The way children deal with questions shows how their early speech output differs from adult input. Although approximately 10% of the adult's speech to the child is **wh**-questions, the child postpones these function words. When children do begin to ask questions they typically preserve the noun/verb phrase order of English syntax, "What I can eat?" Although approximately 90% of auxiliaries used by maternal models in declarative sentences are contracted ("We'll go out now."), the child uses uncontracted forms in the early learning period ("We will go out now"). In other words, the young child conceptualizes the syntactic structure of the language and creates rule-governed speech.

The disparity between *content* (open-class) words and *functor* (closed-class words) is further support that an innate mechanism of language is influencing language acquisition, along with environmental input. Although functor words (conjunctions, prepositions, and verbal auxiliaries) make up more than half the words in adult conversation, the child is able to screen out the content words to produce telegraphic speech. "Your Teddy's in the car" is reduced by the child to "Teddy car." An analysis of stressed syllables and words in continuous speech may explain how selections are made initially by the child from the models heard. Stressed morphemes help the child identify the things and actions within a given context. This association learning of words and meanings suggests top-down storage of a lexicon which is organized by categories to be accessed later.

The child's order of content word production is concrete noun, followed by action verb, followed by verbs that encode mental states, and finally be adjectives. As Gleitman (1986) pointed out, the lexical categories (verbs, adjectives, and nouns) are all heard early in life; but the child almost invariably acquires the names of familiar objects first. Adjectives, which encode the properties of things, are produced much later. The child clearly learns from the language heard (English, Spanish, or Arabic), but the preordered development of language is not explained solely by the linguistic environment to which the child is exposed. Nor are the morphemic and syntactic properties a young child selects during speech acquisition and explained by the more general principles of cognitive development learning.

To summarize, the search for the unit, or element, the neural system uses to process speech has produced numerous theories, but not consensus. Three different bottom-up strategies have been discussed: (1) phoneme as the natural unit of speech, (2) distinctive features theory, and (3) the motor theory of speech perception. Evidence for top-down strategies of word perception have been explained: (1) syntactic influences on word perception and (2) morphemic influences on speech acquisition. The challenge for consumers of this research is to discover the conditions under which students are likely to use phonemic knowledge as the unit of processing and when prosodic knowledge dominates perception.

Comprehending the Speech Stream

Prosodic knowledge is the information a listener obtains from the patterns of tone, accent, and voice modulation of continuous speech. The unresolved discussions between bottom-up and top-down theorists have produced a dilemma in which levels of processing need to be conceptualized and defined. Phoneme perception and feature detection are required for speech perception at the peripheral (lower) levels of processing, while word recognition is required for comprehension of speech at the cortical (higher) levels. The several functions that occur between these points of initiation and interpretation are not yet clear. Acoustical representation in the organ of Corti certainly is not at the word level and prosodic interpretation almost certainly uses meaning units as well as acoustical segments. Some promising discussions of *phases* in the speech processing sequence may provide closure to this topic.

PHASES IN SPEECH REPRESENTATION

The first phase in speech perception is that which converts sound wave patterns into the CNS code. Neuropsychologists call this transduction. In the language of information processing this phase is called transformation, or peripheral auditory analysis. New techniques of psychophysics are used to measure the signals leaving the ear through the auditory nerve. Selective responses to simple speech signals, such as steady-state vowels, stop consonants, and VC syllables have been recorded. This work has identified important properties in the discharge patterns of hair cell axons that correspond to the acoustic attributes of speech sounds. This *psychoacoustic representation* technique is aimed at describing the acoustic features that human speakers produce naturally.

A different technique for peripheral analysis has been to create a psycho-physical model (artificial language) that incorporates known facts about hearing in humans (Pisoni & Luce, 1987). One technique produces "snapshots" of three-dimensional wave patterns at 10-msec intervals along acoustical band widths of ⅓ or ⅙ octave. The spectral display from this analysis is not unlike the waveform patterns of speech sound stimuli passing over the ribbons of hair cells in the Organ of Corti. Such mechanical constructions, based on properties of the human peripheral analysis, have encouraged researchers to try to build better hearing enhancers for the partly deaf—electronic aids that discriminate speech sounds rather than merely increase loudness. Although this research has created spectral formats of speech attributes, researchers have yet to duplicate the perceptual processing of signals by the central nervous system.

The second phase of lexical processing has been outlined as the *initial contact phase* during which the listener employs some representation of the auditory input to make contact with the lexicon (Frauenfelder & Tyler, 1987). Again, experts do not agree on the nature of the representation that makes contact nor when the contact is made. Different suggestions about the nature of *contact representations,* have been proposed; the spectral template of speech (Klatt, 1980); an abstract linguistic unit (Pisoni & Luce, 1987); or accented syllables (Grosjean & Gee, 1987). The *amount of speech* required for entry to the word bank is important because the longer the stretch of speech symbols required for contact, the longer the delay in accessing meaning. First-contact entries to the lexicon are favored, therefore some models cite the first syllable of a word as providing primal information for lexical access.

Following initial contact and activation of a subset of the lexicon, the selection of one intended entry occurs. Almost certainly the familiar action potential of the neurons to produce patterns of inhibition and excitation are involved in the selection, perhaps by association links to other storage areas where confirming experience resides. Some writers propose a "search" model for entry selection within a subset of the lexicon (Bradley, 1980); others prefer a "cohort" model in which failure to match results in decay of the action that is not confirmed (Marslen–Wilson, 1984). The end point of the selection phase is defined at the precise moment that the intended word is recognized.

Word recognition. In experimental tests listeners recognize words in isolation or in context. The point of recognition frequently occurs before the entire word is heard. As reported, the appropriate words may be recognized when the signal is distorted or incomplete. The exact point of word recognition is determined by its physical properties (length, stimulus quality), its intrinsic properties (segmented representations), its semantic quality, and the number of competing members in the cohort. Most experts agree on two points: that the acoustic signal is recognized categorically and sequentially. The segment of the sequence that activates a word may be a feature, phoneme, or syllable. Some experts insist that the propositional unit (the meaning unit) is the key to lexical access.

Higher-order analysis. The final phase in the sequence to match auditory signal and verbal meaning is referred to as *lexical access.* The listener's goal is to tap the stored knowledge associated with a word so that an utterance can be interpreted. This storage is assumed to include knowledge of phonology, syntax, semantics, and pragmatics. Some researchers believe that all information is accessed simultaneously (cohort model); some believe access precedes recognition (search model); and some believe access and recognition are a single process. Word processing at the level of syntax and semantic analysis is considered "high-order" thinking and requires the attention and conscious participation of the listener.

A neuropsychological sequence for processing language is compatible with the theory of phases. Following reception of auditory representations in the superior temporal lobe, the lexical access occurs by relay to Wernicke's area, which is built from associative connections and is organized as schemata. The categories of storage may be genetically ordered, such as having a predetermined place for names, another for action words, and another for descriptors. Higher-order analysis would require stored knowledge for affects, color, rhythm, warmth, texture and other multisensory facets that personalize language. These meanings from long-term memory storage in the different sensory systems come together in the tertiary integration areas, the primal location being the angular gyrus of the left hemisphere. Its function is to integrate the multiple associative linkages to words or propositions. The sequence of sound signal processing is governed by the relay system of the auditory analyzers; therefore, the phases from peripheral stimulation to lexical access must be serially ordered within the neural pathways. The sequence would seem to be (1) reception of the CNS code at the cortical level, (2) access to meanings at the lexical association level, and (3) reference to the tertiary (multimodal) level for resolution of ambiguity, enrichment of language, review of related experience, and higher-order analyses. The interior frontal areas of the temporal lobe have affective linkages to the amygdala and the limbic circuit. The posterior of the temporal lobe expands and interconnects with billions of neuronal linkages to somatic and visual systems.

PROCESSING BY PROSODIC STRUCTURE

A team of linguists, Grosjean and Gee (1987) argued that speech perception is based on prosodic units rather than on the word units of dictionaries and written language. They proposed that continuous speech is processed and accessed by the patterns of stressed and unstressed syllables rather than by sequential one-word-at-a-time accessing of the lexicon. Instead, the listener makes use of the alternating patterns of weak and strong syllables to make separate and parallel analyses. Strong, or accented, syllables are picked out of the stream of speech for lexical search (one at a time). Weak syllables are identified through an analysis of phonological and morphemic rules and their prosodic relationship to accented syllables. To illustrate the hypothetical processing of a sentence, the weak (w) and strong (s) syllables are identified: **I** (w) **put** (s) **the** (w) **bun** (s) **in the** (w,w) **bag** (s). The word *put* would be identified by a listener from its emphasis in the prosodic representation and the lexical search would begin to locate its meaning. Possibly a cohort of words containing a stressed "put" would be searched. Unstressed *I* and *the* would be interpreted by their relationship to the stressed word, or syllable. The listener would be helped by prior knowledge, syntactic rules, present context, and feedback from the lexical search. The authors emphasize that recognition of the accented syllable often precedes recognition of the unaccented syllable that precedes it in the flow of speech. Following this two-level analysis, the next accented syllable *bun* would be picked out for the next lexical search.

Despite this brief presentation of the Grosjean and Gee model, several features are apparent in their theory of access: (a) Prosodic structure, not the word, determines the analysis. (b) Words need not be processed in sequence, but in clusters of syllables. (c) Content and function words are not differentiated in this system, but are processed like other words according to their stress patterns. [The authors note, however, that most functor words are not accented in running speech.] (d) An interaction of top-down and bottom-up strategies are used; as unaccented syllables are held up for morphological information from accented syllables.

DEVELOPING THE LEXICON
TO BE ACCESSED

Simple meanings are learned in the context of the baby's need fulfilling environment. "Here is your juice," says caregiver, extending the bottle. Later baby will say, "ju" or "wawa," consistent with the contents of the bottle. Again the contiguity in time and the attention of the infant assures that word heard, word produced, and object seen are associated and stored in memory. Juice tasted and hunger satisfied are reinforcing. The uncrowded brain of the infant processes and stores hundreds of meaningful, language-related, need-fulfilling experiences each day.

When the child extends one-word sentences to telegraphic speech the focus is still on meaning and a lexicon of content words continues to grow. Caregiver says, "We are going for a ride." Toddler says, "We go ride," picking up not only the essential content of the sentence, but also the accented segments of adult speech. (*We're going f'r a ride.*) The telegraphic speech of young children does not imply they do not hear beyond the accented content words. During the third year a child may emphasize the functors for a time, saying, "Daddy, *we went for a ride,*" not unlike the beginning reader who pronounces word by word for a time. The lexical storage area is different for words that name than for action words, which very likely contributes to their separate organization in the lexicon.

According to a developmental explanation of word storage, the one-syllable word can be affixed, usually with unaccented prefixes or suffixes. The one-syllable word "ride" becomes the accented morpheme of "rider," which can be expanded much later to "riderless." Words like riderless require an extended time for comprehension in reading, which is to be expected because of the added morpheme and the additional time required to process a negative. The tree-like branching of the neural fibers (biological processes) is consistent with a lexical storage system that is built gradually from context-laden and reinforced experiences. The conceptual fit between the normal acquisition of propositional speech (Gleitman, 1986), the prosodic structure theory for processing speech (Grosjean & Gee, (1987) and the potential of the neural system for associating cross-modal experience with spoken words is quite remarkable, and together they postulate only some of the possibilities for understanding spoken language.

Since most speech is context-oriented, it is likely that most access entries are as direct as the branching which grows with the experience. **Deer**, in context of a Bambi story, and **dear** as a term of endearment require no search for the appropriate alternative. There is some evidence that the accented syllable has limited numbers of matches (cohorts) to be sorted through within the lexicon. Huttenlocher and Zue (1983) found that when words are classified by the stress pattern, combined with the phonetic transcription of the stressed syllable only, the average class size is only 3.8 words to be searched. By these criteria 17% of words are unique and 38% belong to a class of five words or fewer. If one considers context of an utterance also, it would appear that many spoken words are accessed directly. The cohorts to be analyzed would be few in number. Most spoken word meanings may be derived and accessed from a growth-organized lexical structure, assembled gradually from the words experienced in a context of social communication.

The development of word finding in children 6 to 14 years old has shown that the lexical access to words produced in speech is based in semantics (Weigel–Crump and Dennis, 1986). The ability to produce names was determined when subjects were presented with an experimental arrangement of four conditions: (a) riddles [given in sequential lists], (b) rhymes [I'm thinking of . . .] (c) semantic description, and (d) pictures. An analysis of errors in naming showed that younger children lacked hierarchical organization of classes and they named associations rather than target words. Older children's errors were closer to target in terms of semantic criteria. Errors in naming pictures were generally real words, phonetically accurate, and bearing a semantic relationship to the correct names. Sex of subjects was not significant for riddles or rhyming, but girls excelled in both accuracy and latency when naming pictures. This study shows a semantic influence at the level of word production that is independent of the phonemic features of the words. The next section relates auditory skills of word recognition and word production to reading.

LEARNING THE ALPHABETICAL CODE

When listeners translate the words they hear into meanings, the stressed, single-syllable words probably are accessed directly, assuming that the words are real and familiarized by past experience. Readers, however, need to translate the word they see in print into its counterpart in the auditory lexicon. For beginners, this translation requires that the letter representations (graphemes) be paired in near-perfect correspondence with the phoneme representations of words familiar in speech. A strong positive relationship exists between children's awareness of the phonemic and syllabic structure of speech and their success in learning to read in the first grade. Further, a deficiency in phonological awareness in a kindergarten child may be predictive of difficulty in learning to read in the first grade. A strong, highly specific relationship has been reported between young children's knowledge of nursery rhymes and the development of phonological skills (Maclean, et al., 1987). Alliteration and rhyming both correlate with early reading skills, even when IQ and social background are controlled (compensated) statistically.

Longitudinal studies have shown that children's deficits in phonological processing skills remain with them through the primary schoolyears (Jorm, Share, MacLean, & Matthews, 1986). In an intensive assessment program involving British children, Ellis and Large (1987) followed 5-year-olds for 3 years, testing them over time on 44 variables of reading and associated skills. At termination, three groups were extracted for comparison: Group A, subjects having *specific reading disability* (high IQ, low reading skills); Group B, *good readers* (IQs similar to group A, achievers in reading); and Group C, subjects having *generalized reading deficit* (lower IQs and low reading). Data were analyzed retrospectively to describe the developmental patterns of the different abilities from the beginning of reading acquisition. Group A was found to vary from their better reading peers in only a few variables: Phonological segmentation, short-term memory, and naming. Group A was deficient in visual processing when compared with group C (generalized deficits); however, the major discriminator of specific reading disability was phonological processing. These patterns of ability were replicated at each age from 5 to 7 years old. The authors criticized research designs which fail to measure the full range of skills related to reading and fail to follow skill development during the critical years of reading acquisition.

Auditory processing deficiencies that accompany severe reading deficiencies apparently continue into adolescence. Byring and Pulliainen (1984) examined 34 subjects (the index group) who were selected for poor spelling. They were compared with 34 controls on a series of neurological and psychomotor tests. Although the groups did not differ in many factors, the control group was superior in phoneme manipulation tasks and in auditory (nonverbal) sequential information processing. The index group was inferior, also, in fine motor control of the left hand. The investigators interpreted their results in terms of a deficit in information processing in the left hemisphere.

Phonological Perception

Most children have learned to construct adult variations of sentences before they enter kindergarten or first grade. Their words are spoken as wholes and they may not discriminate the phoneme segments that correspond (approximately) to the alphabet. *Phonological perception* is the ability to perceive speech sounds, not as discrete noises, but rather in terms of their functional identity in the phonological system. Before children can learn the essential correspondence between particular phonemes (auditory representations) and their graphemes (visual representations), they must be able (1) to segment, or break down a word into its phonemic elements; (2) blend phonemes into recognizable words; and (3) employ the prosodic structure of speech to recognize word boundaries. Most of the research knowledge has been obtained from comparisons of auditory abilities in children who succeeded and those who failed in beginning reading.

The segmentation and speech perception skills of disabled readers was reported by Snowling, Goulandris, Bowlby, & Howell, (1986). Two control groups were given the same series of single-syllable words and nonwords: a CA (chronological age) group matched for age, but reading at normal levels; and an RA (reading age) group matched for reading level, but younger than the index group. When noise interference was used with the word signal, reading-disabled subjects performed as well on repeating high-frequency words, but they were inferior to the CA controls on repeating low-frequency words and inferior to both control groups when repeating nonwords. The investigators suggested that children with specific reading disabilities have difficulty with nonlexical procedures involved in verbal repetition, including phoneme segmentation. They take longer to consolidate new words; thus their verbal memory and reading processes are compromised.

PHONEME–GRAPHEME CONVERSION

Children who are poor readers have difficulty in short-term processing of stimuli that lends itself to phonetic coding. Brady, Shankweiler, and Mann (1983) assessed auditory perception tasks in good and poor readers at the third-grade level. Poor readers were less sensitive to phonetic cues, such as rhyming and nonrhyming; and made significantly more errors when listening to speech in noise; but they did not differ from good readers in perception of speech without noise nor in perception of nonspeech sounds. The investigators concluded that poor readers have a perceptual difficulty that is specific to speech, and that their short-term memory deficits are specific to the auditory processing tasks.

When reading disability persists into adulthood, a high incidence of speech perception deficit is found within the group (Lieberman, Meskill, Chatillon, & Schupack, 1985). Developmental dyslexic subjects show a high deficit in vowel perception. They made significantly more errors (22%), than a control group when asked to identify the place of articulation of stop-consonants [b], [d], and [g] in CV syllables. Poor phonetic perception characterized in the index group, but not all individuals within it. Some subjects were high in vowel errors and low in consonant errors. The investigators emphasized that their disabled adult readers had different perceptual deficits, rather than a general auditory deficit.

The ability to segment spoken words and the ability to combine phonemic units to produce words are different prereading skills which are found at different levels of competence in individual children (Belmont, 1974; Chall, Roswell, & Blumenthal, 1963; Williams, 1984). *Phonemic blending* is the ability to synthesize a word auditorily when the phonemic parts are pronounced in sequence. The child who pronounces the sound of each letter in sequence and cannot pronounce the word may have been taught by the synthetic method, but has not yet learned to synthesize. The distinction between the analysis a listener makes and that required of a reader was explained by Belmont. When language exists as an auditory-vocal system, each word does not need to be analyzed into its component parts. Once reading instruction begins, letters and words must be dealt with in terms of their phoneme–grapheme composition so that appropriate sound–letter and sound–word connections can be made. Whole words must be analyzed into their auditory elements (phonemes) in order to relate them to their appropriate visual counterparts. Also, the child must learn to start with the visual symbols and synthesize (blend) the phonemic elements into the sound patterns of whole words. These complex visual-auditory analyses, syntheses, and translations make new developmental demands on the auditory processing system. Most children can learn to blend by "saying it faster." A child whose problem persists may need to be retaught letter combinations within syllables; such as, consonant blends presented with a vowel, **CCV** (fly, stay, blow, tree) or **VCC** (off, ask, inn, and). The use of real and familiar words is important in helping the child make this transition.

One promising line of research in segmentation, name retrieval, and alphabet mapping has been to provide different training conditions for experimental groups, using pretest-posttest changes in word recognition to determine the relative contributions of different factors. Vellutino and Scanlon (1987) conducted a series of studies with second- and sixth-grade students, matched for age, grade, and reading ability. In one study, poor readers performed significantly below good readers on both pre- and posttests of "phonemic segmentation ability." Results further indicated that name retrieval and alphabetic mapping are important determinants of skill in word identification and that deficiencies in either skill will cause reading disability. The researchers suggested that dysfunction in phonological coding may be a common factor underlying deficiency in both name retrieval and alphabetic mapping. This research is interesting because it isolates phonological coding as instrumental in the visual processing of both letters and words. Aaron (1985) studied grapheme–phoneme conversion in college students who still remained disabled readers. The group of 15 adults of average and superior intelligence revealed a deficiency in decoding which apparently was not related to the "g" factor, or general intelligence. The investigator proposed that phonemic processing is a subroutine that operates to limit reading comprehension.

CONCEPTUALIZATION OF PROSODIC STRUCTURE

The prosodic characteristics of spoken language are conveyed in print by diacritical markings of syllable division and accent. Comparisons of continuous speech in different languages has shown that *stress pattern recognition* of syllables influences the word recognition strategies of readers. Katz and Feldman (1981) reported a series of experiments in which they looked for evidence of syllable effects on word recognition in fifth graders, college students, and Serbo–

Croatian (Yugoslavian) adult readers. In the fifth-grade study, skilled and average readers were asked to pronounce printed word lists of four types: two-syllable words and pseudowords that had been altered by slash marks at regular syllable divisions or at irregular (incorrect) division. Their conclusion was that children recognize words, in part, by means of syllables within words. American college students did not appear to use syllabic information in processing the words, suggesting a shift away from the surface phonological coding that children used. The investigators suggested that English-speaking adults use a predominance of direct visual codes in word recognition. Serbo–Croatian readers, also college students, were chosen for comparison because their language is based on a consistent surface phonological code, called in this study *shallow orthography* which contrasts sharply to the complex, deep orthographic relation to the surface phonetics of English. In Yugoslavian adults, results showed a significant slowing of responses when syllable division was irregular. Phonological coding for them continued to be the mode of word recognition and they were automatic and extremely rapid in the process. The investigators suggested that as reading ability matures, phonological coding is supplanted by non-phonological codes that are more efficient in English in terms of speed accessing the mental lexicon. A somewhat different interpretation might be that mature English readers use the morphological root, or word stem, for fast recognition of words.

Beginning readers are helped significantly by an awareness of the syllabic structure of words (Mann & Liberman, 1984). Some investigators use the concepts of "onsets and rimes" to specify children's perception of syllables (Treiman, 1985). *Onset* is the initial consonant or consonant cluster and *rime* is the vowel and any following consonant(s). Apparently children use both elements when perceiving spoken syllables. Jackson and Kelly–Ballweber (1986) found that the ability to perceive stress patterns in words could not be predicted from the audiograms of hearing-impaired young adults, suggesting a different processing mechanism for the reception of sound signals and the perception of word syllables.

The potential effect of phonological processing on silent reading of word patterns that are difficult to pronounce was investigated by McCutchen and Perfetti (1984). They found that tongue-twister sentences took longer to read silently than neutral sentences. The investigators suggested that concurrent vocalization may play a role in memory. The tongue-twister effect may occur because cognitive capacity is required in a system with a limited capacity. Taken together, these studies suggest that awareness of the prosodic structure is strongly related to beginning reading success, but becomes a diminishing factor as readers become efficient in processing the phonemic structure.

Laterality Effects in Speech Perception

Normal right-handed adults generally exhibit better recall of verbal material presented to the right ear than verbal material presented simultaneously to the left ear (Broadbent & Gregory, 1965). The advantage shifts to left-ear recall when the dichotic listening task is changed to nonverbal material, such as musical themes or environmental sounds (Kimura, 1967). Studies which compared poor readers with normal reading controls have shown differences in the processing of dichotic signals. Dermody, Mackie, and Katsch (1983) reported that children 10 to 13 years old showed no between-group differences when items on a dichotic trial were requested singly, but differences emerged favoring good readers (a) when responses required two phonetic items and (b) when dichotic stimuli were separated by as much as 500 or 1,000 msec. The investigators imply neurological factors in auditory processing were involved. They consider dichotic tasks a useful procedure for investigating them. Dichotic listening investigations, which show a right-ear advantage for both phonetic and word signal processing, have been interpreted as behavioral support for lateral asymmetry in the brain (Pisoni & Luce, 1987). These same studies are considered evidence of specialized neural mechanisms for processing speech.

Chapter Summary

Auditory perception is the individual's immediate interpretation of sound stimulation. Hearing acuity depends on the efficient functioning of the ear, the auditory nerves, and the brain mechanisms that process the sounds. Speech perception is the complex process by which spoken language is segmented into discernible bits of sound wave energy, transduced into the electrochemical code of the CNS, and finally transformed into the representations of language. During speech development children learn to structure syntax, which is transferred to similar contexts. In similar ways they learn the relationships between phonemes and graphemes and conceptualize that written language is a system of rules which have exceptions. The auditory skills that readers need are of two types: (1) bottom-up strategies which focus on the acoustic elements of words, and (2) top-down strategies which focus on meaning units, such as morphemes, propositions, or whole words. Research has shown a positive and consistent relationship between early reading achievement and phonological perception, phoneme–grapheme conversion, and conceptualization of the prosodic structure.

8 Visual Perception of Print

Fluent reading is a process of scanning words to obtain meaning. The eyes function to produce visual signals for the brain to interpret. Earlier chapters have indicated the importance of a language base for gaining meaning from print, of auditory perception that provides a bridge between hearing words and comprehending them, and of motivation to read. When children are beginning to read, they spend time and energy learning to discriminate visual differences. Even earlier, they learn to focus on the printed page with the vague idea that the strange marks they see have a kind of magic locked inside—the fascination of stories they ask to hear again and again.

Reading takes place in the brain where print is interpreted. *Visual perception* is the process by which light energy from the environment is internally organized into meaningful signals. Neuropsychologists describe *visual perception* in reading as the process that begins with retinal detection of simple word features and continues through the processing of word patterns in the visual cortex (Johnson, 1981). *Perception of print* occurs as early as the child can discriminate "farm" and "from" on the printed page. Understanding the physical events that lead to perception suggests why reading is both a visual and a linguistic process. Understanding the process by which print (a symbolic sign system) is perceived is much more complicated than knowing how objects are represented. The first section of this chapter deals with the human system for visual analysis. Subsequent sections discuss the role of visual perception in learning; the relationship of visual processes and reading disabilities; and finally the conditions for rapid reading.

THE VISUAL ANALYZER

The human eye responds to photic energy from a limited range of the light spectrum—about 350 to 760 nanometers. The eye is the peripheral apparatus which shapes the light rays for analysis by the retina and transduces light energy to the elecrochemical code of the central nervous system. Major pathways from eye to cortex connect with affective and cognitive systems on their way to visual reception centers in the occipital lobes. The anatomy of the eye consists of three parts: (1) the *extrinsic muscles* which move the eyeballs, (2) the *optic system* of internal structures which focus incident light rays, and (3) the *receptor cell layers* located in the retina.

Anatomy of the Eye

The human eye is an active organ which adapts to different light intensities, different viewing distances, and even to its own anatomical imperfections. The two eyes move together to follow a line of print by reciprocal control from the autonomic nervous system (ANS) and the CNS.

EXTRINSIC MUSCLES

Each eye is equipped with three sets of muscles which move the eyeballs in coordinated up-down, left-right, and rotational directions (Fig. 8.1). Each muscle is attached to the bony structure in which the eye is situated. The saccadic movements of reading are executed by action of these muscles. Distant objects are viewed with the conjugate positioning of the two eyes by the controlling muscles. When near-point vision is required, as in reading a book, the muscles cause the eyes to converge. The closer the object, the greater the *convergence* that is required. *Binocular depth perception* is possible because the two eyes generate slightly different images of the object to be interpreted in the brain.

THE OPTIC SYSTEM

The eye is a system of tissues and fluids that combine to bend light rays to focus on the retinal layers at the back of the eyeball, where light energy is transduced to

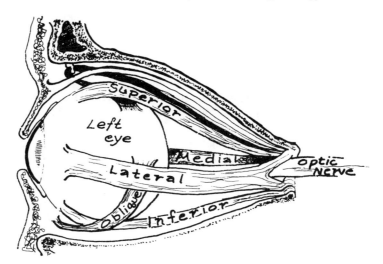

FIGURE 8.1. Extrinsic muscles of the eye. Lateral and medial muscles control left-right movement; superior and inferior muscles control up-down movement; oblique muscles control circular movement (drawing by Donna Thompson).

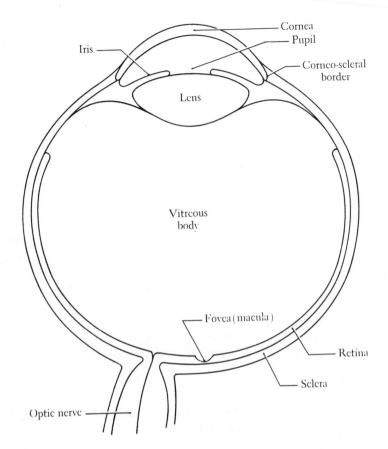

FIGURE 8.2. *Cross-section of the eye. Light passage is influenced by the lens, the cornea (a half-lens) and three bodies of fluid.*

the electrochemical code of the nervous system. The eyeball, almost spherical in shape, is enclosed in a fibrous sheath called the *sclera* or white of the eye (Fig. 8.2). At the front of the eye this connective and opaque tissue merges into a transparent tissue called the *cornea*. In normal vision light reflected from an object passes through the cornea and the aqueous *humor* (a watery fluid) then on through the pupil of the iris. The *pupillary aperture* is a circular opening to the lens. Like the aperture of a camera, its size can be altered to control the amount of light that enters by the *iris*, a pigmented disk that identifies people as brown-eyed, blue-eyed, or some blend of these colorations. When light is intense, *constriction* of a circular muscle attached to the iris results in the smallest possible opening to the lens. Relaxation of the muscle causes *dilation* of the pupil, which may become as much as 17 times the size of minimal aperture. Reduction in pupil size increases the sharpness of the retinal image by eliminating peripheral light rays to the eyes. The pupil appears black because the observer sees all the way through the structures of the eye to a dark *chloroid coating* that lines the sclera. Certain drugs, either applied as drops or taken internally may result in pupillary dilation. An innovative psychologist used photographs in which pupil size was graphically increased to test sexual arousal in subjects, an indication of affective linkages to visual events in the eyes.

The *lens,* a crystalline body, is the major structure for bending light rays to converge, or focus, on the retinal layers at the back of the eyeball. Although transparent to light rays, the lens is an ultrastructure of circular fibers, like the layers of an onion, and a network of horizontal fibers to interlock them. The lens is suspended within a circular body, the *ciliary muscle,* that surrounds the rim of the lens. Three rings of hair-like filaments, called *zonales,* project from the ciliary muscle and attach to the equator of the lens. The shape of the lens is controlled by these rings of nonelastic filaments arranged like spokes around the equator of the lens (Koretz & Handelman, 1988). When the eye is focused on infinity (20 or more feet), the sphincter-like ciliary muscle relaxes and therefore expands, or increases in diameter to its maximum. As the muscle expands it pulls the zonules taut, causing them to pull on the lens, thus increasing its equator and flattening it. This is the *unaccommodated condition* that is just right for focusing a distance image on the fovea. When the eye focuses at near-point the ciliary muscle contracts, reducing the size of its opening, lessening the stress on the zonules and reducing the diameter of the lens. The lens recovers to a more relaxed (thicker) state, achieving the near-point focus needed for reading. The relaxation process is called *accommodation.*

The degree of accommodation that is possible is a function of the contractile power of the ciliary muscle, the elasticity of the lens, and the action of the cornea (a half-lens). Behind the lens is a large cavity filled with *vitreous humor,* a transparent gelatinous mass. The light refraction which occurs as the rays pass through the boundaries of the three chambers containing aqueous and vitreous humor is on the order of 1.33, approximately the refractive index of water. Vitreous humor also has the important function of supplying nutrients, derived from lymph, to the cells of the retina.

In some persons the eyeball is shorter from the front to back than the lens system is designed to accommodate. At resting state, the rays focus behind the retina to produce a blurred image, a condition known as *hyperopia,* or farsightedness. Most children have excellent accommodation systems, but as adults reach middle age, their ciliary muscles become less flexible and the internal structure of the lens weakens. Accommodation for reading is made easier for them with bifocal lenses for near vision. When the eyeball is abnormally long, the lens tends to focus the image in front of the retinal layers, causing *myopia,* or nearsightedness. This problem, common among children, is genetically determined, but it usually does not occur until the growth spurts of ages 8–10, 12–14, or 16–17 (Van Donge, 1971). When light rays pass through the lens they are reversed and inverted, as in a camera lens, so that the image is reflected upside down and backwards.

THE RETINA

The action of the optical system produces a focal image on the *retina.* This innermost layer of the eye extends over about two-thirds of the interior surface of

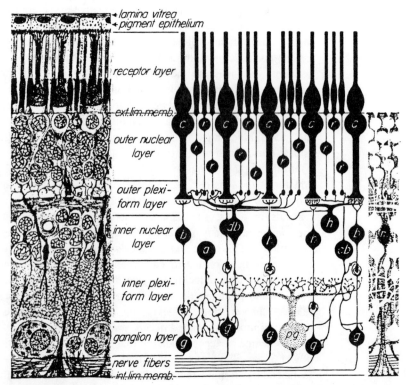

FIGURE 8.3. Layers of the retina. Vertical section at left is photograph of stained tissue. Schematic representation shows cones (c) and rods (r) in outer layers; amacrine cell (a), bipolar cells (b), ganglion cells (g), horizontal cells (h), and parasol ganglion cell (pg) in inner layers from E. G. Walls, Factors in human visual resolution. *Journal of the Optical Society of America, 33,* 487, 1943.) [By permission of the Society.]

the eyeball. The central and most sensitive area of the retina is the *fovea,* or macula. The surface of the retina is interrupted by an opening, slightly to the nasal side of the fovea, where neurons from the retinal cell layers exit to form the optic nerve.

Ten retinal layers are arranged concavely at the back of the eyeball; therefore light passes through the connector cells and their fibers to reach the light-sensitive receptors in the rods and cones. The retina resembles cortical tissue from which it was phylogenically derived (Fig. 8.3). Working inward, the layers of the retina are as follows. (1) a *pigmented layer* of cellular tissue covers the retinal cells and cuts down stray light that might otherwise penetrate the sclera. (2) The *outer segment layer* of the *rods and cones* detects light energy. (3) An *outer limiting membrane* controls the chemical environment of the sensors. (4) The *outer nuclear layer* consists of cell bodies of the rods and cones. (5) The *outer plexiform layer* is where signals from rods and cones synapse with connector cells. (6) The *inner nuclear layer* contains horizontal, bipolar, and amacrine cell bodies and their processes. (7) The *inner plexiform layer* consists of synaptic connections to ganglion cell bodies. (8) This is the *ganglionic layer* where visual input is consolidated. (9) The axons of ganglion cells form a layer of optic nerve fibers and target the opening where they exit. (10) An inner limiting membrane controls the chemical environment of the connector cells. The process by which the rods and cones generate the signals which the brain understands is the first step in the extraordinary sequence by which humans see language.

Photoreceptors

Vision begins in the *receptors* (2) with the conversion of units of energy, called photons, into signals the retina can process and the brain can interpret (Schnapf & Baylor, 1987). Humans have two types of receptors: rod cells and cone cells. The cone system functions in high-intensity light to provide rich detail and color perception. The rod system is so sensitive that it overloads in bright light, but mediates vision in shades of dark-light during poor illumination. The area near the macula (fovea) is saturated with cones, performing detailed vision such as that needed for discrimination of letter and word shapes. The proportion of rods decreases toward the periphery, until their distribution on the retina is entirely rods. There are more rods (130 million) than there are cones (7 million) for each eye. Much of the retina is a mosaic in which the two systems complement each other. The cones yield high acuity but poor sensitivity, whereas the rods yield poor acuity but high sensitivity. The print of books is perceived at or near the fovea.

The *rod cell* is divided into two parts that have specialized functions (Fig. 8.4A). The outer segment detects light. It is cylindrical in shape and holds a stack of some 2,000 disks, arranged like coins in a tube (Stryer, 1987). The disks are assembled in the inner segment of the rod and move outward continuously toward the end of the rod where they disintegrate, a few each day. Each disk is enclosed in a plasma membrane in which two-part molecules, *rhodopsin,* are embedded. One part, the protein *opsin* is a string of amino acids whose form is seven helical coils, standing side by side across the plasma membrane. Rhodopsin's second component, a *retinal* molecule, threads through the middle of opsin's coil. When stimulated by light, retinal changes its shape setting off a series of chemical exchanges. The signal cascades down the outer membrane of the rod cell and exits through the synaptic terminal. The enzyme *transducin* mediates the conversion of light into electrical impulses by the process *transduction.* Generally, one photon activates one rod cell and a mosaic of excitation and inhibition in neighboring cells presents an image of the outside world to the brain.

The *cone cell* is distinguishable by its tapered outer segment. Instead of disks, the layers in cones are formed by folds in the cell membrane (Fig. 8.4B). The folds are studded with specialized pigment molecules consisting of an opsin molecule and one of three variations of the retinal molecule. The three opsins represent three different, "pigment preferences," each responding to a different wavelength (Land, 1977). The maximum absorption of "blue" cones is at wavelengths near 440 nm, of "green" cones near 535 nm, and of "red" cones near 570 nm (Fig. 8.5). The probability that a cone will fire, or signal a response, is increased as the quanta of wavelengths nears the preferred region of sensation.

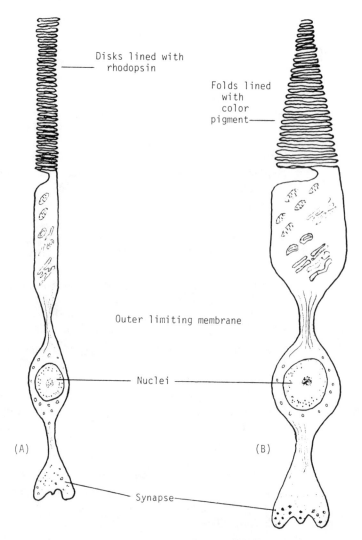

Disks lined with rhodopsin

Folds lined with color pigment

Outer limiting membrane

Nuclei

(A)   (B)

Synapse

FIGURE 8.4. *Cross-section of rod (A), and cone (B). Rhodopsin and color pigment, assembled near inner segments, move steadily upward, renewing the supply as cells degenerate at apex. Outer limiting membrane stabilizes rods and cones. Impulses exit at synaptic bodies.*

Rhodopsin, the sensing molecule in rods, preferentially absorbs photons, or *quanta*, in the region of 505 nm.

Color perception depends upon the combined signals from the three cone systems (Atrens & Curthoys, 1982). For example, light wavelengths of 490 nm will cause absorption in different amounts by blue-, green- and red-sensitive cones. Color vision in humans is phylogenically advanced and provides aesthetic experience in addition to survival skills. Color labeling is learned by association of the brain's encoding of cone stimulation and the linguistic counterpart re-

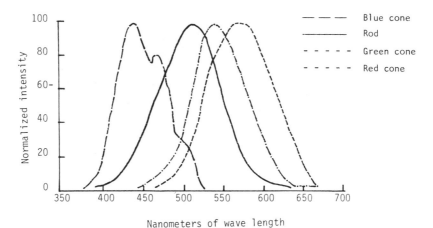

FIGURE 8.5. *Relative values of rods and color-sensitive cones along visual-sensitive continuum. Blue cones peak at 430 nm, rods at 505 nm, green cones at 535 nm, and red cones at 575 nm.*

ceived in the left hemisphere. Objects reflect light of certain wavelengths, whether in dim or bright light. At twilight the human eye sees only shades of gray because the rod system can function at low thresholds while the cone system cannot.

Genetic errors in the trichromatic system of cones accounts for the three main types of color blindness. Each is caused by the absence of one or more types of cone receptors. Individuals without "green" preference cones do not discriminate red and green. Persons who have no retinal cones see only shades of black and white and are referred to as *rod monochromatic*. Such individuals have provided useful data on how images are perceived in the absence of color discrimination, since rods are sensitive at a single wavelength region.

Color detection is an inherited, recessive trait, which is sex-linked and most commonly expressed in males. About 2% of the male population is red-deficient, while about 6% are green-deficient. One in 250 women is red/green-deficient. Traditionally color perception was tested by asking the subject to sort tufts of colored wool into groups of like colors. A red/green deficiency would make it impossible for the person to discriminate red, orange, yellow, and yellow-green. Sets of charts are now used, such as the Stilling or Ishihara tests, which require the subject to recognize a number or a letter buried in a mass of multicolored dots that selectively discriminate the three different cone types.

Print perception does not require color vision. However, lack of color perception is a handicap when the child is being taught a color-coded phonic system or trying to follow directions for coloring an illustration. Teachers should be alert to the possibility (indeed, the probability) of color deficiency within the class. Children find ways of adapting by discriminating colors by their value and intensity, without being aware they see color differently from most people. A second grader, Benjy, was issued a new box of crayons. When he colored his lawn red, classmates reacted with surprise. For him the experience was negatively reinforcing, despite the teacher's praise of his unique and well-composed drawing. The next time Benjy used crayons, he was observed showing a crayon to his neighbor who pointed out the name of the color, printed in caps on the wrapper. After that Benjy checked the label and colored the grass green. He was referred to the school nurse, who ordered a color perception test. He lacked color discrimination of green and red, presumably having only blue-sensitive retinal cones. Ernest Hemingway is said to have been "color blind" and used only obvious color references in his powerful descriptive passages.

Transducers

Light energy is converted to neural energy through the interaction of outer and inner segments of the rods and cones. Like most cells the membrane that surrounds receptors forms a barrier that separates fluids having different concentrations of ions. In retinal cells an *external limiting membrane,* layer 3, protects the separate environments of the outer and inner segments of the rods and cones. The resting state of the cell is characterized by a stable electrical differential, therefore a lack of impulses leaving the cell.

In darkness a continuous flow of ions, the *dark current,* moves through the pores, or gates, of the outer membrane of photoreceptors (Schnapf & Baylor, 1987). Inside the outer segment of the rod, the concentration of sodium (Na+) ions is high, while inside the inner segment the concentration is potassium (K+) is high. When a photon of light activates rhodopsin (or the opsins of cones), the pores are allowed to close, the influx of positive sodium ions is blocked, and the internal voltage of the cell becomes more negative. When the internal voltage is reduced to a critical level it hyperpolarizes, sending an electrical pulse down its axonal fiber. The brighter the light, the greater the number of cells that respond. Rods produce a detectable signal at the synapse when a single photon is absorbed by a single molecule of rhodopsin (Stryer, 1987). Rods pool their photocurrent. Cones require a greater light intensity to produce a response 100 times smaller and 4 times faster than rods. Continuous visual transduction involves a switching to the rod system when light is dim. We all have experienced temporary blindness when moving from bright light to semidarkness during the transition from cone to rod vision.

Conductors

The electrical current that is generated in the receptors is processed at the level of the retina. The information from about 140 million rods and cones must be reduced to the capacity of 1 million fibers that leave the retina via the optic nerve cable. Each rod and cone nucleus has synaptic terminals in an organized network of inner nuclear cell bodies.

Horizontal, bipolar and amacrine cells are distinguishable in the specialized structure of the retinal layers. There rods pool their signals from the different receptive fields for comparison (Fig. 8.6). Signal transmission is by direct electron transfer, therefore the current is amplified. *Horizontal cells* are laterally connected and are inhibitory. They inhibit hyperpolarization in surround cells to increase visual contrast. *Bipolar cells* are described by their name—they have

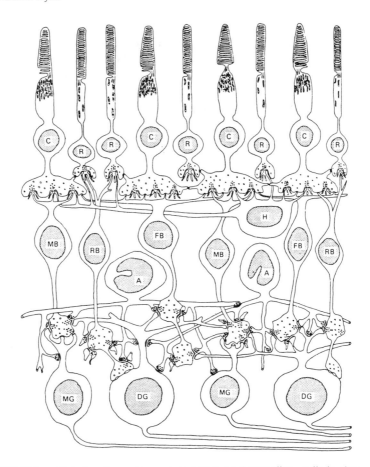

FIGURE 8.6. Details of receptor, connector, and ganglion cells in the retina. Bipolar cells form synapses with both amacrine and ganglion cells. Horizontal and amacrine cells act to inhibit bipolar and ganglion cells. Receptor cells: (c) cone, (r) rod; connector cells: (mb) midget bipolar, (fb) flat bipolar, (h) horizontal, (a) amacrine, (mg) midget ganglion, and (dg) dyad ganglion synapse (from Dowling & Boycott, *Proc. Roy. Soc.* (Lond.), © 1966, pp. 80–111. By permission of the Royal Society and the authors).

dendritic and axonal processes that look alike. They are excitatory and function in cooperation with horizontal cells to enhance pattern vision. *Amacrine cells* are laterally connected. One function is to modify intense responses by depolarization of the ganglion cells, inhibiting an energy overload or a signal of excessive duration.

Ganglion cells consolidate all the sensory information from the eyes for conduction via the optic nerve to the brain. They are specialized connector cells that form the outer layer of the retina. The axons of the other cell types (receptors, horizontals) synapse on ganglion cells. Red cones have a one-to-one connection to ganglion cells via many coordinating connections in the inner nuclear layers. Typically, many rod cell fibers combine in the inner nuclear layers and converge on a single ganglion cell. Ganglion cells are excitatory and operate by depolarization, that is, they send their messages by the familiar spiked pulses. The familiar sequence of sensory input to the brain has been repeated in the visual analyzer: reception and transduction in the sensors followed by conduction over neural cables to appropriate areas of the posterior cortex.

To summarize, the visual input system is activated by the light that falls on the rods and cones, changing light energy to neural impulses. These coded impulses are consolidated in the ganglion cells that form the outer layer of the retina. Axons from these ganglion cells bundle together to form the optic nerve, the major pathway for visual signals to the cortex. Other major pathways convey messages from the motor areas of the frontal lobes and the tertiary areas of the parietal lobe to control eye movements.

Neurology of Vision

Vision is the result of an intricate process that transforms the retinal image in the eye into a perception in the brain (Hubel, 1963). Ganglion cells respond selectively. Some of them are activated by changes in luminosity (the intensity of light) which is important in registering contrasts of dark and light, color definition, and object identification. Other ganglion cells respond to edges, lines, curves, and circles (the features of letters). An image is consolidated in the ganglion cells by the interaction of excitation in certain cells and inhibition of neighboring cells in the layers that feed the ganglia. Martin and Lovegrove (1984) reported that disabled readers are less sensitive than normal readers to letter-like contrasts when luminance is altered.

PATHWAYS TO THE OCCIPITAL LOBES

The principal pathway of the optic nerve is by way of the *optic chiasm* to the lateral geniculate body and from there to the occipital lobes (Fig. 8.7). Left and right visual fields are divided into nasal (near the nose) and temporal (near the temple) areas. Nasal fibers cross into the optic chiasma, while temporal fibers continue without crossing to the *lateral geniculate bodies*. These structures contain a receiving cell for each axon arriving from the retina. Layers 1 and 2 receive information from the rods, layers 3 and 5 receive information from cones on the opposite retina, and layers 4 and 6 receive information from the same side. Cells are organized into columns as well as layers. They interact to coordinate vision from the two eyes for specialized responses such as stereopsis, binocular fusion, and contour orientation (Berkley, 1984). All six layers join in the tracts to the visual cortex where the images from the two eyes are evaluated.

Secondary tracts lead through the optic chiasma to synapse in two *superior colliculi* and two *accessory nuclei*. The superior colliculus interconnects all areas of the cortex with the mesencephalic nuclei in the "old" brain, which is the principal mechanism in arousal. Visual input can thus alert the person to the need to attend. Also, the superior colliculus via its efferent fibers can energize the neural system for whatever response is needed. Input fibers to these bodies from the auditory and somatic systems seem to indicate the control of saccadic move-

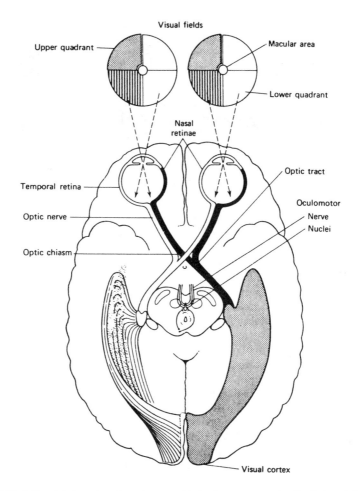

FIGURE 8.7. Major visual pathways. Light from upper half of visual field falls on the inferior half of the retina. Light from temporal half falls on nasal half of retina, while light from nasal half falls on temporal half of retina. Impulses travel through optic chiasma, lateral geniculate body, and optic radiations to reach visual cortex (from Truex & Carpenter, *Human Neuroanatomy*, 6th Ed. © 1969 The Williams and Wilkins C., Baltimore).

ments within the superior colliculus. The internal aspects of arousal and attention in learning to read have attracted the interest of reading researchers (Samuels & Miller, 1985). A modest level of arousal, neither so low as to produce sleepiness nor so high as to produce agitation, is most conducive to learning. The *accessory optic tracts* have connections to the hypothalamus and thalamus, which has direct relays to and from the visual cortex. The thalamic relay is believed to be important in the focus of attention to significant visual stimuli, following the arousal and orientation that is directed from lower centers.

RIGHT AND LEFT VISUAL FIELDS

Retinal stimulation from the right visual field (RVF) arrives in the visual cortex of the left hemisphere. By presenting visual images to one side of a screen at a time, the *visual half-field procedure,* the superiority of the left hemisphere for processing words has been demonstrated in 90% of right-handed people and 60% of left-handed individuals (Bryden, 1982). Word recognition is more accurate and faster in the RVF (relayed to the left hemisphere) than in the left visual field. Boles (1985) suggested the RVF superiority may be explained by the language dominance of the left hemisphere. In a lexical decision task, Chinese university students were asked to choose the real character that represented a word or a semantic category from a foil. The students showed superiority of the RVF on both tasks (Leong, Wong, Wong, & Hiscock, 1985). When asked to pick the real character from a set of mirror images, a grapheme decision, no laterality superiority was shown.

Visual field effects for processing function words, compared with content words, was investigated by Chiarello and Nuding (1987). Function words (where, also) were processed more slowly in the LVF, but content words were processed with similar accuracy (absence of errors) and latency (reaction time) in either hemisphere. The authors suggested that function words are less accessible to the right hemisphere because grammatical judgments presumably are processed in the left hemisphere. Many content words represent, and can produce, visual images. When imageable words were used in horizontal and vertical arrangements, Howell and Bryden (1987) found vertical word reading was not significantly different on left and right visual fields. The investigators concluded that word imageability has no visual-field differences. Some inconsistent results among investigators have lead to lively discussions and prolific research on the mode of word recognition.

In a series of experiments Bub and Lewine (1988) demonstrated that word length has profound (negative) effect on the recognition of words presented to the LVF, but a much weaker effect when presented to the RVF or to the fovea (center visual field). Vertical reading was found similar in both visual fields, but it required double the reaction times of horizontal reading, presumably because subjects were required to encode letter by letter, rather than by more efficient scanning of whole words. Left-handers, as a group, were less consistently lateralized than right-handed students. Some support was found for LVF strength in recognizing concrete, high-imageable words and greater strength of RVF in recognition of abstract, low-imageable words. The researchers suggest that the hemisphere specialization of visual word processing may occur short of cognitive processing of word meanings. The asymmetry of the visual fields shown by their data is consistent with models of lexical access to the two visual cortices. Analysis by sequential encoding of individual letters is accessed in the right visual cortex, while the multiple letters of whole words have direct intrahemispheric access to the left visual cortex. Beginning readers (and very poor readers) may be compelled to access visual memory on a letter-by-letter process, while adult proficient readers employ a direct process that maps whole-word representations.

VISUAL COMPONENTS OF READING

Humans are equipped by phylogeny with two systems which are basic to learning to read: (1) efficient visual perception at near-point and (2) the understanding of a spoken language. By the end of infancy, 18 months to 2 years old, normal children reared in a literate environment have acquired both of these prerequisites for reading, although there may be conceptual, social, and economic reasons for delaying their formal instruction. Reading is an ontogenic accomplishment, a complex skill to be learned by intervention through teaching. A child must learn to extract meaning from print or writing by bringing together a visual, two-dimensional code and the auditory, linear code of speech. This is not ordinary seeing.

Discrimination of Letter Information

A number of models have been proposed to reflect the different integration processes involved in word identification (Chapter 9). Typically, these information-processing models identify visual processes as input and semantic or lexical products as output (Seymour, 1986). In an abbreviated version of Johnson's model (1981) the visual components of print perception are (1) retinal stimulation, (2) feature detection and encoding, and (3) serial assembling of visual-perceptual pattern units. The first step includes the relay of undifferentiated visual signals from the retina by way of optic pathways to the central processing mechanisms. At the second step, encoding, the simple features of print (diagonals, curves, and straight lines) are fused into higher-order perceptual patterns combined from contiguities, intersections and other junctures. The third step, serial assembly, involves the ordering of subword clusters into units, words being the most likely perceptual unit. At this point the representation of a word would be a set of pattern assemblages conforming with the letters of the word; the simple features would have been lost. This visual assemblage would not, as yet, be integrated into cognitive or linguistic-level interpretations.

In Johnson's model a transition from "uninterpreted perceptual encoding" to "cognitive word-level representation" is a qualitative change, learned by association with the acoustic (oral word) memory storage. A direct interpretation of this model is that letter-by-letter processing, if it occurs in mature reading, is perceived automatically and in assembled patterns, and both processes occur prior to comprehension. Beginners may process letters differently, and they must learn to sequence the visual patterns within words according to the rules of the culture.

Although it is more productive for preschool children to be exposed to actual letter forms than simpler graphic representations, research often employs letter-like forms to reduce the effects of past learning. Gibson, Gibson, Pack, and Osser (1962) used 12 letter-like forms as standards and then varied them experimentally. One variation was to change a straight line to a curve, the feature distinction between V and U. Another change was a series of rotations from 45 to 180 degrees, as the transformation of W to M. The third variation was either to close or to break the figure, as when O becomes C. The final pattern change was

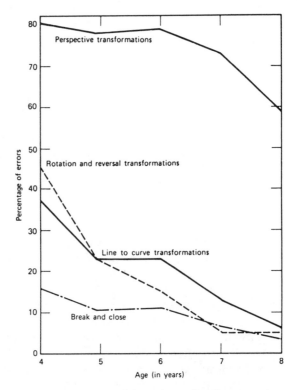

FIGURE 8.8. Transformations of three letter-like forms and perspective. Decrease in perceptual errors occurred with age (from Gibson, "Perceptual development." In Stevenson H. W., Kagan J., & Spiker C.C., (Eds.) *Child Psychology, The 62nd Yearbook of the National Society for the Study of Education.* University of Chicago Press, 1963).

called perspective transformation, when a figure was shown from different points of view (Fig. 8.8). The investigators found (1) 4-year-old children already discriminated the break and close transformations at a high level of accuracy, (2) Children improved markedly from age 4 to age 8 in rotation and reversal transformations, and (3) Children made similar improvements in line to curve transformations. Gibson speculates that these differences are related to the importance of similar discriminations in real life such as the distinction between open and covered objects. In typical school experience the child encounters many letter forms similar to those Gibson tested, hence it is not surprising that 8-year-olds make few errors on letter-like transformations. Perspective transformations are not needed for reading, nor for identification of objects in illustrations.

The relationship of visual perception and skill in learning to read was studied in Spanish children ages 4.5 to 9.5 years by Cordero (1986), whose age range was similar to Gibson's sample. The study found that the correlations between visual perception abilities and reading success were strong in the preschool and first grade, but became weaker as the children progressed to fourth grade. The results suggest that (1) By age 9 nearly all letters were recognized by poor as well as good readers, and (2) The effects of a poor start (because of lack of letter discrimination) would not be revealed as a factor by the measures taken at the later ages.

SIZE OF THE PERCEPTUAL UNIT

The *size of the unit* that is discriminated at the coding step has received much attention. The smallest unit for word recognition may be the distinctive features of a single letter, such as the two vertical lines, joined by a horizontal bar to make **H**, an important discrimination from N, as in Nell. Successive levels of unit size are the single letter, the letter clusters or digraphs (**ch**ip, enou**gh** and b**oy**), the syllables (se/man/tic), the affixes (**con**textual), and the root or morpheme (con-**textu**al). The largest units are the whole word, and the familiar phrase (come to, in love). One of our first graders said, "I remember **look** because it has two eyes in the middle." When two eyes in the middle also say **book** or **good**, the child must learn a heavier load of visual cues or learn the sound–letter associations.

The size of the unit used in recognizing words varies according to the skill of the reader, the reader's purpose, and prior knowledge of the material (LaBerge & Samuels, 1974). Beginning readers who are learning by synthetic rather than whole word methods attack words letter by letter until larger units, including whole words, are recognized automatically. Readers who are taught a sight vocabulary, followed by word analysis, use a variety of cues to remember the more complex patterns of the whole word. Letter-by-letter word recognition may be the dominant word attack strategy for some time while more varied cues are being learned.

Some children taught the "holistic" or sight word approach may concep-tualize the sound–letter system with very little direct instruction. Ehri (1988) studied the way young children learn to recognize words from the beginning. Kindergarten children were given a 40-word recognition test and grouped ac-cording to the number of words known: prereaders (0–1), novices (1–11), and veterans (11–36). Subjects were given practice with (a) words in simplified phonetic spelling and (b) words that achieved visual distinctiveness without letter-sound correspondence. Posttest results showed that novices and veterans learned to read the phonetic spellings more easily than the visual spellings, while the opposite was found in the prereaders, who learned visually distinctive words more easily. According to the author, the invented phonetic spellings did not inhibit the children's progress in learning to spell and read, who recommended consistent phonic systems for early writing.

Timko (1983) compared simultaneous presentation versus successive presen-tation of letter-pairs to kindergarten children. He was interested in whether their learning of confusable letters was enhanced more by a classical (contiguity) association strategy, or by an operant (reinforcement) association model. No significant differences were found between his groups in learning visual discrimi-nation of letters. Our own inclination would be to introduce confusable letters in different lessons, establishing multiple cues for one letter first, to avoid alternate choices of look-alike letters. After that the second letter might be introduced, using different multiple associations. If confusion remains, writing the letters (a features focus) might be tried.

WORD UNIT HYPOTHESES

Researchers remain divided about the ways mature, or independent, readers perceive print, whether by words, by length of focal span, or by morphemes (meaningful units). By experience and tradition, many investigators assume the word is the perceptual unit favored by readers. The tools for observing what people do with their eyes when they read are technically advanced, compared with Huey's eyecup and rolling drum. Cathode-ray cameras and computerized tachistoscopes now record the eye movement of adult readers. Automated latency measures compare the time requirement for different levels of processing in different individuals. Samuel, Van Santen, and Johnston (1982) reported that letters are seen more accurately under tachistoscopic viewing when they are part of a word. Single letter words, I and a, are recognized less well than the same letters when incorporated into words up to three and four letters.

The *word unit hypothesis* was tested by McConkie et al. (1982). Their view was that visual information is acquired in chunks of letters, consistent with the visual area of a single fixation. By this hypothesis, word identification during reading is facilitated as information about the next word is acquired in the peripheral vision during fixation. Sixteen college students served as subjects to determine whether peripheral facilitation was taking place during reading. Short text was read on a cathode-ray tube as the eye movements were monitored. The results indicated that words were read only when directly fixated, and that there was no facilitation from prior peripherally obtained information about the words. The word-unit hypothesis of print perception was supported in this study.

The *morpheme unit hypothesis* states that units such as prefixes, suffixes, and roots of words are processed more efficiently than letters or whole words. Visualized by its morphemic structure, de**sign**er is more directly processed, than seen initially as de/sig/ner. Taft (1985) found support for perception by morpheme as the preferred unit in word recognition. In a series of experiments Schvaneveldt and McDonald (1981) demonstrated that semantic context facilitates the encoding of words when related to the context. Haber and Schlinder (1981) found that adult readers were less likely to detect misspelling in function than in content words and were more likely to detect misspellings that changed the shape of a word. These studies imply that proficient readers give selective attention to visual information that contributes to meaning. Certainly the reader who focuses on structural analysis whenever appropriate has comprehension advantages over readers who use single letters or syllables consistently.

Visual Sequencing

Left-to-right ordering of words printed or written is a necessary approach to reading in English. The sequencing of words is necessary to match the syntax the child knows from having learned to speak in sentences. The correct ordering of graphemes within words is essential if access to the child's lexicon, the oral vocabulary, is to occur. The better the sequential match between visual and auditory forms of words, the more efficiently the comprehension of print is likely to be learned. The child develops the visual competence to perceive the spatial world, but must be taught the arbitrary ordering of printed language, which happens to left to right in English.

Directional preference refers to the tendency of individuals to scan in left-to-right or right-to-left order. In reviewing a series of studies, Nachshon (1985) reported the habits of English, Hebrew, and Arabic students when asked to reproduce visual symbols presented as single characters or in arrays; in directional or in nondirectional displays. English readers tended to produce the characters according to left-right directionality; Hebrew writers showed a right-left preference: and Arabic students showed stronger right-left preferences than Hebrew readers. It was hypothesized that these differences are due to differential reading and writing habits acquired in school. When experimental conditions were altered to elicit responses based on hemispheric asymmetry, substantial support was found for directionality in reading and writing, while subjects retained the effects of nature over nurture in the hemisphere organization of certain other behaviors.

In a study using bilingual subjects, Tramer, Butler, and Mewhort (1985) reported the role of the right hemisphere in scanning. Tachistoscopic presentations to left- or right-visual fields were made to adult readers. A RVF superiority was found for English characters, while the opposite, a LVF superiority was found for Hebrew characters. When English letters were used in a procedure that required scanning, there was a strong RVF superiority. When a spatial clue was given to bypass scanning, there were no visual-field differences. Together these studies show the versatility in readers to use both training and hemisphere specialization to perform new tasks.

Automated visual sequencing refers to the rapid processing of visual symbols in reading. Independent of language comprehension, rapid reading requires efficient blending of letters to create syllables, blending of syllables to create words, and ordering words correctly to create sentences. Pavlidis (1986) would also include the automated sequential movements of the eyes from one syllable or word to the next. Samuels and Kamil (1984) emphasized the importance of automaticity at the visual recognition level for a reader to maintain attention to meanings at the comprehension level. Jackson and McClelland (1981) showed that skilled college readers process visual information faster than less-skilled college students, even when the symbols are novel and the experiment utilizes nonlinguistic forms of visual encoding. Others have reported a "speed–accuracy tradeoff" in which the rapid reaction times of individuals may predict lowered accuracy (Wickelgren, 1977).

An important question for teachers and clinicians is whether repeated exposures to words, such as flash card drill, prolific reading, and rereading enhance the automatic recognition of whole words. In a study of relearning words and pictures, MacLeod (1988) selected items that had been "learned" on a short-term basis and "forgotten" after time periods of 1 to 10 weeks. He used a recall test to measure the *savings in relearning* by comparing items exposed originally and not recalled with control items. A relearning advantage held for *recall* of pictures, words, and word-picture cross-referent items. Relearning savings did not hold for *recognition* tests. The author suggested that relearning assists in the retrieval of information. Perhaps repeated visual experience has effects short of word recall, which patient teachers exploit in first-grade classrooms until automatic recall is learned.

The child who has participated in storybook reading, probably has learned to enter a book from its front cover and to proceed with the left-hand page, followed by the right-hand page. Fisher, Bornstein, and Gross, (1985) tested kindergarten and first-grade children of normal intelligence on left-to-right orientation, letter production, the *Gates–Macginitie Readiness Skills Test,* and a reading achievement test (*Iowa Basic Skills Primary Battery*). For testing visual orientation a delayed matching-to-sample, two-choice test was used. Unlike most readiness tests, these items provided the ceiling needed for this age group. The study found that orientation skills correlated with reading achievement at both grade levels, and with letter production in the kindergarten group. The investigators proposed training programs for different subgroups of reading-disabled children, with remediation based on such different deficiencies as immature spatial coding strategies or a neurologically based inability to distinguish left and right.

Preschool teachers who write descriptive comments on children's paintings, dictated by the young artists, are teaching the left-to-right orientation. Some kindergarten children need extended guidance to sequence to the right when writing their names. First-grade teachers may need to monitor certain children to assure that the writing is begun on the left margin. Children who do not learn left-to-right orientation with these kinds of guidance should be referred to a specialist who can determine the cause of the problem.

Isolation of Words in Text

Letters tell the reader the sequence of phonemes that make a word. When the child conceptualizes that particular words require an invariant membership and ordering of letters, attention to those letters is likely to occur. Berninger (1986) administered visual, linguistic, reading, and spelling tests to 45 children at the end of kindergarten and again at the end of the first grade. She was interested in the normal diversity of prereading abilities in children free from known pathologies. She found individual differences in three visual skills: selective attention to letter information, memory for a component letter, and memory for whole words. The measures were reliable over a year of formal instruction in reading; and they correlated with word decoding and encoding at both kindergarten and first-grade levels. Individual differences were found in two linguistic measures that were reliable and valid: phonemic analysis and vocabulary understanding. The investigator concluded that reading disabilities were not related solely to individual differences in language, but to visual differences as well.

Attention to letters, as opposed to attention to words, is a much discussed but unresolved issue. Having taught many children to read from the beginning, the authors are persuaded that children, in the beginning, approach words in the way they are taught. Most children have the capacity to learn a hundred or more words by sight, without being taught letter-by-letter analysis. A few children, 10% to 20% make very limited progress unless they are taught to attend to letters and the associated sounds. Some children discover the significance of letter–

sound relationships, without benefit of instruction, while most beginning readers do not. Children taught by synthetic methods—the local-to-global approach—gradually learn to recognize whole words at one fixation and to read a line of print with their eyes saccading in advance of their oral reading of the words.

Since the advent of *Sesame Street,* children almost universally know that letters make words and they know the boundary of words in sentences. Less is known about how words in context are processed visually. Brady (1981), among others, has confirmed that readers isolate words in text at the very beginning stages of reading. Some investigators have found evidence of letter migration from one word to another (Moser, 1983), suggesting visual perception of letters or letter clusters. Others have reported evidence of word recognition that is influenced by linguistic parameters or prior knowledge (Woodley, 1987). Some of these processes may involve access of the word image to the lexicon, which is stored and normally organized in the hemisphere of the input from the RVF. Beyond the understanding that printed words stand for speech, certain visual prereading skills are essential: (1) the ability to identify letters as parts within words, (2) the left-to-right orientation of English writing, and (3) the understanding of a relationship of whole words to sentences.

VISION AND READING DIFFICULTIES

The human eye is extraordinarily adaptive to the visual requirements of reading. Visual defects, such as those identified in the first section on the physiology of the eye, are compensated in the three-dimensional surround by input from other senses which is integrated in the brain. The distinction between seeing and perceiving is quite clear-cut in the case of M.B., a boy 10 years old, who was enrolled in the authors' summer reading clinic by his mother. M.B. was legally blind. Unreported to us he had some knowledge of Braille which he had learned at a boarding school for the blind. The mother was less than forthcoming about his school program and expressed the desire to have M.B. learn to read in the "normal" way. During the several weeks it took to clarify the situation, we learned the problem was primarily visual acuity and not print perception. M.B. was minimally retarded, not surprising in a child whose opportunities for visual learning were thus restricted. He loved reading and books. In our program, his material was retyped in large print on light green paper of dull texture, which he perused through thick lenses. His word attack was unusual. He spelled a word and then pronounced it, often without help from the instructor. Most surprising was his rapid progress in learning a sight vocabulary; his long-term memory for the words he identified so laboriously was quite remarkable. His problem appeared to be in the eyes and not in the central processing mechanism.

Visual perception irregularities are found in about 20% to 40% of a population of disabled readers, although some studies report percentages outside this range. Lack of consistent terminology and selection criteria make it difficult to evaluate research on the relationship of visual perception and reading disability. Vision-based causation may be described as visuoperceptual, visuomotor, visuospatial, or visuotemporal; this leaves the reviewer to question whether the groups being described are comparable. Another dilemma for the consumer of reading disability research is that frequently it compares "good" or "normal" readers with "poor readers," thus the differential diagnosis is lacking that would indicate whether or not there is a visual basis for the problem. If the experimental group includes subjects with language or perceptual-motor deficits, any visual effects that might be present are diluted or eliminated in group data. Despite these limitations, an extensive literature exists from which some well-measured and carefully reported studies cover three problem areas: (1) Are the erratic eye movements of poor readers the cause or the result of reading disability? Do practice exercises improve reading? (2) How do individual differences in the duration of a visual image affect reading? Does 20/20 vision mean perfect perception of words? (3) How does the brain coordinate the binocular information across the hemispheres? Do reversals in beginning writers spell p-a-n-i-c?

Eye Movement Control

Javal (1879) reported that during reading the eyes do not move continuously along a line of print but proceed through a sequence of short, rapid jumps (saccades), and pauses (fixations). The main visual function of the saccade is to bring word-letter images onto the fovea (Pavlidis, 1986). Information is taken into the retina during fixations, which account for about 87%-95% of total reading time (Tinker, 1958). Fixation time is limited somewhat by a reduction in acuity shortly before, during and shortly after a saccade to avoid smearing of the image (Volkman, 1976). Rhythmic eye movement patterns correlate highly with reading efficiency; therefore some experts use eye movement evaluations in the diagnosis of reading disability.

SACCADIC PATTERNS

Eye movements are photographed by capturing light reflection on the cornea. Current technology uses a videocamera, fitted with a sensor, to focus on the eye of the subject. A user-comfortable infrared light, directed on one eye of the subject, produces a corneal reflection. An electronic converter changes the corneal reflection to a digital representation of the pupil outline. A microcomputer produces a record of the subject's point of regard on a video display terminal, which shows continuous text in the amount of about half of this paragraph. A programmed computer then calibrates various factors, including head position, to produce a map of the reader's saccades, fixations, regressions, and return sweeps while reading the text.

Pavlidis (1981) analyzed the eye movement patterns of normal, backward, and dyslexic readers. He reported that most dyslexics show erratic eye movements which differ from control groups in several respects: (1) Dyslexics as a group are inferior in sequencing both lines of print and digits when compared with the control groups. (2) Backward readers show the normal staircase pattern of fixations when reading easy (recreation level) material, while dyslexics show the same erratic patterns in both easy and difficult material. (3) Normal readers do not show erratic patterns when the material is increased from easy to frustration levels; they merely read slower. (4) Sequencing is a problem for dyslexics independent of the sensory mode, whether auditory, visual, or cross-modal.

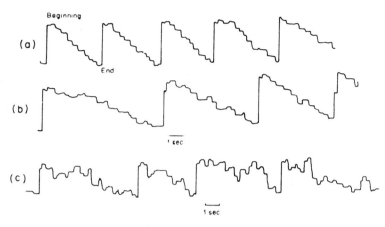

FIGURE 8.9. *Eye movement patterns. Horizontal lines represent fixations. Vertical lines represent movements, or saccads. (a) Record of a normal reader showing successive movements and fixations which form a staircase pattern. Inverted steps represent regressions, which are infrequent and normal. (b) Record of a retarded reader, who makes more forward and regressive movements than a normal reader. (c) Erratic movements of a dyslexic. Regressions are frequent, sometimes clustered, and of greater than normal magnitude (from G. Th. Pavlidis in Dyslexia: Its Neuropsychology & Treatment, p. 99, © 1986, Wiley).*

Pavlidis cited three possible interpretations for his results, suggesting that erratic eye movements may be caused by poor oculomotor control, or a deficit in sequential ordering, or faulty feedback between them. He concluded that the erratic eye movements shown by many poor readers are a symptom of a more profound disability and not the result of poor reading.

Some success has been reported in differentiating language-based and vision-based reading disability through the use of eye movement patterns. Rayner (1986a) compared the patterns of three adults: (a) a proficient reader with (b) an adult dyslexic who showed a language deficiency (a discrepancy in favor of Performance Scale over the Verbal Scale IQ scores on the WAIS); and (c) an adult dyslexic whose IQ was similar to B's but having Performance and Verbal Scales that did not differ significantly. Subject A showed the normal staircase pattern (Fig. 8.9), with typical regression and return sweeps. Subject B showed what Rayner called "a partial staircase pattern," in which the steps are interrupted by numerous regressions backward over material in an effort to identify unknown words from context. Subject C showed a number of "reverse staircase patterns," in which there are clusters of right-to-left saccades. Subject C was described as having a visual-spatial processing deficit. Rayner presented evidence that the eye movement patterns of subjects such as B, who have language-processing disability, are similar to immature readers at a similar level of competence. The pattern is different for subjects with a visual-spatial processing disorder. They show a higher percentage of return sweep inaccuracies and more numerous right-left reversals.

Some recent investigators have not agreed with the Pavlidis's conclusions that erratic eye movement patterns and reading disability are symptoms of a more profound disability. Rayner (1986b) supported the hypothesis in an analysis of five studies, all completed in the 1980s. He speculated that the investigators showed inconsistent results because each had drawn from populations who differed initially because of the selection procedure. Different professionals, whose specializations differ, are likely to attract clients whose characteristics are weighted toward the investigator's specialization and do not comprise a random population, even of reading-disabled clients. Such populations are likely to vary in group characteristics.

Aware of the problem of different types of reading disability, Pirozzolo (1983) separated his dyslexic subjects into "language deficient" and "visual-spatial deficient" and compared both subgroups with normal readers. The most striking result was that even normal readers, as a group, did not show the efficient staircase pattern that is seen in many textbook examples; but made regressions and return sweep inaccuracies of the kind poor readers are expected to make. However, normal readers were more versatile than either of the dyslexic groups in adapting their eye movements—the fixations and durations—to changes in the difficulty of the material. Both visual-based and language-based disability groups showed more regressions than normals, particularly when reading easy materials. Visual-spatial dyslexics showed significantly more inaccuracies on the return sweep than did the other groups. This attempt to subgroup problem readers is a step toward more consistent research results in future studies. One question arises in interpreting this work: whether a Performance Scale-Verbal Scale discrepancy of 10 IQ points is an adequate indicator of a visual-based disability, especially in the absence of other confirming observations.

ISSUE OF PRACTICE EXERCISES

The evidence has accumulated that poor readers show erratic eye movement patterns when reading instructional level material. Practice exercises to improve eye movement patterns by improving the child's ocular motility have been attempted (Goldberg, Shiffman, & Bender, 1983). The investigators examined the eye movement patterns of 50 reading-disabled children and a matched number of controls, using an electronystagmograph. This machine compares changes in the electrical potential of the eye during ocular movements. The study revealed decreasing eye movement rhythmicity with increased difficulty in reading materials (4th-to-12th-grade readability levels). A follow-up experiment demonstrated immediate improvement in eye movement patterns on the part of one student who first showed the myograph tracings of a "disabled reader." By teaching him the unknown words of a selection, prior to reading his eye movement patterns became normal. The authors concluded that no direct improvement in reading may be anticipated from eye exercises; that ocular movements are controlled by the brain and not by the eyes. They conceded that a program of simultaneous tutoring and training may result in improvement through a combination of reading-skill development, relaxation during reading, and positive reinforcement. Metzger and Werner (1984) also concluded from a review of the research in ophthalmology, optometry, and psychology that no evidence has been found to support a relationship between visual training and the remediation of reading disabilities.

Image Persistence

Iconic persistence is the sensory after-effect which follows short exposures of the eyes to light. In reading it is the brief internal representation of visual words no longer present in a fixation. Researchers measure persistence as the time interval between the flash of one visual pattern and the subject's ability to see the next stimulus. The neural mechanism must recover from one activation in order to register the presence of the next exposure. Individual differences in the persistence of the iconic image have been found to affect the reading process significantly.

VARIABILITY IN HUMANS

Høien (1982) established a norm for iconic persistence in normal reading subjects. He projected two letters in sequence, each one for 20 msec; then the interval between the exposures was increased until the second letter could be identified, a measure of the recovery time required for the neural mechanism to begin processing the second signal. A comparison of this norm with the average interval for each dyslexic subject enabled him to identify groups of brief and prolonged persisters. Those having time scores within two standard deviations from the mean were the moderate persisters. At one end of the curve ($-2SD$) were those with short persistence scores (10% of the sample) and at the other extreme ($+2SD$) were those with iconic persistence that was longer than normal (40%). Half (50%) of the disabled readers were within criterion range on this characteristic. The three groups were compared with a control group of normal readers. Letters were presented tachistoscopically under different experimental conditions, using a mask to vary the conditions. Short imagers required less time to overcome the mask than moderates or normals, while persistent imagers required significantly longer recovery times before perceiving the stimulus letter. When the masking occurred between letters, moderates were similar to controls on mean values, but their variance was greater. Long persisters had the highest values (required the most recovery time), which was about twice as long as the short persisters. When letter contour contrasts were reduced, the subjects with iconic persistence of long duration separated even farther from the comparison groups in visual recognition tasks. A lengthy recovery time, following word viewing, is certain to slow the reader and result in unfavorable comparisons with normal readers.

INSTRUCTIONAL ADAPTIONS

Høien (1982) discussed the implications of a lengthy iconic persistence. Synthetic methods (putting letters together to make words) demands rapid identification of parts and produces interference from one letter to the next. A more rewarding approach for this group would be the word/picture (analytic) method in which whole words could be processed with no greater interference than single letters. Since bright light increases persistence, seating away from the windows is suggested for students with prolonged iconic imagery. Since contrast increases persistence, gray on gray increases legibility for them. For the unusually brief imagers the synthetic (sounding) method is recommended. This study did not include reading achievement as a variable, which the investigator cites as research that is still needed. Levels of the neurotransmitter *acetylcolinestrase* in the blood may be related to the latency of the visual image, which future researchers will want to determine.

Slow reading has become the hallmark of disabled readers, many of whom never recover completely from their early struggles with word recognition. The education system can become much better than it is at finding poor readers early and providing them with a sustained program directed toward their particular disability. One of the adaptations that schools could make is the acceptance of slower reading, particularly for science content, in favor of *quality reading*. Our interviews with former reading-disabled students suggests some self-selection on their part of math and science courses over literature or social science.

Information Across Eye Fixations

Binocular vision is the perceptual result of a comparison and/or combination of light signals from the two eyes. When a person reads, binocular vision performs at least three important functions: the near-point convergence required for clear focus, the sequential ordering of the visual patterns of words, and the rhythmic control of saccadic eye movements. Unless the two eyes work together, the iconic traces from one eye may not fuse with the cortical image of the other. Information from the weaker eye may be suppressed by the dominant eye, or the eyes may take turns in processing the visual images. It is deceptively simple to interpret vision in reading as two-dimensional because the alphabet is mapped that way. Sequencing did not emerge as a problem for psychological investigation until recently because of evidence that words and sentences were already ordered by the temporal sequencing of speech. The left lobe was assumed to hold the schemata for concepts of time, including the temporal ordering of language. Binocular vision is now believed to be the mechanism for visual sequencing. Skill in visual sequencing may be one of the important differences between beginners and proficient readers.

DEVELOPMENT OF BINOCULAR VISION

Two-dimensional, spatial mapping is present at birth and visual experience is not necessary for the elaboration of the axons and dendrites that process visual information at this level. Complex binocular vision, on the other hand, has been found to be strongly influenced by experience during critical periods in development. A subset of cells having slightly different locations on the two retinas, have axonal connections to the same binocular cells in the visual cortex (Barlow, Blakemore, & Pettigrew, 1967). It is the function of these cells to compare the images from the two eyes and to make perceptual interpretations such as identifying an object from its visual features, or identifying a word from its contours. Current hypotheses of the complex binocular processes that humans use in word reading comes from animal studies of the development of binocular vision, from grouped-case studies of children of different ages whose visual disabilities have been corrected, and from psychophysics.

Tracking and Contour Selection

Tracking, or *directional movement selectivity,* is the ability to follow a moving object across the visual field. In preliterate *Homo sapiens* the distant tracking of game or of an enemy was as likely to be in a right-to-left direction as left-to-right. This survival mechanism seems to be the substrate for eye movements in reading and the direction they sweep must be learned according to the rules of a particular culture. Since the neural structures for binocular vision are not functioning at birth, large numbers of cells in the visual cortex must become responsive to information from both eyes by environmental stimulation and growth. When young mammals, usually kittens or primates, are deprived of normal visual experience, the gross capability of tracking develops, but the finely tuned abilities of selectivity in directional movement and of visuomotor coordination are faulty (Berkley, 1984). Activation of many cells is needed for normal binocular tracking.

Complex *contour vision* refers to the capacity to recognize objects and thus form a coherent and meaningful visual representation. Contour perception is the ontogenitically acquired mechanism by which words and letters are discriminated (Berkley, 1984). Research on the binocular contributions to contour perception is difficult to perform and even more difficult to interpret. When the vision from one eye (monocular vision) is manipulated by experimentally depriving the other eye, *binocular competition* may take over control and "capture" neuronal growth destined for the deprived eye. Another effect of contrived deprivation is that the functioning eye may suppress the cortical growth and perceptual activities of the deprived eye. The combined effects of suppression and competition are difficult to separate experimentally. Experts believe that both competitive and suppressive mechanisms may be operating in binocular contour vision.

Temporal Vision and Sequencing

In accounting for the developmental differences between the two-dimensional spatial mapping, which appears with maturation by a genetic program, and the more complex binocular functions that require environmental stimulation, two visual systems have been discovered in mammals (Berkley, 1984). A subsystem of x-cells, which mature by phylogenic programming, respond to spatial targets and analyze spatial contrast. A different subsystem of y-cells is concerned with temporal components of vision, such as flicker and movement. Y-cell functions are more complex and require nature–nurture interaction for development. Both systems have independent pathways which arise in the retina and remain essentially independent until they reach the visual cortex. Monocular deprivation

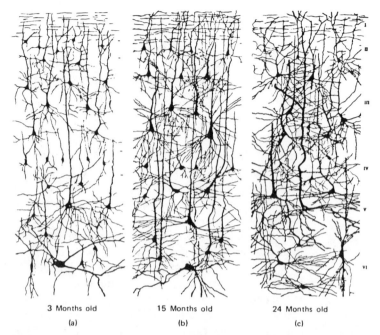

3 Months old   15 Months old   24 Months old

(a)   (b)   (c)

FIGURE 8.10. *Visual cortex of infants. Arborization of neurons at (a) 3 months, (b) 15 months, and (c) 24 months old (selected from Conel, (a) 1947; (b) 1955; and (c) 1959. By permission of Harvard University Press).*

appears to disrupt the development of y-cell pathways, while having little effect on the x-cell subsystem.

Periods of sensitivity are bounded by the time at which a mechanism begins to respond to particular stimuli and ends at the time the system is no longer responsive to environmental stimulation for growth. Complex binocular vision develops postnatally and is strongly influenced by visual experience during critical periods of infancy and early childhood (Fig. 8.10). Studies of experimentally deprived animals have established a critical period during which environmental stimulation is required for the development of generalized binocular acuity. Neurobiologists have projected the critical period for directional tracking and visual representation from the kitten (3–4 months) to the child (5–8 years). Periods of sensitivity are determined by introducing deprivation at various ages. The neurological abnormalities resulting from the deprivation are found primarily in the visual cortex, to some extent in the lateral geniculate nucleus, but not appreciably in the eye.

Infants who experienced abnormal binocular input (uncorrected stabismus, monocular occlusion, or large differences in optical properties between the eyes) have been diagnosed as deficient in binocular vision (Spear & Tong, 1980). The period of sensitivity for normal development of binocular vision in humans has been investigated by following the recovery of children following corrective surgery for strabismus (Banks, Aslin, & Letson, 1975). In these cases the two eyes have been relaying different sets of signals to the brain since birth and correction means the proper alignment of the eyes for the first time. The degree of interocular transfer following correction for strabismus falls off rapidly from age 2 to 6 years and levels off by age of 8. The critical period for contrast sensitivity appears to be shorter than the time frame for binocular vision in general. These are complex perceptual abilities which are dependent on experience during early childhood, abilities which the school reading program takes for granted in its beginning pupils.

LATERALIZATION AND EARLY INSTRUCTION

Laterality is the ability to differentiate left and right. It is seen behaviorally in the ability to distinguish left-right body images, asymmetrical objects presented in mirror image, and letters or words that have reverse counterparts, such as d and b. A relationship exists between left-right confusion, cerebral lateralization, and severe forms of reading disability (Belmont & Birch, 1965). It is important to remember, however, that many disabled readers show normal development of left-right differentiation, and many accomplished readers exhibit atypical brain lateralization. Because of maturational lag or lack of experience with written language some children enter the first grade without having acquired the binocular processing skills that more typical preschoolers have achieved automatically. Lateral confusion usually improves markedly during the first year of reading and writing instruction. The section which follows explains how some individuals may perceive visual symbols in reverse and suggests some established practices to prevent the problem from turning into a reading disability.

Reversals of Letters and Words

Reversals of single letters, of words within sentences, or of entire passages are all symptoms of a deeper problem in visual perception. *Mirror image reading* and writing are examples of full text reversals. Kindergarten and first-grade teachers expect to observe some reversal tendencies in a few of their beginning pupils. Clinicians expect to find reversals in a small percentage of their disabled readers. Some adult dyslexics may show reversals so subtle they are missed, such as the reversal of a middle syllable in a multisyllable word. Specialists who treat eyes often receive patients who believe their tendency to "plug in backwards" is caused by abnormal vision and can be corrected by lenses. Many laypersons, including some in the media, think of reversal tendencies as synonymous with dyslexia. It is more accurate to think of reversals and mirror image perception as symptomatic of one form of visual dyslexia, and the reversals of most beginning readers as a sign they have not yet learned to approach printed English consistently from left to right. The processes by which the brain reverses and reorders print bilaterally (across the commissures of left and right hemispheres) is interesting and important in understanding all reading.

RH to LH Visual Transfer

Bilateral asymmetry is not a problem when viewing large or distant objects; but words must been seen at near-point vision when reading a book and words are not symmetrical. The fusion system of the two eyes tolerates a 5-degree inaccuracy for ordinary stereopsis; but only ¼ degree is tolerated in fusing the images of fine print. In the early stages of learning to read the visual system normally transfers a retinotopic pattern of words and letters from the right to the left hemisphere (via the commissures) where LH can decide what they mean. As the child learns to read well, LH teaches RH some knowledge of shapes of letters and words; at which stage the signals of some sight words may no longer need to be retinotopically organized.

According to Stein and Fowler (1982), the positioning of the eyes is important in avoiding a confused image, and the information to the left hemisphere about the position of the eyes at fixation is necessary for the perceptual system to compensate for mirror-image effects during commissural transfer. They proposed a model to show the pathways of binocular perception. Normally, the image of a word is received in the right visual field of both eyes. (Recall that 11 or 12 letters are viewed to the right and only 3 or 4 to the left of fixation.) The image is transferred across the optic chiasm and received in the left hemisphere, where the word bank is located and grapheme–phoneme associations are made. A right-eye dominant person who is LH-dominant for language is likely to learn to process print without difficulties arising from binocular perception.

When print is viewed in the LVF, the hemispheric transfer from both eyes arrives in reverse form to the right visual cortex, but homotopic connections across the hemispheres are believed to compensate during cross-hemisphere transfer by reversing the mirror image from RH (Fig. 8.11A); thus both images of **d** arrive in the right visual cortex as **b** and are corrected to the original orientation, perhaps by homotopic commissural relays to the angular gyrus. It *receives* messages from the occipital visual areas and from the eye movement control centers in the superior colliculus. The angular gyrus *projects* to motor control centers in the frontal eye fields, to the cerebellum and also to Wernicke's (speech interpretation) area in the temporal lobe. One function of the angular gyrus is to bring together signals from the two retinae and registration of eye position from eye movement control centers. Interhemispheric transfer is potentially confusing and the real-life interpretations of words must be established in the mechanisms for bilateral perception. As Stein and Fowler propose, the parietal lobe receives signals about eye movements in the opposite half of a visual space. When the eye moves to the right, signals about eye position are relayed to control centers in LH, while retinotopic signals remain in RH. In this undesired condition, a letter appearing in the left visual field would be projected to the right hemisphere, where the letter could be seen but could not be interpreted, nor its position known because that information resides in the left hemisphere (Fig. 8.11B). The authors consider *eye position control* to be critical in beginning reading. In normal fixations most of the visual field is to the left. For children with reversal problems, Stein and Fowler recommend that written material always be viewed in the right-half field and thus presented to the left hemisphere until eye position control has been established. When reading becomes proficient, the potential for confusion is avoided because precise knowledge of eye position is known to LH and the mirror effect is automatically compensated. When a young child persists in copying letters in reverse, the teacher is cued that the directional dictates of English have not been learned.

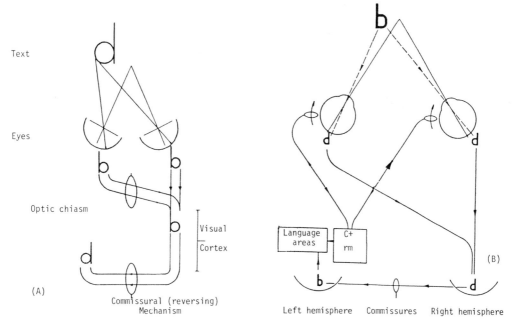

Text

Eyes

Optic chiasm

Visual
Cortex

(A)

Commissural (reversing)
Mechanism

Language
areas

C+
rm

(B)

Left hemisphere   Commissures   Right hemisphere

FIGURE 8.11. Interhemispheric transfer of **b** and **d** in two potentially confusing conditions. (a) Image of "d," seen in RH as "b," may be compensated (corrected) on arrival in LH by homotropic commisural connections. Eye position must be known to LH if mirror image confusion is to be avoided. (b) Movement of eyes pointing to right is registered in LH. Retinal signals from LVF are registered in RH. Visual signal cannot be read; knowledge of position and word knowledge remains in LH (from Stein & Fowler, pp. 51–52. In Y. Zotterman (Ed.), *Dyslexia: Neuronal, Cognitive, and Linguistic Aspects.* © 1982, Pergamon Press).

Eye Dominance and Monocular Occlusion

Monocular preference is the tendency of one eye to be dominant for sighting. The typical person is right dominant for sighting, listening, and walking with major controls in the left hemisphere. *Crossed dominance* is a condition in which left and right preference is mixed. In disabled readers the incidence of crossed eyedness and handedness is much more common than in the general population. The stronger eye is usually dominant, but for a few individuals the weak eye is dominant. Monocular preference is established in early infancy, and perhaps before birth. Goldberg, Shiffman, and Bender (1983) are among those who hold the view that right-hand preference is usually associated with left cerebral dominance. They do not accept the view that lateral dominance or poorly defined laterality are related to reading disorders.

A different view is held by Stein and Fowler (1985), who found unfixed dominance in approximately 60% of their "visual dyslexics," and in only 1 of 80 normal reading subjects. They used the Dunlop (1972) test to look for "disordered fixation during convergence," "failure of hemisphere dominance," and "unstable eye position." By occluding (patching) the left eye, they assured that visual input would be right-eyed and the major input would be to the left hemisphere, where language meanings are assumed to be stored. Their disabled readers, thus treated, gained 13 months in reading progress during the 6 months of the experiment, while nonoccluded dyslexic controls gained 4 months. The results were criticized on the basis that the patches children wore labeled them as experimental; therefore they may have received special help from teachers that nonidentified children did not. The study was repeated, using a larger sample, a more restricted definition of the visual anomaly, and a double-blind design during treatment. All visual dyslexic subjects were fitted with glasses, half of them randomly selected for occluded left lenses and half with untreated lenses. After a 6-month treatment period, 51% of the children who wore occluded lenses had converted to fixed-reference vision, compared with 24% of the group who wore untreated lenses. The treated group advanced 6 months in reading achievement, while the untreated group regressed by 0.4 months. According to the authors, the children who received occlusion treatment but did not improve were found to have both phonic and sequencing errors. The authors caution that lack of fine binocular control is not the only cause of dyslexic's problems. The use of monocular occlusion to correct immature binocular control appears have been successful when the subjects were appropriately selected for poor vergence control, uncomplicated by language-based dyslexia or other symptoms.

Computer-assisted Instruction

The use of microcomputers for visually impaired preschool children has been successful in teaching them to identify letters and digits and to discriminate prepositions (Rettig, Shaklett, & Wyrsch, 1987). Of particular interest to clinicians was that eye tracking was taught by this device. Cassady (1985) reported the improvement of a boy who was both vision- and language-disabled. During a 6-week summer session using a computer, his visual memory of letter sequences improved. He learned to write. His renewed confidence resulted in improved peer relationships. Research is needed on the relative effectiveness of different types of programs for subgroups of reading-disabled children. When poor letter sequencing or letter reversal is a problem, the precise control of text and the immediate feedback make the microcomputer a valuable learning instrument.

PROCESSING CONTEXTUAL PRINT

The ease of reading, and to some extent the rate of reading, is related to the legibility of the print and the design of the format. Some typefaces and some colors are easier to read then others. Newspaper publishers spend millions of dollars to change typefaces in order to increase the ease with which the paper can be read, even though the differences in the typefaces are all but unobservable to the casual reader. Extensive study has been directed at analyzing the comparative difficulty of different typefaces and other visibility options for readers. Books for children in the primary grades are usually set in sizes not deemed necessary or desirable for adult readers.

Rate of Reading

Almost everyone wants to read rapidly in order to obtain more information in the time available. Some commercials promise rates of 1,000 or more words per minute (wpm) without loss in comprehension. Students, managers, and administrators are attracted by the notion that they can accomplish their reading tasks in one-fourth the time they now spend in order to have the three-fourths time for more pleasurable pursuits. There are superreaders, who have learned to read at enviable rates, without benefit of special training in speed reading. Fortunately a considerable amount of researcher's attention has been focused on rate of reading with comprehension.

SUPERREADERS

Rapid reading is a facile interaction between visually processed print and the activation of existing linguistic knowledge. One way to study extraordinary reading rates is to observe the characteristics of naturally fast readers. Masson (1985) reviewed the research to describe the differences between superreaders and typical, or less skilled, readers. First, fast readers make fewer fixations and gain more information from each fixation than average readers, indicating that the *visual span of perception* is greater.

Second, fast readers as a group appear to have *greater speed of access to memory codes* than slow readers. This finding holds when the element of practice is negated by testing visual patterns that are unique to all the subjects. When subjects are asked to match a novel visual pattern to a three-letter name, rapid readers again have a natural advantage. Rapid recognition of stored visual patterns is assumed to be a causal factor in rapid reading of sentences. However, comparisons which combined rapid-word recognition and text comprehension have not been conclusive, perhaps because the correlations between rate of free reading and comprehending are low and unreliable.

Third, fast accurate readers can hold greater numbers of propositions (meaning units) in working memory while integrating them with the words being processed. The *greater span of the working memory* is seen in strong correlations between the number of sentences comprehended while holding test-significant information in the working memory (Daneman & Carpenter, 1980). Findings which come from text processing and include measures of comprehension are persuasive evidence that superior readers are especially efficient at coordinating storage and process functions.

Fourth, reading comprehension is significantly correlated with the comprehension of oral language during listening. This *general language comprehension ability* shows up as more rapid integration of words into phrase units on the part of rapid readers when adults are divided on the basis of reading rate. However, slower readers do as well in the integration of higher order language processes. Graesser, et al. (1980) found their fast and slow readers did not differ on *macrostructure* variables, processes which interrelate sentences and organize the passage as a whole. On *microstructure* variables (number of words, syntactic complexity, and number of propositions within a sentence) slow readers took significantly longer to execute the analyses than fast readers did. Fast and slow readers were equally adept at macrostructure operations that required the integration of information from multiple sentence text. Masson (1985) pointed out a speed–accuracy tradeoff. When the study defines groups of readers on the basis of both accuracy of comprehension and reading rate, the characterization changes. Fast readers who comprehend accurately are distinguished (from other fast readers) by their focus on the macrostructure. Slow comprehenders focus their processing on the microstructure level. Rapid reading alone does not make a super reader if comprehensive interpretation is a criterion.

SKIMMING, SCANNING, AND SPEED READING

Skimming is defined as a skill by which the reader moves rapidly through text to locate particular information or to gain the gist of a selection. Readers whose previous information or world knowledge is comparable to the text may skim to locate potentially new information that may be contained there. Former President John F. Kennedy may have accomplished his famous reading of three newspapers each morning by skimming the second or third accounts of an event. A student, writing a term paper, skims to locate a particular discussion, then reads in detail for clarification or confirmation of an idea to be developed. Elementary schoolchildren are taught skimming skills by proving their answer: "Find the place where—." When interrupted unexpectedly, most readers must skim to relocate their place in the text.

Scanning is the visual pursuit along lines of print to locate a particular letter or feature of print. Researchers employ scanning when they ask subjects to "count all the t's," for example. Tramer et al. (1985) found equal but opposite visual field advantages in English and Hebrew readers on a scanning task. Some editors become so efficient at spotting a misspelling or a misprint that they can find them by scanning. The readers of this book may locate the definition of a term more quickly if they have noted the italics that usually identifies a concept when first introduced. The distinction between scanning and skimming is not always clear as the examples suggest, but both are skills which readers acquire because of the limitations of the visual and perceptual systems for processing print.

Perceptual Limitations

Reports by researchers have revealed the number of letters a reader can take in during one fixation and the kinds of perceptual maneuvers they perform to read without processing each letter. Visual acuity is best at the fovea, which extends as much as 2 degrees (of a circle) on either side of the macula. The *parafovea,* which surrounds the fovea, extends perhaps several degrees farther and is less acute. Beyond these areas is the *periphery,* which has a limited function in reading fixations. A perceptual span of 4 letter positions to the left and 12 to the right of fixation has been observed in proficient reading by adults during eye movement studies (Taylor, 1981). Such a span of 16 letter positions involves the use of peripheral vision, which is limited to seeing gross characteristics of words, such as configuration, initial or final letters and spaces. From the duration of fixations it appears that experienced readers look at long words, which are usually content words, to distinguish the shorter function words. *Processing units,* the text included in a forward fixation, vary with the purpose of the reader and the difficulty of the material. Latency, the time for processing a unit, increases with irregular spelling, as when reading **colour** when the reader's expectation is color. Underwood and McConkie (1985) showed that readers fail to detect letter substitutions within words when they appeared more than three letter positions to the left of the fixated letter, or more than seven to the right.

Evidence of phrase span reading, taking in a phrase unit in a single fixation, has been reported in subjects as young as 7 (Taylor, 1981). In a series of experiments, Rayner (1986a) studied the perceptual span of schoolchildren in the second, fourth, and sixth grades. Beginning readers used a slightly narrower perceptual span (11 letter spaces) compared with adult subjects (14 to 15 letter spaces). Children devoted more time to foveally fixated words than experienced readers. Rayner concluded that the size of the perceptual span is not the cause of beginner's slow reading rates. Rayner presented his stimulus words in a moving window, which may account for greater letter spans in adults than some investigators have found, a methodology that may have affected the children's scores as well. In addition to limitations in the visual span of readers, there are limitations to the rate of processing printed words in the brain.

Temporal Constraints

The eyes can execute a series of controlled saccads across print at about 250 msec each (Tinker, 1958), an average of less than two words can be recognized at a single fixation, and the lexical accessing with full comprehension requires about 239 msec for extended technical passages (Just & Carpenter, 1980). Calculating from these constraints Masson (1985) has estimated that the maximal rate of reading could be 800–900 words per minute and reading rate beyond that would involve skipping many of the printed words. The major constraints would appear to be on the time needed for accessing and organizing meanings, rather than on the time needed for visual recognition. Speeded text presentation has resulted in reduced memory of the material. Some training for increased rate has resulted in reduced comprehension. The rate of speech comprehension is correlated with the rate of reading comprehension, but exercises to increase the listening rate by using compressed speech have failed to make enduring changes in rate of reading with comprehension.

Proponents of *speed reading* claim to teach new skills that will enable ordinary readers to comprehend in excess of 1,000 words per minute (wpm). Just, Carpenter, and Masson (1982) compared a group of college students who had recently completed a speed reading class with a group who were instructed to read fast (identified as skimmers), and another group who were instructed to "read normally." Extended texts were used: a selection from *Reader's Digest* and excerpts from *Scientific American*. Results showed that normal readers read on the average of 240 wpm, speed readers at 700 wpm, and skimmers at 600 wpm. Part of the difference in reading rate occurred because normal readers used a fixation gaze of 330 msec, compared with the speed readers 233 msec and the skimmers 221 msec. The normal readers fixated 64% of the words, while speed readers fixated 33% and the skimmers 40%. Although speed readers sampled the text more uniformly than untrained skimmers, the normal readers were more selective in fixating on content and important words than were either of the rapid reading groups. The results of comprehension tests of normal readers, speed readers, and skimmers showed a consistent advantage for normal readers. The only advantage to speed readers appeared when comprehension questions were on the easier narrative material as opposed to difficult, technical material and when the questions were categorized as general rather than factual. The speed readers did not use an exotic scanning strategy, nor did they show a wider perceptual span. Their advantage was primarily conceptual, they increased their study skill for prereading and learned better inference strategies for combining existing knowledge and text. When reading difficult material for new information the tradeoff for rapid reading is lowered comprehension.

Chapter Summary

The visual features of words are captured by light-sensitive cells in the retinas where rods and cones perform two functions: *photoreceptors* absorb photons and use their energy to activate a series of chemical exchanges; *transducers* convert photic energy into the electrochemical code of the neural system. The topological pattern of excitation and inhibition in the cells of the retina resembles the real-world image, except that it is registered in reversed and inverted order, like the image behind the lens of a camera. The topology is preserved, through synaptic junctions in the midbrain, until arrival at reception centers in the visual cortex. Poor visual acuity is rarely the cause of poor reading, but clear vision adds to the comfort and rate of reading. Research on *iconic persistence* has revealed individual differences which serve as a warning that diagnosis is urgently needed in treating reading disability and in selecting subjects for research. Binocular skills, such as mapping, are present early in life, having developed by genetic programs, while the more finely tuned binocular abilities require experience at critical periods for their ultimate development. Most people can improve the speed with which they read with comprehension, although some of the claims to develop reading rates of several thousand words per minute seem questionable on physiological grounds. Skimming and scanning have valid functions for readers, but the tradeoff is reduced comprehension and increased reliance on prior knowledge.

9 Integration of Sensory Systems

No single sensory system functions in isolation. Visual and auditory systems, which are activated during reading, have been explained separately in order to clarify their unique functions during communication (Chapters 7 and 8). Sensory input must be integrated in the central nervous system to generate perceptual ideation (representation) and to initiate the appropriate motor responses. Learning to read the first language is superimposed on a linguistic system already in place as speech. Auditory functions in reading are well documented and widely accepted. Less understood is the integration of somatic, or bodily, senses in learning to read and in comprehending print.

Most of the research on reading has emphasized the visual or auditory modalities rather than the body senses, such as the somatic, vestibular, kinesthetic, and tactile analyzers. Each of these systems is as independent of the other as are the visual and auditory systems; however, much of the literature on reading treats the deep senses together as one. These discussions may appear under the rubric of *somatic* or *haptic* sensory systems. Some instructional approaches, such as the *kinesthetic method* of Grace Fernald (1943) focused on the simultaneous use of multisensory input and output. The effectiveness of the Fernald approach for severely disabled readers probably is due, in part, to the feedback the learner gets from his or her own sensorimotor responses. This feedback becomes integrated sensory input, which provides new sensorimotor data that are reinforced. In this chapter the integrative processes of reading are treated in three parts: (1) The sequential ordering of the symbolic communication through the input, mediation, and output systems; (2) The different theoretical explanations for how printed words gain access to the word bank, or lexicon; and (3) The failure of some aspect of integration in reading disability, or dyslexia.

SEQUENCING THROUGH NEURONAL ORGANIZATION

Like the central nervous system (CNS) with its division of receptor, connector, and effector neurons, the integration of the sensory systems can be considered as

TABLE 9.1. Flow of Neural Activity in Communication

Flow of Neural Activity in Communication

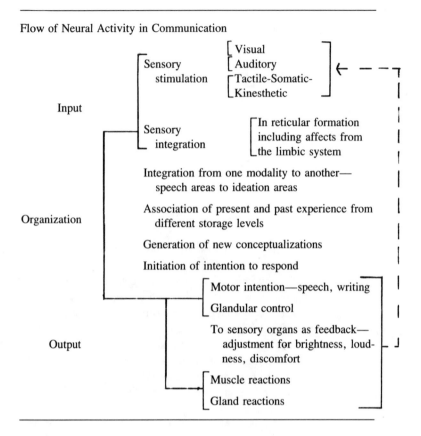

a three-stage sequence of input, mediation, and output processes. The flow of neural activity in linguistic processing is complicated by the continuous feedback from each modality within the system. The forces of sound, light, and pressure that impinge on the individual can be measured mechanically, but the interpretations a reader makes depend on the integrity of the input, the memory store of past experiences, and the organization within the CNS.

The relationship of input, organization, and output is outlined in Table 9.1. *Input* is the data from all the sensory systems that is transmitted to the CNS in the form of electrochemical impulses. Input and organization overlap in the functions of the reticular system where the coded signals are received, selected, and integrated to represent the external world. An important part of experience at this level is the affective loading that comes from the limbic loop, where pleasure and punishment components are generated and stored.

Organization of intellectual processes, or *mediation,* involves the interaction of billions of connector cells which form the major part of the brain. Mediation is the work of the neurons that lie between the ascending and descending neurons of the CNS. This intricate mechanism must be hard-wired for converting sound signals into the phonemes of speech and light signals into word patterns. Learning to read requires the integration of visual ideation of space, location, and figural relations with associated language components.

The assumption that readers who lack skills in one modality (vision) may develop compensatory skills in the other modality (audition) has not been supported by neuropsychology, at least not during the stages of learning to read. Hare (1977) identified children who had scored poorly on the *Frostig Developmental Test of Visual Perception,* but were learning to read successfully by second grade. The children were administered two subtests of the *Illinois Test of Auditory Discrimination,* the reading section of the *Wide Range Achievement Test,* and the paragraph-meaning part of the *Standard Achievement Test.* The findings supported the importance of modality integration. Analyses showed that auditory memory played a small part in both word recognition and paragraph reading. The ability to blend sounds predicted paragraph meaning better than it predicted word recognition. These children's performance in both modalities was generally weak; none of the 77 subjects was strong on any of the auditory tasks, which were as deficient as visual tasks. Compensatory auditory skills had not developed and integration occurred at similar levels in both modalities. This study points up the need for identifying and strengthening a modality weakness, rather than relying on the child to compensate through the stronger modality.

Reading involves the association of present and past experiences from different storage levels of the cortex. Some of the organizing functions of the CNS are the formation of conceptualizations from the multitude of associations within the reading experience. The brain must organize sound–letter associations into a system of rules. A lengthy text must be outlined, synthesized, summarized, or otherwise restructured to fit existing schemata. The conceptualization of affects associated with particular reading experiences makes some persons ludic readers, some research scholars, and others avoiders.

The intention to respond to the print of a book is initiated in the forebrain, where it can be measured, prior to a meaningful response. The sequence of single-word processing can be observed in positron emission tomographic (PET) studies, based on changes in blood flow during brain activity (Petersen et al., 1988). The mechanisms of intention—primarily the premotor cortex with its interconnections to the limbic system—is a waystation between mediation and action, or output.

The initiation of motor responses involved in reading, writing, and speaking is organized in the cortex of the forebrain. *Output* is the muscular or glandular response to motor-intention mechanisms, which includes, but is not limited to, overt behavior. Covert output, which is difficult to observe, feeds processed information back into the system as new input. This organization of input is an important source of learning. Some responses occur without conscious direction. The pupils of a reader's eye dilate in response to the amount of light coming through the windows. The feedback from eye position enables readers to correct the mirror image of visual symbols during transfer from the (dominant) right hemisphere to the left-hemisphere areas of language. During oral reading the loudness of the presenter's voice is adjusted to the body language of the listeners. The integrative processes are much more complex in mature readers than in children.

Input Systems of Communication

The neural activity of activation and reaction, that once was assumed in theoretical models, has now been measured as electrochemical impulses in specific pathways and areas of the brain. Television provides a simplified example of the mechanical aspects of receiving and integrating a message. In transmission the picture is broken down into scanned electrical impulses at the same time that the sound is coded electrically. In the home receiver the picture and the sound are reconstituted, reintegrated, and projected in an approximation of the original form. In the human system the input is encoded in much the same way as television signals are coded; however, having reached the central processing system codes are regrouped and rearranged so that new and complex patterns incorporating past storage emerge. The human brain not only codes, stores, and retrieves the visual effect, but it integrates auditory and somatic sensory input. Integration of input requires that the individual deal with many sources of data at the same time, much of which is irrelevant and must be screened out. To a large degree, the selection of competing input is based on past learning.

AROUSAL RESPONSE TO MULTIPLE INPUT

The screening mechanisms at the mesencephalic level of the reticular formation (hypothalamus and thalamus) shield humans from overstimulation. Normally the activation level regulates the input at a manageable volume for processing and responding (Chapter 2). An unexpected surge or reduction in the volume of input from any one of the senses alerts the person to a change in the environment. Arousal can also result from a low input volume from several senses at once. Integration of multisensory input combines the impact of stimuli and leads to arousal at a lower level than would be required from a single modality. Evidence from electrode analysis indicates that undifferentiated neurons within the reticular formation can be stimulated by input from different sensory modes. Each arousal creates a fresh opportunity for the individual to orient to the source of the change, to evaluate the data from the different senses, and to focus attention on the input that seems important.

When a person is reading fluently at a steady rate and comes to a word that is unfamiliar, a change occurs in the flow of visual input through the reticular formation to the cortex. An arousal state has been produced within the system. The reader may go to the dictionary, attack the word structurally, or reread the context for meaning clues. A response from the several possibilities must be selected. Control of attention to particular stimuli shifts to the thalamic part of the brain stem. Arousal is of short duration, but it provides the impetus for an individual to refocus attention on new and important elements in the environment.

Gaining and sustaining attention is the teacher's primary task. Within a reading group one child may attend to the picture being shown by the teacher while simultaneously listening to the words that explain it. Another child may attend to the picture, see a boat there and compare its lines with his father's boat. A highly distractible child may have heard and attended to the lunch cart in the hall. From the teacher's point of view, the input for all the children was an association of the picture with story vocabulary, but there were important differences in what was being learned. It is relatively easy for teachers to control the stimulus material, but it is difficult to control the meaning of the material, the private motivation of the child, and hence the direction that attention will take.

INTEGRATION OF AFFECTIVE LOADING

The words, phonemes, phrases, and ideas that make up the cognitive content of reading are linked to the previous emotional experiences of the reader. These pleasant and unpleasant affects that were stored in the past bring feelings of pleasure or displeasure to the present text. When an affect, associated through limbic connections, has a punishing effect the learner is likely to direct his or her attention elsewhere—to avoid the situation mentally—if physical escape is not possible. Pleasure linkages draw and sustain attention because the learner wants the experience to continue. When the affects are linked to two or more modalities, the associations are strengthened and the learner has more than one cue to retrieval.

Organization within the System

Even simple reading at the primer level requires numerous mediating actions: (1) linkages between the different modalities, (2) retrieval of past experience, and (3) interaction of association learning and conceptualization. Reading, by definition, requires a meaningful internal response to printed symbols. Malfunctioning in any of the integrative mechanisms interferes with learning unless effective ways are found to facilitate mediation, either through the learner's own adaptation or through exceptional teaching, or both.

LINKAGES BETWEEN MODALITIES

In normal development the stimulation of sensory experiences and the genetic inheritance interact to build neural connections between the different areas of the brain that analyze sensory input. Major pathways have been traced which make cross-cortical linkages from visual, auditory, and motor receiving areas to the *angular gyrus,* the tertiary area where modalities are integrated in communication functions. Ayres (1968) suggested that the somatic and vestibular systems preceded the visual and auditory systems in the phylogenic development of the species. If the newer modalities have been gradually added to the neurological system, rather than substituted, functioning in the cortex may depend on the integration of deep senses not yet investigated. Reading requires the highly integrated activity of all primitive systems on which vision and hearing are built. Much work remains to be done before the interdependence of sensory systems in recall of sensory experience during comprehension is understood. Reading research has focused on auditory-visual interaction primarily, and on visual-motor interaction to a lesser extent.

Auditory-visual Integration

When evaluating the effect of auditory processing on visual word processing, it is important to distinguish between beginning readers, independent readers, and disabled readers. Good readers in grades two and four learn to recognize familiar words from visual input alone and simultaneously expand and consolidate the spelling–sound correspondences (Backman et al., 1984). However, Woodley (1987) studied the influence of linguistic knowledge when university students read connected text. A tachistoscope was used to examine the nature of visual perception in relation to the ability of subjects to apply their knowledge of written language in text comprehension. The stimulus materials were printed lines that ranged from meaningful text to nonsense figural sequences. The Goodman model was used for analysis along two dimensions: (1) the degree to which the reports of text were complete and accurate, and (2) the degree to which subjects applied knowledge of written English in reporting the material. The results showed that the more individuals were able to apply their knowledge of language, the more rapidly and accurately they were able to perceive and report the material. These two studies, which seem to be inconsistent, point up the need to consider the reading stage, the learner characteristics, and the cognitive demands of the task when drawing conclusions about the interaction of the auditory and visual modalities.

A developmental study of elementary-school boys, from second to sixth grades, showed that competence in auditory-visual functions was positively related to reading achievement at all grade levels, especially in tests of word knowledge (Kohn & Birch, 1968). When the relative importance of auditory and visual intrasensory skills and the audiovisual cross-sensory integration skills were studied in first-grade boys, the cross-modal task emerged as the best single predictor for two key reading measures (word attack subtest and total reading score). Derevensky (1977) reviewed the literature on cross-modal functioning and reading achievement. He concluded that sensory integration and cross-modal functioning are related to reading success and that the degree of this relationship depends on developmental level, socioeconomic background, task requirements, and sex of the subjects.

Studies of sex differences have been particularly difficult to evaluate. For example, a study of fifth graders by Rae (1977) reported sex differences in favor of girls in the auditory-visual integration skills in reading. Ward (1977) obtained significant correlations between auditory-visual integration and reading achievement in a sample of British third and fourth graders. In this study, sex was not a significant contributor to the relationship between reading ability and integrative skills, although IQ was a significant factor.

Lovell and Gorton (1968) compared backward readers with normal readers on a battery of tests, including two that measured auditory-visual integration (A-V) and sound–symbol association. Their 100 subjects, ages 9 and 10, were all in the average range on individual intelligence tests. On tasks which required nonreading interaction between visual and auditory functions, the backward readers were significantly lower then the normal readers. Further analysis of the scores from poor readers showed strong, positive correlations between A-V integration and language age; between A-V integration and reading age; and between sound–symbol association and language age. Lack of auditory-visual integration was apparent in poor readers, aside from learned responses to reading.

Auditory and visual modalities have been studied in combination with dimensions of space and time. Willette and Early (1985) selected normal and reading-disabled groups of children from 6 to 13 years old for a complex combination of three modality inputs: visual-temporal, auditory-temporal, and visual-spatial-temporal. The required response to each of three tasks was vocal temporal output. Normal readers were superior to reading-disabled children on all tests of the ability to reproduce stimulus patterns in the vocal temporal mode. The spatial dimension, when added to the visual-temporal combination resulted in superior scores, compared with other modality combinations. However, auditory temporal input was superior to visual temporal input in tests without the added spatial cues. The study shows the advantage in pattern recognition tasks that accrues from combined modality effects. The disadvantage some children reveal in the ability to make such integrations is predictive of reading difficulty. At the secondary-school level, Levine (1983) found that diagnostic reading groups showed differences from normal readers in processing bisensory information (auditory and visual). Although the relative importance of the visual and auditory modalities may shift at different stages in reading, or with different approaches to instruction, continuous integration of visual and auditory signals is known to take place between seeing and reading print.

Visual-motor Integration

When a child is able to control a pencil, as in drawing a picture, but is unable to reproduce an abstract visual form, the disability probably arises in the interaction between the visual analyzing system and one or more of the motor initiating mechanisms. In their comparison of backward and normal readers, Lovell and Gorton (1968) included a visual-motor Gestalt test. Visual models were presented on cards, and each subject was asked to draw reproductions which were then scored with respect to size, shape, and relationship. The importance of visual-motor integration showed up in an analysis of a cluster of factors which were highly correlated: auditory-visual integration, spatial orientation, left-right discrimination, and motor performance. The investigators identified this pattern of performance as dependent on the integrity of central processes.

RETRIEVAL OF PAST EXPERIENCE

The recognition of words in reading, the recall of related experiences, and the reconstruction of knowledge in comprehension are each processes of integration that depend in part on the retrieval of stored experience. Normally this retrieval occurs automatically when the stimulus word(s) activates the neurons that lead to appropriate areas and cells. *Semantic priming* is a technique which presents subjects with a cue, or meaning bias, prior to exposure to a stimulus, so that linguistic influences on perception can be studied. Swinney, Onifer, Prather, and Hirshkowlitz (1979) used semantic priming to study lexical decisions in the processing of words and sentences across sensory modalities. Their college subjects were influenced by both auditory and visual information in making lexical choices. By processing auditorily presented words prior to visual exposures, recognition of visual words was facilitated in items that were related semanticly. Also, lexical decisions were facilitated when a visual word appeared immediately following a related word within a sentence. The procedures used in lexical decision experiments, demonstrated the automaticity of semantic retrieval in response to visual stimuli.

First-grade children were the subjects in a study of auditory and visual matching of trigrams within and across modalities. Crawford and Fry (1979) found significant correlational relationships between auditory-visual, visual-auditory, and auditory-auditory input-output modes. Memory span contributed to auditory scores. Vocabulary and visual memory were the best predictors of visual-auditory task performance. Visual-auditory performance was the best predictor of reading achievement. The investigators suggested that teaching techniques which increase the learner's meaningful participation in the processing of symbolic material are likely to be more effective in recall than techniques that lack meaningful linkages between cue and response. Multisensory involvement facilitates later recall of meanings. When readers build their own responses, the learning is more accessible and more functional.

ASSOCIATION LEARNING AND CONCEPTUALIZATION

There is some physiological evidence that the layers of neurons in the cerebral cortex have differentiated functions that are related to associative and conceptual functions (Chapter 4). A network of axons and dendrites forms linkages between the several layers of cell bodies in the cortex. The cells that are activated during association learning seem to be concentrated in the third and adjacent layers. The fourth to sixth layers, and in some areas a seventh layer, have a concentration of cell bodies that are activated during conceptual processes. Sarkisov (1966) described the layers as important in secondary thought processing, or reflection, and suggested the stellate cells were involved.

Research on conceptualizations in language or reading processes is meager when compared with research on conceptual development in science and mathematics. Piaget's theory of cognitive development, especially his description of operational thought, has stimulated research on concepts, or structural knowledge, of volume, area, number, weight, space, and time (Wallace, 1965). After surveying hundreds of studies on conceptualization, Wallace noted that language plays an important role in conceptualization, but further work is needed to trace the interdependence of language and nonlanguage thought. Many examples of conceptual thought, as contrasted to associative learning, are found in very young children, particularly when nonlanguage manipulative items are available for them to demonstrate a conceptualization. On the other hand adults perform many tasks at the association level that could be conceptualized (pp. 220–221). A concluding note was that psychological processes involved in conceptualization probably will be identified with certainty only when neurophysical researchers are able to identify the neural activity that is distinctive to conceptual thought (p. 235).

Motor Integration During Output

Studies of the behavior of readers rely primarily on the output or response of subjects to reconstruct theoretically what happened during mediation. Although schemata for motor activity are stored in the cortex, output depends on subcortical connections for the initiation and modification of responses. Fine motor skills, such as those required for accommodation to near-point vision, have become semiautomatic in most children by the time they begin reading. However, saccadic movements across the line of print are subject to modification and improvement throughout the reading life of a person. Simple motor activities that accompany reading, such as place keeping and page turning, produce sensory associations that help to keep the process intact and to sustain it.

MOTOR RESPONSE TO AUDIOVISUAL STIMULI

The initial stimulation of the output neurons have been difficult to observe in humans because voluntary activities arise through an interaction of the forebrain cortex and the diencephalon (Chapter 2). In language functions, including reading and writing, the tertiary speech area is involved. Penfield (1969) located this area anterior to motor control areas along the Rolandic fissure and extending into the central fissure that divides the two hemispheres. Eccles and Robinson (1984) suggested bilateral control of language motor functions from the tertiary speech area in LH and a similar area located in RH. This bit of anatomy becomes significant when investigators try to describe the motor response to auditory and visual stimuli during reading.

Katz (1974) compared the perceptual responses of normal and poor readers to a wide variety of experimentally controlled tasks: (a) reaction times to sequences of lights and tones; (b) ability to track auditory, visual, and combined A-V stimuli (sometimes called monitoring); (c) discrimination of auditory and visual material varying in meaningfulness; (d) memory for aurally and visually presented words and digits; and (e) ability to learn meaningful material presented auditorily and visually. Results showed poor readers differing on all perceptual measures from normal readers. A major finding was that poor readers doubled their reaction times when required to shift modality from stimulus to response. They were inferior to normal readers in retaining sequence during recall, in monitoring or tracking a stimulus, and in differentiating auditory and visual stimuli. Poor readers were prone to attentional lapses on visual material; but their difficulty was greater in auditory functioning when the task involved serial learning and complex memory. Although this study involved Black male children, both good and poor readers, the implications for perceptual latency and modality shifts in all children are suggestive.

Children who are unable to direct and sustain attention have attracted the interest of neuropsychological researchers. Ackerman, Anhalt, Dykman, and Holcomb (1986) used tapping responses to compare groups of children with problems and a control group of normal readers. The experimental groups were reading-disabled (RD), nonhyperactive; and two groups of attention-disordered: nonhyperactive (ADD) and hyperactive (H). Reading-disabled groups were inferior to other groups in memory tasks involving acoustic and semantic associations. All three groups differed from controls in memory for low-imagery, as opposed to high-imagery words. These task variables were second to age and the WISC–IQ in predicting reading grade level. The investigators theorized that attentional disorders impede the automatization for these tasks that normal readers enjoy. Together these studies show that output, as measured by latency of motor response is related to the multisensory processing of visual material.

HAPTIC SENSES AS FEEDBACK SYSTEMS

The body senses, both near senses such as touch and deep senses such as kinesthetic, have afferent (input) terminals in many parts of the cortex. Piaget (1969) was explicit, as well as eloquent, in describing the dynamics of selective assimilation by self-directed manipulations of the environment, based primarily on the developmental level of the individual and the level of accommodation to each experience. The taking in, or assimilating, of sensory information changes the person so that cognitive structures are altered and the interaction with the environment is different. It is important to remember that the neural system uses sensory data from within the organism as well as from without to formulate the response patterns recognized as motor activity.

Motor experience has been used to teach children phoneme–grapheme correspondence at the beginning stages of reading. Impressed with the way manual signing sustained the participation of hard-of-hearing children, Koehler and Lloyd (1986) experimented with fingerspelling to teach normal children the spelling and vocabulary skills. They cite the advantages: (1) Visual symbols are easier to attend to, then auditory symbols; (2) Consistency of representation is greater in visual/manual symbols than in auditory/vocal stimuli; and (3) Temporal duration of visual symbols can be extended without distortion; and (4) Visual/motor signs are more easily associated with visual referents than are spoken symbols. The investigators report some important benefits to young learners. The visual cues reinforced the importance of sequence and phoneme segmentation. Although evaluative data are lacking, the technique might be tried and tested for dyslexic children who need help in sequencing, and distractible children who are unable to sustain attention.

INTEGRITY OF THE NEURAL SYSTEM

The integrative functions that occur within the CNS during reading point up the importance of normal functioning and raise questions about the possibility of malfunctioning when normally intelligent children have difficulty learning to read. Lovell and Gorton (1968) clarified some of the inconsistencies reported previously on the relationship of neurological functions and reading disability. Their factor analyses of backward and normal readers showed very different clusters of abilities in the two groups. Among poor readers, 46% of the variance in reading age was accounted for by *lack of neurological integrity*. This was described as a syndrome of the CNS having little relationship to IQ, but related to specific reading disability that often included writing. This factor was comprised of measures of auditory-verbal integration, rotation of abstract designs, spatial orientation, left-right discrimination, and motor performance. Within their poor reading group these abilities were correlated with reading ability, but in the good readers there was a lack of positive relationship. While all children must acquire left-to-right processing of print, good readers learn to do this easily and under a variety of instructional approaches.

Lateral Awareness

A high correlation exists between left-right discrimination of body parts, auditory-visual integration, and language age. Belmont and Birch (1965) published a milepost study of poor readers and matched controls which focused on laterality functions. They distinguished between lateral dominance and *lateral awareness*. They found significant differences between their groups on tests of left-right orientation. "Lateral confusion" was associated with reading performance but not with verbal or IQ measures.

Hicks (1981) studied reversal errors in reading, often considered a symptom of lateral confusion, in children 6 to 10 years old. Measures of inter- or intra-modality integration were administered to four groups of 12 subjects each: beginning readers, retarded readers, dyslexic children, and normal readers. The four tasks required matching an auditory stimulus to an auditory target (A-A), a visual stimulus to a visual target (V-V), an auditory stimulus to a visual target (A-V), and a visual stimulus to an auditory target(V-A). The results indicated that beginning readers made more errors on the V-V task, the retarded made errors on all the tasks, the dyslexics made more errors on the cross-modal tasks (A-V and V-A), and the normal readers made almost no errors. The investigator interpreted these results as support for the Birch and Belmont thesis. She hypothesized that failure in intermodality integration is a major cause of reading failure.

Sequencing Within and Between Words

The ordering of words is essential to comprehension; the ordering of letter representations within words is essential to word recognition. How children learn to sequence printed words is not clear because they seem to acquire left-to-right reading in English or right-to-left reading in Persian with equal facility. One explanation could be that linguistic sequencing is hard-wired, or built into the developmental organization of the brain; that sequencing in speech becomes the inherent structure for sequencing in reading. Putting words or parts of words in the correct order is a temporal relationship which the child demonstrates when learning to talk. Correct spatial-visual relationships are required of the learner when attempts are made to interpret words on paper. Of major concern is how and when sequencing of visual language occurs and why it is delayed in some children.

Visual sequencing was investigated by Whipple and Kodman (1969), who studied children's learning rate in a task requiring the discrimination of symbols presented in sequence. Their subjects were 60 retarded readers who were matched with 60 normal readers. Both groups were screened for speech, hearing, and vision. On three tasks of perceptual learning, each involving the discrimination of visual symbols presented in sequence, the retarded readers were significantly poorer than the normal readers in number of errors on first trial, number of total errors, and number of trials to criterion performance.

In a series of studies on visual processing in beginning reading, Berninger (1987) reported differences in serial processing of letters in words between groups of kindergarten nonreaders and first-grade readers. Her nonreaders remembered a word more accurately than a letter in a word, showing visual origins of the word superiority effect (WSE). First-grade readers remembered a word faster than a letter in a word, which they remembered faster than a letter sequence in a word, again suggesting early origin of WSE. The memory studies were revealing. At the end of kindergarten only memory for a whole word and memory for a letter in a word were correlated with measures of reading achievement. However, by the end of the first grade, all the memory tasks for whole word, letter in a word, and *letter sequence in a word* were correlated with reading achievement. When looking at the relationship between gain scores on five measures of visual processing and word decoding skills, only memory for a letter sequence in a word correlated significantly with two tests of word decoding: the *Slosson Oral Reading Test* and the *Gates MacGinitie Vocabulary Reading Test*. The investigator suggested that serial processing is unique and qualitatively different from other kinds of visual processing in reading. Tentative evidence was produced that visual sequencing of print is acquired during the early stages of learning to read.

The studies on sensorimotor integration in reading have several implications for teachers: (1) The functions of the different modality systems must be integrated if the input-mediation-output sequence is to result in successful reading. (2) Individuals differ with respect to modality strength in learning, and early experiences which strengthen perceptual weakness would seem to be favored. (3) Laterality preference appears to be unrelated to reading ability, but confusion of left and right, or spatial disorientation, may be related to difficulty in beginning reading. (4) Perceptual organization in the forms needed for reading can be taught. (5) Specialized practice tasks should be as directly related to the reading act as the learner is able to perform with success at the time.

THEORIES OF LEXICAL ACCESS

Current models for the recognition of visual words are numerous, sophisticated, complex, and conflicting. Despite these difficulties, it is not possible to proceed very far into current research on reading theory and practice without some understanding of the concepts, the terminology, and the accepted principles of word recognition. The central problem, or goal of this research, is to find out how the printed word (or morpheme, or proposition, or sentence) is translated to the word bank of meanings stored in the brain. To put the question succinctly, How do printed words access the lexicon?

Models of Word Recognition

Despite the unsettled atmosphere of current research, important progress has been made, particularly in explaining the responses of mature readers to visually presented words. These studies are accumulating at a monumental pace, in part because of the importance of literacy in the future development of nations. Unfortunately it may be some time before similar focus is given to sensory integration during contextual reading, to the changing processes of children learning to read, and to typological differences among disabled readers.

LIMITATIONS OF CURRENT MODELS

There are major limitations in available models. (1) The subjects for the research, almost without exception, are college students who represent a population of superior readers with exceptional lexical assets. The strategies used by mature, proficient readers do not necessarily describe the decoding strategies of children and ordinary readers. (2) Most models are based on single-word processing by controlled experimental procedures that call for correct identification of a *target word* when presented with two words or letter strings. In normal reading the parameters are controlled by the reader, whose recognition strategies may differ in important ways from those observed in the laboratory. (3) Most models depend on tachistoscopic presentation. These conditions inject motor responses for button pressing and unreal lexical decisions that are remote from any purposeful reading of text. (4) Experimental conditions that meet the criteria of precision usually require the subject to make associative responses to paired-word items as opposed to rule-governed, semantic decisions of text translation. Nevertheless, potentially important hypotheses have been proposed in the lexical access models, which should be tested to resolve the genuine conflicts among them.

LEXICAL INSTANCE MODELS

A recent volume of *Reading Research* (Besner, Waller, & MacKinnon, 1985) presented the issues and some of the major models that researchers are testing. This section reviews three examples of "lexical instance" models, followed by a more detailed treatment of the "parallel coding" system proposed by Carr and Pollatsek in the same volume.

The major distinction which separates lexical instance models of word recognition from others is their reliance on specific instances, or particular stimuli, to trigger word identification. The processing is assumed to be sequential and associative. One example of a lexical instance model is the *logogen,* or *word detector* model, proposed originally by Morton (1969). The visual stimuli of a word are fed into a system of stored representations to locate a one-on-one match between the logogen and its word. These bits of sensory information cumulatively reach the threshold level of a number of detectors. Words that are visually similar, such as **talk**, **task**, and **balk**, are activated and a decision, or choice, must follow. The data show that lexical decisions are made in favor of (a) recency of exposure to the word, usually during experimentation; and (b) frequency of the word, usually based on published word lists. Reports favoring the logogen process appear frequently in the literature.

Another and more recent form of lexical instance theory has retained the concept of detector activation, but has shifted to the morpheme, rather than the word, as the activator (Carr & Pollatsek, 1985). The *lexical search models* are important because the morpheme as a meaning unit becomes the focus of the inquiry as distinguished from the physical signal of speech. The search model opens new possibilities in understanding the processing of multisyllable words. For example, a word such as "unyielding," would be stripped (by the reader) of its prefix and searched as **yield.** The familiar suffix -**ing** and the negating prefix -**un** would also be processed as semantic units, completing the comprehension task by a morphographic approach. This theory of word recognition is much closer to the top-down, biologically conceived theory of speech perception proposed by Gleitman (1986) than to the bottom-up detection of the logogen model.

Taft (1985) proposed a lexical instance model which prescribed the first syllable of the stem of the word as the syllable of access. This syllable, which is both orthographically and morphologically defined, was called BOSS for *basic orthographic syllabic structure*. His experiments were based on tachistoscopic presentation of pairs from which a variety of lexical choices were required. For example, the BOSS syllable in final, **fin**, would constitute the access to finalize, finality, confine, infinitive, finicky, finish, and so on. Taft pointed out that **fin** is the Latin root conveying the concept of "termination". He would have children taught groups of words from the BOSS as a way of enriching their facility with words. Taft admits that a single access code account may be overly restrictive, but he insists that text as well as single words are probably processed in this form-driven manner. A counteranalysis would point out that many of his examples appear insensitive to the phonological cues on which all young readers depend to some extent. For example, the regular pronunciation of the CVC syllable **fin** calls for a short sound of the **i** vowel, a verbal cue which fits only half of the examples provided. The BOSS theory of word study might be more productive for students whose rules of phoneme–grapheme correspondence are in place.

The mechanics of research, which make possible the precise measurement of a single reading response, have the advantage of isolating processes from the undefined and multiple factors of text reading. Those who take the view that word recognition is an interactive process involving several senses and more than one level of brain functioning are particularly sensitive to the potential lack of fit between hypotheses which assume visual control of the process and those who consider language as the basis for printed word comprehension. Rayner (1983) showed that eye movements are sensitive to the information needs of the cognitive processes involved in reading. Banks, Oka, and Shugarman (1981) concluded that inner speech is an important part of mental processing in normal reading. Seidenberg (1985) departed from the conventional wisdom in his field to declare major differences between single-word reading and reading words in context.

A PARALLEL CODING MODEL

Parallel coding means that two or more pathways to the lexicon, such as morphological and phonological, may function simultaneously or they may alternate. The *Parallel Coding System (PCS)* proposed by Carr and Pollatsek (1985) is one of the most comprehensive models for several reasons: (a) It incorporates other models into a system of parallel processing. (b) It recognizes both associative knowledge and structural knowledge in accessing words. (c) It allows for the extension of single-word recognition to the processing of contextual print. (d) It is potentially conceivable in terms of mechanisms for language processing within the CNS.

The PCS model features three parallel systems or pathways from the visual registration in the retina to conscious word recognition in the working memory (Fig. 9.1). Two pathways are processes of visual code formation: one is a direct *visual/orthographic* pathway to whole word meaning; the other is a *visual/orthographic/morphemic* pathway that routes through a center where meaning-dictated decomposition is mediated. The third system, *phonological recod-*

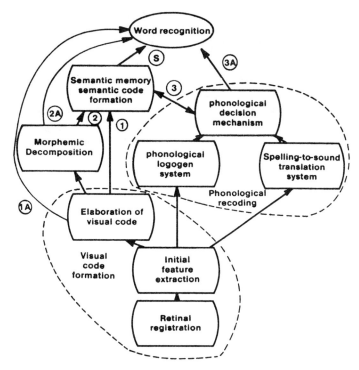

FIGURE 9.1. PCS model got parallel pathways in lexical access. Oval represents conscious word recognition: Working memory. Two pathways show processes of visual code formation: Route one is visual/orthographic; two is visual/orthographic/phonemic. The third pathway is phonological recoding. Each route has an alternate route, suggesting at least six potential routes of access to the lexicon (From Carr & Pollatsek, 1985, Academic Press).

ing, proceeds by visual feature extraction, then splits into two pathways, one functioning on the principles of paired-associate learning, the other on the rule-governed translation of grapheme to phoneme.

The supporting evidence for three parallel systems is impressive but lengthy. The investigators call on the neurologically based distinction between *surface dyslexia* and *deep dyslexia* to support their distinction between phonological and visual processing systems. Surface dyslexics generally appear to have their pho-nological recoding pathways intact; they pronounce words and pseudowords with facility while they have great difficulty with semantics. Deep dyslexics, on the other hand, have a direct and undisturbed pathway to word meaning but have great difficulty with the phonological recoding system. They also have difficulty with function words (as contrasted to content words), with derivations, and with morphemic decomposition. Carr and Pollatsek recognize the lack of a third parallel processing route in this familiar dichotomy of dyslexia. However the three-way typology often reported among developmental dyslexias, as described in the next section, will show additional subtypes within the dyslexic groups.

Visual/orthographic Route

The PCS model proposes as the most direct word recognition strategy a pathway from *retinal registration* of the visual signal to *feature extraction* to *visual code formation* to *semantic code formation,* terminating in conscious *word recognition* in the working memory. An alternate route (1A) would bypass the semantic code formation. The distinction between the first pathway and its alternate can be understood in an example from text reading. The reader, having been introduced to a prospective visit to Grandfather's house may subsequently process "Grandfather's" by the visual/orthographic route, but may skip "to" or use the alternate bypass, since its semantic interpretation may not be needed. When pronouncing sight words during a flash card drill, children may be "reading" by this direct visual/orthographic pathway and not necessarily be activating the "working memory of meaning" implied in the PCS model.

Visual/orthographic/morphemic Route

The second visual pathway leads from retinal registration through feature extraction and elaboration on the visual code. However, the additional information from morphemic decomposition may be needed for word recognition. Continuing the example, "to Grandfather's house" we have a recency association favoring grandfather when, according to the text, grand**mother** emerges from the house in her apron. The reader may require a morphemic breakdown (pathway 2) of a compound word, grandmother, cued by the semantic information obtained from "apron." If the reader was cued immediately by the visual/orthographic/morphemic information from the compound word "grandmother," the semantic memory may be bypassed and the word accessed by the alternate pathway 2A.

Phonological Recoding

The third system of word processing, the auditory approach, begins with retinal registration and visual feature detection, but relies on phonological recoding, rather than elaborated visual coding. Route 3 enters the phonological logogen system, proceeds through the phonological decision mechanism, assesses the semantic memory, and then recognizes the word. Continuing the text of a visit to the country, the reader may need to resort to a phonological processing route and reread the hxxxx word when the phrase "to Grandfather's hxxxx **stable**" is encountered. A phonological decision will be verified in a semantic memory that a horse and not a house will be found in the stable, then pathway 3 leads to word recognition. When the reader learns that grandfather has recently purchased a hackamore, our reader must resort to spelling-to-sound translation (3A) and perhaps to the dictionary for a new entry in his lexicon. These three pathways to word recognition, each with an alternate short circuit, propose pathways within the system for processing a variety of word recognition options. Carr and Pollatsek emphasized that their model is tentative and they invited further testing and discussion.

In a challenge to their assumptions of direct visual access, Perfetti, Bell, and

Delaney (1988) argued that phonological routes are activated automatically during visual lexical access. In automatic activation, phonetic information would become available very quickly as part of visual access to the lexicon. Such activation would be *prelexical,* meaning that auditory information may be part of the recognition process. The activation results from excitatory links between graphic word forms and phonetic word forms, between letters and phonemes, and between grapheme sequences and phoneme sequences. The activation could occur both bottom-up from letter and phoneme units to words and top-down from words to letters and phonemes.

Perfetti and his colleagues used a target word printed in lowercase letters followed by a backward mask, printed in all capitals, to determine the influence of different masks on word recognition. The target words were exposed so briefly that supporting information was needed to identify the target words. For example, the target word **hear** would be followed by a graphemic information (**HEOR**), or phonemic information (**HEER**), or a control having very little overlap with the target (**FODE**), each in randomized order. The college undergraduates who participated were able to identify words significantly more often when masking information (graphemic or phonemic) was given than under control conditions. More important, the correct answers following the graphemic mask (45%) were exceeded by correct answers following the phonemic mask (55%). The interpretation of the investigators was that graphemic effects reflect the contribution of particular abstract letter information while phonemic information is associated with meaning.

The phonemic effect contains phonetic values of the graphemes and of the word itself; the negative effect of masking is reduced because phonetic codes are already activated by the incomplete identification of the target. The results suggest that a phonetic activation occurs nonoptionally and prelexically during lexical access. The investigators propose that a high degree of phonetic activation always occurs during lexical access, which presumably serves comprehension and memory as well as speech production. The Perfetti research brings into question the direct visual accessing of single words during text comprehension. The flexibility of the Carr and Pollatsek model may be more applicable to single-word processing within context than it is to single-word tachistoscopic presentation.

Semantic Context Effects

Some evidence has been presented that printed words are recoded to inner speech. To the extent that this occurs on a continuing basis during reading, the organization of meanings in the speech lexicon would seem to be a valid departure for researching continuous reading effects. Seidenberg (1985) points out that lexical access involves semantic, phonological, and orthographic codes. He proposes a postlexical process in which selection, elaboration, and integration of information is necessary for the purpose of comprehending text. The structure of actual texts, particularly the sentence, makes it difficult to predict how a reader will process a particular word, especially when the text is complicated or personal.

MULTISENSORY PROCESSES IN DYSLEXIA

Most studies of reading disabilities among children and adults have applied three criteria for selecting the subjects with reading disability: (1) adequate intelligence (average or above), (2) a significant lag behind schoolmates in reading achievement, and (3) adequate opportunities, such as cultural support at home and regular attendance at school. This definition by *exclusion* rules out children for study whose reading failure may be based on some recognized causal factor such as intermittent school attendance. Educational and psychological assessment, not neurological criteria, has been the basis for selection in most studies of developmental dyslexia (Ellis, 1984). This section focuses on developmental dyslexia, a reading disability differentiated from the more general classification of learning disabilities.

James Hinshelwood (1917) is credited with an early description of a condition he called *congenital word-blindness*. This concept implied a dysfunction in visual perception or visual processing. Later Orton (1937) associated reading, writing, and speech problems in children with an etiology of *neurological* conditions. His discussions implied a language-based difficulty to be distinguished from sensory acuities of vision and hearing. Almost from the beginning, two approaches to explaining the condition were pursued; the one which began with the visual perception of words, the other rooted in language processing. To this time, visual-based and auditory-based models of dyslexia have been researched widely, but their relatedness has not been resolved adequately.

Despite his controversial stance, Orton has been joined, during the last half-century, by investigators from diverse professions. The diagnosis and instruction of children who experienced unexpected and unusual difficulty in learning to read has produced a monumental literature that is sometimes seen as conflicting and confusing because the concepts are drawn from different disciplines. A few examples of these different contributions are: neurology, Geschwind, (1974); pediatrics, Mattis, French, and Rapin, (1975); psychology, Rayner (1986a); genetics, Pennington et al. (1983); educational psychologists, Keogh and Babbitt (1986); child development, Olson, Kliegel, Davidson, and Foltz (1985); and psycholinguists, Marshall and Newcombe (1973). Fortunately for today's student, these different writers seek to understand a common etiology in the human brain.

When evaluating this literature for possible application it is necessary to note the populations from which subjects are drawn and what questions the researchers were asking. For example, children identified in a "language experience program" of reading instruction are likely to be identified by irregularities of speech or language development. A specialist in visual disorders, who sees a high proportion of children who are referred because of poor reading, is likely to look for visual causes of the disability. High school subjects may integrate visual and auditory signals differently than second graders do; therefore the diagnoses of their problems may differ.

The cutoff point at which a student is defined as a poor reader determines the incidence of reading disability in a school population and the rate of "illiteracy" in the general population (Goldberg, Shiffman, & Bender, 1983). According to

Critchley (1981), approximately 10% of the school population reads less well than they should; a part of these are dyslexic. Naidoo (1981) reported that in England about 4% of the population is dyslexic, independent of time, method, and location of the study. In all countries where investigations have been reported, a small percentage of bright children from good homes and good schools have experienced severe difficulty in learning to read and to spell. These reports come from various countries and languages, including Norway (Gjessing, 1982); the Netherlands (Bakker & Schroots, 1981); and Scotland (Ingram, Mason, & Blackburn, 1970). Some investigators specifically rule out children with structural brain defects and minimal brain dysfunction (MBD) (Critchley, 1981), while others include children of good intelligence with minimal impairments that are assumed (by the investigator) not to be causal factors (Gjessing, 1982).

Despite the persistence of some dyslexic characteristics into adulthood, a large school district in Washington state achieved success in teaching children with reading disabilities, particularly if the diagnosis is made early and specialized instruction is given. When diagnosed in first or second grade, 82% of these schoolchildren were reported to have recovered from a significant disability to grade level achievement in reading. In this study of 10,000 pupils, successful intervention dropped off to 46% when the problem was not diagnosed until third grade; to 42% when diagnosed in fourth grade; and to 10% and 15% when the diagnosis took place in the fifth or seventh grade. Competent diagnosis, early in the primary grades is the first step toward saving large numbers of children from educational handicaps. Many school programs for the reading-disabled do not distinguish dyslexics from the learning-disabled, or the emotionally handicapped. A clarification of diagnosis is needed if better treatment is to be achieved.

Definition

Herbert Spencer, the British philosopher, suggested that human opinion passes through three stages: (1) unanimity of the ignorant, (2) disagreement of the inquiring, and (3) unanimity of the wise. Clearly the experts on reading disabilities are in phase 2 of this sequence. In writing this section we have tried to spare the reader much of the controversy, and instead to report the major lines of investigation, whether from studies of "reading disability," "learning disability" or "dyslexia." The term *dyslexia* is most commonly used among professions within medicine, neuropsychology, and clinical psychology. Educators in the United States tend to study reading disability within the broader category of learning disability.

Dyslexia is a medical term: *dys,* the Latin for "poor or inadequate" and *lexia,* meaning "words of language" or the lexicon. During a recent search we found more than 2,000 articles on dyslexia and at least a dozen recent books with dyslexia in the title. One classification on which most neurologists agree is the distinction between acquired and developmental dyslexia. *Acquired dyslexia* refers to the condition in which an individual who once had learned to read has lost the ability through some form of brain damage, such as stroke, which affected the language-processing areas. *Developmental dyslexia* describes individuals who experience great difficulty in learning to read initially, despite educational opportunity and cultural encouragement.

Experts approach the topic from different assumptions when they define dyslexia. One group supports the *unitary approach,* which assumes that a particular dysfunction exists in dyslexics which differs only in *degree of impairment* between individuals. Such a neuropsychological deficit slows, or distorts, symbolic processing in ways that impede learning to read or to spell. The second group assumes a dichtomous approach in which (a) the LH language processes may be disrupted, indicated by a low Verbal IQ; or (b) the RH visual processes may be disrupted along pathways to the lexicon, indicated by low scores in visual-symbolic skills. The result of either deficit is poor cross-hemisphere communication. The third approach recognizes three or more subtypes of dyslexia: usually two auditory forms (a) language disorders and (b) articulatory/graphomotor disorders; and (c) visuospatial perceptual disorders (Mattis, French, & Rapin, 1975). By implication, the "typology" model requires an openness to new categories, a search for a specific cause, and differential treatment based on that etiology. Some clinicians take an eclectic approach. They attempt a multifactoral diagnosis, examining their students on a variability of measures that have a correlational relationship with reading achievement. Without adequate diagnosis as the precursor to treatment, a program is not likely to be individualized to the extent that most dyslexic persons need.

Like many educators, Rawson (1981) prefers to avoid the term, dyslexia, and to refer to the affected children as "language different." She encourages teachers and counselors to look for potential advantages in the cognitive profiles of poor readers and to discover their talents in spatial, inventive, or artistic abilities. The problem with an avoidance classification is that dyslexics whose spoken language is relatively proficient may not be identified as dyslexic until the optimal period for a corrective program to be effective has passed. Also, the child with the low IQ, who needs a much slower and more structured program of instruction, may be misdiagnosed as "language different." Rawson aptly calls for clinical appraisal of the whole configuration of symptoms and test findings, and the avoidance of single indicators to identify a reading problem.

The World Federation of Neurology has proposed a definition which is sufficiently inclusive to function in educational, research, and clinical settings. *Dyslexia* is a disorder manifested in learning to read, despite conventional instruction, adequate intelligence, and sociocultural opportunity; dyslexia is dependent on fundamental cognitive disabilities which are frequently of constitutional origin. A great deal of progress has been made in identifying some of the cognitive strengths and weaknesses that characterize dyslexic individuals and some of the critical differences that help to subgroup them.

This section is concerned with the neuropsychological aspects associated with different types of developmental dyslexia. Cruickshank (1986) pointed out that professionals from the several disciplines who work at understanding the complex causality of dyslexia do not have a problem of terminology. They regard all learning as neurologically based and dyslexia as a form of learning disability related to reading. A discrepancy between general intelligence and the ability to recognize and interpret words seen visually, or heard auditorily, is viewed as the result of a neurophysiological dysfunction. Cruickshank emphasized that dyslexia, whether mild, moderate, or severe is a complicated CNS problem that requires interdisciplinary diagnostic effort and skilled, individualized treatment.

Types of Developmental Dyslexia

Some writers view developmental dyslexia as primarily a linguistic disorder (Shankweiler, Smith, & Mann, 1984). Thus behind each dyslexic child is a history of developmental disorder in the acquisition of speech: delayed articulation, late onset of speech, or poor access to word meanings. The causal factor may be found in an irregularity of growth in the language processing areas of the brain (Galaburda, 1982, Geschwind, 1974). Some investigators have found language development disorders in each of their subjects and have concluded that reading disorders are an extension of speech disorders (Tracy, 1983). In a comprehensive work, Tomatis (1969) concluded that audition is the only cause of dyslexia. Ellis and Miles (1981) described dyslexia as a deficiency in lexical coding. However, they broadened the scope of their "unitary dysfunction" theory when they focused on the different features in word perception: visual, phonological, semantic, and articulatory. They suggested that a disabled reader could show faulty perception in one or a combination of these different mechanisms. Again, by implication, the extreme variability shown by disabled readers during different experimental conditions calls for differential corrective instruction.

AUDITORY DYSLEXIA; THE "LANGUAGE DIFFERENT"

Linguistic-based disability in learning to read has been called *phonological dyslexia* by Ellis (1984), *dysphonic reading* by Boder (1973), *specific developmental dyslexia* by Ingram, Mason, and Blackburn (1970), and *deep dyslexia* by Marshall and Newcombe (1973). A distinction has been made between "Chinese" readers, who rely so exclusively on whole word approaches that they lack word analysis skills, and "Phoenicians," who remain so dependent on phonic mediation that they fail to acquire an adequate sight vocabulary (Baron & Strawson, 1976). "Chinese" types represent the dyslexia form that is linguistically based, indicating a disability in auditory processing and the prolonged reliance on visual word perception. Sight reading breaks down as the vocabulary requirement expands to many words with similar configuration while phoneme–grapheme associations remain weak. Phonemic, or auditory-based dyslexia is marked by poor discrimination of sound related letters, problems with sound blending, and omissions of letters in complicated words.

Language-based Disorders

Some typologies distinguish between "language disorders" and "articulatory/graphomotor" disorders. Mattis, French, and Rapin (1975) described the language-disorder syndrome as a combination of *anomia* (a difficulty in recalling the names of things) plus one or more of the following: (a) below average verbal comprehension, (b) poor sentence imitation (repeating verbatim), and (c) poor phoneme discrimination. Mattis also recognized articulatory/graphomotor and visuospatial types of dyslexia, which we will describe.

Olson, Kliegel, Davidson, and Foltz (1985) analyzed the coding skills, regularity effects, and spelling errors of large groups of poor readers versus superior readers. Their stimulus words were visually presented pairs, some requiring phonological processing to identify the real word and some requiring orthographic processing. The primary difference between the groups was on the phonological coding. Younger readers used a phonological route primarily, while older poor readers shifted to an orthographic route, although their orthographic approach differed from good readers in important ways. Poor older readers processed smaller units (letter groups), spelled phonologically, showed lower word knowledge (Verbal IQ) and used "plodding" eye movements. These researchers rejected a typological interpretation of their findings; instead they proposed a developmental model in which reading style is a continuous measure, based on a normal probability curve of phonological skill and verbal intelligence. Although often quoted in the reading-disability literature, this study was made up of superior readers having a WISC–R IQ mean of 113, while the "disabled" readers averaged a WISC–R IQ of 102, meaning that some of the results may reflect verbal intelligence differences, rather than symptoms of dyslexia. Also, many of their subjects fell within normal ranges on the standardized reading and spelling tests of the PIAT, indicating the inclusion of x number of normal readers described as disabled. Both Phoenician and Chinese types seem to have shown up in these data, as well as some "visual" differences in the eye movement patterns of superior and poor readers. For children with phonological processing weakness, the investigators recommended a delay in reading instruction or, considering the unreality of this suggestion, they proposed special auditory training for some children early in the reading experience.

Articulatory and Graphomotor Discoordination

A second syndrome of auditory dyslexia has been described as a group of children having speech articulation difficulties without observable language disorders (Mattis et al., 1975). Their naming, speech reception and sound discrimination skills are within normal ranges. Their disability is lack of fluency in speech production, poor coordination of articulatory and graphomotor functions, inadequate sound-blending, and poor visual-motor integration. Twenty-eight percent of the Mattis sample fit the language-disorder syndrome; 48% fell into the articulation graphomotor discoordination group; and 14% were classified as visual perception disabilities, thus accounting for 90% of their total sample in the three subgroups.

Gjessing (1982) made a typological classification of a sample of 100 disabled readers. He was looking for language-based and visual-based disability subtypes and reported that 45% of them were auditory dyslexics. The major difficulty among this group appeared to be language reception and interpretation. The sex ratio was 10 : 1 males—a higher proportion of males than is usually reported in developmental dyslexic populations. Most language-based types had relatives with reading problems, either on the maternal or the paternal side of the family. Gjessing also found a small group (10%) which he described as both auditorily and visually impaired for reading. He insisted that their numbers were few, implying the need for very thorough diagnosis. He found in them a history of trying to learn reading but unable to learn phonics (auditory dyslexia) and unable to remember words by sight (visual dyslexia). These were the most difficult of the subtypes to teach. It might be noted that this group could be misclassified as either visual or auditory dyslexics, whichever happened to be the focus of the study.

In a controlled laboratory comparison of groups of good and poor readers, Ellis and Miles (1981) found *impairment of lexical encoding* in poor readers. When the stimulus was visual and the mediation period was interrupted by a mask, differences were significant. The investigators matched their groups for IQ, sex, and age (10 to 14). They used a tachistoscope to present symbolic material, followed by a masking stimuli, followed by the required response in either visual or auditory output. They found no differences between good and poor readers when processing visual images that were not named and could not be labeled readily. There were no differences in speed of visual coding, capacity to mediate symbols, or rate of image decay. Dyslexics were significantly less capable than normals in processing those visual symbols having a potential for verbal labeling, in general naming ability, in short-term memory for verbal material, in lexical or articulatory encoding and in articulatory name coding. They were relatively slow at naming colors, letters, and pictures. Their greatest and most consistent impairment was in the lexical encoding of visual events. The authors suggested that younger children may be different, citing developmental delay in language as a possible factor.

VISUAL DYSLEXIA: VISIOSPATIAL IMPAIRMENT

Vision-based reading disabilities have been described as *visuoperceptual disorder syndrome* (Mattis, French, & Rapin, 1975); a *dyseidetic* form of dyslexia (Boder, 1973); *surface dyslexia* (Marshall & Newcombe, 1973); and *primarily visuospatial* dyslexia (Fried, et al. 1981). These writers recognize a subtype of reading disability which is distinct from language or auditory-based dyslexia. Mattis et al. (1975) compared three groups: dyslexic children, brain-injured children who were good readers, and normal readers. They described the visual-based syndrome of dyslexics as children with significantly poorer left-hand than right-hand coordination. This careful control of experimental groups produced some interesting results. The language and blending skills of the visual dyslexics were intact and comparable with normal readers. Like the brain-damaged group, the visual-based dyslexics were poor at figure drawing and construction tasks; factors that were not considered causal in poor reading since the brain-damaged group were selected good readers. The dyslexics were found to be poor on visual retention (the Benton Test); however, they made similar scores to normal readers when the exposure time of words was increased from 10 to 30 sec for each trial. Visuoperceptual disorders were found more frequently in groups of young children than among older subjects, suggesting that researchers who focus on older subjects might find a lower incidence of the visual disability syndrome. This finding appeared to confirm the role of right-hemisphere processing of visual symbols in the early stages of reading and the concomitant importance of maturation in cross-hemisphere communication.

Differences between auditory-linguistic and visuospatial subtypes of dyslexia were found in British children 8 to 16 years old (Thompson, 1982). Using the *British Ability Scales,* significant differences were found on Speed of Information Processing, Recall of Digits, and Block Design Level and Power. These measures could be used to identify visual dyslexics in reading clinic groups.

Three different syndromes of visual dyslexia have been identified in sufficient numbers to concern practitioners. First, the *eye movement syndrome* is observed in erratic eye movements, poor oculomotor control, deficits in sequential ordering, or faulty feedback between the two processes (Pavlidis, 1981). Legein and Bouma (1981) compared the response latencies of normal and dyslexic readers. The groups did not differ in recognition of single letters, or in articulation efficiency. However, dyslexics were significantly slower to respond when the letters were imbedded in a sequence of symbols, when the number of letters was extended, or when the stimuli were presented to parafoveal vision. Working from a linguistic model of information processing, the authors concluded that the primary source of difficulty for dyslexics was the translation of visual items to the speech code.

In a second form of visual dyslexia, *lack of positional control,* may result in the child's failure to achieve the cross-hemisphere transfer of visual word forms to the language areas for interpretation. This is a perceptual problem observed in a reversal of letters or mirror image writing (Stein & Fowler, 1982). Most dyslexics show 20/20 vision when tested by ophthalmologists, some of whom discount visual factors as causes of reading disability. Three possibilities, based on position control, have been suggested for individuals whose reading disability is vision-based: disordered fixation during convergence, failure of hemispheric eye dominance, or unstable eye position.

The third form of visual dyslexia is caused by *prolonged eidetic imagery.* Høien (1982) reported that 40% of a sample of vision-based dyslexics showed iconic persistence of durations more than 2 standard deviations beyond normal. This condition slows reading because the eyes cannot respond to a subsequent signal until the previous image has disappeared. Prolonged eidetic imagery extends the time a reader takes to complete a sentence and increases the demands on the working memory for achieving comprehension.

The lack of consensus among experts concerning the etiology of dyslexia can be discouraging to practitioners. In an effort to place alternative conceptualizations of dyslexia in perspective, Vellutino (1977) examined four prevalent explanations for specific reading disability in children: (1) deficiencies in visual processing, (2) deficiencies in intersensory integration, (3) dysfunction in temporal-order perception, and (4) deficiencies in verbal processing. He found the strongest evidence, both direct and inferential, in support of the verbal processing deficit. He viewed reading as a linguistic process, with verbal recoding into the natural language as basic reading. Given adequate visual acuity, the perceptual organization of alphabetic characters is largely determined by the child's ability to cross-reference and integrate the visual and linguistic components of words and word parts. In this complex process, the aspects of language are dominant, including semantic, syntactic, and phonological. Poor readers, whose dysfunction is linguistic, need learning experiences which emphasize the internal structure of words. It should be emphasized that dysfunction in visual perception is not recognized as a viable hypothesis in many studies because the question is not asked and data are not computed. Nevertheless, Vellutino makes his point that reading is a linguistic process and that the *majority of disabilities* are based in one or more aspects of language.

ATYPICAL PATTERNS OF BRAIN ORGANIZATION

Professionals who study the evidence from the neurosciences tend to accept the probability that the group of disabled readers defined as dyslexic are brain-wired in ways that are different from the general population. Neurosurgeons have made important inroads in matching brain injuries to particular language disabilities, but such direct evidence is meager in developmental dyslexia. Some indirect evidence of atypical functioning in readers with dyslexic characteristics has been reported. Also, researchers have shown renewed interest in the heritability of dyslexic characteristics that dates back at least to Hinshelwood (1917).

Evidence from Brain Activity during Reading

When dyslexics process symbolic stimuli in ways that are different from normal subjects, an inherited tendency is suspected. Fried, et al. (1981) used event-related potentials (ERPs) to demonstrate clinical subgroups in dyslexic boys. They compared 13 clinic children and normal readers on wave-form differences on words versus musical chords. Normal readers and visualspatial dyslexics had greater word versus chord wave-form differences over the left than the right hemisphere. Dyslexics whose reading difficulties were related to auditory-verbal processing deficits did not exhibit this asymmetry. The investigators interpreted their results as supportive of the hypothesis that auditory-verbal dyslexics had failed to develop normal left-hemisphere specialization.

Lovrich and Stamm (1983) measured ERPs in reading-disabled and normal 12-year-olds during tasks of selective and sustained attention to auditory signals. The task was to attend to two tone-pip series of differing frequencies presented dichotically, one to each ear. Infrequent signals of varying pitch were interspersed in each series. Button-pressing responses were used to indicate signal counting. No major group differences were found for the behavioral measures of button-press response to selectively attended signals, vigilance, motor coordination, lateral preference, and dichotic listening. The investigators concluded that attentive abilities appear intact in children with reading disability; therefore, this measure could be used to distinguish them from hyperactive children, who are unable to sustain attention during this task.

In a study of brain activation during narrative text reading, Hynd and Grant (1988) used regional cerebral blood flow (rCBF) measures to compare two subtypes of dyslexics with normal reader controls. Subjects were two dyslexic adults, one "deep" or dysphonetic, and one "surface" or dyseidetic; and two controls were matched for age and sex to the two dyslexics, and a third control for establishing test–retest boundaries. Differences between two dyslexic subtypes and between dyslexics and controls were confirmed by regional brain activation patterns. In the deep dyslexic less brain activation was noted during reading in both hemispheres than in the control, although there was profusion in Broca's area and a lowered RH activation compared with at-rest levels. In the surface dyslexic there was lowered gray matter activity in the RH but similar levels of LH activity, compared with the normal control. Two unexpected results occurred in the fluent readers: (a) An unusual increase in the blood flow to the central-posterior cortex was observed in the both hemispheres. This suggests motor-input integration during continuous reading, which is a different result from tests of one-word recognition and semantic choices based on word pairs. (b) When a narrative passage was used to facilitate brain activation, significant activity occurred in the right hemisphere in normal, fluent readers; in certain areas exceeding LH activity. The investigators urge further research into the unique patterns of cortical functioning in subtypes of developmental dyslexia.

Evidence of Heritability

The genetic factor in dyslexia has been pursued in three ways: (1) by *pedigree analysis,* in which incidents of reading disability are traced in familial histories; (2) by *twin studies* in which monozygotic and dizygotic twins are compared for environmental and genetic effects; and (3) by *gene mapping,* in which attempts are made to locate the string of DNA on a chromosome that codes for this particular cluster of behaviors. The evidence for a genetic cause for dyslexia first accumulated about midcentury when it was noted that certain families had aggregates of learning disabilities. Silver and Hagin (1966) uncovered the major difficulty in tracing the dyslexic phenotype when they examined 24 persons who, 10 years previously, had experienced difficulty in learning to read. Fifteen of their subjects had become good readers while 9 had not. In tests of visual-motor, auditory, and tactile functions, both groups showed the same deficiencies in nonreading tasks. When Finucci (1978) reviewed the literature, she concluded that, despite the imprecision of the case study approach, pedigree studies convincingly demonstrated the familial nature of reading disorders. Twin studies are based on the knowledge that monozygotic twins, whose genetic patterns are identical, and dizygotic twins, whose genes are as dissimilar as those of other siblings, share a very similar rearing environment. When identicals are alike in ways that nonidenticals differ, the heritability hypothesis is supported. Hermann and Norrie (1958) studied reading disability in 45 sets of twins, of whom one or both had the problem. Of 33 pairs who were dizygotic, 19 were of the same sex, but in only 4 sets did both twins have a reading disability. By contrast, 12 monozygotic pairs, all experienced difficulty learning to read. This 100% correspondence, compared with 33% among dizygotic twins, was persuasive evidence that genetic inheritance was an important factor.

Harris (1982) studied that genetic effects of auditory-visual integration on reading achievement in 109 twin pairs of first- and second-grade children of whom 57 pairs were monozygotic. The measures included general intelligence, auditory memory, auditory patterns, visual-spatial patterns, and reading achievement. The results provided evidence (generally significant) for heritable variation in reading achievement and auditory-visual integration measures. The integration aspect emerged as a more potent factor in reading achievement than the auditory memory or visual-spatial abilities considered separately. Data on family environments revealed that exposure to and emphasis on intellectual and cultural activities also promoted reading achievement.

The evidence from familial histories and twin studies prompted a search for a gene that may be responsible for dyslexia. Smith, Kimberling, Pennington, and Lubs (1983) located a gene associated with specific developmental reading disability on chromosome 15. They used a procedure called *linkage analysis,* which is based on the nearness of the target gene to other "marker" genes whose genetic transmission and location are known. In this research a blood sample was drawn which contained 21 genotyping markers. The inheritance of these markers was compared with the transmission of reading disability using a linkage computer program designed for this purpose. The investigators were able to identify affecteds and nonaffecteds among nine family groups (80 individuals) on the basis of psychological tests used in reading diagnosis. This procedure of linkage analysis provided independent evidence of an autosomal dominant gene linked to the disability. These studies point up the complexity of this issue, where one of the most intriguing questions remains: What are the environmental factors that induce some dyslexics to learn to read normally while others remain handicapped?

Practitioners who ignore the influence of perceptual or neurological factors in reading difficulties are likely to emphasize the environments of home, school, or community as faulty. A legitimate concern seems to be the responsibility of the educational system for teaching children to read who are normally intelligent generally, but atypical in their perceptual and cognitive processes. When a series of teachers fail a particular child it is more fruitful to ask "why" than "who"? It is possible to argue, as we have throughout this book, that early failure, with its residue of negative affective associations, is handicapping to both the child and his teachers long after any delays in language acquisition have been corrected by development.

Chapter Summary

This chapter focused on research that related auditory, visual, and somatic processes of reading and learning to read. Numerous models have been proposed to explain how the visual signals from printed words access the speech-based lexicon in the left hemisphere. Some models, particularly the logogen and lexical search models, assume a bottom-up process in which features of printed words (visual or morphemic) trigger the search for representations in the lexical storage areas. Other researchers favor a more complex system of parallel processing in which visual and phonological elements interact. The advocates of top-down, or parallel, processing tend to favor meaning, or semantic features as the primal elements in lexical recognition of words. Dyslexia was defined as a disability in translating visual language into linguistic meanings. Hard-wiring (genetic) explanations, as opposed to soft-wiring (environmental) explanations are accepted by a majority of the researchers who are close to this problem. Individuals with dyslexic characteristics are teachable in settings which assure both their progress with effort and their privacy.

IV Diagnosis, Testing, and Evaluation

A test of [conceptualization], however, can never conclusively establish the identity of such hypothetical constructs with the psychological processes involved. . . It seems to me an inescapable conclusion that such certainty will only be achieved if, and when, neurophysiology provides a reliable description of the neural bases of conceptual behavior. . . . If based on meticulous observation. . . [hypothetical constructs] may assist the neurophysiologists in their highly complex task.

—J. G. Wallace (1965, p. 235)

10 | Individual Analysis for Reading Improvement

Reading is a private venture; learning to read is a joint venture. Reading improvement is directly related to the student's level of motivation, which in turn will be strengthened or weakened by ability, effort, and the difficulty of the task. In most instances, improvement of the poor student's motivation requires both a positive change in reading activities along with the improvement of reading skills. This chapter examines the reader's private world, the factors important to that world, and the informal guidelines for diagnosing points of reading difficulty.

PRIVATE WORLD OF THE READER

Why do some children consider reading pleasurable while others perceive it as painful? Why do some children learn to read with ease while others struggle? What combination of factors—cognitive and affective—create the world of the student who is motivated for reading?

The world each person perceives is unique. Various life experiences construct a separate, private world for each individual. Personal experiences, a student's successes and failures, establish a self-concept and reflect personal identity. Encouraged by peers, parents, and teachers, the student has a chance to become more independent, more selective, and more interpretive in real-life experiences, and more interested in broadening a world understanding through reading.

Personal growth is grounded on the quality of past and future choices; the irreversibility of past choices remains a reality. The inability of a person to live through both of two alternative choices is obvious, hence, adolescents who decide to play football at the park rather than read a book may increase their football skills but not their skill in reading. If reinforced by a successful football game and punished by an unpleasant reading experience, an individual will begin to interpret his or her place in the real world as an athlete rather than as a scholar. The choices that students make are influenced by the social milieu in which parents and teachers play a significant role.

Parents can help children choose between the needs of their private world and
273 the expectations of the external world. Adults influence a child's choice to read in

a number of ways: (1) They can instill early enjoyment of books by holding the infant (as young as 6 to 8 months) and sharing brightly colored picture books on a regular basis. (2) Their children's experiential background will be expanded by taking them on nature walks, excursions to the zoo, and trips to the library. They can fill their home with books brought or borrowed and toys which teach. (3) They can model communication skills through conversation, discussion, and explanation. (4) During the early years caregivers need to keep continually apprised of their child's physical well-being, including vision, hearing, and general health.

Reluctant readers cannot escape the effects of past choices, thus both they and their teachers need to accept present realities and build upon the skills that have been acquired. Telling a reluctant reader to change behavior patterns does not erase the deficits from past underachievement, nor does it present the constructive alternatives to effect positive change. The reluctant reader who exerts effort to improve needs encouragement for small gains. Psychological theory can help the teacher or clinician understand how students define their goals and can create opportunities to tailor instruction to meet the individual needs of each reader.

MOTIVATION BY ATTRIBUTION

Motivation is the term used to describe the impetus and drive of a person toward purposeful behavior. Tolman (1932) developed a theory of motivation wherein the individual used prior information to develop an expectation of a future goal. The expectancy itself was hypothesized to serve as an incentive which aroused, initiated, and drove a specific behavior. Theories such as his, where motivation is viewed as acquired and goal directed, are helpful to instructors who are expected to motivate students into productive learning.

Weiner (1972) developed a functional theory of motivation based on attributions. *Attributes* are the psychological qualities ascribed to a person; *attributions* are the causes of events as inferred by the individual. Weiner's theory lays a foundation for understanding why children behave as they do and provides a logical framework for building motivation to enhance learning. Individuals act. Whether they continue the activity is based on prior experience and the emotional reactions resulting from those experiences.

Individuals use personal history, social norms, performance patterns, and time spent at task to make causal inferences about themselves and their behavior as a basis for generating future goals (Weiner, 1986). The child's history of success or failure determines the choice of attribution that is selected to explain feelings. For example, a child who consistently feels successful learns to believe that success is based on ability; a child who is moderately successful learns that success can occur often, is not random, and may be attributed to effort. Unfortunately, a child who consistently fails in reading learns to attribute failure to a lack of ability.

The affective reactions to success or failure were summerized by Weiner (1986): (1) as influenced by how the person thinks, (2) as seen in positive or negative terms, (3) as varied in intensity, and (4) as preceded by self-analysis of the situation. These internal responses give rise to different external behaviors: Success is related to happiness and satisfaction while failure is related to unhappiness and sadness. Of the attributions reported in the literature, three are major and relevant to a psychology of reading: ability, effort, and task difficulty. Individuals infer the cause of an action from emotionally based attributions and then decide if similar behavior is warranted in the future.

Dimensions of Control

Motivation, according to attributional theory, is learned by children's inferences about the causes of their successes and failures. Children ask themselves "why" questions. "Why do I read so poorly?" "Why does the teacher choose to display other children's stories and not mine?" Causal inferences in response to these questions are distributed along three dimensions: stability/instability, controllability/uncontrollability, and internal/external (Table 10.1).

The *stability/instability* dimension sets an expectancy of future outcomes based upon the individual's perception of his or her innate capacity for success. The child who concludes that reading failure is based on lack of ability, a stable condition, projects similar reading failure in the future, and is unlikely to put forth the effort to alter that expectancy. However, if a child views reading failure as due to effort, an unstable condition, then the failing behavior may be perceived as amenable to change (McMahan, 1973). Of the three attributes described, ability is generally considered stable by psychologists and effort and task difficulty are considered unstable. However, ability may be perceived as unstable whenever learning is perceived as possible, and effort may be perceived as stable whenever a child is labeled "lazy" (Weiner, 1980).

The *controllability/uncontrollability dimension* may lead to anger or guilt. The controllable attribute is effort; guilt occurs if failure is attributed by the student to a personal lack of effort. The uncontrollable attributes are ability and task difficulty; anger occurs if the failure is attributed by the student to poor teaching. Punishment of a whole class by the teacher is usually ineffective and destructive because most students do not have an opportunity to change their behavior and gain satisfaction. Frustration or anger over tasks that the child cannot complete may emerge as hostility toward the teacher or may be turned

TABLE 10.1

		Causal Inferences		
		ability	effort	task difficulty
Dimensions	Stable	x		
of Control	Unstable		x	x
	Controllable		x	x
	Uncontrollable	x		
	Internal	x	x	x
	External			

inward. Pleasure and punishment can be externally controlled through grades, gold stars, or money. Such incentives may be effective if students are able to meet the expectations of the teachers by doing extra work and on completion find the work rewarding. It can, however, lead directly to withdrawal from the learning situation when students believe that their best effort cannot meet the teacher's expectations. Teachers frequently evaluate students along the controllability/uncontrollability dimension. Compassion and pity are given to students whose behaviors are judged as beyond their control. The child who fails an exam because of an extended illness will not be criticized as harshly as the child who fails an exam because other activities interfered with study. Teachers can be too sympathetic toward certain students who consistently fail, by simplifying the curriculum or giving too much assistance, either of which removes the student from the responsibility for learning.

The *internal/external dimension* is closely related to the traditional concepts of intrinsic and extrinsic motivation. Failure attributed to lack of ability leads to shame, failure attributed to lack of effort leads to guilt, and both attributions lead to a negative self-image. The internal attributes are ability and effort; the external attribute is task difficulty. Reinforcement may be perceived as contingent on the action of others or may be construed as one's own. Rotter (1954) coined the term "locus of control" to refer to an individual's perception of the source of responsibility for personal behavior. Research has substantiated that students who are high in internal locus of control have better grades than students of the same intelligence whose perception of control is low (Nowicki, Duke, & Crouch, 1978). If failure is caused by a lack of effort, praise and blame can be effective. The result of a reinforcement pattern in which certain pupils regularly receive praise and other regularly receive blame is a continuation of the damaging affects for those already feeling guilt and shame.

Attributions and their relationship to the dimensions of causality may be summarized as follows:

1. Ability is stable, uncontrollable, and internal.
2. Effort is unstable, controllable, and internal.
3. Task difficulty is unstable, uncontrollable, and external.

Attributional analysis points to the importance of combining the dimensions of ability, effort, and task difficulty to ensure that the learner perceives success as stable, controllable, and internal. The expectancy of success determines the direction and intensity of motivation.

Role of Expectancy

A task is motivated by an anticipation of success. In attributional theory, expectancy plays an important role in how to proceed with a given task. Students are highly motivated when their task is neither be too easy nor too difficult (Slavin, 1986). Most learners need to feel that they can be successful if they exert a maximum effort. When instructors award everyone an A, they do not instill pride because no effort is required; instructors who award too few As do not maximize student effort because the probability of success is considered too remote by many of the students. This notion of expectancy is hypothesized to be a mediated process where learners consider their ability, the needed effort, and the difficulty of the task before attempting school-related work.

An *incentive,* often linked closely with internal and external reinforcement, incites people to action. Several key aspects of the successful use of incentives is related to motivational theory. To illustrate, Doug was doing satisfactory work as far as reports from school were concerned, but he found no joy in reading. He did not read in his free time. So his father agreed to pay him a quarter for each chapter that he read. As a result of this incentive Doug read to his father a book of 26 chapters, a chapter each night, and went halfway through a second book. Eventually his father was forced to spend an evening away from home, and it was agreed that Doug could read a chapter as usual, tell his father the story the next morning, and collect his quarter. This experiment was a success, and the same arrangement was made the next night, with the proviso that more than one chapter might be read. On this basis, Doug finished the book in one evening and collected $2.50. Doug's father then suggested that he might like to read another book, just for the fun of it. Doug accepted this challenge and read several books in the series. During this process he increased his reading rate, expanded his vocabulary, and discovered the joys of reading. The use of an incentive, the quarter, was effective in getting the process of reading started and in continuing it long enough to enable other kinds of motivation to become operative. Incentives were effective because Doug had sufficient ability to complete the task, because he considered the size of the task as reasonable, and because Doug considered monetary gains as fair compensation for his effort.

Research Support for Attributional Theory

High-ability subjects attributed successful completion of a task to effort and the absence of luck, while the same subjects attributed failure to complete a task to lack of effort or bad luck (Neale & Friend, 1972). In another study, Ames (1978) reported that fifth graders with low self-esteem did not respond favorably even when their own outcomes were successful. They experienced few successes in reading and did not see a relationship between their lack of success and their actions. They apparently attributed failure to their lack of ability without giving credit to themselves for their achievement.

Spontaneous verbal descriptions have been used to examine attributions associated to achievement success (Diene & Dweck, 1978). After separating their subjects into categories of "helpless" or "mastery-oriented" on the basis of an achievement responsibility scale, the children were asked to voice aloud their thoughts as they performed an experimental task in which failure was assured. Those children categorized as "helpless" did not view failure as related to effort, whereas those categorized as "mastery-oriented" expressed effort-related descriptions. Brunson and Matthews (1981) repeated this "think aloud" research with college students grouped into "competitive achievement strivers" and "less competitive." The "less competitive" group primarily voiced a lack of ability.

CRITICAL FACTORS IN MOTIVATION

The concept of motivation as an acquired behavior is based on the individual's feeling of success in making an effort to understand the world. The private world of the reader is enhanced as life experiences are evaluated. Children and adults will develop and improve their reading skills as they conceptualize the conditions relating to ability, effort, and task difficulty. The child's level of ability is important to know and to consider so that instructors will establish reasonable expectations which neither frustrate nor inhibit the reader's desire to learn.

Ability

Ability is the power to perform a designated, responsive act without further training; it may be potential or actual, native or acquired. At a given time and under given conditions, ability is considered a stable attribute which is important when planning a reading activity. Intellect and memory are two global aspects of ability which are important when considering task difficulty for curriculum planning.

INTELLECT

A positive correlation exists between success in reading and intelligence as expressed in IQ. High intelligence generally results in proficient readers and low intelligence is associated with poor readers. However, some children with high IQ scores do not become good readers and some children with limited ability achieve good reading skills. Ekwall and Shanker (1988) emphasize that despite the relationship between IQ and reading performance, the correlation of the intelligence scores of 70% of the population within the range of 85 to 115 do not correlate significantly.

The predictive value of IQ is reduced when high-IQ learners have severe reading problems, and when slow learners show adequate understanding of printed word forms at the level of the basic reading skills being taught. Intellectual information regarding the student is helpful to teachers and clinicians when tailoring the reading program for the 15% of children who fall on either side of the middle range. Low intelligence will lead to failure if instruction is not adjusted to meet the slower pace of learners.

MEMORY

Cognitive psychologists traditionally categorize memory as short-term (STM) or long-term (LTM). However, some researchers have identified a *working memory* as the mediator between immediate and stored information. Mediation is essential in the comprehension of continuous discourse but is not consolidated into a permanent memory trace (Chapter 3). The concept of working memory has not penetrated most of the literature on the psychology of reading. Long-term memory provides the meaning for words we see for understanding the material being read. Poor readers spend too much time processing encoded information, and do not have sufficient time to put processed ideas into memory storage (Lesgold & Perfetti, 1981). Reading requires the ability to identify words and then to manipulate them in a working memory while a sentence is being processed for meaning. For example, some children become quite successful in decoding and rely on their decoding skills to sound again and again the common words that they should recognize quickly by sight. The ability to remember words quickly and visually is necessary to accomplish comprehension of a sentence within the limits of working memory. The memory for sight word patterns can be developed in young readers by reinforcement.

In every reading class, several students will be found who fail to transfer decoding skills to independent reading, who are deficient in long-term memory, and who process material without comprehension. Serena, a second grader, was atypical in that she could not remember words after many exposures. She would repeatedly fail to distinguish went-want, come-came, horse-house. She forgot words taught in the preparation period. On a reading aptitude test, she did much better in paragraph meaning than on word recognition. Her intelligence was measured at the high end of the normal range. Children like Serena with a weakness in long-term memory need specialized help. They need to learn to see the pattern of letters within the whole word, to focus on the parts that make it unique, and to use kinesthetic tracing to help them remember how words look.

Effort

Teacher and clinicians frequently use phrases such as "he is a hard worker" or "she is a conscientious student" or "she doesn't seem to try" or "he has the potential to do better." Psychologists often qualify the results of a test session by referring to the scores as attenuated, which means that the child did not settle down and may possibly do better under different testing circumstances. The attribute being referred to is *effort,* which is the internal striving to complete a given task. McClelland and Atkinson (1948) coined the term *achievement motivation* to describe individuals who strive for success and choose goal-oriented activities. Achievement-oriented students want to succeed, increase their efforts if they experience failure, remain at a task longer than others, and attribute failure to a lack of effort rather than to poor instruction or to the difficulty of a task. Achievement-oriented readers have positive attitudes about reading and project a positive self-concept.

Learned helplessness describes children who believe that they have no control over the learning process and have experienced multiple failures in attempting to negotiate a pleasurable environment. They perceive effort as having little effect on desired outcomes and consequently they show a decrease in effort and persistence (Greer & Wethered, 1984). Learned helplessness results in students' pessimism about their future and less effort is spent on tasks, compared with achievement-striving children (Thomas, 1979). Two manifestations of effort culminate in aspects of attitude and self-concept.

ATTITUDE

An *attitude* is formed by an affective framework that predisposes an individual toward, against, or away from reading activity. The movement away from a source may be associated with feelings of aggression, hostility, and apathy. The attitudes themselves, positive or negative, probably are not genetically predisposed but are probably learned. The reinforcement in reading is positive if the parents and teachers recognize each new step in the child's progression in learning. The reinforcement is negative if peers make derisive facial expressions or snicker when the child responds inappropriately. Children soon sense their status as readers when they compare themselves with others whose reading is superior. A positive attitude toward reading does not mean that reading will take place, rather it means that actions such as reading are more likely to occur (Gagné, 1970).

A basic contributor to attitudinal development is the home environment. Setting high goals for success, desiring to finish school, and selecting college preparatory classes has not been characteristic of low socioeconomic families. Project Head Start focuses on this target population as more than 90% of the Head Start families have poverty-level incomes. However, the 450,000 children currently enrolled represent only about 15% of all qualified children (Washington & Oyemade, 1985).

The foundation of the pupil's attitude toward learning, particularly reading, may be partly linked to the language patterns modeled within families. Conversations between the parents and their young child teach the basic syntactic patterns, vocabulary, and concepts needed to begin reading successfully. Families who produce good readers have been found to stress the importance of school, are democratic in child-rearing techniques, foster attitudes of independence, and value communication (McGinnis & Smith, 1982). The child's attitudes culminate in an overall view of how they perceive that others perceive them.

SELF-CONCEPT

Self-concept consists of the person's own summation of his or her personality. The typical adolescent wants to project certain images such as "athletic," "smart," or "attractive" and does not want to project images such as "wimpy," "dumb," or "unattractive." Once established, a person's image is reinforced as it is evaluated by others. Kevin, a 3-year-old, was attending a preschool which was part of a child development program in a high school. Most of Kevin's "teachers" were enrolled in courses related to Piagetian psychology. Kevin had learned enough about the reading process to sit in the library and amaze the students with his reading prowess. With each change of class or period, Kevin could be found in the library corner of the preschool absorbing the positive strokes of each new set of "teachers." The concept Kevin had of himself was that of a reader. It was not mere coincidence that his father was a teacher and his mother was a school counselor. Chris, on the other hand, was a large, well-coordinated, physical 5-year old who was the class leader in outside play. The image Chris had of himself was that of an athlete; his father, not coincidentally, was an Olympic steeplechaser.

In part, self-concept develops from the perceived difference between individual self-evaluation and his or her evaluation by others. Teachers unwittingly function as builders of the self-concept of their students. In judging a student's success on the basis of role expectation and role performance, a self-evaluation is imposed on all students. A student of low ability may be doing well when he or she earns C grades, and this success should be acknowledged.

Children can develop a poor image of themselves as readers, and can project that image to teachers with whom they come into contact. The teacher who acquires a child labeled disruptive, lazy, and unmotivated may unconsciously find information which supports that image. Teachers who make a conscious effort to built favorable attitudes toward reading impart that reading is informative and enjoyable. If children perceive teachers as caring, impartial, and effective, their attitude toward them and their acceptance of the information they impart will be more favorably received.

Self-concept is associated with reading achievement. This relationship is a double-edged sword as academic performance directly influences self-concept. School success increases the development of a positive self-image and failure increases the development of a negative self-image (Braun, Neilson, & Dykstra, 1976). Children come to school expecting to learn to read, if this doesn't happen then feelings of guilt, shame, and frustration may develop. Separation in positive versus negative self-esteem and reading progress occurs by the end of the primary grades or earlier (Shapiro, 1979). This means that many children who begin school believing they will be successful, may become discouraged quickly. If they attribute their failures to lack of ability, they are likely to give up easily, be inattentive, and show signs of insecurity.

Task Difficulty

The failure of teachers to direct curriculum to the individual needs of students may be the most important cause of reading disability (Bond & Tinker, 1973). By the sixth grade, the reading levels of one-third of the students fall between grade levels 2.5 and 5.3 and one-third fall between grade levels 6.7 and 9.5—a variation of 7 grades. Teachers faced with classrooms of 30 children find their greatest challenge is meeting this tremendous variation in ability and skill. Teachers typically feel successful because two-thirds of the students (the grade-level third and the above-grade-level third) survive in the current instructional system.

The individual needs of students can be addressed in the following ways. First, students at the far ends of the continuum require identification and prescription which focus on their unusual skills differences. Second, a match must be found between the student's reading level, and the material which is neither too frustrating nor too simple. Third, curricula can be adapted which emphasize content, and de-emphasizes drill or purposeless reading. Fourth, essential phonic skills and comprehension strategies both need to be sequenced according to their difficulty for some students. Distaste for reading is remarkable in view of the many ways in which reading is intrinsically reinforcing. Analysis of task difficulty can turn failure into success. Two important aspects of task difficulty related to program implementation are: (1) The pupil's inability to break the code and (2) Punishment loading connected to the act of reading.

INABILITY TO BREAK THE CODE

The decoding system seems so obvious to teachers that children may be expected to absorb it from exposure to print. Most children need the teacher's help in making sense out of the decoding system. The child who does not bridge the lesson in skill building to the reading task is likely to feel confused. If the child's lack of learning is an unspoken secret between him or her and the teacher, the student can avoid disclosure only by avoiding reading. Throughout the decoding process children need verification that they are correct or they are incorrect. The predictable and systematic aspects of decoding need to be understood and the irregularities need to be faced systematically.

Considering the number of sound–letter associations in decoding, some form of record keeping may be essential to give both teacher and child security in their progress. For many children uncertainty is worse than knowing they do not know. Through the decades of controversy over phonics instruction, teachers themselves have been subjected to negative conditioning about decoding. These attitudes of insecurity are felt by pupils when teachers must follow systems they do not accept as effective. Teachers need not feel guilty over teaching systematically (Chall, 1967, 1983a).

PUNISHMENT LOADING

For those who have experienced reading failure, the problem is finding a meaningful way of learning that avoids the failure associations of the past. Some reading approaches succeed with problem readers primarily because they differ in obvious ways from previous, unsuccessful approaches. As long a student is progressing, his or her tasks may be different from those of classmates without being punishing. When student associations are primarily unpleasant the inevitable result is a failure syndrome.

Children who know too much sometimes are punished for their precocity, with the result that they avoid classroom participation. The upper third of a typical class are punished by boredom because they already know what is being taught. Gifted children are threatening, particularly when the teacher realizes the planned lesson is inadequate. The reading time for an assignment may vary from 6 minutes for the superior reader to 30 minutes for the slow reader (Robeck, 1958). In any case, the teacher's unspoken irritation with the child who upsets the plan is likely be interpreted by the bright child as punishing.

Because of the breakdown in the taboos about parents teaching their children to read, teachers are faced with increasing numbers of children who already can read well when they come to the first grade. It is comparatively easy to adjust the instruction for advanced as well as disabled readers, if the teacher psychologically accepts the need. To avoid building punishment associations with reading, the teacher who adapts task difficulty to the individual will (1) accept each child where he or she is, (2) provide learning experiences that build competence, and (3) adapt the reading program to the child rather than expect all children to fit one curriculum. School administrators can help teachers by providing above-grade-level materials that make genuine adjustment possible.

INFORMAL ANALYSIS OF READING SKILLS

Instruction for students who failed in reading needs to begin by rebuilding the battered ego of the student. When entering a remedial class or clinic, the poor reader nearly always knows there is a reading problem. Because of strong feelings of inadequacy in reading situations, candidates must be shown respect and given privacy for reading and testing from the moment they come for diagnosis. Important information comes from the skillful collection and analysis of data based on informal assessment. Information collected through interviews presents insights into the private world of the reader which otherwise may be overlooked through formal testing and analysis.

Diagnosis by Observation

Teachers and clinicians have daily opportunities to observe a child's reading behavior. They see students in group settings, in class discussions, and when finishing a written assignment. Teachers can effectively analyze the motivational dimension of readers by (1) studying their behavior while they read, (2) discussing their interests, and goals, and (3) documenting the reading and language development through school records.

The personal nature of student and parent interviews make this procedure a powerful change agent during the diagnostic process. The diagnostician asks questions on a one-to-one basis which may tease out the child's level of acceptance of the reading program. The teacher and the student clarify each other's expectations.

The interviewer needs to be well prepared with open-ended questions. The questions themselves should not interfere with the spontaneity and personal nature of the dialogue. Discussion centering on the student's interests and hobbies is an appropriate icebreaker and a source of valuable information. Whether or not children believe that they have a reading problem or how they perceive their skill in reading relates directly to self-concept and must be pursued indirectly. Questions about the best or worst part of reading in school provides indirect information on the strengths and weaknesses of the student. Review of student interview protocol is helpful at each major step in the diagnosis.

Through years of living with their child, parents can voice details and insights about the difficulties the child has at school. Areas wherein parents can provide information are the following:

1. Family. Is it a two-parent home? Are there cooperative interactions among family members? Is there sibling rivalry?
2. Child's health. Has there been any vision testing? Has the child complained about headaches? Has there been any auditory testing? Have there been frequent colds or ear infections?
3. Reading environment. Does the child read at home? Where does the child do homework? Does the child get assistance with homework?

Parents tend to be understanding of problems the child is experiencing at school and usually they want to help the child overcome academic difficulties. Teachers can elaborate the child's program, outline the school's expectations, and discuss routines to be implemented at home. The teacher can inform the parents of their child's independent reading level and the types of reading material that the child is likely to read with success.

Informal Reading Inventory (IRI)

The *informal reading inventory* is considered by most reading specialists to assess reading habits effectively. An IRI provides an analysis of oral reading inaccuracy, reading comprehension, and listening capacity. While there are a number of procedural variations for administering it, an IRI packet of materials usually includes graded word lists, two parallel passages at each grade level, and a set of questions for each passage. A typical sequence of steps for administration follows:

1. A word recognition level is established using graded word lists.
2. The word lists are used to determine the level at which the oral reading of paragraphs should begin.
3. The student reads each passage orally, advancing through each grade until a frustration level is reached. The reader is asked to retell the paragraph of each reading selection. Following the retelling, comprehension questions are asked.
4. Using the second set of passages, a silent reading comprehension score may be obtained. This step is considered optional except by those who believe that comprehension cannot be adequately examined after an oral reading task. The administrator returns to the beginning reading level and has the student read each of the appropriate selections silently. Questions are asked on each passage until a frustration level is reached.
5. A listening level is established. The administrator begins at the highest comprehension level achieved (either silent or oral) and reads while the child listens. Questions are asked after each passage is read until a frustration criterion is reached.

The results of an IRI provide an estimate of the student's independent, instructional, and frustrational reading levels as well as insights into the types of miscues which may be hindering a reader's progress.

TYPES OF INFORMAL INVENTORIES

Traditionally, teachers and clinicians constructed their own IRIs by selecting passages for oral reading analysis from one of the basal reading series adopted by the school. A series of graded reading sheets was prepared ranging from easy first- to difficult eighth-grade reading levels. Approximately 6 to 10 questions for each passage were also prepared for tapping the student's comprehension of the main idea, vocabulary meaning, and inference skills. Publishers of basal series, basic texts, or trade books usually are willing to allow the duplication of limited selections for this purpose. The material is put in similar type for all levels of difficulty so that the reader has no format cues or pictures to trigger rejection of the selection. Each passage is duplicated, one copy being held by the student and another by the examiner to indicate the student's oral reading errors. Following oral reading, comprehension questions are asked and the answers are recorded.

McKenna (1983) criticized teacher-constructed informal reading inventories because of the variation of readability within a basal text anthology. The readability levels vary from story to story so that it is difficult to discern which part of the text accurately reflects the IRI results. Furthermore, if the teacher chooses multiple selections from one reader to form parallel passages for analysis of both oral and silent reading skills, there is no guarantee that the readability of the selections is equivalent.

Commercially published inventories became popular in the mid-1970s and provide better calibrated passages for assessment although they lack the content validity of the teacher-constructed instrument. Jongsma and Jongsma (1981) examined 10 commercial IRIs and found that they frequently varied with respect to: (1) type of content, (2) use of pictures, (3) directions for administration, and (4) clear descriptions of what constitutes an oral reading error.

Commercial IRIs often do not justify the topic selection although the importance of background knowledge of the passage content is well known (Johnson & Pearson, 1982). A student who reads at the third-grade level may become frustrated with a grade-three selection on an unfamiliar topic but show instructional skill at the fourth-grade level on a familiar topic (Spache, 1981). Research has indicated that a range of 1 to 3 years on readability can exist when a reader is confronted with low or high interest material (Caldwell, 1985).

Text is generally organized into either narrative or expository form. Publishers rarely provide information regarding why a particular number of narrative or expository selections are used and why one form is emphasized instead of another at a particular grade level. Narrative text is generally easier for children to understand yet a logical or consistent balance between the two forms is needed in reading assessments.

ANALYSIS OF ORAL READING

The ability to analyze students' oral reading is critical in determining the instructional level for the student and for identifying deficits. Many students go through the middle grades with little improvement in their reading ability and with increased avoidance of reading because the teachers do not know how to analyze the students' particular needs. Reading improvement, such as that provided in special reading classes or remedial reading clinics, can be achieved for most students by the classroom teacher.

As soon as possible after leaving the student, reactions to the oral reading session should be recorded on an analysis sheet (Fig. 10.1). The student's composure and assurance during conversation should be noted, as well as particular signs of tension, such as fidgeting, throat clearing, avoidance of eye contact, or squirming in the chair. A trained observer easily notices whether a child's composure changes when first confronted with the necessity to read. Different responses during reading, especially when errors accumulate, provide important cues to the reader's affective associations with this activity. These observations are supplemented in subsequent learning situations. The reading laboratory teacher recorded the following qualitative observations for Tarry, whose case study information follows. "Appeared relaxed. Conversation was direct, vocabulary mature. Read in a flat, almost monotonous voice."

The next step in the analysis is to mark the student's reading errors on a clean

Name of pupil_____ Age_____

Reading at level_____ Date_____

Pupil reactions observed_____

_____

Errors

    Stops[a]_____   Substitutions[b]_____

    Repetitions[a]_____   Insertions[b]_____

    Omissions[b]_____   Refusals[b]_____

                                        Reversals[b]_____

                                        Total (b)_____

                                        Minus words counted twice_____

                                        Corrected total

Corrected Total_____ : _____ :: _____ : _____

                         Total Running Words   **Error ratio**

Appropriateness of material_____

Type(s) of difficulty indicated_____

Beginning instruction indicated_____

_____

_____

_____

Causes to be investigated_____

_____

Further testing indicated_____

_____

Remarks_____

_____

_____

[a]Fluency errors.

[b]Errors which interfere with comprehension.

FIGURE 10.1. *Recording sheet: Analysis of oral reading. (From M. C. Robeck & J. A. R. Wilson, Psychology of Reading: Foundations of Instruction, 1974, p. 297)*

copy of the recorded material, using the symbols indicated in Fig. 10.2. Then the total errors are tallied on a quantitative analysis sheet. Fluency errors (stops or hesitations and repetitions) do not necessarily interfere with the student's comprehension of the reading material and are not counted in his or her error ratio. The errors that are likely to interfere with comprehension (omissions, substitu-

Errors:	Symbol:	Example:
Stops[a]	//	At/the/foot/of/the/hills/lay the val/ley. (Tarry read word-by-word; then stopped to sound at the beginning of lay and the middle of valley.)
Repetitions[a]	〰	At the foot of the hills lay the valley. (Hills was repeated and valley was read val-valley.)
Refusals (or words supplied[b])	( )	Its patches of bright fall colors (Tarry did not try to sound patches; was then told the word.)
Substitutions[b]	what	make / ~~made~~ a pretty pattern / ~~picture~~. He listened / ~~landed~~ (Make was substituted for made; pattern for picture.)
Insertions[b]	what ^	to ^ the airplane (To was inserted to make sense in the context.)
Omissions[b]	O	safe(ly) at the edge (Safe was read for safely, omitting the suffix.)
Reversals[b]	←	← of a newly cut field. (For was read instead of *of*. More common reversals Tarry made were was for saw and no for on.)

[a] Fluency errors help to describe the error pattern, but are not counted in the error ratio for determining instructional levels.

[b] Errors that interfere with comprehension are totaled to calculate the error ratio, or the average numbers of running words to each error in word recognition.

FIGURE 10.2. Symbols for recording oral reading errors. (From M. C. Robeck & J. A. R. Wilson, *Psychology of Reading: Foundations of Instruction*, 1974, p. 299)

tions, refusals or aided words, reversals) make up the total errors. To determine the error ratio, the total number of running words in the selection is divided by the total number of words not recognized. If the student makes more than one error on the same word, the additional errors are subtracted so that each word not read correctly is counted only once. Tarry's corrected total of missed words was 45; (250/45) is approximately 1 : 5, or one word recognition error per five running words (Fig. 10.3).

DETERMINING THE LEVEL OF INSTRUCTION

The criteria for selecting reading materials for students are based on their error ratio, effectiveness in comprehension, fluency in oral reading, and the purpose of the reading activity. The levels that need to be distinguished in reading programs

Name of pupil Tarry (assumed name) Age 12 years and 1 month

Reading at level   2.6 (Spache)   Date

Pupil reactions observed Appeared relaxed. Open, mature conversation. Read in flat, monotonous voice.

Errors

Stops[a]	38	Substitutions[b]	32
Repetitions[a]	19	Insertions[b]	3
Omissions[b]	5	Refusals[b]	12
		Reversals[b]	3
		Total (b)	55
		Minus words counted twice	-10
		Corrected total	45

Corrected Total   45 : 250   ::   1:5
                   Total Running Words   Error ratio

Appropriateness of material frustration level

Type(s) of difficulty indicated Lack of word attack skills

Beginning instruction indicated Easy material, high interest level. Vowel combinations, consonants in medial and final positions, syllabication of two syllables. Sight recognition of basic service words.

Causes to be investigated Early lack of auditory, visual discrimination.

Further testing indicated WISC, Roswell-Chall, Durrell-Sullivan Achievement-Capacity, auditory discrimination perhaps followed by audiometer check.

Remarks 4/4 comprehension. Many substitutions of words similar in length, like beginning sound. Uses context to go back and correct. Phrases meaningfully. Substitutions make sense. Normal eye-page position.

[a]Fluency errors.

[b]Errors which interfere with comprehension

FIGURE 10.3. *Example: Analysis of oral reading. (From M. C. Robeck & J. A. R. Wilson, Psychology of Reading: Foundations of Instruction, 1974, p. 300)*

are: (1) frustration level, (2) instructional level, (3) independent reading, and (4) listening level (Fig. 10.4).

Frustration level, for most students, is reached when the oral reading error ratio is 1 : 10, 1 error of every 10 words read. Experienced reading teachers learn to recognize frustration in readers, even though some students have long since learned to mask frustration and others have become habituated to their own labored reading. Symptoms of tension associated with reading are usually ob-

Classification	Error Ratio	Comprehension Ratio	Characteristics of Oral Reading	Purposes
Frustration level	1:10 ± 5	1/2 or less	Poor rhythm and phrasing Unnatural voice Observable tension	Analysis and evaluation
Instruction level	1:20 ± 5	3/4	Good phrasing and expression Faster silent than oral (3.0+) Good progress with teaching	Development of skills: word recognition comprehension
Independent level	1:100	9/10	Good phrasing Relaxed tone and posture Control of concepts, organization	Information Enjoyment
Listening level		3/4	Teacher reads the material Child uses vocabulary in speech	Informal appraisal of reading capacity Vocabulary development Background information Evaluation of listening skills

FIGURE 10.4. *Criteria for Appraising Oral Reading.* (From M. C. Robeck & J. A. R. Wilson, *Psychology of Reading: Foundations of Instruction,* 1974, p. 301)

servable in the error pattern through a technique that we will explain. The frustration level is characterized by such a high incidence of recognition failure that reading can hardly be a rewarding experience for the student. The only legitimate purposes for putting students through frustration-level reading are diagnosis and evaluation.

A comprehension tally of one-half correct answers, or fewer, is indicative that the material is too difficult, even for instructional purposes. The characteristics of oral reading—observable tension, poor rhythm and phrasing, and an unnatural voice—give clues to reading problems. Sometimes the rate of reading is considered an important factor, but how important this weighs in the appraisal will depend on the reader's own feelings and purposes. Rate improvement may be an objective of some reading programs, but not for the student who is struggling with word recognition skills.

Instructional-level reading is characterized by an error ratio of approximately 1 : 20, 1 error for every 20 words, when the child is reading new material orally. When the purpose of reading instruction is to improve word-recognition skills, it is vitally important to provide some challenge and some need for learning unacquired skills in order to maintain motivation.

The minimum acceptable comprehension ratio is three out of four questions answered correctly, including some that go beyond literal translation to more complex understandings. Desirable characteristics of oral reading at this level are good phrasing and expression, good progress after teacher guidance, and (at third grade or above in readability) silent reading that is faster than oral reading. The purpose of reading at the instructional level is to develop reading skills, usually in both word recognition and comprehension.

Independent level is characterized by an error ratio not much greater than 1 : 100, one error for every hundred words read. If reading material is much more difficult than that, as is often the case in required reading for science or literature, the teacher may need a preparatory lesson on difficult vocabulary and preview the organization of the content. A comprehension ratio of 9 of 10 questions answered correctly is desired.

The purposes for independent reading are to gain information and for enjoyment. Self-directed reading is likely to lead to further reading by choice, if the experience is inherently rewarding. To assure a pleasurable reading experience, students need to be taught how to self-select at the independent level and how to locate the resources that satisfy their need to know (Chapter 15). The teacher may need to make a judgment about the appropriateness of difficulty levels, based on the student's emotional response to errors and on his or her skills in coping with unfamiliar words. This is important when the material falls between an instructional and an independent level.

Listening level means the grade or age level for understanding material read to the student. Sometimes the listening level, or comprehension level, is considered an indication of the student's capacity for reading the language. When the teacher reads the material to the student, the student should be able to answer three of four varied question types, including some that require synthesis or interpretation. The teacher needs preplanned questions in order to include an appropriate sampling of comprehension skills. In answering, the child should be able to use at least some of the difficult vocabulary from the selection. The purposes for establishing a listening level are many, including informal testing for reading capacity, vocabulary development, providing foundation material, and evaluating instruction in listening skills. Observing the listening level of a students may be the teacher's first clue that they are reading far below his or her potential.

Tarry's error ratio was 1:5, one word recognition error for five running words, when reading at approximately 2.6 grade level. By these criteria he was reading within the frustration range. Even though he appeared relaxed, this kind of reading experience is wearing and offers little, if any, inherent motivation. Material that is much easier should be found for his reading lessons (Fig. 10.3). The teacher needs to coordinate various criteria when making the initial judgment about instructional level. The final decision is based on how the student is observed to respond to the material and to the type of reading difficulty that further analysis reveals.

Classification of Reading Disabilities

This section describes several syndromes of reading failure, based on observations in the reading laboratory at the University of California at Santa Barbara over a 5-year period. The research on disability types began with clinical descriptions of disabled readers who showed similar error patterns. As soon as 20 subjects were identified who showed similar symptoms, a "group diagnosis" was undertaken for the following purposes: (1) to describe the reading syndrome more precisely and (2) to look for commonalities in background and in intellectual functioning. Three groups were identified in sufficient numbers to warrant this kind of analysis: readers who lacked word-attack skills; readers who showed extreme tension associated with reading; and children who lacked motivation for reading. Classroom teachers will recognize one or two of their pupils as fitting these descriptions.

LACK OF WORD-ATTACK SKILL

Of a clinic population of 156 students (ages 6 years and 8 months to 19 years), 67, or 42%, showed simple lack of word analysis skills when reading orally from unfamiliar context (Robeck, 1963). All subjects appeared relaxed in the reading situation. Fluency errors represented about half of the total, with stops or hesitations twice as frequent as repetitions. Subjects tended to phrase well at times; but they lapsed into some word-by-word reading when recognition errors accumulated.

Almost half the errors were on word recognition, with substitutions more frequent than refusals. The substitutions were usually words having the same beginning sounds and similar configurations, and they made sense in the context. Refusals occurred when the reader seemed to have no cue available or when a substitution did not fit the word following. Repetitions occurred when the reading did not make sense, or when context cues to unfamiliar words were needed. Subjects frequently stopped both before and after a substitution. Children who had training in phonic analysis often produced the first sound or syllable and then waited to be told.

EXTREME TENSION ASSOCIATED WITH READING

Twenty reading clinic children were identified for group diagnosis on the basis of observable tension symptoms that were associated with reading but did not characterize their nonreading activities. All readers in this group showed observable tension, even when reading at or near their instructional level; their error ratio deteriorated rapidly as they read further through the selection, and it deteriorated even further when the difficulty of the material was increased. Although all subjects showed a compulsion to continue reading, some readers showed a tendency to stop after a mistake and to continue without correcting; others tended to stop after a mistake and make multiple repetitions of previous parts of sentences they felt sure of. The error patterns were very different in tense readers from those who merely lacked word-attack skill, even though the error ratios were similar. Fluency errors made up half of the total indicating frequent repetitions; substitutions were words with like beginnings and configurations that usually made sense in the context.

LACK OF MOTIVATION

Readers who lack skill in word recognition over an extended period of time may become tense about their reading deficiency or they may develop a lack of motivation for reading. Inadequate success or negative learning toward reading produces attitudes that complicate the diagnosis and impede the reading improvement program. Attitudes about reading, like attitudes generally, may be directed toward, against, or away from activities that require reading. All three of these behaviors indicate a lack of motivation. Although the attitudes differ in kind and degree, students who lack motivation are prone to accept information about reading that is derogatory and to reject or ignore information that is complimentary. In contrast to the tense reader, who often devalues himself or herself, the student who lacks motivation for reading becomes oriented away from reading activities. The tense reader may want to move away from reading, but fear loading makes such overt activity too dangerous. Tense readers try to please adults who want them to learn to read, perhaps by trying too hard. The student who lacks motivation toward reading shows up in the reading program as a reluctant reader, a careless reader, or an active avoider.

Reluctant Readers. These students are usually found in the regular classes because they function well enough in their school placement to get through assignments that require reading. Reluctant readers are neither skillful nor disabled. They read very little, which hinders their progress toward becoming efficient readers, and they are likely to have developed other important and compelling interests (Noland & Craft, 1976).

Teaching techniques are more likely to work for this group when they focus on the content than when they call attention to the readers' inadequacies. Matching the reader's interests with appropriate materials is important. Library skills should be taught early in the program, so the learner can follow an interest promptly. This type of reader can be motivated to work hard and long for information which serves personal needs. Small mistakes made in reading should be ignored and word analysis skills should be taught as the need becomes apparent to the learner. When turned on by interest in the content, the reluctant reader often becomes a self-directed reader who improves rapidly in his overall reading achievement. Success with the reluctant student has convinced many teachers that all students should be motivated this way—that "reading is caught, not taught." Unfortunately, reading teachers encounter many students who lack not only motivation for reading but also the decoding skills needed to gain positive reinforcement from the content.

Careless Readers. Over half of the group of children initially identified for lack of motivation for reading were found to have serious deficiencies in reading skills. Most careless readers are poor readers who do not seem to care whether they improve or not. They submit to reading, are friendly, but do not try.

As individuals, careless readers develop no consistent error patterns, make errors on both easy and difficult words, make corrections sometimes and at other times not, miss words in some sentences that they recognize in another context. Possibly the best cue to identifying them is an improvement in error ratio as the material becomes more difficult by one or two grades in readability. Matt, age 17, a recognized expert at surfing, was given the Gray Oral Reading Paragraphs with error ratios at the indicated grade levels: 6th—1:9, 7th—1:13, 8th—1:18, 9th—1:8, 10th—1:7, 11nth (his grade placement in school)—1:4. Classroom materials at the eighth-grade level could be handled efficiently by Matt. Quite frequently the comprehension ratio also goes up for careless readers when the selections become as difficult as they can manage, but fall off rapidly beyond an instructional level.

The following observations of students who lack motivation are typical: read in a monotonous voice, very careless about word endings, sometimes make up their own phrase, not concerned about mistakes, sometimes correct but not always correctly, do not really try. The causal factors sometimes associated with this reading disability are a replay of causal factors for other types of disabled readers. In order of incidence, for 20 unmotivated readers the factors were: poor auditory memory, lack of social skills, low self-esteem, minimum entrance age, poor visual memory, frequent interruptions in schooling, prolonged high-fever illness, delayed articulation, lack of auditory discrimination, distractable, recurring illness, tonsil-adenoid removal, family pressure to succeed in school, mixed lateral dominance, delayed physical maturation, poor personal adjustment, lowered vitality, diagnosed brain damage, poor motor coordination, respiratory ailments. A total of 131 factors were identified, indicating that a mean of 6-plus potentially impacting conditions had converged in the 20 children, 14 of whom were classified as readers who did not care. Considering the tendency for students whose reading disability is prolonged to slide into a more ego-saving status of the careless reader—poor reading ceases to matter. Pressure to improve by techniques which have already been rejected can force them into becoming hostile, active avoiders.

Hostile, Overt Avoiders. The unmotivated or careless readers may become a self-directed avoiders, if pressed to improve their reading in the absence of improved motivation to learn. Bing, age 10, attended the reading clinic for three semesters, with little improvement in his reading skills. He was the second of five children and the only boy. His father was principal of a four-room country school, where they lived on the grounds. Bing had many friends and owned several animals. His clinic teacher tried to find material that appealed to these interests but was unsuccessful. Bing would come in with a smile on his face and some diversionary object under his arm. His teachers gradually lost confidence in their ability to help him. The school and the home agreed to press Bing for better performance in reading. After almost a year of work, the clinic teacher's entry in the daily log read, "Bing was hostile. Didn't even try to use what he knows." Four years of failure seemed at the time to be irreversible; both teachers and parents seemed to have missed the chance to help Bing become a reader.

Chapter Summary

Reading is a private venture affected by the learner's past experiences and choices. Learning to read is a joint venture; teacher and parents play dominant roles by creating opportunities to assist the child in developing useful skills and positive attitudes. Motivation, an aspect of the reader's private world, can be defined by Weiner's theory of attributions. Ability, effort, and task difficulty are attributes which provide both a theoretical and practical framework when teaching to improve attitude and self-concept.

Informal diagnosis includes systematic observation and interpretation of data by professional judgment. Parent and student interviews are valuable techniques for collecting information regarding student perceptions of the reading curriculum.

Informal reading inventories estimate oral reading accuracy, comprehension, and listening capacity. The error patterns of disabled readers suggest specific tests needed for further diagnosis and estimate the levels at which instruction in skill building should begin. An analysis of the reader characteristics enables the teacher or clinician to classify the problem so that immediate judgments can be made about retraining.

11 Tests for Analysis and Evaluation

Reading progress is measured and difficulties are assessed in order to take the most logical steps when instructing students. Tests help professionals construct reasonable hypotheses and explanations of a student's progress. They are a primary source of information for determining what factors may be causing a particular reading problem. Chapter 10 described informal assessment procedures used to examine the characteristics of typical readers. References were made to tests which are commonly used by teachers to analyze the strengths and weaknesses of readers. In this chapter, reading tests are examined in some detail, particularly with those used in psychological assessment. Many of these tests are administered by psychometrists; however, their results must be interpreted and understood by teachers and other specialists.

Tests provide valuable information about a student's learning ability and achievement. A single test battery which provides all the data needed would be ideal. Such an instrument would be inordinately long; therefore teachers and instructors must be selective. The tests in this chapter are grouped into three broad categories referred to as criterion-referenced, norm-referenced, and dual-purpose.

Criterion-referenced tests are used to pinpoint specific skill deficits in a particular area, such as reading. They cover a relatively narrow range of topics and provide sufficient information for students and teachers to project a learning program. Criterion-referenced tests measure the effectiveness of the interaction between curriculum and students so that cognitive weaknesses can be strengthened (Stodolsky, 1975). These tests concentrate on essential competencies which are developmentally appropriate to the age and grade. *Norm-referenced tests* compare individuals and schools with their counterparts in schools in the norming population. These tests need *adequate* norms and moderate to high reliability and validity. *Dual-purpose tests* combine the depth and specificity of coverage provided in criterion-referenced tests along with reports of norms, reliability, and **294** validity. Results from these dual-purpose instruments can be functional in both planning a curriculum and comparing the progress of individual students with a population.

TESTING FOR DECISION-MAKING

Educators analyze, interpret, and use test data as part of a rationale for making judgments about students and their curriculum. Cognitive strengths and weaknesses are determined by examining many children of the same age and grade in order to provide a basis for understanding the child's academic needs. Tests provide information when a student needs to be: (1) referred to professionals other then the classroom teacher, (2) screened for further testing, (3) classified for special programs, (4) assessed further, and/or (5) instructed by a program which differs from the standard curriculum (Salvia & Ysseldyke, 1985).

Norm-referenced tests are employed for referral, screening, classification, and placement decisions. Teachers refer students to other professionals, such as counselors, school psychologists, and speech pathologists, when they suspect a child is achieving below his or her potential in academic, behavioral, or cognitive development. Test information is used to verify the nature of a student's difficulties and to answer the question: Does the child need additional help from school personnel? Individually administered intelligence tests, for example, are often used to confirm mental abilities or developmental deficits.

Special education faculty frequently want to identify a small number of "at-risk" students from the larger classroom. Screening tests usually answer the question: Does the child need further testing to identify skill deficits? Which tests should be used and how frequently they should be administered is usually an administrative decision, but the results need to be relayed to other staff members. Those students scoring in the lowest 20% on a screening instrument should be referred for further selective or diagnostic testing. Group-administered intelligence tests, reading readiness tests, and achievement tests are for screening.

Classification decisions are required when assigning children into regular classrooms, special education, resource rooms, and speech classes. Test information is needed to answer the question: Is the child eligible for special services? Individually administered intelligence tests identify children with special needs such as the intellectually gifted and talented, the mildly retarded, or the developmentally delayed. Decisions of this impact require tests that are individually administered and have been developed by stringent criteria.

Decisions regarding the progress of individual pupils answer the question: Is a child making expected gains? Achievement or diagnostic tests may be appropriate, depending on whether the purpose is to assess overall achievement or to examine skill attainment. Intelligence tests may be used to place cognitive growth into perspective. A child who scores poorly on a reliable intelligence test would not be expected to make the same magnitude of gain over a period of time as one who scores significantly higher on the same test.

Tests used in making planning decisions are needed to tailor the curriculum or assist specialists to specify individual goals. Instructional planning decisions answer the question: What reading groups or remedial programs might best benefit each child? Criterion-referenced tests are constructed to evaluate the extent to which goals have been realized and to establish future objectives.

CRITERION-REFERENCED TESTS FOR ANALYSIS

Unfortunately, more information is needed for certain children than is available through regular testing programs. Criterion-referenced tests pinpoint why a particular student has a reading problem and what specific skill weaknesses exist. The *Prescriptive Reading Inventory Reading System* and the *Brigance Diagnostic Inventories* are two exemplary tests described in this section.

Diagnostic Test Batteries

The *Prescriptive Reading Inventory Reading System* (PRI/RS) (CTB/McGraw–Hill, 1980) measures the mastery of objectives in reading and language arts from kindergarten through grade 9. The reading diagnostic tests assess four skill areas: oral language and comprehension, word attack and usage, comprehension, and reading applications. There are five levels of the test which estimate mastery of 171 objectives. The skills measured include sound/symbol recognition, phonic analysis, structural analysis, translation, and literal, interpretive, and critical comprehension. Also, an interpretive handbook provides instructional exercises that can be used to teach in needed skill areas.

Five types of assessment can be summarized from the test data: (1) Individualized Diagnostic Maps, which show pupil mastery of specific reading objectives, (2) Class Diagnostic Maps, which profile the performance of a class with reference to specified objectives, (3) Class Grouping Reports, which identify students who may be grouped together for similar instruction, (4) Individual Study Guides, which match reading objectives assessed in the PRI with page numbers in basal series, (5) Program Reference Guides, which match each basal series in its entirety to each objective assessed.

The *Brigance Diagnostic Inventories* (Curriculum Associates, Inc.) are three batteries of tests which can be administered to plan instruction, especially for children with special needs. Each inventory is similar in format and consists of criterion-referenced skill items, and assesses the mastery of a specific skill area.

The *Diagnostic Inventory of Early Development* (1978) tests 98 skills. For children of mental ages less than 7, it has 11 subscales: (1) four preambulatory motor sequences, (2) thirteen gross motor sequences, (3) nine fine motor sequences, (4) eleven self-help sequences, (5) three prespeech sequences, (6) ten speech and language sequences, (7) thirteen general knowledge and comprehension sequences, (8) five readiness sequences, (9) eleven basic reading sequences, (10) seven manuscript-writing sequences, and (11) twelve mathematical sequences. The *Inventory of Basic Skills* (1977) tests 140 skills of children in grades kindergarten through six. There are four subscales: readiness, reading, language arts, and mathematics. The *Diagnostic Inventory of Essential Skills* (1980) is for students from grades 7 to 11. It has two forms, A and B, and contains nine rating scales, which assess health practices, health attitudes, self-concept, general attitude, personality, responsibility, self-discipline, job interview preparation, and communication. The 165 skills measured are divided into academic and applied areas. The academic skills examine oral reading, comprehension, functional word recognition, word analysis, reference skills, graphic representation, writing, spelling, numbers, arithmetical functions, computation of whole numbers, fractions, decimals, percent, measurement, metrics, and math vocabulary. The applied skills are in health and safety, vocational training, food and clothing, and communication and telephone.

Matching the Test to the Curriculum

Recently a principal of an elementary school requested advice on how to measure the skills being taught in a reading program newly adopted by the district. She was concerned that the current assessment, a basal series criterion-referenced test, might not assess the new program fairly. She realized that the match between the coursework and the test used to measure pupil progress is important. In particular, the question being raised was: Does the criterion-referenced test cover both the new curriculum and the instructional delivery? This principal assumed that the children's progress in a new program, which contained a strong component of language arts, would not be accurately assessed by the current means of assessment. The new focus on children's writing might not be adequately measured.

The match between test content and curriculum materials is referred to as *curricular validity;* and the extent to which the test content was taught is called *instructional validity* (Mehrens & Lehman, 1987). The utility of criterion-referenced tests lies in the guidance they provide the professional when formalizing an instructional plan tailored to the needs of particular students. For example, many basal reading series use criterion-reference tests to measure gains against minimum standards as designated by scope and sequence. The effectiveness of such programs, however, as they relate specifically to an individual is not easily measured. When students fail to master the objectives of a criterion-referenced test, it is difficult to determine if the failure was caused by poor instruction, inadequate test items, or inappropriate mastery levels (Gronlund, 1973).

Another problem with this type of test is that it typically assesses an extensive number of skills, overwhelming a teacher with 30 children to be taught. The *Prescriptive Reading Inventory,* for example, measures mastery of 171 objectives so that determining which skills should be selected for instruction is truly a monumental task. In addition, a potential trap for teachers using a criterion-referenced testing system is that they may focus so heavily on isolated skills that they are diverted from teaching reading as an enjoyable accomplishment.

Improvement in reading based on criterion-referenced systems has considerable support (Levine, 1983). For knowledge about how students are doing in a skill area, criterion-referenced measures are valuable. For knowledge about how students compare with national standards, a normed measure should be used.

NORM-REFERENCED TESTS
FOR EVALUATION

Norm-referenced tests are used to evaluate student performance. These test scores are interpreted to indicate an individual's relative standing in a specific group. They are effective in measuring subject areas where mastery is never fully attained, as in reading comprehension or in vocabulary knowledge (Sax, 1974). Tests are normed by administering selected items to a large sample of subjects who represent a reference group. When administering a normed test, individual scores are compared with scores made by the reference group. High, average, or low scores reflect how others with a similar backgrounds scored on the same test. Valuable test results and accurate interpretations are rooted in the quality of the instrument. The value of the instrument to the student is based on the interpreter's understanding of the technical aspects of the standardization.

Statistical Concepts for Test Selection

Misuse and misinterpretation of test scores have caused controversy regarding their value in education. Misuse of intelligence tests, in particular, may unfairly label and consequently stigmatize a child. Key concepts, which help the professional interpret normed test results, require an understanding of: (1) norms, (2) types of scores, and (3) reliability and validity.

NORMS

Norms are based on large samples of subjects representing a defined population from which an individual's score can be compared. Common factors in developing a representative sample are: age, grade level, gender, socioeconomic status, geographical location, race, and date of norms (Salvia & Ysseldyke, 1985). Age is an indicator of physiological and cognitive maturation which relates to motor development, perceptual-motor tasks, and prior knowledge. Grade level is an estimate of past instruction which reflects directly on the amount of time spent in school. Gender is critical because certain physiological and cortical growth patterns of males and females are different. Socioeconomic status, the academic and occupational attainment of the parents, relates to acculturation. Geographical location is critical because individuals living in some regions have limited opportunities and unique value systems. Race can become an important factor in sampling whenever it defines a cultural group. And finally, the date of norms is meaningful because current populations differ from those of 20 years past.

In constructing a norm-referenced test, items are administered to various types of subjects in the same proportion as they exist in the regular population. The items are given to a large sample size to ensure stability and representativeness. If the criteria are clearly defined and are representative of the individual or group being tested, then meaningful and accurate inferences of individual groups may be made within the statistical limitations of the test.

Standardized test construction requires subjects in sufficient numbers to produce a normal distribution (Fig. 11.1). The normal curve is a hypothetical distribution of the total population which is represented by a bell-shaped curve, where most scores are clustered around the center with fewer and fewer scores appearing at the extremes. The probability curve indicates that in a normal distribution 50% of the population falls above the mean score and 50% below the mean score. The normal distribution can be used to screen students who are significantly below or above average.

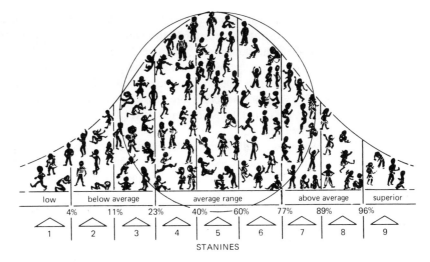

FIGURE 11.1. Normal curve displaying population distribution.

A frequent misuse of norm-referenced tests, occurs when school officials unintentionally, and sometimes intentionally, skew the curve to mislead the public. Parents and others want the test results of the students, their classes, and the schools to be located in the top half of the curve. By teaching how to take a test or by inserting skills at a lower grade level, curriculum is manipulated to improve scores. Since these same advantages may not have been given to those in the norming sample, schools would be increasing scores and improving their image but by invalidating the test norms. Inflated test scores may superficially improve a school's image but do not generate the information needed by staff to make meaningful decisions.

TYPES OF SCORES

The *mean* is an arithmetical average of a group of scores. It is derived by summing all of the scores and dividing by the number of scores used. *Dispersion* is a way of numerically indicating how spread out a set of scores are in relation to the mean. The *standard deviation* is an index of dispersion. In a normal distribution, 68% of the scores are dispersed within one standard deviation of the mean. In a test, with a mean of 100 and a standard deviation of 15, 68% of the test takers would score between 85 and 115. If scores are beyond 2 standard deviations below the mean in either direction, 2.27% of the population is designated. Individuals who fall more than 2 standard deviations below the mean may likely need enrichment or remediation in the area being tested (Fig. 11.1).

The *raw score* is the total number of items answered correctly on a test or subtest from it is converted by a standardized scoring procedure. Raw scores are usually converted into: (1) percentiles which describe the relative standing of an individual by percentage, (2) stanines which describe an interval indicating an individual's general position on the normal curve, and (3) developmental scores which usually make individual comparisons related to age or grade.

Percentiles are numbered between 1 and 99, which indicates a student's relative performance compared to the norm group. A score at the 60th percentile means that the student did better than 60 and less well than 39 of 100 students in the norming group. Percentile ranks are generally easier to understand than other standard scores, but an important caution is warranted. A score of 50% is average and not a poor score, as it refers to the person's rank and not the percentage of the items answered correctly. In fact, half of the individuals fall at or below this rank.

Stanines are divisions of the normal curve where possible scores are divided into nine segments along the base of the normal curve—the standard nine. A stanine of 5 straddles the mean, stanines 1 to 3 are below average, stanines 4 to 6 are average and stanines 7 to 9 are above average. When tracking students was popular, high school students scoring in stanines 4 to 6 on a standardized test were placed in a vocational track while those scoring in stanines 7 to 9 were placed in a college preparatory track. Advocates of this measure point to the fact that this single-digit scale is simple, convenient to use, and minimizes the importance of small score differences. However, this measure may be too general. Jason scored at the 69th percentile (6th stanine) and was tracked to a vocational program. His best friend, Harvey, scored at the 71st percentile (7th stanine) and was tracked to a college preparatory program. Even precise scores are only one indicator when counseling.

Two types of *developmental scores* represent age equivalents and grade equivalents. *Age equivalents* hypothetically compare mental and chronological age in deriving IQ scores. Two children of chronological ages 7 and 9 have an identical mental age score of 8–5. The 7-year-old, Ginger, is in the second grade with an IQ of over 120; the 9-year-old, Susan, is in the fourth grade with an IQ of less than 95. Since both have a similar mental age, their reading age might be comparable even though they might be evaluated very differently by their teachers, and both require special considerations for the school.

Grade equivalents represent a level of achievement considered average for a particular grade and month of the school year within a grade. The score infers the existence of an objective standard of achievement for every month of each school grade. It is sometimes misinterpreted by parents whose children score at a grade higher than their current standing. Howard, a 7th-grade student with a grade equivalent score indicating 10th grade, may not be able to work at the 10th-grade level. Rather, Howard's score reflects what the average grade-10 student would score on the test designed for seventh graders. See Fig. 11.2 for a graphic representation of the types of scores typically presented in standardized test manuals.

RELIABILITY

Reliability refers to the accuracy of a test. Does the score truly represent the examinee's ability? The *reliability coefficient* expresses the amount of confidence the examiner can have in the obtained measurement, if the test were taken on different occasions, would the scores on each occasion be comparable? There are three basic types of reliability coefficients reported in the manuals of reading

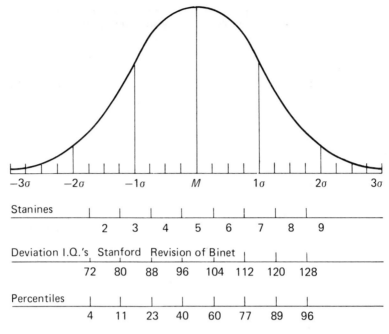

FIGURE 11.2. Normal curve illustrating types of standard scores.

tests: (1) *Test–retest reliability* is a correlation between two successive measurements of the same test following a time delay of the second test. (2) *Alternate-form reliability* is a correlation between two successive measurements of parallel forms of the same test. (3) *Split-half reliability* is a correlation derived by dividing the items of the test into two equivalent halves and correlating the scores of each half.

VALIDITY

Validity refers to whether or not the test content conforms with the purpose of the test. To evaluate validity, the designer must clearly define what is being measured. Three types of validity are cited. *Content validity* is premised on logic. The sample of test items is judged by experts as appropriate and complete. A clear definition of each idea must be made if meaningful conclusions are to be drawn. This type of validity is frequently cited in achievement tests. *Criterion-related validity* is derived by comparing the test results of a sample set of scores with another established criterion measure. It is extremely important to establish criterion-related validity for tests used to confirm a referral or to reclassify a placement. A school district who wants to validate a school readiness test might validate it against the Stanford–Binet if mental age is important or the *Metropolitan Readiness Test* if readiness is important. *Construct validity* is the extent to which a test measures a theoretical trait or characteristic. Many tests base their validity on logic, researched variables, and expert opinion. Usually tests measuring abstract concepts such as creativity or personality are justified in this manner. The strength of the reliability and validity coefficients must be taken into account if users are to feel confident in their application.

Taking the technical information of norm-referenced tests into consideration, two categories are considered: (1) *intelligence scales* which provide predictive information for referring, classifying, and making pupil progress decisions and 2) *standardized achievement tests* which assess what information students already know.

Intelligence Scales

Intelligence testing began in 1904 when compulsory education in France mandated that children be assigned into special classes only after the medical and psychological evaluations. Binet in 1905, with his assistant Simon, developed a series of tasks that bright children would pass and less able ones of the same age would fail. They constructed the first instrument designed to measure intelligence. The Binet scales were imported to the United States and translated into the Stanford–Binet Intelligence Scales in 1916, 1937, 1960, 1972, and 1986. Since Binet's original work, a number of intelligence measures have been developed, many based on different theoretical constructs of intellect. Current definitions of intelligence have been translated into assessment of four areas: learning ability, spatial, conceptual, and sequencing (Reisman & Payne, 1987). The composite scores of the total instrument are expressed in terms of mental age or IQ.

Subtests which attempt to measure *spatial tasks,* such as "Pattern or Picture Completion," "Block Design," and "Object Assembly," require students to use visual-motor skills to copy patterns, to trace a line through a maze, or to reconstruct patterns from memory. Such subtests clue the examiner to important learner characteristics. Does the learner focus on the important aspects of a visual task? Does the learner have good visual discrimination skills? How well does the learner draw inferences and make hypotheses from visual relationships? Can the learner organize parts into a meaningful whole and recognize each part as a section of the whole?

Through subtests such as "Generalization," "Similarities," "Analogies," "Comprehension," and "Abstract Reasoning," different types of *conceptual tasks* are measured. The student makes judgments based on experiential knowledge, interpersonal skills, and relationships between ideas. These subtests help answer questions such as: How well does the student form relationships and concepts? How well does the student move from specific to abstract?

Performance subtests such as "Digit Span," "Picture Arrangement," "Coding," and "Sequencing," are indicators of the child's ability to pay attention and concentrate. Digit Span requires the student to process numerals in order; Picture Arrangement requires the ordering of events of a story; Coding is a measure of learning a new symbolic system. *Sequencing* may be a separate subtest or a combination of one or more of the above. Sequencing is highly correlated with an individual's ability to process print.

Learning ability refers to the student's recall and utilization of experiential or worldly knowledge (Kaufman, 1985). The examiner is responsible for knowing when a test is inappropriate, based on cultural biases that may affect the student's ability to understand the relationships between ideas and to deduce implicit meanings. Learning ability is often expressed in the composite scores of the total instrument as mental age or IQ.

Individually Administered Intelligence Tests

Three of the most respected individually administered intelligence tests are the *Stanford–Binet, Fourth Edition,* the *Wechsler Scales,* and the *Kaufman Assessment Battery for Children* (K–ABC). The standardization and technical qualities of these measures generate information which is valuable for placement and referral decisions. Individually administered intelligence instruments are generally more reliable, allow the test administrator to make qualitative interpretations beyond the test scores and often create less anxiety to the subject. Administration and interpretation of these three tests requires training and experience specific to the test. An experienced psychometrist will know what follow-up tests are needed to confirm any hypotheses that have been generated.

STANFORD–BINET INTELLIGENCE SCALE:
FOURTH EDITION

The newest version of this test is the *Stanford–Binet Intelligence Scale: Fourth Edition* (Thorndike, Hagan, & Sattler 1986) which was based on R. B. Cattell's (1963) theory of intelligence. Cattell defined intellect as either fluid or crystallized. The fluid aspect is general in its scope; it allows an individual to complete many tasks concurrently and is culture-free, abstract, and nonverbal. The crystallized aspect is more specific, related to culture and a person's ability to respond accurately to specific tasks (Cattell & Horn, 1978). Based on this model, the Fourth Edition covers three types of abilities: (1) crystallized abilities include verbal and quantitative reasoning, (2) fluid-analytical abilities include abstract and visual reasoning, and (3) short-term memory includes memory for beads, sentences, digits, and objects.

Technical standards: The instrument was normed on a nationally representative sample consisting of subjects ranging from 2 to 23 years of age. Internal consistency reliability coefficients for composite scores range from .95 to .99. The Technical Manual reports several concurrent validity studies examining gifted, learning-disabled students, and mentally retarded students. Initial findings by independent researchers indicate that the Stanford–Binet Fourth Edition will yield similar IQ scores to the WISC–R for the learning-disabled population (Phelps, Bell, & Scott, 1988). Since this is a new instrument, more comparative studies may be anticipated.

WECHSLER INTELLIGENCE SCALES

David Wechsler created the original Wechsler–Bellevue test, which developed into the *Wechsler Adult Intelligence Scale–Revised* (WAIS–R), the *Wechssler Intelligence Test for Children–Revised* (WISC–R), the *Wechssler Preschool and Primary Scale of Intelligence* (WPPSI). These three tests have been considered particularly useful for diagnosing reading difficulties because they generate separate IQ ratings for performance and verbal abilities.

Wechsler (1949, p. 1) defined intelligence as "the aggregate or global capacity of the individual to act purposefully, to think rationally and to deal effectively with his environment." He saw the overall pattern of intellectual functioning as more important than the parts from which it was constructed, although he departed from the global concept when he separated and normed 12 subtests. Under some circumstances unusual ability in one facet of intelligence did not compensate for deficiency in the total configuration. Wechsler considered drive and incentive to be critical elements of behavior and saw performance tests as carrying a partial loading of these elements in effective intelligence.

WAIS–R

The *Wechsler Adult Intelligence Scale–Revised,* a revision of the 1955 WAIS, is designed for adults aged from 16 to 74 (Wechsler, 1981). Matarazzo (1985) considered this the best standardized test designed for the individual assessment of adults. The 11 subtests are organized into Verbal and Performance Scales. They can be administered separately or together to yield a Verbal IQ, a Performance IQ, and a Full-scale IQ. A criticism by Kaufman (1985) is that it does not have a sufficient number of easy items.

Technical standards: The reliability of the WAIS was determined by the split-half technique. Coefficients for Verbal IQ ranged from .95 to .97, for Full-scale IQ from .96 to .98, and for Performance IQ an average of .93. Subtest reliabilities are excellent as average values exceed .80 for 9 of 11 subtests. Validity data are lacking in the WAIS–R manual. The authors assumed that validity can be assured from the numerous studies done on the 1955 version.

WISC–R

The *Wechsler Intelligence Scale for Children–R* is designed to measure the ability of children 6 to 17 years old. Lubin, Larsen, and Matarazzo (1984) report that this test is the second highest psychologically based cognitive test in use, the only one administered more widely was the WAIS. This suggests the wide clinical use of both tests.

Technical standards: Split-half reliability coefficients range from .91 to .96 on the Verbal IQs, from .95 to .96 on the Full-scale IQs, and .89 to .91 on the Performance IQs. Test–retest reliabilities are reported for all subtests of the WISC–R in the test manual and range from .63 to .95. Concurrent validity was established by examining the relationship between performance on the WISC–R and other measures of intelligence.

WPPSI

The *Wechsler Preschool and Primary Scale of Intelligence* is specifically for children between the ages of 4 and 6 ½. The format of the WPPSI for young children follows that of the WISC–R, although the examiner is given greater freedom in order to maintain rapport with the child. There are 11 subtests, 10 of which are required when computing an IQ. While the verbal scale is similar to the WISC–R, certain adaptations have been made for young children. A subtest called "Sentences" is substituted for "Digit Span." With the increased emphasis on prevention of reading difficulties the WPPSI offers an untapped potential for prediction for children at-risk in reading. Sattler (1982) reviewed the literature and found that the WPPSI has excellent standardization qualities, provides useful diagnostic information, and has interesting test items for young children.

Technical standards: The WPPSI was normed on children stratified on the 1960 census. Internal-consistency is reported as split-half reliability coefficients from .93 to .95 for verbal IQ, from .91 to .95 for Performance IQ, and from .96 to .97 for Full-scale IQ. Validity studies have compared the WPPSI to the Stanford–Binet, yielding a correlation of .81. With ethnic, minority, and lower socioeconomic children, the WPPSI is more variable than for white, middle-class children (Freeman, 1985). The Wechsler Scales have been the tests of choice for assessing general intellectual competence.

Kaufman Assessment Battery for Children

An individually administered test designed to assess intelligence (learning potential and style) and achievement for children 2 ½ to 12 ½ years of age is the *Kaufman Assessment Battery for Children* (Kaufman & Kaufman, 1983). The test provides information for (1) psychological and clinical assessment, (2) psychoeducational evaluation of exceptional children, (3) educational placement and planning, (4) preschool assessment, and (5) neuropsychological assessment. The K–ABC consists of 10 subtests which generate three administered scales and one supplementary scale. Intelligence measures are derived from the Simultaneous Processing Scale, the Sequential Processing Scale, and an optional Nonverbal Scale. Both the Simultaneous and Supplementary Scales can be combined to form a Mental Processing Scale. Achievement, defined as the ability to process information and apply it to real-life situations, is determined from the Achievement Scale.

The theoretical underpinning of the K–ABC is that information is sequentially or simultaneously processed. Concern with the differences in culturally atypical children has led to a Nonverbal Scale, which is designed to measure the intelligence of deaf, hearing-impaired, speech or language-disordered, autistic, and non-English-speaking children. The K–ABC has received mixed reviews. Major strengths include a theoretical bases in brain functioning, excellent manuals for clinical application, and an analysis of psychological significance of the different scores. It has been criticized because of incomplete normative data, lack of long-term stability or reliability data, and a lack of clarity on how to use the sociocultural norms (Mehrens, 1984).

Technical standards: Scaled scores are reported by chronological age. Like the Wechsler Scales, the K–ABC scales are combined to generate a mean of 100 and a standard deviation of 15. The subtests have a mean of 10 and a standard deviation of 3. National and sociocultural norms provide a fair assessment of children from different racial, ethnic, and socioeconomic backgrounds on the Mental Processing Scale and Achievement subtests. Split-half coefficients on the Mental Processing Scale ranged from .84 to .95 across the different age categories. Achievement subtests ranged from .97 to .70 and the reliability on the composite exceeded .90 at all ages. Split-half coefficients ranged from .92 to .63 on the Mental Processing subtests. The composite scales are generally reliable while the subscales are less so.

Group-administered Intelligence Tests

Group intelligence tests are used primarily for making screening decisions. They can be given to a large number of students at one time, can be quickly administered and easily scored. They provide general information about the capability of students at class, school, district, and national levels. Group intelligence tests do not have the technical standards for making placement and classification decisions.

A group-administered intelligence test, such as the *Slosson Intelligence Test* (1981), is frequently given by teachers and other curriculum specialists. Such tests, because they are group-administered and because their technical qualities are not strong enough to classify students, have been popular in screening gifted students. Many states require that before a student is placed into a gifted program the student must be assessed by a standardized individual intelligence measure (Sattler, 1982). Before such expense is arranged, screening procedures such as group intelligence and group achievement tests are used.

The *Slosson Intelligence Test for Children and Adults* (SIT) is a general mental ability measure whose items range from .5-month level to adulthood. The SIT has a question-and-answer format wherein the administrator asks a number of short-answer questions. The areas covered include Math, Reasoning, Vocabulary, Auditory Memory, and Information. This is an untimed test that generates a mental age, IQ, percentile rank, and stanine. The developer suggests that the test is appropriate for different populations, including infants, blind, hard of hearing, organic brain-damaged, emotionally disturbed, and those with physical handicaps. IQs derived from group tests are suitable for group research but not for individual placement.

Technical standards: The SIT was normed on a New England sample ranging from 2 to 18 years old. The SIT reports test–retest stability coefficients. Criterion-related validity is based on high correlations between the SIT and the Stanford–Binet. The SIT is a widely used, quick estimate of intellectual ability that can be used for screening by professionals not trained in giving individual psychological tests. The reliability and validity are suspect and the information about its technical adequacy is limited. Oakland (1985) cautions examiners about estimating the IQs of mentally retarded and gifted children, and suggests avoiding this measure when considering individuals with auditory and visual acuity disabilities.

Standardized Achievement Tests

The purposes of achievement tests in reading are to assess the progress of students from kindergarten through junior college. Two types of achievement tests are survey batteries and reading readiness inventories. Survey tests identify those students who are having difficulty and should be given a reading diagnostic test.

SURVEY BATTERIES

Survey batteries provide comprehensive estimates of the students' normative performance on core subjects: spelling, reading knowledge, vocabulary, arithmetical reasoning, arithmetical computation, science, and social studies. Such a battery has the advantage of having all subtests normed on the same sample population. A pupil's performance in reading can be compared directly with achievement in other subject areas. The *Metropolitan Achievement Tests* (1984, 1986) and the *Stanford Achievement Test Series* (1982) are reviewed.

The *Metropolitan Achievement Test,* 6th Edition(MAT) (Harcourt, Brace, & Jovanovich) utilizes a two component system—the *MAT Survey Test* (1984) and the *MAT Reading Diagnostic Battery* (1986). The *MAT Survey Test* provides general evaluation of the students' skills in Reading Comprehension, Mathematics, Language, Social Studies, and Science. It is both norm- and criterion-referenced and can assess students from grades K to 12.9. Test administration is from approximately 2 to 4 hours. It is used for screening, monitoring the class performance, and evaluating the overall program. The *MAT Survey Test* uses reading items selected from the diagnostic battery.

The *MAT Reading Diagnostic Battery* examines visual discrimination, letter recognition, auditory discrimination, sight vocabulary, recognition of consonant and vowel sounds, vocabulary in context, word part clues, rate of comprehension, skimming and scanning, reading comprehension, and an optional writing test. It is designed for the classroom teacher or reading specialists for planning and evaluating curriculum. There are six levels, from grades K.5 to 12.9. It takes approximately 1 to 4 hours to administer.

Technical standards: Both fall and spring norms were developed using more than 200,000 students in each standardization. Six types of scores are derived: percentile ranks, grade equivalents, normal curve equivalents, performance indicators, and instructional reading levels. Reliability varies between the intermediate and advanced levels where coefficients are above .80 and the primary and elementary levels where about half are above .80. Validity is based primarily on expert opinion.

The *Stanford Achievement Test Series* (SAT) (1982) consists of editions for grades K to 1; grades 1 to 9; and grades 8 through community college. All tests are group-administered and are norm- and criterion-referenced. There is a Basic Battery and a Complete Battery. The Basic Battery includes a reading assessment part which examines Sounds and Letters, Word Study Skills, Word Reading, Sentence Reading, Reading Comprehension, Vocabulary, Listening Words and Stories, Listening Comprehension, Spelling, and Language/English. The Complete Battery includes an optional writing test. The examiner can choose to administer either battery or any of the major test areas separately. This is a comprehensive assessment of reading and its relationship to the language arts.

Technical Standards: Most of the tests were standardized for spring and fall administration. Raw scores can be transformed into stanines, grade equivalent scores, percentile ranks, age scores, and various standard scores. Results can be interrupted for individual student record sheets, class profiles, analyses of each student master of objectives, and local norms. The Stanford series was validated by curriculum specialists, teachers, and minority-group professionals for cultural or ethnic bias.

READING READINESS

Reading readiness tests are norm-referenced achievement tests administered to children in kindergarten, or as they enter the first grade, to predict their initial school success and to identify weaknesses essential for reading. Reading readiness assumes that certain skills in reading should be developed before formal instruction. If certain skills are lacking (e.g., visual and auditory discrimination), these should be strengthened and compensated for prior to reading instruction. These tests help identify some students who are unlikely to succeed in reading based on developmental delays and/or environmental factors. Information generated from such tests can determine the most appropriate intervention at the earliest possible time.

The *Metropolitan Readiness Test* (MRT) (1986) is an excellent instrument for estimating reading readiness. It is a group-administered battery of skills that requires three sittings of approximately 30 minutes each. A practice test is included and should be given before the MRT is administered. There are two levels of assessment. Level 1 is designed for the beginning or middle of kindergarten, and level 2 for the end of kindergarten or the beginning of first grade. Level 1 assesses auditory memory, beginning consonants, letter recognition, visual matching, and school language and listening. Level 2 assesses quantitative language, beginning consonants, sound–letter correspondence, visual matching, finding patterns, school language, listening, quantitative concepts, and quantitative operations. The MRT is a comprehensive and useful instrument for screening beginning readers.

Technical standards: Raw scores can be transformed into percentile ranks, stanines, scaled scores, and normal curve equivalents. Internal consistency of composite scores range from .70 to .90. Validity is weakened by the limited number of items in each area tested and the manual warns the examiner that separate test scores should only be viewed as suggestive.

Dual-purpose Tests for Analysis and Evaluation

Dual-purpose diagnostic reading tests focus on skills specific to the reading process and facilitate individual examination of those skills by comparing the scores of successful and unsuccessful readers with a population sample. By combining the qualities of norm-referenced tests with the skill emphasis of criterion-referenced tests, an instrument is created which can be effective in analyzing skill areas and evaluating skill deficits.

Norm-referenced tests are of minimal value in making instructional decisions since knowing how a child's skill level compares with others provides little specific information to the teacher about instructional content. Criterion-referenced reading tests help educators to determine a student's specific skill needs and appropriate instructional plans. These tests assume: (1) That reading can be broken into component subskills, (2) That test items can be devised to measure those subskills, and (3) That this information can be effectively utilized for instruction. This section reviews the *Diagnostic Reading Scales* (1981), the *Stanford Diagnostic Reading Test* (1984), and the *Woodcock Reading Mastery Tests* (1987).

The *Diagnostic Reading Scales* (DRS) were constructed by George D. Spache (California Test Bureau). Scaled from grades 1 to 7, the materials are appropriate for junior and senior high students who are deficient in reading skills. There are three sections: word recognition lists; oral and silent reading of paragraphs; and a section that assesses word recognition and phonics. The first section of the test includes oral reading of vocabulary lists which the examiner marks to describe the nature of the subject's response: (1) guesses at the word as a whole, (2) spells it letter-by-letter, (3) uses phonic methods of attack, (4) identifies shorter words within the word, or (5) refuses and expects the teacher to supply the word. Word lists are used a lot for a grade-level estimate of the student's instructional level and sight word vocabulary.

The second section of the test has the subject read orally from graded paragraphs, beginning at the level indicated by the vocabulary test. Using the diagnostic technique described in Chapter 10, the reading is scored for insertions, omissions, substitutions, reversals, repetitions, and aided words. Explanations to the teacher for marking and scoring are clear and useful. Questions, both literal and inferential, are asked to check the subject's comprehension. The same series of graded samples may be used to obtain a silent reading level. Speed of reading is calculated by timing the silent-reading passages. The teacher continues by orally reading to the student to determine his or her reading capacity.

The third section supplies word analysis and phonics tests. These are initial consonants, final consonants, consonant digraphs, consonant blends, initial consonant substitution, initial consonant sound, auditory discrimination, short and long vowel sounds, r-controlled vowels, vowel diphthongs and digraphs, common syllables, and blending. With knowledgeable interpretation, these tests provide added insights into perceptual deficits as well as instructional gaps.

The Spache scales are administered individually and require some experience on the part of the examiner to record. The diagnostic battery enables the teacher to obtain an analytical view of an individual's responses which hinder reading.

Technical standards: The 1981 version was normed on 534 students in grades 1 through 8, with consideration to gender differences and minority groups. Information on test–retest reliability are reported only for grades 1 and 2, with about half of the coefficients exceeding .80. Discussion of test validity are reported from earlier test editions.

The *Stanford Diagnostic Reading Test* (SDRT) is a group-administered test whose scores can be interpreted as either norm- or criterion-referenced. There are four levels: (1) grades 1 to 3, (2) grades 3 to 5, (3) grades 5 to low high school students, and (4) grades 9 to 12. The skill domains sampled are: auditory vocabulary, vocabulary, auditory discrimination, phonetic analysis, structural analysis, word parts, word reading, reading comprehension, reading rate, scanning and skimming, and fast reading.

Technical standards: The SDRT was normed on a stratified sample of about 30,000 students in the fall of 1983 and on about the same number in the spring of

1984. Raw scores can be transformed into criterion-referenced scores called Progress Indicators which indicate whether or not a student has mastered a particular skill. Norm-referenced scores include percentile ranks, stanines, grade equivalents, and scaled scores. Internal consistency coefficients for most subtests at exceed .80. Alternate-form reliability coefficients range from .66 to .78. Content validity is judged by comparing the test items with typical curricular content.

The *Woodcock Reading Mastery Tests* (WRMT) (1987) is a battery of six individually administered tests for examining skill development in reading with students in kindergarten through college. The six reading areas are covered: (1) Visual-Auditory Learning, (2) Letter Identification, (3) Word Identification, (4) Word Attack, (5) Word Comprehension, and (6) Passage Comprehension.

Technical standards: Norms were constructed on approximately 6,000 students. The sample was collected in 60 school districts and was based upon community size, race, region, and ethnic origin. Raw scores for each of the subtests can be converted to three different options for interpreting criterion-referenced scores; norm-referenced scores including grade equivalent, age scores, percentile ranks, and standard scores. A "Relative Performance Index" is a score transformation which reflects changes in a pupil's proficiency and presents an index at different levels of difficulty. A typical result might indicate a student reading at third-grade level with 80% accuracy while reading at second-grade level with 95% accuracy. A total score is generated by combining the six subtest scores, providing a reliable index of skill development. Internal consistency reliabilities on all six areas exceed .80. Content validity is based on expert opinion and test construction procedures; concurrent validity correlations between the *Woodcock Reading Mastery Tests* and the *Woodcock–Johnson Psychoeducational Battery* is high.

Individualized Educational Plan (IEP)

The Education for All Handicapped Children Act, P.L. 94–142, dictates that a handicapped child's education must be individually appropriate. The Individual Educational Program requires each child in the program to have a written statement devised by a local education agency or an intermediate education agency to meet his or her unique needs. The statement shall include the child's present level of educational performance, annual goals, specific educational services and regular educational services, and evaluative procedures and schedules.

In developing an IEP, a number of individuals must be included: someone other than the teacher qualified to supervise a child's special education, the teacher, one or both parents, the student when possible, and others at the choosing of the parents or agency. This group will prepare individualized student assessment for classification, prescription of an instructional program, and continued program evaluation.

Individualized intelligence tests have been criticized for assigning a disproportionate number of minority students to special education programs (Turnbull III, 1986). Such tests may be insensitive to variations of language and socioeconomic status. For these reasons, individualized IQ tests are preferred over group IQ tests, and legally, testing as a single criterion is necessary but insufficient for classification. Along with IQ tests, the child's socioeconomic background and his or her adaptive behavior are considered.

By examining the foundation of an IEP, the importance of both criterion- and norm-referenced tests becomes evident. Both types of tests are necessary in developing an instructional program unique to a student, evaluating the program by formative procedures, and classifying students as having special needs. By dovetailing the strengths of both types of tests, wise educational decisions can be made.

Chapter Summary

Tests provide valuable information for making decisions about a student's learning ability and achievement. Criterion-referenced, norm-referenced, and dual-purpose tests were discussed in terms of the types of decisions they can be helpful in making. Criterion-referenced tests are important in planning a curriculum to meet a student's specific skill needs. Norm-referenced tests aid in evaluating a student's performance. Dual-purpose tests combine the qualities of both criterion-referenced and norm-referenced tests.

The IEP represents the value of the different tests as they are used in analysis and evaluation to meet student needs. The care which goes into making the IEP warrants its consideration by classroom teachers. While test data are valuable, it needs to be tempered with insights that go beyond the testing situation.

12 Responsibility for Reading Development

This chapter differentiates the roles of individuals responsible for reading instruction from the view of the educational psychologist. The goal, or overall purpose, of a program is to make the learner increasingly cognizant of the reading objectives and eventually self-directing in achieving them. The preschool child's accountability is slight and the traditional role of the school has been significant. As students mature and attain metacognitive control, responsibility for reading shifts to the students themselves.

A more systematic reading program than has been followed in the past is needed if every student is going to achieve literacy and use reading for further cognitive development. The task of complete literacy is likely to be achieved only if the points of decision are delineated and the persons accountable are designated. A model showing the different parts of the program and the people involved is shown in Fig. 12.1. The flow sheet is a simplified map of the accountability of adults and students for objectives, program selection, instruction, and evaluation.

QUESTIONS OF RESPONSIBILITY

Traditionally schools have been seen as responsible for developing a literate society. Literacy has been defined in different ways: by the number of years in school, by a level of performance on a norm-referenced test, or by a defined set of competencies (Park, 1981). Others have defined it as the level where individuals can read any material they so choose to read (Bormuth, 1982). At a minimal level, literacy is the functional ability to read the forms and instructions necessary in an industrial society. In any case, instruction is intended to help individuals who, for whatever reason, never learned to become skillful enough to read for their own purposes and to be able to continue to improve with practice. Many writers are concerned with growing numbers of illiterate people at both the national and international levels (Carroll & Chall, 1975). It is, however, a sensitive topic inasmuch as illiteracy is related to cultural, social, political, and economic issues. This section addresses four questions of responsibility: (1) Who

312

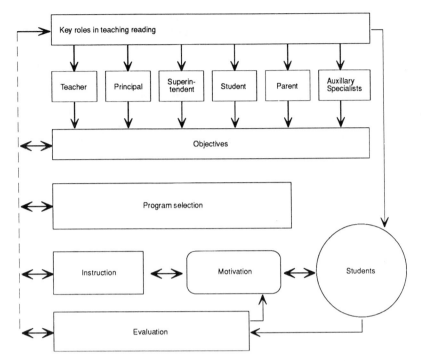

FIGURE 12.1. *Key components for a reading programs. The focus at all points of decision is on students, for whom improvement in reading behavior is the goal. While students themselves are important components, instructional change is an inherent step to improve their motivation and achievement.*

is responsible for literacy? (b) What is the priority? (c) What is the community's commitment? (d) What is the student's role?

Who Is Responsible For Literacy?

An immediate response to this question of responsibility is the teacher. This is only a partial answer, however, because in the school system there are many constraints put on the teacher by principals, superintendents, auxiliary specialists, and other personnel. In addition, the parents and students themselves affect the outcomes by their attitudes toward reading. They must shoulder some of the responsibility for poor performance, just as they have a right to share the credit for reading successes.

In an honest system of accountability, the auxiliary staff must be assessed for the function they carry in the reading program. The most immediate member of the auxiliary personnel is the reading specialist. How do the schools measure the reading specialist's contribution to the improvement of students' reading skills? Perhaps the principal is less directly involved than the reading coordinator, but many principals unwittingly make the teaching of reading either easier or more difficult, depending on the priorities they convey to teachers. Such a simple thing as protecting the teacher from interruption during reading time may make in-

struction more effective. Curriculum coordinators, directors of elementary instruction, and superintendents all influence reading, depending on how they see
their own functions. When the teacher must make reports and attend meetings
that do not contribute directly to teaching, reading instruction is less, rather than
more, effective. In holding the schools accountable for reading instruction, direct
measures of the contributions of administrative personnel should be attempted.
In-service programs such as Teacher Expectations and Student Achievement
(TESA) and Time On Task have proven helpful to both teachers and principals.

The contribution to reading proficiency that is made by the counselor or
school psychologist may be direct. Ideally the school psychologist helps students
who have reading problems unwind the emotional turmoil that may be blocking
their reading proficiency. When systems for measuring accountability are put
into effect, the contributions of the counselor and the school psychologist should
be measured and the desirability of continuing the services appraised.

In addition to the responsibility of the school personnel, the family and the
student bear responsibility for the success or failure of reading instruction. It
appears that: (a) families contribute more to functional knowledge from home
and community than from the school, (b) good readers come from homes that
encourage positive attitudes toward learning, and (c) siblings can be a valuable
source of informal tutoring (Sartain, 1981). In homes where reading is part of the
value structure of the student, there is less chance for reading failure.

What Is the Priority?

In schools where the superintendent and, in particular, the principal, believe that
reading is the most important facet of the entire program, reading instruction will
probably be done well in most classes (Brandt, 1987). If they believe music,
dramatics, or field trips have the highest priority, then they will probably be
given the most attention. The priority of reading is reflected in the amount of
time devoted to reading instruction, the proportion of the budget for materials,
and the quality of the auxiliary staff.

What Is the Community's Commitment?

Closely related to the issue of priority is that of program funding. When reading
instruction is a high priority, the budget usually is relatively generous, but when
other activities have higher priorities than reading the funding usually goes to
them. Substantial funding makes different reading approaches possible for children with unique educational needs. Adequate funding means the availability of
different kinds of books, telebinoculars for screening suspected vision problems,
consultant fees for the teachers, special classes for remedial instruction, and
computer-assisted instruction when requested. The decisions about reading budgets are usually made by administrative staff. Teachers frequently fear accountability because they foresee, with some justification, a demand for a Mercedes–
Benz level of performance with only a Volkswagen level of financial support.

When committing the resources necessary for complete success in reading,
other programs may get less support than they deserve. Monetary resources are
not limitless but, more important, the student's energy and purpose are not
limitless either. Compromises must be made. Probably a greater commitment to
reading skills in the primary grades would reduce the time necessary for develop-

mental reading instruction during the later schoolyears. Certainly there are minimal levels of competence that, having been reached, assure fluency and continued reading success with comparatively small expenditures of energy. When the commitment to reading is not sufficient to ensure children success at a fluency level during the primary grades, a great deal of effort is necessary to provide remediation for them.

Students who achieve fluency at the level of mass media tend to improve their reading during absences from schooling, while otherwise their skills deteriorate (Gray, 1969). Physical and mental handicaps as well as ethnic, cultural, economic, and language differences of students often create barriers which require additional funding to employ teaching specialists and to provide for special equipment, materials, and supplies.

What is the Student's Role?

It is difficult to teach reading to students who are actively resisting the instruction. On the other hand, it is difficult to prevent dedicated students from learning whatever they feel committed to learn. Many children learn to read before they go to school, with little apparent expenditure of energy and minimal teaching on the part of parents or siblings. At the same time many children fail to learn to read in school in spite of able and dedicated teaching. They come to school ready to resist reading, or they learn to resist reading instruction soon after they arrive. The final accountability lies with the student, who ultimately is responsible for his or her own success.

OBJECTIVES

Objectives are the stated levels of functioning in decoding and encoding skills, in reading comprehension, and in the use of printed materials. The kinds of questions a study committee or a teacher must deal with in planning objectives for the accomplished reader are: Do you want readers who follow directions, or who question authority? Do you want them to see hidden meanings; to be skeptical of advertising? Is oral reading a communication skill or is it merely a way the child displays recognition of certain words? What is the relationship of ability to the school's choice of objectives for each student? What is the student's role in determining objectives? The objectives describe the reading behavior toward which the program is focused.

Different reading programs seek different results. In order to have a systematic reading program, the objectives must be formulated in detail. When goals are explicit, the evaluation can be made with assurance that those who are teaching and those who are measuring the results are operating on the same wavelength. While the need for harmony between reading instructional objectives and evaluation seems self-evident, many districts do not use tests that measure the stated objectives of the reading program.

What Kind of Readers?

Most curriculum planners would claim that they would hope to train a reader who is perceptive and understanding—one who could read with skill and see the hidden meanings in the material. Thoughtful analysis indicates that many influential people do not want the general populace to read this well. Much advertising is based on the assumption that most people will be misled by material that is technically honest but structured so that erroneous conclusions may be extrapolated. Menthol cigarette commercials, which picture an idyllic countryside, hope to imply that smoking this brand will transport the smoker to a beautiful surrounding. No one is really expected to believe such far-fetched ideation, but the effectiveness of the advertising is based on the affective interpretation that, in some unknown way, smoking makes the world beautiful.

Some school personnel are not anxious to have students develop into readers who question authority, although the emphasis on critical interpretation has been part of the instruction since the launching of Sputnik. Second thoughts about whether such critical reading is desirable seem to be evident. The Army, among others, hopes inductees will read and follow directions. The ability to read well enough to follow directions is a minimal level of reading competence, which many would consider insufficient as a final goal.

A question arises: Is the building of objectives the right of the superintendent, principal, teachers, parents or the children themselves? Many members of the community are unhappy with the level of reading success achieved by the children. Most of these critics do not question the objectives and tacitly assume these are set for the highest possible development of the children rather than to produce a docile and tractable populace. However, there are those who believe that the highest reading objective set for their children by the school is the skill to follow orders given by superiors.

Is Oral Reading a Goal?

For many years the reading ability was judged by how well students read orally. And, in fact, oral reading is necessary in the primary grades to verify word analysis. Young children need their reading to be heard in order to receive feedback on their accuracy. As was pointed out in Chapter 10, one of the best ways of analyzing reading difficulties is to record the student errors as different passages are read orally. And finally, many people enjoy reading aloud to each other or for an audience. Definite needs exist for some people to be able to read orally, including those who become radio or television announcers, those who read Scripture in church, and those who read parts for a play. However, most reading is done silently for content rather than orally for effect. Consequently, as the reader matures, more and more time needs to be spent reading material silently.

What Is the Student's Role?

Children often know that they want to read, but they have very little knowledge of the wealth of experience that can be gleaned from learning to read interpretively, or from understanding the intention of the author. Should students be free to decide that all they want is surface meaning? Many children come from homes where reading is not important. Many avoid learning to read for one reason or another. Is the decision not to read one that should be respected by the teachers and the school? Eventually, many students seek out speed reading or effective reading courses and attend them at some inconvenience and expense to themselves. Under these conditions, the students determine their own reading objectives; they buy or fail to buy instruction because they believe the particular improvements in reading will or will not be helpful to them.

PROGRAM SELECTION

After the objectives of a reading program have been established and the responsibilities of the different school personnel for reading instruction have been pinpointed, decisions must be made about the policies that the teacher will follow. *Program selection* is the step at which the choices of programs are determined. These choices limit the teacher's alternatives as to method and material.

How far down shall the reading program extend? Will there be a reading program in the kindergarten? How far up shall the program extend? Will there be a reading program in high school? For the college-bound? For the poor readers?

Will there be distinct programs for the different abilities of students? Must the student fit into the program, or will alternatives be provided for individual cognitive styles and levels of functioning? Will classes be sectioned according to levels of reading achievement, or will a range of materials be supplied to each class in each subject?

What are the alternatives in beginning reading instruction? Do teachers select the approach(es) to be used in their own class? Is the district committed to synthetic methods in which sounds and letters are taught first? If so, is the teacher given an option of several synthetic approaches? Is there an administrative commitment to analytical methods, which start with words, phrases, and sentences to be the basis for the sound–letter association?

What are the alternatives for reading in the upper elementary grades? Is reading taught as a skill? Is the reading curriculum exclusively wide reading of the student's own choice? Are power and speed developed systematically?

Will specialized material be used district-wide, or at the teacher's discretion? Does the reading specialist work with students or with teachers? What are the alternatives for the failing student? Correction in the regular developmental program or remedial reading? Who will teach the skills for reading specialized subject material? What is the role of the student in program selection? The decisions made about programs determine, to a large extent, the guidelines within which the teacher must function when teaching reading.

When Should Instruction Begin?

Only a few years ago, in almost all American schools the automatic response to the question of when to begin reading was, "When the child reached the mental age of 6 ½ years." This self-evident truth has never been self-evident in some countries, where vast differences in reading achievement are found whether reading instruction begins at age 5, as in Great Britain, or age 7 as in Sweden (Harris & Sipay, 1985). Researchers have found that under certain conditions children are able to read between the ages of 3 to 6 (Durkin, 1970). Mental age, evidently, is not as important as concern for recognizing and adjusting to individual limitations and needs (Durkin, 1989).

Many kindergartens are now incorporating initial reading activities into their programs that have evolved from the language experiences of a reading culture. Many prekindergarten programs, such as Head Start, are including reading readiness activities. *Sesame Street* teaches numerals, letter names, and introductory reading activities. Almost all federally funded programs are stressing language development, with the active assumption that it is basic to later reading success. There is increasing evidence that the very early home environment—when the child is under 2 years of age—has either an accelerating or a depressing effect on future reading success (Harris & Sipay, 1985).

How Long Should Reading Continue?

In recent years many colleges and universities have instituted reading courses for students who have difficulty in reading well enough to master the academic courses they are taking. Nearly all junior colleges have such courses which are often mandatory for students who score below acceptable levels on entrance tests. Only 30 years ago, few high schools offered formal courses in reading and almost no university considered it.

Should Programs Reflect Different Abilities?

Pupils differ in preparation, ability, and background, requiring that programs be built on their strengths and minimize their weaknesses. Ideally an individual prescription could be written for each student who could then achieve success in the most efficient way. People do differ in intellect, just as they differ in the ability to perform physical feats. Some children who are doing poorly are stimulated to greater efforts when placed in classes with more successful students, but others are overwhelmed by the competition they see. On the other hand, many gifted students are reluctant to perform at their potential level if this is above the performance of most of the class.

The setting up of remedial classes constitutes an exaggeration of the problems incurred through class sectioning. However, there are students unable to read well enough to participate in the curriculum of their grade. They cannot keep up with a class that is studying the interpretation of poetry when they cannot decode the selection. Remedial reading classes need to be structured on the assumption that they are temporary—that blocks that are handicapping learners can be removed. It is destructive to operate on the assumption that an individual is hopeless and can never learn to read. Almost as damaging is the supposition that there is really no problem and the child can continue without differentially designed help. The reality is that many young people need remedial reading instruction whether there is a specific program, whether it will be preventive or corrective, or whether it is correlated with a developmental program.

At the secondary level, decisions about reading are often jockeying for a position in the student's schedule. If reading is a separate subject, what will it replace in the schedule? Will credit earned apply toward high school graduation? Also, long ignored is the fact that teachers of mathematics, science, history, and other content areas must be held accountable for students learning the knowledge of words, terms, and phrases unique to their particular subject. Many colleges require a content-area reading course for students seeking certification as second-ary school teachers.

INSTRUCTION

Instruction is the most significant interaction in the system for improving read-ing. The ingenious teacher can provide materials not conceived of by program planners and can assume responsibility for aspects of reading improvement if provided sufficient support for supplies, secretarial assistance, and/or a teacher aide. A creative, self-directing teacher might then attain freedoms that go beyond the guidelines of the curriculum. Objectives prescribed in the reading plan are achieved at the instructional step, or not at all. What is the interaction between the classroom teacher and the specialized reading teacher? Which is responsible for pupil motivation regarding reading and learning to read? What is the role of parents in reading instruction? Where in the system is there reinforcement for teacher?

Determining accountability, setting goals, selecting programs, and evaluating results are all designed to improve instruction. A crucial ingredient of instruction is the involvement of students so they are motivated to seek their own solutions in word attack or in the integration of symbolic writing. The central relationship of instruction to other parts of the system is shown in Fig. 12.1.

Progress is often more covertly assumed than overtly measured. The final achievements in decoding skills and in sophisticated reading occur by a finite number of steps. The professionals, the parents, and the learner need to know where the learner is on the continuum of proficiency. In the early stages of reading, especially when these occur before school, the instruction should be informal and almost casual from the point of view of the child. By the time children reach the second grade, they should be able to conceptualize the dis-tance they have already come toward mastery of skills basic to effective reading. The most direct way for them to know their progress is to use a reading skill chart that shows intermediate steps. The child can keep track of the mileposts such as knowledge of the beginning consonant sounds, long vowel sounds, short vowel sounds, blends, alternatives for sound patterns, and the expressive interpretation of punctuation marks. These skill analyses allow the teacher to individualize reading in meaningful ways and motivate students who can see their progress toward learning the skills specified.

At later stages, similar records of comprehension are useful—perhaps struc-tured to show association-level learnings, conceptualizations, and creative self-direction. This self-evaluation suggests to the student how progress from literal to interpretive reading is made by seeing the implications in the author's writ-ings. Record keeping need not be onerous or time consuming as students keep these records themselves, the teacher avoids a great deal of work but, more important, the child is motivated to push to new levels of success.

Will the Specialist Serve Teacher or Student?

Ideally all who teach in the elementary school should be specialists in reading so that they can do what is needed without outside help. In reality, many elementary-school teachers have had only one or two courses and limited experience in teaching reading. Under these circumstances, teachers can handle the reading instruction for the average competent learner in the class but they lack specialization for helping and adapting to highly gifted readers. One approach, but the one that is difficult, is for the specialist to teach a group of poor readers within the classroom setting while the regular teacher participates as a team member, possibly teaching other students, but available to discuss what the specialist is doing. After school the specialist meets with the teachers from several classrooms to discuss new materials and methods. Under this plan, the regular teacher would, after substantial instruction, be phased into handling the remedial instruction. For a time the specialist would supervise the teacher's handling of typical problems, but gradually this activity would be phased out and the specialist would move on to help other teachers. The reading specialist also needs to do the diagnostic work that is difficult or impossible in a class situation. Some children need help, at least on a temporary basis, in a removed environment. This procedure is patterned after the postdoctoral residency of physicians.

What are the Alternatives for Beginners?

In general, the approaches to beginning reading fall into either analytical or synthetic methods, although many variants of each are possible, and eclectic systems have evolved. Gray (1969), who classified the reading methods used in 45 countries, defined the variants of both methods.

SYNTHETIC METHODS

The psychological process of synthesis means combining the detailed elements of language (sounds of letters and syllables) into larger units (words, phrases, and sentences). In reading, the letters are put together to form phonemes, which are associated with the appropriate graphemes. Eventually the phonemes are used to form words, which, in turn, build sentences. This system is logical and was popular a century ago. For some children the process of synthesis is most appropriate and the one most likely to lead to successful learning. Initial emphasis on phonic and syllabic elements are characteristic of current systems based on the synthetic method.

ANALYTICAL METHODS

Analysis refers to the mental process of breaking larger units into their constituent elements. In the analytical approach to reading the child starts by learning words, phrases, or sentences that have meaning and are later broken down into their sound parts. In general, this approach starts with stories that the child learns by a whole, or global, approach. After mastering a sight vocabulary, the child learns the common parts out of which the context has been formed. In early enthusiasm for the sight method the analysis was neglected and many children learned only the word-attack skills, which they discovered intuitively. Almost certainly, no one approach is entirely satisfactory for all children in a classroom.

ECLECTIC APPROACHES

The exclusive application of synthetic or analytical methods led to the development of systems that combined both methods. The first part teaches words within text (analysis) and the second part teaches letter sounds in words and combines letters to form new words (synthesis). In many schools little attention is given to decoding skills beyond the third grade, although there are usually designated periods for reading. Frequently children read stories or passages and answer questions based on them. The stories get longer, the vocabulary is more difficult, and for most children the rate of comprehension goes up. New reading systems stress the importance of instruction at the level of need.

Three levels of instruction have been identified. The point at which the reader can determine content is identified as literal. When the reader integrates and/or relates the material with personal experience, it has become interpreted. When the reader understands the significance and implications of the author, the third level has been attained.

Who Evaluates a Program?

Evaluation is the process for determining whether education objectives have been met. Evaluation is interwoven with each step and supplies input for each decision. Also, evaluation is the step that launches such activities as a fresh determination of responsibility and a revision of objectives. Students and all accountable staff are participants in evaluation, hopefully at the planning level. How does evaluation alter the objectives? How does evaluation alter the program selection? How does evaluation alter instruction? How does evaluation alter the accountability of the different people? How does teacher behavior contribute? How is it measured? How is teacher interaction improved? How can evaluation help order the priorities? The ultimate effect on the student is the most important criterion of evaluation.

The purpose of evaluation is to assess the success of the tactics that have been followed and to help in the redefinition of goals. Keeping records of learning successes, suggested in the section on instruction, is a potent form of evaluation and feedback to both the pupil and the teacher. Most of the evaluation of reading progress is informal, although the more highly specified the objectives become, the more clearly the evaluations can be made. At times it is desirable to stand back and get a larger picture of the way the whole program is going. Some of the achievement tests detailed in Chapter 11 can be used for this purpose. Consideration should be given to the kind of comprehension on which instruction has focused so that the test selection can give information about what has been taught rather than what might have been taught. Students who have learned to keep their own performance records can find ways of using outside reading assignments and free reading opportunities to master skills and comprehension abilities. They can become more nearly free agents, which requires the teacher to be sensitive to the progress students are making on their own. The self-directing pursuit of reading achievement should be actively encouraged, which means that some objectives that the teacher had in mind will need to be deferred. when readers are functioning independently, their progress is likely to be rapid and satisfying to both them and their teachers.

All individuals who are held accountable for the success of the reading program should be provided with the evaluation information that will make their contribution more certain. The principal cannot keep up with daily evaluations for each class member but periodic information about class progress is essential. In general, this information should be available to all administrators while there is still time to make constructive changes.

COMPONENTS OF READING PROGRAMS

In the following sections, an attempt is made to provide some answers to the questions raised about improving reading programs from under age 3 to adulthood. A flow chart is provided that pinpoints key components and indicates personnel who should be involved in determining the strengths and weaknesses of a reading program. Evaluation techniques are suggested, and types of performance that might reasonably be expected are outlined. Levels that require somewhat different patterns and emphases in reading instruction include the following: (1) Initial Reading, (2) Learning to Read, (3) Reading to Learn, and (4) Mature Reading. This sequence of instruction is consistent with the five *Stages of Reading Development* by Jeanne Chall (1983b).

Initial Reading

Chall (1983b) defines the initial reading in two stages. In Stage 1, the pupils understand the basic principles of reading: they know the letters in the word, "cat" are not the same and in "can," and they know when they make a mistake when reading. The end of this stage is characterized by the child's understanding of the spelling system. Stage 2 is a consolidation of Stage 1 as reading is used to practice and confirm what is already known. Attention is typically directed toward decoding skills and high-frequency sight-word recognition. In many kindergartens reading instruction is introduced as part of language experience. Labels are commonly used to help children identify objects in the room, their own shelves or lockers, often their own desks. The sensible approach is an individualized program during which the children who are ready begin learning to read and other children continue with language development activities, discrimination learning, and games that help them with left-to-right sequencing. Considering what is known about individual differences, it is evident that for some children, prereading tasks should continue into the first grade. In view of the learning sequences needed for beginning reading, the first phase of the ungraded primary school might combine one or two grade levels with kindergarten, say K–1 or K–2, so that the transition to first grade is made smoothly.

Reading instruction in the kindergarten evolves from informal language activities, such as labeling, to reading experience charts and simple books. When the child's reading passes from the phase of casual word recognition into formal skill development, it is desirable to have different approaches available that are compatible with individual intellectual styles. The children who are structure-oriented and who often develop reading disabilities under the analytical methods may need a program that emphasizes the synthetic approach. It may seem wildly idealistic to suggest that different kinds of reading programs go on in the same classroom for different children but this organization is outlined precisely in Chapter 13. For differential teaching to be a success, certain changes may be necessary; (1) The availability of beginning reading materials that are geared to different instructional techniques, (2) Ways of determining the differential strengths of the children, (3) An understanding on the part of the teacher trainers of the value of the differential programs, (4) A supportive attitude on the part of the administration toward differential teaching, and (5) The allocation of sufficient teacher time to reading to make the program a success. Each of these topics will be expanded upon.

In most school districts a basic reading series is provided along with several supplemental texts and workbooks. A new outlook by the superintendent's office will suggest in-service training to help teachers make the transition to the new approaches. These changes are not expensive but are time consuming when first introduced. Books and materials for one reading approach are similar in price to books and materials in another series, so that it costs little more to order 20 copies of one title and 5 each of two others instead of 30 of the first title.

The cognitive styles of children can be observed rather easily by noting a child's comparative strengths on conceptualization tasks as compared with his or her association-level learning tasks. Children who see structure quickly pay less attention to details and are likely to carry this pattern into reading. They need a method that capitalizes on the organization of detail into syntactic and lexical structures.

Differential instruction in reading is likely to become district policy only with strong backing from the superintendent and building principal. Unless the change is instituted with careful planning that includes parents, they are likely to ask questions that are difficult for teachers or administrators to answer. Both need to know through evaluation how successful they are with new programs and how they can be modified to improve learning.

In order to teach everyone at the primary level to read successfully, sufficient time must be allocated to the task, even at the expense of some content areas. Even with expert teaching, some children will not become independent readers during the primary grades. If the classroom teacher is able to analyze the difficulty and reverse the failure patterns before they become entrenched in the children, failure in the middle grades can be largely eliminated.

Evaluation. At the kindergarten-primary level evaluation is an ongoing process. Children are first identified as ready to begin informal reading activities. Differential evaluation of the strengths of the child is needed to identify the kind of beginning instruction he or she should have. The problems of those having difficulty in spite of the improved earlier steps should be analyzed so that deficits can be eliminated. Children should be identified who need to continue beginning reading past a time that would be wise for the bulk of the children.

Accountability. The building principal must be held accountable for instituting a reading program that functions differentially in the classroom. In some schools responsibility is shared with the elementary curriculum coordinator and the reading specialist, who would be primarily instrumental in getting the program initiated. Once the program is operating, the teacher receives feedback at each evaluation point and should be held accountable for the success of the children (Fig. 12.2).

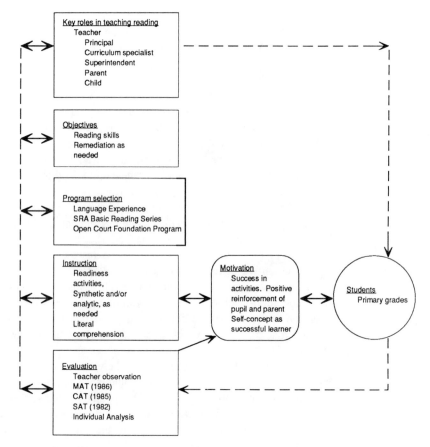

FIGURE 12.2. *Responsibility for the stage of initial reading.*

Learning to Read

Stage 3 students are characterized by Chall (1983b) as using reading to gain new knowledge and information. The reader is required to decenter when comprehending different events and places that occur in the world. Toward the end of this stage, the reader moves closer to reading at the level where popular adult magazines and fiction can be read for enjoyment. Most children will have mastered the basic skills of reading by the time they enter the upper elementary grades, where the task is one of deepening the word analysis and comprehension skills that were started earlier. Much of this in-depth reading is concerned with interpretation and understanding the author's meaning beyond the factual details. Instruction for this level stresses conceptualization of relations within the reading material, understanding the ways authors put words together for different effects, and making inferences clear (Chapter 14). Reading experiences at this level will produce students who read more deeply than story action—for their own satisfaction and insight. Wide reading is typical, but comprehensive reading requires direction from the teacher.

Realistically a few children in the middle grades will not have mastered the skills at an independent reading level or in material they find satisfactory. It will continue to be the responsibility of the teacher to analyze the nature of reading deficits of these children and to help them achieve the competence that typical of earlier grades. New, intensified programs in reading instruction should be as different as possible from approaches in which the student did not succeed earlier.

Evaluation. Both the informal feedback the teacher observes during instruction and the standardized tests that give a profile of the student's higher reading skills are included in the evaluation at this level. For the failing student, oral reading analysis followed by appropriate diagnostic tests is the most useful evaluation procedure to determine the problems that need to be overcome. Screening tests that are used in primary instruction are satisfactory to check the progress of skill development. When a new program is instituted, testing programs should be revised to evaluate the success in achieving the new objectives.

Accountability. The classroom teacher assumes primary accountability for successful reading instruction. The materials are not highly specialized at this level and generally are available if the teacher exerts a reasonable amount of pressure to obtain them. Remedial instruction might be delegated to a reading specialist but, if one is not available, the responsibility and the privilege fall to the classroom teacher (Fig. 12.3).

Reading to Learn

Stage 4, according to Chall (1983b), requires the reader to deal with more than one point of view, the ability to manipulate layers of facts and concepts from other points of view. By secondary levels, reading traditionally falls under the heading of English—a fusion of reading, composition, spelling, and grammar. In English classes, reading is for literary appreciation rather than for skill development. The emphasis notable in the upper elementary grades on reading for interpretation and on understanding the author's significance is carried to new depths. Starting in the 1960s, a trend emerged of having courses on reading per se, in addition to the course in English, because many students were not reading well enough to handle comfortably the social studies, science, mathematics, and other subjects that assumed competence in reading. The courses in reading that have been instituted have been called either developmental or remedial, although both have had large components of correction within them.

Evaluation. The junior high/middle school grade levels are typically more impersonal than in the elementary grade levels. the difference hinges primarily on the greater number of students (about 150) The teacher meets each day if the school is departmentalized. Under the circumstances, it takes longer to know student names and longer to know the difficulties a particular student may be having. When used with the publisher's analyses, tests, such as the *Metropolitan Achievement Tests* (1986) and the *Stanford Achievement Tests* (1982), are helpful to teachers in English, Developmental Reading, and Remedial Reading. Further diagnosis, usually on a referral basis, may be necessary to pinpoint the specific difficulties of particular students.

Accountability. For establishing the necessary programs, accountability must fall on the principal. The counselors should be held accountable for seeing that

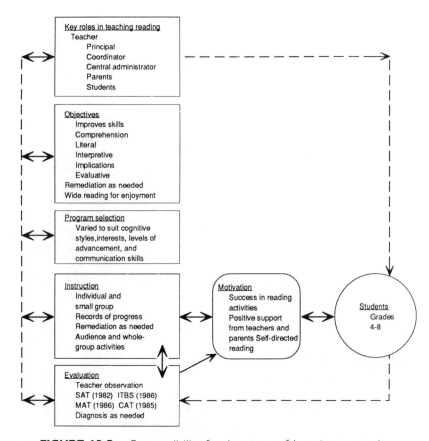

FIGURE 12.3. *Responsibility for the stage of learning to read.*

the students who need remedial instruction are placed in remedial reading. The reading or English teachers are accountable for the progress of the students once they are placed into their classes. Teachers in social studies, science, and mathematics should share in the process of identification and should channel their suspicions of reading difficulties to the counselors, who can arrange for testing. They should also accept responsibility for teaching vocabulary and inquiry models appropriate to the content they teach. By junior high/middle school, all of the children in school have reached a level of maturity that enables them to learn to read, if carefully taught. In any system of accountability, those involved should be expected to see that all students who leave these middle grades have functional competence as readers (Fig. 12.4).

Mature Reading

Chall (1983b) defines the reader at Stage 5 as having the ability to interpret material by constructing ideas based on a high level of abstraction and to create one's own truth from the truth of others. Literary criticism, or advanced interpretation, is the familiar operating style. The same forces that led to the introduction of reading courses in the junior high/middle school years have been

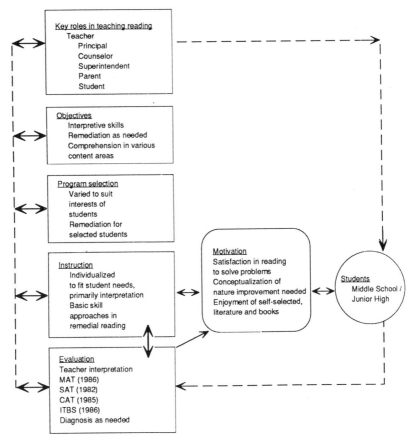

FIGURE 12.4. *Responsibility for the stage of reading to learn.*

effective in establishing similar courses in the senior high school. A small proportion of the students attain Chall's Stage 5. Most of the reading taught in high
school is labeled remedial, where emphasis is put on vocabulary improvement
and comprehension in content areas. Developmental reading is occasionally
offered to college-bound students who are taught speed reading along with the
research and analytical skills.

Evaluation. The format for evaluation is similar as in the junior high/middle
school and high school years. The need for screening tests becomes more apparent at secondary levels than at other levels because of the large numbers of
students each teacher sees. Testing on a differential basis helps establish individual instructional goals for students. Some of the newer computer analyses of
these difficulties, such as established by *Stanford Achievement Tests* (1982), can
be used to counsel students into programs where they can function reasonably.

Accountability. Teachers and principals should be held accountable for seeing
that reading classes are established and qualified teachers are assigned. Second-
level responsibility is: (a) On the programming committee to establish reading
classes at times accessible to the students who need special reading instruction,

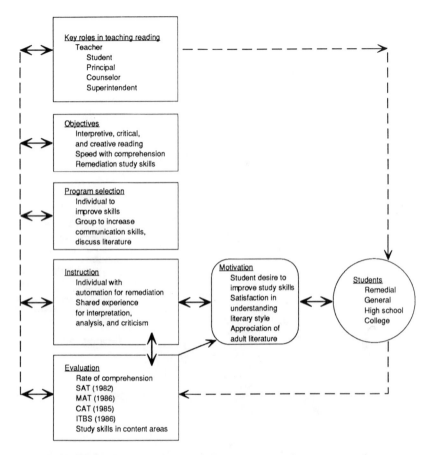

FIGURE 12.5. *Responsibility for the stage of mature reading.*

(2) On the counseling staff to help the students select the programs they need, (3) On the subject teachers to see that their instruction improves the functioning of the student as a reader, and (4) On the student, who is ultimately the most involved person in the program (Fig. 12.5).

COMPUTER-ASSISTED INSTRUCTION

Large numbers of microcomputers were made available to the public schools in the 1980s. Over the past 10 years, computers have been used at all levels for instructional delivery and by administration. Appropriate applications have been found for: administrative record keeping, testing, drill and practice, and word processing.

Administrative record keeping. School districts are using computers for: (a) accounting, payroll, and employee records, (b) attendance, grades, and student records, and (c) course timetabling (Watts, 1981). Computers can easily manage an accounting system which provides levels of data regarding planning and budgeting. Student anecdotal records can be efficiently and safely stored and quickly retrieved. Course schedules can be projected, generated, and changed to be effective in helping forecasting staffing needs, changing the curriculum, utilizing facilities, or the estimating the impact on budgets.

Testing. Computers perform test-scoring and record keeping functions. Standardized tests, requiring the use of scan sheets for students responses, process and store results, and produce both statistic-based and narrative reports for teachers and parents. Interpretation and prescription is usually and wisely regarded as a staff responsibility. One type of software program helps teachers write their own tests through a format generalized by the program. The student takes the test on the computer where the results are processed, stored, and reported to the instructor. Many drill-and-practice programs include evaluation of student progress both during and after an instructional program.

Drill and practice. Early classroom application typically has reflected drill-and-practice activities in areas of alphabet recognition, word building, spelling, word meaning, affix usage, rate improvement, and grammar skills. Publishers found this type of program relatively easy to create and less likely to be pirated than more complex programs. As more and more microcomputers saturated the home and school markets, publishers began risking more money on the research and development of more costly programs. Tutorial programs developed in which the program adjusted content, level, and/or rate based on student performance. Simulation exercises were developed in which generated real-world situations and allowed teachers and students to role play their decisions. Interactive fiction is a derivative of simulation programs, wherein students both create and complete stories; also they devise their own stories from computer-generated story fragments. Other interactive programs require the students to use references, such as encyclopedias and almanacs, in order to complete the narrative.

Word processing. In and of themselves, computers cannot improve writing skills. They serve and encourage writing in many ways: (1) Editing is easier. (2) Errors are less intimidating. (3) Storage of drafts on a disk is convenient. (4) Writers with poor penmanship are not penalized. (5) The spell checker and the on-line thesaurus improves spelling and increases vocabulary. The next section examines specific computer applications in initial reading, comprehensional logic, and futuristic reading access.

Initial Reading

Computers are appropriate for preschool and even day-care centers (Lewis, 1981; Piestrup, 1981). Shade et al. (1983) found that preschool children are capable of operating the standard keyboard with minimal instruction, exchanging diskettes, and working together with minimal supervision. Instead of being an isolating activity as critics originally feared, computer activity has been found to encourage mutual consultation, cooperation, and collaboration. Computers create an environment where children become active learners as they sense their control of the content displayed on the screen. Children build self-esteem as their control is tempered by software which is patient and encourages work at an independent level (Nieboer, 1983).

Computer learning facilitates trial-and-error reasoning, reflective thinking, and visual discrimination often through imagery. Computer programs were found productive for slow learners because they can move at their own pace, repeat each step continuously, and be inconspicuously reinforced by the feedback. Gifted children are helped as they can move rapidly through program levels of increasing difficulty until they are challenged. Scott (1986) recommended a sampling of selected programs related to beginning skill development. These reading programs relate to: prereading (e.g., *Sticky Bear ABC,* by Weekly Reader), decoding and word attack (e.g., *Reader Rabbit and the Fabulous Word Factory,* by the Learning Company), reading for meaning (e.g., *Tiger's Tales,* by Sunburst), sight vocabulary (e.g., *Richard Scarry's Best Electronic Wordbook Ever,* by CBS), and writing (e.g., *Magic Slate,* by Sunburst).

Reader Rabbit and the Fabulous Word Factory (1986) exemplifies software geared to appeal to initial readers. The objectives of this program are: increase vocabulary, improve spelling, develop spatial awareness, and enhance memory and concentration skills. The program uses four game formats:

1. The Sorter Game: Where words are put on shelves that match the target pattern. Patterns can be changed by pressing a single key so that adapting the game to fit the needs of the child or lesson is easy.
2. The Labeler Game: The middle and ending letters are grouped together and the player places a letter under the picture to make a word. By pressing a single key a different set of pictures appears.
3. The Word Train Game: Words which differ by just one letter are put in a train car.
4. The Match-up Game: Pupils play concentration by matching pictures, words, or pictures with beginning letters.

Color, sound, and graphics add to an inherent student motivation to complete the activities. There is flexibility in controlling program difficulty and this provides a challenge for beginning readers, as well as for those more advanced. A number of high-quality programs to reinforce initial skills provide students with an interesting, playful, and exciting way to learn and reinforce important beginning concepts in reading.

Comprehensional Logic

The basis of comprehension is learning how to think critically, to make inferences, and to do problem solving. Some programs accomplish this through traditional means along the lines of direct instruction. These programs may use techniques, e.g., CLOZE, to reinforce important skills. One program, for example, used literature as a basis from which selected words and letters were deleted from high-interest passages of age-appropriate literature. Books accompany the diskettes and documentation. Another program has students learn to apply skills, like recall, main idea, skimming for a word, and inferential thinking, to different content areas. Students typically read a paragraph and answer questions on a multiple-choice format, and records are automatically keep for teacher and student perusal. Interesting formats, material, and reinforcement can make these programs attractive to students.

Many programs exist which foster comprehension development quite ingeniously by teaching thinking through interactive problem solving. *Gertrude's Secrets* (1984) is designed for children in elementary grades. It helps pupils follow directions, develop accurate sequencing, use deductive reasoning, infer and categorize patterns and rules, discover multiple solutions, and learn to think creatively. Students learn to discriminate between objects, classify objects by attributes, and establish rules and common relationships which link objects and sets of objects.

Gertrude's room has three doors which lead to three types of puzzles: array, loop, or train. The pupil has the freedom to roam through the rooms and decide which room to "play" in. It is technically easy to work in Gertrude's world, but there is plenty of room for comprehensional logic. The reading child is given creative-thinking exercises by working in the shape edit room and with exercises related to Venn diagrams. The pupil must think predictively as he or she must learn to anticipate what will happen next.

Computers in the Future

Computer technology in the future will include software programs and hardware adaptations which will enable clear and precise speech production. Currently, speech synthesizers and speech digitizers need to improve voice quality and overall utility. Speech synthesizers translate text into English phonemes. Anything that is spelled phonetically can be spoken through the computer.

Talking Text Writer (1986) and *Talking Text Speller* (1987) by Scholastic allow students to type onto the screen anything they want, in phrases and in sentences. *Talking Text Writer* reads back what is on the screen in a relatively articulate voice. The accompanying speller presents and says words to the student from either standard lists or from the student's own lists. The computer says the word and asks the student to spell it correctly. The drawback with speech synthesizers is that only one voice can be heard and speech quality over extended passages is poor.

Speech digitizers utilize prerecorded human sounds which are converted into a digital signal. Many different voices are distinguishable and subtle tones and stress patterns are discernible. Unfortunately, few computers can make use of this process and little software has been developed using this format. In the future, speech technology will enable computers to talk to students through their own programs so that even those unable to read can make full use of the computer (Blanchard, Mason, & Daniel, 1987).

Computers in the future will use compact disks (CDs) for optical storage and will use digital data to make them compatible with computer translation. CDs, which hold vast amounts of information, can store both text and video information. A single CD disk can store approximately 250,000 pages of text. Since all that is needed is the computer, the CD disk, and the CD player, the latter two being reasonably priced, this configuration appears to be the direction of future information storage and retrieval in the schools. A student can have access to the complete library at the push of a button!

Chapter Summary

The responsibility for reading involves identifying those individuals who play a key role in the program and then holding them accountable for satisfactory performance. Since reading is only one part of the curriculum, decisions must be made about the relative importance of reading and other activities. High levels of performance at low levels of support cannot reasonably be attained.

Decisions about the kind of reader wanted and the abilities that are to be taught must be made at the highest level of administration. Once the objectives have been specified, it is necessary to select a program, or, more realistically, different programs that will help all children achieve reading fluency. The actual instruction needs definition, with particular emphasis on the approaches needed for success in achieving the skills of reading.

The primary function of evaluation is to supply feedback to the students, the teachers, and the administrators about skills achieved and learning still needing to be accomplished. The nature of reading instruction, the locus of accountability, and the means of evaluation change as the student progresses through the school system. The accountability shifts, as the child grows into adulthood, from that of the teacher to the learners themselves.

Computers can play an influential role beyond that of administrative record keeping and test scoring. Computers may help students practice skills ranging from word analysis to comprehensional logic. In the future speech digitizers and compact disks will significantly expand the area of reading instruction and writing by computer.

V Learning-Motivation Theory Applied

The presence of a problem that demands the formation of concepts cannot in itself be considered the cause of the process, although the tasks with which society faces the youth as he enters the cultural, professional, and civic world of adults undoubtedly are an important factor in the emergence of conceptual thinking. If the environment presents no such tasks to the adolescent, makes no demands on him, and does not stimulate his intellect by providing a sequence of new goals, his thinking fails to reach the highest stages, or reaches them with great delay.

—L. S. Vygotsky

333

13 Positive Solutions for Individual Differences

ORGANIZING THE SOCIAL STRUCTURE

Organization of the reading program within the classroom is the responsibility of the teacher. Teachers in self-contained classrooms usually have some freedom in the amount of time given to reading instruction, in the periods of the schoolday it will be taught, in how much reading is emphasized in other curricular areas, and in the materials or approaches selected for a particular class. When the reading program is departmentalized, however, an individual teacher may have little influence over the organizational structure of the total reading program or the basis for assigning a particular student to particular classes. Although the creative-self directing teacher can find ways to give students freedom within a rigid administrative system, a flexible classroom organization is conducive to individualized instruction.

Affective Considerations

Whereas organization does not assure good instruction, order is necessary if each student is to have an opportunity to learn. Five criteria are crucial in making decisions about the framework and personality of a reading program. The first criterion is that learners have a right to read under conditions which will enhance, rather than destroy, their self-esteem. Students often suffer because their poor reading is made apparent to others unnecessarily.

The reading teacher's greatest challenge is to create a class structure which gives individuals maximal opportunity to learn in their own way. This does not necessarily imply one-to-one instruction. At one extreme, the reading program can be individualized completely, providing each of 30 students about 2 minutes of the teacher's hour; at the other extreme, all 30 students can do the same reading task at the same time, utilizing the collective benefit of the teacher's guidance for the entire hour. Every conceivable plan between these two extremes has been tried in an effort to allow for individual differences in learning, while at the same time making the teacher available to more children for longer periods of **335** time.

The teacher needs to give at least as much conscious attention to the social factors as to the cognitive factors when organizing the reading program. Learning in groups has its positive aspects, both for society and for the individual. The child's role is extended beyond the family when blending in with a group of peers at school. Learning to function as an individual, under group conditions, becomes more and more important as people of the world face greater interdependence with one another.

The learning arrangement must be one that preserves and protects the respect of each learner, regardless of his or her reading level. A child's visible reading performance should not cause the loss of respect of classmates; otherwise, the learner will lose self-respect and may turn to other ends to gain status. When a student's level of performance is so low that he or she cannot function within the range of the class in any reading activity, the remedial class may be a constructive placement. Temporary classroom groupings, focusing on a particular skill to be learned or an objective to be achieved, helps to avoid the discouragement most children feel when they are assigned to the "low" group. By focusing on individual progress in skills earned, by helping children keep track of their progress, and by frequent changes of books, the slower readers can work as a group with high motivation and without stigma.

From the beginning reading stages, the teacher should be able to select from a variety of books and shift materials readily by preparing each group to handle each lesson in a satisfying way. Differences in readability can exist in each classroom without highlighting these differences in such obvious ways as giving one group a book that another group has previously read. High-interest books with mature formats are available, even at a readability level of first grade. Poor readers, like adopted children, may *know* their status but need not be reminded of it in public. If they are valued for their effort and realize they are progressing, students need not be the best in the class to be able to enjoy reading.

The second criterion used in organizing the reading program is that affective objectives must be planned differentially, allowing for the different motivation patterns of individuals. Twenty-five years ago, Krathwohl, Bloom, and Masia (1964) outlined affective objectives that can be taught and evaluated in the schools. A hierarchy of personal involvement begins at the receiving or attending level and proceeds through levels of increasing commitment to a personalized value complex.

At the *receiving level,* the student displays awareness, then a willingness to receive, and finally a selected attention to the content or activity, although at an uncritical level. An example in communication skills is the children's selective attention to stories read to them. The antithesis of the desired behavior was David, a 7-year-old nonreader, who put his hands to his ears when the clinic teacher tried to read to him. Older students might still function at the receiving level in some reading tasks, but more commonly they "turn the teacher off" through controlled attention to something else. By focusing on its rhythm, the kindergarten teacher's goal might be "to help children become aware that poetry is fun to hear." If the initial receiving experiences are pleasure producing, or satisfy a student's felt (though not necessarily cognizant) need, students are likely to try the second step in the affective sequence of responding.

In Krathwohl's terminology, *responding* means active participation through a sequence of acquiescence, willingness, and satisfaction. The teacher's affective objective for students might be to interest them in a particular short story to the extent that they would enter into a follow-up discussion. This success implies some knowledge on the part of the teacher of their present interests. Many students are acquiescent enough to go along with whatever the teacher asks, but some do not, particularly if they are acculturated to values that are antagonistic to those of the school.

Valuing is the affective level at which the student internalizes the worth of things—activities, objects, beliefs, or attitudes. In this category individuals first accept a value, then through their choices show a preference, followed by a commitment of some duration. Like the preceding categories, receiving and responding, valuing may function at the association level. A child may read an entire series of books by a particular author, without having conceptualized why they give pleasure or why they fit into a particular organization of values.

Organization of a value system represents the conceptualization of value relationships. When values have been organized into a system, students are likely to see how new experiences fit (or do not fit) into their affective structure. At this step, readers are likely to withstand considerable pressure without changing beliefs and to accept difficult school assignments if considered relevant. The student who values a knowledge of current affairs is likely to have conceptualized the function of reading in gaining this knowledge. The teacher is in a position to support this self-image by reinforcing this student as a person who knows current events. Teachers seldom state their affective objectives explicitly, but many teachers have stimulated certain students who became fascinated by the discipline itself and built it into their value structure.

Characterization by a *value complex* means that the person knows who he or she is and makes decisions from an internally consistent philosophy of life. Such individuals are committed to a particular role in life and are able to arrange at least part of there activities to support the value complex. This category corresponds to the self-direction level in the learning-motivation model (Chapter 2). What students select to read is part of the role in which they see themselves—as a future engineer, architect, or teacher of political science, for example.

How the teacher sees the function of reading in the lives of the students will determine to a large extent the kinds of reading experiences provided in the classroom. If teachers see children in the role of their own cultural values, their reading program is likely to promote discussion, criticism, and self-selection. If teachers see their students as factory workers, they will probably promote word recognition and functional reading. At all stages the teacher must recognize the reading-related abilities children have and accept their interests as valid.

The third criterion for organization is that the reading program extend the cognitive, or thinking, abilities of each learner. Teachers who are familiar with Guilford's intellectual operations can give children experience in thinking beyond cognition and memory to convergent and divergent thinking (Chapter 5). Teachers who want to encourage the conceptualizations that are generalizable to new situations will find it necessary to rethink many of the recommended techniques for teaching reading by association and to encourage students to put the bits and pieces into meaningful relationships. To accomplish this, time for interaction with students must be built into the daily schedule.

The fourth consideration is that freedom be built into the sequence by giving students increasing responsibility for their own programs. At the kindergarten-primary level this means a scheduled time for choosing and carrying out activities that encourage self-direction. By the middle grades most pupils should have learned how to identify an interest in science or social science and to locate and read what is available in the library on the topic. Older students should have acquired an openness to new forms of literature and the ability to make critical judgments.

The fifth criterion is that the reading program be selected to fit the cognitive style of the individual child. Unfortunately, students usually must fit the system, whatever methodology happens to be used in the classroom to which they are assigned. The different cognitive styles of learners and the different value associations they bring to school call for a flexibility that skillful teachers use to provide many kinds of reading experience. These considerations—the right of children to retain self-esteem, the need for affective objectives, the possibility of extending cognitive skills through reading, the opportunity to learn self-direction and the individual differences among learners—all require a classroom organization that is flexible.

Goal Structures

By designing lessons skillfully, teachers can control the type of interdependence required of students to complete a learning activity. The interdependence among students, or *goal structure*, has been categorized as cooperative, competitive, or individual (Johnson & Johnson, 1987). Goal structures give purpose and justification to different types of organizational arrangements. All three goal structures are valuable when used judiciously, and teachers' selection of goal structures over time will be reflected by the cognitive processes of their students.

COOPERATIVE

Lessons, based on *cooperative goal structures,* are structured so that students must work together to complete a shared goal. Cooperative grouping is grounded on the concept that when groups are rewarded, students will help each other learn new material (Slavin, 1986). Cooperative goal structures extend the notion of group activity to include: (1) Individuals within the group must perceive themselves as interdependent with other group members. (2) Positive verbal exchanges are made among group participants, (3) Individual accountability is essential, although expectations may differ among group members, and (4) Students must be taught social skills that are necessary for developing positive relationships (Johnson & Johnson, 1987).

Learning activities based on cooperative goal structures assist students in learning both values and skills from each other and encourage positive attitude building as the group unit is responsible for an overall assignment. Egocentrism is reduced as children work and learn by solving problems with the help of other students and from their perspectives. Peer relationships act as a motivating, autonomy-building influence when students learn to hold each other accountable for both the behavior and the final product. According to Johnson and Johnson (1987), the relationship between cooperative goal structures and interpersonal processes is characterized by intrinsic motivation, high expectations for success, and a strong commitment to learning.

Cooperative goal structures are most appropriate for tasks which are conceptual, lend themselves to problem solving, and require decision making. The more creative and divergent the answers need to be, the more functional this goal structure becomes. For example, a cooperative group technique related specifically to reading is called the "Cooperative Integrated Reading and Composition" (CIRC). This is a procedure developed around four student teams, each consisting of two pairs of students from two different reading groups. Team members take turns reading stories to each other, helping each other with comprehension skills, including writing (Madden, Slavin, & Stevens, 1986). This type of grouping pattern is supported by Good and Marshall (1984), who found that most low-achieving students would be better off receiving more instruction in heterogeneous groups than what is typically used in the classroom.

COMPETITIVE

Lessons, based on *competitive goal structures,* are designed so that students challenge each other, working for individual success by doing better than others. Competition is particularly effective for assignments requiring drill and practice, recall, and review. Activities need to ensure that all students feel they have an equal chance at success of winning and that they do not perceive failure or losing as too defeating. Most students view school as competitive, American children become more competitive as they remain in school, and urban children more competitive than rural children (Johnson & Johnson, 1983).

Teachers who overuse this type of goal structure encourage students to see themselves as "winners" or "losers." The competitive goal structure promotes interpersonal processes which are extrinsically motivating, generate high or low expectations for success, but may foster a low commitment to learning. Pupils who continually see themselves as "losers" form a low self-concept and feel incompetent. The competitive process can be a valuable structure as long as it is used with caution and with respect to each child's emotions and feelings. Competition, defined in personal terms, can be motivating as children try to improve upon their own scores when trying to make personal bests. Mr. J., a junior high teacher, summed assignment and test scores each week and seated students according to the number of points earned. David was always the last student in the last row.

INDIVIDUAL

In an *individualized goal structure,* the learner works toward the completion of an assignment without any interaction with other students. While the basis of instruction is to tailor curriculum to the needs of each student, it has been defined in different ways. Traditionally, it meant that students self-selected the reading material, determined the rate of time to complete the reading, contracted with the teacher for the amount and type of work expected, and conferenced with the teacher for evaluation and encouragement. Individualization from this perspective has been found to work well with highly intelligent, self-motivated learners; and with some teachers who are dedicated and possess exceptional organizational skills.

Carroll (1970b) related individualization to a unique definition of aptitude. He did not define aptitude in terms of achievement, but as the *amount of time* it took a student to learn a given task. It simply took less capable students longer to learn the same material and perhaps in smaller steps as the more capable. This optimistic perspective suggested that theoretically some part of almost any task could be geared to almost all students. Bloom (1976), using this definition as a basis, developed what has become known as "mastery learning." The assumptions to mastery learning are: (1) *Each* student will work at his or her own rate in a tailored sequence of skills, (2) *Each* student will demonstrate a degree of mastery, (3) *Each* student will be self-motivated and self-directed, (4) *Each* student will practice problem-solving processes, and (5) *Each* student will self-evaluate his or her progress (Joyce & Weil, 1986). Individualization from this perspective has been found most effective with disabled and low-income learners.

Johnson and Johnson (1987) report that individualized goal structures fail to promote interpersonal communication and group interaction. There is no exchange and sharing of information or ideas. The interpersonal process is marked by extrinsic motivation, by lack of sustained interest and persistence at tasks, and by a low commitment to learning.

All three goal structures need to used by the successful teacher. Depending on the nature of the task and the learners involved, instruction is improved when the type of interdependence among children is planned. Teachers can use lessons based on a cooperative goal structure when they attempt to foster divergent thinking, want brighter students to model questions for others, or hope to encourage groups to interact through dialogue and mutual respect. Teachers can use lessons based on competitive goal structures when they judge grades to be important, when students view grades as important, and when poor grades are not being used to damage student self-esteem. Teachers can use an individualized goal structure when they want students to define their own interests and goals through self-selection and foster autonomous learning, or to tailor a program to a particular student's skill needs.

Grouping with a Purpose

Elementary teachers typically construct 3 to 5 groups per classroom with usually 6 to 10 students per group (Cazden, 1982). A number of reasons are cited for grouping: (a) Oral reading, initially, is necessary for evaluating children's use of context and word analysis skill, (b) Children with significant ability differences can be grouped to meet particular reading needs, (c) Skill deficits, particularly with young readers, may be addressed more efficiently, and (d) Different group interests can be met efficiently. Some groups are formed among different teachers of the same grade; some groups are formed within the classroom; some groups are homogenous or heterogeneous by ability and/or skill need.

INTERCLASS VS. INTRACLASS GROUPING

Interclass ability grouping, sometimes referred to as between-class grouping, is popular among teachers who believe it is an effective technique for meeting individual academic differences. Two second-grade classes, for example, may be divided for reading by placing the lower reading groups in one room and the more advanced reading groups in the other. Research indicates this type of grouping may slightly benefit those assigned to the advanced class, but at the expense of lesser benefits to those assigned to the lower groups (Rosenbaum, 1980). *Intraclass ability grouping,* also referred to as within-class grouping, is most common in elementary-school reading programs. Typically, a reading teacher will have three to four groups designated by reading skill, each group in a different reader, and proceeding at their own rate. Slavin (1986) found that ability groups, where small numbers of students are placed in each group, learned more than those classes that did not use grouping techniques.

Several explanations partly explain why intraclass ability grouping has been found more effective than interclass ability grouping. First, intraclass ability grouping allows for the adjustment and placement of students based on observation as well as test scores, where interclass ability grouping is frequently based on test scores alone. Second, homeroom teachers apparently try to accelerate the growth of their less capable students, thus demanding more; while teachers who receive a group of "low" students from another classroom often make limited demands from them. Third, intraclass grouping permits students to identify with their class, while frequently interclass grouping promotes identification of status with the reading group.

HOMOGENOUS VS. HETEROGENEOUS GROUPING

Homogenous groups are students grouped together on a common trait such as interest, skill deficit, or ability. Typically, however, homogenous groups are created when a small number of students are working at the same ability level. *Heterogeneous groups* are students grouped together on the basis of differences, usually based on students with varied mental or skill abilities. Research has reported mixed results as to which procedure is most effective.

Homogenous ability groups have been ineffective in part because of low-ability groups have few positive role models, teachers frequently communicate low expectations, and, since these students are typically immature and inattentive, teachers usually spend considerable time addressing behavioral problems (Good & Marshall, 1984). Furthermore, low groups are given less time to spend on answering questions and in engaging tasks, and teachers spend more time dealing with their inability to attend (Hiebert, 1983). With respect to content, low groups are given more word-recognition and decoding instruction.

On the other hand, in working with high groups, teachers have been found to allow fewer interruptions, offer more flexibility in procedures and assignments, and plan more individualized activities (Shavelson & Stern, 1981). High groups spend more time on comprehension activities, and do more silent reading than oral reading. Alpert (1974) examined the high and low reading-group sessions of

15 different second-grade classrooms. She reported that teachers used a variety of reading material and emphasized meaning more when working with the high group than with the low group. Eder (1981) found that students having the most difficulty learning to read were placed into groups where the social interaction was most disruptive. Eder also found that low students spent about twice as much time not attending to the lesson as the high group and found that teacher managerial acts were about three times more frequent with low groups than with high.

Many studies have shown that small-group instruction facilitates the use of greater variety of materials, encourages more individualized attention to students, and provides more positive feedback (Stallings, 1975). Groups will remain as flexible as possible when both diagnostic assessment and observation are ongoing to encourage movement. Effective instruction used different goal structures as a basis for grouping and varies the types of groups implemented over a given period of time. Pupils should remain in heterogeneous groups as much as possible but, when appropriate, small-group instruction by skill or ability is very effective (Good & Marshall, 1984).

ORGANIZING THE TIME AND SPACE

Learning for many children is hindered by the artificial barrier between kindergarten, where one is not expected to read, and the first grade, where every child is expected to do so. The community that provides no prereading for its children is often the same community that requires a strong academic program for first-grade children. A clinical look at the children who are beginning to read reveals a chronological age range from 4 to 7 years or greater. By these ages children have developed attitudes toward reading; these attitudes encourage a classroom organization which provides many opportunities for children to reveal their feelings to adults without having to rely on a language. Group instruction needs to be organized with approaches that allow children to begin reading at different ages and that are individually appropriate.

Kindergarten

Whether reading by children should be taught in kindergarten has been an issue since the 1960s. Some writers are opposed to early reading in the belief that normal, or intellectually average, children should not learn to read until age 6 ½. Some experts have considered reading in kindergarten unnecessary, or risky, for the child because inappropriate methods might be used when teaching, or as an intrusion in the child's total development. Other writers have favored kindergarten reading and have suggested particular approaches for teaching it, such as early writing for reading, computer-assisted instruction, phonetic instruction, language experience, and Montessori education. The schools have been urged to introduce reading opportunities earlier on the grounds that widespread social changes, such as television, computerization, and urbanization, have resulted in earlier development of communication skills in children. Here, a long-neglected suggestion by Gates (1937) needs renewal: The different characteristics of readiness observed in individual children need to be used to determine the kind of programs provided and the timing of those programs.

Reading instruction for children under 6 needs to reflect the child's need for a trust relationship, for unending novelty in perceptual experiences, and for sufficient continuity in this experience to integrate the bits and pieces of the environment. Because of the high proportion of children who, in some respects, are not ready to read, a classroom organization is needed that provides opportunity, without tension and pressure. The language-experience approach, for example, builds the need to read, without placing demands for particular levels of achievement. Advanced kindergarten children are more able to stay with 15 or 20 minutes of reading on a regular basis than are unready first-grade children. There are few reading activities that are right for all the children in a heterogeneous kindergarten or first grade. Lessons given to small groups and regularly planned within the activity period can be adapted to children grouped for their common needs, whether they are being read to, are having reading charts or are discussing story sequences in books without words. The major hazard in kindergarten reading comes from whole-group approaches, which are too easy for some and too difficult for others.

Ungraded Primary

Schools with an ungraded primary program are often designed to encourage teachers in the selection of differential approaches to beginning reading, especially when the kindergarten is incorporated into the early primary program (Goodlad & Klein, 1970). Although departure from the age-grade structure never assures an individually planned curriculum, an ungraded reading program gives the teacher freedom to rearrange the schedule or regroup as often as necessary to increase the independence of readers. However, an organizational structure that eliminates grade designations, only to section classes into "level," often establishes a structure that is less flexible than traditional self-contained grade.

A fully utilized ungraded primary plan has several advantages for individualizing the reading program: (1) Children progress individually and are moved whenever different study materials are indicated. When transfers are made frequently, these changes are innocuous compared with the trauma of once-a-year assignments to new grades and rooms. (2) Teachers are aware of a range of differences that are real but less apparent than in a sectioned class. Teachers plan for individual needs but recommend transfer for children whose growth rates put them outside the range of competence of their group. (3) Children have 2 to 4 years to complete the traditional 3-year program, or 3 to 5 years to complete the kindergarten-primary program skills requirement sequence in reading without gaps. Focus is on reading accomplishment and individual progress, rather than on grade level, which is assumed to reflect, but often does not, the child's level of achievement. (4) Continuous progress through school removes the pass–fail stigma from pupils who move more slowly that the average child. Reading failure accounts for 70% to 90% of nonpromotion in the primary grades (Silberberg & Silberberg, 1977), where the alternatives are repeating a grade or going on to a placement that will mean daily failure, both of which are damaging to the poor reader. (5) The nongraded reading situation facilitates the use of materials according to the interests and needs of children, rather than by grade designation. The use of many approaches is not necessarily assured by a flexible

	Group I	Group II	Individualized Group
Period A	Teacher-directed instruction	Choice time	Independent work or self-selected reading
	Word recognition, comprehension, or corrective lessons	Self-selected activities, as indicated for other groups	Includes all children who do not fit into group programs
Period B	Independent follow-up	Teacher-directed instruction	Choice time
	Assigned desk work	Word recognition and comprehension skills	Self-selected activities and creative work
Period C	Choice time	Independent follow-up	Teacher guided individual reading
	Art and construction Science projects Creative writing Music-math Free reading	Assigned desk work	Programmed, individualized, or language sequence

FIGURE 13.1. Flexible grouping—between I and II, or in and out of individual reading—enables the teacher to provide for individual differences in motivation and achievement. As children become independent readers and responsible choosers, two of the three periods can be shifted to individual and cooperative formats.

organization. However, the teacher's familiarity with many systems and the freedom to select from several reading programs can accomplish choice for children within rigidly organized schools.

A flexible plan for incorporating the reading schedule into the daily program is shown in Fig. 13.1. This arrangement gives each child a time to work with the teacher, a time to work independently in lesson-related reading, and a time to work on areas of personal interest. The three periods may be broken by recess without disruption of the sequence.

Teacher-guided reading: The teacher-directed period is used to introduce new skills, to observe reading behavior, and to guide the child in evaluating independent work. In a typical primary setting the teacher might give the Period A group a carefully structured linguistic program, such as *Open Court,* or one of the basal series that progresses in small steps, such a *Scott–Foresman.* The Period B group might move faster by using a more difficult series with fewer repetitions in vocabulary and larger steps in decoding, such as the *Ginn Basal Readers.* If the group already knows the basic associations for word identification, it might profit from a conceptual-creative emphasis, such as Martin's *Sounds of Language Series.* The Period C group, shows as individualized, might be based on one of many different approaches, including one based on literature. The group might include children whose reading achievement level was too low for them to fit into either of the other groups, a new pupil whose reading needs were being observed, independent readers who temporarily need wide reading instead of skill development. The advantage of a multiple-approach reading program is that individual children are not placed in an unsuitable program. They can be shifted to a new approach whenever they are not responding to the daily instruction.

Independent follow-up work: The dreariness of much independent work comes from it being too monotonous, having too many pages, or being unrelated to the reading content, or out of sequence in the child's skill development. When the desk assignment follows the reading group work, it is possible to plan independent work that grows out of the story content and follows immediately after it is discussed. Deskwork that calls for thinking, decision making, and uniqueness is likely to be more satisfying to most children than routine association–recall responses. Assignments that combine words and pictures enable young children to express complex ideas for which their writing alone is not yet adequate. Workbooks are useful and can save both teachers' and children's time. When used to develop a particular skill, consistent with the particular needs of a pupil, workbooks can give children a chance to show their learning in an independent setting. Practically all children need changes of pace and changes of assignment to keep their interest high. When the child's activities away from the teacher are divided between assigned and self-selected activities, the tendency toward busy-work assignments is lessened.

Freedom to choose: Children should be able to count on having part of each day to plan and pursue an activity of their own choosing. Most kindergarten children are taught to decide what they will do at work time, assemble their materials, complete their commitment, and clean up after themselves. By expanding the options available to children, the choice time can become one of the most valuable learning periods in the schoolday. A sign-up sheet, containing a list of activities, each previously routinized, reduces the planning time needed and provides a record of the child's contract. Creative art, crafts, free reading, library research, science experiments, and many other projects can be conducted simultaneously, if the children are held responsible and the number of children working away from their desks is limited. Choice time should be for all, not limited to the children who finish their reading in a hurry.

Reading to Learn

Most elementary schools provide developmental reading classes for all students, whether the highest class is sixth, seventh, or eighth grade. Assuming that the child comes to the fourth grade having already learned the basic skills for decoding and information getting, the middle grades are the optimal time for extending comprehension skills and learning different functions for reading. Many students, perhaps one-fourth of the typical class, do not read well enough to handle grade-level materials independently. They need structured lessons of the kind provided of primary schoolchildren in learning to read and teacher guidance in reading to learn the content of other subjects. A larger part of the class, perhaps one-half, know the basic word-attack skills well enough to handle the words in their speaking vocabularies, but have not mastered the more difficult skills of syllabication, encoding, and attacking new words. These children can all learn the skills needed to function in high school if a systematic program is provided that continues the skill-building process in word identification and conceptual reading. The students in the top quarter of the class, typically those who are fluent in word recognition and literal comprehension, need to read for various purposes and to learn to apply different kinds of reading competence to those functions (Chapter 14).

Monday (or any day of the week, as scheduled by the librarian): Library Day
Tuesday through Thursday:

Adapted Program	Developmental Program	Individualized Program
Teacher directed Word recognition skills Vocabulary preparation Story setting Motivation Directed reading	Self-preparation of content Silent reading Begin follow-up work	Read self-selected books and prepare reports or Read story selection and do follow-up
Independent work period Silent reading Follow-up activities (comprehension check)	Teacher-directed group work Evaluation and follow-up Rereading Discussion of story materials	Any reader who does not fit in adapted or developmental groups may work in individualized program
Choice of work Library reading Unit work Report preparation Word games	Follow-up activities Library reading Choice of work or creative activity	Individual reading conferences, and Occasional group work for teaching need skills, sharing books, and so on

Friday: Drill games
          Choric Verse
          Book reports: demonstrations, dramatizations, exhibits
          Audience reading: selections, plays, poems, books

FIGURE 13.2. Weekly Reading Schedule (grades four to eight).

Weekly schedule for reading: The classroom organization for reading in grades four through eight needs to be stable enough for regular lessons in developmental reading but flexible enough for library periods outside the classroom and for other reading-related activities. The weekly reading plan shown in Fig. 13.2 is adaptable to self-contained classrooms and to the reading period of a departmentalized school.

Monday is shown as library day, but any other day may be scheduled for the weekly trip to get new books. Most children will need instruction in the location and use of library resources. A few students regularly choose books that are too difficult for them to read. Some of these students acquire psychological payoff from carrying around an impressive looking book, while others have reading interests beyond their reading competence. In these cases the teacher must do some discreet counseling over a period of time, perhaps at first by making suitable books available in the classroom. Some students regularly select books that are much easier than their achievement level would indicate they could be reading. Students need not be discouraged from reading simple material part of the time for relaxation and enjoyment. Adults, including teachers, seldom do all of their reading at their peak level of vocabulary and comprehension. However, students who choose all of their library books at a superficial level need encouragement to develop new interests. Providing sets of paperbacks, which a group of students can read simultaneously and discuss, is one way to get good readers who are intellectually lazy to stretch themselves.

In the upper grades, reading groups are more casually organized than in primary grades, and meet with the teacher for direct instruction less frequently. The flow chart indicates at least one scheduled meeting with the teacher each week for each student, either individually or as part of a group. Students who require daily guidance might be put on a prescriptive plan that could be followed systematically, but independently. Students who need more help than this plan allows, should probably be assigned to a special reading class for diagnosis and remediation.

On Friday, or on another regularly scheduled day, the whole class meets for culminating or audience activities. If given special attention by the teacher, this period can be the most enjoyable part of the school week. Here the focus is on initiative, imagination, and creative production on the part of the students. As in other self-directed activities, students develop their own criteria for the worthiness of the presentation. Mrs. C., a young primary teacher who found herself teaching reading to seventh-grade classes, used this plan to stimulate reading improvement. Book reports became so important to the students that every Friday was taken up with unusual ways to tell about books: dramatizations, dioramas, posters, puppetry, and oral reading. The class adopted a single criterion: that the report reflect the content of the book. Another teacher, Mr. A., was an artist in choric verse. His classes were introduced to poetry, drama, and essay through regular Friday sessions in choric reading. Many teachers have discovered that poor readers, with preparation, could function at a self-directed level in this kind of class.

Arrangement for Older Students

When entering junior or senior high school, students typically enter a world of five or six class periods, each given to a separate subject; or they enter a core curriculum with language arts and social studies given in a block and the other subjects studied on a period schedule. An estimated 80% to 90% of the student's study activity is reading. Although the average reading ability of adults in the United States is between seventh- and eighth-grade level, minimal reading ability of eighth- to ninth-grade level is considered necessary for successful achievement in high school. Typical elementary-school graduates may read avidly, but have not reached their potential as readers, nor are they likely to do so on their own. In the 1980s many high schools have added developmental and remedial reading courses to the regular schedule.

David Russell (1961) distinguished between the developmental-functional aspects of reading programs and the recreational-enrichment aspects. *Developmental reading* is the part of the program in which the improvement of reading skill is the major purpose. At the high school level, the mechanics of reading are involved: increasing the sight vocabulary, developing good eye-movement habits, increasing speed and fluency, and reading difficult selections orally (Heilman, Blair, & Rupley, 1986). *Functional reading* is studying to obtain information; it is reading to learn, in contrast to learning to read. Secondary students are expected to understand a history assignment without the teacher's daily guidance in preparing a bibliography, locating relevant information, or summarizing what is read. They are expected to read classical literature in its original form, rather than in adaptations. To succeed in mathematics, the high school student must be able to read a story problem and understand what it says. Teachers of the separate subjects should teach the specialized vocabulary of their disciplines, but the generalized abilities of functional reading are likely to have greater transferability to new disciplines when taught in developmental reading classes.

Recreational reading often declines during the high school years for most students; therefore, the teacher faces a challenge in trying to develop a love of literature in the students. The affective objectives of the courses in both developmental reading and English literature, if stated, usually focus on the development of appreciation of great books and the refinement of reading tastes. Extension of the reader's interest to drama, poetry, and long novels is the conscious goal of the teacher. Planning between teachers of reading and teachers of English is needed to give community to programs and to assure pleasurable learning for the student. The developmental reading program is likely to have its appeal diminished if the recreational-enrichment aspects are confined to courses in literature.

ORGANIZING THE CONTENT

Reading systems are structured according to the reading skills that are considered important, rather than according to the learning process used by the student. In this section some of representative programs for teaching reading are classified by the kinds of learning the student is likely to do because of the nature of the material. The evaluations are based on the probable tendency of the readers to function at the association, conceptualization, or self-directed level. While some students go beyond the level of the instruction, many persist in functioning with a psychological set toward reading that has been created by the teacher.

Before adopting a reading approach, teachers need to make several decisions. The first choice must is whether to use incidental or systematic teaching, one following the interests of the child and the other being systematically planned learning. The second choice is whether to use a synthetic approach (phonics) or an analytical approach (global). Only after these choices are made can the third choice be made, that is, what reading materials will be used.

Focus on Association Learning

The classification of approaches to beginning reading encompasses the stages from the introduction of decoding and/or recognition of whole words to the stage where the child can read paragraph material independently. Much beginning reading exposes the child to associations between oral and aural word forms. The methodology implies level 1 learning in the common descriptions of "Look, Say" versus "Phonic" approaches. Conceptualization is always possible, but an instructional approach is classified as association learning unless the system was planned toward particular conceptualizations on the part of the children and shows the teacher ways to recognize conceptual learning when it occurs. Two systems, *Distar* and *Open Court Foundation Program,* are intended to exemplify association-based programs.

DISTAR

Direct Instructional Systems (1982) is a direct instruction method which teaches a particular response to a particular stimulus, followed immediately by teacher reinforcement. The material and the prescribed interaction are designed to help disadvantaged children make up their learning deficiencies. The published material consists of a teacher's presentation book and guide, spelling test book, storybooks, and a cassette demonstrating how to pronounce the sounds and how to present tasks from the program. *Reading Mastery I* focuses on basic decoding and comprehension skills—reading letters, words, and stories both aloud and silently; *Reading Mastery II* expands basic reading skills, including decoding difficult words and answering questions. *Language I* gives instruction on word knowledge, foundations of thinking, and oral language skills; *Language II* emphasizes reasoning skills, following directions, and meanings of words and sentences.

Cognitive learning: Distar is taught at a rapid pace, which assures automatic responses to the stimuli presented by the teacher. In reading, the children learn the sound–letter association, then how to blend sounds by "saying it fast." They practice "spelling" by prolonging the phonemes, then they practice writing words that they have learned to sound in the reading sequence. They learn to recognize words phonically prior to reading them in sentences and short stories. This highly structured system is particularly suited to slow-learning children and to children whose language usage is limited to restricted codes.

Affective learning: The immediate and maximum use of feedback is reinforcing to many children who would feel confused and isolated in the language arts discussion of a typical primary classroom. Children who have suffered previous reading failure often respond to a structured program, such as *Distar,* with new confidence. The presentations are geared to the lowest member of the group, thus providing a high percentage of successful responses that the teacher continues to reinforce. The structure in the program assures that the children will not be confused or frustrated by inconsistencies. The teacher feedback includes such remarks as "You're a smart kid," "Good learning," and "Keep on saying it." These reinforcers build improved self-images for young children whose security is still within their own families, and for older children who have experienced reading failure.

Role of the teacher: The authors of Distar hold the teacher accountable for the pupil's failure to learn to read. Since the teacher's role is programmed precisely, including the affective interaction between teacher and children, the programmers might be held accountable by the teacher, if the system is followed faithfully. Self-direction for either teacher or children, if it happens, must take place outside the instructional system as the teacher's behavior is designated with no allowance for creativity (Aukerman, 1984). The skill and ingenuity of the professional teacher is needed in at least five ways: (1) to decide which children need this kind of program, (2) to observe the progress of children, including the affective learning, and make changes to other approaches as needed, (3) to help children transfer *Distar* skills to other language situations, (4) to teach children to look for inherent structure in unstructured settings, and (5) to plan self-directed learning of some skills. Teachers who have a broad knowledge of different theories about learning will not find it difficult to build on the associations children learn in stimulus–response approaches.

OPEN COURT FOUNDATION PROGRAM
(1982)

This program is the beginning sequence of the Open Court Publishing Company's basal reader series, known for its strong phonic elements. The program is very traditional with many structured routines. The purpose is to teach the language arts through skill development in reading and writing and through exposure to literature. The children's material includes readers, practice cards, anagrams, and records or tapes. Lessons are presented to the whole class with the expectation that the learning will be stimulating to good readers, but not too difficult for poor readers.

Cognitive learning: The basic approach is multisensory, with careful selection of the bits of information to be associated and careful control of the sequence to avoid distractors. Prereading abilities, taught at the kindergarten level, have been built downward from the beginning reading program, which is basically synthetic in method. The primary-grade instruction of the full program goes through six steps: sounds of letters, blending, dictation, proofreading, composition, and literature. Associative-level learning is observed in teaching the sounds of letters. The whole class does follow-up dictation in individual workbooks, first writing letters, then words, then sentences. The vocabulary is carefully controlled to avoid irregularities in sounding.

Affective learning: The affective experience of the reader has been considered at two points: the multisensory appeal of the materials and the attitudinal content of the literature. Stories, poems, fables, and other literary classics are presented throughout the series. In this, as in cognitive learning, the instruction is designed to build chains of associations from small to larger units of language. By control of the content and sequence, the inductive learning of basic relationships is assumed.

Role of the teacher: The program is preplanned for the teacher, lesson by lesson, with little decision making required. Skill is needed, however, in helping the children maintain their interest on a long-term basis throughout the extensive writing practice in workbooks and the memorization of poems. Teachers who consider conceptualization an important step in learning will invent ways to use a well-planned sequence to encourage children to discover and verbalize the relations within language and to express themselves in their writing and reading.

Focus on Conceptual Learning

The conceptual level of beginning reading implies the learner's ability to think within the structure of the language itself. Graphemes, the basic units of printed words, can be taught as associative counterparts to phonemes, the basic auditory unit, or to morphemes, the basic meaning unit. Graphemes can also be related structurally to whole words in ways that enable the student to recognize the same grapheme in other situations. Basically the conceptual approach builds understanding of the relationships with the language as a whole by teaching the child to generalize from selected particulars and to apply the generalization appropriately.

Teaching sight–word vocabulary is usually a form of stimulus–response learning. It is difficult to teach service vocabulary, such as "through," "where," and "from," as sight words and impossible for the beginner to sound them. When the focus in on the structural relationship of the word to the sentence, the child can conceptualize the structure of language and learn the word through use because it has a function in speaking, writing, and reading.

Many primary-level stories have the potential for children's conceptualizing the author's message, which needs to be encouraged. However, the necessity to learn decoding skills tends to pre-empt the author's attention from the importance of starting conceptual reading early. Under the guidance of a concept-oriented teacher, most association-based learning can be brought into relationship with the larger structures of syntax and phonics. Likewise, producers who build conceptualizations into their materials are likely to be thwarted in their purposes by the teacher who rewards children for thinking in specifics, without the constant search for larger meanings.

A conceptually focused program is the *SRA Basic Reading Series* (1976). The general goal is to teach decoding inductively while also teaching comprehension. The sequences use linguistic groupings of sound–spelling relationships that the child learns to translate from printed words into spoken words. According to Aukerman (1984), this program surpasses the traditional linguistic approaches in that reading is more interesting and entertaining. The series includes readers at six levels (A through F), each having pupil workbooks, teacher's guides, tests, and instructional materials. Additional selections are provided for children who need extra practice.

Cognitive learning: The child starts with learning the sounds of letters through a controlled exposure to sequenced sound–spelling patterns. Word-attack, word recognition, comprehension, fluency, and expressive reading are incorporated into a carefully developed sequence of sound–spelling relationships. Children can move through the basic program as rapidly as they are able, and into the *Comprehensive Reading Series* (Grades 2 to 6).

Affective learning: The revised material was designed to increase appeal to children by using colorful illustrations, humorous selections, and a fair representation of women and minorities. Oral reading utilizes natural sentences and easy-to-read type. Self-direction is limited in that the program emphasizes the discovery of structure in language and stops short of creative use of language.

Role of the teacher: The SRA program is highly technical but not individually constructed for differences in perceptual and language readiness. The program is for "average" children, so the teacher will need to determine which children are likely to find this approach rewarding. The teacher will need to help some children to build motivation for reading and to teach them the functional use of the written language.

Focus on Self-direction

Some teachers have reasoned that reading should be learned naturally, as socialization creates a need for reading. Such systems vary in detail, but the central principle is freedom from imposed structure for both the teacher and child. Teachers can, of course, impose their own words on the child and their own timing for word analysis. However, language-experience approaches to reading are intended to be individualized and unstructured.

A system described by Stauffer (1970b) is representative. His method incorporates beginning reading into the communication skills of writing, reading, speaking, and listening. The sequence begins with the child's wanting to write something or the teacher's recording the child's remarks about a picture or an experience. The particular content and the initiative for writing are the child's own. Initially the children create the language of individualized experience approaches, and the teacher creates the charts, sentence strips, words cards, and story collections that children read. A variety of children's books are needed—first for listening and browsing, later for individual reading.

Cognitive learning: The focus is on self-direction from the beginning. Children create their own stories, which are recorded by the teacher and read back by the child. Gradually children learn to write and illustrate their own stories. This is read to the whole class in an evaluation setting. Children are encouraged by the teacher to read stories to each other. The teacher covers and labels collections of papers for the library corner. Sometimes children compile their own book: a collection of reports, stories, and poems written over a period of time.

Affective learning: The motivation for reading emerges from the child's self-expression in a school setting. Communication with peers is assumed to be inherently rewarding. Children who are articulate and learn writing skills easily get immense satisfaction from this "natural" approach to reading. Some young children, still egocentric in their social orientation, are even less interested in the activities of children with whom they do not identify than they are in storybook people whom they enjoy imitating.

Role of the teacher: The responsibility for teaching each child to decode, comprehend, and interpret reading material is the teacher's own. The teacher of the language-experience approach to reading needs to be highly skilled in bringing all children into full participation in all activities, knowledgeable about the structure of language, and in the difficulty of the elements of the decoding–encoding sequence.

Comprehensive Reading Systems

The publishers of basal reading series have developed full-range systems of instructional material from which the teacher selects a program for small groups of learners. These systems often de-emphasize or eliminate grade-level designations and allow the teacher flexibility to branch out from a core program to give students additional help on a selective basis. The increased time that is required of teachers to keep track of individual learning and to differentiate tasks for students is compensated through the provision of a variety of components that teachers, especially primary teachers, are expected to make themselves.

Ginn Reading Program (1985, 1989) is an example of a system which draws from a range of experts on reading, such as Clymer (senior author), Torrance (creativity), Shuy (linguistics), McCullough (developmental reading), Ruddell (research) and others, to design the program. The kind of learning that takes place depends on the style of interaction, the questioning techniques, and the lesson structure the teacher has learned to use in the classroom. Ginn currently has two primary programs. These are: (1) *Ginn Reading Program* which is built on the strengths of the original Ginn Program. The goal is to teach all children to comprehend, enjoy, and use written language. The four skill strands are comprehension, decoding, vocabulary, and life and study skills. Supplementary materials include card sets, big books, wall charts, worksheet masters, Hispanic support components, and parent/home activity sheets. (b) The *World of Reading Program* is Ginn's newest K–8 reading series. It utilizes the building-block approach to teaching reading which is recognition and introduction, recall, exercise, and practice or application. This program emphasizes teaching reading through fine literature and award-winning authors.

Cognitive learning: The level of learning that takes place will depend on the cognitive style of pupil and the way the lessons are structured by the teacher. According to this system, decoding is learned by discovery of sound–letter relationships, which is common to words selected from the material, such as the /ar/ correspondence in barn, Harvey, car, farmer, and garden (Clymer, 1970). Decoding is a means by which children focus on literal and inferential comprehension. The transfer of word-attack principles to story reading is facilitated by the overlapping vocabulary of comprehension and decoding activities.

Creative self-direction: The development of creative reading is proposed specifically in the lesson objectives through guided thinking, such as sensing ambiguities and finding unique solutions to problems. Given this kind of encouragement and freedom to choose their own reading-related activities, children become self-directed readers long before decoding, as a separate program, is mastered.

Role of the teacher: Professional reading teachers will have little difficulty in transferring from a phonic orientation to a linguistic approach to decoding. The teacher's guides have identified the important ideas in each selection, the specific objectives for comprehension and word attack, and ways to adjust to individual needs. By leaving the responsibility of decision making to the teacher, this tool will be effective in the hands of the practitioner who can take advantage of its flexibility. Like earlier basal readers, there are many more activities suggested than a group of readers will want or need to pursue. What the teacher omits from a lesson plan may be as important in keeping individual children interested as the procedures selected to teach. The shift to levels breaks the grade-age barrier only if teachers accept the responsibility of identifying the instructional level, as each student develops new skills each day. Teachers who value their own self-direction will appreciate the literary value of the content from the beginning, and the integration of phoneme-grapheme principles as the means, rather than the purpose, of reading.

Chapter Summary

Reading programs are organized for group instruction in order to extend the services of teachers and material resources to as many students as possible in the most cost-efficient manner. The best organizational plans provide the greatest flexibility for individuals to learn in ways that are best for them and toward goals that fit their lives. Primary- and upper-grade schedules for reading should provide each child with times for teacher-guided instruction, independent work, and self-directed activity. Classroom organization should provide group and individualized instruction on a flexible basis. Representative systems for teaching reading were discussed according to the level of learning that was emphasized by their authors.

14 Thought Processes in Conceptual Reading

The purpose for advanced reading is to conceptualize the content and significance of what the author has written. Comprehension, an active process, lies not in the material alone but in the interaction of the author's message with the reader's prior background and experience. Conceptual reading is loaded with the individual's own interpretations and extrapolations, often incorporating meanings beyond those conceived by the writer. Many readers who have learned the techniques of code breaking still function at simplistic levels of comprehension. Nearly all students need help from the teacher in learning how to construct deeper meanings and to appreciate more fully an author's multiple messages.

Much of the effort in beginning reading instruction is necessarily given to code-breaking systems and to improving a learner's techniques. It has been argued that once the skill to change graphemes into morphemes has been learned, the proficient reader should be able to interpret the meaning inherent to all material. However, even gifted students can learn to read more perceptively when they are stimulated by adroit questioning and when they have learned how to monitor their own cognitive processes. Students need comprehension instruction that is specific and designed to organize their reading.

Although uncertainties about the basic processes and instructional approaches to reading comprehension have existed for a long time, a considerable research effort has occurred since the mid-1970s (Pearson & Gallagher, 1983). For the past 15 years, a branch of cognitive psychology called information processing has produced a multitude of models for analyzing connected discourse. Some examples of text-analytical models are schemata, frames, scripts, and story grammars. These techniques, coupled with a construct called metacognition, a mental process in which readers monitor their own understanding of text, provide data-based procedures for researching conceptual comprehension.

Several powerful studies indicated a lack of classroom instruction in comprehension. Durkin's (1978–1979) descriptive study examined how well comprehension was being addressed in the elementary classroom. She and her co-workers observed 40 intermediate grade teachers for about 300 hours during the course of a schoolyear. They found that fewer than 50 minutes of the 300 hours (less than a quarter of one percent) contained any instruction on how to improve comprehension strategies. If the major purpose of reading is to obtain meaning from text, surely instruction regarding this process needs to be seriously confronted.

In this chapter, three contemporary aspects of conceptual reading are presented: (a) how comprehension occurs, (b) the types of thinking that follow reading, and (c) the procedures used when teaching students to read in depth. Schema theory is used as a backdrop for understanding concept formation, storage, and retrieval. Comprehension has been considered either as a series of subskills, which are described in traditional taxonomies, or as a single skill which is centered in the general ability to reason. Teaching procedures are grounded on two approaches, one in which teachers ask pupils different types of questions and the other in which pupils monitor their own comprehension processes and derive their own questions.

COMPREHENSION

E. L. Thorndike (1917) stated: "Reading is thinking" (p. 310). Coming from a connectionist psychologist, this often cited remark indicated his belief that reading extended beyond word recognition. Some 54 years later, R. L. Thorndike (1973–1974), reviewed the current literature addressing this issue and found additional support to his father's notion that even ". . . the act of answering simple questions about a simple paragraph . . . includes all the features characteristic of typical reasoning" (p. 323). Thinking, or more particularly the application of intelligence, is essential in obtaining meaning from written material. A theoretical framework explaining the nature of intelligence is crucial when laying a foundation to the comprehension process. A foremost contributor to a theoretical understanding of intellectual development was Jean Piaget.

The Structure of Knowledge: Jean Piaget

Piaget emphasized that cognitive development is a process of construction which results from the learner's interactions with the external world. Piaget (1971) defined intelligence from a biological orientation conveyed by the word *equilibrium*. In this context, equilibrium implies a conciliatory and growth-producing adjustment between two factors; a person's mental actions (cognitive structures) and the environment. According to developmental theory, human beings do not inherit cognitive structures, although they do inherit the reflexes for interacting with the environment. As individuals respond to environmental demands, they incorporate into their internal actions only those facets which can be assimilated, that is, which fit into existing cognitive structures. Simultaneously, there is a compelling need for individuals to react and adapt to the reality and the novelty of the external world. The result of this accommodation to the environment causes thinking and creates structures for increasingly abstract thought.

Structures become integrated through a process called *organization* (Piaget, 1952). Organization is the biological necessity of humans to arrange experiences into coherent systems. Piaget called the cognitive structure, which becomes an organized pattern of behavior, *scheme*. The term, scheme, has been translated into English as *schema* and has been used by cognitive psychologists to describe how knowledge is organized and maintained.

Information Processing in Cognitive Psychology

Cognitive psychology examines how the mind works, including processes of perception, memory, thinking, learning, reasoning, language, and comprehension. *Information-processing* psychologists have attempted to study cognitive functions by focusing on complex rational behaviors and by viewing the individual as an active seeker and user of information. In recent years, their perspective has become the dominant theory used to study cognitive processes in reading (Lachman, Lachman, & Butterfield, 1979). Psychologists who focus on information processing include social psychologists, developmental psychologists, and neuropsychologists. They hypothesize that schema (plural schemata) is the primary unit of knowledge from which incoming information is integrated, stored, and retrieved from memory. All the information an individual uses to interpret external reality contributes a total set of schema. The schemata instantiated at any moment constitute the accuracy and depth of the interpretations being made. *Schemata-driven structures* represent the generic concepts which provide a memory foundation for understanding objects, events, sequences, and actions (Rumelhart & Ortony, 1977).

Reading specialists attribute the relationship between thinking, reading, and remembering to Bartlett (1932). He applied Piaget's theories on the acquisition of knowledge by extending to reading comprehension the notion that memory is organized by schemata. In his original work, *Remembering: A Study in Experimental and Social Psychology,* Bartlett asked English subjects to memorize an unfamiliar North American Indian story called "The War of the Ghosts." The subjects were asked to recall this passage at repeated intervals of time. There was a tendency for the subjects to distort and change the style of the passage over successive reproductions. As predicted by Bartlett, these changes made the passage read more and more like traditional English folktales rather than Indian legends. For example, in the original passage, the death of an Indian was marked as "something black came out of his mouth"; one English subject reported this event as the Indian "foaming at the mouth."

Bartlett described the constructivism of memory as a process of rationalization. He alluded to schemata in discussing how rationalization gives text an appropriate mental framework (context) and makes details meaningful by connecting parts of the material which at first appear disconnected. In "War of the Ghosts," his subjects altered the surprising, jerky, and seemingly inconsequential form to an orderly, English-oriented narration. They omitted or changed all of the elements that left the reader puzzled, and provided specific associative links to clarify their understanding of the text. During recall the subjects applied rationalizations to the Indian tale, as a whole, through remarks indicating that the story was not English or that it was a dream. Also, they substituted familiar details, such as "boat" for "canoe," "rowing" for "paddling," "peanut" for "acorn," "cat" for "bush cat," and "cabin" for "Kashim." Bartlett's work on memory provided the framework for his constructive theory of comprehension.

THE CONSTRUCTIVE THEORY
OF COMPREHENSION

Constructivism hypothesizes that the reader needs to go beyond explicit information to perceive, comprehend, and recall an author's message (Paris, 1975). A basic tenet of this theory is that situations described from the linguistic input of print embody more information than from the linguistic input alone (Barclay, 1973). The meaning generated from a sentence, paragraph, or story adds up to more than the independent meanings of the words. Once print is integrated and linked to prior knowledge, readers do not remember the original form of information, but they synthesize new information with their own prior knowledge to generate integrated ideas. This reconstruction and integration of ideas form the basis of memory (Pezdak, 1980). To constructivists, the important concerns in reading comprehension are word meaning, context interplay, and memory retention.

Word meanings are not fixed but are determined by the context in which they are found (Weaver, 1980). In examining the characteristics of standardized vocabulary tests, Dolch and Leeds (1970) found that only the most common definition of a word was used. The tests tended to omit certain classes of words: (a) *Hononyms,* which have the same spellings but come from different roots, such as the word "box." (Box can mean a container, to strike with an open hand, and a small shrub used in gardens.) (b) *Derived meanings,* which originate through analogy or application. (Box can refer to a container full of apples or a box seat at a theater.) (c) *Figurative meanings,* which connote symbolic interpretation. (Boxed in means that there is nowhere to escape.) Conceptual readers recognize the multiple meaning of words and readily shift to a new definition when one meaning does not fit the schematic structure.

Context-dependent interplay represents the relationship between linguistic input and prior knowledge (Bransford & Johnson, 1972). Objects become meaningful as a function of their relationships with other objects. In the sentence, "The woman has a tear in her eye," the meaning of "tear" is clear in relation to the word "eye." "Tear" has a totally different meaning in the sentence, "The woman has a tear on her blouse." Comprehension occurs as readers interpret the interaction between objects, actions, and events. Moreover, skilled comprehenders use their knowledge about this interactive relationship to improve their reading.

In a study involving fifth graders, Steiner, Weiner, and Cromer (1971) hypothesized that unskilled comprehenders have difficulty using contextual cues to improve their reading skills. The investigators used two groups, one skilled and one less skilled. Prior to reading a selection, both groups were provided the extra context of an aural summary to facilitate word identification. Each subject read a story in four conditions: single-word mode with and without supplementary information and paragraph mode with and without supplementary information. The skilled readers were expected to use the summary to reduce their word identification error rates. Results opposite of those anticipated occurred as skilled readers made substantially more errors when provided supplementary contextual information than without. The high error rate of less skilled comprehenders' remained the same when supplementary information was used. These researchers concluded that good comprehenders take advantage of the supplementary information (prior knowledge) to reduce their attention to words, while less skilled readers continued to ignore supplementary material and focused on decoding.

Memory retention is based on the reader's ability to combine isolated ideas into integrated ones when recalling material. People tend to remember their own reconstruction of a prior mental activity (Paris & Lindauer, 1976). An important study which demonstrated how young readers acquire, construct, and retain information was conducted by Paris and Carter (1973). Second- and fifth-grade children generated inferences after orally reading a set of sentences. The students each read aloud a list of three acquisition sentences which they were told to remember, then participated in a diversionary task which required them to sort blocks for 5 minutes. Finally they were given a set of recognition sentences to which they were to respond "yes" or "no" if they had heard the same sentence. An example of an acquisition set was:

> The bird is in the cage (4).
> The cage is under the table (5).
> The bird is yellow (6).

The most reasonable inference to be made from this set of sentences is that the bird is under the table. The corresponding set of recognition items were:

> The bird is inside the cage (25).
> The cage is over the table (26).
> The bird is under the table (27).
> The bird is on top of the table (28).

Sentences 25 and 27 were semantically congruent with the acquisition set with 27 being a true inference. These second and fifth graders responded consistently that they remembered the true inference statement. These results support the constructivist notion that children retain information that is implied.

SCHEMATA AS A STRUCTURE OF COMPREHENSION

Samuels and Eisenberg (1981) presented a model of memory based on schemata. They define schemata as active processes of a well-defined structure which can be diagrammed. The diagram consists of subschemata indicated as a network of *nodes* and *links* (Fig. 14.1). Each node represents a single concept and is linked to a number of other nodes. For example, the concept "restaurant" includes information common to all restaurants, such as menus, tips, and waiters; "restaurant" also links information general to other businesses, such as purchasing, sales, and overhead.

Schemata allow the reader to "fill in" gaps not specified in text. If the author says that the child is *brushing* his teeth, the type of brush is known—not a paint brush or hair brush—even though that information is not specified. Charac-

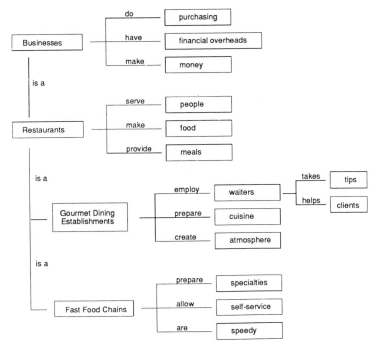

FIGURE 14.1. The concept of "restaurant" is illustrated by a network of nodes and links characteristic of schemata.

teristics of schema were summarized by LaBerge and Samuels (1974) as: (a) Schemata are embedded in one another such as "restaurant" is embedded in the concept of "business." (b) They create *slots* to be filled in by the reader from past experience, such as how to "operate a computer" by inferring from the use of a typewriter. (c) They are generic so that the concept "speed" can apply to many different objects in many different situations, including the use of the drug so nicknamed. Concepts are clarified through a network of information stored in long-term memory. Comprehension can be viewed as consisting of selecting the schemata and confirming that they reasonably account for the material being read. Proficient comprehenders find the schemata that best fit or account for all of the incoming information.

Knowledge-based Schemata

When the constructive theory of comprehension is applied to written discourse, schemata have been classified as either knowledge-based or text-based. To comprehend a passage, the reader needs schemata to define the purposes of reading, to identify the organizational structure of the material, and to recognize when key concepts are presented. According to McNeil (1984), these qualities are part of the reader's background knowledge about reading. *Knowledge-based schemata* are the mental units of structure by which people carry meanings formed from past experience, and from which linguistic input serves to help individuals reconstruct and modify their previous knowledge of the world (Bransford, Barclay, & Franks, 1972).

Prior knowledge provides a common experiential framework between the reader and the author. Consider how difficult it is to understand the political satire in *Gulliver's Travels* unless the history of 18th-century England is known. In Book 1, Gulliver set sail for the East Indies when a storm wrecked his ship. He swam to shore where he collapsed from exhaustion. Upon awakening he was astonished to find humans no more than 6 inches tall, called Lilliputians. Eventually Gulliver befriended them and visited their country's capital. There the Principal Secretary of Private Affairs discussed with Gulliver the war that existed between Lilliput and the neighboring island, Blefusca. The basis of the conflict was a religious question of whether the faithful should break their eggs on the big end (Big Endians) or the little end (Little Endians). The Blefuscudians broke their eggs, in the traditional style, at the big end. The Lilliputians lost 11,000 soldiers and 40 ships over this dispute.

At one level of interpretation, *Gulliver's Travels* is an entertaining and humorous novel about a man's unusual adventures to strange lands. To those versed in English history, however, it is a powerful satire regarding British life and history. The egg issue is ridiculous until it becomes clear that it symbolizes the issue behind "holy wars" of the late 17th century between Catholic France and Protestant England. The egg breaking refers to differences in the breaking of bread in communion. The Big Endians are therefore Catholic, and the Little Endians are Protestant. Jonathon Swift satirizes English politics, human morality, and contemporary philosophers. Analysis based on prior knowledge of English history allows the reader to interpret more closely the different levels of intent.

No matter how explicitly writers communicate an implicitedness exists which necessitates the use of prior knowledge by the reader. Comprehension suffers when readers do not make maximum use of their prior knowledge (Bransford and Johnson, 1972). Students with a high knowledge background on a selection recall more information, provide more elaboration of events, and express the material more accurately than low-knowledge individuals (Spilich, Vesonder, Chiesi, & Voss, 1979). Teachers can improve comprehension by helping students to recall and articulate relevant information prior to reading the material.

Text-based Schemata

Readers are likely to focus on text-based strategies rather than personal knowledge, when they encounter unfamiliar material. With difficult passages, readers may need to attend more to word meaning, forfeiting the benefit of contextual and syntactic clues. *Text-based schemata* are informational units built upon the organizational patterns of *narrative prose* such as stories and folktales. Forms of narrative prose, for example, can be described in an hierarchical series of categories, arranged in a logical sequence (Mandler & Johnson, 1977). A typical sequence begins with a *setting* which introduces the protagonists and provides information about the place, time, and context from which the story will develop. The *episodes,* which unfold may include some or all of the following: (a) Initiating events where protagonists reveal their goals, (b) Internal responses which psychologically motivate characters toward that goal, (c) Attempts by characters to reach that goal, (d) Consequences which indicate their failure to attain that goal, and (e) A reaction in response to their failure or attainment of that goal. Children learn to construct text-based schemata for narrative prose by listening to stories, and by experiencing causal relationships and action sequences among other individuals. Proficient readers use story organization to focus on certain aspects of incoming information, to attend to what has gone on before, and to determine when a part of a narrative needs to be put to memory (Kieras, 1978).

McConaughy (1980) asked adults and children to read several stories and then to write summaries highlighting what they thought were the main points of the text. The youngest children summarized the beginning and ending components of the story focusing on settings, initiating events, and conflict resolutions. Their responses indicated comprehension at the recall level, a type of response dependent on *simple descriptive schemata*. Older children made inferences by supplying meaningful information that logically fit in the story and supplied explanations for actions and events. This level of response, because of the amount of conceptual interpretation, was classified as *information-processing schemata*. Adults explained the motivational and psychological causes behind protagonists' actions using *social-inference schemata*. McNeil (1984) postulates that teachers of children in the early grades may be able to draw out inferences about motivation after the literal aspects of a story have been discussed.

Whereas narrative writing is concerned with characters, actions, events, and their dynamic relationships, *expository writing* addresses the presentation of facts, comparisons, and explanations (Aulls, 1978). Text-based schemata, used to help readers structure incoming data, are more predictable in narrative than in expository writings. Because material in expository form is most often found in the content areas such as science, history, or English, readers often have limited experiential information to relate to these subjects. The less definitive expository form includes a topic sentence, supporting information, and usually a concluding sentence. But while the topic sentence consistently occurs as the initial sentence of a paragraph to signal the subject, the main idea which signals the most important statement may be found anywhere in the paragraph and may even be implied. In order to understand expository material, the reader must differentiate specific and general topics, define relationships between the main topic and subordinate topics, and learn to compare and evaluate evidence that support the main ideas presented.

Based on schema theory, conceptual comprehension may proceed inductively or deductively. According to induction, the reading process is data-driven from the recognition of letters and words. Using data-driven strategies, the reader contributes word analysis skills to the process. The reader begins with little information about the content and the print is processed until the information is understood.

According to deduction, the reading process is concept-driven by strategies determined from the reader's knowledge of text organization and prior experience (Freedle & Hale, 1979). Good comprehenders are hypothesized to use concept-driven strategies, such as prior subject information or context clues, to help integrate written material while poor readers rely heavily on text-driven strategies such as decoding. The more background information readers have, whether the material is expository or narrative, determines the type of strategy they can utilize to improve their comprehension.

A Polarization of Views: Subskill or Unitary Process

The nature of the skills needed to understand what is read continues to be speculative. Educators and researchers have continued through the years to create taxonomies of skills and to demonstrate their validity and uniqueness. Two directions have evolved in the literature. One supports the idea that comprehension consists of a set of distinguishable subskills and the other supports the idea that comprehension represents a unitary, general ability. In the 1940s, Davis (1944) analyzed student scores on the *Cooperative Reading Comprehension Tests* and concluded there were nine distinguishable skills in comprehension. Thurstone (1946), by reanalyzing Davis's correlations explained them as a single factor. In the 1970s, Davis (1971) continued to argue that comprehension is composed of separate, isolable skills but supported only four: (a) word knowledge, (b) drawing inferences from the content, (c) recognizing a writer's purpose, attitude, tone, and mood, and (d) following the structure of a passage. Still, others continued to insist that comprehension exists as a single aptitude (Thorndike, 1973–1974).

Whether comprehension is a series of subskills or a unitary skill is important because the point of view of the teacher determines the didactic approach used in the classroom. A teacher using the subskill approach is likely to ask questions of increasing difficulty modeled by one of the current taxonomies. On the other hand, a teacher using the unitary approach, attempts to develop students' reasoning ability by helping them formulate their own questions with the expectation that this ability generalizes. This polarization of views exists because of the difficulty involved in measuring the learning of a silent and complex skill.

Problems in Measuring Comprehension

Comprehension occurs at a number of cognitive levels that are integrated with the reader's prior knowledge and experience. To study comprehension, researchers frequently divide this process into distinct factors in order to verify and measure those subskills essential to comprehension. Problems which confront researchers are: (a) which unit of analysis should be used: words, sentences, or longer units, (b) how to separate memory and comprehension from the interaction, and (c) how to isolate the subskill(s) under consideration from the reader's prior knowledge.

UNIT OF ANALYSIS

Comprehension materials need to be uniformly controlled for structure, difficulty, and organization (Eamon, 1978–1979). In the past researchers have used different units of analysis for measurement. At the word level, the reader must comprehend the meaning for each word (Vygotsky, 1962); at the sentence level, the reader assembles a group of words to form an idea (James, 1890); and at the paragraph and story levels, ideas are integrated to form the meaning of the total passage (Mandler & Johnson, 1977). Furthermore, each level of comprehension interacts with other units: words within sentences and sentences within larger segments. How to develop a consistent and replicable method of constructing items which are syntactically and semantically similar is difficult. Within story selections complex ideas can be stated simply and simple ideas can be made complex by altering sentence structure (Thorndyke, 1977). In the past, a wide variety of units such as words, phrases, sentence length, and vocabulary density have been used in an effort to control text across selections. None of these units has been completely successful (Meyer, 1975).

The proposition is frequently used as the unit to count when measuring reading comprehension. *Propositions* are ideational units with a syntactic structure similar to simple sentences. The proposition consists of a relational word such as a verb which determines the relationship between other words in the proposition known as arguments (Lachman et al., 1979). "She reads books" is a proposition in which "reads" is the relational word linking the arguments, "She" and "books." The use of propositions is promising because: (a) Young children lack an awareness of many linguistic structures apart from meaning, and (b) Skilled readers use the largest possible unit to obtain meaning (Gibson & Levin, 1975). Standardizing a unit to analyze different selections of text is needed to be able to generalize the results of different research projects.

MEMORY AND COMPREHENSION

Most research to date has imposed a memory task on readers to measure their comprehension skill. A format generally used to identify and examine comprehension subskills is: (a) To present to the subject some type of material such as word lists, sentences, passages, or stories, (b) To remove that material, and (c) To test through memory tasks such as direct recall, probed recall, or recognition (Stein & Glenn, 1979). During *direct recall,* subjects attempt to recite everything they have read. *Probed recall* tests more than literal recollection by requiring subjects to answer particular types of questions. Recognition is measured by objective tests in multiple-choice and true/false formats. There are two basic difficulties involved with these memory-related tasks. First, because the material is not remembered does not necessarily mean that it was not understood. For example, older children may remember more information than younger children not because they understand more but because older children may have better mnemonic strategies and more experience in anticipating the kinds of questions that are likely to be asked. Second, the subject's response bias may play an important part in the way in which questions are answered. Children may perceive differently than the researcher what ideas are valuable and consequently may put to memory material which is not pertinent to the questions being asked. An important and often perplexing job facing researchers is to justify why some questions are asked and others are not.

PRIOR KNOWLEDGE

Comprehension involves integrating new ideas and concepts initiated from text into existing cognitive structures or knowledge-based schemata. Many skills such as being able to draw inferences require the reader to go beyond the explicit meanings of written text. According to linguists, the same passage or selection on a topic may be understood in different ways depending upon the reader's background. Even at the word level, meaning is dependent on how familiar it is in the reader's repertoire of experiences with that word. Vocabulary is greatly determined by the richness and depth of experiences and by labeling and filing those experiences to make them flexible when recalled from many and varied conditions (Dale, 1969).

While prior experience is a critical consideration when investigating comprehension, it is difficult to determine and control experimentally. A traditional means of measuring comprehension is a standardized test. However, the researcher finds it difficult to know whether the reader's responses to test questions are a result of textual information or prior knowledge. Tuiman (1973–1974), examined a number of basic achievement tests including the *Iowa Test of Basic Skills* and the *Metropolitan Achievement Test*. He found that none of these tests predetermined the information subjects brought to the item as distinct from information presented in the passages. Since the reader was given a choice of four answers, chance score on these tests was calculated at 0.25, while the average correct response of subjects who responded to the items without reading the accompanying passages ranged from 0.32 to 0.50. How to control for the reader's prior knowledge and experience in testing situations is a major obstacle.

Selective Use in Teaching

Because of the measurement difficulties, debate continues on whether the process of comprehension is a unitary skill or a series of subskills. The focus on subskills has produced a number of taxonomies offering the reading teacher a basis to form different types of questions in an orderly fashion. The focus on reading as a unitary skill stresses lessons to students on how to monitor their own learning and form their own questions. Based on the goals of the teacher, the abilities of the students, and the atmosphere of the class, both approaches may be used effectively to teach conceptual reading.

SUBSKILL APPROACH TO COMPREHENSION

Subskills are categorical descriptions of the ways readers interpret text. It is critical that teachers know the cognitive outcomes of reading in order that they select techniques that instruct children to think more clearly. In an effort to identify the subskills to be included in a curriculum, Rosenshine (1980) examined comprehension skills that were common to five popular reading textbook series. He synthesized these skills into three general areas:

1. *Locating details*—paraphrasing, recognition, and matching.
2. *Simple inferential skills*—understanding words in context, recognizing cause-and-effect relationships, and comparisons and contrast.

3. *Complex inferential skills*—recognizing main ideas or topics, drawing conclusions, and predicting outcomes.

Rosenshine's categories were based on increasing complexity. Such a hierarchical organization characterizes the taxonomies published in the 1950s and 1960s and which continue to be taught. A *taxonomy* is a hierarchical classification of skills which assumes that each level requires a different degree or kind of interpretation.

Bloom's Taxonomy

An extensive literature describes the different types of thinking that occur after reading. The most famous taxonomy regarding comprehension is Bloom's *Handbook on Educational Objectives: Cognitive Domain* (Bloom, Engelhart, Furest, Hill, & Krathwohl, 1956). Bloom and his collaborators divide the cognitive domain into intellectual abilities which can be applied to reading instruction. The knowledge level, which is the foundation to higher levels, is defined as literal, direct recall of information. In conceptual comprehension, the higher intellectual abilities involve organizing and reorganizing content at five successive levels: comprehension, application, analysis, synthesis, and evaluation.

COMPREHENSION

To Bloom, comprehension requires the student to use knowledge to indicate understanding. Three kinds of increasingly difficult comprehension tasks are defined: translation, interpretation, and extrapolation. *Translation,* as an educational objective, requires the reader to change knowledge from one symbolic form to another. In the primary grades, a child might draw a picture to illustrate an important event from the story. Older students might write a paragraph to make a geometrical proof. *Interpretation* requires the student to identify the major ideas in a communication and to understand the relationships between them. One example of interpretation is the ability to relate the subsections of a chapter to each other and to prior knowledge in order to reconstruct a shorter version of the chapter. *Extrapolation* requires the student to take given information and build upon it. The reader fills in the gaps or reads between the lines of a written presentation. Before readers can carry out an extrapolation, they must first translate and interpret the material. Many errors of comprehension are due to extrapolation which is carried beyond the limits to which the communication was intended.

APPLICATION

Application requires students to apply the skills and abilities they have developed to solve problems. The individual applies knowledge and understandings to a simulated or real situation. In comprehension, students are able to use material when specifically asked; in application, they demonstrate what they can be done with knowledge. A student who builds a computer from its component parts must apply a great deal of reading knowledge to assemble it properly. Most of what the reading teacher does in the classroom is an application of life experiences, formal training, and self-education, as well as an application of learning theory, methodology, and life experiences. Some examples of objectives which illustrate the process of application are:

> The ability to apply social science generalizations and conclusions to actual social problems.
>
> The ability to predict the probable effect of a change in a factor on a biological situation previously at equilibrium.
>
> The ability to relate principles of civil liberties and civil rights to current events.
>
> The ability to apply the laws of trignometry to practical situations. (Bloom et al., 1956, p. 124)

ANALYSIS

Analysis is the process of breaking down text into its elements, relationships, and organizational principles. *Analysis of elements* requires the reader to inspect material closely for unfounded assumptions. A philosophy student studies the assumptions on which any particular philosophy is grounded. Once these assumptions are accepted, the philosophy is usually constructed so well that it is logically unassailable. Because many widely divergent philosophies exist, each being a logically integrated whole, indicates a need for analysis of the premises on which any philosophy is based. Students need instruction in "distinguishing facts from hypotheses" and "distinguishing a conclusion from the statements that support it" (p. 146).

Analysis of relationships indicates how the elements in a communication fit together logically. When editors check to see that the headings in a piece of writing are parallel in construction, they are analyzing relationships. The statement, "As teachers' salaries rose, the consumption of alcohol increase," implies a cause-and-effect relationship but analysis reveals that the two parts of the statement are independent and not necessarily related.

Analysis of organizational principles means examining the structure and organization of the message. A student's determination as to whether a piece of poetry was or was not a sonnet depends on the ability to recognize the elements, to see the relationships between the elements, and determine whether organizational principles of the composition met the criteria of a sonnet.

SYNTHESIS

Synthesis is the process of taking parts of text and putting them together into a complex whole. The category of synthesis is listed under the general term: production of a unique communication, production of a plan, and the derivation of a set of abstract relations.

Production of a unique communication conveys an experience or message to others as evidenced by an essay, a poem, a play, or a musical production. *Production of a proposed set of operations* refers to whether a plan which is carried out is germane to a task. An objective, important to the teacher, would be preparing a set of lesson plans. A test for this objective would involve the completeness in lesson coverage, the thoroughness with which probable contingencies have been anticipated (such as the need for audiovisual aids), and the provisions it makes for meeting the needs of individual students. *Production of a set of abstract relations* finds the student building a classification system or generating new propositions for given data or theories. The intellectual act in this synthesis is the production of logically consistent schemata. Piaget's stages represents synthesis of his psychology of cognitive development.

EVALUATION

Evaluation, the highest category of Bloom's taxonomy, uses standards or criteria to make a judgment. It is the ability to judge an idea or event in terms of internal values or external criteria. Teachers of necessity employ evaluation every time they grade a set of essays. This task is performed with greater reliability if their criteria represent professional standards and are formulated before grading.

Bloom's taxonomy is a useful hierarchy of intellectual operations that can be used to structure the questions used to teach conceptual reading. While researchers argue that learning a subskill at one level may not transfer to a more sophisticated level, the value of each skill stands on its own merit. Those who have taught reading know that students often find analysis an easier process than synthesis, suggesting the importance of asking both types of questions. This taxonomy applies especially well to reading comprehension in different subject areas.

Barrett's Taxonomy

One of the most elaborate descriptions of reading is the *Barrett Taxonomy, Cognitive and Affective Dimensions of Reading Comprehension* as reported by Clymer (1968). Barrett's taxonomy has been popular because it was designed for the classroom. He describes five major levels, each of which is subdivided for descriptive purposes. The principal levels are (a) literal comprehension, (b) reorganization, (c) inferential comprehension, (d) evaluation, and (e) appreciation.

Barrett hypothesizes that *literal comprehension* may involve either recognition or recall and that thinking activities may range from simple to complex. In all cases, comprehension is focused on points that are explicitly stated by the author. Guides to aid the student in reading may consist of questions that ask for details, comparisons, sequences, main ideas, cause-and-effect relationships, and character traits. Questions that require recall (short-answer format) would be more difficult for students than the same questions cast in recognition (matching format), although both are likely to test learning.

In *reorganization,* the reading material is a basis for (a) classifying people, places, and things into categories, (b) outlining the material read, (c) summarizing the principal ideas in the passage, and (d) synthesizing ideas from more than one passage. Creating an outline of the text is a reorganization skill that many children from grades four to eight lack. Organization is an essential study skill for retaining and understanding different subject matter. All of these responses require conceptual thinking beyond Barrett's level of literal comprehension.

Inferential comprehension requires readers to go beyond the text and to use their own experience and background to (a) infer supporting details, (b) infer main ideas that are not explicitly stated, (c) infer sequences either between incidents in the reading or after the passage terminates, (d) infer comparisons between characters, (e) infer cause-and-effect relationships, (f) infer character traits, (g) predict outcomes, and (h) interpret figurative language. A suitable activity might be reading a part of a passage and then predicting the outcome. The accuracy of the prediction is checked by what follows when the passage is read. The principal difference between literal comprehension and inferential comprehension depends on whether the information to be comprehended is explicitly stated or has been inferred by the learner.

Evaluation involves the student reading to make judgments, either by given criteria or personal values. Evaluation may be checked by asking students to decide (a) whether the incidents could really happen, (b) whether what is written is fact or opinion, (c) whether the information is based on valid and adequate sources or on internal consistency and completeness, and (d) whether the material is appropriate to the characterization. Older students may be asked to make value judgments of the worth, desirability, or acceptability of the actions of characters within a passage. Evaluation involves the student's conceptualization of the criteria and has overtones of cognitive, rather than affective, responses.

Appreciation involves both emotional and intellectual components since the reader is asked to respond to questions concerning literary form and aesthetic impact. The suggested activities for students are that they (a) verbalize their emotional responses to the content, (b) identify with characters or involve themselves in incidents, (c) react to the language used by the author, and (d) describe their feelings about the author's ability to use words to create vivid images. Although this level of criticism seems sophisticated, such personal evaluation should be encouraged in children's responses to literature. Appreciation requires affective conceptualizations on the part of the student.

Barrett emphasizes the role of questioning as a stimulus to creating different kinds of reading experiences. One advantage of the taxonomy is that it breaks the different levels of conceptual reading into subdivisions that make possible a pinpointing of objectives. The more explicitly the objectives can be defined, the greater the probability that they will be taught and measured. This taxonomy defines goals more explicitly than do most descriptions of the reading process. The interactions of reasoning and written text produces qualitatively different thoughts. Bloom's and Barrett's taxonomies are both models which describe levels of thought. The goal of the teacher is to urge students to move to the highest level attainable.

Elaboration of a Subskill:
Inferential Thought

Making inferences is a subskill which has come under considerable scrutiny in recent years by psycholinguists. Nicholas and Trabasso (1980) examined inferential thinking by defining it as the ability of the reader to understand the relationship between propositional units of text. To illustrate the importance of inferential thinking, this example was presented:

1. Mary had a little lamb. Its fleece was white as snow.
2. Mary had a little lamb. She spilled gravy and mint jelly on her dress.
3. Mary had a little lamb. The delivery was a difficult one and afterwards the vet needed a drink. (p. 216)

The "Mary had a little lamb" sequence demonstrates how inferences play a crucial role in transmitting thoughts. According to Nicholas and Trabasso (1980), inferences help the reader to: (a) specify word meaning, (b) identify the context of a passage, (c) anticipate the causes and consequences of upcoming events, and (d) predict, from the organizational structure of prose, the nature of upcoming syntactic information.

Inferences help to specify the meaning of words which typically have multiple interpretations. Although the words and their location are identical in the first sentence of the "Mary had a little lamb" sequence, the meaning of the first sentence is altered by its relationship to the second sentence. The noun, lamb, had three interpretations: (a) a normal lamb, (b) a roasted lamb, and (c) a neonate. The verb, had, had three interpretations: (a) ownership, (b) consumption, and (c) parturition. And the adjective, little, represents the three relative sizes: a small but fully developed lamb, a newborn lamb, and a slice of lamb.

Inferences help the reader to identify the context in which the events of the passage occur. In one context, Mary probably lived in the country where sheep are raised. In another context, Mary was probably dining at a social event which the meal was formal and she was wearing a dress. In the last context, Mary was a ewe giving birth to a lamb, presumably in a barn or in a veterinarian's office.

Inferences help the reader to anticipate the causes and consequences of events. When Mary is dining, the reader can surmise the conditions necessary to prepare and serve a meal as well as the physical and psychological consequences of spilling gravy and jelly on her dress. When Mary is the name of a ewe, the reader can surmise the physical surroundings of the delivery and the veterinarian's psychological need for a drink afterwards.

And finally, inferences help proficient readers reduce their dependence on graphophonic information by maximizing the use of syntactic and semantic structures through expectation or prediction. The good reader uses the organizational conventions of language to minimize the processing limitations. Stories, which are clearly written and organized, in a format which conforms with the structure typically used are better remembered than those that are less well written. Researchers have demonstrated that children's recall of short descriptive passages were influenced significantly by the logical order within the story's sequence of events and actions (Danner, 1976; Stein & Glenn, 1979).

From the preceding description of inferences, the teacher can understand the importance of asking students a variety of questions at different levels. The teacher can instruct students how to use context to derive word meaning, create settings, and to anticipate the causes and consequences of character behaviors. As each subskill is analyzed, it becomes clear that questioning strategy is an essential instructional component to a reading curriculum.

Teaching Based on the Subskill Approach

The most effective learning occurs through careful planning and execution of lessons. Some proponents of the subskill approach suggest that learning is built from small increments to a larger understanding. When teachers write their course objectives as subskills, they sharpen their own definitions of thought processes to make learning more coherent.

Planning, according to the subskill approach, is easily justified when grounded on a recognized theoretical foundation. Those favoring a this approach divide comprehension into specific areas. Planners, however, find it difficult to select the most important subskills to be taught because various authors and textbooks present different priorities. A list of important competencies are needed as guidelines to track student progress. Adapting a taxonomy may result in a checklist from which subskills are selected for a specific group of students. Robeck and Wilson (1974) divided comprehension into three broad categories: literal, interpretative, and evaluative comprehension. A breakdown of their checklist follows in Table 14.1.

In *literal reading,* the reader is guided to recall factual information. Teachers can help children identify major points and facts at whatever skill level the student has attained. Nearly all reading that a lawyer does is literal, but this requires more sophistication than the interpretive or evaluative reading that a high school student does.

Interpretive reading extends the author's meaning based on past experience to include such interpretive skills as classifying, synthesizing, and inferring. Experienced adult readers interpret almost automatically and with little awareness that the comprehension of what the author is saying is being supplemented. When children are being taught comprehension skills, this extension of the meaning is not automatic, partly because they do not have the background to make viable interpretations. Unless taught, they may not be aware that such extensions are acceptable. Instruction for reading comprehension that is well designed can dramatically improve the student's functioning. Questions that stimulate interpretation usually call for information not explicitly stated in the material: "Who do you think . . . ? Why . . . ? Supposing . . . ?" The importance of conceptualizations to undergird the learning can foster a significant part of the reading teacher's repertoire. Learning to make inferences requires that students distinguish between a synthesis of the author's literal message, which is a conceptualization of lines read, and their own inferences, which are conceptualizations of what is between the lines.

Hansen (1981) compared second-grade students' ability to make inferences when they were taught 10 basal stories using three different instructional treatments. The *strategy treatment* required teachers to ask the students to predict what they would do and what the story characters might do when confronting situations similar to those in a story. In this treatment, teachers guided students through the story to compare their predictions. The *inferential-questioning treatment* was similar except that all of the questions asked in guided reading were inferential. The *traditional-based treatment* asked students to read a selection and then were presented a set of questions, about 80% literal and 20% inferential. When asked inferential questions, subjects taught by either the strategy or

TABLE 14.1 Student Self-evaluation of Reading Comprehension

Name _____ Reading Material _____

	Association	Conceptualization	Creative Self-direction
Literal comprehension	1	2	3
Details			
Main ideas			
Sequences			
Comparisons			
Cause-and-effect relationships			
Character traits			
Interpretive comprehension			
Classify details			
Classify events			
Classify characters			
Synthesize early and late materials			
Infer details			
Infer main ideas			
Infer sequences			
Infer comparisons			
Infer cause-and-effect relationships			
Infer character traits			
Evaluative, or critical, comprehension			
Note extrapolations			
Appropriateness of evidence			
Evidence fact			
Evidence fancy			
Analysis of contradictions			
Emotionally toned adjectives			
Non sequiturs			

Under *associations* mark page numbers where the point occurs (more than one possible per square).

Under *conceptualizations* check if you made any about the material being considered.

Under *creative self-direction* check if you used something from this reading selection while reading another. Use numbers and footnotes to record.

Use separate set of three columns for each reading.

inferential-questioning treatments, surpassed those taught by the traditional-basal treatment. From these results, it was concluded that the ability to answer interpretative questions such as inferences was enhanced by direct teaching.

Evaluative reading uses interpretive reading as a basis from which judgments are made, a skill which is particularly important in reading advertisements, contracts, and position papers. Both children and older students need to be taught to read critically those materials in which the author's purpose is to persuade, proselytize, or motivate the reader. Students can begin by identifying the author's purpose: to sell designer jackets, justify a sales tax for school support, or convert to a new religion. The neophyte reader of propaganda materials needs to learn to make judgments about the adequacy of the evidence, about its appropriateness in the context, and about its validity. The instruction for this kind of reading starts at the association level, where the teacher helps the reader to distinguish between the literal statement and the writer's position.

Systematic analysis will often show authors espousing contradictory positions in the same selection. Some writers use emotionally toned adjectives either to support or to destroy a position. Often the author will use a non sequitur, which is an inferential statement that does not follow from the premises. When shown examples of these kinds of errors, students generalize evaluative criteria to other materials.

Taxonomies form a basis from which some teacher manuals and curriculum guides are prepared. The subskill approach presupposes a teacher-oriented curriculum that directs student thinking to successively higher goals. This organization is somewhat different from the student-oriented processes proposed by the unitary approach.

UNITARY APPROACH TO COMPREHENSION

Many authorities argue that comprehension cannot be broken into distinct subskills but exists as a single aptitude (Spearitt, 1972). A teacher, viewing comprehension from this perspective, is concerned with readers' making their own interpretations and generalizations. Philosophically, this idea was stated as early as 1913 by Huey who said ". . . until the insidious thought of reading as word pronouncing is well worked out of our heads, it is well to place emphasis strongly where it really belongs, on reading as thought getting, independently of expression. "

Reading: A Thinking Process

Wolfe (1968) indicated that the efficient reader does not just recall words but actively participates in a process of collecting and solving problems. Even in the upper grades, a number of students possess good decoding skills and can recall the words of a passage accurately, yet they cannot answer beyond the level of literal comprehension. These students have a limited appreciation of the many messages an author usually communicates.

Wolfe depicted the levels of thought made by the proficient reader, reflecting the interaction of the reader's background, the text, and the cognitive effort that must be made when reading.

Level 1: *Associative thinking*—the immediate thoughts related to an experience.

Level 2: *Concept formation*—the process of forming a definition to a problem.

Level 3: *Problem solving*—the process of examining a task and problem to find a self-satisfying solution.

Level 4: *Critical thinking*—the process of forming judgments based on significant facts and/or correlated ideas.

Level 5: *Concentrative thinking*—the in-depth process of making implications after significant facts and correlated information have been examined; a process often characterized by the formation of opinions.

Level 6: *Creative thinking*—the in-depth process of reacting to another's ideas or one's previous ideas to produce new ideas. . . . She concluded that ". . . those who read think, and those who think read" (p. 6)!

Some educational psychologists find it difficult to dichotomize this thinking as a unitary approach as theoretically distinct from Bloom's taxonomy as a subskill approach. The concept of reading as reasoning incorporates the individual's own awareness of cognitive processes and the self-regulation of those processes. Self-awareness and self-control over one's thoughts in problem solving is called *metacognition* (Flavell, 1976). One form is *metacomprehension,* the ability of readers to adjust their thinking for more effective understanding. In conceptual reading, metacomprehension strategies are aroused when expectations about the text are not confirmed or when unfamiliar concepts occur too frequently to be ignored. Proficient readers demonstrate metacomprehension by using different strategies of self-monitoring: (a) By knowing the parameters of a given task. Understanding the purpose for reading, and consciously adjusting speed and attention to fit these task demands improves comprehension (Flavell & Wellman, 1977). (b) By knowing when to identify important aspects of text and focusing on those rather than on insignificant details. The practice of continual self-questioning helps to determine whether one is following the author's message (Wong, 1985). (c) By knowing one's personal skills and strengths in monitoring text. Sophisticated readers take corrective measures when failures in comprehension are detected (Brown, 1980).

Failures in monitoring comprehension can occur at the word level, at the sentence level, and at the integration of sentences and paragraphs into a whole story. Collins and Smith (1982) suggested that readers risk misunderstandings in reading by: (a) ignoring the word or words that are the source of difficulty, (b) suspending judgment on the misunderstanding hoping that it will be clarified later, (c) rereading the sentence or paragraph looking for a revised interpretation, (d) rereading the previous context to re-evaluate the presented information, and (e) referring to an expert source such as a parent, dictionary, or secondary source. These metacomprehensive responses may or may not be beneficial, which exemplifies the importance of monitoring one's own interpretations. For example, ignoring words may or may not affect comprehension. It is the point at which contextual clues are insufficient to generate meaning that a reader must know to change strategies. Rereading a chapter or paragraph is a common strategy that is valuable only if the problem which caused the lack of concentration, is corrected a strategy which assumes attentiveness. College students, trying to understand Piagetian texts in their original translations, often use a secondary source as a helpful introduction.

Teaching Based on the Unitary Approach

Teaching from the unitary perspective focuses on methods which help students learn to interpret text by themselves. Metacomprehension strategies are *planning* how to approach the material, *predicting* what needs to be remembered and how long this task will take, *guessing* before the solution is obvious, and *monitoring* when one is not reaching the planned goals (Brown, 1980). Skills in self-questioning instruction are emphasized and have been shown to be effective in improving comprehension.

McNeil (1984) warned that traditional tests measuring particular skills may not be helpful in understanding the process of comprehension. Vocabulary and comprehension items make it difficult to determine if the reader is having problems with the language in the material or with the questions being asked. He suggested the following questions to determine whether pupils have the prerequisites to read for meaning: (a) Do students attempt to make sense of the material read or do they focus on decoding? (b) Do students modify their reading strategies for different purposes, such as skimming for impressions or scanning for details? (c) Can students distinguish important information from less significant details? (d) Can students determine if the descriptions of characters match their behaviors? (e) Do students realize when statements are untrue when compared with their knowledge of the world? (f) Do students recognize when they understand what they are reading and when they do not? (g) Do students know what to do when they do not understand what they are reading? Some research in teaching students to activate relevant prior-knowledge appropriate to self-questions appears to produce better comprehension than teacher-generated questions (Craig & Lockhart, 1972).

ACTIVE COMPREHENSION

Having readers directly involve themselves in monitoring the text has been called active comprehension (Singer, 1978). Poor readers may not generate clarifying questions because they are unaware of their importance. They lack a sensitivity to critical textual elements and an understanding of the value in self-checking their comprehension. Cohn (1969) found good readers were active participants in the reading process while poor readers were passive. He graphically described the mental involvement during reading about the proper way to carve a leg of lamb. His good readers questioned the meaning of words and manipulated the alternatives so that they *understood* what was implied. Ideas were checked for internal consistency with reality as the reader knows it. He suggested that students need to be taught to ask themselves: "Do I know what this sentence means?" "What is the antecedent of this pronoun?" "What is the relationship between the characters?" "What is the main idea in this passage?" One of the best-known active comprehension techniques, which is particularly appropriate for use with expository forms of writing, is the SQ3R approach.

SQ3R

The SQ3R approach was developed by Robinson (1961). This system advocates a five-step process, in which the SQ stands for *survey* and *question;* and the 3R symbolizes *read, recall,* and *review.* Children can be taught to use SQ3R techniques in the upper elementary grades and even to modify the way they apply the techniques to different study materials.

Survey. This means looking over the selection to see what the material is about. Reading the first paragraph of chapters, skimming the subheadings, and reading the summary constitutes a survey. The point is to form a conceptualization of what the chapter is about so that the pieces can be fitted into a structure, rather than remaining as isolated bits of information. Before buying a new textbook, older readers often check the table of contents and index to survey the topics to be covered and the authors who have contributed.

Question. The second step is to formulate questions representing the major headings of the chapter and write them down in a notebook. By changing the headings into a question, attention is focused on the main idea. The transformation of format requires at least a minimal understanding of the chapter and involves the reader.

Read. When materials are being read for study purposes, a moderate amount of concentration is required. Keeping in mind the question that the heading has become and trying to answer this question fits the details into a conceptual framework as the reading progresses.

Recall. At the end of each section, covered by a question, the student writes the answer in a notebook. The student's own words constitute his or her conceptualization of the content. At first students will need to look back over the section they have just read in order to locate points they should have picked up but missed. With practice in keeping the question in mind as they read, they will become more adept at the formulation of the summary statements.

Review. The final step is to read over the notes for the whole chapter and then, from memory, write a summary statement or paragraph that delineates the contents and provides an excellent outline of the chapter.

DR–TA

Stauffer (1975) formulated a group instruction technique for active comprehension known as a Directed Reading–Thinking Activity (DR–TA). This process approach is particularly useful in comprehending reading narrative forms of literature. The assumption is that conceptual reading skills and appropriate emotional understandings are determined by students' actions on the text and their interactions among each other. DR–TA groups of 8 to 10 students to encourage their dialogue. Everyone reads the same material at the same time. The purposes for reading are declared by the students as they learn to ask questions. Answers are discussed and supported as feedback develops the authenticity of the predictions and responses. The teacher asks questions which require children to interpret and make inferences from what they have read. The primary objective of group DR–TA training is in critical reading.

A typical reading lesson begins by asking for predictions based on title clues. As the lesson develops, predictions are requested for the first page, the first half of the story, and then five-sixths of the way through. The purpose of this silent reading procedure is to control the amount of information children use. DR–TA encourages both divergent and convergent thinking. Students learn to evaluate information and to read just their hypotheses to fit additional information. The teacher's role is to draw each student into active participation with questions such as "What do you think will happen next?" and prompts such as "Read on and find out." Throughout most of the story, divergent thoughts are common as children make many predictions, convergent thinking occurs toward the end of the story as information focuses on the appropriate outcome.

Chapter Summary

Reading is a thinking process which requires the reader to construct meaning actively by relating text to past experience. A branch of cognitive psychology, information processing employs constructivism in researching the processes of memory, thinking, and comprehension. The notion that comprehension is an active, constructive process suggests the need for teachers: (a) To access students' background knowledge before having them read a story, (b) Provide supplementary information if necessary to clarify implied messages, and (c) Instruct students how to relate their background knowledge to text information.

Proficient readers use their knowledge of language and composition to structure their thoughts. Narrative and expository are different forms of writing which have particular qualities. The teacher can help students comprehend information more effectively by teaching them how to recognize the unique characteristics of different forms of writing.

Two theoretical bases are used by teachers to formulate lessons. The subskill approach divides comprehension into a hierarchy of skills and the unitary skill approach hypothesizes a single aptitude when defining comprehension. The subskill approach gives the instructor more control over the types of questions being asked when a story is presented. The unitary approach is process-oriented and relies heavily on the students' ability to learn to formulate their own questions and to monitor their own understandings.

15 | Creative Reading and Writing

I wanted to write a poem
that you would understand
For what good is it to me
if you can't understand it?
But you got to try hard—

William Carlos Williams, from "January Morning"
in *I Wanted to Write a Poem* (1958)

All reading embodies an element of creativity. Readers bring part of themselves and their background to the interpretation of what the author has written. At least part of the extrapolation that readers make when they tackle a reading task is unique. This process can be seen in the use of context clues where the unknown word must have a certain meaning in order to fit the thought being projected by the author. This extension of the author's idea is carried forward without particular awareness on the reader's part and becomes apparent only when the psychological process of extrapolation is examined. Readers use the materials produced by authors to stimulate their own thinking and often their own writing. This extension of meaning beyond the author's intended message, perhaps in conscious opposition to the author's purpose, requires intent and self-direction on the part of the reader.

Creative readers are self-directed; they engage themselves in cognitive and affective responses that go beyond comprehension of the author's message to satisfy purposes of their own. It is important for these readers to know where the author's ideas end and their own ideas begin. This chapter was written for persons who enjoy reading literature and for the teachers of mature students. The first section concerns competent readers who are also creative persons. The second section categorizes the subject-area disciplines into three types of reading which require distinctive reader talent: semantic-logical, symbolic-mathematical, and empathic-mystical. The final section views literary criticism as one **377** way to launch a writing program from reading or literature classes.

READING POWER AND
THE CREATIVE RESPONSE

The relationship between reading and writing proficiency has interested scholars for two centuries, yet the nature of this relationship has resisted precise description. English teachers, by predisposition and professional choice, tend to value the aesthetic appeal of literature and to avoid the quantitative reporting that experimental psychologists produce. Educators from disciplines outside the literary arts tend to think of reading and writing competence as someone else's domain. The paucity of research on this topic has been addressed in the 1980s by a revival of qualitative research, as opposed by quantitative experiments; this opens new opportunities for theory-based discussion and hypothesis testing in the language arts. Widespread attention has been given to fostering written language through children's literature (Newkirk, 1987; Phillips, 1987); integrating writing and reading instruction (Raphael & Englert, 1988); organizing the classroom for reading-writing activities (McVitty, 1987); and to interrelating English and reading (Squire, 1987b). Most reading/writing research has been criticized by Belanger (1987) as a tinkering with methods in the absence of theoretical models.

Positive research findings were cited by Belanger (1987) in the persistence of statistically significant correlations between reading and writing across a broad range of subjects, measures, and experimental settings. However, experiments have failed to show improvement in writing performance as a result of reading treatments and vice versa. The most promising treatments have been those which teach prose structure and story schemata and the least successful are those which teach general reading and writing skills and expect automatic transfer. These results invite the interpretation that skill teaching relies heavily on associative learning, while understanding of structure and schema fosters conceptualization and, therefore, transfer of learning. Research is needed to examine the psychological processes by which readers become engaged sufficiently to want to put their responses in writing.

Initiation of Self-direction

Children who experience early success in reading are likely to read on their own volition, without pressure to do so from adults. The exploration activities of prereading have elements of curiosity, playfulness, and initiative which characterize the older creative reader as well. Learning the decoding skills and achieving automatic recognition of a working vocabulary lacks the spontaneous enjoyment of picture-storybooks, yet the child's interest and momentum can be sustained with successful and reinforced skill building. The stages of reading development, proposed by Chall (1983b), describe two periods which we have identified as particularly amenable to self-directed reading: Stage 3, which typically is achieved during the upper elementary grades and Stage 5, which characterizes the mature college reader.

BASIS FOR NEW IDEAS

Having achieved decoding skills and reading fluency at earlier levels, the stage 3 child has the power to become independent in seeking out materials that satisfy personal interests and goals. The children begin by learning the subject matter of the middle grades and some of them seek increasingly more complex fiction, biography, and nonfiction to read on their own volition. The schools provide access to a library of books and periodicals, free time for reading, and recognition for supplementary reading outside of school. Curiosity beckons the pre-adolescent to the adventure story recommended on TV, the magazine article on how to grow thin on good food, and a novel featuring teenage characters. In these ways older children who read widely experience new feelings and learn new attitudes. Stage 3 children read more books by their own volition than at any other time in their lives as students. Through new interests and the desire for new information they enter the world of adult materials; through self-directed reading they generate a base of prior knowledge for the greater demands of high school.

One of the hazards of self-participation in reading is the tendency on the part of some readers to be diverted from the author's message to ideas that are only tangentially related to the selection. The eyes may continue to focus systematically on the printed words but very little of the message comes through. When the reading is assigned for a well-defined purpose, these mental excursions obstruct efficient work, even though the private ideas that are stimulated by the author's words may start a whole new form of creativity. Readers who learn to define the purpose of their reading will build appropriate habits of interpretation. They should be able to distinguish when reading to acquire background information, when generating new ideas for an assignment, or for the pleasure of manipulating ideas.

BASIS FOR HYPOTHESIZING

The ultimate in independent and responsible reading is viewed in this text as level three learning—the fusion of affective and cognitive conceptualizations in self-directed and unique productivity. The level 3 reader is prepared by commitment to a value system and by comprehensive reading practices to generate hypotheses as an outcome of reading research. Robeck and Wilson (1974) explained

> Scholarly research or creative work, by definition, goes beyond what has already been written. A preliminary step is careful reading to learn what is already known in a field to establish the platform from which to generate new knowledge. The nature of the creative process is not different from that of the self-direction advocated for young children, but it is more sophisticated in that the creativity moves beyond knowledge already established. The basic reading is difficult since many, if not all, possible sources must be searched and interpreted. Concomitant with search reading, many possible hypotheses are formulated by the creative reader, which can potentially be tested. Most of these are discarded as further reading shows they have already been tested and confirmed or invalidated. Sometimes hypotheses are eliminated through further reading, because they are logically incompatible with established sources, although occasionally it is desirable to reexamine accepted ideas by questioning their validity. This kind of reading requires an openness, or a questioning attitude, that probes the basis on which conclusions had been substantiated. Creative readers, aware of the time of writing, may know of later evidence that calls for reopening the question. (p. 535)

Chall (1983b) described the Stage 5 reader as needing to value the work, as taking a qualitative approach as opposed to the quantitative reading of the high school years (stage 4). Having achieved competence, high school students can comprehend different subject areas, recognize technical words, manipulate abstract terms, vary their reading rate according to purpose and report a multiplicity of views without really integrating them (pp. 51–52). These stage 4 skills are basically those of the comprehensive reader, functioning at the level of conceptualization (Chapter 14). Chall describes the stage 5 reader as being able to integrate, reconstruct, and relate the world view to one's own. It is the personal response to the reading that characterizes stage 5. Scholarly readers must dare to have a viewpoint; but in doing so they open themselves to opposition and rejection. Chall sees a counterpart in the stage 0 child who approaches books with openness, daring, and natural use of language. Some college students continue to function at stage 2 or 3 in certain subject areas when lacking the prior knowledge and the reading competence of stage 4. A student may be a stage 5 reader of Shakespeare while functioning at lower stages in physics or geology. The transition to stage 5 will occur if colleges and graduate schools expect and teach for it and the community rewards independence and innovation.

Factors in Creative Reading

The task of exploring a relationship between creative writing and reading is made difficult, according to Holmes (1963), because the products of a science must be tied together with the methods of an art. He reported an experiment which analyzed the different subabilities that enabled some students to develop into "powerful readers." The subjects were the 108 verbally brightest and 108 of the verbally dullest students from an original sample of 400 high school students. A substrata factor analysis of 54 variables revealed that vocabulary is fundamental to the process of power of reading in all groups. Further, the low verbal group showed a greater dependence on vocabulary (50% of the variance) than did the average group (38%) and the high verbal group (20%). Verbal analogies were also predictive of reading power, revealing 17%, 16%, and 14% of the variance in the three groups. Factors such as listening ability, tone intensity, mechanical interest, and study planning provided lesser amounts of variance. Since the study accounted for only 52% of the variance in power of reading for the high group, the intriguing question was: What other strengths were being utilized? From his knowledge of poetry, Holmes interpreted the results of the experiment in terms of the *depth of meaning* that readers with exceptional power brought to the task. Their concepts were enriched with deep emotional experience, symbolic appreciation, value-based interpretation, and imagination. Their conception of analogies, metaphors, and similes were concrete and personal. The conclusion was that having to write, especially having to write poetry, sensitized students toward an appreciation and understanding of all that is read and alerts these students to great concepts, ideas, and words.

The reader is never dissociated completely from the context. Lubbock (1962) expressed this involvement when he wrote:

> The reader of a novel—by which I mean the critical reader—is himself a novelist; he is the maker of a book which may or may not please his taste when it is finished,

but of a book for which he must take his own share of responsibility. The author does his part, but he cannot transfer his book like a bubble into the brain of the critic; he cannot make sure that the critic will possess his work. The reader must, therefore, become, for his part, a novelist, never permitting himself to suppose that the creation of the book is solely the affair of the author. (p. 2)

Imagination is the bond that hold author and reader to a common purpose.

RESPONDING TO DIVERSE DISCIPLINES

The expansion of knowledge makes it increasingly difficult to test the findings of one discipline against another. The hypothesizing process is dissimilar in the same ways that reporting of the material is different. Among the ways of knowing are: (1) Semantic-logical reading, which evaluates the content for logical consistency, (2) The symbolic-mathematical reading, which is the basis for the statistical testing of hypotheses, and (3) The empathic-mystical reading, which makes possible the understanding of written messages on religious beliefs and life-styles. Semantic-logical thinking, used in *historical research,* will be expanded in this section. Symbolic-mathematical reading has evolved over the last century as the foundation for *experimental research.* Empathic-mystical reading, which has been suspect by many scholars who are locked into their own major concerns, has become increasingly popular in such pursuits as sensitivity training, psychoanalysis, and varieties of religious experience.

Semantic-logical Reading

The method of historical research requires evaluative reading of material that throws light on a particular era or problem. The primary sources of knowledge are dispersed in archives, private collections, and libraries. Alton, a high school senior, was learning how to write a research paper in his English class. At first, he thought he would write a history of Santa Barbara, but his teacher persuaded him that an exhaustive study of this topic would be too time consuming. After some exploratory reading about the city's founding in 1704, he decided to limit his topic to a history of the courthouse. By the time he had finished the assignment, he had been to the land registry office to trace the ownership of the land assembled for the site. He had visited the courthouse to experience its Hispanic splendor and obtain a brochure containing the highlights of its history. He had gone to the archives of the Supervisors to read the records of public debates that preceded the letting of contracts. On a hunch that one of the architects might still be practicing, Alton visited him and was allowed to see the file of sketches and specifications. He found the numerous change orders particularly informative. Using the dates from the brochure he was able to locate relevant issues in the stacks of the local newspaper. These primary sources would not have been located without initiative, persistence, and a well-defined goal. To exploit the material required all the reading skills he had practiced in school—surveying, skimming, rapid reading, study reading, locating, note taking, and documenting. Interwoven with these reading techniques were the mediating processes of evaluating, synthesizing, generalizing, and thus creating a meaningful structure. While the chronological organization Alton followed is the most obvious, other forms of organization are common. The kind of research students have in mind will determine the steps their reading searches will take. The reading students do on their own helps them crystallize their thinking and their writing.

Creative readers approach the literature of a discipline with different emphases according to their private purposes. The interpretations will be conceptually harmonious, that is, better understood, if a reader grasps the author's orienting framework early. Some ways of organizing semantic-logical writing are by (1) chronology, (2) philosophy, (3) political resolution of conflicts, (4) evolution of ideas, (5) analysis of trends, and (6) increments of complexity.

CHRONOLOGICAL ORGANIZATION

One of the simplest ways of organizing historical material is by chronology, that is according to the date of publication. Many research summaries are also ordered on this basis. The reader can discover this structure readily and an interpretation of the material is made easy by proceeding from present to ancient sources or from antiquity to the most recent publications. Typically the students who write dissertations include a chapter that reviews the literature. A chapter that appears episodic and disjointed to the reader can be put in a meaningful framework, if the parts are ordered chronologically. Even elementary children, doing their first reports, can learn to look for a chronological order within the sources they are reading. The chronological arrangement of data may be the best way to create a meaningful framework to provide an inherently rational relationship for multiple sources.

Assigned to teach a college freshman course that integrated composition, history, and reading, Kelder (1988) used a chronology of related events to help students connect them with their own lives and ways of looking at the world. Primary-source documents personalized history for them and provided the basis for explaining the significance of an event and redefining words in historical context. After reading John Stuart Mill's essay, "On Liberty," students wrote essays on their own conformity to a group and how public opinion affected their lives. They examined current controversies, such as the religious conflict between Sunni and Shiite Muslim sects, and offered their own suggestions in writing. The students were helped to see how discourse can sharpen meanings and shape world views.

PHILOSOPHICAL ARGUMENT

The essence of philosophical structure is logical organization and integration. An example is the controversy between Leibnitz and Voltaire about this being the best of all possible worlds. Leibnitz (republished, 1936) presented three premises that he accepted as self-evident truths: There is a God, the nature of God embodies complete wisdom, and God exemplifies complete goodness. Since the world exists, it followed logically that God had created it, that He had known the alternate organizations of the world, and that He had necessarily chosen the best of the possibilities.

In his attack on this philosophical construct, Voltaire (1761) used satire rather than philosophical argument. He marshaled the atrocities of the current wars, the tragic disasters of the Lisbon earthquake, and the sadism of the Spanish Inquisition to challenge Leibnitz's philosophical formulation of a "best possible world." Voltaire's writing was crisp and lucid, many more people read his *Candide* than the prosaic *Monadology* by Leibnitz. Frequently, readers are distracted from examination of both sides of a question by the brilliance of a particular author's style rather than by the logic of his message.

The emotional versus the logical argument can be discerned in the popular press as pro-and-con arguments for smoking cigarettes and marijuana. People regularly read the arguments about the certain linkage of cigarette smoking and lung cancer, presented in coldly logical terms. However, when marijuana is considered, the argument changes subtly; since there is at this time less proof that marijuana has any specific, identifiable damaging effect, it therefore must be good and should be legalized. The fact that it took several centuries to establish the causal relationship of cigarette smoking and lung cancer is ignored in parallel arguments about marijuana. Young readers should be encouraged to distinguish between logical fallacy and logical inconsistency and to analyze whether the premises appeal to emotional predispositions or logical argument.

POLITICAL RESOLUTION OF CONFLICTS

Strategies for interpreting the social sciences often revolve around the political decisions that resolved the conflict or problem being analyzed. Serious readers find rather quickly that most controversies are resolved on the basis of economic or political power rather than on the basis of logical inference. In school, teachers show their power by saying, "You do it because I said so," and principals say, "It is school policy." Employers say, "This is the way I want it done." There may or may not be logical underpinning for the decisions and, on occasion, it is possible to point to logical inconsistency in an array of decisions that are promulgated. Creative readers can ferret out the power base that makes the decision effective even if unwise.

As a political-sociological fantasy, *Animal Farm* (Orwell, 1954) has little significance unless read creatively. The struggle for dominance takes place between different animal groups who think they have the formula for creating the good life. The pigs emerge victorious because of their numbers and their repression of nonutilitarian activities. They establish control over the farm in ways that give them plenty to eat, while not missing the cultural values they never knew existed. Student activists of the 1960s and 1970s read *Animal Farm* creatively and built analogies to the power structure that preserves the establishment. They shouted "Pig" at policemen who, at the time, were unaware of the point of reference or its meaning. Secondary students who are exposed to this book are able to create the implications it raises.

Great writers tend to resist the consignment of their art to social or political comment, yet they are sensitive observers of life and reveal this in their writing. Symbolic representation has been used by literary geniuses to give depth and power to their ideas. Fantasy as a literary form cannot be understood unless read creatively. Henry James relied on the creative response of the readers to define his novels as art. The symbolic poetry of Theodore Rhoetke, William Carlos Williams, and Dylan Thomas, was intentionally created with the idea that the reader would interpret the symbolism in a personal way, thus becoming a partner in the aesthetic experience. Nathaniel Hawthorne and other writers in the Gothic tradition used deliberate ambiguity that required readers to draw their own conclusions about events within a plot. Each of these writers was accused, at one time or another, of raising political issues in their art or criticized on the ground that they threatened the establishment.

EVOLUTION OF IDEAS

Some ideas are centuries in the making. The monotheistic idea that permeated the Old Testament, the Talmud, and the Koran gradually evolved as prophets and priests read and discussed the religious writings available to them. Sometimes an idea requires centuries of evolution, while at other times a great scholar looks across the centuries to conceive a new structure. Darwin, in the *Origin of the Species,* portrayed the biological unity of all living species. Freud viewed the continuity of emotional development from infancy to old age as continuous differentiation from primitive instincts. Piaget saw similar continuities in cognitive development of human beings from the reflexive activity at birth to the formal operations in problem solving.

Students of Piaget's construction of cognitive development find reading him extremely difficult if they start by reading Piaget directly, without a knowledge of his whole structure of stages and periods. Olga, a graduate student in child psychology, disdained reading *about* anybody and wanted to "read Piaget". After reading for a week she reported, "Yes, I have read hundreds of pages. I find him very interesting, but I can't tell where he is going." After she had learned that each of Piaget's periods of development followed a sequence from trial-error groping through cause–effect thinking to a culmination in intentional manipulation, Olga was able to read any part of his work with understanding. The intellectual structures in the first period are sensorimotor; in the middle periods they are symbolic representations and concrete operations; and in the third period they are logical abstractions in relation to each other. When this structure is grasped any one theme can be read in the context of the entire construct.

ANALYSIS OF TRENDS

Books that project from present trends require imaginative reading because they picture a world that does not exist. Aldous Huxley, in *Brave New World,* projected trends into a future society that controlled heredity and produced satisfied workers to do the chores as well as creative superior beings. Optimists tend to read and identify with the master race while pessimists project themselves into roles they do not want to accept. This picture of a brave new world of perfect nutrition from tablets and population control by radiation is attractive to some people but frightening and repulsive to others. Malthus's dire prediction of the population explosion and consequent mass starvation has haunted generations of readers, even though agricultural research has continuously pushed the specter a few years further into the future. Toynbee's *Outline of History* used the cyclical rise and fall of empires to project the future of the United States. Marx analyzed trends toward concentration of power and predicted a world ordered according to his socialist doctrine. Children's books on space travel are analyses of trends in transportation and require imagination from the reader.

Semantic-logical thinking is an inherent contribution of the reader in all complex discourse of literature and the social sciences. Teachers of the content areas can help students discover the overall structure of the discourse they are assigned and to seek the author's purpose in writing. Oral discussion of issues and conflicts can stimulate the students to construct their own responses to the ideas of the authors. Konopak et al. (1987) reported that writing was used successfully to enhance students' learning of content and to extend their cognitive processes in analysis and synthesis.

Symbolic-mathematical Reading

During the last 150 years, the language of mathematics has become increasingly crucial as a way of communicating about the reality of the world. The ability to read this language depends on facility that comes with understanding and freedom for the reader to modify what is written in the same way creative readers modify semantic content. Differential predictions of engineering grades in college have shown English grades in high school to contribute a negative weighting, whereas high school English grades have a high positive weighting for future grades in liberal arts (Dvorak, 1960). Readers who have developed unusual strength in semantic forms of communication may find it difficult to gain comparable satisfaction in the use of symbolic language. The day-to-day work of engineers requires them to read symbolic language for ordinary communication.

Mathematics as a basic language of thought first developed in the physical sciences. Creative reading of symbolic-mathematical material is essential background for productive thinking within this field. Snow (1964), among others, has delineated the essential dichotomy between the worlds of the literary scholar and the physical scientist. Fluency in creative reading in one field does not assure fluency in the other field, and it is presumptuous for the person who knows how to read one language to assume theirs is the only one worth knowing.

THE LANGUAGE OF EXPERIMENTAL RESEARCH

Statistics was developed as a tool for experimental research in the technology of agriculture. Fisher (1930) developed the basic concepts when he experimented with crop improvement in agronomy plots. The control of fertilizer, moisture, and seed strains was less complete than similar research in the chemistry lab. The need to average uncontrolled variables stimulated Fisher to develop the probability theory in statistics. The language of statistics, as a branch of mathematics, is still evolving in its application to nonparametrical situations. As the experimental approach has expanded to psychology, sociology, and education, the assumptions on which agricultural statistics were founded are distorted by biasing factors which require new ways of treating data. A specialized vocabulary has evolved that attempts to translate symbolic terms into semantic forms. The handling of the multiple array of data, with subordinate variables, led to the development of computer systems for analyzing the relationships within the language of mathematics.

THE QUANTIFIED LANGUAGE OF SOCIAL SCIENCE

The power of statistical language has converted many disciplines from descriptive to quantified ways of designing research. In the biological sciences the change is noticeable in the way research on Mendel's laws of heredity is reported. The old descriptive account of the number of sweet peas of each color to be expected from crossing has been superseded by complex mathematical probabilities that predict the multiple effects of chromosomal contributions. In psychology and education, mathematical models of learning, which are developed for individual sets of data, epitomize the use of symbolic language (Atkinson, 1965). Political science and sociology have moved toward quantified descriptions of group behavior.

The study of linguistics—the science of language—has become an influence in the pedagogy of reading. Different approaches to research on linguistics illustrate the difference between semantic and symbolic languages as bases for communication. Chomsky (1968) described generative grammar from the point of view of a rationalist rather than an empiricist in that he used intuitive information in linguistic, rather than statistical, analysis of word forms. An empirical approach is typified by Bennett's (1969) statistical measure of a stylistic trait in *Julius Caesar* and *As You Like It*. He uses a mathematical model to question whether both dramas were written by the same author. He finds that this method of analysis establishes a high degree of probability that the same author wrote both plays, even though they are quite different in plot and purpose. Readers who are concerned about challenges to Shakespeare's authorship might find Bennett's analysis difficult, and perhaps unrewarding. Readers who learn to function in both semantic and symbolic language will find it possible to extend their thinking by transposition from one world to the other. Computers, which are also used to create music and to translate one language into another, may turn out to be a bridge of understanding between symbolic and semantic systems.

THE CREATIVE WRITING APPROACH

A symposium, dedicated to explore the technical necessity for increased number of creative scientists, was summarized by Maugh (1974). He defined creativity as that "ill-defined state of mind which allows the investigator to forge anomalous or apparently unrelated facts into bold new chains of theory." Scientific innovation was, for him, essentially a preverbal process, and the necessity of translating the process into words alters the perception of the process. A major theme emerged from the discussions—that a scientific advance has two stages: (1) the generating of many ideas and (2) the criticizing of those ideas to determine which are worthwhile and which are worthless. Consensus was that the ability to generate new ideas was the innate part of creativity and that the development of a critical faculty in creativity can be nurtured by education. Young authors, in proposing a third level of learning—creative self-direction— reject the first proposition; but they choose to pursue the second which concerns teaching critical thinking.

The Maugh symposium reasoned that the best way to develop creative scientists was through a master–apprentice relationship with an outstanding research scientist. Lacking Nobel-quality scientists in numbers sufficient to staff the high schools of the world, they proposed to teach the second aspect of scientific innovation by *teaching criticism of creative writing.* The instructor begins the course with the assumption that the students have some creative writing ability, then teaches them how to distinguish good writing from bad. By teaching how to avoid the banal and the trivial, science would profit from this kind of education.

Empathic-mystical Reading

Mystical, religious, or allegorical literature deals with the knowledge of intuition and demands extraordinary responsiveness from readers. The empathic reader fashions the emotions of authors who write of experiences that are conveyed indirectly. Sensorial language and common experience are emphasized to give reality to the deeper meanings the writer intends to communicate. Semantic forms are used to express nonsemantic ideas and to put into words the under-standings and feelings that are easily conveyed wordlessly in direct contact. Restricted code language is often used to express emotional meanings within a group who share meanings not common to the larger culture. Some Black liter-ature, such as Cleaver's *Soul on Ice,* has its primary impact because the reader is able to feel the emotions that are being portrayed. Poets and novelists, such as Theodore Rhoetke in *Shape of the Flame* and Lewis Carroll in *Through the Looking Glass,* write on more than one level with multiple meanings only avail-able to the perceptive reader. Rhoetke's readers get a visual and auditory experi-ence on one dimension and the psychological trauma of homosexuality on an-other. Carroll's readers discover a children's fantasy in which people grow large or small by taking a pill, while at another level a political satire is aimed at the ruling classes of his country, and on a third level society's overuse of stereotypes is criticized. This subsection considers (1) some qualities of human sensitivity which foster empathic communication, (2) the mystique of religious literature, and (3) some efforts to project scientific knowledge into an unknown future.

SENSITIVITY TOWARD OTHER PEOPLE

People differ in their affective sensitivity just as they differ in their cognitive intelligence. When the schools consistently define and value affective goals, they will discover and reward talent in individuals who read nonverbal content and translate it into words. Creative people tend to be sensitive to the feelings of others in their environment. They have learned to interpret small cues in the behavior of others, such as quick glances between two people that reveal shared meanings. The sensitivity that avoids prying and the compassion that lifts a burden without too much talk are known to many readers. Plays and movies portray sensitivities by adroit use of silence. A reader must supply his or her own pauses and construct the nonverbal happenings to get a similar effect.

Sensitive readers see themselves in the characters portrayed in literature, which makes them vulnerable to self-criticism. The more open they are to the experiences of protagonists, the greater the possibility that they can be hurt by the author's subtle damnation of weakness. Egos that are insensitive are protected from experiencing both the pain and the ecstasy of life portrayed in literature. The creative reader of Greek tragedy identifies with the heroes and heroines by getting caught up in their drama. The playwright encourages identification with characters who are high-born, good, beautiful, and perfect except for one flaw in their character. In the end, the tragic protagonists become the victims of their own weakness, which costs them their lives. A negative experience is likely to result from a surface reading of Greek tragedy, whereas the creative reader experiences a catharsis, which the playwright intended—a washing away of guilt feelings or an emotional purging followed by rejuvenation. The nature of this experience explains why some readers go back and reread tragedies while other readers shun this form of literature.

RELIGIOUS AND MYSTICAL LITERATURE
Ancient societies were held together as much by the cohesion of their beliefs as by their economic interdependence. Native American Indians communicated their culture through mythology, songs and dances, and their visual arts. The myths, orally transmitted, conveyed a oneness with nature and the continuity of life in the hereafter. A heritage of mythology evolved in ancient Greece in the fables of Aesop, with their folk wisdom derived from animals personified. The prophets spoke in parables, using familiar episodes to teach a lesson in moral conduct. Medieval Christians invented the *mystery play* to represent Biblical events, which later were produced by craft guilds, who took them to the marketplace in the form of *miracle plays* or *morality plays*. In these ways religious leaders communicated their ideas to populations who were not literate in forms they understood. Religious works will continue to be produced and read as long as curious readers seek a spiritual significance beyond their own knowledge and understanding.

College curricula have made available a vast literature in mysticism, both Christian and Eastern. Some students read the writings of ancient mystics, anticipating that their new insights may be as germane to decision making, or more so, than conclusions based on statistical experimentation. This willingness to try to understand man's relationship to God (Theos, Allah, Khuda, Kami, or Brahma) as being a valid interest is an outgrowth of the expanding understanding of empathic language.

These varied literary experiences that have participated an awareness of the possibility for communion with other people and communion with God are part of the same cloth of life. Students who have been indoctrinated to be skeptical of all forms of communication that cannot be objectively measured and statistically treated are likely to find mystical-empathic literature unsettling and unreal. Nevertheless, there are many ways of knowing and no language has exclusive hold on the interpretation of reality. Human societies extend their cultural heritage in constructive ways by being aware of the potential as well as the actual.

SCIENCE AND THE FUTURE
Innovative thinkers are predisposed to speculate, to extrapolate, and to hypothesize the unanswered question of human existence. Experimental scientists are

most comfortable in the time frame of present knowledge and verifiable evidence, dating to Roger Bacon in the 13th century. Certain branches of the physical sciences have explored the past with impressive results, for instance, geology and archaeology, but not without professional opposition to each innovative hypothesis. Scientists who risk speculation about the future are especially vulnerable, even when such ventures follow a lifetime of solid research. Karl Pribram, *Language of the Brain* (1971), was taken less seriously by some psychologists following his proposal of a holographic model for the brain's organization of memory storage. David Loye, in *The Sphinx and the Rainbow* (1983), brought psychology and neurology together in a bold discussion of how mind and brain project future events and raised yet again the old question about a "stream of consciousness."

Later in the nineteenth century William James, the psychologist, made the ingenious observation that consciousness "does not appear to itself chopped up in bits" and suggested the metaphor of a river, or stream. "Let us call it the stream of thought, of consciousness, or of subjective life" (1890). Wilder Penfield, a neurosurgeon, described a possible mechanism for this "experiential record" in a courageous book, *The Mystery of the Mind* (1975). Penfield wrote of a "racial memory" that humans share with animals, of an "acquired memory" consisting of words and nonverbal concepts, and of a third important form of memory: the "experiential memory, and the possibility of recalling the stream of consciousness with varying degrees of completeness" (p. 63). He located the site of consciousness and its activation in the gray matter at the top of the brain stem, then surrounded the area with question marks in his figures, indicating that the anatomical circuits are yet to be established (Fig. 15.1). Penfield admitted in writing that for 30 years he had been on a search for the "place of understand-

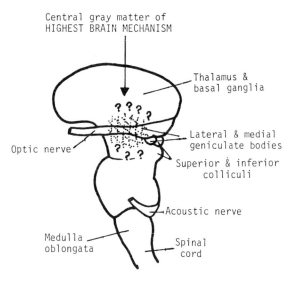

FIGURE 15.1. Hypothetical location of highest brain mechanism. Question marks indicate that detailed circuits are yet to be established. (From Penfield, *The Mystery of the Mind,* p. 38, © 1975 Princeton University Press).

ing," the location of those neuronal circuits which are most intimately associated with the initiation of voluntary activity and with the sensory summation prerequisite to it" (p. 112). He hypothesized a "physical basis of mind," but he left open the question of a relationship between mind and an "outside spirit." "Science has no such answers" (p. 115). Creative scientists will one day test the Penfield hypothesis; creative readers will continue to struggle with the larger question of spirituality.

READING TO WRITE

Creative reading stimulates in many people a desire to write their own interpretation of experience. The impulse to create is generated by the interaction between the reader's conceptualization of the worth of the author's theme, the persuasiveness of the writing, and the worthiness of the reader's own interpretive responses. When students conceive their ideas as distinct and worthy, putting them on paper is a relatively easy step to be taken. From this point of view, style and grammar are tools of less importance than the ideation; student writers are freed from apprehension about technique through confidence in the worth of their ideas. In this chapter the focus has been on the psychological contact between creative reading and productive writing. The concern has been the bond of communication between author and reader. This final section begins with recent attention in classrooms to teaching writing from instruction in reading, the second part presents literary criticism as a way of integrating writing and reading, and the final part invites a master poet to express his concerns about the prostitution of art in an uncomprehending society.

Exposition and Narration

This discussion of self-directed reading and creative writing has encompassed both expository writing, which can be innovative and exciting, and narrative writing, which gave birth to literary criticism. Fourth-grade children make an intuitive separation between these forms as "real" or "made-up," perhaps because the writing comes either from a context of subject matter or of story reading. Some children write fluently when reporting a student trip, but experience a block when the task involves imagery or fantasy. Liliane's inhibition was the opposite. She wrote stories almost daily of episodes in the life of an imaginary friend, Sally, and slipped the papers under the blotter on the teacher's desk. When asked to write a report of a visit to the museum of natural history, the words failed her. Asked by the teacher what Sally might have done at the museum, she created an imaginative account that was enriched by the vivid reality of her observations. The confidence gained in either form of writing transfers to the other when children's opportunities to write are frequent.

Writing and reading can be integrated, regardless of the reading material, according to Raphael and Englert (1988). They describe both reading and writing as complex cognitive processes which share three similar strategies: planning (prereading and prewriting); drafting (writing or guided reading); and revising (modifying and extending or postreading). They recommend an environment which emphasizes writing for real purposes and real audiences, provides frequent opportunities to share one's writing, and allows for extended writing and evaluation. Their focus was on specific strategies which enhanced both reading and writing.

Kellogg (1988) investigated the effect of three strategies for improving the efficiency and quality of university students' writing. The writing process included collecting information, planning ideas, translating ideas into text, or reviewing ideas and text. Translating ideas into text referred to the actual language production—lexical selection and sentence construction. The hypotheses were based on the cognitive concept of limited attentional capacity. The strategies for reducing attentional overload were (1) preparing a written outline, (2) composing a rough draft, and (3) formulating a mental outline. The results showed no beneficial effort from writing a rough draft. Both mental and written outlines eased attentional overload by allowing the writer to focus processing time, though not cognitive effort, on the single process of translating ideas into print.

Literary Criticism

Literary criticism is taught by everyone who teaches reading; whether students learn to make good judgments or not, they will make judgments about what they read. High school English teachers are aware of the role of analysis in the interpretation of literature. Elementary teachers are less likely to have studied literary criticism as part of their preparation for teaching, although their potential effectiveness in building taste is important. Their attitudes toward particular books are read affectively by the children as well as the praises conferred in book reviews. Criticism itself has become an art form. English teachers may not think of themselves as literary critics, yet they function in this role when choosing materials to be read, phrasing questions to be asked, and evaluating student productions.

THE TEACHER-CRITIC

Affective knowledge is central when judging literature and when teaching appreciation, because the emotional response must be the student's own. Aesthetic feelings cannot be supplied in a foreword to a book, an overview by the teacher, or a critical essay. The teacher must encourage students to make their own emotional responses if their appreciation is to endure. Initially selections should be chosen that are not too complicated and have some element that touches the reader rather directly. For instance, reading sections of *Alice in Wonderland* can call forth responses of amusement on the part of the child. The simple theme and rhythm of a ballad, such as *The Wreck of the Hesperus,* enables students to feel sympathy without having to work too hard at analyzing the form. One professor, a critic in his own right, demonstrated how to teach poetry to a high school class by beginning with jingles that titillated the students because of the punch line. He quickly moved on to reading parts of *The Shooting of Dan Magrew* as an exciting experience. By this time the class was ready to analyze how the pace and mood of the writing was achieved.

If students are to develop judgment in reading literary works, they must have practice in analysis and criticism. The conclusions they reach must be respected as valid for them at that time and in the same way that other creative responses are accepted. A high school English class on its final examination was given two poems to be analyzed and judged. Which poem is better? Why? In preparation for the exam, the class had been told they would be given two poems, one good and the other bad; they should be able to tell the difference on the basis of rhyme patterns, rhythm, onomatopoeia, alliteration, meaning, and so forth. Without the poets being identified, the following poems were reproduced.

The Tyger

Tyger! Tyger! burning bright
In the forests of the night,
What immortal hand or eye
Could frame thy fearful symmetry?

In what distant deeps or skies
Burnt the fire of thine eyes?
On what wings dare he aspire?
What the hand dare seize the fire?

When the stars threw down their spears
And water'd heaven with their tears
Did he smile his work to see?
Did he who made the Lamb make thee?

Flower in the Crannied Wall

Flower in the crannied wall,
I pluck you out of the crannies,
I hold you here, root and all, in my hand,
Little flower—but *if* I could understand
What you are, root and all, and all in all,
I should know what God and man is.

The students who saw Blake's vivid imagery and conceived his symbolism identified *The Tyger* as the better poem. They were graded zero on the question without regard to their written analyses. The students who preferred Tennyson's explicit morality received a high score on the question. If the teacher had conceived of the students as having a right to make a judgment on the basis of their own emotional response and their ability to support their choice with rational argument, all the students could have been reinforced for their efforts.

THE AUTHOR-CRITIC

Writers sometimes enrich the literature by their own discussions of the creative process. Williams (1950) defined analysis as a process by which a complete reading of a poem is attained. He deplored "murdering by dissection," an apt phrase for a physician, and recommended the use of comparison as a way of teaching the use of words, both for their meanings and for their emotional content. English and reading teachers will find his distinction between vivid and sensorial description useful in helping students make the same distinction. D. H. Lawrence (1928) was an effective critic of the critics who reviewed his work. He objected to a purely rational approach to literature and pointed up to the need for emotional awareness in judging a work of art. He said, "Literary criticism can be more than a reasoned account of the feeling produced upon the critic by the book he is criticizing. . . . The touchstone is emotion, not reason." He considered a person rare who had the force and complexity needed to be a responsible critic. Although many critics are scholastically educated, according to Lawrence, few are emotionally educated to deal artistically with the emotional meaning of the work. A good critic needs the flexibility to know what he or she feels and to respond affectively.

Rational Criticism

A discipline that some critics impose on themselves is to interpret the text of the work by eschewing extrapolations that cannot be supported by examples from the text. Beardsley (1970, p. 89), in *The Possibility of Criticism,* appealed for standards in judgment and decried the critic who strayed into "literary history, political deep thinking or psychoanalysis." He deplored critics who project themselves by going beyond the text to create affective interpretations that are irrelevant to the author's purpose. Beardsley showed how necessary it is for the emotion in the event to be consistent with the syntax, meter, and diction. In the terminology of the psychology of reading this limitation on "affective interpretation" can be understood as conceptualization of affects in the learning-motivation model (Chapter 2). The conceptualizations that enable a student to judge a poem have to do with the sense of artistic coherence of the various parts, including meaning, and its structure.

The literal evaluation of rational criticism has a place in children's initial acquisition of literary genre, particularly early departures from objective reality, such as science fiction and fantasy. Schechter and Schechter (1987) observed 30 fifth graders over the course of a year to investigate their sequential acquisition of the constitutive elements of the two forms of children's stories. Notations were made of the relationship between the lesson format, the literacy environment, and the evolution of the children's writing. Using dimensions such as true–untrue or possible–impossible, the children's notions of story genre were acquired. The teacher and the research credited multimedia exploration and pedagogical strategies with the children's conceptualization of literary genre.

Projective Criticism

A different approach to criticism—far afield from the textual analysis of Beardsley—is the psychological analysis that intentionally goes beyond the work itself to project what the author may have been saying, perhaps unconsciously. Critics who are psychoanalytical in their reading tend to see literature as an expression of the inner life of the writer, representing a kind of self-therapy that reveals subconscious concerns through symbolism. Some highly regarded authors, such as Kafka, Joyce, and Anderson, were psychologically oriented themselves. Their writing was so obscure that most students required orienting explanations from an instructor. The critics who also were reading Freud became biographers and interpreters of one or more great writers. In this kind of psycho-analytical criticism much of the comment was filtered through the critic's own background.

Some reader-critics became writers whose own contribution was exemplified in historical research, unique interpretations and excellent writing. A primordial example of the writer-critic was Leon Edel, who became the Western world's leading authority on the life and work of Henry James (Hellman, 1971). Edel's publications include a five-volume biography of James, several collections of the original plays, novels, and short stories encased in scholarly interpretation, and thousands of personal letters selected and arranged into books. Edel's scholarly obsession took him to the places James had lived in America and Europe. His early interest in James has been attributed to a common background of life in pioneer America, interrupted by extended sojourns with their respective families in European capitals. Edel considers his first papers on James, written as a graduate student, as sophomoric. However, he read James well enough from the beginning to sustain an interest and to become a creative biographer in his own right. His critics are those who object to analysis "from inside out" rather than in terms of external reality. James, himself, has been credited with introducing the "stream of consciousness" novel, an idea that seems to have evolved from discussions with his brother, William James, the renowned psychologist. Edel has been criticized in the *Psychiatric Quarterly* for going beyond his training, cautioning its readers that Edel's wife's training as a psychoanalyst did not qualify him (Hellman, 1971, p. 43).

The dichotomy between textual and psychological interpretation is to some extent semantic. Those who have learned to read empathic-mystical literature see emotional and intrapersonal meanings in the text that may be missed by readers who are attuned only to semantic-logical interpretations. The flexible reader can shift from one kind of interpretation to another, depending on the nature of the literature being read and the purposes as conceptualized.

THE STUDENT-CRITIC

Reports from field studies have indicated an extraordinary focus on peer sharing, review, and evaluation in the reading-writing programs. Phillips (1987) investigated whether children's literature might be used to foster written language development at the first-grade level. Her subjects wrote and read poetry, fairy tales, and fantasy. Compared with other first-grade classes, the "literature group" wrote in longer selections with greater fluency and higher literary quality. Raphael et al. (1987) emphasized peer editing and publication, and/or instruction in text structure in a program of expository composition. All students in the text structure instruction significantly increased their ability to summarize information and both treatment groups increased their writing skills.

Existing research was utilized to design a program for older students, based on the points of contact between reading and writing: context concerns, main idea structure, organizational strategy, and sentence structure (Bratcher–Hoskins, 1986). Students were taught these relationships between reading and writing to guide discussions and peer reviews of the writing. Reagan (1986) described a program for combining reading instruction with writing instruction which included mapping, summarizing, synthesizing, and critiquing assigned readings. At all grade levels it is important for instructors to emphasize the positive analytical criticism that professional artists endow on one another and to minimize negative comments that do not contribute to improvement of the product.

Concerns of a Poet

William Carlos Williams, physician and poet, was an avid reader whose life in the hospital and the library intermingled in his poems. His great American poem, *Paterson,* is concerned primarily with the relationship of the writer to society. Williams was concerned with developing a poetic form that would reflect his abstraction of the oneness of Paterson, the man, and Paterson, the city. "I had to invent my form, if form it was. I was writing in a modern occidental world; I knew the rules of poetry . . . but I decided I must define the traditional in terms of my own world" (Williams, 1958, p. 74). The setting of *Paterson Book III* (Williams, 1963, pp. 118–138) is the library.

> A cool of books
> will sometimes lead the mind to libraries
> of a hot afternoon, if books can be found
> cool to the sense to lead the mind away.

The library was a depository of other people's ideas. As a reader, Williams cut away much of the original verbiage in order to find the thought that fed his imagination. He feared the seductive quality of books to lead the writer away from his or her own expression into accepting the thoughts of another.

> A library—of books! decrying all books
> that enfeeble the mind's intent
> Beautiful thing!

As a poet, Williams was concerned that writers not prostitute their art in order to live. He made his own living by practicing medicine and financed the publication of the first four of the Paterson volumes.

> They have
> maneuvered it so that to write
> is a fire and not only of the blood.

> The writing is nothing, the being
> in a position to write (that's
> where they get you) is nine-tenths
> of the difficulty: seduction

> or strong arm stuff.

Williams's third major concern was communication, how to get his ideas across to the people he knew and loved. He was distressed when the poem he had labored to deliver was not understood.

Is it a dirty book? I'll bet

it's a dirty book, she said

Or, Geeze, Doc, I guess it's all right
but what the hell does it mean.

In trying to reveal the complex relationships of persons to their outer world, Williams described life in physical terms. His search for artistic integrity, unlike the Victorian concept of the beautiful virgin, was a search for beauty encased in sordid everyday life. He was haunted by literary beauty covered by decadent words.

Take off your clothes,
(I said)

Haunted, the quietness of your face
is a quietness, real
out of no book.

Your clothes (I said) quickly, while
your beauty is attainable.

These concerns, first to find a form that revealed his times, second to retain his freedom as a thinker, and third to communicate truth, became the preoccupations of his life as a writer.

Williams is a prime example of one who moved from creative reading to creative writing. If the goals of the reading program include writing at a creative, self-directing level, the relationship between reading and writing and between self-actualization and writing need to be experienced as early in the school life as possible.

Chapter Summary

All reading for meaning involves some creative interpretation. Picture-book pre-readers, independent fluent elementary-school readers, and mature college readers all represent stages in development which are amenable to creative responses to printed literature. Many different functions are served in creative reading, including building bases for new ideas and for hypothesizing theories to be tested.

Semantic-logical reading is the basic orientation of historical and philosophical research. To function well with this kind of literature the reader must learn to organize many sources into a single system. Some forms of organization are by chronology, philosophy, political resolution, evolution of an idea, analysis of trends, and increments of complexity. Symbolic-mathematical reading is the basis for communicating empirical research. The ability to read in this area includes sophistication in the language of statistics, which has gradually spread from the physical sciences through the biological sciences to the social sciences. Empathic-mystical reading has increased in volume and importance, and the emotional content of intercommunication has become a subject for scholarly concern. Sensitivity toward other people and training in sensitivity to one's own feelings are generating a literature of their own. The mystic religions, particularly those of the East, are being seriously studied in schools and colleges.

Literary criticism is an art form in its own right. Adherents to diverse interpretations base their analyses primarily on literal versus psychological interpretation. One of the functions of reading instruction is to help students read critically for both content and style. Beardsley epitomized the highly skilled critic who is dedicated to the interpretation of the context as the source of information. Edel was an equally able critic who emphasized the importance of psychoanalytical bases for understanding the works of the psychological novelist Henry James.

Creative reading often eventuates in creative writing. William Carlos Williams was an example of a reader who developed his own writing form, who maintained his literary integrity by supporting himself and his writing by practicing medicine, and was sometimes distressed because he was misunderstood. Teachers at all grade levels can start students toward self-fulfillment through reading and writing.

References

Aaron, P. G. (1985). The paradoxical relationship between intelligence and reading disability. *Perceptual and Motor Skills, 61*(3, pt. 2), 1251–1261.

Ackerman, P. T., Anhalt, J. M., Dykman, R. A., & Holcomb, P. J. (1986). Effortful processing deficits in children with reading and/or attention disorders. *Brain and Cognition, 5*(1), 22–40.

Ainsworth, M. D. S., Blehar, M. C., Waters, E., & Wall, S. (1978). *Patterns of attachment.* Hillsdale, NJ: Lawrence Erlbaum Associates.

Albert, D. J. (1966). Memory in mammals: Evidence for a system involving nuclear ribonucleic acid. *Neuropsychologia, 4,* 79–92.

Alkon, D. L., Lederhendler, I., & Shockimas, J. (1982). Primary changes of membrane currents during retention of associative learning. *Science, 215,* 693–695.

Allen, M., & Wellman, M. (1980). Hand position during writing, cerebral laterality and reading: Age and sex differences. *Neuropsychologia, 18,* 333–340.

Allport, F. H. (1924). *Social psychology.* Boston: Houghton Mifflin.

Alpert, J. L. (1974). Teacher behavior across ability groups: A consideration of the mediation of Pygmalion effects. *Journal of Educational Psychology, 66*(3), 348–353.

Alvermann, D. E. (1982). Reading achievement and linguistic stages: A comparison of disabled readers and Chomsky's 6- to 10-year olds (ED 212 994). *Resources in Education.*

Ames, C. (1978). Children's achievement attributions and self-reinforcement: Effects on self-concept and competitive reward structure. *Journal of Educational Psychology, 70,* 345–355.

Antonova, G. P. (1967). Uchet Individual' Nykh Osobennostei Myshleniya Uchashchikhsya v Protsesse Obucheniya. *Vaprosy Psikhologic, 13*(2), 89–100.

Armitage, S. E., Baldwin, B. A., & Vince, M. A. (1980). The fetal sound environment of sheep. *Science, 208,* 1173–1174.

Arnold, M. B. (1984). *Memory and the brain.* Hillsdale, NJ: Lawrence Erlbaum Associates.

Athey, I. (1982). The affective domain reconceptualized. *Advances in Reading/Language Research, 1,* 203–217.

Atkinson, R. C. (1965). *Introduction to mathematical learning theory.* New York: Wiley.

Atrens, D. & Curthoys, I. (1982). *The neurosciences and behavior.* (2nd ed.) Sydney: Academic Press.

Aukerman, R. C. (1984). *Approaches to beginning reading.* New York: Wiley.

Aulls, M. W. (1978). *Developmental and remedial reading in the middle grades.* Boston: Allyn & Bacon.

Ayres, A. J. (1968). Reading: A product of sensory integrative process. In H. Smith (Ed.), *Perception & Reading* (pp. 77–82). Newark, DE: International Reading Association.

Backman, J., et al. (1984). Acquisition and use of spelling-sound correspondences in reading. *Journal of Experimental Child Psychology, 38*(1), 57.

Baddeley, A. D. (1966). Short-term memory for word sequences as a function of acoustic, semantic and formal similarity. *Quarterly Journal of Experimental Psychology, 18,* 362–365.

Baddeley, A. D. (1983). Working memory. In D. E. Broadbent (Ed.), Functional aspects of human memory. *Proceedings of a royal society discussion meeting* (pp. 73–86). January 26–27. London: The Royal Society.

Bakker, D. J., & Schroots, H. J. F. (1981). Temporal order in normal and disturbed reading. In G. T. Pavlidis & T. R. Miles (Eds.), *Dyslexia research and its application to education.* Chichester, England: Wiley.

Banks, M. S., Aslin, R. N., & Letson, R. D. (1975). Sensitive period for the development of human binocular vision. *Science, 190,* 675–677.

Banks, W. P., Oka, E., & Shugarman, S. (1981). Recoding of printed words to internal speech: Does recoding come before lexical access? In O. J. L. Tzeng & H. Singer (Eds.), *Perception of print: Reading research in experimental psychology* (pp. 137–170). Hillsdale, NJ: Lawrence Erlbaum Associates.

Barclay, J. R. (1973). The role of comprehension in remembering sentences. *Cognitive Psychology, 4,* 229–254.

Barlow, H. B., Blakemore, V., & Pettigrew, J. D. (1967). The neural mechanism of binocular depth discrimination. *Journal of Physiology, 193,* 327–342.

Barnes, J. A. Jr. (1983). An analysis and comparison of reading and writing levels of 3rd, 5th, and 7th grade students as measured by readability formulae. *Dissertation Abstracts, 45/01,* 1756–A.

Baron, J., & Strawson, C. (1976). Use of orthographic and word specific knowledge in reading words aloud. *Journal of Experimental Psychology: Human Perception, 2,* 386–393.

Bartlett, F. C. (1932). *Remembering: A study of experimental and social psychology.* Cambridge, England: Cambridge Press.

Bateman, B. (1968). The efficacy of an auditory and visual method of first-grade reading instruction with auditory and visual learners. In H. Smith (Ed.), *Perception and Reading,* pp. 105–111. Newark, DE: International Reading Association.

Bauer, R. H., & Emhert, J. (1984). Information processing in reading-disabled and nondisabled children. *Journal of Experimental Child Psychology, 37*(2), 271–281.

Beardsley, M. C. (1970). *The possibility of criticism.* Detroit: Wayne State University Press.

Beaumont, J. G. (1983). *Introduction to neuropsychology.* Oxford, England: Blackwood Scientific Publications.

Becker, W. C. (1986). *Applied psychology for teachers: A behavioral approach.* Chicago: Science Research Associates, Inc.

Belanger, J. (1987). Reading achievement and writing proficiency: A critical review of research (ED 282 180). *Resources in Education,* October.

Belmont, I. (1974). Requirements of the early reading task. *Perceptual and Motor Skills, 38,* 527–537.

Belmont, L., & Birch, H. G. (1965). Lateral dominance, lateral awareness, and reading disability. *Child Development, 36*(1), 57–71.

Bennett, P. E. (1969). The statistical measurement of a stylistic trait in *Julius Caesar* and *As You Like It.* In L. Dolezl & R. W. Bailey (Eds.) (pp. 29–41), *Statistics and style.* New York: American Elsevier.

Benson, D. F. (1981). Dyslexia and the neuroanatomical bases if reading. In F. J. Pirozzolo & M. C. Wittrock (Eds.), *Neuropsychological and cognitive processes in reading,* pp. 69–92. New York: Academic Press.

Benson, D. F. (1982). Language processing. *In the proceedings of the symposium on The brain: Recent research and its educational implications,* pp. 103–114. Eugene: College of Education, University of Oregon.

Berkley, M. A. (1984). Preceptual development and physiology. In M. S. Gazzaniga (Ed.), *Handbook of cognitive neuroscience.* New York: Plenum Press.

Berlyne, D. (1965). *Structure and direction in thinking.* New York: Wiley.

Berninger, V. W. (1986). Normal variation in reading acquisition. *Perceptual & Motor Skills, 62,* 691–716.

Berninger, V. W. (1987). Global, component, and serial processing of printed words in beginning reading. *Journal of Experimental Child Psychology, 43,* 387–418.

Bertelson, P. (1986). The onset of literacy: Liminal remarks. *Cognition, 24*(1–2), 1–30. Amsterdam: Netherlands.

Besner, D., Waller, T. G., & MacKinnon, G. E. (Eds.) (1985). *Reading research: Advances in theory and practice* (Vol. 5). Orlando, FL: Academic Press.

Best, C. T. (1985). *Hemisphere function and collaboration in the child.* New York: Academic Press.

Biemiller, A. (1970). The development of the use of graphic and contextual information as children learn to read. *Reading Research Quarterly, 6,* 75–96.

Bigelow, G. S. (1967). Global versus analytic cognitive style in children as a function of age, sex and intelligence. *Dissertation Abstracts, 28*(3–A), 295–305.

Black, F. W. (1974). Self-concept as related to achievement and age in learning-disabled children. *Child Development, 45,* 1137–1140.

Blanchard, J. S., Mason, G. E., & Daniel, D. (1987). *Computer applications in reading,* (3rd ed.) Newark, DE: International Reading Association.

Blom, G. E., Waite, R. R., & Zimet, S. G. (1970). A motivational content analysis of children's primers. In H. Levin & J. P. Williams (Eds.), *Basic studies in reading,* (pp. 188–221). New York: Basic Books.

Bloom, A., et al. (1981). Relationship between intellectual status and reading skills for developmentally disabled children. *Perceptual and Motor Skills, 53*(3), 853–854.

Bloom, B. S. (1976). *Human characteristics and school learning.* New York: McGraw-Hill.

Bloom, B. S., Engelhart, M. D., Furest, E. J., Hill, W. H., & Krathwohl, D. R. (1956). *Taxonomy of educational objectives: The cognitive domain, Handbook I.* New York: Longman.

Bloom, F. E., Lazerson, A., & Hostadter, L. (1985). *Brain, mind and behavior.* New York: W. H. Freeman.

Bock, J. K., & Brewer, W. F. (1985). *Discourse structure and mental models* (Tech. Rep. No. 343). Washington, DC: (ED 263 532).

Boder, E. (1973). Developmental dyslexia: A diagnostic approach based on three atypical reading-spelling patterns. *Developmental Medicine and Child Neurology, 15,* 663–687.

Bogatz, G. A., & Ball, S. (1971). *The second year of*

Sesame Street: A continuing evaluation (Vol. 1). Princeton, NJ: Educational Testing Service.

Boklage, C. E. (1981). On the distribution of nonright-handedness among twins and their families. *Acta Geneticae Medicae et Gemellologiae, 30,* 167–187.

Boles, D. B. (1985). The effects of display and report order asymmetries on lateralized word recognition. *Brain and Language, 26*(1), 106–116.

Bond, G. L., & Tinker, M. A. (1973). *Reading difficulties: Their diagnosis and correction.* New York: Meredith Corp.

Bormuth, J. R. (1982). Literacy is rising, but so is demand for literacy. In L. Reed & S. Ward (Eds.), *Basic skills: Issues and choices* (Vol. 1 pp. 183–190). St. Louis: CEMREL.

Bower, B. (1985). Taking food from thought: Fruitful entry to the brain's word index. *Science News, 128*(6), 85.

Bower, B. (1988). The brain in the machine. *Science News, 134,* 344–345.

Bradley, D. (1980). Lexical representation of derivational relation. In M. Aronoff & M. L. Kean (Eds.), *Juncture.* Saratoga, CA: Anma Libr.

Brady, J. V. (1958). Ulcers in executive monkeys. *Scientific American,* October, 95–100.

Brady, M. (1981). Toward a computational theory of early visual processing in reading. *Visible Language, 15,* 183–215.

Brady, S., Shankweiler, D., & Mann, V. (1983). Speech perception and memory coding in relation to reading ability. *Journal of Exceptional Child Psychology, 35*(2), 345–367.

Brandt, R. (1987). On leadership and student achievement: A conversation with Richard Andrews. *Educational Leadership, 45*(1), 9–16.

Bransford, J. D., Barclay, J. R., & Franks, J. R. (1972). Sentence memory: A constructive versus interpretive approach. *Cognitive Psychology, 3,* 193–209.

Bransford, J. D., & Johnson, M. K. (1972). Contextual prerequisites for understanding: Some investigations of comprehension and recall. *Journal of Verbal Learning and Verbal Behavior, 11,* 717–727.

Bratcher–Hoskins, S. (1986). Teaching written language: Points of contact between sophisticated reading and writing (ED 270 755). *Resources in Education,* November.

Braun, C. (1986). Reading/writing connections: A case analysis (ED 266 403). *Resources in Education.*

Braun, C., Neilson, A. R., & Dykstra, R. (1976). Teacher expectations: Prime mover or inhibitor? In B. L. Courtney (Ed.), *Reading interaction: The teacher, the pupil, and the materials* (pp. 40–48). Newark, DE: International Reading Association.

Britton, J. (1987). *Writing and reading in the classroom* (Tech. Rep. No. 8). Washington, DC: Office of Educational Research and Improvement (ED 287 169).

Broadbent, D. E. (1958). *Perception and communication.* London: Pergamon Press.

Broadbent, D. E. (1962). Attention and the perception of speech. *Scientific American, 206*(1), 143–151.

Broadbent, D. E. (1983). *Proceedings of a royal society discussion meeting,* January 26–27. London: The Royal Society.

Broadbent, D. E., & Gregory, M. H. P. (1965). On the interaction of S-R compatability with other variables affecting reaction time. *British Journal of Psychology, 56,* 61–67.

Brown, A. L. (1980). Metacognitive development and reading. In R. J. Spiro, B. C. Bruce, & W. F. Brewer (Eds.), *Theoretical issues in reading comprehension.* (pp. 453–481). Hillsdale, NJ: Lawrence Erlbaum Associates.

Brown, R. (1973). *The first language: The early stages.* Cambridge, MA: Harvard University Press.

Brown, R., & Bellugi, U. (1964). In Eric H. Lenneberg (Ed.), *New Directions in the study of language* pp. 131–161. Cambridge, MA: MIT Press.

Brown, R., & Byrd, C. C. (1984). Reading expectancy and regression formulas (ED 240 538). *Resources in Education,* July.

Brown, R. M., Sanocki, T., & Schrot, D. (1983). Phonemic coding in marginally competent readers. *Journal of General Psychology, 109*(1), 87–94.

Bruner, J. J., Goodnow, J., & Austin, G. (1956). *A study of thinking.* New York: Wiley.

Brunson, B. I., & Matthews, K. A. (1981). The type A coronary-prone behavior pattern and reactions to uncontrollable stress: An analysis of performance strategies, affect, and attributions during failure. *Journal of Personality and Social Psychology, 40,* 906–918.

Bryden, M. P. (1982). *Laterality: Functional asymmetry in the intact brain.* New York: Academic Press.

Bub, D. N., & Lewine, J. (1988). Different modes of word recognition in the left and right visual fields. *Brain and Language. 33,* 161–188.

Buffery, A. W. H., & Gray, J. A. (1972). Sex differences in the development of perceptual and linguistic skills. In C. Ounstad & D. C. Taylor (Eds.), *Gender differences: Their ontogeny and significance* London: Churchill-Livingstone.

Buschke, H. (1974). Spontaneous remembering after recall failure. *Science, 184,* 579–581.

Byers, J. L. (1961). *Strategies and learning set in concept formation.* Doctoral dissertation, University of Wisconsin.

Byring, R., & Pulliainen, V. (1984). Neurological and neuropsychological deficiencies in a group of older adolescents with dyslexia. *Developmental medicine and Child Neurology, 26*(6), 765–773.

Caldwell, J. A. (1985). A new look at the old informal reading inventory. *Reading Teacher, 39,* 168–173.

Cameron, J., Livson, N., & Bayley, N. (1967). Infant vocalizations and their relationship to mature intelligence. *Science, 157,* 331–333.

Carafoli, E., & Penniston, J. T. (1985). The calcium signal. *Scientific American, 253*(5), 70–78.

Carbo, M. (1988). The evidence supporting reading styles: A response to Stahl. *Phi Delta Kappan, 70*(4), 317–322.

Carr, T. H., & Pollatsek, A. (1985). Models of word recognition. In D. Bresner, T. G. Waller, & G. E. MacKinnon (Eds.), *Reading Research: Advances in theory and practice* (Vol. 5), 1–82. Orlando, FL: Academic Press.

Carroll, J. B. (1970a). The nature of the reading process. In H. Singer & R. B. Ruddell (Eds.), *Theoretical models and processes of reading* (pp. 292–303). Newark, DE: International Reading Association.

Carroll, J. B. (1970b). Problems of measurement related to the concept of learning for mastery. *Educational Horizons, 48*(3), 71–80.

Carroll, J. B., & Chall, J. S. (1975). *Toward a literate society.* New York: McGraw-Hill.

Cassady, J. K. (1985). Jason's reading—and liking himself better. *Academic Therapy, 21*(2), 159–165.

Cattell, R. B. (1963).Theory of fluid and crystallized intelligence: A critical experiment. *Journal of Educational Psychology, 54,* 1–22.

Cattell, R. B., & Horn, J. L. (1978). A cross-social check on the theory of fluid and crystallized intelligence with discovery of new valid subtest designs. *Journal of Educational Measurement, 15*(3), 134–164.

Cazden, C. B. (1982). Contexts for literacy: In the mind and in the classroom. *Journal of Reading Behavior, 14*(2), 413–427.

Chall, J. (1967). *Learning to read: The great debate.* New York: McGraw-Hill.

Chall, J. (1983a). *Learning to read: The great debate* (rev. ed.). New York: McGraw-Hill.

Chall, J. (1983b). *Stages of reading development.* New York: McGraw–Hill.

Chall, J. (1989). Learning to read: The great debate 20 years later. *Phi Delta Kappan, 70*(7), 521–538.

Chall, J., & Peterson, R. (1986). Influence of neuroscience on educational practice. In S. L. Friedman, K. A. Klivington, & R. W. Peterson, (Eds.), *The brain, cognition, and education* (pp. 287–318). Orlando, FL: Academic Press.

Chall, J., Roswell, F. G., & Blumenthal, S. H. (1963). Auditory blending ability: A factor in success in beginning reading. *Reading Teacher, XVII,* 113–118.

Chan, K. S., & Cole, P. G. (1987). An aptitude-treatment intraction in a mastery learning model of instruction. *Journal of Experimental Education, 55*(4), 189–200.

Changeau, J. (1974). Some biological observations relevant to a theory of learning. From Colloques Internationaux du Centre National de al Recherche Scientifique, No. 206. *Current Problems in Psycholinguistics,* 281–288.

Chiarello, C. (1980). A house divided? Cognitive functioning with callosal agenesis. *Brain and Language, 11,* 128–158.

Chiarello, C., & Nuding, S., (1987). Visual field effects of word orientation and imageability on visual half-field presentations with a lexical decision task. *Neurophysiologia, 25*(3), 539–548.

Chomsky, C. (1968). *The acquisition of syntax in children from 5 to 10.* Cambridge, MA: MIT Press.

Chomsky, N. (1957). *Syntactic structures.* The Hague: Mouton.

Chomsky, N. (1965). *Aspects of theory of syntax.* Cambridge, MA: MIT Press.

Chomsky, N. (1968). *Aspects of the theory of syntax.* Cambridge, MA: MIT Press.

Chomsky, N. (1970). Phonology and reading. In H. Levin & J. Williams (Eds.), *Basic studies on reading.* New York: Basic Books.

Cioffi, J., & Kandel, G. L. (1979). Laterality of stereognostic accuracy of children for words, shapes and bigrams. *Science, 204,* 1432–1434.

Clark, M. M. (Ed.) (1985). New directions in the study of reading (ED 270 733). *Resources in Education,* November.

Clymer, T. (1968). What is reading? Some current concepts. In H. M. Robinson (Ed.), *Innovation and change in reading instruction* (pp. 7–29). Chicago: National Society for the Study of Education.

Clymer, T. (1970). *Reading 360.* Boston: Ginn.

Cohen, R. L., Netley, C., & Clarke, M. A. (1984). On the generality of the short-term memory/reading relationship. *Journal of Learning Disabilities, 17*(4), 218–221.

Cohn, M. L. (1969). Structured comprehension. *Reading Teacher, 22*(5), 440–444.

Collins, A., & Smith, E. E. (1982). *Teaching the process of reading comprehension* (Tech. Rep. No. 182). Champaign, IL: Center for the Study of Reading, University of Illinois, September.

Comrey, A. L., Michael, W. B., & Fruchter, B. (1988). J. P. Guilford. *American Psychologist, 43*(12), 1086–1087.

Condon, W. S., & Sander, L. W. (1974). Neonate movement is synchronized with adult speech: Intractional participation in language acquisition. *Science, 183,* 99–101.

Connell, D. R. (1986). Writing before reading (ED 260 413). *Resources in Reading,* January.

Corballis, M. C., & Beale, I. C. (1976). *The psychology of left and right.* Hillsdale, NJ: Lawrence Erlbaum Associates.

Cordero, J. A. (1986). The relation of visual perception to reading: Evolutionary data using the reversal test. *Infancia Y Aprendizaje, 34,* 101–111.

Coren, S., & Porac, C. (1977). Fifty centuries of right-handedness: The historical record. *Science, 198,* 631–632.

Corso, J. F. (1981). *Aging sensory systems and perception*. New York: Praeger.

Craik, F. I. M., & Lockard, R. S. (1972). Levels of processing: A framework for memory research. *Journal of Verbal Learning and Verbal Behavior, 11,* 671–684.

Crawford, J. H., & Fry, M. A. (1979). Trait-task interaction in intra- and intermodal matching of auditory and visual trigams. *Contemporary Educational Psychology, 4*(1), 1–10.

Critchley, M. (1981). Dyslexia: An overview. In G. T. Pavlidis & T. R. Miles (Eds.), *Dyslexia: Research and its application to education,* (pp. 1–11). Chichester, England: Wiley.

Crowell, D. C., & Hu-pei Au, K. (1981). Developing children's comprehension in listening, reading, and television viewing. *Elementary School Journal, 82*(2), 129–135.

Cruickshank, W. M. (1986). Foreword. In G. T. Pavlidis & D. F. Fisher (Eds.), *Dyslexia: Its neuropsychology and treatment*. Chichester, England: Wiley.

CTB/McGraw Hill. (1980). *Prescriptive reading inventory reading system* (PRI/RS). Monterey, CA.

Culp, M. B., & Span, S. (1985). The influence of writing on reading. *Journal of Teaching Writing, 4*(2), 284–289.

Curtis, C. K. (1983). Relationships among certain citizenship variables. *Journal of Social Studies Research, 7*(2), 18–28.

Dale, E. (1969). Vocabulary measurement: Techniques and major findings. *Elementary English, 42,* 895–901, 948.

Daneman, M., & Carpenter, P. A. (1980). Individual differences in working memory and reading. *Journal of Verbal Learning and Verbal Behavior, 19,* 450–466.

Danner, F. W. (1976). Children's understanding of intersentence organization in the recall of short descriptive passages. *Journal of Educational Psychology, 68,* 174–183.

Davis, F. B. (1944). The factorial composition of two tests of comprehension in reading. *Journal of Educational Psychology, 37,* 481–486.

Davis, F. B. (Ed.) (1971). *The literature of research in reading with emphasis on models*. New Brunswick, NJ: Iris Corporation.

Dean, R. S. (1977). Effects of self-concept on learning with gifted children. *Journal of Educational Research. 70,* 315–318.

DeCasper, A. J., & Fifer, W. P. (1980). Of human bonding: Newborns prefer their mother's voices. *Science, 208,* 1174–1176.

Degrosky, D. S. (1982). Television viewing and reading achievement of seventh and eighth graders (ED 215 291). *Resources in Education,* September.

DeHirsch, K., Jansky, J. J., & Langford, W. S. (1966). *Predicting reading failure*. New York: Harper & Row.

Dermody, P., Mackie, K., & Katsch, P. (1983). Dichotic listening in good and poor readers. *Journal of Speech and Hearing Research, 26*(3), 341–348.

Derevensky, J. L. (1977). Cross modal functioning and reading achievement. *Journal of Reading Behavior, 9*(3), 233–251.

Diack, H. (1960). *Reading and the psychology of perception*. New York: Philosophy Library.

Diagnostic Inventory of Early Development. (1978). Subtest of *Brigance Diagnostic Inventories*. Billerica, MA: Curriculum Associates, Inc.

Diagnostic Inventory of Essential Skills. (1980). Subtest of *Brigance Diagnostic Inventories*. Billerica, MA: Curriculum Associates, Inc.

Diagram Group. (1982). *The brain: A user's manual*. New York: Pedagree Book.

Diagnostic Reading Scales. (1981). Monterey, CA: CTB/McGraw–Hill.

Diamond, M. C. (1984). Age, sex, and environmental influences. In N. Geschwind & A. M. Galaburda (Eds.), *Cerebral dominance* pp. 134–146. Cambridge, MA: Harvard University Press.

Diamond, M. C. (1985). Neurodevelopment: From the fertilized egg to the fully developed cerebral hemispheres. *Workshop of the California Neuropsychological Services,* San Rafael, CA, August 9.

Diene, C.I., & Dweck, C. S. (1978). An analysis of learned helplessness: Continuous changes in performance, strategy, and achievement cognitions following failure. *Journal of Personality and Social Psychology, 36,* 451–462.

Direct Instructional Systems (DISTAR). (1982). Chicago, IL: Science Research Associates, Inc.

Dolch, E. W., & Leeds, D. (1970). Vocabulary tests and depth of meaning. In R. Farr (Ed.), *Evaluation of reading* (pp. 254–262). New York: Harcourt, Brace, & World.

Dooley, M. S. (1988). Dialogue journals: Facilitating the reading–writing connection with native American students (ED 292 118). *Resources in Education,* August.

Dowling, J. E., & Boycott, B. B. (1966). Organization of the primate retina: electron microscopy. *Proceedings of the Royal Society, B. 166:* 80–110.

Duane, R. M. (1986). A study of tenth and eleventh grade students who failed the New Jersey minimum basic skills test in reading (ED 267 393). *Resources in Education,* August.

Duffy, F. H., McAnulty, G. B., & Schachter, S. C. (1984). Brain electrical activity mapping. In N. Geschwind & A. M. Galaburda (Eds.), *Cerebral dominance* pp. 53–73. Cambridge, MA: Harvard University Press.

Dunant, Y., & Israel, M. (1985). The release of acetylcholine. *Scientific American, 252*(4), 58–66.

Dunlop, P. (1972). Dyslexia—the orthoptic approach. *Australian Orthoptic Journal, 12,* 16–20.

Dunn, R., & Dunn, K. (1978). *Teaching students through their individual learning styles: A practical approach.* Reston, VA: Reston.

Dunn, R., Dunn, K., & Price, G. (1975). *Learning style inventory.* Lawrence, KS: Price Systems.

Dunn, R., & Price, G. E. (1980). The learning style characteristics of gifted students. *Gifted Child Quarterly, 24*(1), 33–36.

Durkin, D. (1966). *Children who read early.* New York: Columbia University Press.

Durkin, D. (1970). *Teaching them to read.* Boston: Allyn & Bacon.

Durkin, D. (1978–1979). What classroom observations reveal about reading comprehension instruction. *Reading Research Quarterly, 4*(14), 481–533.

Durkin, D. (1980). *Teaching young children to read* (3rd ed.). Boston: Allyn & Bacon.

Durkin, D. (1989). *Teaching them to read.* Boston: Allyn & Bacon.

Dvorak, A. (1960). *Differential prediction of college grades.* Presentation to California Education Research Association. Santa Rosa, CA.

Dworkin, P. H. (1985). *Learning and behavior problems of school children.* Philadelphia: W. B. Saunders.

Eamon, D. B. (1978–1979). Selection and recall of topical information in prose by better and poor readers. *Reading Research Quarterly, 2*(XIV/2).

Early, M. (1960). Stages of growth in literary appreciation. *English Journal, 49,* 161–167.

Eccles, J., & Robinson, D. N. (1984). *The wonder of being human.* New York: Free Press.

Eder, D. (1981). Ability grouping as a self-fulfilling prophecy: A micro-analysis of teacher-student interactions. *Sociology of Education, 54,* 151–162.

Ehri, L. C. (1983). How orthology alters spoken language. In J. Downing & R. Valtin (Eds.), *Language awareness and learning to read,* (pp. 119–147). New York: Springer Verlag.

Ehri, L. C. (1988). Movement in word reading and spelling: How spelling contributes to reading (ED 287 154). *Resources in Education,* March.

Eimas, P. D. (1974). Linguistic processing of speech by young infants. In R. L. Schiefelbusch & L. L. Lloyd (Eds.), *Language perspectives: Acquisition, retardation and intervention* (pp. 55–73). Baltimore: University Park Press.

Eimas, P. D. (1975). Speech perception in early infancy. In L. B. Cohen & P. Salapatek (Eds.), *Infant perception,* New York: Academic Press, pp. 193–231.

Eisenberg, R. (1965). Auditory behavior in the human neonate: Methodological problems and the logical design of research procedures. *Journal of Auditory Research, 5,* 159–177.

Eisenberg, R. (1976). *Auditory competence in Early life: The roots of communicative behavior.* Baltimore: University Park Press.

Elkind, D., & Weiss, J. (1967). Studies in perceptual development III: Perception exploration. *Child Development, 38,* 553–556.

Ekwall, E. E., & Shanker, J. L. (1988). *Diagnosis and remediation of the disabled reader* (3rd ed.). Boston: Allyn & Bacon.

Ellis, A. W. (1984). *Reading, writing and dyslexia: A cognitive analysis.* London: Lawrence Erlbaum Associates.

Ellis, N., & Large, B. (1987). The development of reading as you seek so shall you find. *British Journal of Psychology, 78*(1), 1–28.

Ellis, N. C., & Miles, T. R. (1981). A lexical encoding deficiency. In G. Th. Pavlidis & T. R. Miles (Eds.), *Dyslexia research and its application to education I.* Chichester, England: Wiley.

Entwistle, N. J. (1988). Motivation factors in students' approaches to learning. In R. R. Schmeck (Ed.), *Learning strategies and learning styles.* pp. 21–51. New York: Plenum Press.

Entwistle, N. J., & Ramsden, P. (1983). *Understanding student learning.* London: Croom Helm.

Epstein, A., Giolas, T. G., & Owens, E. (1968). Familiarity and intelligibility of monosyllabic word lists. *Journal of Speech and Hearing Research, 11*(2), 435–438.

Epstein, J. J. (1978). Growth spurts during brain development: Implications for educational policy and practice. In J. S. Chall & A. F. Mirsky (Eds.), *Education and the Brain.* pp. 343–370. Chicago: University of Chicago Press.

Erdl, J. (1968). Evoked potentials, neural efficiency and IQ. *Paper presented at International Symposium for biocybernetics.* Washington, DC, February 8.

Erdl, J. (1972). Goodbye IQ, hello EL (Ehrl Index). Phi Delta Kappan interview. *Phi Delta Kappan,* October, 89–94.

Erikson, E. H. (1963). *Childhood and society.* New York: Norton.

Evans, R., et al. (1986). The effects of sentence combining instructions on controlled and free writing and on scores for standardized tests of sentence structure and reading comprehension (ED 269 739). *Resources in Education,* October.

Fairweather, H. (1982). Sex differences: Little reason for females to play midfield. In J. G. Beaumont (Ed.), *Divided visual field studies of cerebral organization* (pp. 147–194). London: Academic Press.

Fantz, R. L. (1966). Pattern discrimination and selective attention as determinants of perceptual development from birth. In A. H. Kidd & J. L. Rivoire (Eds.), *Perceptual development in children* (pp. 143–173). New York: International Universities Press.

Feagans, L., & Short, E. J. (1984). Developmental differences in the comprehension and production of narratives by reading disabled and normally achieving children. *Child Development, 55*(5), 1727–1736.

Fernald, G. (1943). *Remedial techniques in basic school subjects.* New York: McGraw-Hill.

Field, H., et al. (1967). Response of newborns to auditory stimulation. *Journal of Auditory Research. 7*(3), 271–285.

Field, T. M., Cohen, D., Greenberg, R., & Woodson, R. (1982). Discrimination and imitation of facial expression by neonates. *Science, 218,* 179–181.

Finucci, J. M. (1978).Genetic considerations in dyslexia. *Progress in Learning Disabilities, 4,* 41–63.

Fisher, C. B., Bornstein, M. H., & Gross, C. G. (1985). Left-right coding and skills related to beginning reading. *Journal of Developmental and Behavioral Pediatrics, 6,* 279–283.

Fisher, R. A. (1930). *Statistical methods for research workers.* Edinburgh, Scotland: Oliver and Boyd.

Flanders, J. P. (1968). A review of research on imitative behavior. *Psychological Bulletin, 69,* 316–337.

Flavell, J. H. (1976). Metacognitive aspects of problem solving. In L. B. Resnick (Ed.), *The nature of intelligence* pp. 231–235. Hillsdale, NJ: Lawrence Erlbaum Associates.

Flavell, J. H., & Wellman, H. M. (1977). Metamemory. In R. V. Kail, Jr., & J. W. Hagan (Eds.), *Perspectives on the development of memory and cognition* (pp. 3–33). Hillsdale, NJ: Lawrence Erlbaum Associates.

Foss, D. J., & Swinney, D. A. (1973). On the psychological reality of the phoneme: Perception, identification, and consciousness. *Journal of Verbal Learning and Verbal Behavior. 12,* 246–257.

Fowler, C. A. (1981). Some aspects of language perception by eye: The beginning reader. In Ovid J. L. Tzeng & H. Singer (Eds.), *Perception of Print: Reading research in experimental psychology* (pp. 171–196). Hillsdale, NJ: Lawrence Erlbaum Associates.

Fox, B. & Routh, D. K. (1980). Phonemic analysis of severe reading disability in children. *Journal of Psycholinguistic Research, 9,* 115–119.

Franklin, D. (1984). Crafting sound from silence. *Science News, 126*(16), 252–254.

Fransson, A., (1977). On qualitative differences in learning: IV—Effects of motivation and test anxiety on process and outcome. *British Journal of Educational Psychology, 47,* 244–257.

Frauenfelder, U. H., & Tyler, L. K. (1987). The process of spoken word recognition: An introduction. *Cognition, 25,* 1–20.

Freedle, R., & Hale, G. (1979). Acquisition of new comprehension schemata for expository prose by transfer of a narrative schema. In R. D. Freedle (Ed.), *New directions in discourse processing* (Vol. 1) (pp. xv–xix). Norwood, NJ: Albex.

Freeman, B. J. (1985). *Buros ninth mental measurements yearbook.* Lincoln, NE: University of Nebraska Press, pp. 1725–1726.

Fried, I. et al. (1981). Developmental dyslexia: Electrological evidence of clinical subgroups. *Brain and Language, 12,* 14–22.

Friedlander, B. Z. (1967). *The effect of speaker identity, inflection, vocabulary and message redundancy on infants' selection of vocal reinforcers.* Paper presented at the Society for Research in Child Development. New York, March.

Gaddes, W. H. (1981). An examination of the validity of neuropsychological knowledge in educational diagnosis and remediation. In G. W. Hynd & J. E. Obrzut (Eds.), *Neuropsychological assessment and the school-age child* pp. 27–84. New York: Grune & Stratton.

Gagné, R. M. (1970). *The conditions of learning* (2nd ed.). New York: Holt, Rinehart, & Winston.

Galaburda, A. M. (1982). Neurological aspects of language and dyslexia. In Y. Zotterman (Ed.), *Dyslexia: Neuronal, cognitive, and linguistic aspects.* Oxford, England: Pergamon Press.

Garai, J. E., & Scheinfeld, A. (1968). Sex differences in mental and behavioral traits. *Genetic Psychology Monographs, 77,* 169–299.

Gardiner, J. M. (1983). On recency and echoic memory. In D. E. Broadbent (Ed.), Functional aspects of human memory. *Proceedings of a Royal Society discussion meeting, pp. 29–44.* January 26–27. London: Royal Society.

Gardner, H. (1986). Notes on cognitive development. In S. L. Friedman, K. L. Klivington, & R. W. Peterson (Eds.), *The brain, cognition and education* pp. 259–284. Orlando, FL: Academic Press.

Garger, S., & Guild, P. (1984). Learning style: The crucial differences. *Curriculum Review, 23,* 9–12.

Garner, R., & Reis, R. (1981). Monitoring and resolving comprehension obstacles: An investigation of spontaneous text lookbacks among upper-grade good and poor comprehenders. *Reading Research Quarterly, 16*(4), 569–582.

Gates, A. I. (1922). *Psychology of reading and spelling with special reference to disability.* Contributions to Education, No. 129, Bureau of Publications. New York: Teachers College, Columbia University.

Gates, A. I. (1937). The necessary mental age for beginning reading. *Elementary School Journal, 37,* 497–508.

Gates, A. I. (1940). A further evaluation of reading readiness tests. *Elementary School Journal, 40,* 577–591.

Gates, A. I., & Russell, D. H. (1938). Types of materials, vocabulary burden, word analysis, and other factors in beginning reading. *Elementary School Journal, 39,* 27–35, 119–128.

Gavel, S. R. (1958). June reading achievements of first-grade children. *Journal of Education, 140,* 37–43. Boston: Boston University.

Gelfand, S. A. (1981). *Hearing: An introduction to psychological and physiological acoustics.* New York: Marcel Dekker.

Gersten, R. M., et al. (1981). The relationship of entry IQ level and yearly academic growth rates of children in a direct instruction model: A longitudinal study of over 1500 children (ED 202 595). *Resources in Education.* Washington, DC.

Gersten, R. M., & Maggs, A. (1982). Teaching the general case to moderately retarded children: Evaluation of a five-year project. *Analysis and Intervention in Developmental Disabilities, 2*(4), 329–343.

Gertrude's Secrets. (1984). Menlo Park, CA: Learning Company.

Geschwind, N. (1974). *Selected papers on language and the brain.* Norwell, MA: Reidel.

Geschwind, N. (1979). Specializations of the human brain. *Scientific American, 241*(3), 180–189.

Geschwind, N. (1982). Disorders of attention: A frontier in neuropsychology. *Philosophical transactions of the Royal Society of London,* Series B.

Geschwind, N. & Behan, P. (1982). Left handedness: Association with immune disease, migraine, and developmental learning disorder. *Procedures of the National Academy of Science, 79,* 5097–5100.

Giannitrapani, D. (1969). EEG average frequency and intelligence. *Electroencephalopgraphy and Clinical Neurophysiology, 27,* 480–486.

Gibson, E. J., & Levin, H. (1975). *The psychology of reading.* Cambridge, MA: MIT Press.

Gibson, E. J., Gibson, J. J., Pack, D., & Osser, H. (1962). A developmental study of the discrimination of letter-like forms. *Journal of Comparative Psyhsiological Psychology, 55,* 897.

Gima, S (1982). The effects of word potency, frequency, and graphic characteristics on word recognition in the parafovia field (ED 214 138). *Resources in Education,* August.

Ginn Reading Program. (1985, 1989). Lexington, MA: Ginn.

Gjessing, H. J. (1982). Function analysis of reading and writing behavior: A methodological approach to improved research in reading disability. In Y. Zotterman (Ed.), *Dyslexia: Neuronal, cognitive, and linguistic aspects.* Oxford, England: Pergamon Press.

Gladstone, M., & Best, C. T. (1985). Developmental dyslexia: The potential role of interhemospheric collaboration in reading acquisition. In C. T. Best (Ed.), *Hemispheric function and collaboration in the child* pp. 87–118. New York: Academic Press.

Gladstone, R. (1988). *U.S. illiteracy: An economic time bomb. Santa Barbara News-Press,* February 22. Santa Barbara, CA.

Glaser, K., & Eisenberg, L. (1956). Maternal deprivation. *Pediatrics, 16,* 626–642.

Glees, P. (1988). *The human brain.* Cambridge, MA: Cambridge Press.

Gleitman, L. R. (1986). Biological preprogramming for language learning. In S. L. Friedman, K. A. Klivington,

& R. W. Peterson (Eds.), *The brain, cognition and education* pp. 119–149. Orlando, FL: Academic Press.

Glick, S. D., & Shapiro, R. M. (1984). Functional and neurochemical asymmetries. In N. Geschwind & A. M. Galaburda (Eds.), *Cerebral dominance* pp. 147–166. Cambridge, MA: Harvard University Press.

Goeders, N. E., & Smith, J. E. (1983). Cortical dopaminergic involvement in cocaine reinforcement. *Science, 221,* 773–775.

Goldman, H. K., Shiffman, G. B., & Bender, M. (1983). *Dyslexia: Interdisciplinary approaches to reading disabilities.* New York: Grune & Stratton.

Goldstein, D., & Dundon, W. D. (1987). A longitudinal comparison of systems used to identify subgroups of learning disabled children (ED 278 683). *Resources in Education,* June. Washington, DC.

Good, T. L., & Marshall, S. (1984). The organization of instructional groups. In P. L. Peterson, L. C. Wilkinson, & M. Hallinan (Eds.), *The social context of instruction* (pp. 15–38). Orlando, FL: Academic Press.

Goodfriend, P. (1984). The effect of cognitive organization ability on reading (ED 237 963). *Resources in Education,* October.

Goodlad, J. I., & Klein, M. F. (1970). *Behind the classroom door.* Belmont, CA: Charles A. Jones.

Goodman, K. S. (1965). A linguistic study of cues and miscues in reading. *Elementary English, 42,* 639–643.

Goodman, K. S. (1976). Reading: A psycholinguistic guessing game. In H. Singer & R. B. Ruddell (Eds.), *Theoretical models and processes of reading* (pp. 497–508). Newark, DE: International Reading Association.

Goodman, Y., & Burke, C. (1972). *Reading miscue inventory kit.* New York: Macmillan.

Gordon, H. W. (1984). Dyslexia. In R. Tarter & G. Goldstein (Eds.), *Advances in clinical neuropsychology.* New York: Plenum Press.

Gordon, H. W., & Carmon, A. (1976). Transfer of dominance in speed of verbal recognition to visually presented stimuli from right to left hemisphere. *Perceptual Motor Skills, 42,* 1091–1100.

Graesser, A. C., Hoffman, N. L., & Clark, L. F. (1980). Structural components of reading time. *Journal of Verbal Learning and Verbal Behavior, 19,* 135–151.

Gray, W. S. (1937). The nature and types of reading. In *The teaching of reading: A second report* (pp. 23–38). Thirty-sixth Yearbook, Part I, of the National Society for the Study of Education. Chicago: University of Chicago Press.

Gray, W. S. (1956). *The teaching of reading and writing: An international survey.* Chicago: Scott, Foresman.

Gray, W. S. (1960). *On their own in reading* (2nd ed.) Chicago: Scott, Foresman.

Gray, W. S. (1969). *The teaching of reading and writing* (2nd ed.). Paris: United Nations Educational Scientific and Cultural Organization.

Greer, J. G., & Wethered, C. E. (1984). Learned help-lessness: A piece of the burnout puzzle. *Exceptional Children, 50,* 524–530.

Gregorc, A. F. (1982). *Gregorc Style Delineator.* Columbia, CN.

Gronlund, N. E. (1973). *Preparing criterion-referenced tests for classroom instruction.* New York: Macmillan.

Grosjean, F., & Gee, J. P. (1987). Prosodic structure and spoken word recognition. *Cognition, 25,* 135–155.

Group Embedded Figures. (1971). Palo Alto, CA: Consulting Psychologists Press, Inc.

Guilford, J. P. (1967). Creativity and learning. In D. B. Lindsley & A. A. Lunsdaine (Eds.), *Brain function IV: Brain function and learning.* Berkeley and Los Angeles, CA: University of California Press.

Guilford, J. P., & Tenopyr, M. L. (1969). Implications of the structure-of-intellect model for high school students. In W. B. Michael (Ed.), *Teaching for creative endeavor* (p. 27). Bloomington: Indiana University Press.

Haber, R. N., & Schlinder, R. M. (1981). Error in proof-reading: Evidence of syntactic control of letter processing. *Journal of Experimental Psychology, 7,* 573–579.

Hall, R. W., & Moon, C. E. (1986). Effects of familiarity, reading level, and practice on dual-task verbal processing (ED 269 716). *Resources in Education,* October.

Hallahan, D. P., & Reeve, R. E. (1980). Selective attention and distractibility. In B. K. Keogh (Ed.), *Advances in special education* (Vol. 1). Greenwich, CT: JAI Press.

Hansen, J. (1981). The effects of inference training and practice on young children's reading comprehension. *Reading Research Quarterly, 16,* 391–417.

Hare, B. A. (1977). Perceptual deficits are not a cue to reading problems in second grade. *Reading Teacher, 30*(6), 624–628.

Harris, A. J., & Sipay, E. R. (1985). *How to increase reading ability* (8th ed.). New York: Longman.

Harris, E. L. (1982). Genetic and environmental influences on reading achievement: A study of first- and second-grade children. *Acta Geneticae Medicae et Gemillologiae: Twin Research, 31*(1–2), 64–116.

Harris, L. J. (1985). Teaching the right brain: Historical perspective on a contemporary education fad. In C. T. Best (Ed.), *Hemispheric function and collaboration in the child,* pp. 231–270. New York: Academic Press.

Hebb, D. O. (1949). *The organization of behavior.* New York: Wiley.

Heilman, A. W., Blair, T. R., & Rupley, W. H. (1986). *Principles and practices of teaching reading* (6th ed.). Columbus, OH: Merrill.

Hellman, G. T. (1971). Profiles (Leon Edel). *The New Yorker,* March 13, p. 43.

Hermann, K., & Norrie, E. (1958). Is congenital word blindness a hereditary type Gerstmann syndrome? *Psychiatrica et Neurologia, 136,* 59–73.

Hess, E. H. (1956). Space perception in the chick. *Scientific American, 195*(1), 71–80.

Hicks, C. (1981). Reversal errors in reading and their relationship to inter- and intramodal functioning. *Educational Psychology, 1*(1), 67–79.

Hiebert, E. H. (1983). An examination of ability grouping in reading instruction. *Reading Research Quarterly. 18,* 231–255.

Hilgard, E. R. & Bower, G. H. (1975). *Theories of learning* (4th ed.), Englewood Cliffs, NJ: Prentice-Hall.

Hinshelwood, J. (1917). *Congenital word-blindness.* London: H. K. Lewis.

Hitch, G. J., & Halliday, M. S. (1983). Working memory in children. In D. E. Broadbent (Ed.), *Functional aspects of human memory,* (pp. 87–102). *Proceedings of a Royal Society discussion meeting,* January 26–27. London: Royal Society.

Høien, T. (1982). Iconic persistence and reading disabilities. In Y. Zotterman (Ed.), *Dyslexia: Neuronal, cognitive and linguistic aspects.* Oxford, England: Pergamon Press.

Hobson, A., & Brazier, M. A. B. (1980). *The reticular formation revisited.* New York: Raven Press.

Holmes, J. A. (1957). The brain and the reading process. In *Claremont College Reading Conference Twenty-second Yearbook.* Claremont, CA: Claremont College Curriculum Library.

Holmes, J. A. (1960). The substrata-factor theory of reading: Some experimental evidence. In *New frontiers in reading. Proceedings of the fifth annual conference of the International Reading Association.* New York: Scholastic Magazines.

Holmes, J. A. (1963). *Creative writing and power in reading.* Invited address before the International Reading Association, Miami, May 1–4.

Holmes, J. A. (1970). The substrata-factor theory of reading: Some experimental evidence. In H. Singer & R. B. Ruddell (Eds.), *Theoretical models and processes of reading* (pp. 187–197). Newark, DE: International Reading Association.

Holmes, J. A., & Singer, H. (1961). Substrata-factor differences underlying reading ability in known groups. *Report of a Cooperative Research project to U.S. Office of Education.* Contract Nos. 538, SAE 8176, & 538 SAE 8660.

Horowitz, D. (1984). The psychobiology of parent–offspring relations in high-risk situations. In L. P. Lipsitt & C. Rovee–Collier (Eds.), *Advances in infancy research* (Vol. 3 pp. 1–22). Norwood, NJ: Albex.

Howell, J. R., & Bryden, M. P. (1987). The effects of word orientation and imageability on visual half-field presentations with a lexical decision task. *Neuropsychologia, 25*(3), 527–538.

Hubel, D. H. (1963). The visual cortex of the brain. *Scientific American,* November.

Hubel, D. H. (1985). Normal physiology and architecture of the monkey visual cortex. The ever-changing brain. *Workshop of the California Neuropsychology Services.* Meeting in San Rafael, CA, August 11.

Huey, E. B. (1908). *The psychology and pedagogy of reading.* Cambridge, MA: MIT Press.

Hull, C. L. (1943). *Principles of behavior.* New York: Appleton–Century–Crofts.

Huttenlocher, D., & Zue, V. (1983). *Phonotactic and lexical constraints in speech recognition, 3,* 157–167. Working papers of the speech communication group.

Hynd, G. W., & Grant, W. W. (1988). Pediatric neuropsychology. In Hynd, G. W., Hynd, C. R., Sullivan, H. G., & Kingsbury, T. B., IV (Eds.), *Regional cerebral blood flow (rCBF) in developmental dyslexia: Activation during reading in a surface and deep dyslexia.* New York: Grune & Stratton.

Ingram, T. T. S., Mason, A. W., & Blackburn, I. (1970). A retrospective study of 82 children with reading disability. *Developmental Medicine and Child Neurology, 12,* 171–181.

Inhelder, B. (1969). *Intelligence and memory.* Lecture at American Educational Research Association, March, Los Angeles.

Inhelder, B., & Piaget, J. (1958). *The growth of logical thinking from childhood to adolescence.* New York: Basic Books.

Inventory of Basic Skills. (1977). Subtest of *Brigance Diagnostic Inventories.* Billerica, MA: Curriculum Associates, Inc.

Jackson, M. D., & McClelland, J. L. (1981). Exploring the nature of a basic visual-processing component of reading ability. In O. J. L. Tzeng & H. Singer (Eds.), *Perception of Print: Reading research in experimental psychology* (pp. 125–136). Hillsdale, NJ: Lawrence Erlbaum Associates.

Jackson, P., & Kelly–Ballweber, D. (1986). The relationship between word and stress pattern recognition ability and hearing level in hearing-impaired young adults. *Volta Review, 88*(6) 279–287.

Jacobson, E. (1932). Electrophysiology of mental activities. *American Journal of Psychology, 44,* 677–694.

Jakobson, R., Fant, R. C., & Halle, M. (1967). *Preliminaries of speech analysis: The distinctive features and their correlates.* Cambridge, MA: MIT Press.

James, W. (1890). *The principles of psychology.* New York: Holt Rinehart, & Winston.

Javal, E. (1879). Essai sur la physiologie de la lecture. *Annales D'oculistique, 82,* 242–253.

Johnson, D. (1986). Remediation for dyslexic adults. In G. T. Pavlidis & D. F. Fisher (Eds.), *Dyslexia: Its neuropsychology and treatment.* New York: Wiley.

Johnson, D. J., & Pearson, P. D. (1982). *Teaching reading vocabulary,* (2nd ed.) (pp. 249–262). New York: Holt, Rinehart, & Winston.

Johnson, D. W., & Johnson, R. (1983). The socialization and achievement crisis: Are cooperative learning experiences the solution? In L. Bickman (Ed.), *Applied social psychology, Annual 4,* (pp. 119–164). Beverly Hills, CA: Sage.

Johnson, D. W., & Johnson, R. T. (1987). *Learning together and alone* (2nd ed.). Englewood Cliffs, NJ: Prentice–Hall.

Johnson, N. F. (1981). Integration processes in word recognition. In O. J. L. Tzeng & H. Singer (Eds.), *Perception of Print: Reading research in experimental psychology* pp. 29–63. Hillsdale, NJ: Lawrence Erlbaum Associates.

Johnson, S. (1982). Listening and reading: The recall of 7- to 9-year olds. *British Journal of Educational Psychology, 52*(1), 24–32.

Jongsma, K. S., & Jongsma, E. A. (1981). Commercial informal reading inventories. *Reading Teacher, 34,* 697–705.

Jorm, A. F., Share, D. L., MacLean, R., & Matthews, R. (1986). Cognitive factors at school entry predictive of specific reading retardation and general reading backwardness. *Journal of Child Psychology and Psychiatry, 27*(1), 45–54.

Joyce, B., & Weil, M. (1986). *Models of teaching* (3rd ed.). Englewood Cliffs, NJ: Prentice-Hall.

Just, M. A., & Carpenter, P. A. (1980). A theory of reading: From eye fixations to comprehension. *Psychological Review, 87,* 329–354.

Just, M. A., Carpenter, P. A., & Masson, M. E. J. (1982). *What eye fixations tell us about speed reading and skimming* (Eye-lab Technical Report.) Carnegie-Mellon University.

Kampwirth, T. J., & Bates, M. (1980). Modality preference and teaching method: A review of the research. *Academic Therapy, 15,* 597–605.

Kagan, J. (1971). *Change and continuity in infancy.* New York: Wiley.

Kagan, J., & Kogan, N. (1970). Individuality and cognitive preference. In P. H. Mussen (Ed.), *Carmichael's manual of child psychology* (3rd edition) Vol 1, (pp. 1273–1365). New York: Wiley.

Kandel, E. R., & Schwartz, J. H. (1982). Molecular biology of learning: Modulation of transmitter release. *Science, 218,* 433–443.

Kane, M., & Kane, N. (1979). Comparisons of right and left hemisphere functions. *Gifted Child Quarterly, 23*(1), 157–167.

Katz, L., & Feldman, L. B. (1981). Linguistic coding in word recognition: Comparisons between as deep and a shallow orthography. In A. M. Lesgold & C. A. Perfetti (Eds.), *Interactive processes in reading* pp. 85–106. Hillsdale, NJ: Lawrence Erlbaum Associates.

Katz, P. A. (1974, May). Audiovisual shifting and reading achievement. Presentation to the Preconvention Conference of the International Reading Association. *Brain functions in reading and reading disability,* New York City.

Kaufman, A. S. (1976). Do normal children have flat ability profiles?, *Psychology in the Schools, 13,* 284.

Kaufman, A. S. (1985). *Buros ninth mental measurements yearbook.* Lincoln, NE: University of Nebraska Press, 1699–1703.

Kaufman, A. S., & Kaufman, N. L. (1983). *K–ABC Kaufman assessment battery for children, administration and scoring manual*. Circle Pines, MN: American Guidance Service.

Kauffman, J. M. et al. (1987). Characteristics of students placed in special programs for the seriously emotionally disturbed. *Behavioral Disorders, 12*(3), 175–184.

Keefe, J. W. (1982). Assessing student learning styles: An overview. In *Student Learning Styles and Brain Behavior* pp. 43–53. Reston, VA: National Association of Secondary School Principals.

Keefe, J. (Ed.). (1986). *Profiling and utilizing learning style*. Reston, VA: National Association of Secondary School Principals.

Kelder, R. (1988). Entering a discourse community: Writing as a mode of learning in a content course (ED 286 210). *Resources in Education*, February.

Kellogg, R. T. (1988). Attentional overload and writing performance: Effects of rough draft and outline strategies. *Journal of Experimental Psychology: Learning, Memory and Cognition, 14*(2), 355–365.

Kendler, H. H., & Kendler, T. S. (1962). Vertical and horizontal processes in problem solving. *Psychological Review, 69,* 1–16.

Keogh, B. K., & Babbitt, B. C. (1986). Sampling issues in learning disabilities research: Markers for the study of mathematics. In G. T. Pavlidis and D. F. Fisher (Eds.), *Dyslexia: Its neuropsychology and treatment* (pp. 9–36). Chichester, England: Wiley.

Kershner, J. (1978). Lateralization in normal 6-year-olds as related to later reading ability. *Developmental Psychobiology, 11,* 309–319.

Kershner, J. R. (1985). Ontogeny of hemispheric specialization and relationship of developmental patterns to complex reading skills and academic achievement. In C. T. Best (Ed.), *Hemispheric function and collaboration in the child* (pp. 327–360). New York: Academic Press.

Kieras, D. E. (1978). Good and bad structure in simple paragraphs: Effects on apparent theme, reading time, and recall. *Journal of Verbal Learning and Verbal Behavior, 17,* 13–28.

Kimura, D. (1961). Cerebral dominance and the perception of verbal stimuli. *Canadian Journal of Psychology, 15,* 166–171.

Kimura, D. (1966). Dural functional assymetry of the brain in visual perception. *Neuropsycholgia, 4,* 275–285.

Kimura, D. (1967). Functional asymmetry of the brain in dichotic listening. *Cortex, 3,* 163–178.

Kirby, J. R. (1988). Style strategy and skill in reading. In R. R. Schmeck (Ed.), *Learning strategies and learning styles*. New York: Plenum Press, pp. 229–274.

Kirk, U. (1983). *Language and the brain*. New York: Academic Press.

Kirk, U. (1985). Hemispheric contributions to graphic skill. In C. T. Best (Ed.), *Hemispheric function and collaboration in the child* (pp. 191–221). New York: Academic Press.

Klatt, D. H. (1979). Speech perception: A model of acoustic-phonetic analysis and lexical access. *Journal of Phonetics, 7,* 279–213.

Klatt, D. H. (1980). Speech perception: A model of acoustic phonetic analysis and lexical access. In R. A. Cole (Ed.), *Perception and Production of Fluent Speech* (pp. 243–288). Hillsdale, NJ: Lawrence Erlbaum Associates.

Klivington, K. A. (1986). Building bridges among neuroscience, cognitive psychology, and education. In S. L. Friedman, K. A. Klivington, & R. W. Peterson (Eds.), *The brain, cognition and education,* (pp. 3–15). Orlando, FL: Academic Press.

Koehler, L. J. S., & Lloyd, L. L. (1986). *Using fingerspelling/manual signs to facilitate reading and spelling*. Paper presented at the biennial conference of the International Society for Augmentation and Alternative Communication, Cardiff, Wales, September 22–24.

Koffka, K. (1935). *Principles of Gestalt psychology*. New York: Harcourt Brace Janovich.

Kohler, W. (1940). *Dynamics in psychology*. New York: Liveright.

Kohn, D., & Birch, H. G. (1968). Development of auditory-visual integration and reading achievement. *Perceptual and Motor Skills, 27,* 459–468.

Kolers, P. A. (1968). Introduction. In E. B. Huey *Psychology and pedagogy of reading* (pp. xiii–xxxix). Cambridge, MA: MIT Press.

Konopak, B., et al. (1987). Reading and writing: Aids to learning in the content areas. *Journal of Reading, 31*(2), 285–306.

Koob, G. F. Riley, S. J., Smith, S. C., & Robbins, T. W. (1978). Effects of 6-hydroxydopomine lesions of the nucleus accumbenssepti and olfactory tubercle on feeding, locomotor activity, and amphetamine anorexia in the rat. *Journal of Comparative and Physiological Psychology, 87,* 772–780.

Kooney, S. T., & Murphy, M. (1983). Message plausibility and children's ability to monitor their own comprehension. *Research in Education*, September.

Koretz, J. F., & Handelman, G. H. (1988). How the human eye focuses. *Scientific American, 259*(1) 92–99.

Krashen, S. D. (1973). Lateralization, language learning, and the critical period: Some new evidence. *Language Learning, 73,* 63–74.

Krathwohl, D. R., Bloom, B S., & Masia, B. B. (1964). *Taxonomy of educational objectives: The affective domain*. New York: David McKay.

Krupski, A. (1980). Attention processes: Research, theory, and implications for special education. In B. Keogh (ed.), *Advances in Special Education* (Vol. 1). Greenwich, CT: JAI Press.

Kuhl, P. K., & Meltzoff, A. N. (1982). The bimodal perception of speech in infancy. *Science, 218,* 1138–1141.

LaBerge, D., & Samuels, S. J. (1974). Toward a theory of automatic information processing in reading. *Cognitive Psychology, 6,* 293–323.

Lachman, R., Lachman, J. L., & Butterfield, E. C. (1979). *Cognitive psychology and information processing: An introduction.* Hillsdale, NJ: Lawrence Erlbaum Associates.

Land, E. H. (1977). The retinex theory of color vision. *Scientific American, 237*(6), 108–128.

Lassen, N. A., Ingvar, D. H., & Skinhj, E. (1978). Brain function and blood flow. *Scientific American, 229*(4), 62–71.

Lawrence, D. H. (1928). *John Galsworthy, Scrutinies by various writers,* Col. By Edgell Rickword, (pp. 51–72). London: Wishart.

Lederhendler, I., & Alkon, D. L. (1986). Implicating casual relations between cellular function and learning behavior. *Behavioral Neuroscience, 100*(6), 833–838.

Legein, C. P., & Bouma, H. (1981). Visual recognition experiments in dyslexia. In G. T. Pavlidis & T. R. Miles (Eds.), *Dyslexia research and its application to education* (pp. 165–175). Chichester, England: Wiley.

Leibnitz, G. W. Von. (1936). The monadology. In B. Rand (Ed.), *Modern classical philosophers* (pp. 199–214). New York: Houghton Mifflin.

LeMay, M. (1984). Radiological, developmental, and fossil asymmetries. In N. G. Geschwind & A. M. Galaburda (Eds.), *Cerebral Dominance* pp. 26–42. Cambridge, MA: Harvard University Press.

Lenneberg, E. H. (1967). *Biological functions of language.* New York: Wiley.

Leong, C. K., Wong, S., Wong, A., & Hiscock, M. (1985). Differential cerebral involvement in perceiving Chinese characters: Levels of processing approach. *Brain and Language, 26,* 131–145.

Lesgold, A. M., & Perfetti, C. (1981). Interactive processes in reading: Where do we stand? In A. Lesgold & C. Perfetti (Eds.), *Interactive processes in reading* (pp. 387–407). Hillsdale, NJ: Lawrence Erlbaum Associates.

Levine, D. U. (Ed.). (1985). *Important student achievement through mastery learning programs.* San Francisco: Jossey–Bass.

Levine, M. J. (1983). The effect of task parameters in diagnostic reading groups. *Psychology in the Schools, 20*(3), 276–283.

Levy, J. (1980). Cerebral asymmetry and the psychology of man. In M. C. Wittrock (Ed.), *The brain and psychology.* New York: Academic Press.

Levy, J. (1982). Children think with whole brains: Myth and reality. In *Student Learning Styles and Brain Behavior* (pp. 173–184). Reston, VA: National Association of Secondary School Principals.

Levy, J., & Reid, M. (1976). Variations in writing posture and cerebral organization. *Science, 194,* 337–339.

Levy, J., & Reid, M. (1978). Variations in cerebral organizations as a function of handedness, hand posture in writing, and sex. *Journal of Experimental Psychology: General, 107,* 119–144.

Lewin, K. (1935). *A dynamic theory of personality* (Tr. K. E. Zener & D. K. Adams). New York: McGraw–Hill.

Lewis, C. L. (1981). A study of preschool children's use of computer programs. In D. Harris & L. Nelson–Hern, *Proceedings of the Third National Educational Computing Conference* (ERIC Document No. ED 207 526). Denton, TX: North Texas State University.

Lezak, M. (1982). The cerebral hemispheres. In M. C. Robeck & R. Sylwester (Eds.), *The brain: Recent research and its educational implications. Conference Report.* Eugene, OR: University of Oregon, College of Education.

Lezak, M. D., & Newman, S. P. (1979). *Verbosity and right hemisphere damage.* Paper presented at the Second European Meeting of the International Neuropsychological Society. Noordvijkerhout, The Netherlands.

Liberman, I. Y., Liberman, A. M., Mattingly, I. G., & Shankweiler, D. (1980). Orthography and the beginning reader. In J. F. Kavanagh & R. Venezky (Eds.), *Orthography, reading, and dyslexia.* Baltimore, MD: University Park Press.

Lieberman, P., Meskill, R. H., Chatillon, M., & Schupack, H. (1985). Phonetic speech perception deficits in dyslexia. *Journal of Speech and Hearing, 28*(4), 480–486.

Lindsley, D. B. (1938). Electrical potentials of the brain in children and adults. *Journal of Genetic Psychology, 19,* 285–306.

Loban, W. (1964). Stages in the acquisition of standard English. In R. W. Shuy (Ed.), *Social dialects and language learning* (pp. 77–104). Champaign, IL: National Council of Teachers of English.

Lorenz, K. (1965). *Evolution and modification of behavior.* Chicago: University of Chicago Press.

Lorenz, K. (1969). Innate bases of learning. In K. H. Pribram (Ed.), *On the biology of learning.* (pp. 13–93). New York: Harcourt Brace & Jovanovich.

Lovell, K., & Gorton, A. (1968). A study of some differences between backward and normal readers of average intelligence. *British Journal of Educational Psychology, 38*(3), 240–248.

Lovett, M. W. (1987). A developmental approach to reading disability: Accuracy and speed criteria of normal and deficient reading skill. *Child Development, 58*(1), 234–260.

Lovrich, D., & Stamm, J. S. (1983). Event-related potential and behavioral correlates of attention in reading retardation. *Journal of Clinical Neuropsychology, 5*(1), 13–37.

Loye, D. (1983). *The sphinx and the rainbow.* Toronto: Bantam Books.

Lubbock, P. (1962). On the reader's involvement. In R. W.

Stallman and R. E. Watters (Eds.), *The creative reader* (2nd edition) (p. 2). New York: Ronald Press.

Lubin, B., Larsen, R. M., & Matarazzo, J. D. (1984). Patterns of psychological test usage in the United States: 1935–1982. *American Psychologist, 39,* 451–454.

Luria, A. R. (1973). *The working brain: An introduction to neuropsychology.* New York: Basic Books.

Luria, A. R. (1976). *Cognitive development: Its cultural and social foundations.* Cambridge, MA: Harvard University Press.

McCarthy, P., & Schmeck, R. R. (1988). Students' self-concepts and quality of learning in public schools and universities. In R. R. Schmeck (Ed.), *Learning strategies and learning styles* (pp. 131–156). New York: Plenum Press.

McClelland, D. C., & Atkinson, J. W. (1948). The projective expression of needs: II The effect of different intensities of the hunger drive on thematic apperception. *Journal of Experimental Psychology, 38,* 643–658.

McConaughy, S. H. (1980). Using story structure in the classroom. *Language Arts, 57,* 157–165.

McConkie, G. W., et al. (1982). Perceiving words during reading: Lack of facilitation from prior peripheral exposures (ED 217 400). *Resources in Education,* November.

McCutchen, D., & Perfetti, C. A. (1984). The visual tongue-twister effect: Phonological activation in silent reading (ED 240 533). *Resources in Education.*

McGinnis, D. J., & Smith, D. E. (1982). *Analyzing and treating reading problems.* New York: Macmillan.

McGlone, J. (1980). Sex differences in human brain asymmetry: A critical survey. *Behavioral and Brain Sciences, 3,* 215–263.

McKenna, M. C. (1983). Informal reading inventories. A review of the issues. *Reading Teacher,* November, 168–173.

McMahan, I. D. (1973). Relationships between casual attributions and expectancy of success. *Journal of Personality and Social Psychology, 28,* 108–114.

McNamee, G. D. (1982). The social origins of comprehension skills at the prereading level (ED 214 116). *Resources in Education,* August.

McNeil, J. D. (1984). *Reading comprehension.* Glenview, IL: Scott, Foresman.

McNeill, D. (1970). The development of language. In P. H. Mussen (Ed.), *Carmichael's manual of child psychology* (pp. 983–1060). New York: Wiley.

McVitty, W. (Ed.) (1987). Getting it together: Organizing the reading-writing classroom (ED 278 043). *Resources in Education,* June.

Maclean, M., et al. (1987). Rhymes, nursery rhymes and reading in early childhood. *Merrill–Palmer Quarterly, 33*(3), 255–281.

MacLeod, C. M. (1988). Forgotten but not gone: Savings for pictures and words in long-term memory. *Journal of Experimental Psychology: Learning, Memory and Cognition. 14,* 195–212.

Maccoby, E. E., & Jacklin, C. N. (1974). *The psychology of sex differences.* Stanford: University of Stanford Press.

Madden, N. A., Slavin, R. E., & Stevens, R. J. (1986). *Cooperative integrated reading and composition: Teacher's manual.* Baltimore, MD: Johns Hopkins University, Center for Research on Elementary and Middle Schools.

Maestas, L., & Croll, V. J. (1985). The effects of training in story mapping procedures on the reading comprehension of poor readers. *National Institute of Education* (Tech. Rep. No. 352). Washington, DC.

Malinowski, P. A. (1988). The reading–writing connection: An overview and annotated bibliography (ED 285 138). *Resources in Education,* January.

Mandler, J. M., & Johnson, N. S. (1977). Remembrance of things parsed: Story structure and recall. *Cognitive Psychology, 9,* 111–151.

Mann, V. A., & Liberman, I. Y. (1984). Phonological awareness and verbal short-term memory. *Journal of Learning Disabilities, 17*(10), 592–599.

Mann, V. A., Shankweiler, D., & Smith, S. T. (1984). The association between comprehension of spoken sentences and early reading ability: The role of phonetic representation. *Journal of Child Language, 11,* 627–643.

Marshall, J. C. (1988). The lifeblood of language. *Nature, 331,* 560–561.

Marshall, J. C., & Newcombe, F. (1973). Patterns of paralexia: A psycholinguistic approach. *Journal of Psycholinguistic Research, 2,* 175–199.

Marslen-Wilson, W. (1984). Function and process in spoken word recognition. In H. Bouma & D. Bouwhuis (Eds.), *Attention and performance: Control of language processes.* Hillsdale, NJ: Lawrence Erlbaum Associates.

Marslen-Wilson, W. D., & Welsh, A. (1978). Processing interaction and lexical access during word recognition in continuous speech. *Cognitive Psychology, 10,* 29–63.

Martin, F., & Lovegrove, W. (1984). The effects of field size and luminance on contrast sensitivity differences between specific reading disabled and normal children. *Neuropsychologia, 22*(1), 73–77.

Massaro, D. W. (1974). Perceptual units in speech recognition. *Journal of Experimental Psychology, 102,* 199–208.

Masson, M. E. J. (1985). Rapid reading processes and skills. In G. E. MacKinnon & T. G. Waller (Eds.), *Advances in theory and practice* (Vol. 4, pp. 183–230). Orlando, FL: Academic Press.

Matarazzo, J. D. (1985). *Buros ninth mental measurements yearbook.* Lincoln, NE: University of Nebraska Press, 1703–1705.

Mattis, S., French, J. H., & Rapin, I. (1975). Dyslexia in children and young adults: Three independent neuropsychological syndromes. *Developmental Medicine and Child Neurology, 17,* 150–163.

Maugh, T. H. 2d, (1974). Creativity: Can it be dissected? Can it be taught? *Science, 184,* 1273.

Mazaux, J. M., & Orgogozo, J. M. (1982). Analysis and quantitative study of language disorders in lesions of the left thalamus: Thalamic aphasia. *Cortex, 18*(3), 403–416.

Mehrens, W. A. (1984). A critical analysis of the psychometric properties of the K–ABC. *Journal of Special Education, 18*(3), 297–310.

Mehrens, W. A., & Lehman, I. J. (1987). *Using Standardized Tests in Education.* New York: Longman.

Menyuk, P. (1971). The acquisition and development of language. Englewood Cliffs, NJ: Prentice-Hall.

Metropolitan Achievement Tests. (1986). San Antonio, TX: Psychological Corporation.

Metropolitan Readiness Test. (1986). San Antonio, TX: Psychological Corporation.

Metzger, R. L., & Werner, D. B. (1984). Use of visual training for reading disabilities: A review. Pediatrics, 73, 824–829.

Meyer, B. J. F. (1975). Identification of the structure of prose and its implications for the study of reading and memory. *Journal of Reading Behavior, 7,* 7–47.

Miles, T. R. (1983). *Dyslexia: The pattern of difficulties.* Springfield, IL: Charles C. Thomas.

Miller, E. (1979). First-grade reading instruction and modality preference. *Elementary School Journal, 80*(2), 99–104.

Miller, G. A. (1956). Information memory. *Scientific American* (reprint). San Francisco: W. H. Freeman.

Milner, B. (1965). Visually-guided maze learning in man: Effects of bilateral hippocampal bilateral frontal and unilateral cerebral lesions. *Neuropsychologia, 3,* 317–338.

Monroe, M. (1937). *Reading aptitude test.* Boston: Houghton Mifflin.

Morell, P., & Norton, W. T., (1980). Myelin. *Scientific American, 242*(5) 88–118.

Morton, J. (1969). Interaction of information in word recognition. *Psychological Review, 76,* 165–178.

Moser, M. C. (1983). Letter migration in word perception (ED 232 144). *Resources in Education,* December.

Moskowitz, B. A. (1978). The acquisition of language. *Scientific American, 239*(5) pp. 92–108.

Murphy, H. A. (1943). *Evaluation of specific training in auditory and visual discrimination on beginning reading.* Doctoral dissertation. Boston: Boston University.

Nachshon, I. (1985). Directional preferences in perception of visual stimuli. *International Journal of Neuroscience, 25*(3–4), 161–174.

Naidoo, S. (1981). Teaching methods and their rationale. In G. T. Pavlidis & T. R. Miles (Eds.), *Dyslexia research and its applications to education.* Chichester, England: Wiley.

Neale, J. M., & Friend, R. M. (1972). Attributional determinants of reactions to performance in academic situations. *Perception and Motor Skills, 34,* 35–40.

Nell, V. (1988). The psychology of reading for pleasure: Needs and gratification. *Reading Research Quarterly, 23*(1), 6–50.

Newkirk, T. (Ed.). (1987). Only connect: Uniting reading and writing (ED 281 223). *Resources in Education,* September.

Nicholas, D. W., & Trabasso, T. (1980). Memory and inferences in the comprehension of narratives. In F. Wilkening, J. Becker, & T. Trabasso (Eds.), *Information integration by children* (pp. 243–265). Hillsdale, NJ: Lawrence Erlbaum Associates.

Nickerson, R. S. (1981). Speech understanding and reading: Some differences and similarities. In O. J. L. Tzeng & H. Singer (Eds.), *Perception of print: Reading research in experimental psychology* (pp. 257–289). Hillsdale, NJ: Lawrence Erlbaum Associates.

Nieboer, R. A. (1983). The relationship between memory span and processing speed. In M. P. Ornstein, J. P. Das, & N. O'Conner (Eds.), *Intelligence and learning.* (pp. 179–183). New York: Plenum Press.

Noland, R. G., & Craft, A. P. (1976). Methods to maturate the reluctant reader. *Journal of Reading, 19,* 387–391, February.

Nowicki, S., Duke, M. P., & Crouch, M. P. D. (1978). Sex differences in locus of control and performance under competitive and cooperative conditions. *Journal of Educational Psychology, 70,* 482–486.

Oakhill, J. (1984). Inferential and memory skills in children's comprehension of stories. *British Journal of Educational Psychology, 54,* 31–39.

Oakland, T. (1985). *Buros ninth mental measurements yearbook.* Lincoln, NE: University of Nebraska Press, pp. 1401–1403.

Olds, J. (1960). Differentiation of reward systems in the brain by self-stimulation techniques. In E. R. Ramey & D. S. O'Doherty (Eds.), *Electrical studies of the unanesthestized brain* (pp. 17–51). New York: Harper & Row.

Olds, J., & Milner, P. (1954). Positive reinforcement produced by electrical stimulation of septal area and other regions of the rat brain. *Journal of Comparative and Physiological Psychology, 47,* 419–427.

Olson, R. K., Kliegel, R., Davidson, B. J., & Foltz, G. (1985). Individual and developmental differences in reading disability. In G. E. MacKinnon & G. G. Waller (Eds.), *Reading Research: Advances in Theory and Practice* (Vol. 4), pp. 2–64. New York: Academic Press.

Open Court Foundation Program. (1982). LaSalle, IL: Open Court Publishing Co.

Orton, S. T. (1937). *Reading, writing, and speech problems in children.* New York: W. W. Norton.

Orwell, G. (1954). *Animal farm.* New York: Harcourt Brace & Javanovich.

Paris, S. G. (1975). Integration and inference in children's comprehension and memory. In F. Restle, R. M.

Shiffrin, N. J. Castellan, H. R. Lindman, & D. B. Pisoni (Eds.), *Cognitive theory* (Vol. 1) (pp. 223–246). Hillsdale, NJ: Lawrence Erlbaum Associates.

Paris, S. G., & Carter, A. Y. (1973). Semantic and constructive aspects of sentence memory in children. *Developmental Psychology, 9,* 109–113.

Paris, S. G., & Lindauer, B. K. (1976). The role for inference in children's comprehension and memory for sentences. *Cognitive Psychology, 8,* 217–227.

Park, R. (1981). A critical review of developments in adult literacy. In M. Kamil (Ed.), *Directions in reading: Research and instruction* (pp. 279–289). Washington, DC: National Reading Conference.

Pask, G. (1988). Learning strategies, teaching strategies, and conceptual or learning style. In R. R. Schmeck (Ed.), *Learning strategies and learning styles* (pp. 83–100). New York: Plenum Press.

Patten, M. D. (1983). Relationship between self-esteem, anxiety, and achievement in young learning disabled students. *Journal of Learning Disabilities, 16,* 43–45.

Pavlidis, G. Th. (1981). Sequencing, eye movements and the early objective diagnosis of dyslexia, In G. T. Pavlidis & T. R. Miles (Eds.), *Dyslexia research and its application to education* (pp. 99–163). Chichester, England: Wiley.

Pavlidis, G. Th. (1986). The role of eye movements in the diagnosis of dyslexia: In G. T. Pavlidis & D. F. Fisher (Eds.), *Dyslexia: Its neuropsychology and treatment* (pp. 97–110). New York: Wiley.

Pavlov, I. P. (1927). *Conditioned reflexes.* London: Oxford University Press.

Payne, M. C., & Holtzman, T. (1983). Auditory short-term memory and digit span: Normal versus poor readers. *Journal of Educational Psychology, 75*(3), 424–430.

Pearson, P. D., & Gallagher, M. C. (1983). The instruction of reading comprehension. *Contemporary Educational Psychology, 8,* 317–345.

Pellegrini, A. D. (1983). Identifying casual elements in the thematic-fantasy play paradigm (ED 227 965). *Resources in Education,* August.

Penfield, W. (1969). Consciousness, memory, and man's conditioned reflexes. In K. H. Pribram (Ed.), *On the Biology of Learning* (pp. 127–168). New York: Harcourt, Brace, Jovanovich.

Penfield, W. (1975). *The mystery of the mind.* Princeton, NJ: Princeton University Press.

Penfield, W., & Evans, J. (1935). The frontal lobe in man: A clinical study of maximum removals. *Brain, 58,* 115–138.

Penfield, W., & Roberts, L. (1959). *Speech and brain mechanisms.* Princeton, NJ: Princeton University Press.

Pennington, B. F., et al. (1983). Developmental continuities and discontinuities in famial dyslexia. In R. Emde & R. Harmon (Eds.), *Continuities and discontinuities in development* pp. 123–151. New York: Plenum Press.

Pennington, B. F., Johnson, C., & Welsh, M. C. (1987). Unexpected reading precocity in a normal preschooler: Implications for hyperlexia. *Brain and Language, 30*(1), 165–180.

Perfetti, C. A., Bell, L. C., & Delaney, S. M. (1988). Automatic (prelexical) phonetic activation in silent word reading: Evidence from backward masking. *Journal of Memory and Language, 27,* 59–70.

Petersen, S. E., Fox, P. T., Posner, M. I., Mintun, M., & Raichle, M. E. (1988). Positron emission tomographic studies of the cortical anatomy of single word processing. *Nature, 331,* 585–589.

Pezdak, K. (1980). Arguments for a constructive approach to comprehension and memory. In J. Danks & K. Pezdak (Eds.), *Reading and understanding.* Newark, DE: International Reading Association.

Phelps, L., Bell, M. C., & Scott, M. J. (1988). Correlations between the Stanford–Binet: Fourth Edition and the WISC–R with a learning disabled population. *Psychology in the Schools, 25,* 380–382.

Phillips, L. M. (1987).Using children's literature to foster written language development (ED 276 027). *Resources in Education,* April.

Piaget, J. (1952). *Origins of intelligence in children.* New York: W. W. Norton.

Piaget, J. (1959). *The language and thought of the child.* London: Routledge & Kegan Paul.

Piaget, J. (1969). *The theory of stages in cognitive development* (Sylvia Opper, trans.). An address to the CTB/McGraw–Hill Invitational Conference on Ordinal Scales of Cognitive Development, Monterey, CA: CTB/McGraw-Hill, February.

Piaget, J. (1970). *Structuralism.* New York: Basic Books.

Piaget, J. (1971). *Biology and knowledge.* Chicago: University of Chicago Press.

Pickles, J. O. (1982). *The physiology of hearing,* London: Academic Press.

Picton, T. W., Stuss, D. T., Klivington, K. A., & Marshall, K. C. (1986). Attention and the brain. In S. L. Friedman, K. A. Klivington, R. W. Peterson (Eds.), *The brain, cognition, and education* (pp. 19–79). Orlando, FL: Academic Press.

Piestrup, A. M. (1981). Preschool children use Apple II to test reading skills programs (ED 202 476). *Resources in Education.*

Pinel, J. P. J., & Treit, D. (1983). Conditioned defensive burying paradigm and behavioral neuroscience. In T. E. Robinson (Ed.), *Behavioral approaches to brain research.* Oxford, England: Oxford University Press.

Pinnell, G. S. (1988). *Success of children at risk in a program that combines writing and reading* (Tech. Rep. No. 417). Washington, DC: Office of Educational Research and Improvement (ED 000 036).

Pirozzolo, F. J. (1983). Eye movements and reading disability. In K. Rayner (Ed.), *Eye movements in reading: Perceptual and language processes.* New York: Academic Press.

Pirozzolo, F. J. (1985). Neuropsychological and neuroelectric correlates of developmental reading disability. In C. T. Best (Ed.), *Hemispheric function and collaboration in the child* (pp. 309–326). New York: Academic Press.

Pirozzolo, F. J., & Wittrock, M. C. (Eds.). (1981). *Neuropsychological and cognitive processes in reading.* New York: Academic Press.

Pisoni, D. B., & Luce, P. A. (1987). Acoustic-phonetic representations in word recognition. *Cognition, 25,* 21–52.

Pitts, S. K. (1986). Read aloud to adult learners? Of course. *Reading Psychology, 7*(1), 35–42.

Posner, M. I. (1982). Cumulative development of attentional theory. *American Psychologist, 37*(2), 168–179.

Posner, M. I., & Freidrich, F. J. (1986). Attention and the control of cognition. In S. L. Friedman, K. A. Klivington, & R. W. Peterson (Eds.), *The brain, cognition, and education* (pp. 81–103). Orlando, FL: Academic Press.

Pribram, K. H. (1971). *Languages of the brain: Experimental paradoxes and principles in neuropsychology.* Englewood Cliffs, NJ: Prentice-Hall.

Rae, G. (1977). Relation of auditory-visual integration to reading and intelligence. *Journal of General Psychology, 97*(1), 3–8.

Ramsden, P. (1988). Context strategy: Situational influences on learning. In R. R. Schmeck (Ed.), *Learning strategies and learning styles* pp. 159–184. New York: Plenum Press.

Rankin, E. (1978). Rates of comprehension flexibility: A new measurement procedure. *Twenty-Seventh Yearbook of the National Reading Conference.* New York: Wiley.

Raphael, T. E., et al. (1987). The impact of text structure instruction and social context on student comprehension and production of expository text (ED 275 990). *Resources in Education,* April.

Raphael, T. E., & Englert, C. S. (1988). Integrating writing and reading instruction (ED 294 175). *Resources in Education,* April.

Rawson, M. B. (1981). A diversity model for dyslexia. In G. Th. Pavlidis & T. R. Miles (Eds.), *Dyslexia research and its application to education* (pp. 13–33). Chichester, England: Wiley.

Rawson, M. B. (1986). Developmental stages and patterns of growth of dyslexic persons. In G. T. Pavlidis & D. F. Fisher (Eds.), *Dyslexia: Its neuropsychology and treatment* pp. 3–8. Chichester, England: Wiley.

Rayner, K. (1986a). Eye movements and the perceptual span in beginning and skilled reading. *Journal of Experimental Child Psychology, 2,* 211–236.

Rayner, K. (1986b). Eye movements and the perceptual span: Evidence for dyslexic typology. In G. T. Pavlidis & D. F. Fisher (Eds.), *Dyslexia: Its neuropsychology and treatment* pp. 111–130. New York: Wiley.

Rayner, L. (Ed.). (1983). *Eye movements in reading: perceptual and language processes.* New York: Academic Press.

Reader Rabbit. (1986). Menlo Park, CA: The Learning Company.

Reagan, S. B. (1986). Teaching reading in the writing classroom. *Journal of Teaching Writing, 5*(2), 177–185.

Reed, D. W. (1970). A theory of language, speech, and sorting. In H. Singer & R. B. Ruddell (Eds.), *Theoretical models and processes of reading* pp. 217–238. Newark, DE: International Reading Association.

Reisman, F. K., & Payne, B. D. (1987). *Elementary education.* Columbus, OH: Merrill.

Restak, R. (1979). *The Brain: The last frontier.* New York: Doubleday.

Rettig, M., Shaklett, E. U., & Wyrsch, M. (1987). Microcomputer applications with visually impaired preschool-aged children. *Journal of Visual Impairment and Blindness. 81*(3), 120–122.

Robeck, M. C. (1958). *An analysis of the responses of retarded, average, and superior readers to identical story material.* Unpublished doctoral dissertation, University of Washington.

Robeck, M. C. (1963). Readers who lack word analysis skill. *Journal of Educational Research, 56*(8), 432–434.

Robeck, M. C. (1965). Types of reading disability. In J. A. Figurel (Ed.), *Reading and inquiry* (ED 298-300). Proceedings of the International Reading Association.

Robeck, M. C. (1968). *Acceleration: Programs for intellectually gifted pupils.* Sacramento, CA: California State Department of Education.

Robeck, M. C. (1988). *High IQ children with severe reading difficulties: A followup study 25 years afterward.* Report to the California Educational Research Association meeting in San Diego, November 17–18.

Robeck, M. C., & Wilson, J. A. R. (1974). *Psychology of reading: Foundations of instruction.* New York: Wiley.

Robinson, F. P. (1961). *Effective study* (rev. ed.). New York: Harper.

Robinson, H. (1972). Visual and auditory modalities related to methods for beginning reading. *Reading Research Quarterly, 8,* 7–39.

Rosenbaum, J. E. (1980). Social implications of educational grouping. *Review of Research in Education.* Washington, DC: American Education Research Association.

Rosenshine, B. (1980). Metacognitive development and reading. In R. J. Spiro, B. B. Bruce, & W. F. Brewer (Eds.), *Theoretical issues in reading comprehension* (pp. 535–554). Hillsdale, NJ: Lawrence Erlbaum Associates.

Rosenzweig, M. R. (1986). Multiple models of memory. In S. L. Friedman, K. A. Klivington, & R. W. Peterson (Eds.), *The brain, cognition, and education,* pp. 347–371 Orlando, FL: Academic Press.

Rothman, J. E. (1985). The compartmental organization of the Golgi Apparatus. *Scientific American, 253*(3), 74–89.

Rotter, J. (1954). *Social learning and clinical psychology.* Englewood Cliffs, NJ: Prentice-Hall.

Rudel, R. G. (1985). Hemispheric asymmetry and learning disabilities: Left, right or in-between? In C. T. Best (Ed.), *Hemispheric function and collaboration in the child,* pp. 275–305. New York: Academic Press.

Ruggiero, V. R. (1988). *Teaching thinking across the curriculum.* New York: Harper & Row.

Rumelhart, D. E., & Ortony, A. (1977). The representation of knowledge in memory. In R. C. Anderson, R. J. Spiro, & W. E. Montague (Eds.), *Schooling and the acquisition of knowledge* pp. 99–135. Hillsdale, NJ: Lawrence Erlbaum Associates.

Russell, D. H. (1956). *Children's thinking.* Waltham, MA: Blaisdell.

Russell, D. (1961). *Children learn to read* (2nd ed.). Boston: Ginn.

Sagi, A. (1981). Mothers' identification of infant cries. *Infant behavior and development, 253*(3), 74–89.

Salvia, J., & Ysseldyke, J. E. (1985). *Assessment in Special and Remedial Education* (3rd ed.). Boston: Houghton Mifflin.

Samuel, A. G. (1981). Phonemic restoration: Insights from a new methodology. *Journal of Experiential Psychology: General, 110,* 474–494.

Samuel, A G., Van Santen, & J. R., Johnston, J. C. (1982). Length effects in word perception. We is better than I but worse than you or them. *Journal of Experimental Psychology, 8,* 91–105.

Samuels, S. J., & Eisenberg, P. (1981). A framework for understanding the reading process. In F. J. Pirozzolo & M. C. Wittrock (eds.), *Neuropsychological and cognitive processing in reading* (pp. 31–67). New York: Academic Press.

Samuels, S. J., & Kamil, M. L. (1984). Models of reading process. In P. D. Pearson (Ed.), *Handbook of reading research* pp. 185–224. New York: Longman.

Samuels, S. J., & Miller, N. L. (1985). Failure to find attention differences between learning disabled and normal children in classroom and laboratory tasks. *Exceptional Children, 52,* 358–375.

Santastefano, S., Rutledge, L., & Randall, D. (1965). Cognitive styles and reading disability. *Psychology in the Schools, 11*(1), 57–62.

Sarkisov, S. A. (1966). *The structure and functions of the brain.* Bloomington: Indiana University Press.

Sartain, H. W. (1981). Research summary: Family contributions to reading attainment. In H. Sartain (Ed.), *Mobilizing family forces for worldwide reading success* pp. 4–18. Newark, DE: International Reading Association.

Sattler, J. M. (1982). *Assessment of children's intelligence and special abilities* (2nd ed.). Boston: Allyn Bacon.

Sawusch, J. R. (1986). Auditory and phonetic coding. In E. C. Schwab & H. C. Nusbaum (Eds.), *Pattern recognition by humans and machines: Vol. 1, Speech perception* pp. 51–88, Orlando, FL: Academic Press.

Sax, G. (1974). *Principles of educational measurement and evaluation.* Belmont, CA: Wadsworth.

Schechter, M., & Schechter, S. R. (1987). *Children's acquisition of literary genre: Science fiction versus fantasy* (SF 068 743). Toronto: Department of Education.

Scheibel, A. B. (1980). Anatomical and physiological substrates of arousal: A view from the bridge. In J. A. Hobson & M. A. B. Brazier (Eds.), *The reticular formation revisited* (p. 63 ff). New York: Raven Press.

Scheibel, A. (1985a). *The rise of the human brain.* Workshop on the ever changing brain. California Neuropsychological Services meeting in San Rafael, August, 9.

Scheibel, A. (1985b). *The brain grows up and grows old.* Summer workshop of the California Neuropsychology Services, San Rafael, August 9.

Schlesinger, J. M. (1982). Receptive language in infant need for subtle techniques. In *Steps to language.* Hillsdale, NJ: Lawrence Erlbaum Associates.

Schmeck, R. R. (1988). An introduction to strategies and styles of learning. In R. R. Schmeck (Ed.), *Learning strategies and learning styles,* (pp. 3–19). New York: Plenum.

Schnaph, J. L., & Baylor, D. A. (1987). How photoreceptor cells respond to light. *Scientific American, 256*(4), pp. 40–47.

Schvaneveldt, R. W. & McDonald, J. E., 1981. Semantic context and the encoding of words: Evidence for two modes of stimulus analysis. *Journal of Experimental Psychology, 7*(3), 673–687.

Schwab, E. C., & Nusbaum, H. C. (Eds.). (1986). *Pattern recognition by humans and machines, Vols. 1 & 2, Visual perception.* Orlando, FL: Academic Press.

Scott, S. (1986). Curriculum planner. *Teaching and Computers,* November/December, 58.

Seidenberg, M. S. (1985). Time course of information activation. In D. Besner, T. Gary Waller, & G. E. MacKinnon (Eds.), *Reading research: Advances in theory and practice, 5,* pp. 199–252. Orlando, FL: Academic Press.

Seymour, P. H. K. (1986). *Cognitive analysis of dyslexia.* London: Routledge & Kegan Paul.

Shade, D. D. et al. (1983). Microcomputers: A close look at what happens when preschool children interact with age-appreciation software (ED 243 608). *Resources in Education.*

Shankweiler, D., Smith, R. T., & Mann, V. A. (1984). Repetition and comprehension of spoken sentences by reading-disabled children. *Brain and Language, 23*(2), 241–257.

Shapiro, J. E. (1979). Developing an awareness of attitudes. In J. Shapiro (Eds.), *Using literature and poetry effectively,* (pp. 2–7). Newark, DE: International Reading Association.

Sharon, S., & Calfee, R. (1977). The relation of auditory, visual and auditory-visual matching to reading performance of Israeli children. *Journal of Genetic Psychology, 130*(2), 181–189.

Shavelson, R. J., & Stern, P. (1981). Research on teachers' pedagogical thoughts, judgments, decisions, and behavior. *Review of Educational Research, 51,* 455–498.

Silberberg, N. E., & Silberberg, M. C. (1977). A note on reading tests and their roles in defining reading difficulties. *Journal of Learning Disabilities, 10,* 100–113.

Silva, P. A., et al. (1985). *Journal of Child Psychology and Psychiatry and Allied Disciplines, 26*(3), 407–421.

Silver, A. A., & Hagin, R. A. (1966). Maturation of perceptual functions in children with specific reading disability. *Reading Teacher, 19,* 253–259.

Simner, M. (1969). *Response to the newborn infant to the cry of another infant.* Paper presented to the Society for Research in Child Development, meeting in Santa Monica, CA, March.

Simon, H. A. (1986). The role of attention in cognition. In S. L. Friedman, K. A. Klivington, & R. W. Peterson (Eds.), *The brain, cognition and education* pp. 105–115. Orlando, FL: Academic Press.

Sinatra, R. (1982). Learning literacy in nonverbal style. In *Student Learning Styles and Brain Behavior* pp. 203–211. Reston, VA: National Association of Secondary School Principals.

Singer, H. (1970). A developmental model of speed reading in grades three through six. In H. Singer & R. R. Ruddell (Eds.), *Theoretical models and processes of reading,* pp. 198–218. Newark, DE: International Reading Association.

Singer, H. (1978). Active comprehension. *Reading Teacher, 31*(8), 901–908.

Singer, H. (1984). Learning to read and skilled reading: Multiple systems interacting within and between the reader and the text. In J. Downing & R. Valtin (Eds.), *Perception of print,* pp. 193–206. New York: Springer–Verlag.

Skinner, B. F. (1953). *Science and human behavior.* New York: Macmillan.

Skjelfjord, V. J. (1976). Different ways of viewing pupil readiness for learning to read. *Scandanavian Journal of Educational Research, 20*(3), 105–121.

Slavin, R. E. (1986). *Educational psychology: Theory into practice* (2nd. ed.). Englewood Cliffs, NJ: Prentice–Hall.

Slobin, D. I. (1982). Universal and particular in the acquisition of language. In E. Wanner & L. R. Gleitman (Eds.), *Language acquisition: The state of the art* pp. 308, 430, 527n. New York: Cambridge University Press.

Slosson Intelligence Test. (1981). East Aurora, NY: Slosson Educational Publications.

Smith, F. (1971). *Understanding reading: A psycholinguistic analysis of reading and learning to read.* New York: Rinehart & Winston.

Smith, F. (1973). *Psycholinguistics and reading.* New York: Holt, Rinehart, & Winston.

Smith, S. D., Kimberling, W. J., Pennington, B. F., & Lubs, H. A. (1983). Specific reading disability: Identi-

fication of an inherited form through linkage analysis. *Science, 15,* 1345–1347.

Snow, C. P. (1964). *Two cultures and a second look.* New York: Mentor Press.

Snow, D. P., & Coots, J. H. (1982). *Sentence perception in listening and reading* (ED 208 388). Washington, DC: National Institute of Education.

Snowling, M., Goulandris, N., Bowlby, M., & Howell, P. (1986). Segmentation and speech perception in relation to reading skills. *Journal of Experimental Child Psychology, 41*(3), 489–507.

Sokolov, E. N. (1960). Neuronal models and the orienting reflex. In M. A. B. Brazier (Ed.), *The central nervous system and behavior* pp. 187–276. New York: Josiah Macy.

Sommerhoff, G. (1974). *Logic of the living brain.* London: Wiley.

Spache, G. D. (1981). *Diagnosis and correction of reading disabilities.* Boston, Allyn & Bacon.

Spear, P. D., & Tong, L. (1980). Effects of monocular deprivation on neurons in the cat's lateral suprasylvian visual area. *Journal of Neuropsychology, 44*(3), 568–584.

Spearitt, D. (1972). Identification of subskills of reading comprehension by maximum likelihood factor analysis. *Reading Research Quarterly, 8,* 92–111.

Sperry, R. W. (1970). Perception in the absence of the neocortical commissures. *Perception and Its Disorders.* Res. Publ. Assn. Research Nervous Mental Disease, XLIII, pp. 123–138. Baltimore: Williams & Wilkins.

Spilich, G. J., Vesonder, G. T., Chiesi, H. L., & Voss, J. F. (1979). Text processing of domain-related information for individuals with high and low domain knowledge. *Journal of Verbal Learning and Verbal Behavior, 18*(3), 275–290.

Squire, L. R. (Ed.). (1987a). *The dynamics of language learning: Research in reading and English* (ED 280 080) August. Washington, DC: Office of Educational Research and Improvement.

Squire, L. R. (Ed.). (1987b). Discussion at the mid-decade seminar on the teaching of reading and English (ED 274 967). *Resources in Education,* March.

SRA Basic Reading Series. (1976). Chicago: Science Research Associates, Inc.

Stahl, S. A. (1988). Is there evidence to support matching reading styles and initial reading methods?: A reply to Carbo. *Phi Delta Kappan, 70*(4), 317–322.

Stallings, J. (1975). Implementation and child effects of teaching practices in follow through classroom. In *Monographs of the Society for Research in Child Development, 40*(Series No. 163), 1–119.

Stanford Achievement Tests. (1982). San Antonio, TX: The Psychological Corp.

Stanford Diagnostic Reading Test. (1984). San Antonio, TX: The Psychological Corp.

Stanovich, K. E., Feeman, D. J., & Cunningham, A.

E. (1983). The development of the relation between letter-naming speed and reading ability. *Bulletin of the Psychonomic Society, 21,* 199–202.

Stanovich, K. E., Nathan, R. G., & Vala-Rossi, M. (1986). Developmental changes in the cognitive correlates of reading ability and the developmental lag hypothesis. *Reading Research Quarterly, 21,* 267–283.

Stauffer, R. G. (1969). *Directing reading maturity as a cognitive process.* New York: Harper & Row.

Stauffer, R. G. (1970a). Reading as cognitive functioning. In H. Singer & R. B. Ruddell (Eds.), *Theoretical models and processes of reading,* (pp. 124–141). Newark, DE: International Reading Association.

Stauffer, R. G. (1970b). *The language-experience approach to the teaching of reading.* New York: Harper & Row.

Stauffer, R. G. (1975). *Directing the reading-thinking process.* New York: Harper & Row.

Stein, J. F., & Fowler, S. (1982). Towards a physiology of visual dyslexia. In Y. Zotterman (Ed.), *Dyslexia: Neuronal, cognitive and linguistic aspects* (pp. 51–52). Oxford, England: Pergamon Press.

Stein, J., & Fowler, S. (1985). Effect of monocular occlusion on visuomotor perception and reading in dyslexic children. *Lancet, 2*(8446), 69–73.

Stein, N. L., & Glenn, G. H. (1979). An analysis of story comprehension in elementary school children. In R. D. Freedle (Ed.), *New directions in discourse processes, Vol. 2: Advances in discourse processes.* Hillsdale, NJ: Lawrence Erlbaum Associates.

Steiner, R., Weiner, M., & Cromer, W. (1971). Comprehension training and identification for poor and good readers. *Journal of Educational Psychology, 62,* 506–513.

Steinschneider, A., Lipton, E. L., & Richmond, J. B. (1966). Auditory sensitivity in the infant: Effect of sensitivity on cardiac and motor responsivity. *Child Development, 37,* 233–252.

Stellar, J. R., & Stellar, E. (1985). *The neurobiology of motivation and reward.* New York: Springer–Verlag.

Sterling, E. G., & Bell, E. (1930). The hearing of school children as measured by the audiometer and as related to their school work. *Public Health Report, 145,* 1117–1130.

Stevens, C. F. (1979). The neuron. In *The brain, a scientific American book* pp. 15–25. San Francisco: W. H. Freeman.

Stevenson, A., et al. (1988). Achievement in the writing to read program: A comparative evaluation study. *Resources in Education* (ED 293 147), September.

Stevenson, H. W., Kagan, J., & Spiker, C. C. (1963). *Child Psychology, The 62nd Yearbook of the National Society for the Study of Education.* Chicago: University of Chicago Press.

Stewart, E. D. (1981). Learning styles among gifted/ talented students: Instructional technique preference. *Exceptional Children, 48*(2), 134–137.

Stodolsky, S. S. (1975). What tests do and don't do. In V. Perrone (Ed.), *Testing and evaluation: New news* pp. 13–17. Washington, DC: Association for Childhood International.

Stryer, L. (1987). The molecules of visual excitation. *Scientific American, 257*(1), 42–49.

Swinney, D. F. A., Onifer, W., Prather, P., & Hirshkowlitz, M., (1979). Semantic facilitation across sensory modalities in the processing of words and sentences. *Memory and Cognition, 7*(3), 159–165.

Taft, M. (1985). Morphographic approach to decoding. In D. Besner, T. G. Waller, & G. E. Mackinnon (Eds.), *Reading Research: Advances in Theory and Practice* (Vol. 5), pp. 83–123. Orlando, FL: Academic Press.

Talking Text Speller. (1987). Jefferson City, MO: Scholastic Software.

Talking Text Writer. (1986). Jefferson City, MO: Scholastic Software.

Tartter, V. C. (1986). *Language processes.* New York: Holt, Rinehart, & Winston.

Taylor, D. C. (1969). Differential rates of cerebral maturation between sexes and between hemispheres: Evidence from epilepsy. *Lancet, 2,* 140–142.

Taylor, I. (1981). Writing systems and reading. In G. E. MacKinnon & R. G. Waller (Eds.), *Reading research: Advances in theory and practice* (pp. 1–51, Vol. 2). New York: Academic Press.

Thomas, A. (1979). Learned helplessness and expectancy factors: Implications for research in learning disabilities. *Review of Educational Research, 49,* 208–221.

Thompson, M. E. (1982). The assessment of children with specific reading difficulties (dyslexia) using the British Ability Scales. *British Journal of Psychology, 73*(4), 461–478.

Thorndike, E. L. (1913). *Educational psychology: The psychology of learning* (Vol. 2), New York: Teachers College.

Thorndike, E. L. (1917). Reading as reasoning: A study of mistakes in paragraph reading. *Journal of Educational Psychology, 8,* 323–332.

Thorndike, R. L., (1973–1974). Reading as reasoning. *Reading Research Quarterly, 9*(2), 135–147.

Thorndike, R. L., Hagan, E. P., & Sattler, J. M. (1986). *Stanford-Binet intelligence scale: Fourth edition.* Bensenville, IL: Riverside.

Thorndyke, P. W. (1977). Cognitive structures in comprehension and memory of narrative discourse. *Cognitive Psychology, 9,* 77–110.

Thurstone, L. L. (1946). Note on a reanalysis of Davis' reading tests. *Psychometrika, 11,* 185–188.

Tietjens, E. (1934) Moving. *Child Life Magazine.*

Timko, H. G. (1983). Effects of differential criterion levels on the discrimination of letter. *Journal of Experimental Education, 51,* 203–205.

Tinker, M. A. (1952). *Teaching elementary reading.* New York: Appleton–Century–Crofts.

Tinker, M. A. (1958). Recent studies of eye movements in reading. *Psychological Bulletin, 55,* 215–231.

Tinker, M. A. (1963). *Legibility of print.* Ames, IA: Iowa State University Press.

Tolman, E. C. (1932). *Purposive behavior in animals and men.* New York: Appleton–Century–Crofts.

Tomatis, A. (1969). *Dyslexia.* Ottawa, Ontario: University of Ottawa Press.

Torgeson, J. K. (1982). The learning disabled child as an inactive learner: Educational implications. *Topics in Learning and Learning Disabilities, 2,* 45–51.

Torrance, E. P., & Rockenstein, Z. L. (1988). Styles of thinking and creativity. In R. R. Schmeck (Ed.), *Learning strategies and learning styles* 275–290. New York: Plenum Press.

Trabasso, T., & Nicholas, D. W. (1980). Memory and inferences in the comprehension of narratives. In F. Wilkening, J. Becker, & T. Trabasso (Eds.), *Memory and inferences in the comprehension of narratives* (pp. 215–242). Hillsdale, NJ: Lawrence Erlbaum Associates.

Tracy, J. M. (1983). *An analysis of the linguistic and reading comprehension abilities of severely reading disabled school-aged children. Unpublished doctoral dissertation, University of Oregon.*

Tramer, O., Butler, B. E., & Mewhort, D. J. (1985). Evidence for scanning with unilateral visual presentation of letters. *Brain and Language, 25,* 1–18.

Treiman, R. (1985). Onsets and rhymes as units of spoken syllables: Evidence from children. *Journal of Experimental Child Psychology, 39*(1), 161–181.

Truex, R. C., & Carpenter, M. B. (1969). *Human neuroanatomy, 6th ed.* Baltimore: Williams & Wilkins.

Tuiman, J. J. (1973–1974). Determining the passage dependency of comprehension questions in five major tests. *Reading Research Quarterly, 9,* 206–223.

Tunmer, W. E., Herriman, M. L., & Nesdale, A. R. (1988). Metalinguistic abilities and beginning reading. *Reading Research Quarterly, 23*(2), 134–158.

Turnbull, H. R., III (1986). *Free appropriate public education.* Denver: Love.

Underwood, N. R., & McConkie, G. W. (1985). Perceptual span for letter distinctions during reading. *Reading Research Quarterly, 20*(2), 153–162.

Vacca, J. L., Vacca, R. T., & Gove, M. K. (1987). *Reading and learning to read.* Boston: Little, Brown.

Valenstein, E. S. (1980). *The psychosurgery debate.* San Francisco: W. H. Freeman.

Van Donge, N. W. (1971). Visual problems in the classroom. In J. A. R. Wilson (Ed.), *Diagnosis of learning difficulties.* New York: McGraw–Hill, pp. 37–60.

Vellutino, F. R. (1977). Alternative conceptualizations of dyslexia: Evidence in support of a verbal-deficit hypoth-

eses. *Harvard Educational Review, 47*(3), 334–354.

Vellutino, F. R., & Scanlon, D. M. (1987). *Facility in name retrieval and alphabetic mapping as co-determinants of skill or lack of skill in word identification.* Paper presented at the Biennial meeting of the Society for Research in Child Development. Baltimore, April 23–26.

Vernon, M. D. (1957). *Backwardness in reading: A study of its nature and origin.* Cambridge, England: Cambridge University Press.

Volkmann, F. C. (1976). Saccadic suppression. In R. A. Monty & J. A. Senders (Eds.), *Eye movements and psychological processes.* Hillsdale, NJ: Lawrence Erlbaum Associates.

Voltaire, F. M. A. D. (1761). *The history of candide or all for the best* (Tr. by A. B. Walkley). London: Chapman and Dodd.

Vosniadou, S., & Ortony, A. (1984). *Sources of difficulty in the young child's understanding of metaphorical language* (Tech Rep. No. 290). Washington, DC: National Academy of Education.

Vygotsky, L. S. (1962). E. Hanfman & G Vaker (Ed. and trans.), *Thought and language.* Cambridge, MA: MIT Press. (Original work published 1934)

Walker, H. M. (1983). The social behavior survival skills program (SBS). *Association for Direct Instruction News, 2*(3), 36–37.

Walker, H. M., & Buckley, N. K. (1974). *Token reinforcement techniques: Classroom applications for the hard-to-teach child.* Eugene, OR: E–B Press.

Wallace, J. G. (1965). *Concept growth and the education of the child: A survey of research on conceptualization.* New York: New York University Press.

Walls, G. L. (1967), The vertebrate eye. In D. B. Lindsley & A. W. Melon (Eds.) *The neural basis of behavior* (p. 200). Columbus, OH: Merrill Books.

Walsh, D. J., Price, G. G., & Gillingham, M. G. (1988). The critical but transitory importance of letter naming. *Reading Research Quarterly, 23*(4), 189–200.

Wang, W. S. (1981). Language structure and optimal orthography. In O. J. L. Tzeng & H. Singer (Eds.). *Perception of print: Reading research in experimental psychology* (pp. 223–236). Hillsdale, NJ: Lawrence Erlbaum Associates.

Ward, L. O. (1977). Variables influencing auditory-visual integration in normal and retarded readers. *Journal of Reading Behavior, 9*(3), 290–295.

Warren, R. M. (1972). Perception of temporal order: Special rules for initial and terminal sounds of sequences. *Journal of Acoustical Society of American, 52,* 167.

Warren, R. M. (1982). *Auditory perception: A new synthesis.* New York: Pergamon Press.

Washington, V., & Oyemade, U. J. (1985). Changing family trends. *Young Children, 40*(6), 17–19.

Watson, J. B. (1930). *Behaviorism.* Chicago: University of Chicago Press.

Watson, J. B., & Morgan, J. J. B. (1917). Emotional reactions and psychological experimentation. *American Journal of Psychology, 28,* 163–174.

Watson, J. S. (1969). Operant conditioning of visual fixation in infants under visual and auditory reinforcements. *Developmental Psychology, 1,* 508–516.

Watts, N. (1981). A dozen uses for the computer in education. *Educational Technology.* Englewood Cliffs, NJ: Education Technology Publications, pp. 18–22.

Weaver, C. (1980). *Psycholinguistics and reading: From process to practice.* Cambridge, MA: Winthrop Publishers.

Wechsler, D. (1949). *Wechsler Intelligence Scale for Children, Manual.* New York: Psychological Corp.

Wechsler, D. (1974). *Wechsler Intelligence Scales.* San Antonio, TX: Psychological Corp.

Wechsler, D. (1981). *Wechsler Adult Intelligence Scale—Revised.* Psychological Corp. San Antonio, TX: Harcourt Brace Jovanovich.

Weigel–Crump, C. A., & Dennis, M. (1986). Development of word-finding. *Brain and Language, 27,* 1–23.

Weikert, D. P., et al. (1970). *Longitudinal results of the Ypsilanti Perry Preschool project, final report, Vol. 2.* Washington, DC: HEW, Office of Education.

Weiner, B. (1972). *Theories of motivation.* Chicago: Rand McNally.

Weiner, B. (1980). *Human motivation.* New York: Holt, Rinehart, and Winston.

Weiner, B. (1986). *An attributional theory of motivation and emotion.* New York: Springer–Verlag.

Wender, P. H., Pederson, F. A., & Waldrop, M. F. (1967). A longitudinal study of early social behavior and cognitive development. *American Journal of Orthopsychiatry, 37*(4), 691–696.

Wepman, J. (1968). The modality concept-including a statement of the perceptual and conceptual levels of learning (ED 012 678). *Resources in Education.*

Werner, H., & Kaplan, B. (1963). *Symbol formation.* New York: Wiley.

Wertheimer, M. (1945). *Productive thinking.* New York: Harper & Row.

Wertheimer, M. (1961). Psychomotor coordination of auditory and visual space at birth. *Science, 134,* 1692.

Whipple, C. L., & Kodman, F., Jr. (1969). A study of discrimination and perceptual learning with retarded readers. *Journal of Educational Psychology, 60*(1), 1–5.

Whitmer, J. E., & Miller, M. (1988). The effects of writing on reading abilities: A comparison of first grade writing programs with and without computer technology (ED 298 157), May. *Resources in Education.*

Whyte, S. S. (1987). The connection of writing to reading and its effect on reading comprehension (ED 278 940). July. *Resources in Education.*

Wickelgren, W. A. (1969). Auditory or articulatory coding in verbal short-term memory for English consonants. *Psychological Review, 76,* 232–235.

Wickelgren, W. (1977). Speech-accuracy tradeoff and information processing dynamica. *Acta Psychologia, 41,* 67–85.

Wigfield, A., & Asher, S. R. (1984). Social and motivational influences on reading. In P. D. Pearson (Ed.), *Handbook of Reading Research,* pp. 423–452. New York: Longman.

Wilkinson, A. C. (1982). Children's understanding of written and spoken discourse (ED 207 019) February. *Resources in Education.*

Willette, T. L. & Early, G. H. (1985). Abilities of normal and reading-disabled children to combine the visual and auditory modalities with dimensions of space and time. *Perceptual and Motor Skills, 61*(3, pt. 2), 1285–1298.

Williams, J. P. (1984). Phonemic analysis and how it relates to reading. *Journal of Learning Disabilities, 17*(4), 240–245.

Williams, R. (1950). *Reading and criticism.* London: Frederick Muller.

Williams, W. C. (1958). *I wanted - to write a poem.* Boston: Beacon Press.

Williams, W. C. (1963). *Patterson III.* New York: New Directions.

Wilson, J. A. R., & Robeck, M. C. (1967). *Kindergarten evaluation of learning potential.* Manchester, MO: McGraw–Hill, Webster Division.

Wilson, J. A. R., Robeck, M. C., & Michael, W. B. (1969). *Psychological foundations of learning and teaching.* New York: McGraw–Hill.

Wise, R. A., & Bozarth, M. (1982). Action of drugs on brain reward systems: An update with specific attention to opiates. *Pharmacology, Biochemistry, and Behavior, 17,* 239–243.

Witelson, S. F. (1976). Sex and the single hemisphere specialization of the right hemisphere for spatial processing. *Science, 193,* 425–427.

Witelson, S. F. (1985). On hemisphere specialization and cerebral plasticity from birth: Mark II. In C. T. Best (Ed.), *Hemispheric function and collaboration in the child.* New York: Academic Press.

Witkin, H. A. (1971). *Group Embedded Figures Test.* Palo Alto, CA: Consulting Psychologists Press, Inc.

Witkin, H. A., & Goodenough, D. R. (1981). *Cognitive styles: Essence and origins.* New York: International Universities Press.

Witkin, H. A., Goodenough, D. R., & Karp, S. A. (1967). Stability of cognitive style from childhood to young adulthood. *Journal of Personality and Social Psychology, 7*(3, pt. 1), 291–300.

Witty, P. (1949). *Reading in modern education.* Boston: D.C. Heath.

Wolfe, J. B. (1968). Teaching today's children to think. In J. Downing & A. L. Brown (Eds.), *The third international reading symposium: Today's child and learning to read* (pp. 67–69). London: Cassell and Company, LTD.

Wong, B. Y. L. (1985). Self-questioning instructional research: A review. *Review of Educational Research, 55*(2), 227–268.

Woodcock Reading Mastery Tests. (1987). Circle Pines, MN: American Guidance Service.

Woodley, J. W. (1987). The role of non-visual information in visual perception: An integration of research perspectives (Ed 283 134). *Resources in Education*, November.

Wooldridge, D. E. (1963). *The machinery of the brain.* New York: McGraw–Hill.

Worden, T. W., & Franklin, M. R. (1986–1987). Adapting tutorial techniques to perceptual modalities of deficient readers. *Educational Research Quarterly, 11*(1), 40–48.

Yakovlev, P. I., & Lecours, A. R. (1967). The mylogenic cycles of regional maturation of the brain. In A. Minkowski (Ed.), *Regional development of the brain in early life* (pp. 3–69). A symposium organized by UNESCO and WHO. Philadelphia: Davis.

Yim, C. Y., & Morgenson, G. J. (1980). Effect of iotophoritically applied dopamine on the response of nucleus accumbens neurons to electrical stimulation of the amygdala. *Neuroscience Abstracts, 6,* 447.

Zarry, L. L. (1978). *The effect of videotaped cross-sex-typed career themes on career choices.* Doctoral dissertation, University of Oregon.

Zotterman, Y. (1982). *Dyslexia: Neuronal, Cognitive, and Linguistic Aspects.* Oxford, England: Pergamon Press.

Author Index

Subject Index

Motivation (*cont.*)
  critical factors in, 277
  definition, 38
  dimensions of control, 275
  intrinsic vs extrinsic, 52–53
  mastery as, 52
  negative, 53–55
  neuropsychological basis for, 32–33, 38–51
  relationship to learning, 19
  reward effect, 47–51
  role of expectancy, 276
  teaching, 30
Motor analyzer, 98
Motor area for speech production, 195
Motor control
  eye position and, 236
  levels of, 163–164
Motor gyrus, 163
Motor integration and reading, 98, 194–196
Motor responses
  audiovisual stimuli for, 251–252
  good and poor readers', 251–252
Motor theory of speech perception, 194–196
Mnemonic devices, 98
Multiple meanings, 22–23
Myelination, 151–153
Myelencephalon, 161
Myopia, 211

N

Narration, 109–110
  exposition and, 390–391
Narrative language and reading success, 76
Native American children, 87
Near-point vision, 211
  infant capabilities, 221
Negative motivation, 53–55
Neural activity, observation of, 17–18, 168–169
Neural cells
  changes with learning, 158–160
  communication among, 100
  resting state of, 155–157
  structure of, 148–154
Neural linkages
  babbling and, 73–74
  between modalities, 100, 163
Neural network model for computer design, 80
Neuronal processes, 149–151
Neural system, 15
  changes in learning, 99–100
  integrity in reading skill, 252–254
  microstructure of, 100
Neuroglia, 151, 153
Neurological integrity, 252, 262–263

lateral awareness as, 253
  visual sequencing and, 253–254
Neurons
  connector, 148–154
  effector, 148–149, 151–154
  growth of, 100, 134
  receptor, 148–149, 151, 154
Neurotransmitters, 49–50, 156–158
Neuroscience
  dyslexia and, 260–268
  evidence from, 15–18
Nonreaders, functional definition, 25
Norms, 298–299
Norm-referenced tests, 294
  [**see also** Tests, types of]

O

Occipital lobes, 143
  print perception in, 236
  visual functions of, 162, 218–220
Ocular-motor control, 236–238
Ontogenetic influences
  behavior and, 144
  hearing and, 187–189
  interaction with phylogeny, 144–148
Open Court Foundation Program, 349–350
Operant conditioning, 7–8, 30, 33–34
Operactivity, 79
Optic chiasm, 143, 218–219
Optic pathways, 218
Optic system, 209–211
Orbital cortex
  location of, 164
  personality aspects of, 165
Organ of Corti, 182–183, 185
Organization, neuronal, 244
  association functions, 247–248
  conceptual functions, 250
  integration functions, 247–249
  retrieval functions, 249–250
Orientation and attention, 43–47
Orienting reaction vs habituation, 44–45
Origins of intelligence in children, 38
Orthographic code, 67
Ossicle chain, 180
Outer ear, functions of, 179–180

P

Parafovea, 240
Parallel processing, 4, 256–259
  of print, 256–259
  of speech, 196–197